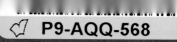

ISBN: 0-226-76975-5

The Irony of Liberal Reason
Thomas A. Spragens, Jr.

The liberal tradition that is heir to and protector of
Western humanism has developed within itself,
ironically, tendencies that threaten humane values.
These self-destructive tendencies, the author shows,
stem from failures within the larger philosophical
tradition undergirding liberalism, especially with
regard to the conception of human reason. The
surviving conceptions of reason within the liberal
tradition—conceptions the author calls "technocratic"
and "value noncognitivist"—not only leave
humanistic ideals and practices largely without support
but often threaten them directly. The liberal quest for a
system of ordered liberty has thereby been weakened,
for its own philosophy has incubated the tyrannical
and anarchistic derangements it hoped to escape or
avoid.

The conclusion reached by the author is nonetheless
a hopeful one. He shows that the philosophical
premises that have proved to be ironically destructive
are dispensable because they are obsolescent. He finds
within contemporary philosophy of science and
post-Wittgensteinian philosophy the basis for a new
conception of the human understanding and of rational
practice that can sustain, rather than subvert, liberal
ideals. *The Irony of Liberal Reason,* then, is a critical
historical analysis leading to a constructive polemic
—"an excursus in therapeutic intellectual history . . .
intended as a piece of conceptual archeology aimed at

Thomas A. Spragens, Jr.

The Irony of
Liberal Reason

The University of Chicago Press
Chicago & London

THOMAS A. SPRAGENS, JR., is professor of political science at Duke University. Among his publications are *The Dilemma of Contemporary Political Theory, The Politics of Motion: The World of Thomas Hobbes,* and *Understanding Political Theory.*

The University of Chicago Press, Chicago 60637
The University of Chicago Press, Ltd., London

© 1981 by The University of Chicago
All rights reserved. Published 1981
Printed in the United States of America
9 8 7 6 5 4 3 2 1   81 82 83 84 85

Library of Congress Cataloging in Publication Data

Spragens, Thomas A., Jr.
    The irony of liberal reason.
    Includes bibliographical references and index.
    1. Liberalism.   I. Title.
HM276.S67   320.5'1   81–3027
ISBN 0–226–76975–5   AACR2

Contents

	Preface	vii
1	Politics, Epistemology, and Liberalism: An Introduction	3
2	"Simple Truths and Infallible Methods": The Emergence of Liberal Rationalism	18
3	The "Moral Sciences" and Liberal Hopes	50
4	The Logic of Domination: The Origins of Technocracy	91
5	*Werkmeister* and Therapists: The Technocratic Legacy	128
6	The Origins of Political Irrationalism	196
7	Custom, Preference, and Will: The Several Faces of Modern Political Irrationalism	256
8	The Quiet Demise of Liberal Reason	311
9	Picking Up the Pieces: Rational Enterprises and Humane Politics	357
	Notes	397
	Index	436

Preface

This study developed from a double sense of disquiet and ambivalence: the first concerning modern liberalism, the other concerning scientific rationalism.

Modern liberalism has served as the principal intellectual force behind progressive and enlightened politics in the West and as a repository for fundamental human values. Any humane political order, I would argue, must take with great seriousness the major concerns and ideals of this tradition: civil rights and liberties, representative institutions, the political role of reason and persuasion, limited government, respect for human dignity and equality. Yet, many programs, ideas, and attitudes that come labeled as "liberal" seem disturbingly at odds with the humaneness that is at the core of liberalism. Some of them embody an arrogant elitism of "the enlightened few"; others verge on a nihilistic dismissal of the very intelligibility of humane moral ideas.

Similarly, the intellectual advance of modern science clearly constitutes one of the most prodigious accomplishments of the human understanding. The procedures, standards, and habits of mind characteristic of the scientific enterprise seem to possess a kind of permanent validity. Yet, some of the intellectual trends closely associated with modern science are also disturbing and peculiar. The attempt to reify scientific inquiry into a kind of applied formal logic, for example, seems both scholastically barren and somewhat peripheral to actual scientific practice. More important, the attempt to elevate this narrow and misleading conception of scientific rationality into a universally applicable norm has been positively destructive of many essential aspects of human culture.

These two apparently distinct sources of disquiet, moreover, turn out on closer examination to be profoundly related to each other, both logically and historically. Modern liberalism was twin-born with scientific rationalism, and both sought to establish their respective beliefs and aspirations on the same basic philosophical assumptions.

The thesis of this book, then, took shape as I sought to understand the reasons for my ambivalence and the nature of the connections between them. Succinctly stated, the argument is that the same liberal tradition that is heir to and protector of Western humanism has developed within itself tendencies that threaten humane values. These self-destructive tendencies in turn stem from failures within the larger philosophical tradition that undergirds liberalism—especially from failures related to this tradition's conception of human reason.

Originally, Enlightenment liberalism was humane but utopian and philosophically incoherent. Time has since eroded its utopianism, and critical reflection has largely resolved its original philosophical incoherence. However, the surviving conceptions of reason—which I shall call "technocratic" and "value noncognitivist"—leave humanistic liberal ideals and practices largely without sustenance and indeed often threaten them more directly.

If cause for dismay, these developments are not, however, cause for despair, for the philosophical premises that have proved to be ironically destructive are proving to be obsolescent. It is therefore now quite possible to begin to transcend the sources of liberal corruption and to resuscitate the humane essentials of the liberal tradition, properly understood.

I seek to contribute to that end through a critical historical analysis that leads to a constructive polemic. My purposes are to identify the key features of the most significant "ideal type" conceptions of politics within liberal rationalism; to explain some of the intellectual dynamics that produced them; to illuminate and criticize their internal weaknesses, their empirical flaws, and their normative inadequacies; and, finally, to suggest the main features of a re-emergent liberal humanism based on a more adequate and contemporary assessment of human reason.

Methodologically, this study should be approached as an excursus in therapeutic intellectual history. It is intended as a piece of conceptual archeology aimed at the diagnosis of problems that confront us and at the exorcism of demons that afflict us. Freud and Wittgenstein provide us with instructive analogies in the structure and goals of their psychoanalytic and linguistic-philosophical enterprises, respectively. Like the fly in Wittgenstein's famous simile, we often entrap ourselves in conceptual and linguistic fly-bottles of our own making. When the ideas involved are political ideas, moreover, the entrapments may be literal as well as figurative. My goal, then,

like Wittgenstein's, is liberation. Because human beings are creatures of history, however, we don't simply fly into our conceptual
and linguistic entrapments; instead, we inherit them. Hence the linguistic approach must be supplemented by retrospective reconstructions like those necessary in psychoanalysis. We need to
discover and to understand the roots of our problems before we can
effectively transcend them, and this means that we must look back
before we can look forward. It makes little sense to speak of putting a
fly-bottle on a psychoanalyst's couch, but some such conflation of
metaphors is requisite to describe the structure of our task.

The product of such a present-oriented inquiry into the intellectual
history of liberalism will, like the reconstructions of psychoanalysis,
necessarily be much more schematic than the actual course that
history followed. The evolution of liberalism, as Harold Laski has
said, "was never direct and rarely conscious. The pedigree of ideas
is never straightforward. Into the development of liberalism there
have entered winds of doctrine so diverse in their origin as to make
clarity difficult and precision perhaps unattainable."[1] This complexity and diversity of the liberal tradition must be respected and
acknowledged. For the sake of self-understanding, however, it is
also necessary to try to sift out of this complexity some of the
persistent and significant ideas that continue to shape many of our
own perceptions and beliefs. Such selective attention to particular
themes in an intellectual tradition may obscure that tradition's full
richness, but it is necessary if we wish to illuminate the tradition's
contemporary impact. Only "by noting the presence of these elements which show greater resistance to change," as Charles Frankel
writes, can we "provide structure and continuity to what would
otherwise be merely a chronicle of the order in which changes have
succeeded one another."[2]

Although this study is chiefly a work of diagnosis and criticism,
the last chapter provides a very sketchy start in the task of reconstruction. In some respects, this sketch might better have been
left to some future time, when it could be more fully developed. It
seemed essential, however, to include it in order to put the earlier
sections into proper perspective. To have omitted any reconstruc-
tive sketch entirely might have left the impression that our fly-bottle
had no escape, and that would have been the opposite of my intent
and belief. For too long the dominant tendencies of Western philosophy have contributed to a situation in which, as Yeats put it, the
worst are filled with passionate intensity while the best lack all conviction. The emerging philosophical landscape, however, should be
viewed by humane liberals as presenting a hopeful prospect, not a
hopeless cul-de-sac.

In the last chapter, then, I state a position more than I make an argument. I invite readers to consider the hopeful implications of recent philosophical developments in light of the problems and failures surveyed in the earlier chapters. My aim is to provide intimations of a conception of liberal rationalism that, unlike previous versions, is both philosophically defensible and politically salutary.

I have tried to make this study both useful to my fellow political theorists and intelligible to a broader circle of readers. Unavoidable perils and difficulties attend any attempt to speak to a heterogeneous audience. However, if each group is willing to be somewhat forbearing in different ways, the problems are not entirely insuperable. In this specific case, I have included some material, especially in the early chapters, that political theorists will find superfluous and unoriginal; I hope they will appreciate that these sections are necessary to give the book synoptic completeness and to make it coherent for the student and the nonprofessional. Likewise, nonprofessional readers will probably find some sections too detailed for their taste; I hope they will appreciate that these sections are often those most likely to be useful to the truly knowledgeable reader.

Finally, a few definitional clarifications might be helpful at the outset to forestall potential misunderstanding or confusion. My use of the term "irony" may confound the literary critic, but it is not idiosyncratic. I mean by "irony" exactly what Reinhold Niebuhr meant by it in *The Irony of American History,* and I can improve little if any upon his elucidation. "Irony," he writes,

> consists of apparently fortuitous incongruities in life which are discovered, upon closer examination, to be not merely fortuitous. Incongruity as such is merely comic. It elicits laughter. This element of comedy is never completely eliminated from irony. But irony is something more than comedy. A comic situation is proved to be an ironic one if a hidden relation is discovered in the incongruity, [for example] if wisdom becomes folly because it does not know its own limits. . . . The ironic situation is distinguished from a pathetic one by the fact that the person involved in it bears some responsibility for it. It is differentiated from tragedy by the fact that the responsibility is related to an unconscious weakness rather than to a conscious resolution.[3]

Niebuhr also adds a comment that is helpful in relating the notion of irony to our therapeutic intent. As he observes, some element of unconsciousness is essential to irony—as it is not to tragedy or pathos. Therefore, once analytic insight eliminates this failure of awareness, the ironic situation dissolves. Those who are implicated in it must either take steps to remedy the situation or else—no longer devoid of the knowledge that invests them with *mens rea*—become involved in outright evil.

The phrase "liberal reason" will also be unintelligible or misleading unless it is understood as a kind of shorthand. Were it not obviously too cumbersome to tolerate, we might instead use the longer phrase "modern, critical, positivistic rationalism insofar as it is implicated in and allegedly related to political standards and aspirations, especially the standards and aspirations of modern liberalism." Those who find peculiar the suggestion that a philosophical account of the nature of the human understanding might be so implicated in and related to political ideas will, I hope, be rather swiftly persuaded that these relationships do in fact exist historically, whatever their logical validity.

Choosing names to designate and characterize the two major second-generation offspring of liberal reason was also problematic. For each there is a philosophical conception of the nature, scope, and distribution of rationality and there is a political orientation based on—or at least tailored to be compatible with—the philosophical conception. For the first offspring I have used the term "technocratic" to refer to both the philosophical and the political ideas. For the second, I have used the term "value noncognitivist" to designate the philosophy and the term "irrationalist" to characterize the politics. I am not altogether happy with either term; but "value noncognitivist" has the virtues of widespread acceptance and relative precision (despite the unfortunate philosophical bias built into the noun "value"), and "irrationalist" identifies the common and problematic property of the several political outlooks it covers.

The Irony of Political Reason is principally a work of synthesis and interpretation. Some of the pieces of the puzzle are—to my knowledge, at least—original. Many others were readily available in some of the excellent monographic literature cited in the text. I almost hesitate to single out specific sources for fear of failing to mention others equally praiseworthy. Nevertheless, some of those whose work was especially valuable to me are Aram Vartanian, Isabel Knight, Charles Frankel, R. V. Sampson, Frank Manuel, E. A. Burtt, Basil Willey, Elie Halévy, Nicholas Lobkowicz, Bernard Crick, Friedrich Hayek, Carl Becker, Philip Rieff, Floyd Matson, Nicholas Kittrie, Grant McConnell, Theodore Lowi, William Lee Miller, Hans Morgenthau, Stephen Toulmin, Norwood Hanson, J. O. Urmson, and Frederick Suppe.

In addition, I owe a large debt to others who have given us their thoughtful and provocative interpretations of the general problems that have concerned me. Leo Strauss, Eric Voegelin, Lester Crocker, Peter Gay, Robert Nisbet, Reinhold Niebuhr, Roberto Unger, Theodore Roszak, Jürgen Habermas, and Michael Polanyi are some of the more important figures in this respect. There are both similarities and differences between these interpretations and my own. At one point I sought to make these comparisons at each relevant juncture. That attempt, however, began to convert the text into a review essay; so I abandoned the effort and will, with some trepidation, leave it to the reader who is so inclined to venture his own comparisons.

Fellowship assistance from the National Endowment for the Humanities gave me time to begin my research for this study, and a Rockefeller Foundation Humanities Fellowship enabled me to complete my work on it. To both agencies I am profoundly grateful, not only for their specific assistance to me but also for their general contribution to humanistic scholarly inquiry in this country. The Duke University Research Council also provided support for this project, and I thank them for their assistance. For their work on the manuscript I also wish to thank Louise Walker, Patsy MacFarland, Patricia Jenkins, Doris Ralston, and Caryn Van Pelt.

The Irony of Liberal Reason

the diagnosis of problems that confront us and at the exorcism of demons that afflict us."

"A ruminative, serious, and provocative book. It is conceptually clear without being simplistic; it is clearly, even gracefully, written; it addresses a compellingly important problem. This book deserves a large audience."—Joseph Hamburger, Yale University

"The combination of Spragens's timely theme and his flawless command of the great tradition in modern European philosophy makes this a very important book. It should be one of those genuinely scholarly works which reach a substantial audience of serious readers outside academia."—Robert Nisbet, American Enterprise Institute for Public Policy Research

THOMAS A. SPRAGENS, JR., is professor of political science at Duke University.

For information on books of related interest, or for a catalog of new publications, please write:

Marketing Department
The University of Chicago Press
5801 S. Ellis Avenue
Chicago, Illinois 60637

1 Politics, Epistemology, and Liberalism: An Introduction

As Hans Morgenthau observed some three decades ago, "the pleasant interlude of the Victorian age has come to an end."[1] The ready optimism and rationalist faith that characterized that era seem distant to us now. Contemporary Western man may retain the hopes and dreams of his Victorian predecessors, but he cannot easily share their serene confidence that these dreams will be realized. Both the politics and the intellectual history of the twentieth century have left thoughtful men chastened and apprehensive, inducing sobriety if not a deepening skepticism.

In political philosophy this change is reflected in the receding hold of liberalism on the modern mind. In some ways the nineteenth century marked the high tide of liberalism as a political creed in the West. Born two centuries before, the liberal world view had graduated from an explicit doctrine to the status of a largely tacit set of assumptions and predispositions. Nineteenth-century liberalism hardly needed to be a conscious theory; it had become almost a habit of mind. As Edmund Stillman and William Pfaff have said,

> the nineteenth, more than the seventeenth or eighteenth, was the Enlightenment century, enjoying the fulfillment, at any rate, of that material faith and that conviction of man's ability to shape and perfect his condition which had originated in the great intellectual revolution of two hundred years earlier.[2]

In recent decades, however, the tenets of liberalism that had been virtually habitual a century before have become subject to serious challenge. Many, indeed, have come to view the wares of liberalism as shopworn and outmoded, having neither intellectual nor emotional appeal. For some, the answer to the vacuum left by the fading of liberalism's charm has been to embrace other seemingly more modern and vibrant political creeds. Marxism has served this function in some instances, although Marxism grew from the same soil as liberalism and has suffered somewhat from the same erosion of intellectual assumptions that has affected contemporary liberalism. Fascism represented a more virulent and radical rejection of the whole liberal outlook, but it was self-consumed by its own demonic incandescence. More prosaic authoritarian regimes, however, continue to exist and to trade on liberalism's decline.

For others, the response has been to depoliticize the aspirations of liberalism. Since it has failed to live up to the promises made in its behalf, the political realm is shunted aside in favor of other forms of human activity. The passions that fueled liberal political enterprises are devoted instead to other kinds of pursuits: to art or to religion or to personal and family life. As Kenneth Keniston put it so aptly, we have seen recently a "privatization of Utopia."[3] In part this trend is salutary, for the tendency of liberalism was to overpoliticize the world—to expect more from politics than it could possibly give. Yet the reaction may have been too extreme. As Keniston says, "the deflection of the Utopian spirit . . . leads to a withdrawal of idealism from the areas of our shared lives that most need a Utopian vision."[4]

Still others, of course, find liberal hopes uncompelling in any form. Instead of "privatizing" Utopia, they abandon it altogether. If the result here were merely a reawakening awareness of the tragic dimension of human existence, it would be a healthy development. However, this abandonment of liberalism's assumptions seems often to slide into a debilitating skepticism.[5] Rather than simply shed the illusions of naïve liberalism, some seem inclined to abandon any grounds for the guidance of political action. Freed from the spell of illusion, they fall prey to political paralysis or even nihilism.

Even those who still hold to the basic liberal vision feel compelled to subject their beliefs to anxious scrutiny. Some conclude that the basic structure of philosophical liberalism is essentially sound and that some modifications will suffice to restore its vitality and contemporary relevance.[6] Other sympathetic critics conclude, as did Paul Tillich, that the philosophical foundations of modern liberal democracy have been shown to be very threadbare indeed under the ideological challenges of recent decades and that more radical philosophical revisions are necessary and appropriate.[7]

Recent years have seen many thoughtful analyses of the difficulties that contemporary liberalism has encountered. And throughout the different facets of the situation a common pattern recurs—a pattern perhaps best designated as "ironic." In several ways the problems facing contemporary liberalism result as much from its successes as from its failures. Many of the more cherished immediate goals of liberalism have been attained, yet the results have not proved satisfactory. The pot at the end of liberalism's rainbow seems to have contained more brass than gold.

Every political theory is, in part at least, the projection of an aspiration into the future. Potentialities of human existence are recognized, and these set the agenda for concrete political programs and provide the motivation for political action. In some respects, this feature of a political theory was especially marked in liberalism, since it looked to posterity with unparalleled anticipation. Later generations were expected to inherit the "heavenly city," to borrow Carl Becker's phrase.[8] The world of medieval Scholasticism, it has been said, was characterized by the comfortable interpenetration of space and destiny.[9] The world of classical liberalism, in parallel but in contrast, was characterized by an exhilarating interpenetration of time and destiny. Men like Condorcet and Priestley could console themselves in the darkest personal circumstances simply by turning their thoughts toward the future. Whatever the folly and frailty of the present, each new day was moving the world closer to felicity and rationality.

But between the idea and the reality have intruded the ironies of history. In many ways the liberal program has been triumphant, but not in the way its progenitors foresaw. Instead, new problems have arisen, often as unintended and unforeseen by-products of liberalism's accomplishments. Success, for liberalism, has by no means proved to be a "bitch goddess," but it nevertheless has certainly not resolved the tensions and conflicts of political life, as had been hoped.

In part, this pattern of irony is simply one of the constants of human experience. Our words and deeds outrun our grasp, bringing consequences we neither desired nor anticipated. Appreciation of this fact of life is a key constituent of the practical wisdom of the politician or statesman. In part, however, the failure of liberalism to anticipate or to deal effectively with many of the problems of contemporary politics is a direct consequence of some rather profound philosophical weaknesses. The "ironic flaw" of liberalism has been the incapacity of its deepest assumptions—ontological, epistemological, and anthropological—to sustain its finest aspirations and ideals.

In some ways, in fact, the philosophical matrix of liberalism not only is unable to sustain its most humane goals but even threatens to undermine them. Some of the more destructive tendencies of modern civilization have been nourished by the very preconceptions that were supposed to have been unambiguously beneficial to the human estate. It is facile and misleading to depict the ideological violence, the allure of totalitarian solutions to political problems, the growth of political irrationalism, and the tendencies toward anomic depersonalization in modern politics simply as atavistic eruptions of barbarism or wholly as the outcome of sociological forces. The causes of such threatening political phenomena as these are complex and tangled. No single explanation can suffice. However, we do need to perceive that some of the more cherished myths and metaphors of the modern sensibility are part of the problem. Western liberalism has its dark side, often unrecognized, which we ignore at our peril.[10]

Thoughtful critics of the liberal tradition in the West have alerted us to many of the more significant theoretical weaknesses of liberalism. The individualism of liberal psychology and sociology, the rationalism of liberal psychology and philosophy, the thoroughgoing secularism and largely uncritical pursuit of a narrowly conceived freedom—all of these fundamental tenets of liberal thought have been shown to be deficient or inadequate in important respects.

Liberalism relied on an image of man that was heavily "rationalistic" in a narrow sense. The enlightened individual could be expected to discern his self-interest with careful reference to a felicific calculus and to behave accordingly. But the belief that man needed only to be freed from his self-imposed tutelage to become a prudently hedonistic bourgeois has proved neither very durable nor very desirable. Both the lower "irrational" components of the psyche—the deeper, darker passions—and the higher "irrational" side of the psyche—the transcendental urges expressed in religion and art—have not been easily expurgatable. Nor has their repression by the forces of liberal rationality proved to be an unambiguous blessing. Instead of serving as midwife for the common good, the narrow rationalism of liberal anthropology has helped produce the hysteria of Freud's Viennese dowagers, the "mechanized petrifaction" of Weber's "specialists without spirit," and the banality of evil that Hannah Arendt saw epitomized by Eichmann. By the middle of this century, then, it had already become rather commonplace, as Hans Morgenthau noted,

> to point out the fallacy of the rationalistic conception of man, to wit, its depreciation of, if not its complete disregard for, the spiritual and emotional aspects of human life. Psychology, sociology, as well as political science in its more advanced contributions, all supported by the religious, philosophic, and historic memory of the race, have well-nigh destroyed this conception.[11]

The idealized goal of the wholly free individual has produced its share of irony as well. Among other things, liberalism wished to free the individual from the restrictions of communal bonds and from captivity to the past. But these forms of liberation seem not to have been an unalloyed blessing. The eighteenth-century liberal looked forward with confidence to the time when "natural" and spontaneous relationships among free individuals would replace the repressive parochialism and artificiality of traditional social statuses, identities, and functions. Traditional society was viewed more or less as Sinclair Lewis's *Main Street* writ large, and its anticipated demise was cause for rejoicing.[12] By the end the nineteenth century, however, some unexpected costs of social mobility were noticed by discerning observers. Emile Durkheim's analysis in his classic study of suicide, for example, attributed part of the problem to the phenomenon of "anomie," a kind of excessive social rootlessness. The attainment of community, then, no problem under the assumptions of early liberalism, has become a persistent concern of recent decades.[13] In similar fashion, the escape from the "incubus" of tradition, to borrow Marx's epithet, has had its unforeseen and undesirable side. Perceptive contemporary psychologists like Kenneth Keniston now find themselves writing about the human need for a sense of historical continuity and a "sense of personal relatedness to the personal past." Without the sustenance of some intelligible relationship with the past (and with the future), Keniston argues, psychic disorientation, alienation, and a compulsive need to be absorbed in the experience of the present moment tend to result. With the advantage of hindsight, he notes the ironic pattern that liberal premises could not anticipate:

> Historical dislocation can bring an enormous sense of freedom, of not being bound by the past, of creating oneself at each moment of one's existence. Yet characteristically a philosophy of absolute freedom, based on a denial of any necessary relationship with the past, is usually a philosophy of the absurd; the signs of this freedom are not joy and triumph, but nausea and dread; and its possessors are not the creators but the Strangers and Outsiders of the universe.[14]

Irony has also attended the characteristic liberal outlook on power in society. Sustained by the happy faith that the hand of nature could produce an optimum social equilibrium, the more optimistic liberals tended to view the exercise of political power as an outmoded vestige of the irrational past. A truly rational political order would relegate the use of force to the status of something resorted to only in exceptional circumstances. Rational men would perceive the coincidence of long-run self-interest and the common good. The coercive power of social authority would be necessary only to curb the acts of those who for some reason deviated from the rational norm. Even

John Locke, who was, as we have been reminded by Sheldon Wolin, attuned to the insecurities and anxieties of life,[15] seemed to believe that only the presence of such deviants (a presence for which he gives no explanation, but which he takes as a fact of life) necessitated the institution of government in the first place. "Were it not for the corruption and viciousness of degenerate men," he wrote, "there would be no need of any other, no necessity that men should separate from this great and natural community, and associate into lesser combinations."[16]

This streak of naïveté concerning the pervasive, if usually latent, function of power in society was, of course, ideologically useful to the bourgeoisie once they had triumphed historically. No greater balm for the conscience could be devised than the identification of one's own political ascendancy with the alleged disappearance of coercion from everyday social life. The relative deprivation, often severe, of the lower classes could be seen as one of those unfortunate but inevitable facts of life beyond the reach of human action. By transferring the social consequences of a capitalist economy to the heading "laws of nature," the problem of power in society could be largely repressed. Hence, as Harold Laski has said, "a doctrine that started as a method of emancipating the middle class changed, after 1789, into a method of disciplining the working class."[17]

Besides obscuring some crucial questions of social justice, the liberal blindness to the reality of power has led to an incapacity to handle it wisely and with a sense of limits. The liberal mind tends to generate manic cycles of excess and complete retreat in the arena of power politics. American liberalism, especially, seems to oscillate between legalistic and pacifistic protestations, on the one hand, and binges of largely unrestrained use of force on the other. Our incursions into the world of power politics are seen as appropriately sporadic and definitive. We want to remain the innocent nation, isolated from the corruption of "old world" politics, and, when we engage in international power struggles, we wish to see them on the scale of Armageddon. If we must dirty our hands, all right—but only in a "war to end all wars" or a war to "make the world safe for democracy." The liberal is uneasy in the gray area between total peace and outright war, perhaps because the categories of the liberal mind cannot make this gray area intelligible. It is therefore not too surprising to find that, as Reinhold Niebuhr has observed,

> the elements in our population which are most prone to defy the limits of power . . . and to seek a resolution of our difficulties by a sheer display of military power, are frequently drawn from a

bourgeois-liberal tradition which was, until recently, unconscious of the factor of power in political life.[18]

Irony has also attended the liberal analysis of the political implications of economic forces. The tendency toward laissez-faire originally came from the perception that politically originated contrivances constituted the most important interference in the operations of the pure market model. Therefore, the early liberals espoused the elimination of state interference, since the free market not only would lead to an economic optimum but also would create a politically advantageous wide dispersion of power. By the latter part of the nineteenth century, however, this prescription was made anachronistic by unanticipated developments in the workings of industrial capitalism. Monopolies, the great impediment to the beneficent consequences of a market economy, no longer were caused solely by political intrusion into the economic realm but instead could be generated internally by the economy itself. The remedy devised to deal with royalist grants of economic prerogative was hardly efficacious against the problem posed by American Sugar or American Tobacco. Indeed, the only answer to the economic and political distortions created by such industrial giants seemed to lie in the countervailing power of the government. State power, the classic enemy for early liberalism, became the only recourse against this new threat to basic liberal goals. The strategic reorientation consummated by the New Deal in this country was neither easy nor unanimous. Adaptation of the liberal program to Keynesian theory and oligopolistic realities has added complicating epicycles to the liberal paradigm. Some, indeed, have preferred to retain the simplicities of Spencer's *Social Statics,* although they now constitute a minority wing within the house of liberalism.

Each of these instances, then, constitutes one facet of the underlying, basic problem of contemporary liberalism, namely, the gradual dissolution of the happy fusion of is and ought—of time and destiny—that characterized classical liberalism. At its outset, liberalism found strength in the congruence it perceived between the world as it ought to be and the world as it was coming to be. The liberal view of reality comfortably sustained liberal ideals. Today, however, the aspirations and ideals of liberalism seem to have become increasingly detached from the modern perception of reality. The *gestalt* has gradually fallen apart. Hence, the contemporary liberal must try to overcome an increasingly wide gap between what he wishes and what he sees. The nature of man and the shape of history seem to collide rather than coincide with the liberal vision.[19]

In some respects, then, liberalism has had to confront the perception of a reality that contradicts its hopes. Even beyond this problem, however, lies another. For in some ways liberal premises themselves have become a stumbling block to liberal aspirations. The contemporary liberal must fight with himself as well as with the world. On top of the problems of reality-orientation are heaped the tribulations of schizophrenia. Assumptions and ideas that were supposed to lead to the fruition of liberalism have instead helped to generate, or at least to sustain, some quite illiberal political paradigms.

This ironic pattern has been manifest especially in the strange career the idea of reason has had in the political sensibility of the liberal West, and it is this aspect of contemporary liberalism that provides the focus for what follows. The problem here is not the failure of empirical man to measure up to the image of "rational man"; the problem lies within the liberal conception of rationality itself.

At first glance, epistemology and politics might seem strange bedfellows. The problems of knowledge—what may man know, how may he know it, who may know it—seem to constitute a peculiarly recondite philosophic concern. Epistemological questions appear to be highly abstract and reflexive, quite removed from the sphere of political beliefs and behavior. Certainly, the relationships between the two are not immediately apparent. Political figures are not likely to keep the writings of Kant, Hume, and Berkeley close by for ready reference.

Further thought, however, suggests that epistemological and political conceptions do have significant points of contact. These points of contact are more latent than manifest, but they are nonetheless present. Men may not seek out epistemological treatises for guidance on immediate political issues. However, their tacit assumptions about the who, the what, and the how of reliable knowledge profoundly shape their basic orientation and attitude toward a whole range of important political concerns.

Both empirical evidence from intellectual history and logical considerations substantiate this contention. Consider first the persistent conjunction in Western thought of epistemological inquiry and profound political theory.

In the Socratic tradition the connection between knowing rightly and doing well is very intimate. One cannot be virtuous without being knowledgeable, and therefore, as Herbert Marcuse has said, for classical Greek philosophy "epistemology is in itself ethics, and ethics is epistemology."[20] From principles of ethics it is only a small step to principles of politics, especially when man is viewed as essentially a political animal. Plato's *Republic*, the first great treatise in Western political philosophy, therefore stands as a virtual monument to the nexus between epistemological and political ideas. The *Republic* is a dialogue about politics, but it is at the same time a searching study of education. Great portions of it focus on the nature and extent of human knowledge and on how those who are capable may best be taught to know the good, the true, and the beautiful. We have received from this first great work of political theory some classic epistemological metaphors, models, and allegories: the allegory of the Cave, the account of intellectual conversion, the image of the divided line, with its levels of knowledge, and the theory of Ideas. And all of these essentially epistemological theories are developed in the course of asking fundamental political questions. Only on the basis of an understanding of knowledge and its pitfalls, Plato suggests, can we make sound judgments about the proper organization of the polis.

Revolutions within the tradition of political theory, moreover, are very often intimately associated with new departures in epistemology. The radically innovative theorist frequently directs part of his critique toward the prevailing assumptions concerning the ways of knowing.

Machiavelli, for example, styled his political essays as a path-breaking departure from the established mode of conceptualizing political life. He had resolved, he related, "to open a new route which has not yet been followed by any one,"[21] and the access to this new route was to be provided basically by two alleged methodological innovations. The first was a new approach to the study of history. Students of politics, Machiavelli complained, had provided so little prudential guidance for the conduct of governmental affairs because they lacked "real knowledge of history, the true sense of which is not known."[22] The virtue of his own work, he clearly believed, was to provide this "real knowledge" that would transform political theory. His second epistemological claim was that the tradition of political philosophy had been misled by a faulty conception of the relationship between Idea and Reality, between truth and imagination. In effect, he argued that Plato's divided line is upside down. Like Marx confronting Hegel, Machiavelli would turn Plato on his head:

My intention being to write something of use to those who understand, it appears to me more proper to go to the real truth of the matter than to its imagination; and many have imagined republics and principalities which have never been seen or known to exist in reality.[23]

Hobbes was even more explicit about the central role a "new science" would play in the formation of his political insights. Galilean science was the model for his science of "politique bodies," and the insights he felt could be gained through this new manner of knowing might enable men to extricate themselves from the political miseries of their "naturall condition." The method of resolution and composition, applied so productively to the problems of physical dynamics, could be adapted to the mysteries of politics, Hobbes believed. In this way men could obtain knowledge of politics by reaching its first principles by resolution; by composition they could then proceed to construct a healthy and viable state.[24]

The Hegelian tradition in political theory, to take a final example, also received decisive inspiration from its understanding of the structure of human knowledge. The model of dialectical logic, a pattern of coming to know through reconciling antagonistic viewpoints, provided Hegel with the format for comprehending political and historical patterns. Or perhaps it was the other way around. In either case, the isomorphism between and the interpenetration of Hegel's epistemological and political concepts are readily apparent. It is not surprising, then, to find that contemporary left-wing Hegelian, Herbert Marcuse, devoting considerable attention to the ideological implications of epistemological assumptions. Reason, properly conceived, he suggests, is not politically neutral; it is instead a "subversive power," and the peculiar entrapment of modern man, he argues, rests in part on the systematic philosophical repression of this basic epistemological truth.[25]

This recurrent overlap of the problems of knowledge with the problems of political theory is not fortuitous. Government, as Madison wrote in the Federalist no. 51, is "the greatest of all reflections on human nature." The problems of political theory, then, tend to take the form of answers to the question What, given the nature of man, is the appropriate way to order political society? The nature of man, in turn, is very importantly defined by his knowing capabilities. Indeed, the very species designation for man, *Homo sapiens*, suggests that the distinctiveness of the human animal rests primarily in his capacity to know. Reflections on human nature, accordingly, must include some basic contentions about the nature and scope of human knowledge. Are political principles matters of knowledge rather than pure expressions of will? If so, who is capable of knowing these principles, and how? Questions like these can hardly be avoided by any thinker who reflects on the philosophical foundations of politics.

Moreover, in politics the reality principle tends to serve as a mediator between "is" and "ought." Those who can be entrusted to act wisely in political matters, that is, are those who have some grasp of the basic realities of political life. No one is likely to place confidence in the political wisdom of those who inhabit private dream-worlds or are prone to hallucinations. From Plato's "cave" to Marx's "trade-union consciousness" to Lippmann's "stereotypes," therefore, the problem of knowledge versus "false consciousness" has been an important one. Truth may not be a decisive political weapon, but it is rarely politically neutral. The urgent attention given to the media, the arts, and the agencies of education by governing elites (especially in totalitarian regimes) testifies to this fact.

Liberal political philosophy and political institutions have tended to place particular importance on the rational and cognitive dimension of politics and have thus taken as the ideal model of political activity the interaction of rational, if self-interested, men. Politics, for the liberal, is therefore seen as properly and fundamentally an enterprise of persuasion, and liberals have accordingly emphasized the development of institutional channels of political persuasion: universal education, free speech, elections, parliamentary debate. If all of these channels are properly developed, the liberal assumption has run, political outcomes will be satisfactory. This faith is reflected in John Stuart Mill's characterization of his father's ideas:

> So complete was my father's reliance on the influence of reason over the minds of mankind whenever it is allowed to reach them, that he felt as if all would be gained if the whole population were taught to read, if all sorts of opinions were allowed to be expressed to them by word and in writing, and if by means of the suffrage they could nominate a legislature to give effect to the opinions they adopted.[26]

Let us summarize the argument to this point. First, the models of epistemology and politics often overlap, and they do so for good reason. Second, the interaction between the image of reason and the ideals of politics has been central to liberal political theory. Third, liberalism as a political world view has lost much of its previous force and credibility. Finally, many of liberalism's problems have been generated, ironically, by the fruition of some its own hopes and by the embodiment of its own premises.

Against this background, the thesis of this book can now be stated. The image of reason that originated in close association with political liberalism and was generally believed to be its great ally has, I shall argue, become instead an indifferent ally at best and, at worst, an outright enemy of liberal aspirations. As the liberal model of reason has developed, it no longer provides sustenance for the hopes of liberalism. In some respects it actually helps to generate and to sustain some highly illiberal political ideas. There seems to be an inner logic to the modern conception of knowledge that makes it structurally disposed, despite humane intentions, to produce inhumane models of political relationships and political activities—models that are tyrannical, nihilistic, or paralytic.

This problem—in keeping with the widespread pattern of irony in the career of liberalism—is internally generated. That is, the problem is not that men (as has often been noted) do not in fact behave in a rational fashion; the problem is what happens when they *do* behave in accordance with the image of reason that arose with political liberalism or at any rate take it seriously as an accurate account of the nature and scope of human knowledge. Liberal reason has turned out to be not very liberal, after all, and perhaps not very rational, either.

The term "liberal reason" is somewhat ambiguous, and not all of its ambiguity can be removed; for I use it here as a "family" term, to borrow Wittgenstein's characterization. That is, "liberal reason" refers to a variety of largely overlapping conceptions of human reason held by the members of an intellectual tradition. Some facets of the ideal-type model of liberal reason are therefore open-ended or perhaps in dispute among its adherents. Nevertheless, the family resemblance is sufficiently strong to warrant the use of a general-category term.

The family members of "liberal reason" are Enlightenment reason, scientific reason, positive reason, and critical reason. The philosophic fathers of the tradition are Descartes and Locke. These two thinkers have their real differences, of course, and they represent different wings of the tradition; but they shared the belief that a new and powerful conception of reason had been developed and that it would have profound political consequences. Enlightenment figures who were devoted to working out some of these consequences could and did look to either man, or to both, for inspiration. They also referred to outstanding exemplars, such as Newton or Galileo, who had allegedly put the new epistemology into practice.

The development of the paradigm of liberal reason, however, has in fact been its dissolution. The new way of knowing was intrinsically incapable of fulfilling the expectations it had aroused. Now that this incapacity has become apparent, the original paradigm has become fragmented. The remaining fragments share some premises derived from their common source, but they differ in other important respects. Each of them, moreover, tends to have political implications that undermine the theoretical foundations of liberalism. As a result, the legacy of the original paradigm of liberal reason has been in some ways strikingly illiberal.

The two principal fragments that have survived the dissolution of the original model I have labeled the "technocratic" and the "value noncognitivist" models of reason. The technocratic conception retains the belief that scientific, critical reason can ascertain principles for governing political and moral action, but it has departed from the earlier conception of liberal reason by regarding access to these truths as limited to a relatively small elite who have mastered the tools of critical reason; the political models generated by this tradition have therefore tended to be authoritarian and tyrannical, in varying degrees. The value noncognitivist conception of reason has retained the idea that true knowledge is certain, precise, and "objective," but it too has departed from the earlier paradigm—by denying that political and moral principles are accessible to reason so conceived.

Neither of these legatees of the original model of liberal reason provides much philosophical support for the humanitarianism of the liberal tradition. The result has been a steady erosion of some of the tacit foundations of liberal government, an erosion that Walter Lippmann tried to describe two decades ago by speaking of the loss of the "tradition of civility."[27] Liberal ideals have lost their vitality, cut off from convincing philosophical roots. Liberalism has come full circle in one important respect, then: previously sustained by a happy confluence of is and ought, it now faces a deep conflict between the two. Originally the prevailing image of human reason seemed a bulwark; the remnants of it have become a threat.

The first two tasks of this study, then, are to substantiate the presence of this ironic pattern in the history of liberal reason and to explain some of the logical dynamics that produced it. This historical and philosophical analysis will then lead into a polemic, for a good case can be made, I believe, that the idea of liberal reason was radically flawed from the outset.

The political expectations the early liberals entertained were unrealistic because they were based, in part, on unrealistic premises about the possibilities of human knowledge. Their descendants have jettisoned some of the more unrealistic epistemological premises and have found themselves drawing some very illiberal political inferences from what was left. But the modifications made by the various heirs of liberal reason have not been radical enough. Our regnant models of knowledge still insist on some of the most fundamental tenets of critical reason, and these are equally unrealistic. We are still encapsulated in one version of what Dewey called the "quest for certainty."

Seeking quixotically to reach the unreachable goal of certain knowledge, modern man has plunged into a cycle of epistemological pride and despair. We imagine ourselves on the threshold of attaining perfect truth and are proud. The next moment we are forced to acknowledge the imperfections of our knowledge and are driven to despair. We demand to know all or we feel that we know nothing. We are Cartesian optimists one day and Humean skeptics the next.

This cycle of mania and depression finds expression in the political realm as well, and, if the preceding argument about the relationship between epistemology and political theory is sound, this parallelism is not by chance. One moment we see ourselves as the masters of nature, including human nature. Through our perfect knowledge of the world we can rebuild it and so escape the vicissitudes of history. Our science can save us. The next moment we are thrown into despair by the failure of our cherished political dreams. We complain that our knowledge is utterly useless to us in our political problems.

To extricate ourselves from this destructive cycle, we need to reexamine its roots. A more adequate assessment of the nature and extent of human reason can, I think, eliminate one important source of the political excesses of the modern West. Sober recognition of the limitations of the human mind should help discourage the political hubris produced by intoxication with the vision of Laplacean omniscience. At the same time, an appreciation of the genuine abilities of the human mind, measured by less than eschatological standards, may prevent the political paralysis brought on by moods of total skepticism.

Because the standard political categories "liberal," "conservative," and "radical" have lost a great deal of their capacity for discriminating political orientations, there may be some danger in characterizing this essay as one that seeks to help reground liberalism philosophically. What especially makes this characterization potentially misleading is the fact that some aspects of classical liberalism, such as its excessive individualism, are not worthy of resurrection. Nevertheless, liberalism has been a principal vehicle of political humanitarianism in the modern West, and it is this humanitarian idealism that cannot be allowed to wither away for want of an intellectual foundation. "When even the ideas of humanitarian liberalism are consigned by the intellectual to the same charnel house that holds the bones of capitalism and nationalism," writes Robert Nisbet, "his emancipation is complete. He is now free—in all his solitary misery."[28] Herein lies the dilemma of modern liberalism.

If they are to command the allegiance of thoughtful people, the classic ideals of humane liberalism need to become grounded once again in philosophical beliefs that themselves command respect; but before that task can be undertaken with reasonable hope of success, it is necessary to understand and to appreciate the nature and causes of the ironies that have attended the career of liberal reason.

2 "Simple Truths and Infallible Methods": The Emergence of Liberal Rationalism

Alfred North Whitehead once remarked that Western philosophy could be regarded as a series of footnotes to Plato. With even less hyperbole it could be said that modern Western philosophy has been a series of footnotes to Descartes and Locke.

Jean D'Alembert, in his *Preliminary Discourse* to the *Encyclopedia*, that magnificent mirror of Enlightenment hopes and self-understanding, sought to identify the principal sources of the *philosophes'* inspiration. Looking back to the intellectual insights and achievements that culminated in the encyclopedic project, D'Alembert concluded that Bacon, Descartes, Newton, and Locke "are the principal geniuses that the human mind ought to regard as its masters. Greece would have raised statues to them, even if she had been obliged to tear down those of a few conquerors to give them room."[1]

In strictly philosophic terms, moreover, Locke and Descartes were clearly the dominant contributors. Bacon contributed more in the way of mood and orientation than he did in the way of doctrine. He sensed and articulated the possibility that a new, this-worldly approach to human knowledge could produce great dividends and lead to the relief of man's estate. He emphasized experimental and "inductive" knowledge and urged men to analyze nature. He sought to reorganize and codify the various sciences. He clearly sounded some notes that were elaborated into dominant themes of the Enlightenment. Yet his own philosophical system, if it can be called that, was tentative, sketchy, and in many ways still entangled in Scholastic concepts that were soon to be rejected. Therefore, D'Alembert, even as he venerated his illustrious predecessor, felt obliged to reproach him gently for "having perhaps been too timid." "He seems," D'Alembert continued,

to have shown a little too much caution or deference to the dominant taste of his century in his frequent use of the terms of the
scholastics, sometimes even of scholastic principles.... After
having burst so many irons, this great man was still held by certain
chains which he could not, or dared not, break.[2]

Newton's impact on the world of the Enlightenment was, of
course, dramatic, pervasive, and profound. Pope's extravagant en-
comium (''God said, 'let Newton be'; and all was light'') reflected
the almost universal adulation of the great English scientist. Yet
Newton's phenomenal influence stemmed from what he did as a
scientific practitioner, not from what he said as a philosopher. He
was the great exemplar and embodiment of the scientific revolution,
not its authoritative metaphysician. He had staggered the minds of
his fellows and captured the public imagination by his discovery of
the calculus, by his demonstration of the utility of mathematical
methods in the natural sciences, and, above all, by his formulation of
the law of gravitation. When it came to his more philosophical
speculations, his writings on natural theology and the like, upon
which he devoted a great deal of attention and concern, his influence
was greatly circumscribed. Indeed, D'Alembert found it necessary
to defend Newton rather obliquely against the charge that his philosophical accounts of his discoveries relied on notions of ''occult
qualities''; and when he considered Newton's ''metaphysics''
D'Alembert speculated that Newton himself ''was somewhat dissatisfied with the progress he had made in metaphysics,'' concluding
that, ''since he has not caused any revolution here, we will abstain
from considering him from the standpoint of this subject.''[3]

Bacon's principal role was that of a forerunner, a kindred spirit,
then. And Newton was the preeminent practitioner, the genius who
demonstrated the incomparable utility and power of the new modes
of inquiry. Locke and Descartes, the remaining two members of
D'Alembert's pantheon, remain as the principal philosophical
sources of Enlightenment rationalism.

The pervasive influence of Locke has, of course, long been emphasized by students of the Enlightenment, and key Enlightenment
figures were themselves quick to acknowledge their indebtedness to
him. D'Alembert credited Locke with having ''created metaphysics,
almost as Newton had created physics.''[4] Condillac and Helvetius
saw themselves as refining and purifying Locke's essential insights.
And Voltaire paid homage to Locke as the wisest, most methodical,
and most exact mind imaginable.[5]

Recent scholars have tended to concur. Paul Hazard, for example,
says of Locke: ''I do not know if there has ever been a dealer in
ideas who, more unmistakably than he, has shaped his century. He

went forth from the schools, universities, the learned circles, the academies, to reach the profane; he became one of the indispensable accessories of the intellectual mode."[6] And Ernst Cassirer has observed that "on all questions of psychology and the theory of knowledge Locke's authority remained practically unchallenged throughout the first half of the eighteenth century."[7]

The other serious claimant to the title of principal philosopher behind Enlightenment rationalism is Descartes. Aram Vartanian, in his excellent study *Diderot and Descartes,* argues that Locke's influence has been overstated while that of Descartes has been correspondingly underestimated. "English philosophy," he argues, "was at best secondary to Cartesian precept in prompting and molding a major segment of Enlightenment thought."[8] The impact of Cartesianism on the Enlightenment is generally obscured because it was downplayed by the *philosophes* themselves. And it was downplayed by the *philosophes* because they wished to distinguish their ideas from what might be termed the "right-wing" Cartesianism of such figures as Malebranche and Bossuet. Malebranche had seized on the features of Descartes's thought—such as his doctrine of innate ideas and his dualism—that the *philosophes* found most objectionable; moreover, he sought, on the basis of these features, to assimilate Cartesianism to the position of the Church. For tactical reasons, then, the *philosophes* were forced to minimize their indebtedness to Descartes, since "Cartesianism" had come to signify a mixture of idealism and fideism that they found repugnant. Rather than contest with the idealists for the role of Descartes's legitimate heirs, these naturalistic Enlightenment rationalists simply styled themselves Lockeans. They could thus retain the aspects of Cartesian thought they found congenial by placing them within the sensationalist and "inductivist" epistemological matrix taken from Locke.[9] From the point of view of the *philosophes* this strategy made good sense. From the point of view of intellectual history, Vartanian insists, the result has been to obscure the extent of Cartesian influence on Enlightenment rationalism.

The crucial point for present purposes is the assimilability of key Lockean and Cartesian ideas about the nature and extent of human cognition. Despite their differences, the British "empiricist" and the French "rationalist" overlap in some of their central beliefs in such a way that it becomes difficult to determine which of them contributed the most to the Enlightenment conception of reason. The rationalism of the *philosophes* actually represented a coalescence of "left-wing" Cartesianism with "left-wing" Lockeanism. "Right-wing" Cartesianism, represented by Malebranche, was rejected, as was "right-wing" Lockeanism, represented by Berkeley. Locke, after all, had his own idealistic and skeptical aspects, which Berkeley had noted and developed; but this side of Locke, like the innatism and deductivism of Descartes, was treated by the Enlightenment mainstream as so much chaff to be separated from the wheat.

Differences exist, of course, between Locke's empiricism and Descartes's rationalism. These differences are important in some areas, and they should not be lost sight of. Yet, considering the whole of their conceptions of human knowledge, and ignoring those parts of their thought that the succeeding generation tended to regard as idiosyncratic, the overlap between their ideas is profound, extensive, and vitally significant. Locke's critique of the Cartesian belief in innate ideas, a critique that generally won out in the Enlightenment, was essentially an internecine battle within a school, not warfare between fundamentally opposed camps. In fact, despite Locke's hammering away at the doctrine of innate ideas in the *Essay,* the actual differences between him and Descartes, even on this issue, are probably much less than is commonly supposed.[10] Descartes allowed that he would be perfectly happy to accept the phrase "innate faculty" as conveying his idea. He once said, for example, that he "never said or thought that the mind has ideas that are innate, in any other sense than that it has a faculty for thinking such ideas."[11] Locke's reflective account of his own position in the Preface to the second edition of the *Essay* is not very different.

> That there are certain propositions which, though the soul from the beginning, when a man is born, does not know, yet, by assistance from the outward senses, and the help of some previous cultivation, it may afterwards come either self-evidently, or with a demonstrable necessity, to know the truth of, is no more than what I have affirmed in my First Book.[12]

Therefore, even this most celebrated difference between Descartes and Locke may be more semantic than real.

The other difference often cited between Lockean and Cartesian epistemology—the contrast between inductive experimentalism and deductive rationalism—is likewise generally exaggerated. As the Vienna Circle has demonstrated in our own century, it is possible to bring these two strands together into a single epistemological model. The "logical" side of logical empiricism, with its formalistic emphasis on hypothetico-deductive explanation, is squarely in the tradition of Cartesian rationalism, while the "empirical" side falls clearly within the tradition of British empiricism. Such a fusion of rationalism and empiricism would probably have come as no surprise to

Descartes himself. For, as Vartanian observes, Descartes had seen no fundamental incompatibility between his procedural recommendations and those of Bacon. "From the standpoint of Cartesian thought," he continues, "there was no conflict between experimentalism and rationalism."[13]

Locke himself was perfectly willing to acknowledge his intellectual debt to Descartes. Lady Masham, who was Cudworth's daughter, reported that Locke had told her that "the first books . . . which gave him a relish of philosophical things were those of Descartes."[14] Locke's contemporaries, moreover, were sensitive to the deep affinity between Locke's thought and that of his French predecessor. In fact, Locke was even accused by some of simply plagiarizing Cartesian ideas. James Tyrrell wrote to Locke that "a friend told me the other day that he had it from one who pretends to be a great Judge of bookes; that you had taken all that was good in it; from Descartes (sic) diverse modern french Authours, not only as to the notions but the manner of connection of them."[15]

The undeniable differences between the empiricist and the rationalist orientations, therefore, should not divert us from the even larger areas of agreement between them in their basic view of the nature and capacities of human understanding. Accounts of the history of modern philosophy tend to focus on the persistent antinomies of the tradition: materialism/idealism, dualism/monism, empiricism/rationalism. But undergirding these debates, indeed generating them, is a common core of ideas that constitutes the fundamental paradigm or disciplinary matrix of the critical tradition in philosophy, and it is this fundamental paradigm that we have in mind when we refer to "liberal reason."

The principal tenets that, taken together, compose this fundamental paradigm of liberal reason can be stated relatively concisely, although each of them will receive further elaboration in the pages that follow. These central contentions are:

1. The assumptions and methods of the previously dominant Aristotelian-Scholastic tradition are mistaken and must be fundamentally revised or supplanted before genuine "natural philosophy" can be possible.
2. The human understanding, guided by the "natural light" of reason, can be and should be autonomous. Moreover, it constitutes the norm and the means by reference to which all else is to be measured.
3. It is possible and necessary to begin the search for knowledge with a clean slate.
4. It is possible and necessary to base knowledge claims on a clear and distinct, indubitable, self-evident foundation.

5. This foundation is to be composed of simple, unambiguous ideas or perceptions.
6. The appropriate formal standards for all human knowledge are those of the mathematical modes of inquiry.
7. The key to the progress of human knowledge is the development and pursuit of explicit rules of method.
8. The entire body of valid human knowledge is a unity, both in method and in substance.
9. Therefore, human knowledge may be made almost wholly accessible to all men, provided only that they not be abnormally defective in their basic faculties.
10. Genuine knowledge is in some sense certain, ''verifiable,'' and capable of being made wholly explicit.
11. Knowledge is power, and the increase of knowledge therefore holds the key to human progress.

All attempts to generalize about a broad school or tradition of thought, of course, are going to be simplified and will not do full justice to the many exceptions that exist. The above sketch is by no means exempt from this disability, and that caveat needs to be entered at the outset. Many thinkers who subscribed to the general outlook in question, for example, dissented on specific issues. However, we are forced to generalize in exploring the historical sources of our own sensibility if our intellectual road map is not to vanish in a welter of detail. Despite exceptions, then, the above sketch provides a reasonably accurate outline of a broad movement of thought. Moreover, the beliefs mapped out were not confined to the relatively few serious thinkers of the tradition but instead became rather widely disseminated among the generally literate public. In this popularized format, still deeply entrenched in the vulgar conception of science, the nuances of the tradition become less important.

The Autopsy of Scholasticism

The common ''negative'' point of departure for the exponents of liberal rationalism was their vehement rejection of the Scholastic tradition. In their view, Scholasticism had contributed little or nothing to human knowledge. If anything, the disputations of the schools, they felt, had been an obstacle to a proper understanding of the world. The Scholastic divines had obscured and confused human inquiry by providing fraudulent or empty answers to misconceived questions. When Descartes pondered the results of Scholastic philosophy, he resorted to an analogy similar to that used by Plato centuries earlier to characterize those who were devoid of reason's light. "They seem to me," he said, "to resemble a blind man who, in order to fight without disadvantage with an opponent who sees, would have him descend to the bottom of a very dark cave."[16] He went on to say that he had

> never observed that previously unknown truth has been discovered by way of the disputations practiced in the Schools.... The very obscurity of the distinctions and principles on which they rely is precisely what enables them to speak with as much confidence as if they had understanding of them, enabling them to hold to them even in the face of the most subtle and skillful opponents—there being no possibility of their being enlightened and thereby refuted.[17]

Hobbes blamed Aristotle himself for the deficiencies of Scholasticism. He fulminated that "scarce anything can be more absurdly said in naturall Philosophy, than that which now is called Aristotle's *Metaphysiques;* nor more repugnant to Government, than much of that hee hath said in his *Politiques;* nor more ignorantly, than a great deal of his *Ethiques*."[18] Descartes and Locke, especially the latter, were kinder toward Aristotle, blaming his followers for the problems they perceived.[19] Wherever the fault lay, however, all of the key seventeenth-century thinkers viewed the Scholastic mode of inquiry as a huge stumbling block to the advance of knowledge. There was, they felt, no health at all in the regnant philosophical tradition of their day. It had to be utterly displaced and a new beginning made. Only in this way could mankind be led out of the cave. As Descartes wrote to one of his acquaintances in 1619, "I propose to give the public . . . an entirely new science . . . by the aid of which I expect to be able to dissipate darkness however dense."[20]

The most glaring incapacities of the Scholastic tradition, of course, were to be found in the very area that concerned the philosophical revolutionaries most directly, namely, "natural philosophy." The natural philosophy of the Schools, Hobbes averred, "was rather a dream than science."[21] "In many occasions," he complained, "they put for cause of Naturall events, their own Ignorance; but disguised in other words." And "for Physiques, that is, the knowledge of the subordinate, and secundary causes of naturall events; they render none at all, but empty words."[22] Locke quite agreed. When he spoke, in his famous image of the "under-labourer," of "clearing the ground a little, and removing some of the rubbish that lies in the way to knowledge,"[23] it was these pseudo-explanations of Scholasticism that made up the "rubbish."

Of particular importance was the characteristic seventeenth-century analysis of the reasons for these explanatory failures of

Scholasticism. Why had so much "rubbish" been produced? What fundamental mistakes had been made to induce such extensive non-sense, which masqueraded as higher learning? What forces were at work to sustain and encourage such "vain philosophy"? The answers to these questions were crucial, for they were to provide the basis for proposed solutions. The diagnosis of the intellectual disease, in other words, indicated the kinds of therapeutic measures that were to be recommended. And these therapeutic measures in turn constituted the core of the epistemological program, and a significant part of the political program, of the Enlightenment.

A major reason that Scholastic natural philosophy was "rather a dream than science" in the eyes of such figures as Hobbes and Descartes was its faulty theory of motion, inherited from Aristotle. The model of motion as the "actualization of potentiality," which shaped the entire Aristotelian cosmology, was the immediate culprit. The immediate task, then, was to reformulate the theory of motion by driving formal and final causes from the realm of legitimate explanation. Motion, following the lead of Galileo, who was in Hobbes's view "the first that opened to us the gate of natural philosophy universal,"[24] was now to be understood inertially, and the Aristotelian complex of final, formal, efficient, and material causes was to be reduced to the latter two. These fundamental conceptual changes constituted an intellectual revolution of stunning proportions and profound ramifications. The whole cosmology of Aristotelianism and Scholasticism had depended on these concepts of change and causality, which were now to be banished from the realm of significant discourse. Our understanding of the world would never be the same.[25]

The diagnosis of the failure of Scholasticism went even deeper, however. The faulty notions of change and causality were the immediate substantive source of the problem. But what more general failures lay behind them? Men could not have been so consistently mistaken for so long on such crucial questions unless their whole approach to knowledge was somehow badly flawed. The errors of Scholastic cosmology were therefore taken as a clear manifestation of even more fundamental procedural failures. Persistent and uncorrected substantive error, in other words, betokened a profound methodological failure. The revolution in cosmology suggested the need for a radically refashioned epistemology.

The attempt to isolate and identify the underlying epistemological defects that had permitted the production and perpetuation of "vain philosophy" focused on four principal alleged sources of error. These sources were partly political, partly linguistic, partly methodological. First, it was held, the power of reason had been inhibited and enchained by forces whose self-interest lay in propagating superstition and blind credulity. Second, the powers of the mind were held to have been enchanted and entrapped by the spell of words, by empty verbiage. Third, human inquiry was easily led astray, it was held, for want of clear rules of method. Finally, it was contended that previous inquiries into the nature of things had been subverted by the lack of any firm foundations for knowledge. Each of these perceived sources of error in turn prompted specific recommendations and projects to remedy the situation and to prevent future recurrences of philosophical distemper.

The Sociology of Error

The first strand of the Enlightenment's critical analysis of past failures was a sociology of error. Reason had been subjugated by authority. Philosophical error had been so tenacious because men relied on what "authorities" had said rather than on their own native intellectual powers. They had gone to texts for enlightenment and had been poorly served. Instead they should have gone to the things themselves, to "nature," for illumination. Condorcet analyzed the problem this way: "the authority of men was everywhere substituted for the authority of reason. Books were everywhere studied more than nature, and the opinions of the ancients instead of the phenomena of the universe."[26] And Locke, in his analysis "of wrong assent, or error" in Book Four of the *Essay,* spoke of men who are "cooped in close by the laws of their countries, and the strict guards of those whose interest it is to keep them ignorant, lest, knowing more, they should believe the less in them."[27]

In part, this corruption of human inquiry was seen as resulting simply from methodological error. Men had the wrong idea about the proper sources of knowledge. However, as Locke's remark about "those whose interest it is to keep them ignorant" suggests, this methodological failure was seen to be encouraged and enforced by political power. Specifically, the church and the political establishment were indicted as institutional bulwarks of the epistemological failure. They had a vested interest in thwarting unfettered rational inquiry, as the liberals alleged with some justification. The church hierarchy was devoted to the preservation of the faith and to the preservation of their own social privileges. Accordingly, they encouraged fidelity to established doctrine and counseled respect for religious authority, and they discouraged as impiety and as a threat to their position all attempts to emancipate rational analysis from accepted theological premises. The political authorities, with their vested interest in the status quo, also were threatened by the subversive possibilities of unfettered critical reason. Accordingly, they had their own interest in circumscribing the range of reason and in defending tradition and custom as sufficient sanction for political arrangements. Condorcet complained that

> Reason was never called upon to decide those matters where there was any real conflict of interests; religion, far from recognizing the authority of reason, claimed to overrule it and glorified in its humiliation; and politics, in deciding what was just, always respected whatever was consecrated by habit, ancient customs, and convention.[28]

One of the important prescriptive implications of this diagnosis, then, was the identification of significant political targets. Freedom of the mind, which was a sine qua non of political freedom, could not be attained until institutionalized constraints upon it were overthrown. As long as clerics and monarchs retained their power to interdict the natural directions of rational inquiry, little progress could be expected: man would never truly be free ''until the last king had been strangled with the entrails of the last priest.'' The liberals' sociology of error introduced a profound political dimension into the program of modern rationalism right at the outset.

It should be noted parenthetically that the political uses and implications of the new rationalism could assume significantly different forms in different political contexts. In eighteenth-century France, political rationalism tended to be radical, since religious dogmatism was implicated with the political establishment. In seventeenth-century England, on the other hand, the principal devotees of revelation and immediate inspiration as the source of political guidance tended to be the radical sectarians. In the hands of both Locke and Hobbes, then, the counsels of rationalism could be levied against the presumed dangers of ''enthusiasm'' in politics. In a similar fashion, significantly different political uses were later to be made of utilitarianism on the opposite sides of the Channel.

Apart from identifying entrenched political obstacles to intellectual progress, the analysis of the previous repression of reason eventuated in admonitions and exhortations to give reason the autonomy it deserved. The ''natural light'' of reason was held to be competent to adjudicate all claims. In Hegel's apt phrase, the world was to be ''stood upon its head.'' As Engels characterized the Enlightenment demands, everything had to ''justify its existence before the judgment seat of reason or give up existence. Reason became the sole measure of everything.''[29] Once the forces and preconceptions that had restricted the free play of the human mind were removed, a new and uncorrupted order, both intellectual and political, could be erected. The goal was clear: "to hasten to build the edifice of reason on the ruins of opinion."[30] To attain this end, men had to overcome their unwarranted intellectual timidity. Intimidated for too long by those who deprecated the capacities of the unaided human intellect, men had to will to be free. Kant's analysis of the Enlightenment message was therefore focused on the need for courage and daring.

Enlightenment is man's exodus from his self-incurred tutelage. Tutelage is the inability to use one's understanding without the guidance of another person. This tutelage is self-incurred if its cause lies not in any weakness of the understanding, but in indecision and lack of courage to use the mind without the guidance of another. Dare to know! Have the courage to use your own understanding; this is the motto of the Enlightenment.[31]

Breaking the "Spell of Words"

A crucial role in the entrapment of human reason, as the epistemological revolutionaries saw it, had been played by what they called "the spell of words." Accordingly, they devoted considerable attention to analyzing the nature of this verbal entrapment and to indicating means of escape from it.

Decadent Scholasticism had indeed reached the point where much of what purported to be "explanation" was composed of empty verbalizing. Misled by the Aristotelian notion of formal and final "causes," many of the Scholastics had offered the kind of answers satirized by Molière, who depicted a doctoral candidate receiving praise for offering "dormative properties" as the answer to "Why does opium induce sleep?" The epistemological revolutionaries of the seventeenth century heaped scorn on this kind of tautological "explanation," and the focus of their criticism was on language. The human mind had been misled and corrupted by words without meaning. Locke devoted the Third Book of his *Essay* to an examination of language and its abuses. He spoke of problems caused by words that "remain empty sounds, with little or no signification, amongst those who think it enough to have them often in their mouths, as the distinguishing characters of their Church or School, without much troubling their heads to examine what are the precise ideas they stand for."[32] Hobbes mocked the "empty words" of the Scholastics relentlessly. "The Writings of the Schoole-Divines," he wrote, "are nothing else for the most part, but insignificant Traines of strange and barbarous words."[33]

This extraordinary and malignant capacity that words apparently had to deceive mankind led these thinkers to use metaphors of bewitchment and entrapment. Words had cast a "spell." They had "entranced" men. They had "bewitched" the human intelligence.

Hobbes relied on metaphors of entanglement, warning that men had become "entangled in words, as a bird in lime-twiggs; the more he struggles, the more belimed."[34] And he conjured an image of man trapped by language that parallels the more recent Wittgensteinian image of the "fly in the fly-bottle." "The errours of Definitions multiply themselves," he wrote; and men

> at last finding the errour visible, and not mistrusting their first grounds, know not which way to cleere themselves; but spend time in fluttering over their bookes; as birds that entring by the chimney, and finding themselves inclosed in a chamber, flutter at the false light of a glasse window, for want of wit to consider which way they came in.[35]

Like Wittgenstein, and for similar reasons, the proponents of the new philosophy envisioned a "therapeutic" function for their work. They hoped to rescue men from their linguistic entanglements, to release them from their verbal entrancement. In fact, the *philosophes* tended to be more optimistic than Wittgenstein on this score. For Wittgenstein the therapeutic enterprise is a continuous one. Language is forever "going on a holiday" and thereby creating confusion. The fly may be led out of one fly-bottle, but he can be expected to fly shortly into another. In contrast, the Enlightenment thinkers hoped for a final and decisive cure. Some were more tentative in their expectations, to be sure. Locke, for example, acknowledged "the imperfection that is naturally in language."[36] But most enthusiasts of the new philosophy were confident of total success. With their new insight, philosophers could free men from the spell of words as a hypnotist releases his subjects from their trance. A snap of the fingers would dispel this form of human bondage forever. The bad magic of those who used insignificant speech to keep other men under control would be destroyed. Helvetius looked forward to the prospect with delight.

> Let precise ideas be annexed to each expression, and the school divine, who by the magic of words, has thrown the world into confusion, will be a magician without power. The talisman, in the possession of which his ability consisted, will be broken. Then all those fools, who under the name of metaphysicians, have for so long a time wandered in the land of chimeras, and who, on bladders blown up by wind, traverse in every direction, all the depths of infinity, will no longer say that they see what they see not, and know what they know not; they will no longer impose on mankind.[37]

What was the basis for this confident expectation of deliverance from verbal confusion? The hope was based principally on the striking intellectual breakthroughs produced by the application of mathematical methods and modes of analysis to thitherto intractable problems. The discoveries of scientists such as Galileo, Kepler, and Newton were produced by way of numbers rather than words. Mathematics and geometry produced precision, clarity, and certainty and thereby became not only the ideal to which all sciences should approach but the principal means for reaching it. The entire age was, as Aubrey wrote of Hobbes, "in love with geometry."[38]

A few voices warned against expecting too much from mathematicizing modes of inquiry. D'Alembert wrote of the mathematical sciences that

> their nature and their number should not overawe us. It is principally to the simplicity of their object that they owe their certitude . . . . Only those [sciences] that deal with the calculation of magnitudes and with the general properties of extension . . . can be regarded as stamped by the seal of evidence.[39]

On the whole, however, these cautionary voices went unheeded. (In some ways this was probably fortunate. Diderot's prediction in *The Interpretation of Nature* that the fruitfulness of mathematics in natural philosophy was approaching its end was seriously in error.) And the ambiguities involved in "mathematicizing" inquiry were given little serious attention. For the most part, mathematics was regarded as the appropriate norm for all knowledge and as a method that admitted of practically universal extension. Testimony on behalf of this view can be found in the writings of most of the major intellectual figures of the seventeenth and eighteenth centuries.

Hobbes spoke of geometry as "the Mother of all Naturall Science,"[40] and he conceived of reason as essentially a kind of mathematical reckoning. "In what matter soever there is place for addition and subtraction, there is also place for Reason; and where these have no place, there Reason has nothing at all to do."[41]

The normative status of mathematicizing forms of inquiry was similarly fundamental, profound, and pervasive in Descartes. The methods and standards of mathematics served him throughout as the model to which all inquiry should conform. By abstracting out the formal patterns of this approach to knowledge from their specific embodiment in the mathematical disciplines he hoped to make them universally applicable. His goal was to develop a "universal mathematics," one that would be a "general science which explains all that can be inquired into respecting order and measure, without application to any one special subject matter."[42] And he counseled that "in our search for the direct road to truth we should not occupy ourselves with any object about which we are unable to have a certitude equal to that of arithmetical and geometrical demonstrations."[43]

The role of mathematics as the paradigm case of knowledge is not as stark in Locke's epistemology. Nevertheless, he also exhibited a strong tendency to conceptualize knowledge by reference to the mathematical sciences. A student of Locke's epistemology has written that the

> perfect intellectual transparency, which appeared to him [Locke] to be possessed both by the primary assumptions of these sciences and by their demonstrations, constituted his ideal of knowledge, and formed the standard by which he tested the worth of all our intellectual possessions. His view of knowledge, like that of Descartes, is throughout dominated by his conception of the mathematical sciences, the revival and development of which constituted the most striking intellectual achievement of the age in which he lived.[44]

Spinoza and Condillac were of like mind. They would have embraced the words of Fontenelle, who wrote, in *On the Usefulness of Mathematics and Physics:*

> The geometric spirit is not so exclusively bound to geometry that it could not be separated from it and applied to other fields. A work on ethics, politics, criticism, or even eloquence, other things being equal, is merely so much more beautiful and perfect if it is written in the geometric spirit.[45]

Cassirer concludes that this belief was the generally accepted view in the Enlightenment. Despite the protestations of occasional dissenters like Pascal, "the eighteenth century grapples with this problem and decides that, as long as it is understood as the spirit of pure analysis, the 'geometric spirit' is absolutely unlimited and by no means bound to any particular field of knowledge."[46]

This widespread acceptance of mathematics as the appropriate formal norm for all areas of knowledge had several significant corollaries. First, it generated a quest for a universal language, or at least for language that would approach the transparency and precision of numbers. Second, the idea of an allegedly universally applicable model of inquiry led to the idea of a unified science. Third, the acceptance of the mathematical norm began to bring into disrepute any discipline that seemed clearly incapable of approximating the geometric ideal.

The hopeful quest for a universal perfected language was to be the means of escape from the abuse of words and the insignificant speech that had undone Scholasticism. Language could no longer ensnare and mislead if it could be reformulated into a kind of verbal algebra. The first requirement would be the establishment of clear and unambiguous definitions, which could serve as axioms. This step was crucial. The success of geometry, as Hobbes expressed it, was due precisely to its ability to affix such clear meanings to its basic terms:

> In Geometry, (which is the onely Science that it hath pleased God hitherto to bestow on mankind,) men begin at settling the significations of their words; which settling of significations, they call Definitions; and place them in the beginning of their reckoning.[47]

Once these names were properly affixed, the rest of the language could be built up, as Hobbes put it, by "reckoning"—that is, by the simple use of accurate deductive logic. By eliminating the confusion and obscurity induced by faulty, vague, or meaningless definitions, a purified language of science could be constructed. Writing to Mersenne, Descartes expressed this hope:

> If someone were to explain correctly what are the simple ideas in the human imagination out of which all human thoughts are compounded, and if his explanation were generally received, I would dare to hope for a universal language very easy to learn, speak, and to write. The greatest advantage of such a language would be the assistance it would give to men's judgment, representing matters so clearly that it would be almost impossible to go wrong. As it is, almost all our words have confused meanings, and men's minds are so accustomed to them that there is hardly anything which they can perfectly understand. I think it is possible to invent such a language and to discover the science on which it depends.[48]

For practical reasons, however, he doubted that such a language would ever come into actual use.

In some versions there would be more than one perfect language. Condillac, for example, believed that it was too much to hope for a single ideal language, but he trusted that each language might be perfected in itself. Leibniz, like Descartes, was more utopian. He envisioned a single ideal language for all the sciences. But whatever differences in detail there were among the several accounts, a common hope united them: that language might become perfected, free from ambiguity and error, by following the lead of mathematics. The "spell" of words would be broken, and the increase of knowledge assured, by the geometricization of language.

The correlative hope was that the sciences might themselves become unified. If all knowledge was essentially one, if all valid inquiry was a form of mathematical analysis, then "science" should be a single mansion. The various pursuits of the mind should be capable of synthesis within a common framework. Bacon had already articulated this hope for the development of a "universal science" in his *Advancement of Learning*. Descartes ardently embraced the same hope, which undergirded his whole epistemological program. Men are "indeed deceived," he admonished, when they study one science independently of the others. They should

> bear in mind that all the sciences are so closely interconnected that it is much easier to study them together than to isolate one from the others. If, therefore, anyone genuinely desires to investigate the truth of things, he should not select some one particular science; all of them stand together and are interdependent.[49]

The enterprise of the French Encyclopedists, of course, was built upon and was the preeminent attempt to embody the "postulate of unity" (Cassirer's term). "The universe," wrote D'Alembert in the *Preliminary Discourse,* "if we may be permitted to say so, would only be one fact and one great truth for whoever knew how to embrace it from a single point of view."[50] Sustained by this conviction as to the fundamental unity of all phenomena, the attempt to comprehend all knowledge within a single framework gathered force. What remained ambiguous in most cases was the exact nature of this unity. And the ambiguity was important. Did the unity consist simply in the common amenability of all phenomena to human reason? Or did it involve the postulation of a more radical ontological unity in all phenomena—i.e., metaphysical monism? Figures such as D'Holbach, Lamettrie, and Helvetius willingly embraced the latter, more radical, form of the postulate of unity. Others drew back from what they perceived as the consequences of taking this step. This intellectual tension within the Enlightenment, it is probably safe to say, has been a persistent one in Western philosophy, and it will reappear in various guises during the course of our study of the political ironies of liberal rationalism.

A third consequence of the "geometric spirit" was the denigration of all aspects of the human intellect and all products of the human mind that resisted assimilation to quasi-mathematical form. The principal obstacle to intellectual progress, as the Enlightenment generally saw it, was not ignorance so much as prejudice and superstition masquerading as knowledge. Mere ignorance was only a void that could easily be filled. Prejudice was a positive hindrance that had to be dispelled.[51] The odyssey of human reason was depicted by the Enlightenment as a tale of the mind's progressive deliverance from fraudulent modes of perceiving the world. Included among these discarded, outmoded forms of "knowledge" were not only outright superstition and prejudice, but myth, metaphysics, theology, and poetry—all forms of discourse that could neither assume the form nor provide the clarity of mathematics. The story, as it was chronicled by Turgot, Comte, Condorcet, and others, was one of the mind's purification by evolution toward a more and more precise and unambiguous—hence abstract—form of reason. Modes of discourse that could not pass muster as "clear and distinct" were not only not of value; they were actually enemies of Enlightenment and had to be cast aside.

The role of imagination in human knowing became suspect. Some of the better minds of the time fully appreciated the value of imagination and warned against its deprecation. Descartes, for example, was quite willing to acknowledge an affinity between poetic imagination and scientific intuition, and Diderot concurred heartily. "Imagination," he said, "is the quality without which one is neither a poet, a philosopher, a wit, a rational being, nor a man."[52] On the whole, however, this kind of appreciation of the imagination was on the losing side of the epistemological debate. The dominant tendency was to perceive imagination as simply a primitive and inferior form of cognition, one that might have been useful earlier but that could now be superseded by more reliable ways of knowing. As Condillac saw it, the empire of the imagination ended when the age of analysis began. The products of the imagination had no truth-value.[53] At best, they had ornamental value; at worst, they were misleading impediments to knowledge. As the Abbé Trublet wrote in 1735,

> the more perfect the reasoning faculty becomes, the more will judgment take precedence over imagination, and the less, in consequence, will poets be held in honor. The earliest writers, we are told, were poets. That I can well believe; they could not very well have been anything else. But the latest will be philosophers.[54]

The poetic and the imaginative modes of thought were suitable for immature minds, but they were intrinsically "fantastical," incapable of being "clarified" and scourged of the mysterious and the ambiguous. Hence, they did not count as knowledge, and men were generally counseled to avoid their seductions. Jean LeClerc warned his readers in 1699 that,

> when you begin reading a piece of poetry, remember you are reading the work of a purveyor of lies, whose aim it is to feed us on chimeras, or on truths so twisted and distorted that we are hard put to it to disentangle fact from fiction.[55]

Hume concurred. Poets, he averred, are "liars by profession."[56]

Simple Ideas and Secure Foundations

The next focus of the seventeenth century's diagnosis of Scholasticism's failure was on the problem of secure foundations. (The first mistake of Scholasticism was its reliance on the dictates of authority rather than the autonomous power of reason; its second error was its entrapment in meaningless verbiage.)

If a system of knowledge is to be stable and trustworthy, it must be well grounded. It must, the rationalists believed, rest on something solid. And, continued the analysis, this sure foundation was precisely what was lacking in previous philosophy. The works of the ancient moralists, Descartes complained, were "palaces arrogantly magnificent, with no better foundations than sand and soft shifting ground." The other sciences were no better off, since they took their principles from philosophy. So, concluded Descartes, the confusions, uncertainties, and endless argumentation within the regnant tradition should have come as no surprise. "Nothing solid can have been built on foundations so unstable."[57]

The search for firm foundations was the heart of the new rationalism's methodological program. Descartes's methodological radicalism was intended to be destructive, but only to a point. He wished to tear down the network of inherited beliefs and opinions, but only because it was already in danger of falling.[58] Like most revolutionaries, he believed that the ultimate outcome of his efforts would be the establishment of a new and better order of things— perhaps even an order that would endure forever. What was true could survive his critical onslaught, he reasoned. Only the jerry-built tenements of pseudo-knowledge would come tumbling down.

Cartesian doubt, then, was not pyrrhonic. He did not expect it to end in skepticism, cynicism, or agnosticism. In a letter written in 1638 he said: "Although the Pyrrhonians reached no certain conclusions from their doubts, it does not follow that no one can."[59] The acids of his critique, he believed, would eat away a great deal, but whatever survived would serve as the solid and trustworthy foundation for his "marvelous science."[60] He had not undertaken his program of systematic doubt in order to emulate the skeptics, "who doubt only for doubting's sake and profess to be always noncommittal; on the contrary, my purpose was solely to find ground of assurance, casting aside the loose earth and sand, that I might get down to rock and clay."[61]

Locke, in his characteristically more modest language, was expressing a similar hope and intent when he described his own methodological program. He styled himself a humble "under-labourer" rather than a dramatic revolutionary, but his goal was basically the same as Descartes's. If he could only remove the "rubbish" that obscured the view, he could help mankind perceive the solid landmarks needed to mark the way of intellectual progress.

In both the rationalist and the empiricist versions of the methodological program, moreover, the *warrant* of reliable foundations of knowledge was the same. Clear and distinct ideas could be taken as self-evident truths. These perceptions that carry the warrant of self-evidence are the "certain seeds of truth with which our souls are naturally endowed."[62] While there may be "some difficulty in rightly determining which [ideas] are those we apprehend distinctly," Descartes concluded, it could be taken "as being a general rule, that the things we apprehend very clearly and distinctly are true."[63] These truths are vouchsafed to us by the "natural light" of our mind, which has been given us by God or by nature. In like fashion, Locke wrote that this

> light, true light in the mind, is or can be nothing else but the evidence of the truth of any proposition; and if it be not a self-evident proposition, all the light it has, or can have, is from the clearness and validity of those proofs upon which it is received.[64]

What, then, were these clear and distinct ideas? What substantive notions could serve as the valid starting point of knowledge? Here the Cartesian answer differed from that offered by Locke and his empiricist followers. For Descartes, of course, the famous *cogito* served as the fundamental truth that was beyond doubt: "We have finally to conclude that this declaration, *Ego sum, ego existo,* is necessarily true every time I propound it or mentally apprehend it."[65] From there, Descartes believed, we could move to the idea of God and His existence: "It is at least as certain that God, who is this Perfect Being, is or exists, as any demonstration of geometry can possibly be."[66] Thence we could proceed to certain principles of the object world, *res extensa:* "And now that I know Him, I have the means of acquiring a perfect knowledge of innumerable things, not only in respect of God Himself and other intelligible things, but also in respect of that corporeal nature which is the object of pure mathematics."[67]

This Cartesian specification of the content of our clear and distinct ideas did not enter the mainstream of Enlightenment thought. His answer seemed too Catholic, too spiritualist, too a priori. It contained too much residue from the past. It was because Locke's orientation at this crucial juncture was deemed superior to that of Descartes that figures such as Diderot, Condillac, Helvetius, and Voltaire styled themselves Lockeans.

Locke shifted the emphasis from the a priori to the a posteriori, from what is given to the understanding to what is found in experience. To be sure, he had his own version of the *cogito.* We know our own existence by infallible intuition. "Experience then convinces us, that we have an intuitive knowledge of our own existence, an internal infallible perception that we are. In every act of sensation, reasoning, or thinking, we are conscious to ourselves of our own being; and, in this matter, come not short of the highest degree of certainty."[68] God, Locke continued, we know by demonstration. As for the rest, we know by sensation.

Locke began, then, by resurrecting the very faculty that Descartes began by doubting—*sensation.* He did not share Descartes's distrust of sense perception, believing with Condillac and Helvetius that the errors and misperceptions of one of the senses were corrected not by the understanding alone but by the other senses. "Sense experience," then, attains the status of a reasonably certain starting point for our knowledge. "The foundations . . . on which rests the whole of that knowledge which reason builds up and raises as high as heaven are the objects of sense-experience."[69]

Despite numerous equivocations, some of which were astutely exploited by Berkeley, Locke seems to have been reasonably confident that sensation provided the mind unproblematically with "simple ideas" that were the atomic components of reliable knowledge. "Nothing can be plainer to a man," he wrote, "than the clear and distinct perception he has of these simple ideas," and elsewhere he stated confidently that "we are sure [these simple ideas] agree to the reality of things."[70]

In any event, it was this apparent confidence in and exclusive reliance upon the senses that impressed Locke's French followers. It was Locke, Condillac wrote in the Introduction to his *Essay on the Origin of Human Knowledge,* who had the "honour of being the first to demonstrate . . . that all our knowledge is derived from the senses."[71] His own inquiry, Condillac believed, was essentially an attempt to refine, systematize, and improve on Locke's basic insight.

The French refinement of Lockean empiricism was basically a fusion of Lockean content with a Cartesian format. Locke's account of the origin of human knowledge in sensations was accepted in simplified form and assimilated to the Cartesian quest to establish a "marvelous science." The *philosophes* thought that the resulting synthesis embodied the virtues of both thinkers and eliminated their defects. Descartes's emphasis on clarity, systematic rigor, and firm foundations could be salvaged from the deductivism, a priorism, and dualism that had corrupted his thought, and Locke's inductivism and empiricism could be sharpened by casting aside the ambiguity and ambivalence he sometimes displayed. D'Alembert, Condillac, and Helvetius sallied forth to seek a new science with the Lockean assurance emblazoned on their shields: "Our simple ideas are all real and true."[72]

This emphasis on the simplicity of the world and of the ideas that reflect it is important and characteristic. The *esprit simpliste,* as Vartanian observes, was "one of the omnipresent prepossessions of the age of *lumières* in the domain (among others) of natural science."[73] Indeed, along with Kant's "Dare to know," another motto of the Enlightenment could have been the admonition: "Simplify!" As Descartes explained, "What alone is required is that we each of us intuit the simples apart from all else, attentively turning upon them the light native to his *ingenium*." In fact, he continued, "the whole of human science . . . consists in this, that we have [clear and distinct] understanding of the manner in which those simple natures combine to compose other things."[74]

Whatever differences Locke and the empiricists who followed him had with Descartes, they agreed with him here. Condillac opined that the proper way to understand the operations of the mind was "to show in what manner they are all derived from one fundamental and *simple* perception."[75] D'Alembert wrote that nature was to be known

> by the art of reducing, as much as that may be possible, a large number of phenomena to a single one that can be regarded as their principle [because] there are but few arts or sciences whose propositions or rules cannot be reduced to some simple notions and arranged in such a close order that their chain of connection will nowhere be interrupted.[76]

And Helvetius made it all sound simple indeed:

> Almost all philosophers agree that the most sublime truths, once simplified and reduced to their plainest terms, may be converted into facts, and in that case present nothing more to the mind than this proposition, *white is white, and black is black*.[77]

Whatever the process was called—"reduction," "resolution," or "analysis"—it all amounted to the same thing. In each case the underlying assumption was "the basic Cartesian assurance that the human understanding might be solidly constructed exclusively out of the simple elements revealed by analysis."[78] In each case the prescribed method was one of intellectual decomposition of a complex whole into the "minimal parts" (Descartes's term) that would constitute the universal "first principles" (Hobbes's term, adapted from Aristotle) of knowledge. And in each case the fruit of this procedure was the same: the foundations of knowledge could be secured. The methodological incompetency in this respect of Scholasticism, which allegedly stood on "soft, shifting ground," could therefore be remedied once and for all.

This quest for secure foundations for human knowledge, beginning with the critique of Scholasticism and moving through Descartes and Locke into Enlightenment empiricism, is enormously important to the subsequent hopes and ironies of liberal rationalism.

The confidence that knowledge could be firmly grounded sustained the optimistic expectation that political conflicts generated by the philosophical conflicts of a prescientific era could be left behind forever. The certitude that their knowledge rested on an unquestionable base produced the dogmatism of technocracy. And the specific content ascribed to the senses by the heirs of Locke and Hume produced the "paradox of the Age of Reason" that in turn has led to political irrationalism. The intellectual pathway followed on this quest deserves, therefore, some emphasis.

This is especially so because, at first sight, it might appear that the journey came full circle. It began with the Aristotelian precept, adopted by Scholastic thought, that nothing is in the intellect that has not entered by the senses. Descartes then challenged this fundamental premise. The senses often deceive us, he observed. True knowledge can be reached only by the understanding, which is independent of the senses and must disentangle itself from them in order to reach full clarity. "Neither our imagination nor our senses can ever assure us of anything whatsoever save so far as our understanding intervenes," he claimed. Even "bodies" are "cognized not by the senses or by the imagination, but by the understanding alone."[79] Furthermore, he contended, we have ideas—like the ideas of God and of the rational soul—that have never been in the senses.

After Locke's criticism of innate ideas, however, the senses underwent a radical rehabilitation. In place of the Cartesian warnings about the deceptiveness of sensation, we find an enthusiastic accreditation of their trustworthiness. Helvetius even said that "the senses never deceive us." If we do receive any misimpressions from the senses, they will be self-correcting. The "united testimony of the senses" will inform us of "the real forms of bodies."[80] And instead of Descartes's insistence that the understanding contains ideas that the senses never apprehended, we find Condillac applauding Locke for demonstrating that "all our knowledge is derived from the senses."[81]

So it seems that we are right back where we started. After a Cartesian interlude, we are back to the Aristotelian account of the origin of knowledge. An epistemological counterrevolution had occurred, and we are back to status quo ante. So it might appear; but appearances can be deceiving. In this case, the counterrevolution was purely formal, for in the interim between the Scholastics and the *philosophes* an ontological revolution had also occurred. Thus the substantive context had changed radically, and when the epistemological question of the foundations of knowledge came back, in its formal full circle, it was actually standing in a different place altogether. Condillac could therefore argue that the Peripatetics, though they used to assume that all knowledge comes through the senses, were nevertheless "so far...from having any certainty of this truth, that not one of them could ever explain it."[82]

As the eighteenth-century empiricists saw it, the Scholastics might have understood *that* we know only through our senses, but they had fundamentally misconceived *what* our senses convey to us. In the Aristotelian formulation of the epistemological process, the senses provided to the mind images of whole existences, such as trees, dogs, and people. The forms of the sensory images, once stripped of their "accidental" attributes, were the substantial forms that together composed the world—the "essences"—and knowledge was made possible by the capacity of the senses to receive the impression of universal forms resident within the particulars. This formulation was virtually unintelligible to the new empiricists. It represented what was literally a "fantastic" account of sensation, for what it contended was sensed—the formal essences, or universals—simply did not exist in the world, and, not being "real," these universal forms could hardly constitute the content of our sensory "data." For eighteenth-century empiricism, what our senses conveyed—indeed, what they had to convey—was impressions of "primary qualities." Since that, and that alone, was what truly existed "out there," that was all that sense "impressions" could possibly be. The "simple ideas" of Locke were the "internal" embodiment of *res extensa*—the "material things" (Locke's term) that composed the world.

The universals that the senses apprehended in the world, then, were not the chimerical forms, essences, and "quiddities" of Aristotelianism but the attributes of "Body": extension, location, and motion. Since all of these attributes, the "primary qualities," were "simple" and clear, sensation could itself be regarded as fundamentally composed of equally clear and simple ideas. All that was requisite for these simple ideas to stand out in clear relief was the elimination of the "obscurantist" and confusing notions with which Scholasticism had clouded men's vision.

The Need for Right Method

The last complaint lodged by the new rationalists against the tradition they sought to supersede was that it was *unmethodical*. Previous inquiry had failed to build solid and lasting knowledge because it had proceeded without explicit procedural rules. This lack of methodological rigor had to be remedied by careful attention to the productive *forms* of inquiry. Descartes was the prototype of those who shared this concern. The very titles of his major essays manifest his focal concern for establishing reliable procedural guides for inquiry. He sought "to seek out and decide on the true method, a method which I could rely upon as guiding me to a knowledge of all the things my mind is capable of knowing."[83] The settled *order* of inquiry was all-important. And this order of inquiry could be and should be, he held, set forth in the form of clear and explicit rules, the observance of which constituted the very essence of human "sagacity." "It is precisely in the due observance of such order that human sagacity almost entirely consists," he insisted. "This is why we maintain that in our inquiries we must proceed methodically."[84]

Since knowledge was basically a unity, moreover, the same method could be employed in all subjects amenable to human cognition. Properly constructed *regulae* could be universal in scope. Descartes hoped that his work exemplified this possibility. As he wrote to Mersenne, "I have also inserted a certain amount of metaphysics, physics, and medicine in the first *Discourse* in order to show that my method extends to topics of all kinds."[85]

Actually, the objection to Scholastic methods was more substantive than formal. The Scholastics had their methods, which were in some cases formalized to the point of sterility. It was simply that these methods were wholly inappropriate to investigate the world as the seventeenth century was beginning to perceive it or to discover what seventeenth-century thinkers wanted to know. Despite the widespread implication that earlier philosophy had gone astray because it was not methodologically systematic and self-conscious, the real difficulty was not *that* it had embodied no methods at all but *what* its methods were. Aristotle as much as Descartes, for example, had insisted that scientific inquiry must begin with those things that are simple and universal—with first principles—but he had a very different impression of what those principles were.

The significance of the methodological self-consciousness of the adherents of modern reason, then, was that it represented the attempt to specify the appropriate means of exploring the new nonfinite, spatialized, exteriorized universe of *res extensa* or "body."[86] The methods articulated in the Aristotelian *Organon* were simply inappropriate to investigate a world of this sort. The Aristotelian mode of inquiry was tailored to be effective only within the stable, finite Greek cosmos,[87] and the abandonment of that world view therefore caused a methodological vacuum.

The precepts listed above attempted to fill this void. The substantive recommendations of the new methodology derived from the beliefs in the autonomy of reason, the possibility of obtaining clear and distinct ideas, and so on. The most basic and widely acclaimed methodological rules, then, were:

1. "Dare to know!" Doubt anything you haven't ascertained for yourself. Don't accept ideas solely on the basis of external authority. Subject all ideas to the "natural light of reason."
2. Always establish firm foundations for your knowledge. Especially be certain that your basic definitions are based on clear and distinct ideas that reflect the "plain truths" of the real world.
3. Reach these foundations by analysis. Resolve and reduce any complex problem into its simple constituent parts. These will be your "first principles."
4. Be systematic and orderly in building any intellectual edifice on these firm foundations. Let the rigor of the "geometric spirit" be your guide here.

Apart from other very general admonitions, which enjoined all that is virtuous in research—for example, Look at all the evidence, Try to be objective, and so on—these were the major constituents of the new "universal method." When Descartes enumerated the rules he had devised to guide his own inquiry, he came up with the following precepts, which, he felt, "would be found sufficient, always provided I took the firm and unswerving resolve never in a single instance to fail in observing them": first, "to accept nothing as true which I did not evidently know to be such...."; second, "to divide each of the difficulties I examined into as many parts as may be required for its adequate solution"; third, "to arrange my thoughts in order, beginning with things the simplest and easiest to know...."; and last, "in all cases to make enumerations so complete, and reviews so general, that I should be assured of omitting nothing."[88]

To summarize very briefly to this point: the seventeenth and eighteenth centuries[89] perceived profound debilities in the whole approach to knowledge they had inherited from the Peripatetics. Most of the leading philosophical thinkers of the period saw as their principal task the development and articulation of a new epistemology and a corresponding methodology, which could replace the older tradition and make good its failures. The principal structural determinants of the new epistemology were the changing ontological and cosmological outlook and the exemplary intellectual achievements of the scientific revolution. The characteristic diagnosis of the sources of the incompetencies of previous inquiry focused on its subordination of reason to authority, its entanglement in verbal snares created by careless definitions, its lack of firm foundations or starting points for inquiry, and its want of settled method. The adherents of the new rationalism sought to remedy these problems by liberating human reason, by providing the clear and distinct foundations and the precise methods that had been lacking, and by transforming language to accord with the model of mathematical "language."

Certainty within Limits

As the fruit of their epistemological revolution, the rationalists anticipated unparalleled intellectual progress. They were, of course, quite vindicated in this expectation, at least insofar as the natural sciences are concerned. Their concrete program for this progress, however, was as questionable as it has been profound in its consequences. In their view, science could proceed by a process of simple and straightforward accretion. Because knowledge had been set on secure foundations and provided with rigorous methods, all science henceforth would be "normal science," in Thomas Kuhn's sense of that phrase. That is, the basic assumptions, premises, paradigm, framework, of science had now been settled, once and for all. Hence, only "puzzle-solving" remained for future generations, and they had the tools to do this unproblematically. Condorcet, Frank Manuel has observed, was "like most of his contemporaries" in this respect. He

> was smugly convinced that problems of scientific theory had all been solved or at least were on the verge of solution . . . . Modern questions in the philosophy of science did not perturb him, and the prospect of accumulating ever more data and of establishing appropriate correlations among them seemed endlessly fruitful.[90]

The endless disputations that had characterized all previous intellectual history could be expected to disappear or at least greatly to subside as science developed. John Stuart Mill could still confidently state this hope in the mid-nineteenth century:

> As mankind improve, the number of doctrines which are no longer disputed or doubted will be constantly on the increase; and the well-being of mankind may almost be measured by the number and gravity of the truths which have reached the point of being uncontested.[91]

This kind of progress seemed reasonable to expect because the new epistemology promised that human knowledge would henceforward be free of obscurity or dubitability. In a word, men could now be certain of their knowledge. They no longer would be merely speculating about the truth, like their predecessors; they could now possess the truth. As Hegel put it, the time had now come for philosophy to "give up the name love of knowledge" and become "real knowledge."

Real knowledge. Truth. Certainty. These would be the essence of the new science. At least, certainty was possible as long as the natural limits of the human understanding were understood and respected. The full theme of positive reason, then, could be said to be "certainty within limits."

Descartes, of course, was the oracle of certainty. Nothing was more important to him than to establish certainty as the hallmark of true science. "All science consists in sure and evident knowledge," he insisted. Anything less was neither worthy of the name knowledge nor properly amenable to fruitful human inquiry. "We reject all modes of knowledge that are merely probable, and resolve to believe only that which is perfectly known, and in respect of which doubt is not possible. . . . It is better, therefore, not to study at all than to occupy ourselves with objects so difficult that, owing to inability to distinguish true from false, we may be obliged to accept the doubtful as certain." We should "concern ourselves only with those matters which can be known with certainty," and the mathematical sciences provide the appropriate norm for that certitude. Thus, "we should not occupy ourselves with any object about which we are unable to have a certitude equal to that of arithmetical and geometrical demonstrations."[92]

Locke seemed, in contrast, to be very conscious of the frailty of human cognition. His argument for toleration stressed this fallibility of the mind. "The necessity of believing without knowledge, nay often upon very slight grounds, in this fleeting state of action and blindness we are in," he counseled, "should make us more busy and careful to inform ourselves than to constrain others."[93] Moreover, he expressed very clear doubts about the possibility that natural science could be anything other than a highly speculative venture: "But as to a perfect science of natural bodies . . . we are, I think, so far from being capable of any such thing, that I conclude it lost labour to seek after it."[94] This sounds more like Vico than like the Locke one encounters in the pages of the Enlightenment, but it is Locke nonetheless. It is a side of Locke that led to Berkeley and Hume. It is not the side of Locke that so inspired the French sensationists.

Nevertheless, Locke set the standards of true knowledge as high as anyone. Knowledge meant certainty for him, just as it did for Descartes. He accepted the norm of demonstrability and insisted on it in numerous contexts. "With me," he wrote, "to know and to be certain is the same thing: what I know, that I am certain of; and what I am certain of, that I know. What reaches to knowledge, I think may be called certainty; and what comes short of certainty, I think may not be called knowledge."[95] In genuine knowledge, Locke held, the "possibility that it may be otherwise" is excluded.[96] "What we once know, we are certain is so; and we may be secure that there are no latent proofs undiscovered which may overthrow our knowledge, or bring it in doubt."[97] He had no intention whatever, he wrote, of "pulling up the old foundations of knowledge and certainty." Instead, he felt that "the way I have pursued, being conformable to truth, lays these foundations surer."[98]

If Locke had some doubts about the certainty of knowledge under the new epistemological dispensation, his *philosophe* followers did not share them. Where he vacillated, they were resolute. Locke's equivocations on this matter they wrote off as "timidities" and "confusions." When these flaws were refined out, the lesson they learned from him was that certainty was attainable so long as the natural limits of the mind were recognized and respected.

These limits of the human mind's scope, moreover, were not seen as severe or threatening. In fact, the circumscription of the understanding that Locke had provided was greeted by his Enlightenment acolytes as a blessing. It was seen as a relief, not a constraint, as a liberation, not a confinement. For *within* these limits lay all that was really worth knowing, including the truths of natural science, about whose absolute reliability they had none of Locke's reservations. Beyond these limits lay simply the "metaphysical" garbage they sought to escape in any case. Far from confining the mind, Locke had in their view freed it from meaningless verbiage. The fence he set up around the boundaries of the understanding simply prevented men from straying beyond the firm ground of *terra cognita* into the swamps of vain philosophy. Good fences, they might have said, make good philosophers.

To borrow a theological term, we might characterize this dominant paradigm of "certainty within limits" as *epistemological manicheanism*. In its relation to the human understanding the world was divided in two. On one side lay the kingdom of light, the land of the intelligible. In it, all was transparent and comprehensible with certitude. On the other side lay the kingdom of darkness, the land of the unintelligible. In it, all was impenetrable to the best efforts of the human mind. Knowledge was absolutely luminous and indubitable. Anything less could not be called knowledge. Any idea involving judgment, any idea that was merely likely or probable, "never amounts to knowledge, no, not to that which is the lowest degree of it."[99]

This dichotomizing approach to problems of epistemology has become deeply entrenched in the modern sensibility. What is known, we suppose, is what is unequivocally and explicitly true, demonstrable, verifiable, proved. Anything else is "opinion," where each may have his say, and where one statement is of equal worth or worthlessness with any other. We begin our epistemological debates with these either-or premises. Is a proposition meaningful or meaningless, we ask? Is ethics cognitive or noncognitive? Is law or the study of politics a science or is it not? Is he an absolutist or a relativist? We rarely pause to ponder where we got the ground rules for these interminable debates.

Despite his consideration of "degrees of assent" in Book Four of his *Essay*, it was Locke who provided some of the most striking imagery of the manichean orientation in epistemology. He recommended that "we confine our thoughts within the contemplation of things that are within the reach of our understandings, and launch not out into that abyss of darkness where we have not eyes to see, nor faculties to perceive anything."[100] The principal objective of his *Essay*, he wrote in his Introduction to it, was to find the "horizon" that "sets the bounds between the enlightened and dark parts of things; between what is and what is not comprehensible by us."[101]

From the seventeenth century to the twentieth, from Locke to the Vienna Circle, from Descartes to the Wittgenstein of the *Tractatus*, this has been a persistent philosophical concern: to provide specific criteria for the identification of this "horizon." The verifiability principle of meaning, considered in its role as a criterion of demarcation, is but the summation of this persistent quest. Voltaire, Hume, and Helvetius all made their own attempts to specify the location of this crucial horizon.[102]

Equally consistent have been the procedural admonitions derived from the underlying manichean presuppositions: Confine yourself to the light; Don't wander out into the darkness; above all, Do not pretend to speak meaningfully about what cannot be said. Wittgenstein captured this methodological corollary of epistemological manicheanism in his justly famous remark in the *Tractatus:* "Was man nicht sagen kann, darüber muss man schweigen" (One must keep silent about that which he cannot say). Wittgenstein's utterance had a certain delphic quality to it. One interpretation suggests that frustration with this stipulation, which seemed inescapable within his premises but unacceptably stringent, led him to unravel the whole view of language and the world to which he had originally subscribed. Locke and Descartes both had offered their own strikingly similar stipulations, however; and their recommendations were quite straightforward and free of frustration. The horizon of the understanding, they felt, was sufficiently wide that its due observance offered no cause for intellectual claustrophobia. Locke could see nothing but good coming from his attempt "to prevail with the busy mind of man to be more cautious in meddling with things exceeding its comprehension; to stop when it is at the utmost extent of its tether; and to sit down in quiet ignorance of those things which, upon examination, are found to be beyond the reach of our capacities."[103] Descartes seemed to feel that little of worth would be lost and a great deal gained by observance of his Rule Eight: "If in any series of things into which we may be inquiring we come upon something which our understanding is unable to intuit sufficiently well, there we must stop short. What follows thereupon is not to be studied; that would be useless labor, and from it we should abstain."[104] Only many years later, after the frontiers of certainty had receded significantly, did such injunctions begin to seem cause for dissatisfaction.

Platonism in a World of Body

The adherents of positive reason agreed with Locke: they had no intention of "pulling up the old foundations of knowledge and certainty" but instead planned to "lay those foundations surer." They were not really being wholly novel in their insistence on the equivalence of knowledge and certainty. They were simpy being more definitive in their hopes, since they were changing the grounds of certainty from (allegedly) unquestionable principles to the clear and distinct perceptions of the autonomous mind.[105] As John Dewey pointed out decades ago, the "quest for certainty" is not of recent origin. "The dream of manifest truth," in the words of Marjorie Grene, "began, in our tradition at least, in the first great synthesis of Western thought, in Greek philosophy."[106] It was a dream embodied in both the Aristotelian insistence on the linear demonstrability of science and the Platonic fascination with the precision of mathematics. The problem with the ancients, as the Enlightenment saw it, was not so much that they failed to seek certainty but that they provided fraudulent bases for the search. This failure the adherents of positive reason believed they could make good.

In their view, Plato (unlike Aristotle) had at least been on the right track in his insistence on mathematics as the key to reliable knowledge. In some respects, therefore, it is possible to see modern rationalism as a resurgence of Platonism in epistemology. Many of the seventeenth-century figures recognized the affinity. Descartes at times used Platonic imagery to convey his ideas, and Hobbes was happy to acknowledge Plato as "the best Philosopher of the Greeks" because he "forbad entrance into his Schoole, to all that were not already in some measure Geometricians."[107] Had Aristotle been similarly discriminating, Hobbes implied, we would have been spared the semantic imbroglios of decadent Scholasticism.

The fundamental epistemological geography of modern rationalism, in fact, can appropriately be seen as a radicalization of the Platonic model of the divided line. Plato's divided line separated *doxa* from *epistēmē*, unreliable belief from genuine knowledge. Modern rationalism did not adopt the ontological bases of this separation in Plato—the distinction between the world of appearances and the world of Forms—but it sought within its own metaphysical presuppositions, just as fervently as Plato did, to establish a clear and sharp boundary between *doxa* and *epistēmē,* a firm line of demarcation between the knowable and the unknowable: within the boundary, a realm of pure light, wholly intelligible to the inquiring mind; beyond the boundary, a realm of utter darkness, wholly opaque to the understanding.

The radical deprecation of the imagination that was characteristic of the new rationalism also recalls a familiar Platonic theme. Just as Hume or Jean LeClerc did later, Plato had seen poets as potentially dangerous deceivers, whose stock-in-trade was a mode of perception devoid of truth criteria. And Plato had, like Condillac, used the analogy of cosmetics to convey the false allure of poetic devices.

The parallels between Plato and the scientific rationalists are not, however, identities. The nature and significance of the mathematical orientation in the seventeenth and eighteenth centuries was different from its nature and significance in Plato's thought because the ontological context was different. Plato's mathematics was Pythagorean. He saw it as a kind of mystical analogue of the cosmic harmonies. The seventeenth century's mathematics was mechanistic rather than mystical. It was the philosophical offspring of Democritus rather than Pythagoras. Hence, what the seventeenth century saw in mathematics was different from what Plato saw. His infatuation with mathematics grew from his belief that it revealed the music of the soul; Hobbes's infatuation with geometry grew from its capacity to illuminate the motion of bodies.

The animus Plato displayed toward poets also was somewhat different from the antipoetic sentiments of modern rationalism. Although he sometimes spoke as though he disdained poetry and the imagination per se, in other places he made it clear that his aim was to discriminate "good" poetry from "bad" poetry, not to eliminate it altogether. His recommendation was that poetry be disciplined, not that it be abandoned as obsolescent. So, here again, the perception of the new rationalism as a resurgence of Platonism against an established Aristotelianism cannot be carried so far that it misleads more than it illuminates.

There is one further parallel between Plato and the new rationalism, however, and it is central to the concerns of this study. Observing it, moreover, can serve us as a transition to the next chapter's focus on the political implications the reformers saw in their epistemological revolution. For Plato, truth was not morally or politically neutral. Knowledge was closely tied to virtue and was also politically therapeutic. Sophistry threatened both the soul and the polis. The good life and the good society needed grounding in philosophic intelligence.

In this respect, liberal rationalism was very Platonic. Diagnostically, it attributed many of the political and moral ills of the day to Scholastic sophistry. Condorcet was perhaps extreme in his opinion that ''all errors in politics and morals are based on philosophical errors, and these in turn are connected with scientific errors,''[108] but he nonetheless reflected a very deep and widespread conviction that the linkage between political and philosophical error was extremely close. This conviction was, in fact, central to the concerns of reformers of very different political coloration. The Enlightenment liberals, for example, saw superstition as the handmaiden of tyranny. Hobbes, on the other hand, condemned it as the inciter to anarchy, writing that the ''doctrine of separated essences, built on the Vain Philosophy of Aristotle, would fright them from Obeying the Laws of their Countrey, with empty names; as men fright Birds from the Corn with an empty doublet, a hat, and a crooked stick.''[109]

The positive and hopeful other face of this belief was the expectation that the triumph of reason would lead to the relief of man's estate. Like Plato, the adherents of the new rationalism offered their knowledge as a crucial resource for political regeneration. Like him, they believed that knowledge and virtue were closely related, and, again like him, they sought to provide to their fellow men not merely intellectual clarity but political therapy as well.

3   The "Moral Sciences" and Liberal Hopes

The new science they were developing was, in the eyes of Locke, Descartes, and their *philosophe* followers, in no sense purely academic. Their intellectual revolution was thoroughly practical in both its motivation and its presumed consequences. The fulcrum of the revolution they espoused was epistemology, but it was the political world, in the broadest sense of that term, that was going to be moved. Archimedes speculated that he could move the world if he could find a vantage point to give him sufficient leverage. As the adherents of the new rationalism saw it, this suggestion was no longer merely a speculative hypothesis. It was a practical possibility.

In the first place, many of the central metaphors and motifs of the new rationalism were profoundly "political" ones. The autonomy of reason and the accessibility of knowledge, to cite two especially important examples, were central components of Enlightenment epistemology in its typical form. But autonomy and accessibility are not only epistemological conditions; they are political situations. And the attainment of a political situation implies some form of political activity. The changeover to a new conception of human knowledge, moreover, constituted a genuine intellectual *revolution*. And even intellectual revolutions cannot take place in an institutional vacuum. Even revolutions of the mind require embodiment. When D'Alembert sought to characterize Descartes's achievement, then, he chose a terminology that was explicitly and unabashedly political. "He can be thought of," D' Alembert said,

> as a leader of conspirators who, before anyone else, had
> the courage to arise against a despotic and arbitrary
> power and who, in preparing a resounding revolution, laid
> the foundations of a more just and happier government,
> which he himself was not able to see established.[1]

This political interpretation of the accomplishments of the epistemological revolutionaries, was not, moreover, a latter-day interpolation by politically minded *philosophes*. The *philosophes* perhaps had their own reasons for emphasizing the political side of the scientific revolution, but they did not create this image de novo out of their own concerns and hopes. The political dimension formed an important part of the self-interpretation of Locke and Descartes. They clearly perceived their own mission to be broadly political in both its impetus and its consequences. They were spurred to their epistemological reflections in part by moral and political considerations, and the enlightenment they sought to provide was presumed to carry with it significant implications for the political affairs of mankind.

Commentators on the Cartesian impact on the Enlightenment have often taken pains to point out the moral and political aspirations and interests that undergirded Descartes's philosophical enterprise. Charles Frankel, for example, has noted the "pronounced moral interest" in Descartes, arguing that "he gave it the place of an ultimate standard in his philosophical system,"[2] and J. B. Bury wrote of "the far-reaching effects on the condition of mankind" that Descartes expected his work would have.[3] The method he was engaged in developing was not, in Descartes's view, suitable solely for the natural sciences. It was a generally applicable method, one that was appropriate for moral tutelage as well. In the words of Vartanian,

> It is a curiously striking fact that the *Discours*, while ostensibly expounding a method suited to natural science, discussed and evaluated this persistently in terms of its importance for the conduct of life. Descartes seemed to be offering simultaneously a method for the explanation of physical events and for the exploration of man's nature and earthly destiny.[4]

Descartes's own account of both the motivations behind his intellectual pilgrimage and the ultimate intent of his new science makes the political and moral thrust of his enterprise quite clear. "Throughout," he wrote in the *Discourse*, "I was obsessed by the eager desire to learn to distinguish the true from the false, that I might see clearly what my actions ought to be, and so to have assurance as to the path to be followed in this life."[5] As for the consequences he hoped his new method to have, his originally proposed title for the *Discourse* stands as testimony. As he described it to Mersenne, the general title would be "The Plan of a Universal Science to raise our Nature to its Highest Degree of Perfection."[6]

Descartes never made very clear the nature of the presumed intimate nexus between his mathematicizing methodology and moral truth. Though it could well have stood some careful examination and justification, he seems to have taken it largely for granted. It does seem, however, that one important basis for his belief in the moral bearing of his new science was his firm belief in the unity of all knowledge. If all the sciences are part of a seamless web, then a method appropriate to one science will be appropriate to them all, and discoveries made in one area will have direct implications in others. In Rule One of *Rules for Direction,* in any case, this seems to be the clear implication of his immediate juxtaposition of the themes of the interdependence of all the sciences and of the practical outcome of his inquiry. "We ought to bear in mind that all the sciences are so closely interconnected that it is much easier to study them together than to isolate one from the others," he admonished his readers.

> If, therefore, anyone genuinely desires to investigate the truth of things, he should not select some one particular science; all of them stand together and are interdependent. What he should alone consider is how best to augment the natural light of reason, not however with a view to resolving this or that difficulty, as propounded in the Schools, but in order that his understanding may guide his will in the choices he has to make on all the various issues by which he is faced throughout life.[7]

Locke likewise was led to his epistemological reflection by moral and political concern. He wrote a great deal, of course, on explicitly political topics, on education, and on religion. It is not always appreciated, however, that his *Essay concerning Human Understanding* also had its genesis in his effort to come to terms with the problem of moral knowledge. In the winter of 1670–71 Locke engaged in discussion with several of his learned friends about the foundations of moral philosophy. From the course of these discussions, which apparently were disturbingly unproductive, he concluded that he must first inquire into the nature and scope of the human understanding. Only when the grounds and limits of knowledge were adequately clarified, he decided, could the kinds of questions that perplexed his discussion group be addressed satisfactorily. He related the history of his undertaking in the "Epistle to the Reader" of the *Essay:*

> Were it fit to trouble thee with the history of this *Essay*, I should tell thee, that five or six friends meeting at my chamber, and discoursing on a subject very remote from this, found themselves quickly at a stand, by the difficulties that rose on every side. After we had awhile puzzled ourselves, without coming any nearer a resolution of those doubts which perplexed us, it came into my thoughts that we took a wrong course; and that before we set our-

selves upon inquiries of that nature, it was necessary to examine our own abilities, and see what objects our understandings were, or were not, fitted to deal with.[8]

Locke's friend James Tyrrell, who was also present on that occasion, reported that the "subject very remote from this" was the problem of the "principles of morality and revealed religion."

This pattern of progression in Locke's intellectual journey, from fundamentally moral and political questions of the grounds of right action back to the underlying epistemological foundations of such claims, was not unusual in seventeenth-century England. Britain was beset in that era by explosive civil divisions that were intimately related to religious divisions in the society. Intellectual currents flowing from the Reformation and, to a lesser degree, from the scientific revolution had helped to create a crisis of authority. On the one hand, a variety of religious sects had sprung up, and they were making extravagant claims to knowledge based upon immediate inspiration and on their own reading of biblical texts. On the other hand, the skepticism and materialism emanating from the Continent posed a different kind of threat, one that was politically less significant but intellectually more formidable than the challenge of the sectarians. From their very different vantage points the "enthusiasts" and the skeptics both seemed to be undermining the very foundations of established religious and social order. Under siege from at least two directions, then, some of the best minds of the day sought to shore up these foundations.

As the seventeenth century wore on, their concern grew. Ultimately, the challenge posed by both the sectarians and the materialists was epistemological. How do you *know*, they asked, that the political precepts and religious doctrines you uphold are true? We know, the sectarians averred, because God has told us, because the Bible has told us, because our consciences have told us. We don't know, said the skeptics, and neither do you. The "moderates," as they might be called, were accordingly driven to provide an epistemological reply. Joseph Glanvill identified the target of their reply in the title of his "Anti-fanatical Religion and Free Philosophy." Robert Boyle joined in with his emphasis on natural religion. The Cambridge Platonists sought to place morality and the basic tenets of natural theology on a certain and demonstrable basis. The English Deists sought to demonstrate the "reasonableness" of Christianity. The basic argument was in each case the same: the human mind may not be competent to know all things, but it can know what is needful for guidance in this life. We need not despair with the skeptics or abandon ourselves to flights of "inspiration" with the enthusiasts. When its scope and limits are properly understood, the natural light of reason can provide solid footing for those who use it properly.

Locke's *Essay*, then, was one significant contribution to this attempt to define and legitimate the role of reason in practical affairs. However far afield he might wander into abstruse speculation in his *Essay*, Locke had some very practical lessons in mind. He was concerned throughout to demonstrate that "God has furnished men with faculties sufficient to direct them in the way they should take, if they will but seriously employ them that way."[9] Though he talked principally in terms of the knowledge of "particular existences" and "material things," he was profoundly concerned with the bearing that all this had on man's knowledge of moral "facts"—of his obligations and responsibilities. "How short soever their knowledge may come of an universal or perfect comprehension of whatsoever is," Locke insisted, men still "have light enough to lead them to the knowledge of their Maker, and the sight of their own duties."[10]

In short, from the very outset of modern epistemology, reason was considered to be of more than purely academic interest. Reason was not purely an intellectual capacity; it was a political force. Reason came in varied guises and assumed varied political tasks. In Locke's England, reason contended with the fantasies of irrationalism. In the *philosophes'* France, reason wrestled the forces of dogmatism and reaction. In Hegel's Germany, reason used its cunning to move decisively toward its self-realization in the world. Whatever role it seemed to assume in different philosophical and political contexts, however, reason was an omnipresent political protagonist. It was not merely contemplative; it was an actor.

What began in Locke, Descartes, and Bacon culminated in Condorcet and Hegel. Modern reason began its political career as a dynamic new method with profound practical possibilities. Within two centuries it achieved its own apotheosis. For Descartes, reason was a potent tool. For Locke, it was a natural light that shone to light man's way in a world that exceeded his comprehension. For Condorcet, reason was an epic hero. It took on a life of its own in his chronicle of the progress of the human mind. Reason became a dramatic persona. Condorecet described its vicissitudes and its struggles almost as if it had a mind and will of its own. "Everywhere during this stage," he wrote, for example,

> we see reason and authority fighting for supremacy, a battle which prepared and anticipated the triumph of reason. . . . Reason, which sometimes leant on authority and was more often opposed by it, wished to know what she could expect from it in the way of assistance and what grounds there could be for making the sacrifices that it demanded of her.[11]

Hegel carried this Enlightenment tendency to personify reason to an extreme conclusion. We may talk as if reason were a persona, he decided, because it is a persona. Indeed, it is the divine persona whose autobiography constitutes the history of the world. We may talk as if it had purposes of its own, because it does have its own autonomous end—an end that will be realized. Reason is not a tool of men; men are the tools of Reason. We don't use it; it uses us. With this ironic twist, we approach one version of the technocratic outcome of modern rationalism, and we must postpone further consideration of this development until the next chapter.

Knowledge and Power, Theory and Practice

Reason was a political force, in the new rationalists' view, because, to cite the Baconian maxim, knowledge was power. Hobbes said it well: if the consequence of science were purely contemplative delight, he wrote, really difficult theoretical inquiry would not be worth the effort. "For the inward glory and triumph of mind that a man may have for the mastering of some difficult and doubtful matter, or for the discovery of some hidden truth, is not worth so much pain as the study of philosophy requires." Knowledge must produce concrete results. "The end of knowledge is power," and "the end or scope of philosophy is, that we may make use to our benefit of effects formerly seen."[12]

The high expectations the seventeenth and eighteenth centuries entertained for the new science derived from their conception of it as a fusion of Aristotelian theoretical and practical science. Aristotle held that some sciences, such as astronomy, could be certain and precise; but these were purely contemplative. Other sciences were practical, such as the study of politics; but these could not attain real certainty or precision. The new science, as its enthusiasts saw it, was a unified whole possessing the virtues of both the Aristotelian theoretical and practical sciences without their limitations. Science, in its new form, could be both certain and practical. It would possess both the intuitive certitude of Aristotelian *noēsis* and the practical force of Aristotelian *phronēsis*. The possibilities of such a combination seemed almost endless.

The new science would be useful to men, relevant to the political order, in several ways—which were not always kept analytically distinct.

First, the new science would, it was hoped, alter the "political" balance between man and nature. The forces of the natural world have always been antagonistic in many ways to the desires and needs of men. The scourges of disease and infirmity, the ravages of plague and famine and drought, the final fact of death, have always been among the principal obstacles to human happiness. As Freud observed in *Civilization and Its Discontents,* the program of the pleasure principle seems to be "at loggerheads with the whole world.... There is no possibility at all of its being carried through; all the regulations of the universe run counter to it."[13] And, of the three principal sources of human suffering that Freud itemized, the first two are natural phenomena: the decay and dissolution of our bodies, and the forces of destruction in the "external world." (The third source, "our relations to other men," is specifically political.) The earnest hope and clear expectation of the reformers was that their epistemological breakthrough would decisively change the balance of power in this war of man with nature.

The new knowledge of nature, as Descartes explained, would no longer be merely "speculative." It would instead be the crucial means by which man could genuinely gain dominion over his old foe:

> In the place of the speculative philosophy taught in the Schools we can have a practical philosophy, by means of which, knowing the force and the actions of fire, water, air, of the stars, of the heavens, and of all the bodies that surround us—knowing them as distinctly as we know the various crafts of the artisans—we may in the same fashion employ them in all the uses for which they are suited, thus rendering ourselves the masters and possessors of nature.[14]

"Thus rendering ourselves the *masters and possessors* of nature." The old biblical authorization in the Book of Genesis, that man shall be entitled to dominion over the things of this earth, suddenly took on new force and meaning. Mastery and possession are radical forms of control. The onset of the new conception of human reason thus had distinctly Faustian overtones. If nature had held men in bondage, now men would reverse the relationship. The alchemists' quest was fueled anew. Bacon, in fact, suggested that the term "natural magic" should be revived and applied to the side of natural philosophy dealing with the "production of effects"— what we would today call technology.[15] Some even dared hope with Condorcet that man's ultimate adversary, Thanatos, might be overcome—that perhaps "the day will come when death will be due only to extraordinary accidents or to the decay of the vital forces, and that ultimately the average span between birth and decay will have no assignable value."[16]

Condorcet and the others who were excited by the prospect of the nascent scientific technology's practical fruits should probably be forgiven for their enthusiasm. From their standpoint, the horizon of possibilities seemed beyond immediate view, and in many ways, after all, they were right. In some areas the accomplishments of modern technology have virtually qualified to be called "natural magic." We have realized the dream of Icarus, flying even to the moon. We have eradicated many of the dread diseases that for centuries destroyed and crippled human lives. We can see across the oceans by television and satellite. We have immeasurably lightened human toil by the use of mechanical power. In all these ways and many more, the burdens, disasters, and limitations placed upon us by nature have been transcended. Descartes, Bacon, and Condorcet, could they return to behold these wonders of the modern world, might justifiably feel that their visions had been fulfilled.

There are ironies even here. We are now beginning to discover that nature will not consent to be mastered and possessed in toto. Human intervention in natural processes cannot escape the limits of ecology, and some of the ecological by-products of technological advance may pose new and more difficult threats to human welfare. The nightmares of Malthus refuse to be completely dispelled; they reappear in both their original form and in new and more subtle ways as well. Moreover, as the mention of ecology reminds us, man is himself in some sense a part of nature, even as he also transcends it. As the capacity for technological intervention in natural processes progressed, therefore, some of the potential paradoxes in the simple image of "man's dominion over nature" began to become manifest.

On balance, however, the hopeful expectations the epistemological reformers associated with the "natural magic" have been borne out. We can never fully escape the peculiarly modern nightmares of Frankenstein, the Sorcerer's Apprentice, or the mad scientist, and the power of man over nature may yet prove to be man's self-acquired means of self-extinction; but few of us would gladly return to the disease-ridden days of the past or to the days when men were themselves beasts of burden. Different ones of us may weigh the ledger sheet differently, and all the results are not yet in, but there is ample warrant to sustain the judgment that Descartes's perceptions of the practical benefits of his new science were essentially accurate if oversimplified.

The political benefits from the new epistemology were expected to be direct as well as indirect. The spread of enlightenment, it was hoped, would produce some crucially important, specifically political dividends. The miscarriages of politics had been caused by distortions in man's beliefs about himself and his world. Condorcet wrote that "all errors in politics and morals are based on philosophical errors, and these in turn are connected with scientific errors."[17] Although Condorcet was extreme in thus attributing *all* political failures to philosophical and scientific error, he was representative in perceiving an intimate connection between the two. Darkness in men's minds had engendered political backwardness; illumination would bring a bright new era of progress and light.

The optimistic assessment of the political consequences to follow the spread of enlightenment, apart from the benefits from increasing control over nature, came in two parts. The first of these relied on the anticipated consequences of the widespread dissemination of the "facts" of political life in the narrow sense of that word. The second depended on the belief that the new reason was capable of apprehending moral "facts" as well.

The Dissemination of the Facts and the Exposure of Political Fraud

The first argument was more straightforward and more unproblematic than the second. A great deal of political repression is facilitated by deception and duplicity on the part of the governing power. The people can be fleeced because they are kept in the dark about what is going on. A monopoly of relevant information is a good guarantee of disproportionate power, and it is an advantage that ruling elites of all sorts have always been reluctant to relinquish. If all the members of society could become aware of the issues and could become informed about who was doing what to whom, they could protect their interests. The systematic exclusion of great segments of society from access to the facts about their political situation deprives them of their rights. The elimination of their ignorance in this respect would be a great leap forward.

It was in this context that the invention of the printing press was regarded as an event of decisive significance. The printed word made possible the dissemination of information on a scale never before approached. In doing so, averred Condorcet, it liberated mankind from dependence on political and religious authority.

> Has not printing freed the education of the people from all political and religious shackles? It would be vain for any despotism to invade all the schools; vain for it to issue cruel edicts prescribing and dictating the errors with which men's minds were to be infected, and the truths from which they were to be safeguarded; vain for the chairs dedicated to the moral enlightenment of the vulgar or the instruction of the young in philosophy and the sciences to be obliged under duress to put forward nothing but opinions favorable to the maintenance of this double tyranny: printing would still be able to diffuse a clear and independent light.[18]

In vain would repressive authority contend against the power of the printed word, in Condorcet's estimation. "How could it be possible to bolt every door, to seal every crevice through which truth aspires to enter?" he asked.

> For though this was difficult enough even when it was only a question of destroying a few copies of a manuscript to annihilate it forever, of proscribing a book or an opinion for a few years to consign it to eternal oblivion, has it not become impossible today, when it would be necessary to maintain an absolutely ceaseless vigilance and an unresting activity?[19]

To us in the twentieth century, who have witnessed the propaganda mills of totalitarianism and the capacity of the press even in free societies to mislead and misinform, it seems a striking lacuna in Condorcet's argument that he does not consider the extraordinary utility the communicative media might have for a repressive regime. He was not troubled by the Orwellian vision of the media as a weapon of political control. When he considers possible governmental threats to the illuminative capacity of the printed word, he thinks solely in terms of negative opposition, of censorship, not in terms of deliberate perversion of the medium, of indoctrination. He tended to discount this possibility, not even giving it careful consideration, because it seemed precluded by some of the other assumptions of the new epistemology. If the truth were genuinely as simple, as clear, as self-evidencing as it was portrayed by Descartes, Locke, and the others, then it needed only a chance to be heard to be accepted. The truth would, on these assumptions, always triumph in the "free marketplace of ideas," as a later age came to call it. It could be defeated only by total suppression; it could not simply be drowned in an ocean of lies and falsehoods.

The spread of "enlightenment" narrowly defined—that is, awareness of the hard facts of political happenings—would create a new and decisive force on the political scene. A "new sort of tribunal had come into existence"[20] through the revolution of the printed word: public opinion. The populace, no longer left in the dark about political events, would be capable of forming a mind of its own. Great things were hoped for from this development. In the first place, as John Stuart Mill observed in his *Considerations on Representative Government,* "it is an inherent condition of human affairs, that no intention, however sincere, of protecting the interests of others, can make it safe or salutary to tie up their own hands."[21] The accessibility of relevant information, therefore, would enable the people for the first time to protect their own interests where governmental policy was concerned. The new awareness level of the public would make their exploitation by their leaders immeasurably more difficult if not impossible. Condorcet, as usual, dared hope for even more.

He envisioned the emergent force of public opinion as Solomon-like in its wisdom. Its judgments would be both just and rational, as well as inexorable. Its influence, therefore, could be expected to be wholly beneficent.[22]

Condorcet's enthusiasm has, of course, not proved to be wholly warranted by the facts of history. For one thing, governments have proved extraordinarily adept at appropriating all of the media of communication and education for their own purposes. Technological revolutions in the transmission of information have probably aided in the consolidation and extension of repressive political authority at least as much as they have aided those who have resisted exploitation. Moreover, the weight of public opinion has contributed to political disasters as well as to political progress. James Mill was still rather unabashedly optimistic over the consequences he anticipated from the ascendence of *vox populi*. His son, influenced by de Tocqueville, began to have second thoughts; and many political scientists today have argued that the vitality of liberal democracy depends largely upon elites, which are more likely to adhere to liberal values than is the public at large. (This latter contention has, in turn, been challenged by other students of politics. It is probably safe to say that this ideologically significant empirical question is still a live issue.)

At the same time, the hopes and expectations of the early liberals on this point have hardly proved wholly unwarranted. The truth does seem hard to stamp out completely. The great difficulties of maintaining a total monopoly over the channels of opinion formation have undoubtedly caused many sleepless nights for political autocrats. In liberal societies, where free speech flourishes, the press has been a constant irritant to and check upon the powers that be. John Mitchell, Jeb Magruder, and the rest of the Watergate crew found to their sorrow that it isn't easy these days to sweep political dirt under the rug, and in dictatorial regimes the seepage of ideas into the public domain when official restrictions are relaxed only briefly may prove to be as explosive as a leaking gas main. The Czechoslovakian uprising of 1968 and the Portuguese coup of 1974 illustrate the constant threat the dissemination of ideas poses to repressive governments of the left or of the right. The vastly widened access to information and the greater political impact of public opinion in the modern world may not have been unambiguous allies of political liberty and progress, but they have in fact assumed a distinctive and important role in the struggle of the governed, in many societies, to protect their legitimate interests and to defend or attain freedom from official coercion. Contemporary liberals have become somewhat disillusioned with this aspect of Enlightenment optimism, but they have no grounds for total cynicism here. On this issue, the early liberals were at least half right.

The Scientific Apprehension of Moral Truths and the End of Misguided Behavior

The new understanding of reason was, however, presumed to have an even more profound direct bearing than this on the conduct of political life. "Enlightenment" meant a great deal more than simply being informed about the everyday facts of politics. It represented also an anticipated revolution in the area of moral knowledge. "Enlightenment" meant not only the spread of truth but the accessibility of Truth with a capital "T". It stood not only for a radical quantitative extension of empirical knowledge but also for a radical qualitative breakthrough in the capacity to ascertain normative truths.

This point needs to be stressed, for it is often obscured by assumptions, now widespread, that then had no currency. The seventeenth and eighteenth centuries had not heard of "value-neutral" science or of the "emotive theory of ethics," even though they unwittingly laid the groundwork for the later articulation of these concepts. As the Enlightenment saw it, the revolution in knowledge would encompass knowledge of the "ought" as well as of the "is." It would guarantee that men who appropriated the new method would be able to know with unprecedented clarity what they should do as well as what was the case. Knowledge was a unity; moral knowledge was thus to be attainable with the same certainty, clarity, and distinctness, the same firm foundations and simplicity, as the rest.

Moral knowledge, in other words, fell within the charmed circle of epistemological manicheanism. It fell within the realm of light. It was not included among the metaphysical debris that could be cast aside with considerable relief as beyond the cognitive capabilities of the human understanding. Man was not to be left in the dark as to his moral and political rights and obligations. Indeed, he would now be enabled to perceive them with a precision never before attainable. As Locke assured his readers in the *Essay*, "the candle that is set up in us shines bright enough for all our purposes." Though limited in scope, man's knowledge is sufficient for obtaining "the conveniences of life and information of virtue."[23]

Almost all the principal figures in the seventeenth-century movement for the establishment of a new science and in the Enlightenment shared this belief. Bacon had already prefigured the pattern when he looked forward in his *Advancement of Learning* to a universal science that would furnish axioms applicable to ethics as well as to physics and mathematics. Descartes agreed. He also conceived of his new method as the foundation of a body of knowledge whose capstone would be moral knowledge. As Charles Frankel has said,

> the notion that moral wisdom was the culminating contribution of the new enlightenment was also foreshadowed by Descartes. The last degree of wisdom, its culminating point, was moral science, which presupposes "a complete knowledge of the other sciences." The medieval notion that knowledge could be completely summed up, together with the Augustinian emphasis that the sum would be moral, was passed down to the Enlightenment by Descartes in the shape of the conviction that moral progress was to be made (and was now possible) by deducing an infallible moral science from the other branches of knowledge.[24]

Hobbes and Spinoza both held a rather somber view of human nature. They certainly did not share the optimism of some of the later Enlightenment figures about progress based on moral improvements in humanity. Yet they, too, clearly believed in the possibility of a moral science. Spinoza cast his writing on ethics in quasi-geometrical form, laying down "axioms" and "postulates" and then "deriving" moral conclusions from them. Hobbes, similarly, spoke of "the science of natural justice," which he felt that he had himself provided for mankind. He contended that he had, in his political works, "put into order, and sufficiently or probably proved all the Theoremes of Morall doctrine, that men may learn thereby, both how to govern, and how to obey."[25] The truths embodied in his theorems, Hobbes believed, would not be self-effectuating; but a sovereign power could "convert this Truth of Speculation, into the Utility of Practice."[26] It was this possibility that gave Hobbes some hope for the deliverance of men from the dangerous predicament into which nature had placed them and that kept his bleak view of man from becoming simply a counsel of despair. Man's situation was grim, in Hobbes's view; but his capacity to produce and comprehend a moral science might save him.

Locke also expressly affirmed his conviction that a science of morals was a possibility. It may confound the expectations of those of us who take our image of "empiricism" from its twentieth-century incarnations, and who are accustomed to hearing Locke referred to as a founding father of the empiricist tradition, to realize that he harbored some fairly profound reservations about the possibility of a natural science but had few doubts about the possibility of a moral science. Therefore it is worth pausing to emphasize this aspect of his epistemological reflections. "Empiricism" is at best a "family word," in Wittgenstein's phrase, and it covers a rather wide range of ideas. Anyone who uses the term without due cognizance of its multiple ambiguities will mislead himself both logically and historically.

Locke took pains to emphasize that his rejection of innate ideas did not entail denying that the mind had innate powers to discern the truth on its own. Many ideas, though not innate, were sufficiently open to the natural capacities of the mind that any man who "makes proper use of the faculties he is endowed with by nature"[27] could perceive them. Certain moral truths fell into this category, and they could be denominated as "natural laws." When the "natural light" of the mind fell upon them, they were readily discernible.

Locke elaborated his belief in the accessibility of moral truths to the natural powers of the mind in the *Essay:*

> I would not here be mistaken, as if, because I deny an innate law, I thought there were none but positive laws. There is a great deal of difference between an innate law, and a law of nature; between something imprinted on our minds in their very original, and something that we, being ignorant of, may attain to the knowledge of, by the use and due application of our natural faculties. And I think they equally forsake the truth who, running into contrary extremes, either affirm an innate law, or deny that there is a law knowable by the light of nature, i.e., without the help of positive revelation.[28]

Locke not only considered that it was possible for the natural reason to apprehend moral truths. He held that these moral truths were clear, simple, and discernible with certainty. Man has certain "definite duties," he said, "which cannot be other than they are." And the necessary truth of these duties was "so manifest and certain that nothing can be plainer."[29] Moreover, he shared the widespread hope that these necessary and plain moral truths might be articulated and organized into a coherent and demonstrable ethical science, one that would approach the certainty of mathematics. "I doubt not," he wrote in the *Essay,*

> but from self-evident propositions, by necessary consequences, as incontestable as those in mathematics, the measures of right and wrong might be made out, to any one that will apply himself with the same indifferency and attention to the one as he does to the other of these sciences.[30]

Later on in the *Essay* he returned to this possibility with a similar apparent confidence:

> This gave me the confidence to advance that conjecture . . . that morality is capable of demonstration as well as mathematics. . . . I

doubt not but, if a right method were taken, a great part of morality might be made out with that clearness, that could leave, to a considering man, no more reason to doubt, than he could have to doubt of the truth of propositions in mathematics, which have been demonstrated to him.[31]

It is not surprising, then, that the same basic hope was very widespread in the Enlightenment; for both the Cartesian and the Lockean sources of Enlightenment thought were in agreement that moral vision was part of scientific truth. The quest for a quasi-geometrical moral science transcended most of the philosophical and political divisions that were important in other contexts. Theists, Deists, agnostics, and atheists, rationalists and empiricists, could all find it possible to embrace this quest. The epistemological manicheanism of their time confronted them with a fairly stark either-or proposition. Either moral truths were part of the corpus of the new science or else they were not knowledge at all. Few were willing to accept a position of complete moral relativism, and they accordingly looked forward to the establishment of a "clear and distinct" morality based on the firm foundations of modern methodology.

On the Continent, Condillac followed the lead of his mentor, Locke. Although he took the weakness of the human understanding as one of his themes, he seemed to have little doubt that moral and political truths are clearly accessible to man's mind. The geometric norm he applied to knowledge in general, moreover, he considered equally applicable in this area. "It seemed to me," he wrote in the opening section of his *Essay on the Origin of Human Knowledge,* "that we might reason in metaphysics and in morals with as great exactness as in geometry."[32] Helvetius expressed a similar view: "In geometry every problem not fully resolved, may become the object of a new demonstration. It is the same in morality and politics."[33] Holbach was aware of some of the difficulties to be overcome before a demonstrative science of politics and morals would be reached. It would, he opined, take a long time and a good deal of experience. Even then, it would probably be possible to find only "general rules," not uniform laws applicable to all times and places. Despite these reservations, his basic hope was quite clear:

> The true principles of Government will be clear, evident, demonstrated, for all those who will have reflected upon these important objects; . . . in going back to the nature of man, one can deduce from it a Political System, a harmony of intimately connected truths, a chain of principles as sure as in any of the other branches of human knowledge.[34]

Chastellux looked forward to the establishment of what he called "andrology," or the science of "man in general." This science would then "serve as the basis of physical and moral medicine, and out of this science would politics be born."[35] Voltaire and Diderot hoped to find universally valid, scientifically ascertainable legal norms. Grotius and Pufendorf sought to establish natural law and the law of nations on axioms that would make them demonstrative sciences. The Physiocrats also saw their own work in this light; they were, in their view, as Laski put it, "doing for matters of social constitution what the great scientists of the seventeenth century had done for the physical universe."[36]

Back in the Anglo-Saxon world, the belief in the possibility of a quasi-mathematical science of morality, articulated by Locke, Cumberland, and the Cambridge Platonists, continued on into the rather different intellectual environment of a century and more later. Tom Paine captured the imagination of many, and terrified the establishment, by his rhetorical appropriation of some of these assumptions on behalf of his democratic passions. He appealed to "common sense" and to "the simple voice of nature and reason," which allegedly had the capacity to discern moral reality with assurance. Like Mackintosh, Godwin, and Bentham, he believed, in the words of Elie Halévy, "that the principles of morals were at once clear, simple, and accessible to common sense, and were a suitable basis for a science."[37]

To be sure, some who thought about the matter had begun to perceive that the assimilation of moral truths to the methods and assumptions of the new science was problematic. D'Alembert, for example, prefigured a later form of empiricism by transposing Locke's doubts about a demonstrable natural science and his confidence in the capacity of reason to demonstrate moral truths. "Certitude is more appropriate to physical objects, the knowledge of which is the fruit of the constant and invariable testimony of our senses," he said. "Moral truths," in contrast, were apprehended by "conscience," which was, together with aesthetic sensibility, a kind of "feeling." "One could call it evidence of the heart," he said, "for although it differs greatly from the evidence of the mind which concerns speculative truths, it subjugates us with the same force."[38] This position, which he had probably not thought through to any real depth, did not in D'Alembert's mind add up to an "emotive theory of ethics" in the contemporary sense of the phrase, but the basic categories of that position are clearly being formulated here. The problem was simple, but there was no readily acceptable answer: if moral truths were not a part of science, then what were they? Most of the seventeenth- and eighteenth-century thinkers who followed Locke and Descartes in their hopes for a "moral science" would have agreed with the anonymous reviewer of D'Alembert's *Discourse* who complained: "Are not the first principles of ethics of an evidence recognized by the light of Reason? Do men have no rule for their action other than conscience? Has M. d'Alembert realized the frightful consequences of such a principle?"[39]

The Problematic Content of the Moral Sciences

Throughout the eighteenth and into the nineteenth century, then, many of the leading social thinkers were absorbed in the enterprise of "moral Newtonianism," as Halévy has called it. This enterprise, which was actually sanctioned and animated by philosophical assumptions considerably antedating Newton, sought to unify and synthesize the moral world, as Newton's theories had unified the physical world, by discovering and articulating some basic principle or small group of principles that would constitute the moral equivalent of the law of gravitation.

When it came time to specify the content of this demonstrative moral science, its proponents became remarkably vague. They offered at best only fragmentary examples, and these examples were either a priori stipulative definitions or purely analytic explications or a combination of the two.

Locke is interesting and instructive in this respect. The several instances in his *Essay* where he asserted the feasibility of a quasi-mathematical moral science occasioned a great deal of interest on the part of many of his readers. They encouraged him, even importuned him, to provide the substance of this new science, not merely to state it as a formal possibility—to give the world the immense benefit of these "self-evident propositions . . . as incontestable as those in mathematics" from which "the measures of right and wrong might be made out."[40] Molyneux, for one, wrote to express his profound desire that Locke would "think of obliging the world with a treatise of morals, drawn up according to the hints you frequently give in the *Essay*, of being demonstrable, according to the mathematical method." James Gibson has described Locke's response:

> To this request, Locke replied that it is one thing to see that morality is capable of demonstrative treatment, and another thing to work out the demonstration; but promised, nevertheless, to turn his thoughts to the matter. Molyneux returned to the point again, and was not the only one who incited him to the attempt. In the end, though Locke was able to assure his correspondent that he had laid by some materials for the purpose, the intention was never carried out. The task, he was inclined to think, was too

great for "one in my age and health." Besides, the gospel containing "so perfect a body of ethics," it seemed to him that "reason may be excused from the enquiry, since she may find man's duty clearer and easier in revelation than in herself"; and that his own time and strength might be better spent "in other researches" in which he found himself "more in the dark."

Gibson comments: "It is probable that Locke realized more fully the difficulties of the undertaking the more he thought about it."[41]

In any case, the few specific examples of demonstrable moral propositions that Locke provided were simply tautologies. For example, he wrote that

> "Where there is no property there is no injustice," is a proposition as certain as any demonstration in Euclid: for the idea of property being a right to anything, and the idea to which the name "injustice" is given being the invasion or violation of that right, it is evident that these ideas, being thus established, and these names annexed to them, I can as certainly know this proposition to be true, as that a triangle has three angles equal to two right ones.[42]

Grant me my premises, he said in effect, and I shall force you to my conclusions. But what were the grounds for the premises? Locke apparently thought they were among those "simple" and "self-evident" ideas that no one could deny. What happened when someone found the premises unacceptable remained a mystery.

The other exponents of a moral science who sought to provide concrete examples of it did no better. In demonstrating his moral "theorems," Hobbes began by stipulating some highly important "definitions" of injustice, for example, as "the not performance of covenant" and liberty as "the absence of impediment." If you will accept his definitions, he can lead you to the conclusions he wants you to accept; but he can do so because the conclusions are already there in the premises. Helvetius argued similarly. Accept the definitions which he stipulates on the ostensive grounds of "clarity," and he can reduce political norms to a science:

> Annex a clear idea to the word probity, and regard it with me as the practice of actions useful to our country. What is then to be done to determine demonstratively what actions are virtuous, and what vicious? Name those that are useful or prejudicial to society. Now in general nothing is more easy.[43]

Hobbes was actually quite clear and candid about the purely analytic quality of his new science of politics. "Reason," he affirmed, is purely formal: "Reason serves only to convince the truth not of fact, but of consequence."[44] Science can be truly demonstrative only because it is a self-contained logical system:

> The end of science is the demonstration of the causes and generations of things; which if they be not in the definitions, they cannot be found in the conclusion of the first syllogism, that is made from those definitions; and if they be not in the first conclusion, they will not be found in any further conclusion deduced from that; and, therefore, by proceeding in this manner, we shall never come to science; which is against the scope and intention of demonstration.[45]

Two complaints against this avowedly analytic conception of moral science, indeed of all science, come immediately to mind; but Hobbes found neither one troublesome. First, one might ask, what are the grounds of these definitions? Obviously, everything hinges upon them. What if men disagree about them? Hobbes didn't seem to find this a real problem. Like most of his fellow adherents to the new epistemology, he seemed to believe that men could apprehend the basic "elements" of reality without difficulty or confusion. In the past, to be sure, they had not been successful in doing so, but this failure was not the result of any intrinsic incapacity of the mind; it was instead the consequence of the positive confusions and errors induced by "vain philosophy." Once these extrinsic obstacles to clear sight had been dispelled, the natural light of the mind would, perceiving reality, quite readily make accurate definitions. As Helvetius put it, "the obscurity of a proposition never lies in the things, but in the words."[46] With the elimination of semantic confusion, allegedly promised by the imminent dissolution of Scholastic philosophy, "the things" in the world would appear quite clearly to the mind via the senses.

Second, one might then protest, what was the point of a purely analytic moral science of this sort? What would be gained from it? For Hobbes, the answer to this one lay in the word "consequences." The relationship between premise and conclusion in science was, in his view, also a relationship between cause and consequence in the real world. By its capacity to derive the consequences of given principles, science could make good the weakness in man's perception that Hobbes believed was the principal cause of political disasters. Men do not choose to have wars; they blunder into them, he said, because they "know not the causes neither of war nor peace." And this ignorance comes about because "none hitherto have taught them in a clear and exact method."[47] Men suffered from a bad case of nearsightedness:

> For men are by nature provided of notable multiplying glasses, (that is, their Passions and Self-love,) through which, every little

payment appeareth a great grievance; but are destitute of those prospective glasses, (namely Morall and Civill Science,) to see a farre off the miseries that hang over them, and cannot without such payments be avoyded.[48]

Science could make good this failure, Hobbes thought. In history, the consequences of actions become visible only later on— and later on may be too late, for by then the actions may be irretrievable and the consequences unavoidable. In logic, consequences become visible almost immediately. A demonstrative science was indeed analytic, but it was not thereby trivial; for it could perform the invaluable service of telescoping the chain of cause and consequence into a readily comprehensible system. Moral science, then, could provide men with the foresight they needed to save themselves from the folly of pursuing their potentially destructive passions.

This was a defensible answer to the problem, but it was one that derived its force from Hobbes's own distinctive conception of human nature. Given his psychology of the passions—man governed immediately by vanity and the lust for power but governed ultimately by the desire to avoid violent death—the capacity to anticipate consequences would be sufficient. Men so "enlightened" would act prudently, "nature itself [in the form of the natural desire for self-preservation] impelling them."[49]

The more common understanding of what a moral science would entail was somewhat different from Hobbes's very interesting version. This more common image—"moral Newtonianism" proper, it might be called—was depicted in terms of *moral vision* rather than foresight. The function of this science would not be simply to predict the necessary consequences of given actions but rather to provide a clear and unambiguous perception of what was good. Reason was to *unveil* the Good just as it was unveiling Nature. No longer would the *agathon* be difficult to discern; no longer would men see the Good "through a glass darkly." The illumination of the new method would penetrate the obscurity that had previously surrounded moral facts, just as it had dispelled the alleged mysteries surrounding natural facts. Enlightenment would dispel the darkness of the moral and political Cave in which men had wandered for so long.

John Stuart Mill gave lucid expression to this hopeful expectation in the nineteenth century, thereby exemplifying the persistence of moral Newtonianism and its imperviousness in some quarters to the inroads of Humean skepticism. As one who had always "regarded the methods of physical science as the proper models for political," he looked forward to a time when "convictions as to what is right and wrong" would be "so firmly grounded in reason and in the true exigencies of life, that they shall not, like all former and present creeds, religious, ethical, and political, require to be periodically thrown off and replaced by others."[50]

The fruits of success of such a moral science would, of course, be enormous. The attainment of a demonstrative science of human order, a scientific delineation of right and wrong, promised to transform politics. It would provide an indisputable standard for the assessment of policies, for one thing; and the ability to determine the right action in a given situation on a rational and objective basis would eliminate the deep and often destructive political strife caused by the presence of widely divergent moral ideals. With objective certainty about moral issues would come the moral *unanimity* of society. A new age of "positive" politics would ensue, an age that would see a true "end of ideology," in the contemporary sense of that phrase. The ideological and religious sources of social divisions would be outmoded, transcended and replaced by the new, universally valid, and objective doctrine.

Building on this certain and permanent scientific basis, which could compel universal allegiance, men could be guaranteed political progress. The new science would guarantee future development. As Frank Manuel put it,

> the mathematicization of the study of man would become a double security against antiprogressive forces, for moral knowledge would find itself protected by the armor of numbers and equations, and moral problems would be removed from the disputes of the marketplace, where they always provoked destructive violence.[51]

If someone complained that he saw little progress toward the establishment of this moral science, there was a ready answer. The moral sciences were still in their infancy. It was just a matter of time. After all, what was needed was an "experimental physics of the soul." Once the experiments had been conducted, once the empirical evidence had been gathered, results would be forthcoming.

The Mixture of Old and New Ideas

In reality, the whole idea of a "moral science" was a logically unstable mixture of old and new ideas. It sought to combine the form of the new Reason with the substance of the old Reason. A moral science would have the scope and content that classical *logos*-rationality had claimed; it would therefore include the perception of the teleological order of human fulfillment. It would, at the same time, have the form and methods of the new "technical rationality"; it would thereby achieve the clarity, certainty, simplicity, and accessibility that this new conception of knowledge seemed to promise.

"*Logos*-rationality" was the participative apprehension of the order of Being. Technical rationality was the detached scrutiny of objects in the world. The proponents of the new science hoped to attain the results of the former through the means of the latter. Or, to put it slightly differently, they hoped to illuminate Nature as it had been conceived in the classical tradition, with its teleological order, by using the beacon light of the new methods. (It seems not to have occurred to them at first that the new conception of reason might not logically be made to perform in this fashion. Instead of illuminating Nature, it might insist on reducing it to its own dimensions.)

The coexistence of the old and the new throughout the seventeenth and eighteenth centuries, however problematic logically, is readily apparent. Descartes, certainly, did not conceive of himself as a moral or religious revolutionary. In fact, he was apparently exceptionally conventional and uncritical in these matters. The provisional code of morals he had drawn up for himself, he reported in the *Discourse on Method*, had, as its first maxim,

> To obey the laws and customs of my country, adhering unwaveringly to the religion in which, by God's grace, I had been educated from my childhood, and in all other matters regulating my conduct in conformity with the most moderate opinions, those furthest removed from extremes, as commonly exemplified in the practice of the most judicious of those among whom I might be living.[52]

In his expressed conviction that "the most moderate" opinions in moral matters were "likely to be the best"[53] he sounded rather like a domesticated Aristotelian pursuing the golden mean within the broad confines of the status quo. He certainly was no radical.

In religious matters Descartes was also very orthodox and subservient to authority. His timidity on this score may well have been partly a function of natural prudence and an aversion to martyrdom. In a letter to Mersenne, for example, where he wrote that he "would not wish, for anything in the world, to maintain [some of his ideas on physics] against the authority of the Church," he added: "I desire to live in peace and to continue the life I have begun under the motto 'to live well you must live unseen.'"[54] However, his religious orthodoxy seems to have been quite sincere and not merely a screen erected for prudential reasons. His personal life was marked by signs of piety and by resolute adherence to the articles of the Catholic faith. He allegedly made a pilgrimage to Loretto as a sign of gratitude for his philosophical discoveries, and he wrote to Mersenne that "I am enraged when I see that there are people in the world so bold and so impudent as to fight against God." As for himself, he had found "an evident proof . . . which satisfies me entirely, and which makes me know that there is a God with more certainty than I know the truth of any proposition of geometry."[55]

Moreover, Descartes had his distinctly mystical side. Rather like Sir Thomas Browne, who was both an enthusiast of experimental science and a deep believer in witchcraft, Descartes found it possible to place great emphasis on the role played by irrational factors like luck, emotion, and divine inspiration in human life. As Karl Stern once wrote apropos of this dimension in Descartes: "Just as a camel loads its body with water for the long desert trip, Descartes carried enough *supplément d'âme* to last for the arid journey of a *mathēsis universalis.*"[56]

In the hands of its creator, Cartesian doubt was not politically or morally radical. Doubt was kept on a tight leash, however absolute it was alleged to be within its legitimate sphere. As we saw earlier, Cartesian doubt was not pyrhonnic. Nor was it agnostic or subversive. Doubt was for Descartes a method, not a stance. It was in no way supposed to lead to "impudence" or rebellion. His critical program, as he said, "had all along been limited to the reform of my own thoughts." It had not been directed at the foundations of the political order:

> Great public institutions, if once overthrown, are excessively difficult to reestablish, or even to maintain erect if once seriously shaken; and their fall cannot but be very violent. . . . Almost always the imperfections are more tolerable than the changes required for their removal. . . . This is why I cannot at all approve of those reckless, quarrelsome spirits who, though not called by birth or fortune to take part in the management of public affairs, yet never fail to be always on the hunt for some new reform. If I thought that in this essay there were the least ground for supposing me to be guilty of any such folly, I should never willingly consent to its publication.[57]

Cartesian doubt later slipped its leash. Descartes had articulated concepts and a style whose heuristic implications he could not fully control. Reason would soon become, as Condorcet would put it, the antagonist of Authority. But Descartes did not plan it that way. So far as he was concerned, reason could be at home within the established moral and political order.

Locke was, of course, more "liberal" and "modern" than his Continental predecessor. He was not a Catholic, and the hand of the Inquisitor did not reach across the Channel. Moreover, the political order in England had moved more rapidly to accommodate the intellectual, economic, and social transformations that had occurred. "Authority," in Locke's later days at least, did not appear to be as flagrantly in conflict with the demands of "reason" as it was on the Continent. At times Locke did conceal some of his controversial views, as when he refused to acknowledge his authorship of *The Reasonableness of Christianity*. However, when he fled England temporarily for refuge in Holland, it was because of specifically political associations, not because of philosophical heresy. When he returned, on the same ship that carried Mary, soon to be queen, he was quite in tune with the emergent conventional wisdom of post–Glorious Revolution England. Indeed, he was one of its leading spokesmen.

The intent to retain established moral truths within the context of the new philosophy is nevertheless quite as evident in Locke as it was in Descartes. In a way, in fact, it is more evident. In Descartes's thought the old and the new seemed simply to coexist without being reconciled. In this respect, as in others, Descartes was dualistic. Locke, on the other hand, was the great synthesizer, even when synthesis was not really a logical possibility. He seemed fairly comfortable in believing that he had reconciled the old and the new in a coherent whole. In his attempt, he glossed over some very deep internal tensions within his thought that were soon to unravel his alleged synthesis. For the time being, however, he unquestionably poured a great number of traditional philosophical beliefs into his new epistemological vessel.

In Locke's view, the new reason in no way undermined traditional beliefs in God or in natural law. Indeed, the existence of both was considered quite "evident." Knowledge of God's existence and of the moral law clearly fell within the scope of the human understanding, in Locke's eyes, however limited that understanding might be in other respects. In the *Essay* he wrote that

> our reason leads us to the knowledge of this certain and evident truth,—That there is an eternal, most powerful, and most knowing Being; which whether anyone will please to call God, it matters not. The thing is evident; and from this idea duly considered, will easily be deduced all those other attributes, which we ought to ascribe to this eternal Being.[58]

Similarly, Locke insisted throughout his life on the existence of a law of nature that "can be perceived by the light of nature alone."[59] This law of nature he described as "the decree of the divine will discernible by the light of nature and indicating what is and what is not in conformity with rational nature, and for this very reason commanding or prohibiting."[60] His basic conception of it seems to have been quite in harmony with traditional natural-law ideas, despite the fact that he was never able to give an adequate justification for it on his philosophical principles, and despite the fact that the content he ascribed to it seemed to become attenuated in his later, more hedonistic, thought. He seemed to perceive no fundamental difference between his idea of natural law and the Aristotelian, Ciceronian, Scholastic, or Platonist notions of it. He cited Aristotle for support of his affirmation of the existence of a law of nature in his *Essays* on that topic. The ideas and terminology in his early Latin treatise on the civil magistrate were sufficiently Scholastic that they could have been "derived directly from St. Thomas or Suarez."[61] The Anglican divine Richard Hooker was a constant and esteemed reference point for him, especially in his *Treatises on Civil Government,* and the Cambridge Platonist Nathanael Culverwel seems clearly to have provided inspiration for Locke's own thoughts on natural law. In short, however innovative his epistemology, Locke evinced little doubt that the human understanding could extend to knowledge of God and to the perception of a natural law that, though eroded somewhat in content, had basically the same substance as the traditional law of nature.

The deep conviction that the new rationalist methods simply provided fuller and more systematic insight into fairly well-established moral and religious truths was very widespread in the seventeenth and eighteenth centuries. Most of the Fellows of the Royal Society in England, for example, felt certain that the new natural philosophy did not and would not come into conflict with the essentials of Christian doctrine. Indeed, they "thought of themselves as simple investigators of God's creation, studying the natural revelation as theologians studied the Scriptural revelation."[62] Samuel Clarke insisted in his thesis for his Cambridge doctor of divinity degree that "no article of Christian faith is opposed to right reason," and John Ray wrote a work entitled *The Wisdom of God Manifested in the Works of the Creation.*

A similar conviction that old truths could rest comfortably in the context of the new rationalism was manifest in more secular circles as well. Grotius sought to ground his conception of law on secular, rational, and scientific foundations, but his conception of the content of that law was not very different from the earlier view. As Cassirer observes, he "advances beyond scholasticism less in content than in method."[63] Thomas Jefferson wrote to Henry Lee that the ideas set forth in the Declaration of Independence were based on principles established long ago by Aristotle and Cicero, among others.[64] And D'Alembert assured his readers that the basic principles of morality and religion were clearly discernible by the mind. "It is therefore evident," he said,

> that the purely intellectual concepts of vice and virtue, the principle and the necessity of laws, the spiritual nature of the soul, the existence of God and of our obligations toward him—in a word,

the truths for which we have the most immediate and indispensable need—are the fruits of the first reflective ideas that our sensations occasion.[65]

In short, for much of the seventeenth and eighteenth centuries the new reason was expected to have the same competence as *logos*-rationality when it came to the "moral sciences." It could be expected, moreover, to reveal largely the same moral truths, only with much greater clarity, certainty, and simplicity. Moral inquiry would be a part of the exploration of "nature," in the wide sense of that word. It would involve the elaboration of more definitive insights into human nature through the "experimental physics of the soul." In doing so, the moral sciences were generally expected to fulfill rather than undermine the aspirations of classical *logos*-rationality to illuminate the order of Being and of man's perfection. This was to be an important feature of enlightenment, which was to be the adversary of irrational "authority" and "enthusiasm" but the friend and ally of moral truth.

The adherents of the new model of reason, therefore, were virtually unanimous in believing that the epistemological revolution would be politically and socially beneficial. The attainment and dissemination of truth and understanding, and the concomitant dispelling of error and ignorance, could in their view have only a positive influence on the conduct of politics. When it came to the actual dynamics of this beneficent influence, however, and to the specific political form it should assume, there was much ambiguity, confusion, and disagreement. Some were not really too concerned with the details; it simply seemed obvious that the epistemological breakthrough had brought more light into the world and that the practical consequences of this new illumination could only be good. Burke was later to defend "prejudice" in politics, but no one was inclined to argue that error, ignorance, and superstition were political virtues.

The Varieties of Moral Newtonianism

Those who tried to think further about the specific political implications of enlightenment were often not wholly clear or consistent in their expectations. As in the underlying conception of a moral science, a great number of old assumptions were mingled with new beliefs. Moreover, these thinkers sometimes followed different and not wholly compatible lines of reasoning simultaneously, either in the conviction that these were mutually reinforcing or else simply unaware that the viewpoints they embraced without distinction were in fact divergent.

As a consequence of this ambiguity, overlap, and confusion, any attempt to disentangle these varied models analytically and to identify coherent accounts of the relationship between intellectual advance and political progress can produce only "ideal types." It is necessary and possible to reconstruct relatively coherent paradigms that were in fact operating in important ways in the political thought of the new rationalists, and representive figures can be adduced whose ideas conformed rather closely to these ideal-type models. However, it should be borne in mind that these models are more schematic and coherent than the more complex and less consistent ideas they seek to sort out and clarify.

With this warning in mind, it is possible to disentangle at least four different conceptions of the political impact and significance of the intellectual revolution that had occurred. In rough order of their appearance, these may be termed (1) politically conservative liberalism, (2) democratic natural-right liberalism, (3) natural-reconciliation-of-interests liberalism, and (4) artificial-reconciliation-of-interests liberalism. The key basis for discriminating among these ideal-type models lies in their differing specifications of the source of political order. The first two models agreed in depicting reason and virtue as the keys to political progress; they differed regarding the direction and process by which reason and virtue would become politically efficacious, the former believing in a "trickle-down" model, the latter in a "percolate-up" model. The third relied on the rationality of nature in concert with a more limited form of human rationality. The final model put the burden of political advance on the deployment of rationally conceived human artifice.

Until around the middle of the eighteenth century, political rationalism assumed a relatively conservative form as far as questions of political organization were concerned. Bacon, Locke, Descartes, and the early *philosophes* in varying ways tended to see the role of reason in terms of enhancement of the existing political order. The achievements and discoveries of the new epistemology would be of great political service, but they did not entail any profound transformation of the usual political relationships. The best strategy for the rationalization of the political order was generally conceded to center around enlightening those who held power. Philosophers could influence kings, and enlightened monarchs could bring peace and happiness to their subjects. Hobbes hoped to persuade some ruler to exercise his sovereignty on behalf of his civil philosophy, and rulers like Frederick and Catherine were eyed hopefully by the early *philosophes*. Political change and progress could be achieved most effectively if brought about from the top downward. Liberalism's early political views were neither very democratic nor very revolutionary so far as distribution of power or the source of political advance were concerned.

Francis Bacon was no democrat. As chancellor of England, he was, of course, a member of the "establishment" himself. However radical and innovative his ideas in the area of epistemology might be, he took a quite traditional view of the necessity of political authority and of its prerogatives. He is alleged to have said that he "did not love the word People." One of his biographers summarized his basic political conservatism: "From first to last, Bacon showed what seemed an inborn reverence for authority and paternalism in government—the Continental idea—which contrasted strikingly with his intellectual originality and impatience where science and education were concerned."[66]

Descartes, as we saw earlier, had no quarrel with authority in morals, religion, or politics. He went to considerable lengths to emphasize that his method of doubt was confined solely to matters of philosophy, and these he tried diligently to quarantine from matters of state. Locke was somewhat more moderate and "liberal", concerned as he was with the limits of a sovereign's authority over his people. The principal impetus to his insistence on the limits of legitimate authority, however, derived more from political circumstance than from philosophical deductions, and in some ways these limits were merely an extension into a new social setting of the medieval principles of constitutionalism—i.e., the insistence that the king was not above the law.

Condillac was basically quite conservative in his political views. He had no problem in acknowledging the legitimacy of the social, political, and economic inequalities that characterized the established order in eighteenth-century France. He even believed that the sovereign had a duty to promote the true religion, and he doubted the notion of progress. In these latter beliefs, however, he was already something of an anomaly.

Some who did believe in the idea of progress were nevertheless quite conservative on the issues of political organization and the distribution of power. The abbé de Saint-Pierre, for example, was even convinced that the best course of action might be to increase the power and authority of government. This, he believed, would be the most effective way to achieve progress, assuming, of course, that those in power became more enlightened. The Physiocrats were largely hostile to democracy, being instead proponents of enlightened despotism. Voltaire tended to prefer monarchy to democracy, thought of parliament as a convention of propertyholders, and had no qualms about the role of class inequalities in society, which he considered inevitable in any case. He was also the author of some of the more withering epithets applied to the common man. While it might be somewhat extreme to say with de Tocqueville that the *philosophes* despised the public almost as much as they despised the deity, it is nonetheless quite clear that passionate attachment to the rationalist intellectual revolution was not considered incompatible with a decidedly nondemocratic political stance.

Toward the latter part of the eighteenth century, however, a discernible shift occurred in the dominant political implications inferred from rationalist premises. A process of political radicalization began. The characteristic political lessons that were drawn from the new epistemology began to become more liberal and democratic and less accommodating to established patterns of authority. The trend was toward greater egalitarianism, greater liberalization, more optimism. The hopeful democratic views of Condorcet, Chastellux, Jefferson, and Paine began to supersede the more elitist outlook of Voltaire, Condillac, and the Physiocrats. Emphasis was placed more and more on the natural rights of all men, and greater store was set by the political role of enlightened public opinion. Reason and virtue were still looked on as the likely sources of political improvement, but were expected to be lodged more widely within the populace as a whole. The ideal of representative government, as both an inherently worthwhile goal and as a potential means to the rationalization of social policy, gained ground rapidly. If the voice of the people was not considered to be the voice of God, it was at least held to promise political progress as it became both more enlightened and more influential.

This process, which might be called the political radicalization of Cartesianism, actually involved several crucial steps, two of which had already been accomplished between 1680 and 1740, roughly speaking. The first step was the gradual sloughing-off of the dualistic, spiritualistic, and innatist aspects of Cartesian thought. This trend, which was part of the mainstream of secularist philosophical thought, also permitted the assimilation of the Cartesian heritage to Lockean empiricist notions, as we saw earlier. This development was largely accomplished by the early part of the eighteenth century. The second major development within this radicalization process, and one that occurred at virtually the same time, was the destruction of the sanctuary Descartes had set up to isolate political and moral doctrines from his critical method. The "left-wing" intellectual heirs of Descartes saw him as untrue to his own principles in this respect. They found quite unconvincing the rather weak theoretical arguments he had offered on behalf of his attempt to place political principles beyond the reach of the method of doubt, and the practical considerations and prejudices that had led him to make the attempt were to them quite unacceptable. For the *philosophes* there could be no intellectual preserves set up against the free exercise of critical reason; the only areas properly "off limits" to reason were those intrinsically beyond its compass, and politics was not among them. This judgment also fitted well with the empiricist notion of an "experimental physics of the soul."

The third step in this radicalizing process—one that came slightly later—consisted in following out more assiduously the democratic notions that were implicit in the new epistemology. This shift was what marked the transition from the more elitist *philosophes* of the first half of the eighteenth century to the more egalitarian *philosophes* of its last half.

Political events, of course, provided the decisive impetus to this last stage of radicalization. The tendency toward political radicalization of the intelligentsia after 1750, especially in France, went hand in hand with the democratic radicalization of rationalism. This important causal role of autonomous historical forces does not mean, however, that the theories were merely Marxist "superstructures," ideologies in the pejorative sense of that term, purely dependent variables without logical force or autonomous influence of their own. It means simply that all political theories have empirical content, reference points in the real world, as well as theoretical concepts. Like the law, they are a combination of logic and experience. New experience provides more empirical grist for the theoretical mill, and important empirical political trends may therefore quite logically impel some changes in a theoretical viewpoint.

This is basically what happened in the case at hand. The political experience of the last part of the eighteenth century began to cast doubt on some of the previously dominant assumptions about the probable political location of reason. The experience of the earlier liberals, from Spinoza to Voltaire, was that not much enlightened political action could be expected of the people, the common men, in any society. They were held—not wholly without cause—to be basically ignorant and superstitious, inclined to support irrational and authoritarian causes, and even prone to turn with fury on their best leaders. Spinoza, for example, had undergone a profoundly sobering encounter with that fury in the Netherlands. Accordingly, like Plato looking for his philosopher-king, they tended to assume that enlightened monarchs were the most likely conduit for reason in political life. This judgment was based on a practical assessment of the empirical possibilities for political progress, and, given the available evidence, it was not an unreasonable inference. In France, at least, this basically Platonic theoretical tendency was undoubtedly reinforced by the practical inclination of the modernizing bourgeoisie to look to the crown for an ally against the reactionary force of the feudal aristocracy.

It was this empirically rather justifiable and historically well-established assumption that the experience of the eighteenth century began to call into question. In England the role of the king was clearly diminishing in significance as Parliament became the dominant institutional force in that country's political life. Since most of the *philosophes*—with a few significant exceptions, such as Rousseau—considered British political forms more advanced than those on the Continent, this British trend toward parliamentary sovereignty helped to change assumptions about the nature and source of political authority in a modern polity. Perhaps the way to an enlightened society was through the ascendancy of a representative body instead of through the education of philosopher-kings.

The contrasting experience of France in the same era contributed to the same conclusions from the other end. If Britain afforded an example of relative progress through diminution of the royal prerogative, the unhappy French situation provided a case of apparent political stagnation under continued royal authority. Kings were not proving very adept as receptors and vehicles of enlightenment. Louis XV and Louis XVI seemed more bent on retarding progress than on abetting it. Perhaps royal authority was, then, an obstacle to the rationalization of politics rather than a principal agent of political reason? Perhaps it trailed public opinion rather than led it? The philosophy of *bons sens* certainly seemed to be quite enthusiastically received by "the people"—i.e., the bourgeois upper echelons of the Third Estate—even as the French monarchs were proving relatively indifferent to it. Perhaps the adherents of the Age of Reason should look to the people rather than to the prince.

This important shift in the expected social source of enlightenment and progress—from above to below, from king to populace—had received sufficient acceptance by the end of the century that Condorcet could almost take it for granted. The evidence of history clearly indicated, he said, that public opinion leads rulers rather than vice versa. Enlightenment begins with philosophers. It is then gradually disseminated among the educated populace. Only later still are those who govern society dragged by the force of public opinion into approving enlightened policies:

> If in the moral and political sciences there is always a large interval between the point to which philosophers have carried the progress of enlightenment and the degree of enlightenment at-

tained by the average man of education (and it is the body of beliefs held in common by such men that constitutes the generally accepted creed known as public opinion), those who direct public affairs and who immediately influence the fate of the common people, under whatever constitution they may hold their powers, are very far from rising to the level of public opinion; they follow its advance, without ever overtaking it and are always many years behind it and therefore always ignorant of many of the truths that it has learned.[67]

This final step in the democratic radicalization of the Cartesian (and Lockean) account of knowledge and its social impact was actually highly consonant with the basic precepts of the new epistemology. Indeed, the late-eighteenth-century adherents of natural-rights democracy could with some justification consider the earlier, more elitist *philosophes* to be men of little faith who had permitted their limited experience to override their logic. Many of the central metaphors and motifs of the new rationalism were profoundly political, and the implications they contained tended to be libertarian and egalitarian.

Take, for example, the absolutely central motif of *autonomy* in the new epistemology. The insistence on the possibility, even the necessity, of intellectual autonomy and self-reliance was an omnipresent theme from Descartes's solitary *cogito* to Kant's injunction to throw off self-incurred tutelage. The capabilities of the unfettered natural light of the mind suggested the importance of intellectual freedom and independence for intellectual progress. Autonomy, however, is clearly a political situation as well as an epistemological precondition. The one could not be wholly abstracted from the other. An important implication of the new epistemology, then, was that men must be *free* to follow the natural light of their intellectual faculties.

The epistemological theme of autonomy, in other words, quite naturally spilled over into the political theme of *liberté*. The connection might be a relatively logical one: minds inhabit bodies; knowing is an act; therefore, political freedom must to some extent accompany intellectual liberation. Or the connection might be looser, merely analogical. Epistemology helped to put the notion of freedom into the air, and politics was not immune from the contagion of the idea. This form of influence may be less specifiable, but it is no less profound.

These political implications of the insistence on intellectual autonomy were quite explicit in the minds of many of the leading exponents of the new mode of reason, from Descartes, who worried about them, to Condorcet, who gloried in them. Locke, for example, clearly set his emphasis on the natural capacities of the mind in a political context. These capacities, he said, had been obscured by those who would

> take [their followers] off from the use of their reason and judgment, and put them on believing and taking them upon trust without further examination: in which posture of blind credulity, they might be more easily governed by, and made useful to some sort of men, who had the skill and office to principle and guide them.[68]

The political and intellectual liberation of mankind would go hand in hand.

Another extremely important political dimension of the new epistemology also fitted quite nicely into the democratic radicalization process, for throughout the new epistemology ran the motif of the universal, or nearly universal, accessibility of the truth. This accessibility seemed to be a logical consequence of the new science's basic features: its simplicity, its self-evident foundations, and its generation from explicit rules of method.

Insistence on the accessibility of knowledge was a persistent theme from the early days of Bacon's "instauration" to very late currents of Enlightenment thought. Descartes, of course, was quite explicit in his conviction that his method would open the pathways of knowledge to even the most humble. His own successes he attributed not to any peculiar excellence in his own mental capacities but rather to his careful observation of proper method. "Good sense," he wrote,

> is of all things in the world the most equitably distributed . . .; the power of judging well and of distinguishing between the true and the false, which, properly speaking, is what is called good sense, or reason, is by nature equal in all men.[69]

Accordingly, he believed that his way to knowledge could be appropriated by anyone:

> Throughout the treatise as a whole our aim will be to follow so carefully the paths which lie open to man and which lead him to truth, and to render them so easy that anyone who has perfectly mastered this whole method, however ordinary his mental powers, may be enabled to see that no path is closed to him which is not also closed to others.[70]

In the eighteenth century this Cartesian faith persisted and intensified. Helvetius echoed the theme of equal endowment and drew the same hopeful conclusion Descartes had reached: "There are no truths contained in the works of Locke and Newton that are not now comprehensible by all men of a common organization. . . . The most sublime discoveries, clearly represented, are conceivable by all."[71]

D'Alembert emphasized the significance of simplicity and method in opening the truth to everyone:

> Hence it is perhaps true that there is hardly a science or an art which cannot, with rigor and good logic, be taught to the most limited mind, because there are but few arts or sciences whose propositions or rules cannot be reduced to some simple notions and arranged in such a close order that their chain of connection will nowhere by interrupted.[72]

And Diderot suggested the populist program that might follow:

> Let us hasten to make philosophy popular. If we want the philosophers to march on before, let us approach the people at the point where the philosophers are. Will they say there are works which will never come within reach of everyone? If they say so, they only show that they are ignorant of what proper method and long practice can do.[73]

If it was true, as Descartes maintained, that the epistemological revolution could "make peasants better judges of the truth about the world than philosophers are now,"[74] then claims of political privilege or distinction on the basis of special intellectual competence lost their force. If the common man could legitimately aspire to be a sage, then he might reasonably expect to be self-governing. As Theodore Roszak has remarked of Descartes's and Bacon's insistence on the wide accessibility of knowledge via proper method, "the seeds of a democratic politics lie hidden therein, a subversive belief in human equality founded upon the prospect of knowledge available to all on a non-privileged, non-classified basis."[75]

The democratic optimism of men such as Condorcet and James Mill was in a sense a new version of two very old and established maxims—the one that holds that the truth makes men free, the other that knowledge is virtue or at least leads directly to it. As Condorcet asked, rhetorically,

> Will not the free man's sense of his own dignity and a system of education built upon a deeper knowledge of our moral constitution, render common to almost every man those principles of strict and unsullied justice, those habits of an active and enlightened benevolence, of a fine and generous sensibility which nature has implanted in the hearts of all and whose flowering waits only upon the favourable influences of enlightenment and freedom? Just as the mathematical and the physical sciences tend to improve the arts that we use to satisfy our simplest needs, is it not also part of the necessary order of nature that the moral and political sciences should exercise a similar influence upon the motives that direct our feelings and our actions?[76]

There is some question about the extent of this belief in the capacity of knowledge to increase virtuous action. Lester Crocker, for example, has written that "Condorcet alone, perhaps, believed in an actual change in character, in improvement of the moral and physical constitution."[77] However, this claim is somewhat misleading. Even Condorcet did not believe that improved knowledge would actually improve man's moral "constitution." As the above quotation makes clear, his conception was that enlightenment would simply permit the "flowering" of the "fine and generous sensibility" that "nature" had already "implanted." Enlightenment would not create good motives; it would simply enable them to become operative. And, in this form, the belief that the spread of knowledge would lead to the proliferation of virtuous action was quite extensively held. Voltaire, for example, who was rather skeptical about the prospects for progress, nevertheless wrote that rational philosophy "is mild, it is humane; it teaches us forbearance and dispels discord; it fosters virtue and makes obedience to the laws agreeable rather than compulsory."[78] And Diderot wrote that the ultimate aim of the *Encyclopedia* was "that our grandsons, as they become better educated, may at the same time become more virtuous and more happy."[79]

It would, in fact, have been somewhat surprising if such an inference had not been drawn, for the suppositions that sustained it were deeply implanted in the inherited philosophical tradition, both on its Platonic and its Aristotelian sides. When Mersenne objected to Descartes's optimism that his new pathway to the apprehension of truth would conduce to virtuous action, Descartes replied by citing the orthodox Scholastic doctrine on the relationship between the will and the understanding. "You reject my statement," he wrote to Mersenne,

> that in order to do well it is sufficient to judge well; yet it seems to me that the common scholastic doctrine is that *the will does not tend towards evil except in so far as it is presented to it by the intellect under some aspect of goodness*—that is why they say that *whoever sins does so in ignorance*—so that if the intellect never presented anything to the will as good without its actually being so, the will could never go wrong in its choice.[80]

It was an assumption carried over almost intact from established tradition, then, that helped to fuel Descartes's expectations about the moral consequences of his methodological innovations.

In parallel fashion, the Platonic tradition had always held that the good, the true, and the beautiful ultimately overlapped. The Truth about the world was orderly, symmetrical, aesthetic, and by means of this balanced and harmonious beauty it exerted an erotic pull on the mind and will of the philosopher, the lover of truth. Just as there were many other transfigured Platonic themes in the new rationalism, this notion of the conduciveness of knowledge to virtue also survived in various quarters. Platonic *erōs* for the *logos* of the cosmic order could and did assume Newtonian form. In one of the foremost popularizations of Newton's ideas, for example, University of Edinburgh Professor Colin McLaurin wrote that the "perfect goodness" with which the movements of the Newtonian cosmos were "evidently directed" constituted "the supreme object of the speculations of a philosopher; who, while he contemplates and admires so excellent a system, cannot but be himself excited and animated to correspond with the *general harmony of nature.*"[81] Plato could hardly have said more of the *agathon*.

Voltaire also had recourse to erotic imagery, of a somewhat less elevated type, when he sought to characterize the attraction of the newly apprehended order of nature upon man's will. He has "Reason" say to "Truth":

> My daughter, I think our reign may be just beginning, after our long imprisonment. . . . That will happen to us which has happened to Nature: she has been covered by an ugly veil and completely disfigured during countless centuries. At the end have come a Galileo, a Copernicus, and a Newton, who have shown her nearly naked and who have made men almost amorous of her.[82]

As time went on, one might go on to add, "Nature" suffered the occupational hazards of an aging striptease artist. By the time Darwin and Freud had pulled off a few more veils, "Nature" had lost her charm, and men began to clamor for a return of the old girl to greater propriety. But that was later.

This somewhat confused, incompletely thought-out superimposition of new form on old substance in the idea of reason was an important contributor to the classic early-modern model of liberal democracy. Some of the most crucial norms of classic liberal democracy were liberty and equality, the sanctity of natural right, the importance of public opinion, and the parliamentary ideals of representative government and persuasion. "Reason" sustained each of these ideals. "Reason" was accessible to all, hence it was egalitarian. It presupposed individual autonomy, hence it was libertarian. It could clearly discern the existence and content of natural right: "We hold these truth to be self-evident." Its spread legitimized the sovereignty of *vox populi*. It would be embodied in the action of representative bodies, who would convene to discern the common good through rational discourse and persuasion.

The democratic philosophy of natural right was, of course, not universally embraced or universally undergirded by rationalist premises. Not everyone was a Jefferson, much less a Godwin, Paine, or Priestley. Nevertheless, the natural-rights philosophy, which had profound roots in the new rationalism, had sufficient credence in the later eighteenth century that Jefferson could be criticized for having put forward "hackneyed" ideas in the Declaration of Independence. Jefferson, appropriately undismayed by this criticism, replied that he had simply undertaken "to place before mankind the common sense of the subject."[83]

The gradual dissolution of the philosophy of natural rights was both cushioned and masked for a long time by the nearly simultaneous emergence of another model, which some have called the "identity-of-interests" model and which I have chosen to call the "natural-reconciliation-of-interests" model. In this view of things, it was not the virtuous will drawn teleologically toward order through its rational apprehension of the Good that would produce the good society. It was, instead, the machinations of nature that would do so. Nature, envisioned as a system of forces that possessed an entelechy toward balance, order, and harmony, would reconcile men's varied individual interests into a coherent and orderly social whole.

The archetype of the natural-reconciliation-of-interests conception of a liberal society is usually considered, with some justification, to be Adam Smith's theory of the "invisible hand." However, the basic idea of the invisible hand was actually quite widely adhered to in his time. Volney characterized nature as the "regular and constant order of events" that conducts men, "without distinction of country or sect, toward happiness and perfection."[84] Tom Paine claimed in *The Rights of Man* that unrestricted economic competition would bring permanent international peace, since war would no longer be in anyone's interest. Jefferson wrote that "so invariably do the laws of nature create our duties and interests that when they seem to be at variance, we ought to suspect some fallacy in our reasonings."[85] Kant's belief in the possibility of "perpetual peace" grew from a similar conception; in his essay of that name he wrote that "one purpose shines manifestly through all her [i.e., nature's] mechanical order: to use the discord of men for producing concord among them against their own will."[86] And Condorcet, with his characteristic clarity and enthusiasm, asked rhetorically,

> how, with all this seeming chaos, is it that, by a universal moral law, the efforts made by each individual on his own behalf minister to the welfare of all, and that the interests of society demand that everyone should understand where his own interests lie, and should be able to follow them without hindrance?[87]

Smith himself softened, and somewhat muddied, his own thought about the social role of the invisible hand by his allegiance to the "moral sense" school. When his thought as a whole is considered, it seems clear that he looked not only to the operations of natural equilibrating forces but also to what he saw as the natural sympathetic and convivial emotions of men to produce social order. For the purposes of ideal-type analysis, Mandeville's *Fable of the Bees* perhaps embodies the natural-reconciliation-of-interests model in its most stark and uncluttered form. In his *Fable,* Mandeville sought to demonstrate that individual selfish and egocentric impulses are spontaneously transmuted into socially beneficent consequences, and that an excess of individual altruism can actually be socially disruptive. From the standpoint of society, at least, admonitions on behalf of individual virtue were at best beside the point.

A great deal of confusion was introduced into much of the political theory of the late eighteenth and early nineteenth centuries by the failure to distinguish clearly these two different conceptions of liberalism. Was the moral basis of a liberal society natural right and the means toward its attainment a human will rationally oriented to self-evident moral and political truths? Or was the moral basis of liberal society instead utility and the means toward its attainment the equilibrating and ordering force of nature? These are quite different conceptions, and, as became more apparent later on, the differences might have significantly divergent practical implications. At the time, however, very few thinkers took any pains to choose decisively or to distinguish carefully between them. Both Voltaire and Diderot, for example, vacillated between a quasi-natural-law ethics on the one hand and utilitarian egoism on the other, and English political thought of the period tended to suffer from the same ambiguity. Elie Halévy has pointed out, for example, how Mackintosh manifested considerable confusion on this issue. "Now, is the principle which Mackintosh sets up against Burke the principle of utility or the 'metaphysical' principle of the Rights of Man? It is impossible to answer this question, for Mackintosh himself does not appear to be aware of a logical divergency between the two principles."[88] Thomas Paine, in similar fashion, seemed to move gradually—and without being fully aware of the transition—from a theoretical stance based on the principle of natural right toward one based more on the principle of utility.[89]

Part of the reason for this apparent casualness and confusion over a very basic and important theoretical issue was that, for many people, the two conceptions seemed to be mutually reinforcing rather than competing. As long as nature was seen as a force at work on behalf of social harmony, a reconciler of private and public interest, it could be seen as simply an alternative route to the same end.

Morally competent reason and the rightly ordered will it engendered should bring men into a well-ordered liberal society; but if reason failed to accomplish this goal on its own, then the machinations of nature would fill the gap. Reason and nature were seen as alter egos in any case. Nature was rational, just as Aristotle had said, and reason was natural. It really didn't matter, then, whether the path to the good society was through reason or through nature. The outcome was believed to be the same in either case.

An undiscriminating adherence to both conceptions of the road toward a liberal society possessed strategic advantages. The natural-reconciliation-of-interests model served as a good position to fall back to whenever one or another of the critical assumptions of the rational common-good model came under attack. For example, as the conception of reason began to narrow and attenuate, the idea that nature was at work to unify divergent private interests into a coherent whole helped to make this diminution of reason seem less problematic. If natural forces operated in this way, man could be merely rational (as in economic "rationality") rather than fully Rational (as in the classical tradition), and this didn't really matter as far as the consequences were concerned. Enlightened apprehension of the good was not really essential; an enlightened apprehension of one's own self-interest would suffice. Nature would do the rest.

Conflation of the two models also gave liberal theory epicyclical reserves for handling the problem of motivation. Many Enlightenment figures, though willing to concede that man had the intellectual capacity to know what he should do, harbored doubts about the capacity of this knowledge to energize the will. Knowledge is one thing, action another. As Saint Paul had lamented, the frailty of human nature is such that men may easily find themselves acting contrary to what they know to be good. Passionate self-interest might thus override a merely intellectual grasp of the principles of virtue. Here, too, the natural-reconciliation-of-interests model supplied a ready answer. On its assumptions, this gap between knowing and doing, the problem of motivation, was no problem at all, because nature acted to conjoin social duty and self-interest. If men simply pursued their own self-interest, they would at the same time, thanks to the natural order of things, be performing their best service to society. It was not necessary, then, to inspire men to altruism and virtue. They needed only to appreciate and to pursue their own selfish interests, and the invisible hand would turn their activity to socially beneficial ends.

Using the principle of utility as a supplement to the natural-rights model provided comfort and security, but it was not free of real dangers; these, however, became evident only somewhat later. Secure in the belief that self-interest rationality was sufficient, liberalism watched the scope of human reason and the psychology of human motivation erode quite dramatically without dismay. The fall-back position seemed satisfactory enough that no alarm sounded when natural-rights philosophy was discarded as "metaphysical." What was not perceived until too late was that the fall-back position was itself vulnerable. What if the social manifestations of nature's operation were not so beneficent? What if nature could not be relied on to transmute self-interest into public interest? Divorced from these cheery assumptions, the principle of utility would become at best systematically ambiguous and empty as a social doctrine. At worst, it might become profoundly illiberal.

This possibility soon became a reality. The optimistic conception of nature as a political deus ex machina was itself subject to erosion, assailed by some as an unwarranted metaphysical notion and condemned by others as without empirical warrant. From that time on, liberalism in the classical sense became a free-floating set of aspirations and hopes rather than a philosophically grounded set of norms and expectations. Cut off from the real sustenance that coherent and convincing empirical beliefs and philosophical ideas can supply, liberalism has had to try to sustain itself by the direct attraction of its ideals.

As the conviction spread that nature might be as incompetent as spontaneous rational will to create a stable and harmonious political order on its own, another model of the new reason's political role was articulated. If nature could not be counted on to arrange things properly, it was up to men themselves to take on this task. If nature was not a self-equilibrating social mechanism, then men must assume an active role to make good this incapacity. Men must become good political mechanics, regulating and manipulating the gears, levers, and pulleys of political events to bring them under rational control. If this task was done properly, in accord with the teachings of the emergent moral sciences, it was believed that the naturally divergent interests of individuals could be channeled into creating a coherent and harmonious public order. Rationally devised artifices could bring the general interest out of a myriad of private interests. This conception of the role of reason in politics might be called the doctrine of the artificial reconciliation of interests.[90]

Actually, the notion of the artificial reconciliation of interests produced a very mixed array of political ideas when it came down to the specific details. These details could be extremely important in practice, and they rested ultimately on some fairly important philosophical differences, often more tacit than explicit. The common thread was the analogy with mechanical contrivance. Social order was to be created by astute social engineering. The crucial question, often answered only by implication, then became: What was engineerable? What could be manipulated, regulated, and controlled, and what were the natural limits on social artifice?

The moderate form of this conception of politics tended to manifest itself in constitution-building. The *Federalist Papers* were an expression of this form of political Newtonianism. The limits nature sets on political possibilities were held to be very real and profound. Human nature, especially, was seen for the most part as a constant that must be accommodated by any sound and rational constitution. The purpose of a constitutional framework was to provide creative outlet for the moral, communal, and altruistic components of human nature while establishing procedural safeguards to prevent the selfish and domineering tendencies in man from producing tyranny or anarchy. This basic view of the nature/artifice relationship in politics is clearly manifest, for example, in the tactics Madison considered appropriate for combatting the baneful influence of "factions." One could not realistically hope to eliminate factions, he said, because they grow directly from attributes of human nature. Any attempt to eliminate them would logically entail attempting to "change" human nature itself, and this could not be done without extinguishing liberty. Madison therefore rejected this option as entirely infeasible and turned to stratagems for containing and controlling the bad consequences that factions could produce for the body politic.

The more radical form of the artificial-reconciliation-of-interests model did not recognize such limitations. If human nature was part of nature in the general sense, why could it not be similarly brought under control? Was there any reason in principle that the "dominion over nature" that Bacon, Descartes, and the rest had promised as the fruit of the new science could not extend to dominion over human nature? Could human nature not be refashioned by those who understood the levers and pulleys that impelled it, by those who understood the science of human motivation, to make it more tractable politically? For the beneficent and scientific legislator, human nature should present no more of an obstacle to the construction of the good society than would any other part of the cosmic mechanism. His knowledge would enable him to divine the requisites of social order and to shape men accordingly.

4 The Logic of Domination: The Origins of Technocracy

When the movement of critical rationalism into political and social theory issued into the enterprise of "moral Newtonianism," Descartes's optimism about the political and moral utility of his method and his belief in the fundamental unity of knowledge had triumphed over his cautious fear about turning the principle of doubt loose in the political arena.

As we have seen, however, "moral Newtonianism" was not a single coherent political program. Within the widespread quest to apply reason to politics in the way Newton had applied it to nature there were sharply contrasting schools of thought. The differences among them were extremely important, not only because they were theoretically significant but because their political implications could diverge dramatically. Often, however, the enthusiasts of moral Newtonianism were themselves insufficiently aware of these internal differences.

Moral Newtonianism$_1$ interpreted the Newtonian order as a moral and ethical order—as a great analogy of harmonious Being. The apprehension of this moral order thus amounted to receiving a revelation about Goodness, and those who received this revelation were in turn presumed to be "enlightened" in a profoundly moral sense. They were "enlightened" in the same way that Plato's philosopher was enlightened when he stumbled out of the Cave and beheld the light of Truth.

Like Plato's philosopher, moreover, the man enlightened by the Newtonian revelation could be expected to be erotically drawn to conform his own soul to that Truth. He would long to be in harmony with the morally beautiful cosmos he perceived. Or, to put it in Aristotelian terms—as Descartes did quite explicitly—man would naturally seek what he, now in a definitive way, apprehended as good. Under this interpretation of the meaning and significance of reason-in-politics-as-manifest-in-Newton, therefore, the problem of motivation was no problem at all. Knowledge, as in classical Greek ethics, could be assumed to produce virtuous action.

Within Moral Newtonianism$_1$, moreover, we can discriminate two alternative and contrasting political viewpoints, resulting from divergent accounts of *who* was presumed capable of apprehending the Newtonian *agathon*. If it was assumed that the implementation of the moral lessons of Reason would most likely come from the conversion of rulers by philosophers, then enlightened despotism was the logical goal. Voltaire and the early eighteenth-century *philosophes* generally took this approach. On the other hand, if one was convinced that common sense or public opinion was more likely to be enlightened than the minds of monarchs, a more democratic natural-rights liberalism could seem logical. Condorcet and Paine wound up taking this direction.

Moral Newtonianism$_2$ read the Newtonian analogy somewhat differently. This school saw the Newtonian order as a vast self-regulating natural cosmos. Its harmony was not so much an ethical as an efficient harmony. It did not so much inspire men to be virtuous as it conspired to produce beneficent results through the working-out of its own laws. The lesson drawn from this interpretation was, then, not so much "Know this and be inspired by it to be good" as it was "Understand that nature works for good in all things, and allow it to accomplish its ends." The great force of Nature, as Newton had revealed, could, in Condorcet's words, bring harmony out of "seeming chaos," converting private vice into public virtue. The path to political progress, accordingly, was the pursuit of "enlightened" self-interest together with a reliance on Nature to do the needful.

Moral Newtonianism$_3$ also read the Newtonian analogy in mechanical fashion rather than the mystical-moral fashion of Moral Newtonianism$_1$. However, in this version the machine was perceived not as a naturally self-regulating machine but rather as a morally indifferent piece of machinery that was amenable to intervention and control on behalf of moral ends. Nature might not, left to itself, bring about political progress. However, because it was a lawfully ordered mechanism, it could be engineered, by those who understood its laws, to produce the desired results. The universe, as revealed by Newton, was a giant piece of clockwork that, with appropriate direction and guidance from the outside, could run very well indeed.

In its moderate version, Moral Newtonianism$_3$ produced an emphasis on constitution-building. The manipulable environment was presumed to be that part of the world external to man in some sense. Social engineering, accordingly, was focused on institutions. Human beings themselves were assumed to possess the autonomy and integrity of moral creatures and therefore were not appropriately subject to direct manipulation—for practical reasons, for moral reasons, or for some combination of the two.

Another and more radical version of Moral Newtonianism$_3$ saw no reason to exempt human beings from its social engineering. Human nature was itself a continuous part of nature; thus it too was a part of the world mechanism that could be tinkered with, if necessary, to achieve desired ends. Man was seen as a machine animated by the passions, passions that were in turn amenable to "artificial" direction by those who understood the laws governing them.

It is this "radical" version of Moral Newtonianism$_3$ that provides the starting point for what we shall call the technocratic tradition. For the technocrats, politics becomes a science instead of a prudential art. It is neither Aristotelian theoretical science nor Aristotle's practical science but rather both of these wrapped up together—a "practice based on theory." The knowledge base for rational political action, that is, was seen as possessing the status of Aristotelian theory without its practical limitations, and the activity of politics was seen as possessing the practical force of Aristotelian *phronēsis* without its uncertainties and ambiguities. Technocratic politics, in short, is, in a very profound sense, "the experimental physics of the soul," practiced on law-governed objects by law-discerning legislators.

In styling particular political theorists as "technocrats," we must remember that we are dealing with an ideal type. Some thinkers will approximate the ideal more fully than others, and even they will not all be of one mind on all issues. A rough genealogy of technocratic thought, however, would probably identify the French moralist and social theorist Claude Helvetius as the first relatively complete technocratic archetype. Helvetius is not generally regarded as a major figure in political theory because of his somewhat limited intellectual stature. This essentially valid qualitative judgment should not, however, obscure the enormous importance of his work, for intellectual stature and historical significance do not always go hand in hand. Even though *De l'Esprit* may be a "weak and unoriginal work,"[1] then, it is nonetheless essential to recall Halévy's admonition that, "However much this book may be forgotten today, it is impossible to exaggerate the extent of its influence throughout Europe at the time of its appearance."[2] The reason it had this enormous impact is also important in our context of ideal-type analysis. It received the reception it did precisely because it carried some very typical ideas to their logical conclusion. As Cassirer remarks, "the influence [of *De l'Esprit*] on the philosophical literature of the eighteenth century is explicable in that the epoch found here a basic element of its thought expressed with pregnant clarity, and indeed with an exaggeration which parodies its thought."[3]

Some technocratic ideas can also be found in some of Helvetius's philosophical precursors, among them such figures as the English "associationist" David Hartley and the Abbé Condillac. Others who followed Helvetius and elaborated technocratic ideas and motifs in somewhat different fashion include Comte, Saint-Simon, Robert Owen, and Jeremy Bentham. Bentham, indeed, happily affirmed his affinity with and his indebtedness to Helvetius. "What Bacon was to the physical world," wrote Bentham, "Helvetius was to the moral. The moral world has therefore had its Bacon; but its Newton is yet to come."[4] (Bentham aspired to the latter role himself.)

Exploring the origins of the technocratic tradition, then, means looking at the logical unfolding of that tradition's characteristic and fundamental ideas from Locke to Helvetius and his followers. Locke provides the philosophical starting point and adumbrates the notion of an "experimental physics of the soul." And, after some help from intervening figures—mostly disciples of Locke—Helvetius brings the technocratic framework into full view with his plan to put the political order into the hands of his "true doctors of morality."

Looking at this development of ideas, we can see how the conceptual foundations of technocracy arose from the refinement and politicization of key epistemological motifs. Models of "knowing activity" that originated with Locke and Descartes were logically purified and freed from ambiguities and limitations. These purified epistemological conceptions were then converted into anthropological models—ideas about human nature. Finally, these anthropological conceptions became the basis for the political roles and functions of technocratic society.

Mind as *tabula rasa:* Purifying Locke's Sensationism

The first epistemological idea to achieve political significance was the *tabula rasa*. Logically refined and analogically extended, this Lockean notion underlies the technocratic depiction of the governed (by contrast with their governors, who, as we shall see later, become conceived *sub specie* the Cartesian *res cogitans*). Those who are appropriately subject to technocratic contrivance, to the "artifices" that aim at the reconciliation of interests, must be both actually and legitimately manipulable. The *tabula rasa* serves as the basis for these essential interpretations.

The development of the *tabula rasa* into one of the central conceptual motifs of technocracy involved three steps: first, Locke's image of the human mind as *tabula rasa* had to be cleansed of the ambiguities and complications with which he clouded it; second, the *tabula rasa* had to come to represent not only the human mind but also the human soul; and third, the emptiness of the soul, so conceived, had to be taken to imply its plasticity.

Locke invited or prefigured each of these steps, but he refrained almost systematically from carrying them to the potential conclusions and applications that others saw rather quickly. Those who styled themselves philosophical Lockeans and who sought to draw these conclusions and make these applications felt like the Baron d'Holbach, who wondered rhetorically:

> How has it happened that the profound Locke, who, to the great mortification of the metaphysicians, has placed this principle of Aristotle [i.e., that nothing enters the mind of man but through the medium of his senses] in the clearest point of view; how is it that all who, like him, have recognized the absurdity of the system of innate ideas, have not drawn the immediate and necessary consequences? How has it come to pass, that they have not had sufficient courage to apply so clear a principle to all those fanciful chimeras with which the human mind has for such a length of time been so vainly occupied?[5]

For Locke, it is true, had cluttered up his *tabula rasa* with sundry reservations and codicils. The mind at birth, he said, should be considered "white paper, void of all characters, without any ideas." It is an "empty cabinet" until it is filled from the outside via the senses.[6] However, he allowed in the second book of the *Essay* that "objects of reflection" stand together with the objects of sensation as "the only originals from whence all our ideas take their beginnings."[7] He spoke at times of natural powers of the mind in a way that made them seem capable of producing new complex ideas on their own.[8] His conception of knowledge as the "agreement of ideas," moreover, seemed to provide a plausible starting point for the conclusions of a George Berkeley. And, in Book Four of the *Essay*, Locke seemed to waffle on the certainty of knowledge gained through sensations, especially by contrast with intuition and reason.

For these sins of indecisiveness and timidity, Locke was chastised by his more single-minded French disciple, Abbé Condillac. Condillac's review of the doctrine that all knowledge derives from the senses runs as follows. The Peripatetics first "assumed" the doctrine, but they did not understand it. "It often happens that a philosopher declares himself on the side of truth, without knowing it,"[9] he wrote; and the Peripatetic enunciation of the doctrine was a case of this sort. "So far were they from having any certainty of this truth, that not one of them could ever explain it, and after a long succession of ages, the discovery was not yet made."[10] Bacon was, in his view, the first to "perceive this truth," and Locke "has the honour of being the first to demonstrate it."[11]

Locke, however, failed, in Condillac's judgment, to complete his assigned task. In particular, Locke's retention of reflection as a separate source of understanding alongside of sensation was unacceptable to him. Locke's failure on this score, Condillac thought, came about because he did not follow through with sufficient rigor and profundity his investigation into the origins of knowledge. "So far is he," wrote Condillac, "from searching deeply into the origin of human knowledge, that he touches the subject but very slightly."[12] This failure Condillac aimed at remedying in his *Essay on the Origin of Human Knowledge* and in his *Treatise on Sensations*. In these works, Condillac argued what he suggests Locke would have recognized had he only considered the matter more fully: that all our ideas come from the senses, from "simple perceptions."

Condillac's argument received widespread acceptance among the *philosophes*. Helvetius, for example, who wrote *De l'Esprit* only a few years later, seemed to assume that it required relatively little argument to assert that all ideas come from sensations. "All the operations of the mind are reducible to judgment," he declared; and "every judgment is nothing more than a sensation."[13] And in his later treatise, *De l'Homme*, he stated flatly that "all the operations of the mind are reducible to sensation."[14]

It is important to keep in mind, moreover, some of the tacit features of this modern conception of the *tabula rasa* that made it distinctive and that contributed to its significance as a construct of philosophical anthropology. These tacit features are often obscured because the adherents of the model directed their polemical arrows against the Cartesian notion of innate ideas. This made sense in the context of the times, but the distinctiveness of their doctrine would have been far more sharply delineated had they contrasted their conception of sense data with Aristotle's. For Aristotelian theory, as Condillac observed, also held that no ideas were in the mind that were not first in the senses. And Aristotle had even used the simile of the blank sheet of paper. But the Aristotelian *tabula rasa* was situated in a finite cosmos ordered by *logoi*. The senses were assumed to be capable of apprehending these *logoi*, or essences, when they were repeatedly encountered in the course of experience. The virgin mind, moreover, though presumed to be originally blank, was also presumed to be appropriately structured to receive and comprehend these essential patterns of reality. In its context of philosophical realism, therefore, the Aristotelian *tabula rasa* was an emptiness of pure potentiality. Though it might be empty *ab initio*, the mind was not without its own essence, which awaited actualization.

The Helvetian *tabula rasa* embodied a much more radical conception of mental emptiness and passivity. In a nominalist universe devoid of ordering *logoi*, sensation was not only the origin of the mind but its essence as well. The Aristotelian mind might begin as a *tabula rasa*, but it was not therefore without very well-defined limits as to what it could potentially come to know. These limits were already embedded in the eternally fixed structure of nature. The Helvetian *tabula rasa* was not subject to such constraint. Born into an infinite universe rather than a finite cosmos, it was empty in a much more radical sense. One knew in advance the essential forms that would eventually fill the empty cabinet of the Aristotelian mind, but the empty mind of modern sensationism might be filled in an infinite variety of ways, depending on the way sensations were combined. The "emptiness" of Aristotle's *tabula rasa* is the emptiness of pure potentiality. The "emptiness" of the Helvetian *tabula rasa* is the emptiness of plasticity.

Man as *tabula rasa:* Emptying the Soul

It is one thing to see the human mind as a *tabula rasa*. It is something else and something more to see the human soul as a *tabula rasa*. The mind, we might say, is filled with ideas. The soul is filled with passions. The mind deals with thought, the soul with action. These things are not identical, surely, and they could therefore quite conceivably be governed by very different principles. Specifically, in the present context, it is perfectly possible to conceive of a being born without ideas who is nonetheless programmed for quite definite actions. Creatures with minds that are empty *ab origine* might be filled with strong predetermined passions or instincts.

In the face of this clear logical possibility, it is striking to observe how easily and almost insensibly the *tabula rasa* was converted from an epistemological model—about mind—into an anthropological model—about the nature of man. This extension occurred, in fact, not so much through any explicit argument as through semantic carelessness or confusion. Either different terms were used interchangeably, as though they were unproblematically identical; or else the same term was used in different contexts, once again asserting an identity that was never demonstrated.

Locke provided an instructive example of the first of these semantic conflations in his *Essay*. There he deployed the concepts "mind" and "soul" almost interchangeably. He displays a slight tendency to use "soul" in an active voice and "mind" in the passive voice—that is, to speak of the mind as "receiving" ideas or impressions and the soul as "thinking." The mind might then seem to be conceived as a storehouse of ideas—a place—and the soul as a faculty—an operative intellectual force. However, even this distinction is not at all carefully maintained and may not have been significant to Locke. For example, he sometimes speaks of the mind as an active force, describing it as "employing itself" and as "coming to reflect on its own operations." Conversely, he sometimes describes the soul in passive terms, as where he speaks of "ideas that are in the soul of a child."[15] The net result is clearly to suggest that mind = soul = man and therefore to invite the reader, however inadvertently, to assume that the soul is as devoid of content as the mind when it comes from the hand of its Creator.

Helvetius likewise conflates the terms mind and soul, ideas and passions. The very titles of his works reflect the parallel with the Lockean pattern, for *esprit* refers more or less interchangeably to both mind and soul, and the subject matter of *De l'Homme* is but a continuation of the former work. More than that, Helvetius reflects clearly how the ambiguity of the crucial notion of "sensation" was also very important in the easy conversion of the *tabula rasa* into an anthropological model. "Sensations" may refer to "impressions," in the sense of "ideas." "Sensations" may also be taken to refer to "feelings," however. And it is apparent from the opening pages of *De l'Esprit* that Helvetius uses the pivotal concept of sensation to cover both ideas and feelings interchangeably. In fact, the operations of the mind, he tells us, being based entirely on "physical sensibility," are "reducible to feeling."[16]

The *tabula rasa* comes to mean, then, not simply that the mind is born as a clean slate but that the mind/soul is born without ideas/feelings. Since there are no innate ideas, there are, by the same measure, no innate passions, motivations, desires, or instincts.[17] Man no longer has the "natural" impulsion toward perfecting himself, toward actualizing his potentiality, that he had—even with his *ab initio* empty mind—in Aristotle's conception. His will does not "naturally tend" toward the good, or at least toward what it perceives as good. Because it is as empty as the mind and subject to being filled up from without, it is determined by efficient causes rather than by the now-discredited final causes. Note, then, the highly significant conjunction that appears almost casually in Helvetius in this context: "All our thoughts *and wills* must then be either the immediate effects, or necessary consequences, of the impressions we have received."[18]

Malleable Man: The Potentially Happy Puppet

It requires only a very short step, then, to give political force to this anthropological model of the *tabula rasa*. All that is needed is to shift the focus from the attributes of a *tabula rasa* to its functional possibilities. The move is from static adjectives, such as "empty" and "blank," to what philosophers of science refer to as dispositional terms, and in this case the key concept is "malleability." When the plasticity and potential manipulability of the *tabula rasa* are emphasized, rather than its actual emptiness, an incipient political program appears. The emptiness invites being filled; for if, according to the just-noted claim of Helvetius, "all our thoughts and wills" are the "immediate effects or necessary consequences of the impressions we have received," then anyone who can control and change these impressions can control and change mankind.

The inference that empty man is thereby also malleable man seems to have been almost effortlessly made. Indeed, although the inference is often made quite explicitly, it is not so much justified by argument as it is accomplished by the accretion of dispositional metaphors. It is in his *Some Thoughts Concerning Education,* for example, that Locke clearly links his claim that the mind is a blank slate at birth with the contention that it is therefore utterly malleable. He does so, in part, simply by adding the more dispositional images of "wax" and "water" to that of "blank paper." His views in that volume, wrote Locke, were "designed for a Gentleman's Son, whom, being then very little, I considered only as white Paper, or Wax, to be moulded and fashioned as one pleases."[19] Earlier in the same work he had said, "I imagine the Minds of children as easily turned this or that Way, as Water it self,"[20] and, for that reason, the education given a child was not only important, it was virtually definitive.

Nevertheless, Locke seemed unwilling to go all the way on this issue. While he held, for example, that education pretty much made the man, Locke was not willing to claim on its behalf the exclusive power of determining the fate of all men. He allowed a 10 percent residual category:

> I confess, there are some Men's Constitutions of Body and Mind
> so vigorous, and well framed by Nature, that they need not much

assistance from others; but by the strength of their natural Genius, they are from their Cradles carried towards what is excellent; and by the Privilege of their happy Constitutions, are able to do Wonders. But examples of this kind are but few; and I think I may say, that of all the Men we meet with, nine Parts of ten are what they are, good or evil, useful or not, by their Education.[21]

In Helvetius, the Lockean metaphors of the waxen mind and the watery will become embodied in the image of the "human puppet." "To guide the motions of the human puppet," writes Helvetius, "it is necessary to know the wires by which it is moved."[22] And elsewhere he writes: "Man is a machine, which being put in motion by corporeal sensibility, ought to perform all that it executes."[23]

In keeping with this unalloyed imagery of passive manipulability, Helvetius exhibits few of Locke's reservations about the power of education. Locke's residual one-tenth of men who are what they are and will be, largely irrespective of their education, does not figure into the calculus of his disciples. David Hartley suggested that like circumstances and like education make all men the same; for example:

if beings of the same nature, but whose affections and passions are, at present, in different proportions to each other, be exposed for an indefinite time to the same impressions and associations, all their particular differences will, at last, be overruled, and they will become perfectly similar, or even equal.[24]

Helvetius expresses the same idea and its possibilities more succinctly and colorfully. "There is nothing impossible to education," he writes; "it makes the bear dance."[25]

The moral Helvetius drew from this conception of human malleability was a very hopeful one. The susceptibility of human beings to modification from the outside opened the prospect of the artificially contrived improvement of all mankind. "If I can demonstrate," he wrote,

that man is in fact nothing more than the product of his education, I shall doubtless reveal an important truth to mankind. They will learn that they have in their own hands the instrument of their greatness and their felicity, and that to be happy and powerful nothing more is requisite than to perfect the science of education.[26]

Hartley seemed more aware of the potential for abuse of social engineering:

The doctrine of association, when traced up to the first rudiments of understanding and affection, unfolds such a scene as cannot fail both to instruct and alarm all such as have any degree of interested concern for themselves, or of a benevolent one for others.[27]

Nevertheless, he too is eager to point out the appealing prospects he sees implicit in his doctrine of malleability. His associationism, he tells us, affords

> some pleasing presumptions; such are, that we have a power of suiting our frame of mind to our circumstances, of correcting what is amiss, and improving what is right.... For thus we may learn how to cherish and improve good [affections and passions], check and root out such as are mischievous and immoral, and how to suit our manner of life, in some tolerable measure, to our intellectual and religious wants.[28]

Such, in brief, was the way the *tabula rasa* became an explicitly political concept. Locke introduced the idea into modern epistemology in 1690, the publication date of his *Essay*. By the middle of the next century it had been cleansed of the ambiguities and reservations he had appended to it. His implicit invitation to use it as an anthropological construct had been accepted and acted upon, and the appropriate political lessons had been adduced from it.

Emptying the State of Nature

Before examining the other components of the technocratic outlook, it is worth a brief digression to observe how this process of politicizing the *tabula rasa* is reflected in the changing image of the "state of nature" during the same period.

The analytical construct "state of nature" first became an important feature of political theories in the seventeenth century. This timing was not adventitious, coinciding as it did with the widespread dismissal of classical philosophical premises. The constructive task of political theory has always been to ascertain what political order is most congruent with human nature. Because "nature" was conceived teleologically in Aristotelian thought, "human nature" was there identified with fulfilled human potentialities. The logical starting point for classical political theory was therefore the completely actualized human being—man in his perfection rather than man in his origins. Moreover, since man was considered naturally sociable, his "nature" could not be considered in abstraction from social institutions.

This pattern changes quite dramatically with the banishment of final causality from philosophical respectability. The quest for the politically crucial touchstone of "human nature" had to assume radically different form. "Natural" man came to mean man *apart from* civil society. Man's "nature" came to refer to those human properties that might be supposed to *antedate* civil society. Hence arose the analytical device—or "experiment," as Rousseau termed it—"state of nature." It was a representation of the "fundamental" attributes of mankind as distinguished "from the changes and additions which his circumstances . . . have introduced to modify his primitive condition."[29] In short, the "state of nature" embodied the attempt to discriminate "essence" from "accidents" in man at a time when the original Aristotelian meaning of these terms no longer obtained. The result was to identify essence with origins rather than end and to search for it in a mythical time prior to the establishment of society.[30]

It is interesting to observe, then, how the content ascribed to this mythical state of nature steadily eroded in the course of the eighteenth century. In the early depictions of the state of nature, its inhabitants, though prepolitical in the narrow sense, clearly possessed recognizably human faces. In the intermediate depictions, these human features became progressively more primitive. Finally, these recognizably human features disappeared altogether, leaving only the empty visage of indeterminate sensibility. Over the same period of time that the *tabula rasa* is refined and converted into an anthropological and political model, the "state of nature"—an anthropological construct with political guidance as its aim—itself turns into a *tabula rasa*. This process of emptying the state of nature, like the other developments noted above, can be taken to begin with Locke (and with his relative contemporary, Hobbes) and to end with Helvetius, with Rousseau falling somewhere in the middle.

The conceptions of the state of nature articulated by Hobbes and Locke in the mid-seventeenth century exhibit some stark contrasts. Hobbes's state of nature, justifiably renowned, is a state of belligerency wherein an individual life is "solitary, poor, nasty, brutish, and short." Locke's state of nature is much more serene and pleasant—a condition of "peace, goodwill, mutual assistance, and preservation." Whatever the substantive differences between the Lockean and the Hobbesian versions of the state of nature, they have one thing in common: their inhabitants are recognizably human. They are endowed with a galaxy of natural passions, whether convivial or bellicose. Moreover, both Locke and Hobbes included reason and a law of nature as important constituent features of the state of nature. In Hobbes, both of these conceptions were severely attenuated from their classical form; in Locke, reason retained many of its classical noetic features, and the law of nature still reflected the presence of some teleological order. In both versions, however, the state of nature was a very human place, even if it was prepolitical in the formal sense. It was still a society, even if not a polity.

For this reason, Rousseau concluded that Hobbes and Locke had both failed in their attempts to divine the natural state of man. They had incorporated into their models of the state of nature passions and practices that could not have antedated social intercourse and that therefore could not properly be considered truly "natural." In his own analysis, Rousseau hoped to avoid committing this "blunder made by those who, in reasoning on the state of nature, always import into it ideas gathered in a state of society."[31] In order to perceive accurately what "the natural man" looked like, said Rousseau, one must try to discern "the first and most simple operations of the human soul."[32] Only these features of man should be admissible as constituent elements of his "nature."

Rousseau was inclined to attribute only two "first and most simple" passions to the human animal as he came from the hand of nature: the desire for self-preservation and natural sympathy. Natural sympathy, the more novel conception of the two, attributed to man "a natural repugnance at seeing any other sensible being, and particularly any of our own species, suffer pain or death."[33] Other capacities and passions attributed to man in the state of nature by previous theorists Rousseau cast aside as later, artificial additions. He denied, for example, that the egoism Hobbes depicted as innate was truly natural. "Egoism," he declared, "is a purely relative and factitious feeling, which arises in the state of society."[34] Only within society would the comparison of the self to others take place, and only on the basis of such comparisons could the notion of eminence, and likewise the quest for it, make any sense whatever. In similar fashion, Rousseau rejected Locke's claim that natural man possessed a faculty of reason that could apprehend principles of a natural law. To make such a supposition, as Locke did, Rousseau noted, would seem to maintain "that mankind must have employed, in the establishment of society, a capacity which is acquired only with great difficulty, and by very few persons, even in a state of society."[35] Locke's contention that the institution of the family was natural was also rejected as an importation of a later social arrangement into the state of nature.

Stripped of his "natural reason," in Locke's sense, and of his egoism, Rousseau's natural man emerges as a primitive. He is not so much the "noble savage" as he is a bucolic beast. He is "rather wild than wicked."[36] "The only goods he recognizes in the universe are food, a female, and sleep: the only evils he fears are pain and hunger."[37] He is "an animal weaker than some, and less agile than others; but, taking him all round, the most advantageously organized of any." "I see him," Rousseau added, "satisfying his hunger at the first oak, and slaking his thirst at the first brook; finding his bed at the foot of the tree which afforded him a repast; and, with that, all his wants supplied."[38]

Just as Rousseau had criticized Locke and Hobbes for retaining artificially, socially induced features of human life in their accounts of the state of nature, so Helvetius criticized Rousseau for the same alleged sin. If the "nature" of man is taken as signifying his original state, and if man begins his earthly career as a *tabula rasa*, then Rousseau, too, had failed to be sufficiently stringent in his analytical quest to divest his natural man of any and all acquired characteristics. Rousseau, said Helvetius,

> thinks (and I think with him) that we are born without vices, because we are born without ideas; but for the same reason we are also born without virtue. If vice be a stranger to human nature, virtue must be a stranger also. Both of them are not, and cannot be any other than acquisitions.[39]

Natural man, Helvetius concluded, really is a blank sheet of paper. He possesses only the passive capacity to register sense impressions and to respond positively or negatively to those he finds pleasurable or painful. Beyond that, he is nothing.

> Born without ideas or character, and indifferent to good and evil, [he] has no gift from nature but corporeal sensibility. . . . In the cradle he is nothing; . . . his virtues and vices, his factitious passions, his talents, his prejudices, and even his self-love, are all acquired.[40]

Conceived metaphysically, the denizen of Rousseau's state of nature was, like so many modern conceptions of man, a ghost in a machine. Rousseau had accepted the Cartesian characterization of animals as automata: "I see nothing in any animal but an ingenious machine, to which nature hath given senses to wind itself up."[41] And man was himself an animal, excepting for his free will and his consciousness of that freedom: "I perceive exactly the same things in the human machine, with this difference, that in the operations of the brute, nature is the sole agent, whereas man has some share in his own operations, in his character as a free agent."[42] Thus Rousseau concedes man-as-animal to the realm of phenomena, in Kant's sense, but prevents him from sinking into the object-world of a mechanistically conceived nature by insisting on his noumenal interior.

But Helvetius will have none of this sentimentalist dualism. Liberty, he insists, is one of those chimeras of superstition and credulous philosophy. He says that "no idea can be formed of the word

Liberty, when applied to the will'' (i.e., it is a meaningless concept); that it ''must be considered a mystery'' (i.e., it is a delusion); that ''it is a subject only proper for theology'' (i.e., for fools); and that ''a philosophical treatise on liberty would be a treatise on effects without causes'' (i.e., a piece of nonsense).[43] Helvetius thereby expels the ''ghost'' from Rousseau's metaphysical conception of man and is left with only the mechanism.

Over the period extending from, roughly, 1650 to 1760, then, the ''state of nature'' was progressively attenuated in content until the faces of its inhabitants were as blank as the *tabula rasa*. Arising after the rejection of classical teleology as an alternative method for ascertaining the ''essence'' of man, the whole conception gradually became obsolete through the process of critical clarification described above. For it became clear that if man were to be conceived as sensation without *telos* (Hume's ''bundle of impressions''), then he would have no real ''nature'' in the traditional sense at all. Looking for man's essence in his origins, the investigators found nothing. As Holbach concluded: ''Man, in his origin, is an imperceptible point, a speck, of which the parts are without form.''[44]

Politicizing the Subject-Object Dichotomy

At first sight, this anthropological reduction of man to the dimensions and attributes of *res extensa* might seem to lead to a fatalistic political dead end. If man is but ''a passive instrument in the hands of necessity,''[45] in Holbach's pregnant phrase, where is his hope? If all his ''motions'' are but the inevitable effects of inexorable natural forces, where is the leverage for change or progress? Is man not simply doomed to accept his fate as the pawn of nature?

Clearly, this conclusion was not the one reached by Hartley, Helvetius, and their disciples. Their message is an optimistic call to action rather than a fatalistic call for resignation. Their lesson is that man can ''make himself.'' Learning that men are ''nothing more than the product of [their] education,'' Helvetius argues, places in their hands ''the instrument of their greatness and felicity.'' And Hartley's lesson was that ''we may learn how to cherish and approve'' our good passions and affections and to ''check and root out such as are mischievous and immoral.''

Buried beneath the faceless abstractions and pronouns in pronouncements such as these lie both the answer to the technocrats' escape from political fatalism and also a profound political problem, which they rarely confront candidly. The political problem might be called the ''we, who?'' problem, and it is endemic to technocracy.

Who is this "man" who is "nothing more than the *product* of his education?" And *who*, then, is the *producer? Who* are the "they" whose hands will hold "the instrument of *their* greatness and felicity"? *Who* are the "we" who "may learn how to cherish and improve" some passions and affections while "checking and rooting out" others? *Who*, in short, are the educators and who the educated? *Who* are the knowers and who are the known? *Who* controls and who is controlled?

Although the solution to these problems is rarely clear (since it remains cloaked in the rhetoric of "man making himself"), it seems to be that we are not really talking about the same people in each case. Instead, one "class" of man is envisaged as educating or improving another "class." And this difference provides the escape from fatalism. For if "man" may be conceived on the one hand as sinking into the passivity of mechanical "nature" (e.g., Holbach's "passive instrument in the hand of necessity"), some other men seem to be exempt from this process of cosmological submergence; indeed, they seem to rise above nature altogether, and they do so by virtue of their knowledge, their perception of the truth. The old adage about "the truth making you free," it could be said, attains truly metaphysical significance under the aegis of technocracy, for the conceptions of both "truth" and "freedom" are radicalized and given extreme force. By attaining scientific truth, one may buy one's freedom from the grasp of a deterministic nature that swallows up the unenlightened.

Aristotle, we might recall, put reason into nature. "When one man said," wrote Aristotle in the *Metaphysics,* "that reason was present—as in animals, so throughout nature—as the cause of order and all arrangement, he seemed like a sober man in contrast with the random talk of his predecessors."[46] In seventeenth-century cosmology, reason is squeezed back out of nature—with significant anthropological consequences. Those men who do not possess reason sink wholly into nature—now a nature of blind mechanical force—while those who are rational escape nature altogether. "Mankind" undergoes the same process of disarticulation as does the cosmos: just as rational nature turns into reason and nature, rational-and-natural man splits into rational "men" and natural "men," the former group being superhuman, the latter group subhuman by previous standards.

This same process of disarticulation can be seen anthropologically as the dissolution of Rousseau's model of man. Rousseau's "ghost *in* a machine" splits up into the two categories of ghosts *and* machines. Some men are machines—passive *automata,* malleable creatures of necessity. Other men are ghosts—spirits who are free agents, self-determiners of their own fate.

Recalling the Cartesian origins of the ghost/machine dichotomy, we can characterize this distinction between two types of men as the politicization of the subject/object dichotomy. Man as machine, as *tabula rasa*, is man *sub specie rei extensae*. And man as ghost is man *sub specie rei cogitantis*. Man as thinking substance rises above, observes, controls, and ultimately "saves" man as extended substance. Such, in a nutshell, are the metaphysics and politics of technocracy.

The line separating "subjects" from "objects" emerges in this way as the major "class distinction" of modernity, far transcending in depth and significance the more mundane Marxist categories of bourgeois and proletarian—however important these may be. As in the Marxist analysis of the origins of classes, moreover, the source of the gulf between "subjects" and "objects" is their differential relation to the mode of production—in this case, however, to the mode of the production of knowledge rather than wealth. The knowers of technocratic politics base their ascendancy over the known on their access to and control of the truth. (Unlike Marxist analysts, however, technocratic theorists depict this dominance as legitimate and benevolent rather than illegitimate and exploitative. This difference should occasion no great surprise, of course; for what is going on here is the fashioning by a well-intentioned, power-seeking intellectual class of their own legitimacy myth. Had the bourgeoisie fashioned the Marxist analysis, we could have expected it to emerge as a tale of moral uplift.)

To call the distinction between rational "subjects" and natural "objects" a class split is actually a bit misleading. The difference between them is greater than that. Classes are distinguishable groups within the same species. But *res cogitans* and *res extensa* are, in a quite literal philosophical sense, different species (substances) altogether. Their contrasting relationship to the means of production of knowledge results not simply in different "accidents" of their existence but rather in their possession of different defining characteristics. "Subjects" and "objects" are different in *essence*. They have different attributes. They embody altogether different modes of life.

Human "objects" are artifacts—whether artifacts of natural forces or of rational contrivance. They are characterized, as we have seen, by their immanence, their passivity, their manipulability, their bondage, their "drivenness"—in a word, by their blind determination by outside forces. They inhabit the "realm of necessity."

The attributes of the "subjects" are exactly the opposite. They possess the features of those who have ascended to the Archimedean point—floating above nature rather than encapsulated within it. They are radically transcendent beings rather than radically immanent creatures. They have shed the contingency and partiality that Aristotelian rational animals possessed in part and that Cartesian objects possessed in their entirety. Instead of being radically determined beings, mere instruments in the hand of necessity, they are radically self-determining. They live in the "realm of freedom."

As they escape the contingency of prescientific life, the Cartesian "subjects" are invested with powers and attributes previously reserved for deities. The key categories here are knowledge, will, and power; the previously divine attributes are, respectively, Laplacean omniscience, Olympian detachment, and the fabricating capability of a gnostic demiurge.

Laplace captured the attributes of Cartesian omniscience in strictly hypothetical terms. *If* someone could look down on *res extensa* and see it clearly and comprehensively, he *could* be presumed to "know it all." By calculating the future consequences of existing vectors of motion, moreover, his knowledge could encompass the future as well as the present. He could know not only what is but what is to be. For the technocratic theorist, this hypothetical possibility is taken to be a real possibility or even an accomplished fact. "Practical difficulties" and "insufficient data" may remain as significant residual problems, but this is the promise of genuinely "positive" knowledge. This is what scientific knowledge is all about: clear and definite comprehension of all the motions of nature, including the motions of man-as-part-of-nature. Leather-tongued as he was, Bentham captured some of the most essential metaphors of this account of transcendent knowledge and its purposes when he explained the significance of his own work. He wrote, said Bentham, so that the legislator might "raise his contemplation to that elevated point from which the whole map of human interest and situations lies extended to his view."[47]

In our account of the conversion of the *tabula rasa* into an anthropological model from its origins in epistemology, we observed how attributes originally ascribed to the mind become attributed to the soul as well. Characteristics of ideas, in other words, are presumed to be assignable to the will of those possessing the ideas. Exactly the same process occurs when *res cogitans* becomes an anthropological model. In the case of the *tabula rasa,* the common feature of ideas and will was passivity. In the case of *res cogitans,* it is "objectivity."

The knowledge possessed by *res cogitans* is objective knowledge:

"pure" in its clarity and distinctness, unsullied by subjective passion, and untainted by immersion within the contingencies of nature. In like fashion, the will of the "moral scientist" is described as free of the partiality of other men. He is "detached" and dispassionate. His learning, writes Helvetius, is a "pure and sacred fire"[48] that purges him of egoism as it delivers him from ignorance. The true moralist, then, meets Kierkegaard's stringent criterion for "purity of heart": he wills but one thing. By his "absolute detachment from personal interest"[49] he can will the common good.

Res cogitans as Technocratic Legislator

Although the scientist as *res cogitans* is "detached" and "objective," he is not supposed to be inactive. His is *not* to be the *vita contemplativa*. For the technocrat, so passive a role would manifest a failure of nerve and of public spirit. Instead, it is the mission of the scientific savant to return from Olympus, to convert his theory into practice, and to make men happy. The Archimedean point, after all, possesses not only elevation but leverage—the leverage to move the whole world.

Res cogitans thus becomes a political figure. Legitimated by his cognitive transcendence and his purity of heart, his task is to fabricate a good political order out of the human matter whose laws are known to him. He is to be a sentimentalized version of that other notable nominalist deity as political ruler—Hobbes's sovereign.[50] Because of his godlike knowledge and dispassion, he meets the superhuman qualifications and has the superhuman capabilities that Rousseau envisioned for the ideal Legislator. "It would take gods to give men laws," wrote Rousseau. The lawgiver should be "a superior intelligence beholding all the passions of men without experiencing any of them." He would be of a substance different from that of other men, "wholly unrelated to our nature while knowing it through and through." He "ought to feel himself capable, so to speak, of changing human nature," for he is to be "the engineer who invents the machine."[51]

Rousseau, it seems clear, was speaking hypothetically: it "would" take gods to give men laws. What Rousseau considered merely a hypothetical ideal, however, Helvetius considered a realizable possibility. A true scientist was indeed a "superior intelligence . . . capable of changing human nature." And what Helvetius described as a real possibility, Jeremy Bentham thought he had achieved in his work and his person. Rousseau stated the qualifications of the technocratic Legislator; Helvetius declared them attainable; and Bentham applied for the job.

The starting point for the work of the ideal Legislator, as Helvetius describes it, is his knowledge of "the wires" that move the "human puppet." Shifting his analogy from the mechanical to the animal, Helvetius marvels:

> What a mass of light does the knowledge of mankind throw upon the several parts of government! The ability of the groom consists in knowing all that is to be done to the animal he is to manage; and the ability of a minister, in knowing all that is to be done in the management of the people he is to govern.[52]

Let the "experimental physics of the soul" begin, he counsels:

> Let philosophers penetrate continually more and more into the abyss of the human heart, let them there search out all the principles of his actions, and let the minister, profiting by their discoveries, make of them, according to time, place and circumstances, a happy application.[53]

Magistrates are to become, in Helvetius's pregnant phrase, the "true doctors of morality."[54] Priests had pretended to this role, but their claim was based on a misconception about the nature and source of virtue. "Virtue . . . is the work of the laws and not of religion."[55] It is the crucial and the proper role of the legislators, then, to "compel men to be virtuous."[56] They accomplish this compulsion by doing what Jeremy Bentham was soon to attempt in much greater detail: namely, by turning a felicific calculus into an applied science. Moral "doctoring" should consist in an appropriate and judicious appending of pleasures to actions desired by the legislators, of pains to actions deemed unacceptable. In short, "morality, politics, and legislation are but one and the same science,"[57] and this science is a therapeutic application of rewards and punishments.

All societies, of course, engage in this kind of enterprise as a matter of necessity. A society that did not do so would be a society without a criminal code and without any means of honoring its heroes. What distinguishes the technocrat's version of the legislative craft, however, is the unbounded scope he gives to his legislator and his hedonistic psychology. Helvetius displays these earmarks, together with some ingenuity, in one of his specific proposals for appending pleasures to socially useful deeds. Since sexual gratification is one of life's keenest pleasures, he suggests, the "true doctors of morality" should not leave it to be indiscriminately distributed. Instead, they should award the favors of the fairest maidens to those who have been of most service to the society—"Nubile Prizes," as it were.[58] Let us suppose, writes Helvetius, that

the most beautiful of the Spartan ladies had been consecrated to
merit; that, being presented naked in the assemblies of the people,
they had been carried off by the warriors as prizes obtained by
their courage; . . . it is certain that this would have rendered the
Spartans still more brave and valiant. . . . Women who everywhere
else seem, like the flowers of a fine garden, to be made only for the
ornament of the earth, and to please the eye, might be applied to a
nobler use . . . and [might] at length become one of the most powerful springs of legislation.[59]

It is not at all clear what the ladies themselves might think about
being thus "consecrated to merit," and perhaps this proposal is
purely fanciful—the sexist fantasy of a notoriously hot-blooded
aristocrat. Nonetheless, it does illustrate the willingness of the
technocrat to subject individuals to exploitation if it serves the purposes of the state. In the "government of all," writes Helvetius with
enthusiasm rather than concern, "the nation is then the despot."[60]

One thing Bentham makes perfectly clear: the technocrat will not
be deterred from such depredations of individuals on the grounds of
natural right. Natural right is one of those meaningless metaphysical
conceptions exploded by scientific analysis. "Natural rights is simple nonsense: natural and imprescriptible rights, rhetorical nonsense, nonsense upon stilts."[61] The critical acids that Condorcet
expected to illuminate the rights of man by dissolving the superstitions that obscured them had instead gone on to destroy the philosophical basis of those rights themselves.

Equally uncompelling would be objections raised on the ground
that people were being deprived of their liberty. These would be
deemed "capricious" and "sentimental" objections in Bentham's
view; hence a rational and systematic moral legislator should ignore
them. Liberty was not included by Bentham among the proper ends
of civil law. Moreover, it is hard to see exactly what meaning liberty
might have for those pleasure-pain mechanisms whose behavior Bentham sought to fashion on behalf of public utility. He aimed to
make his subjects happy; their freedom was not a concern. "Call
them soldiers, call them monks, call them machines, so they were
but happy ones, I should not care."[62]

The other modus operandi of the "doctors of morality," along
with legislation, was to be education. In fact, the two were really
conceived to be one and the same thing by Helvetius and his disciples: "character formation." What the legislator sought to achieve
through his system of laws, the educator should achieve through his
system of instruction. The ends and the means were the same in both
cases. The goal of legislation was not simply obedience; nor was the

aim of education mere illumination. The end was what Locke had mandated in his *Thoughts Concerning Education:* "it is virtue, direct virtue, which is the hard and valuable part to be aimed at."[63] And the means were also essentially the same in both cases: "make" the subject "behave" properly by controlling his "environment." In Helvetius's words, "the science of education may be reduced perhaps to the placing a man in that situation which will force him to attain the talents and virtues required in him."[64]

Although Locke's focus on the cultivation of virtue in education is retained, his residual sense of the ambiguities and limitations of character formation is not. "Children," averred Robert Owen, the English industrialist-reformer,

> are without exception, passive and wonderfully contrived compounds; which, by an accurate and subsequent attention, founded on a correct knowledge of the subject, may be formed collectively to have any human character. And although these compounds, like all the other works of nature, possess endless varieties, yet they partake of that plastic quality, which, by perseverance under judicious management, may be ultimately moulded into the very image of rational wishes and desires.[65]

If virtue is what the technocrat wishes to instill in his "living machinery" (Owen's phrase), and if happiness is what he wishes to achieve for them, what can be said about the content ascribed to these central concepts? Is the technocrat's virtue the virtue of the Platonic soul, Christian goodness, or Renaissance *virtú?* Is his happiness Christian beatitude, Aristotelian *eudaimonia,* or the contentment of a bourgeois gentleman? Very different meanings have been accorded these two fundamental moral notions, so it is important to have some idea of what they signified to the early technocrats.

The general answer to this question seems to be that the technocrats were often rather vague on this issue. They bandied the key concepts of virtue and happiness about without paying careful attention to them, perhaps from dogmatism, perhaps from carelessness, perhaps in some cases from tacit recognition of the tactical advantages of ambiguity. Nevertheless, it seems also safe to say that both the history and the logic of technocracy move in a morally reductionist direction.

As for virtue, undoubtedly the devout evangelical Christian David Hartley assumed that the traditional moral virtues of the Christian tradition were those that should be promoted by the principles of his associationism. Conversely, by the "mischievous and immoral" passions and affections he sought to eliminate he seems clearly to have meant the sinful passions and affections—pride, cupidity, and the like.

Some residues of the traditional virtues remain in Helvetius, but mostly in a rather offhand way. He tells us, for example, that "according to this plan of education, I should be sure that if my son was foppish, impertinent, conceited, or imperious, he would not *remain so long*."[66] His basic conception of virtue, however, is very secular and utilitarian—to an extent that Hartley would surely have found scandalous and even pagan. Helvetius sought, for example, to rehabilitate pride, sensuality, and the love of glory from the disrepute into which they had been cast by Christianity. Self-sacrifice, in the sense of subordination to the public interest, remains a virtue, but self-effacement does not. The "monkish" virtues of humility and asceticism are dismissed as both unnatural and useless. It is both silly and unnecessary for moralists to condemn pride and the love of pleasure and glory, Helvetius contends—silly because it puts them at war with nature, and unnecessary because these passions are not incompatible with a harmonious social order. Indeed, it is by the judicious direction of the love of glory and the judicious dispensation of pleasure that the public interest can best be promoted. We have noted already, for example, Helvetius's proposal for the socially constructive manipulation of the libido. And it is by "inflaming" his subjects with a "passion" for glory that Helvetius would propose to compel his subjects to be virtuous.[67]

For Helvetius, then, the definitive test, when it comes to virtue, is this: if the passion or action is compatible with, supportive of, or directed to the public interest, then it is virtuous; if not, it is a vice. Ultimately, then, the meaning of virtue is "some quality useful to society."[68] And since the public interest was in practice "that of the majority," virtue amounts to exactly the same thing as "justice" in Helvetius's scheme: "the practice of actions useful to the greatest number."[69]

And in Bentham, of course, the utilitarian reduction is complete. Bentham appropriates Hartley's characterization of bad actions as "mischievous"; but "mischief" for him consists not in sinfulness but in violation of the greater-happiness principle. Conversely, the only meaning of virtue—a term Bentham more or less dispenses with entirely—is, as in Helvetius, conducive to the happiness of the greatest number.

What then is this "happiness" that is both the ultimate measure of virtue and the ultimate purpose of the technocrat's social contrivance? Hartley again provides a traditional Christian answer. But this is quickly left behind with the ascendance of the sensationism and mechanistic naturalism implicit in the technocratic rendering of Cartesian and Lockean ideas. For Hartley, who looked foward to a time of "ultimate unlimited happiness," this felicity would consist "in the pure love of God and of His works."[70] But for Helvetius, human felicity consisted in simple hedonistic self-gratification. The legislator's task of making his subjects happy consisted of procuring them "all the amusements and pleasures compatible with the public welfare."[71] And these pleasures, Helvetius tells us, are ultimately sensual enjoyments: "I assert that man being, by nature, sensible of no other pleasures than those of the senses, these pleasures are consequently the only object of his desires."[72]

Bentham's conception of happiness is, as much as that of Helvetius, reducible to pleasure. The test of a good action, then, is its tendency to produce an excess of pleasure over pain. Bentham is not, however, as reductionist as his mentor Helvetius in his understanding of "pleasure." Instead of attempting relentlessly to compress all pleasures into the pleasures of sense, as Helvetius does, Bentham enumerates a variety of types of pleasure in his typical Aristotelian categorizing fashion. He in fact identifies no fewer than fourteen kinds of "simple pleasures" in his *Principles of Morals and Legislation*. However, if he is not reductionist in his account of happiness/pleasure, he can safely be said to exhibit a thoroughgoing relativism regarding the different varieties. For him, pleasure is good per se, whatever its source. Thus the "pleasures of skill" are on a par with the "pleasures of relief," the "pleasures of amity" with the "pleasures of wealth," and the "pleasures of benevolence" with the "pleasures of malevolence." These are Bentham's terms. Translating them, we might say that, morally, Bentham equated virtuosity and detumescence, friendship and avarice, charity and vindictiveness; for, if they are equally pleasurable, all these traits and dispositions are in themselves of equal value. Despite John Stuart Mill's later insistence that utilitarian doctrine did not value a "pig satisfied" over "Socrates dissatisfied," it is hard to find philosophical grounds in Bentham for a qualitative distinction of this kind. To "measure the value" of pleasure or pain, Bentham would consider "intensity, duration, certainty, propinquity, fecundity, and purity," each of which is a quantitative measure ("purity" meant simply "the chance of not being followed by sensations of the opposite kind"). No mention is made of sophistication, maturity, complexity, elevation, or any other conceivable qualitative test. Thus Bentham accomplishes in morals what Adam Smith produces in aesthetics: an amiably philistine destruction of all qualitative distinctions and standards by making everything a matter of "taste."

The Radical Governance of
the *deus faber*

The technocratic vision of politics can now be summarized in the following way: Society should be rationalized by the strategic application of scientific knowledge. From his elevated perspective the scientist is to observe the motions of mankind and infer from these observations the laws of human behavior. Legitimated by his positive knowledge and by his moral disinterest, he can become a "true doctor of morality" who compels men to be virtuous through an experimental physics of the soul. His primary tools are legislation and education, both of which involve controlling the environment in order to attach pleasures to socially useful acts and pains to socially mischievous acts. He need not be inhibited in his work by fear of infringing liberty or natural rights. And his ultimate goal is to achieve a smoothly functioning society that maximizes the pleasure of the human artifacts who inhabit it.

The technocratic tradition gives a peculiarly modern and profoundly radical twist to the idea of governance. Indeed, the technocrat's conception of governance transcends the bounds of the traditional notion of governance altogether. Governance, as he envisions it, is not a form of leadership. It is not a form of representation. It is, instead, a form of creation. The governor-"ghost"-subject relates to the governed-"machine"-object not as one man relates to another but as a potter relates to his clay. Governance is envisioned not as a process of reciprocal—if asymmetrical—interaction but as a process of unilateral control. The technocrat is a maker of society. He assumes the role of demiurge, imposing order and form on the chaos of human nature. The technocratic ruler, in short, is a *deus faber*.

This radical conception of the relationship between governors and governed leads to, and is reflected in, a corresponding transmutation in other important political concepts—especially those of authority and education.

The authority possessed by the technocratic *deus faber* is of a new and radical kind. For the *deus faber* is not merely authorized to govern. Authority is not "vested in" him from other people. Instead, he is himself the *author* of the social order. He is not the "bearer" of the person of his subjects, as even Hobbes's sovereign was conceived to be, so much as he is the creator of these persons. There is thus no logical limit to his power, at least from the will of other men; for he shapes their will rather than receives "informed consent" from it. Rousseau, when speaking of his hypothetical superhuman legislator, recognized that this kind of authority exceeds and is different from previous conceptions of authority. It is "an authority that is no authority . . . an authority of a different order, capable of constraining without violence and persuading without convincing."[73]

In like fashion, the very meaning of the word "education" is transformed under the aegis of technocracy. Placed in a new "language game" governed by new philosophical assumptions, the word loses the original signification manifested by its etymology. The root meaning of education comes from the stems for "to lead" and "out." But this conception of the educational process no longer makes sense if there is believed to be nothing "in" human nature to "lead out." It instead becomes a kind of "placing in," an implantation more than an actualization of potentiality. The role of the educator changes and becomes more radical. He is no longer a midwife for the growth of character but a demiurge who himself fashions that character.

How was it, one might well ask, that the technocratic reformers seemed blind to the negative and destructive potential inherent in their visions of such vast powers of social control? Were they simply dazzled by the beneficent possibilities they dreamed of? Partly. Were they simply so arrogant as to assume they knew what was best for everyone else? No doubt it was partly that too. Beyond these rather everyday human frailties, however, the technocrats remained oblivious of the problem of power for philosophical reasons. "Power" in the usual sense simply did not appear on their conceptual landscape. As they saw it, the far-ranging tasks they assigned to the "true doctors of morality" were neither "political" functions nor exercises of "power" in the traditional sense at all.

Paralleling Rousseau's account of the "different order" of "authority that is no authority," the technocrats saw their scientific legislators as exerting a "power that is no power." "Power" in the usual sense implies the exercise of will and the presence of coercion. But as the technocrats conceived it, neither will nor coercion was involved in their scheme of government. Coercion was not involved because, when one shapes a *tabula rasa*, one inflicts no "violence" on one's material: a *tabula rasa* possesses no autonomous desires or natural entelechy to violate. In addition, many of the technocrats also believed that any enlightened man would perceive his self-interest to coincide with public utility. As Owen predicted:

> When these truths are made evident, every individual will necessarily endeavour to promote the happiness of every other individual within his sphere of action; because he must clearly, and without any doubt, comprehend such conduct to be the essence of self-interest, or the true cause of self-happiness.[74]

Moreover, they did not consider the legislator's will to be a determinant of his actions. He was, as we noted earlier, conceived as wholly disinterested, impartial, and detached—a "pure" heart without any personal axes to grind. It was not he who acted so much as the truth, which acted through him. He was not conceived of as imposing his will on anyone else, because his mandates were not discretionary. In a new and different sense, then, the governance of the technocrat was depicted as "a government of laws, not of men."

(This last sentence was originally written simply as a catchy way to express the assumptions apparently entertained by technocratic thinkers. I find, however, that Comte had been quite explicit on this score: "Scientific polity wholly excludes the arbitrary.... Government by measures replaces government by men. There arises in politics a true law, understood in the real and philosophic sense that the illustrious Montesquieu attached to that phrase.")[75]

By peopling their world with gnostic demiurges on the one hand and artifacts on the other, the technocrats in effect sought to abolish "politics" altogether. Just as they claimed to escape the contingencies of history and the uncertainties of philosophy, just as they radicalized the notions of governance and authority, just as they transformed the meaning of legislation and education, so also the technocrats presumed that the positivity of their science would make politics in the usual sense quite obsolescent. The traditional problems and issues in political life were in their view simply the mark and the curse of a prescientific age. In the rationally ordered "postpolitics" of a nascent scientific era, political problems would disappear; only problems of technique and implementation would remain. In that now classic phrase, the governing of man would be replaced by the administration of things.

One might easily infer from the rather pedestrian and prosaic quality of this phrase—"the administration of things"—that politics under the technocratic regimen would be of limited significance. However natural this inference, it would be mistaken. The "merely technical" character of technocratic governance embodied in this phrase refers to its means, not its ends. It is a phrase designed to signify the "neutrality" and the "objectivity" of the *process* of governance; it should not be construed as suggesting the relative inconsequentiality of its *purposes*. Instead, the old Platonic hope for the marriage of knowledge with power becomes even more intense under technocracy, since the possibilities of reason are seen as even greater.

These possibilities include, indeed, the possibility of perfection. As a result, the technocratic program was, in the eyes of its adherents, not simply the proper heir to the atavistic arrangements of politics; it was also the proper heir to the equally outmoded theological scripts for human salvation. As John Passmore has observed, the technocratic program for human perfectibility marked a new departure in the long theological controversy between Pelagians and Augustinians.[76] The Augustinians insisted that man must rely on God's grace for his perfection. The Pelagians contended that he could be perfected through the assiduous exercise of his own free will. In the soteriology of technocracy, both of these accounts are relegated to the status of prescientific superstition, but the aspiration to perfection is not abandoned; it is simply translated into the new idiom and given a new script. Man is to be perfected neither by divine grace nor by his own free efforts but by the deliberate and skilled contrivance of his fellow man. Specifically, he is to be perfected through the artifices of scientific legislators. *Res extensa* is to be saved through the quasi-divine knowledge and benevolence of *res cogitans*. The modern drama of salvation is peopled by a cast of characters who step from the pages of the *Discourse on Method*.

Phrases such as the one depicting governance as "the administration of things" thus embody one of the most distinctive and important features of technocratic ideology. By packaging soteriological aspirations in neutral and technical language, they manifest what Michael Polanyi has somewhat cumbersomely called "dynamo-objective coupling."[77] This "coupling" is the linkage of intense moral passions with presumed scientific dispassion and objectivity. The moral content and the scientific pretensions of the ideology exist in symbiosis, since each part performs important services for the other: the moral content gives meaning and motivation to the scientific enterprise, and the scientific language gives protection to the moral ends contained within it. The science is thereby saved from irrelevance, and the moral goals are rendered immune to moral challenge: anyone who seeks to challenge technocratic goals on explicitly moral grounds is simply informed that he is being unscientific or that he has misinterpreted the technocratic claims. Put another way, anyone opposing technocratic prescriptions on moral grounds is rebuked for raising "utopian" objections against "scientific" findings.

Hartley therefore bolsters his Christian reformism by purportedly grounding it in his science of associationism; at the same time, the doctrine of associationism is saved from academic barrenness by being infused with evangelical fervor and significance. In like fashion, Helvetius couples his proposed science of human behavior with his majoritarian republicanism, and Bentham links the ostensive science of his felicific calculus with his passionate romanticism. (Mary Peter Mack writes: "The source of Bentham's inspiration was not only scientific, but moral and aesthetic. . . . Indeed, bizarre as it may seem initially, William Blake is Bentham in verse.'')[78] Bentham's judicial prescriptions and his various institutional recommendations are vested with the authority of his Newtonianism, on the one hand; on the other, his turgid catalogues of human dispositions and actions are infused with the urgency and import of his romantic hopes. "Romance . . . the Utopia . . . Romance," he said of his work. "How should it be anything less?"[79]

Bentham's Panopticon:
The Spider in His Web

It was Bentham's prodigious imagination that devised the paradigmatic institution of technocracy: the Panopticon, his model prison.

Bentham's devotion to the Panopticon, it should be emphasized, resulted from no idle whim or passing fancy, for this was one of his most cherished proposals, and it was fully consonant with his philosophical beliefs and his strategy for social progress. For twenty years he sought passionately to gain acceptance of it, and he was still bitterly bemoaning his lack of success with it at the age of eighty-three, fully forty-five years after the idea had come to him. At that advanced age Bentham wrote his "History of the War between Jeremy Bentham and George III," in which he blamed that monarch for an alleged conspiracy against him and his beloved Panopticon. But for George III, he grieved, "all the paupers in the country, as well as all the prisoners in the country, would have been in my hands."[80]

Bentham conceived the architecture of the Panopticon as a rotunda. "The building circular," he wrote,

> the cells occupying the circumference. . . . In the center was the apartment, styled, from its destination, the Inspector's Lodge: from thence by turning round his axis, a functionary, standing or sitting on the central point, had it in his power to commence and conclude a survey of the whole establishment in the twinkling of an eye.

The Keeper could, by this architectural plan, "see all"; hence the name pan-opticon. On the other hand,

> it was considered . . . that the workmen, whose operations were designed to be thus watched, should not be able to know, each of them respectively at any time, whether he was or was not at that moment in a state in which the eyes of the inspector were directed to his person. [Therefore,] by blinds and other contrivances, the keeper [was to be] concealed from the observation of the prisoners, unless where he thinks fit to show himself.[81]

The genius of the Panopticon, then, was its concrete embodiment of the Cartesian subject-object relationship and the conversion of this epistemological situation into a political institution. In the center of the structure sat the Cartesian subject, the Keeper, who assumed the form of, in Bentham's words, "an invisible omnipresence." Around the circumference were housed the Cartesian objects, the inmates, who were visually absolutely accessible to this warden they could not see. As Bentham clearly recognized, moreover, this extreme situation of one-way observation constituted a remarkably effective system of control and domination. So far from causing him dismay, it was this very feature that appeared to him to be "the fundamental advantage" of his proposal. "To be incessantly under the eyes of the inspector is to lose in effect the power to do evil and almost the thought of wanting to do it."[82]

Omniscient and omnipotent, the Keeper was like a deity within his circular world. His little flock could escape neither his gaze nor his control. Once again, Bentham clearly recognized the "divine" attributes and functions of the Warden, and, once again, this recognition evoked his enthusiasm rather than his concern. Although hardly given to frequent scriptural allusions, Bentham placed the following passage from the 139th Psalm at the beginning of his "Panopticon Papers":

> Thou art about my path, and about my bed:
> and spiest out all my ways.
> If I say, peradventure the darkness shall cover me,
> then shall my night be turned into day.
> Even there also shall thy hand lead me; and thy
> right hand shall hold me.

Perhaps Bentham was unworried by the quasi-divine and quasi-totalitarian aspects of his model prison because he intended to occupy the central position himself. He was, after all, willing to put in his claim to be the "most benevolent man who ever lived." "Someone must have been so," he said. "Why not I?"[83] Moreover, his lack of concern over the despotic features of his scheme did not stem from the idea that it would be confined to prison populations, for he offered the Panopticon as an appropriate model also for schools, factories, workshops, and asylums.

When Edmund Burke was shown the plan of Bentham's Panopticon, he reportedly remarked: "There's the keeper, the spider in the web."[84] Although Bentham was allegedly not especially pleased with that comment, it is interesting to note that the same metaphor appeared in the work of his mentor, Helvetius. Writing about the order of Jesuits, Helvetius spoke of their general in these terms: "It is from thence, in the obscurity of his cell, like a spider in the center of his web, that he extends his threads over all Europe, and is by those threads informed of all that passes there."[85] For this arrangement, Helvetius expressed his profoundest admiration. Although he obviously was not enamored of the Jesuits' purposes, he esteemed their form of government as a model worthy of emulation. "The real crime of the Jesuits," he declared,

> was the excellence of their government. . . . It must be confessed that the Jesuits have been one of the most cruel scourges of nations; but without them we should never have perfectly known what a body of laws directed to one end was capable of operating on men.[86]

Actuated by the same principles as Helvetius, Bentham evidently concurred in this judgment. For the genius of his cherished Panopticon was precisely its embodiment of this "excellent government." The "spider in his web," whose efficiently despotic regime Helvetius admired, shed his Jesuitic robes and allegiances and assumed technocratic incarnation in Bentham's "Keeper."

In effect, Bentham's technocratic rendering of the spider-in-his-web form of governance institutionalized the extreme situation more recently depicted by Sartre in *No Exit*. In that play, each of the eyelid-less characters is similarly "incessantly under the eyes of" the other. The differences are two. In Sartre's play the relationship is reciprocal: each is made an "object" by the unrelenting gaze of the other. In the Panopticon the relationship is asymmetrical: the warden is the only subject; the inmates are but objects of observation. The other contrast is that Sartre's play is a parable of hell, while Bentham's institution is offered as the epitome of good government.

Liberalism and Technocracy: Continuity and Change

The technocratic view of politics is an offspring of the liberal tradition. Reflecting its parentage, technocracy exhibits some fundamental continuities with liberalism. At the same time, it clearly diverges from liberalism in equally significant ways—both philosophically and politically. It is important to be clear about both the continuities and the changes and about the reasons behind the latter.

The central continuities between liberalism and technocracy turn around their similar conceptions of human knowledge and its political utility.

First, the technocrats embraced and expanded on the fundamentally positivistic conception of knowledge they found embedded in liberal rationalism. They anticipated the establishment of a secure and incontrovertible base for human knowledge in clear and distinct perceptions. They took over the assumption that the achievements of the mathematicizing sciences were paradigmatic for the progress of knowledge, even if these achievements could only be approximated in other areas. They looked toward the time when knowledge would escape all residual mystifications, become expressed in a language freed from metaphysical confusion and opacity, and advance through a process of steady accretion.

Like the early adherents of liberal rationalism, moreover, the technocrats believed that the realm of positive knowledge included the norms of appropriate human behavior. Both accredited, in other words, the idea of the "moral sciences." Knowledge of true rational morality, as contrasted with the dogmatic prejudices embodied in theologically originated mandates, could be attained by the same means and methods that had produced such dramatic gains in the knowledge of nature. The advance of science would clarify norms as it illuminated phenomena. In the terms of our model of "epistemological manicheanism," the technocrats conceived of moral-political standards of right order as falling within the luminous circle of "objective knowledge," not in the dark beyond of "metaphysics."

In their social theory, similarly, both the early liberals and the technocrats were believers in the politics of "enlightenment." Comte and Helvetius, every bit as much as James Mill and Condorcet, assumed that scientific advance was the principal source and guarantor of political progress. For both groups, history was an epic battle in which scientific reason was triumphing over the forces of superstition and reaction. Reason was the measure of all things, and the "rationalizing" of social order was the primary goal of political action.

In these very fundamental and important respects, then, the technocratic tradition is continuous with the original beliefs and aspirations of its parent, liberalism. The technocrats, however, were driven by both logic and experience to amend the original epistemological model—and therefore the political program based on it—in at least two crucial ways. First, the technocrats began to appreciate and to acknowledge the complexity and the sophistication of scientific reason. This recognition, in turn, affected and changed their understanding of *who* might be among the enlightened and therefore of *how* the rationalization of the political order could proceed. Second, the technocrats began to absorb the pressures from within the new rationalism toward philosophical naturalism. This absorption then led them, in turn, to a somewhat revised conception of the nature and content of the norms ascertainable by "moral science."

The technocratic tradition first departed from early liberalism, then, by circumscribing the number of persons who might be expected to have access to scientific truth. As noted in chapter 3, the belief that the new reason embodied a process of profound *simplification* was an important idea. It was important, not only because it helped to sustain the image of the increasing momentum of scientific progress, but also because it seemed to underwrite democratic expectations in politics. If the peasant of the near future might, as Descartes envisioned, exceed the understanding of the present-day philosopher, then society might become enlightened and democratic at the same time. Descartes himself did not elaborate this forecast. Indeed, since he tended to terminate his philosophical speculations short of considering their possible political and religious significance, he may not have considered it with any care. But these implications were clearly and explicitly developed by others. Certainly, democratic liberals like Condorcet and James Mill regarded the simplicity and accessibility of reason as important to the prospects of democratic government.

Technocratic revisionism recognized that this belief in the potential near-universal accessibility of the truths of scientific reason was unrealistic, for it either misconceived the nature of scientific truth, or it overestimated the capabilities of the untutored mind, or both. This technocratic critique of the epistemological democratism of liberal reason could have been either logical or empirical. The logical criticism would have been that the idea of science as "simple" rested on overly facile analogies, semantic confusion, and unwarranted expectations. In the first place, it was overly facile and therefore misleading to take the discoveries of Galileo and Newton about the mechanics of physical motion as paradigmatic of all scientific discovery. These discoveries had indeed produced a great rush of illumination by a dramatic conceptual simplification that could be expressed in precise and simple formulas, but not all intellectual progress, even in the physical sciences, is like that. Even here, the high hopes of the democratic liberals traded on ambiguities in the concept of "simplification." For although the apprehension of a general pattern behind a large number of superficially disparate phenomena may indeed be a kind of simplification, it does not necessarily follow that it will be simple for an untutored mind to understand or appreciate the general pattern, however economical its expression. The simplicity and economy of expression mask the sophistication of the concepts resident within it. Indeed, the very simplicity of expression may render the content even more enigmatic. $E = mc^2$ is in one sense a very simple formula, but its meaning is not therefore simple to grasp.

The expectation that a clear and simple universal language would be developed—one that on the one hand would suffice to embody all important scientific truths and, on the other, would be intelligible to all men—could not be realistically maintained.[87]

In point of fact, the technocratic departure from the democratic epistemology of the liberals, such as Condorcet and Mill, was probably more empirical than logical. It simply seemed apparent as time went on that the corpus of scientific knowledge was not assuming a form that was easily intelligible to the average man. Those who were scientifically enlightened continued to be a relatively circumscribed group, and they seemed destined to remain a clear minority. Access to the truths of science required both unusual aptitude and a training that not many could undertake. The average individual might, to be sure, attain a primitive grasp of basic scientific ideas, but even then he would be a consumer rather than a producer of these truths. More important, since he would be unable to adjudicate and evaluate these ideas on his own, he would obviously remain quite dependent on the scientists.

Accordingly, the technocratic model revivified the "two truths" doctrine of the early, more elitist *philosophes*. That is, the real, the unvarnished, truth would be accessible only to the few enlightened ones. For the mass of men, the enlightened would fashion a simpler, mythical, account, which would contain only what they could understand—or should understand, for the good of society. In this respect, the "knowledge economy" of the technocratic society would function rather like the society of Plato's *Republic*. The knowing elite, now scientists rather than philosophers, would ascertain the truth and create "noble lies" (i.e., myths) for the consumption of the masses, who were unable to apprehend reality on their own.

Quite counter to the Platonic tendency, however, was the second amendment effectuated by the technocrats upon the original paradigm of liberal reason. This shift—which, like the first, had extremely important political implications—seemed to happen out of direct view, even inadvertently. It concerned the *what* of reason rather than the *who*—the range of reason rather than the access to it.

Specifically, the technocrats arrived at a new conception of what *kind* of norms the new reason revealed. With respect to this question the early adherents of liberal reason had been the Platonists—or the Aristotelians—or the Augustinians. That is, the early adherents of liberal reason carried over the classical conception of the capstone of reason as moral *logos*-rationality. The norms that both Locke and Descartes expected the new reason to establish with new clarity were the traditional teleological truths of human essence. The "science of morals," wrote Descartes, is "the highest and most perfect, which, presupposing an entire knowledge of the other sciences, is the last degree of wisdom."[88]

It gradually became clear, however, that the competence of technical reason did not extend that far. The new reason had the capacity to grasp only existence, not essence; and the existence it could grasp was itself circumscribed to the motions of primary qualities. One possible conclusion to draw from this discovery was that it was necessary to reject the idea of moral cognition, of objective norms, of rational ethics altogether. Many later drew this conclusion, as we shall see shortly. But the technocrats did not abandon the idea of normative truth accessible to the new reason; instead they gradually transformed it to fit the narrowed dimensions of technical reason.

The technocrats, as noted earlier, read the book of nature through the eyes of Democritus rather than Plato. In their universe, therefore, rationally ascertainable norms could not be understood in essentialist or in transcendentally teleological fashion. Instead, the technocrats were logically impelled to perceive the political standards established by scientific reason as tantamount to criteria of a smooth-running and efficient social machine. By understanding political norms in this fashion, the technocrats were able—to their own satisfaction, at least—to reconcile the narrowed and naturalistic content of scientific reason with the moral competence they imputed to it.

As a consequence of these philosophical changes, the technocrats' political program was strikingly different from that of the early liberals—different in both ends and means.

If the techocrats were at one with liberals in their hopes for making society "rational," the specific content of rationalism was very different for them. For the liberals, reason and common sense—freed from their enslavement and corruption by superstition, myth, and dogmatism—were expected to fasten directly and unproblematically on the goals and standards they themselves considered to be "natural" and "self-evident." Central among these self-evident truths were the goals of liberty, equality, justice, and natural rights. Quite different was the technocrats' conception of "rational" social goals. For them, "liberty," "justice," and "rights" were consigned to the realm of metaphysical nonsense—empty and "negative" abstractions without grounding in the world depicted by modern science. Their own goals were the rather vaguely conceived ones of social harmony, organization, peace, and happiness, all of which were conceived to be more consonant with a naturalistic and mechanistic view of the world and of human nature.

And if the technocrats agreed with the liberals in conceiving that political progress would be achieved by the spread of reason, their scientific elitism rendered this process remarkably despotic—even if it was covered over with a heavy gloss of sincere benevolence. The rationalization of social order, in their accounts, was to come not so much through democratic persuasion and accommodation as through the expert social management of well-meaning "doctors of morality." Technocratic praxis assumed not a representational mode but the mode of authoritarian therapeutic intervention. The technocrats offered not a political program in the usual and traditional sense but rather "a grand vision of social preventive medicine" in which the legislator is "the physician of the body politic."[89] And although it is possible to conceive of medical practice in a noncoercive fashion, the technocrats' positivistic conception of science left them quite unconcerned about such niceties as "informed consent." To recall Bentham's phrase, once again, the inhabitants of technocracy were to be *made* (Bentham's emphasis) to behave.

In one sense, then, the technocrats were "counter-revolutionaries," as Hayek suggests.[90] Taken by itself, however, that characterization is both too simple and misleading. Clearly, technocracy is counterrevolutionary vis-à-vis the fundamental principle of liberty, and, as a passionate classical liberal, Hayek tends to view everything from that reference point. It should be equally clear, however, that Bentham's Keeper and Helvetius's Legislator are not simply reincarnations of Louis XIV. However dictatorial these figures may be, they are modern through and through. The philosophical assumptions that purport to legitimize their rule did not exist until the seventeenth century.

Indeed, styling the technocrats as counterrevolutionaries may reinforce the modern self-congratulatory illusion that all distasteful political ideas and events are to be explained as reversions to the past. This delusion was, of course, endemic to the Enlightenment. But we should know better by now—and we surely need to know better. For what the technocrats exemplify is precisely how easily—even how commonly—distinctively modern premises can serve to justify extremely coercive and questionable political practices.

That so decisive a change in political destination was based on philosophical premises nearly identical with their own explains the liberal humanists' dismay and confusion when confronted by the technocratic challenge to their ideals. They were understandably upset by the way their cherished norms of human dignity and political liberty had been so unceremoniously pushed aside, and they were even more distressed to discover their polemical incompetence in the face of this threat. Because the technocratic program had borrowed their own most fundamental philosophical premises, the liberal humanists found it very difficult to gain the theoretical footing they needed to criticize it convincingly. They were faced by their own basic beliefs, carried to conclusions they found both impossible to accept and also impossible to refute.

Diderot's unhappy and bewildered reaction to the work of Helvetius may be taken as the very prototype of this persistent dilemma of modern liberalism. "I am infuriated," he wrote, "at being entangled in a devilish philosophy which my mind cannot help approving and my heart cannot help denying."[91]

He was not alone in his frustration. As D. W. Smith has written of the liberal *philosophes:*

> When they were brought face to face with the extreme rationalistic conclusions of *De l'Esprit,* they were revolted by the discovery that man had been turned into nothing more than a pleasure-pain calculating-machine little different from animals, that man could not be held responsible for his actions, and that all emotions such as love, friendship, and courage, which had seemed to ennoble life, had to be dismissed as illusory. Shocked and bewildered, the philosophers found themselves rejecting a work which had done nothing but develop to extreme limits the sensationalist theories which they had already accepted. They were mystified and angered by their inability to refute rationally an ethical system which they were, in fact, rejecting emotionally.[92]

In the shortsighted fashion of many revolutionaries, both political and intellectual, the *philosophes* had assumed that the destructive impact of their rationalism and their debunking naturalism would remain confined to the doctrines of their Scholastic, feudal, and clerical adversaries. When the children of their intellectual revolution turned on them to devour them, they were, then, ideologically, in real trouble. For they had neither foreseen nor prepared for the necessity of protecting their own humanistic assumptions against the critical forces they had unleashed.

5 *Werkmeister* and Therapists: The Technocratic Legacy

We can now enumerate the central constituent features of the fully developed technocratic political program. These might be termed the identifying hallmarks of technocracy. A political theory or an ideology may properly be labeled "technocratic" to the extent that it embraces or embodies the following ideas:

1. The analytical division of society into two "classes" of people who are radically distinguishable in their relationship to the mode of production of knowledge (to put it in quasi-Marxist form) and who are therefore conceived as radically distinguishable in their mode of being—the "knowers" being depicted as free, rational actors, the "nonknowers" as causally determined functions of their environment.
2. The tendency to see politics—in the sense of a continual process of accommodation among contending interests and conceptions of virtue—as an atavistic form of social organization that should properly give way to administrative regulation based on scientific principles.
3. A doctrine of "authority" in which social power is legitimated by the attainment of scientific credentials rather than by political delegation and which extends to a warrant to "create" or "transform" the very nature of the governed.
4. A tendency to minimize or deny outright the existence of transcendental or moral constraints—such as rights or individual liberties—upon the legislator and to look instead to naturalistic and therapeutic standards.
5. A doctrine of human perfectibility that relies on neither divine grace nor individual effort but instead on the beneficent intervention of rational authorities.

The technocratic perspective is not rigidly circumscribed

by conventional ideological boundaries. On the contrary, it has proved itself compatible with a wide segment of the standard ideological spectrum. In somewhat different ways, liberals, conservatives, radicals, and reactionaries have all found it possible to rely on technocratic conceptions in the context of their divergent orientations. A principal reason that "technocratism," or some such name, has not achieved the status of a distinct ideology in modern politics is the very ubiquity of its fundamental ideas. The actual power and influence of the technocratic model of politics has probably been heightened precisely because it has not stood out as a separate and distinctive orientation.

Part of the purpose of this chapter, then—indeed of this entire book—is to suggest some important inadequacies in our conventional ideological categories. Like Sheldon Wolin's argument in the final chapter of his *Politics and Vision,* the argument of which runs parallel to mine in substance as well as form, my analysis "is intended as an argument against the fetish of ideological interpretation which compels us to look at past theories through constrictive peepholes."[1] If we have not been sharply attuned to the presence and role of the technocratic orientation, the fault lies in part with our conceptual lenses.

The standard ideological categories, though quite useful for some purposes, tend to blind us to important similarities among viewpoints that fall into different categories; equally important, they tend to obscure some highly important differences of viewpoint between schools that are lumped under the same conventional heading. For example, the conventional categories tend to be organized to discriminate among diverging perspectives on economic matters and among contrasting beliefs about the relative natural goodness and equality of men. Thus, Louis de Bonald and Richard Weaver would conventionally be considered right-wing or conservative, Hubert Humphrey and Lester Frank Ward as liberal or progressive, and Michael Harrington and Lenin as socialist or radical. These are important bases for distinguishing different political leanings, and the resultant groupings make good sense in some respects. However, if different criteria were applied—less conventional, perhaps, but focused on equally important issues—the groupings would shift. If technocratic leanings were contrasted with a dedication to a politics of civility, restraint, and human rights, then de Bonald, Ward, and Lenin might well be thrown together and contrasted with Weaver, Humphrey, and Harrington. Certainly, for my part, I would rather be governed by any of the latter than by any of the former; and, as a political theorist, I would consider inadequate any analytical framework that could not account for this eminently defensible preference.

The technocratic model, the contemporary role of which is the focus of this chapter, is, of course, an "ideal type." That is, it is a paradigm built up out of several distinguishable components and refined into a coherent "pure" pattern for purposes of analysis. Rather like the "pure market" of the theoretical economist, therefore, it is rarely if ever found existing in unsullied clarity. In the thinking of even those who have most fully embraced the technocratic idea there are usually some loose ends, which—since their sources are external to the premises of technocracy—create some unresolved tensions within their theories. Helvetius, for example, embodied the technocratic conception of politics quite fully and explicitly, but he also insisted on a free press in his ideal society. Similar features can be found in the thought of Jeremy Bentham or even in the thought of B. F. Skinner, who in most respects comes rather close to advocating technocratic politics in its starkest form.[2]

These "loose ends," it should be added, are of considerable significance, practically as well as theoretically. For they usually serve to soften the otherwise totalitarian implications of the theorist's basic framework. They prevent, in other words, the completion of the dynamics of "technocratic closure"—the tendency of technocratic ideas, if wholly unopposed or unconstrained by other ideas, to generate what Eric Voegelin has aptly termed the "prison fantasies" of the technocratic school.[3]

Every ideal type is something of a caricature, distorting the complexity of reality through unavoidable oversimplification. Nonetheless, any valid and useful ideal type is not a straw man. It is not simply an artificial construction of the analyst. Instead, it is a pattern possessing its own internal "logic" and coherence. The binding force that integrates the various facets of the model into a gestalt comes from within and is not arbitrarily imposed from the outside. The model also, as I tried to indicate in chapter 4, possesses its own dynamic momentum: if the basic premises are accepted, the rest tends to follow.[4]

Because the technocratic model does possess an inner logic, coherence, and momentum, it has the capacity to surface repeatedly in slightly different forms. It is only necessary that its premises remain fundamentally intact. Therefore, someone like B. F. Skinner can, two centuries later, virtually replicate the politics of Helvetius with little if any direct encounter with or debt to the earlier thinker. He need only have the singlemindedness to draw out the implications of an archetypal epistemology that remains very much alive, even if it has receded since the eighteenth century from the status of explicit doctrine to the less visible but perhaps even more powerful role of tacit presupposition.

Once the presuppositions, the hallmarks, and the internal dynamics of the technocratic paradigm have been identified, the contemporary presence of this approach to political life should become apparent. For the tenets of the technocratic ideal, rooted in one reading of the positivistic predispositions of modernity, have been incorporated into many areas of modern social theory and practice. Technocracy is not merely a historical curiosity. It remains a significant force in determining the way that many schools of thought understand the nature of man, his knowledge, and his politics. As such, it has significantly shaped the course of contemporary history.

Historicist Technocracy: Comte

Just as the technocratic conception of politics is capable of crossing standard ideological boundaries, it is also found within different philosophical traditions.

Conventional wisdom identifies Continental historicism and Anglo-American empiricism as divergent intellectual traditions whose adherents regard each other with indifference or hostility. There are, of course, substantial theoretical grounds and significant evidence to justify this conception. To begin with, even the superficial reader has to be impressed by the distinctive and divergent styles of philosophizing produced by these two traditions. They tend to address different kinds of questions, and they utilize strikingly different vocabularies. Therefore, the two schools of thought tend to interact very little. As David Braybrooke and Alexander Rosenberg noted a few years back, "Almost no graduate student doing epistemology or philosophy of science at an English-speaking university is ever exposed to [historicist writings]."[5]

When one of the two traditions deigns to take note of the other, it is, again, almost always to castigate the rival outlook in the strongest terms. Empiricist philosophers from Carnap to Popper have condemned historicist ideas as pseudo-science at best and as dangerous total nonsense at worst. In return, the heirs of the left-wing Hegelians, such as Lenin and Marcuse, have condemned empiricism as a static and sterile manifestation of bourgeois false consciousness.[6]

Nevertheless, it seems quite clear that technocratic conceptions of politics have developed within both of these traditions. Each has produced thinkers skeptical about the scientific apprehension of political norms. But each has also produced thinkers whose political ideas exhibit all the hallmarks of technocratic thought. Indeed, some thinkers have found it rather easy to draw on both traditions, assimilating them into a common vision, to justify their versions of technocracy. Moses Hess is probably the outstanding example of this, but many of the second-generation "young Hegelians" were very receptive to the political ideas of the philosophically positivistic French and English socialists. The two traditions seemed in their eyes mutually reinforcing rather than contradictory.

The crucial conceptual innovations necessary to assimilate technocracy with historicism were accomplished by Auguste Comte. These innovations did not have to await the extensive productions of his philosophical maturity, the *Cours de philosophie positive* and the *Système de politique positive*. They were already clearly apparent in his early essay, the *Plan of the Scientific Operations Necessary for Reorganizing Society*.

The first of these conceptual innovations was Comte's fusion of nature and history, together with the alterations in each of these philosophical symbols necessary to permit their assimilation. On the one hand, Comte historicizes nature: the realm of nature is laid out not merely in space but also in time. Nature grows or becomes; it does not merely exist in a complete and static form. At the same time, Comte "naturalizes" history. History, being now properly understood as nature-laid-out-in-time, must therefore be seen as governed by the workings of natural laws. History is a "phenomenal" realm of natural forces whose patterns of necessary change can be discerned by positive science. Because no one has properly appreciated this fact before, Comte complains, "as yet there exists no true history, conceived in a scientific spirit."[7] Like Machiavelli, who had made a similar complaint, Comte wants to insist that history is governed by natural regularities, "laws," which "true history" should discover. Machiavelli believed these regularities to be patterns of recurrence, based on the eternal sameness of nature, but Comte saw them as patterns of "succession" or progress.

Comte's naturalizing of history carries with it the corollary of historical inevitability. Because history is governed by natural laws, it proceeds on its course essentially "independent of the human will."[8] Historical events are the result of "necessary" rather than "accidental" causes.[9] History follows "a determined and invariable course" and is characterized by "unavoidable transitions."[10]

Comte's second innovation is the reintroduction of teleology into nature. History's "inevitable" course is determined at base by the "instinctive tendency of the human race to perfect itself."[11] The "faculty of self-improvement," which Rousseau held to be one of the two distinguishing features of humanity, turns in Comte into the driving force of history. Thus "the principle of progressive civilization" is one that is "inherent in human nature."[12] It is, to borrow Aristotelian language, man's striving to actualize his potentialities that creates the laws of succession, which in turn create the pre-determined course of historical development.

Comte's final major conceptual innovation is his account, based on these two metaphysical claims about history, of what a "scientific" politics entails. On this question, he very clearly and explicitly draws the distinction between "scientific" and "utopian" politics that is conventionally associated with Marx and Engels. Previous social theorists and reformers, he charges, have misconceived their task and their capacities in a utopian (in the Marxist sense) fashion. They are found "still supposing that social phenomena can be modified at will, the human race having, in their view, no spontaneous impulsion, but being ready to yield to any influence of the legislator."[13]

This belief, that "social events [are] exposed to disturbance by the accidental intervention of the legislator,"[14] Comte holds to be a fallacy based on the outmoded "theologico-metaphysical infancy" of the human mind. It is a fallacy resembling precisely, and for the same reasons, the fallacies of astrology and alchemy, both of which similarly supposed, says Comte, that natural forces could be "arbitrarily" and "accidentally" controlled by the human will. In contrast, the recognition by a mature positivist philosophy that history is as spontaneously law-governed as astronomy and chemistry have found nature to be leads to an altogether different, new, and "scientific" conception of politics.

Scientific politics begins for Comte with the theoretical and positive science of history whose previous absence he bemoans and whose accomplishment is one of his major philosophical goals. The "social physicist" first "observes" the previous course of history, finding in it the regular and determinate laws of succession that govern it. On the basis of this knowledge, he can then obtain a "scientific prevision" of social phenomena "within the limits of exactness compatible with their higher complexity."[15] This capacity for scientific prevision is possible once he has achieved a satisfactory explanation of the past, since the metaphysics and methodology of positivism render explanation and prediction logically isomorphic.

This "determination of the real tendency of civilization" provides, then, "the fundamental datum and positive starting point of general practical politics"[16] in the scientific mode. Because the course of history is predetermined, no one can alter its basic end. "Nevertheless," Comte alleges, "the progress of civilization is more or less modifiable ... within certain limits."[17] Although the scientific practice of politics cannot establish its goals in a purely discretionary manner, it can "accelerate or retard" the course of civilization. Hence its proper role is to "facilitate the definitive transition to the new social state.''[18] To borrow the Marxist analogy, the scientific practitioner of politics may ease the birth pangs of the new order. He ''can harmonize political action with [the real tendency of history] and render as mild, and as short as possible, the crisis that the human race inevitably undergoes during its successive passages through the different stages of civilization.''[19]

Again paralleling the Marxist contrast between scientific and utopian socialisms, Comte explains that the time has only just arrived for the possibility of scientific politics. Previously, neither the intellectual nor the social preconditions for this definitive step existed. The human mind and the various sciences develop in a determinate evolutionary fashion in which no ''interval of any importance [can be] overleaped.''[20] Therefore, a genuine science of politics could occur only after the study of society had moved through its theological and metaphysical phases and entered its positive era. Likewise, the social systems that reflect these different stages of intellectual development must also have reached a definitive stage. The military epoch, based on theological conceptions, and the juridical epoch, based on metaphysical conceptions, must each have done its work in preparation for the final epoch of science and industry. Since both preconditions, the intellectual and the social, had been achieved only in his own day, Comte held, ''it is easy to explain at once why politics could not sooner have become a positive science''; but it is also possible to understand why ''the moment for commencing this great operation has at last arrived.''[21]

Although Comte clearly viewed the eighteenth-century technocratic theorists as utopians, enmeshed in an inadequate metaphysics they could not transcend and deluded in their belief that the discretion of the legislator was almost unlimited, his own philosophy nevertheless bore all the crucial hallmarks of technocracy. ''Politics'' in the usual and traditional sense he believed to be obsolescent. The old pattern of accommodation of interests could now be replaced by a rational ordering of society through posttheoretical practice. The task of organizing social life properly depended on ''raising politics to the rank of the natural sciences.''[22]

Like the earlier technocrats, moreover, Comte understood this new science of politics as a theoretical and positive science that brought to fruition the work of the intellectual revolutionaries of the seventeenth century. He wrote that

> It is time to complete the vast intellectual operation begun by Bacon, Descartes, and Galileo, by constructing the system of general ideas that must henceforth prevail upon the human race. This is the way to put an end to the revolutionary crisis that is tormenting the civilized nations of the world.[23]

This positive philosophy was a science of observation, resulting in laws of resemblance and succession epitomized by the doctrine of gravitation and capable of verification. The establishment of this science would substitute scientific authority for political authority, permitting the emergence of a "radical consensus"[24] in the "social organism." And this consensus produced by the triumph of a positive science of politics would in its turn bring peace and harmony into the heretofore conflict-ridden social arena:

> Under the rule of the positive spirit, again, all the difficult and delicate questions that now keep up a perpetual irritation in the bosom of society, and that can never be settled while mere political solutions are proposed, will be scientifically estimated, to the great furtherance of social peace.[25]

In archetypal technocratic fashion, Comte envisions a pivotal role for his elite class of scientists—the *savants*. Since right practice is consequent to and determined by true theory, and since the *savants* are the custodians of true theory, they are the ultimate authorities of the positive polity. The class of *savant*, moreover, consists necessarily of a select few. "Almost all men," writes Comte, "are naturally unfit for intellectual labor."[26] As a result, the important truths of social physics are "accessible to a very limited circle."[27] Therefore, "the formation of social theories should be confided only to the best-organized minds, prepared by the most rational training."[28] A more democratic and egalitarian approach would not only be impossible; its consequences would be disastrous. "Can it be supposed," Comte asks rhetorically,

> that the most important and the most delicate conceptions, and those which by their complexity are accessible to only a small number of highly prepared understandings, are to be abandoned to the arbitrary and variable decisions of the least competent minds? If such an anomaly could be imagined permanent, a dissolution of the social state must ensue, through the ever-growing divergence of individual understandings, delivered over to their disorderly natural impulses in the most vague and easily perverted of all orders of ideas.[29]

The masses will receive their simplified and watered-down version of the truths of the positive polity through the mediation of the fine arts. Here, says Comte, is the socially useful function of the imagination. It can inspire the people's allegiance to the new social system, but its "direction" must always be subordinated to the truths of scientific observation. Comte then elaborates this basically Platonic view of artistic propriety in a way that could easily be taken as a contemporary account of Soviet "socialist realism" and its role in creating "socialist man." The social utility of the arts, Comte writes,

> consists in presenting a vivid picture of the ameliorations that the new system should bring about in the condition of mankind. . . . Such a perspective alone can induce men to effect the moral revolution within themselves essential for establishing the new system. This alone can repress egotism . . . , draw society from its apathy, and impress on it that active devotedness that is demanded by a social state destined to maintain all the human faculties in constant action.[30]

Finally, Comte exemplifies very clearly both the "dynamo-objective coupling" and the authoritarian-therapeutic orientation intrinsic in the technocratic viewpoint. Illustrative of the former is his insistence on the "objectivity" of his social physics:

> Admiration and reprobation of phenomena ought to be banished with equal severity from every positive science, because all preoccupations of this sort directly and unavoidably tend to hinder or mislead examination. Astronomers, physicists, chemists, and psychologists neither admire nor blame their respective phenomena. . . .It should be the same, in this respect, in political science as in the other sciences.[31]

At the same time, however, he fills his sociology with normative content through his use of interpretive categories like "normal," "determinate," and "definitive." His social physics is "positive" but not at all devoid of prescriptive implications. Instead, its perfection would permit a "rigorous determination, embracing every essential detail, of that system that by the natural progress of civilization *ought* to prevail as the final social system."[32] Thus the normative thrust of Comte's social project and the passions associated with it fuel his sociological theories and save them from academicism. And, in return, the scientific status and emotive "neutrality" he ascribes to his doctrine serve to protect it from any criticisms levied against it on traditional, ethical, or political grounds. Like the true technocrat he is, Comte is a man with a redemptive mission. And his crusade is encapsulated against legitimate controversy and criticisms by the pronouncement that these criticisms are based on misunderstandings and obsolete epistemology.

The result is a therapeutic politics in an authoritarian key. Comte's praxis is, like Bentham's, a "social preventive medicine."[33] "Disturbances . . . in the social body," he declares, "are exactly analogous to diseases in the individual organism, and I have no doubt whatever that the analogy will be more evident . . . the deeper the investigation goes."[34] Accordingly, "political art can pass upwards as medical art has done, the two cases being strongly analogous."[35] And the cure for society's ills is to be administered by the management class, the *industriels*—under the strict tutelage of his philosopher-kings, the *savants*. As for the rest, they should acquiesce in the therapeutic regimen laid on them and be grateful. Once the positive philosophy has put to rest the "anarchic dogmas" of liberty of conscience, equality, and popular sovereignty, the principle of "spontaneous subordination," best exemplified within the family, will reassert itself and become "the type of all wise social coordination."[36] For "stormy discussions about rights," a positive philosophy will "substitute peaceable definition of duties."[37] Thanks to the "eminently organic tendency of the new political philosophy," the citizen will be "regarded as a public functionary whose duties and claims are determined more or less distinctly by his faculties."[38] The "natural subordination of the woman" will be placed "on its right basis."[39] And a "firm alliance between philosophers and proletarians"—one which of course also embodies the "spontaneous" and "natural" subordination of the latter—will emerge to provide "the effective impulse towards social regeneration."[40]

Comte and Hegel

In 1824, two years after the appearance of Comte's *Plan for the Scientific Operations Necessary for Reorganizing Society*, one of his students went to study in Germany. Upon discovering Hegel, he reported to his master that "there is a marvelous agreement between your results, even though the principles are different, at least in appearance."[41]

Comte's pupil was remarkably astute in his observation, right down to its nuances. Certainly the philosophical "principles" of Comte and Hegel are quite "different." Comte wrote—at least up until his post-crisis later work—in a very secular and scientific fashion. He was explicitly antitheological and ostensibly antimetaphysical. Hegel's philosophy, in contrast, was at heart a heterodox theology, heavy with metaphysics. Yet there were in fact some "marvelous agreements" in "results." And, as the pupil's phrase "at least in appearance" suggests, even the principles of the two disparate figures were not entirely dissimilar beneath the surface.

Viewed from the standpoint of what we might call (in a nonreductivist sense) their underlying epistemological myths, the convergence of Comte's positivist historicism and Hegel's idealist historicism seems less than astonishing. Despite their different philosophical language, they—as well as the earlier technocrats—shared a fundamentally similar belief about the new dispensation of reason. Whether they expressed it in secular or quasi-theological terms, they both felt that mankind had hitherto walked in darkness but had now seen a great light. Recent discoveries had resulted in a philosophical *kairos*. The real truth was now based on secure foundations and discernible to those who had eyes to see it. The future destiny of mankind was therefore to acquiesce in or to help bring about the increasing rationality of the world. The theological motifs embedded in this "myth," we might add, provide the basis for Eric Voegelin's revealing if somewhat misleading metaphor of the "gnostic" character of modernity.

Hegel, Comte, and the early technocrats all believed that knowledge, including the political and moral "sciences," could, by virtue of their discoveries, attain the status of Aristotelian theoretical knowledge. This was possible because historical contingency no longer was a factor in their epistemologies. In their different ways, Hegelian, Comtean, and empiricist epistemologies depicted a non-contingent knowing subject and a naturalized object of his knowledge. On the empiricist side, the historical factor was simply ignored, overlooked, or eliminated by virtue of its mathematical paradigm of knowledge. Neither Cartesian "ghosts" nor "machines" dwell in time. An Archimedean point is outside time, and primary qualities are timeless. Hence, true theoretical knowledge, which Aristotle saw as possible only with regard to unchanging objects, was deemed attainable.

The Hegelian account was more complex and sophisticated and did not derive from the geometricizing of all knowledge, which Hegel rejected. Hegel did not overcome historical contingency in knowledge by ignoring time. Instead, he explicitly *ended* time. Knowledge for him could now be true knowledge—"scientific," certain, and complete—because history had reached its fulfillment. Therefore, the knowing subject, specifically Hegel himself, attained the standpoint of eternity. And "history" could now be comprehended like a natural fact because it was now a closed process. Subject and object had grown from a historical process, but both were now "timeless."

Alexandre Kojève elaborates in the following way this relationship between Hegel's view that history "ended in the wars of Napoleon"[42] and his belief in "absolute Knowledge":

> We know that for Hegel this end of history is marked by the coming of Science in the form of a Book—that is, by the appearance of the Wise Man or of *absolute* Knowledge in the World. This absolute Knowledge, being the *last* moment of Time—that is, a moment

without a Future—is no longer a temporal moment. If absolute Knowledge *comes into being* in Time or, better yet, as time or History, Knowledge that *has come into being* is no longer Temporal or historical: it is *eternal,* or if you will, it is *Eternity* revealed to itself; it is the Substance of Parmenides-Spinoza which reveals itself by a *Discourse* (and not by Silence), precisely because it is the *result* of a historical *becoming;* it is Eternity *engendered* by Time.[43]

Hegel therefore believed, in Kojève's words, that "I am not only a thinking being. I am the bearer of an absolute Knowledge. And this Knowledge is actually, at the moment when I think, incarnated in me, Hegel."[44] What is more, he was able to transmit this millennial confidence to his intellectual heirs. As Friedrich Theodor Vischer recalled in a memoir, "We were propelled by a fervent and proud trust that the Hegelian philosophy, which we brought to increasing dominance among the educated youth, gave us possession of the real truth."[45]

In his own distinctive fashion, then, Hegel's account of the eschatological fruition of knowledge through a historical process that had reached its definitive phase ran remarkably parallel to Comte's account of the final triumphant entry of philosophy into its positive stage. And, following upon this profound underlying isomorphism, their philosophies of history were also quite similar.

For both Comte and Hegel, history was the rational development of ideas in time. Because whatever is "real-ized" in history must be rational, and because reason is internally structurally consistent and compelling, it follows that the course of history is in some sense "inevitable." What Hegel expresses in his well-known dictum that "the real is the rational and the rational is the real" Comte tries to convey, not only in his claim that "the new philosophy . . . exhibits as inevitable that which first presents itself as indispensable; and the converse," but in his approving acceptance of what he calls De Maistre's "fine" political aphorism that "whatever is necessary exists."[46]

For both Comte and Hegel, moreover, the upward and rational thrust of historical progress did not proceed in a straight line. Instead it was depicted as developing through a process of resolving self-generated tensions and oppositions. In Hegel, of course, this pattern is that of his dialectic. In Comte, the same process is conceived as an "oscillation" between "organic" stages, which embody coherent principles of constructive order, and "critical" stages, in which the inadequacies and contradictions of the preceding organic stage are uncovered and challenged. "The course of civilization," says Comte, "does not advance in a straight line. It is composed of a series of progressive oscillations, more or less ample or slow, on either side of a mean line, which may be compared with that presented by the mechanism of locomotion."[47]

Finally, since the course of history is, for both Comte and Hegel, predetermined by its intrinsic rationality, their conceptions of the efficacy of human will and effort in history are quite similar. The only individuals whose actions really count are those who are able to intuit the direction of the determining forces and so to swim with the tide. In Hegel, these are the "world-historical individuals" whose "own particular purposes contain the substantial will of the World Spirit." It is theirs "to know ... the necessary next stage of the world, to make it their own aim and put all their energy into it."[48] Comte concurs:

> All men who have exercised a real and durable action on the human race ... have, at every epoch, perceived what were the changes that the stage of civilization tended to bring about. These they enunciated, and proposed to their contemporaries doctrines and institutions in harmony with them. Whenever their conceptions were in accord with the real state of affairs, the changes so foreseen were speedily realized or consolidated.[49]

The judgment of Comte's pupil, that "the identity of results [between Comte and Hegel] exists even in the practical principles, as Hegel is a defender of the governments, that is to say, an enemy of the liberals,"[50] is probably too simplistic. It is noteworthy, however, that in at least two important respects Hegel and Comte drew the same political implications from their philosophies. For both of them, the state or the collective was to be considered prior to or superior to the individual. Hegel considers the state (a term that has a broad meaning for him, closer to "organized social culture" than to "government") "the divine Idea as it exists on earth." Hence "all the value man has, all spiritual reality, he has only through the state." Although the language of means/ends is not entirely proper in this context, Hegel says, it can nonetheless be said that "the state does not exist for the citizens; on the contrary, one could say that the state is the end and they are its means."[51] Comte, in turn, speaks of the "the naturally collective character of human activity" and of "the logical supremacy of collective conceptions," and he sees it as the goal of both individual and social development "to subordinate the satisfaction of the personal instincts to the habitual exercise of the social faculties, ... with the view of identifying the individual more and more with the species."[52]

Just as both Comte and Hegel consider the individual as properly subordinate to the whole, they also interpret the true meaning of human freedom to be the knowledgeable and willing subordination to rational and necessary law. "Knowledge of the law of progress enforces resignation," says Comte. The aim of politics is "to bring our political conduct into harmony with . . . the actual tendency of civilization."[53] Because this "real tendency" is grounded in the human quest for self-fulfillment, such "resignation" to it is positive freedom. The rationality of history, in other words, reconciles freedom with necessity. Hegel expresses the same idea in these words:

> In so far as the state, our country, constitutes a community of existence, and as the subjective will of man subjects itself to the laws, the antithesis of freedom and necessity disappears. The rational, like the substantial, is necessary. We are free when we recognize it as a law and follow it as the substance of our own being.[54]

Historicist Technocracy: Left-Wing Hegelianism

The concrete political implications of Hegel's philosophy, as is well known, were both ambiguous and controversial. It was quite possible to read this philosophy of history in the passive voice, as it were, emphasizing the rationality of the Real and recalling that Minerva's owl took flight only at dusk. Hegel's "right-wing" disciples took this interpretive tack and used Hegel to legitimize their political conservatism.

On the other hand, Hegel's ideas were also susceptible to a much more activist and potentially technocratic interpretation. Like the earlier and more positivistic technocratic theorists, Hegel had provided a rationale for the claim of Absolute Knowledge. He had adumbrated the idea of fundamental "class" divisions—e.g., the difference between the "world-historical" agents of history and the "victims" of history—based on a differential relationship to Reason. And, again like the earlier technocrats, he had (1) subsumed freedom under rationality, (2) suggested that rationality required restraint, and (3) glossed over the element of coercion in this restraint by use of the abstraction "Man."[55] The "left-wing" followers of Hegel, then, developed his ideas along these lines, very much in the way that Locke's epistemology was politicized and radicalized by his "left-wing" disciples.

The forces driving the young Hegelians toward their own version of technocracy were both political and philosophical. The political impetus came from their disillusionment with the increasingly reactionary character of Prussian political life. Although it may have taken both a leap of faith and flight of imagination even in Hegel's day to depict Prussia as the Incarnation of the Idea, most historians agree that the Prussia of 1818 was reasonably progressive in the context of its time. By 1830, however, and increasingly thereafter, Prussia became more reactionary just when the standards of political "enlightenment" were becoming more demanding. The gap between the Rational and the Real in Prussia, then, seemed to be widening rather than diminishing; the "rose" was becoming harder and harder to find in the "cross" of contemporary politics.

The philosophical impetus for the Young Hegelians was provided by the dilemma that confronted all of Hegel's disciples: what was to be the task of philosophy now that the absolute truth about the world had already been revealed in the master's system? Was there anything left to do? Or were Hegel's followers doomed to be nothing but epigones, reciting as mere catechism the finished truths of a completed theory?

One possible solution offered an answer to both dilemmas—the political and the philosophical—simultaneously. Contemplation was no longer the appropriate task of the philosopher: it was now, after Hegel's accomplishments, redundant philosophically, and it was inadequate politically. The Young Hegelians were thus forced toward the conclusion that the future task of philosophy was to *transform itself from theory into practice* and thereby to bring the world into conformity with the norms of reason. Truth had already been attained. What was now necessary was to actualize it in order to make men free. Michelet expressed the new program quite succinctly when he wrote in 1837 that

> as far as thought is concerned, the reconciliation is completed. It only remains for reality to elevate itself from all sides toward rationality, too. . . . The world emerges from thought and is developed further by it. As philosophy teaches us, truth, in order to become ours, has to become our own activity; and by means of truth transformed into activity, we shall reach freedom.[56]

Or, as the Polish Hegelian August von Cieszkowski put it, "that which imagination foreboded and which thought has recognized now has to be actualized by Absolute Will."[57]

The left-wing Hegelians differed among themselves, to be sure, about the actual concrete content of their world-rationalizing practice. For Feuerbach and Bruno Bauer it was conceived as critique: the world could be made more rational by holding its self-destructive illusions up to the light of reason and thereby dispelling them. It was especially important, they believed, to exorcise the alienating mystifications of religion. For Cieszkowski, this praxis was to be constructive reform, whose political directions were left quite vague. For Arnold Ruge, the rather dogmatic and crusading liberal reformism he embodied in his own life was what this praxis was supposed to be. And for Marx and Moses Hess, in their different ways, the praxis of the post-Hegelian philosopher was to issue into the politics of revolution.

Whatever their differences, however, the left-wing Hegelians shared an important common conviction about their activity. All of them sharply differentiated their form of praxis from the mundane prudence of Aristotle. However important practical reason was to Aristotle, he always conceived it as the partial and imperfect activity of a finite creature. Indeed, practical reason he distinguished from theoretical reason in one respect precisely by its intrinsic and inescapable *lack* of certainty. It was a mark of wisdom, Aristotle cautioned his readers, not to demand more certainty of a form of knowledge than its subject matter would allow.

In contrast, the left-wing Hegelians conceived the emergent form of philosophical praxis as *succeeding to the consummation of* theory rather than as *distinguished from* theory. Theirs was a posttheoretical practice. Because it was predicated on a previously understood absolute knowledge, the world-transforming praxis of the philosopher-turned-actor was no longer the heuristic and groping activity of contingent humans. It was instead the actualization of Truth, the materialization of Reason.

The left-wing Hegelians thus developed, on a rather different basis, a conception of rational political action that, in form, virtually replicated Comte's views on the same subject. For both, the appropriate politics for the new era they envisioned was putting-absolute-knowledge-into-effect. Rational politics was practice based on antecedently consummated theoretical knowledge. "In brief," Comte had written, "it is our business to contemplate order, that we may perfect it."[58] Ruge and Cieszkowski would have concurred. As Ruge put it, the present irrationality of the world produces

> unrest, dissatisfaction . . . and the nasty *ought* of *praxis*. Now something has to be done. . . . Just as pure insight is the starting point of thought, the decision to subject reality to this insight is its final point.[59]

The left Hegelians moved in the direction of Comtean historicist technocracy in other respects as well. First, their philosophy became increasingly secular and materialistic, in contrast with the more theological and idealist Hegel and his conservative followers. Second, they began to argue, like Comte, that their absolute knowledge could divine the future course of historical development, at least in outline. Left behind was Hegel's circumspection on this score. Cieszkowski, for example, envisioned the post-Hegelian philosopher as a "historiosopher" who could "construct from the already past section of the whole process of history its ideal totality and, in particular, its still missing future section."[60] Finally, again like Comte, the answer to the problem of reconciling "ought" with "science" and "is" came through investing this projected future with normative status. Since the future was where the immanent telos of history would be reached, normative demands were conceived as grounded upon—indeed, as coterminous with—the scientific apprehension of where history was going. In other words, the same idea that permitted Comte to speak of a government of measures rather than men allowed Marx to escape Stirner's nihilistic rejection of all ideals without surrendering his credentials as a nonutopian scientist.

The protagonist of the left Hegelians' posttheoretical practice emerges, then, as a historicist version of the *deus faber*. The "historiosopher" in action, translating the truth of absolute knowledge into reality, is no ordinary political figure. He is instead, like the *deus faber*, one who fashions the world in the likeness of Reason. He is a "*Werkmeister*," in Cieszkowski's words, "the conscious master builder of his own freedom." He elaborates:

> After humanity has reached true self-consciousness, it must accomplish its very own deeds according to all rules of the art, that is, according to the Idea. This does not mean that Providence ought to abandon history to its fate. Rather, it means that humanity has become mature enough to make its own determinations perfectly identical with the Divine Plan of Providence.[61]

Praxis, Prophecy, and the Transformation of Prometheus

Marx's well-known aphorism that philosophers have hitherto only interpreted the world but that now the task is to change it was not, then, a superficial slogan, a simple call to action. Instead, it embodied Marx's conviction that the time was now at hand for "posttheoretical practice." As early as his doctoral dissertation, Marx offered a prolegomenon for his future efforts by elaborating this conception. At certain axis-points of history, Marx argued, speculative philosophy, having fulfilled its mission, is superseded by practical action based on its success. Philosophy abandons the theoretical attitude and enters history as a "practical person hatching intrigues with the world." Its "heart has become strong enough to create a world."[62]

Given the inconclusive quality of the endless quarrels about "what Marx really meant," it is not really possible to say how far

Marx himself was implicated in the logic of technocracy. The most persuasive commentaries suggest that he was both too sophisticated and subtle conceptually and too committed to genuine freedom to succumb to technocratic closure. Nevertheless, it is significant to note that Marx avoided this pitfall essentially through the combined effect of a crucial ambiguity in his theory and an equally crucial contingency that sheltered it from exposure. The crucial ambiguity turned around the notion of "revolutionary praxis"; the crucial contingency was that his prophecies should be borne out by the course of history.

In tandem, these two ideas—of praxis and historical inevitability—served to distinguish Marx's vision from the technocratic utopia in which all-knowing "scientific" authorities "make" their fellow men "behave" as they should. The doctrine of inevitability implied that nobody made anybody else do anything. It was not any class of human beings that brought progress. It was "History" itself, acting through them. The movements of the dialectic, the violence of the revolution, the emergence of freedom were more akin to natural eruptions like earthquakes than to human contrivances. Moreover, to the extent that conscious human effort was involved, it was the self-transforming activity of revolutionary praxis, not the political coercion of one group changing or coercing another group.

Unfortunately, these two obstacles—the one conceptual, the other "empirical"—standing between Marx's hopes and the technocrat's fantasies, have proved to be exceedingly fragile.

In the first place, the "praxis" of avowed Marxist regimes has turned out to be remarkably indistinguishable from the absolute control and authority of technocratic subjects over the governed objects. One can argue persuasively that this regrettable tendency is a result of the failure of Marx's later disciples to appreciate the important subtleties of Marx's teaching. Certainly those political figures who embrace Marxist formulas as their legitimacy myth have exhibited little concern for or grasp of the finer points of Marx's actual writing. However, Marx surely shares some responsibility for the technocratic realities justified in the name of revolutionary praxis, for even the most devout defender of Marx's humanism would find it very difficult to maintain that Marx's concept of praxis was sufficiently well developed and clearly stated to serve as an effective guide. "Revolutionary praxis" is a slogan with profound hortatory force for Marx, but it hardly attains the status of a clearly defined philosophical concept or of a clearly identifiable form of political activity.

The reasons for this crucial theoretical lacuna in Marx, with its momentous "concrete" significance, are again disputable. But one probable reason is both simple and revealing, namely, that Marx was incapable of elaborating the notion of praxis without making apparent the ultimate incoherence of his philosophy. The peculiar power and appeal of his thought lies, at least in part, in his claim to have reconciled historical determinism with rational exhortations to action and to have reconciled the dispassionate objectivity of "science" with intense moral passions. The notion of praxis stands right at the juncture of these allegedly reconciled aspects of Marx's overall system. It serves as a crucial "bridging" concept to unite these disparate parts of his thought. But since the disparate parts are in fact not logically assimilable, the bridging concept itself is not coherently explicable. Hence Marx's reticence.

Lobkowicz elaborates Marx's difficulties this way:

> Marx has landed himself in a hopeless dilemma which has haunted his more intelligent disciples until today. This dilemma may be summed up as follows: if ideals play no genuine role in history, it hardly is meaningful to speak of *revolutionary* practice and, in fact, to be a revolutionary or even "progressive" at all. Practice in this case is as little "revolutionary" as biological evolution or the movement of stars. On the other hand, if there really exists a truly " 'revolutionary,' critical-practical activity," as Marx suggests in the first of the "Theses on Feuerbach," then not only must it be possible to be guided by some ideals but moreover there must exist some norms, an *ought* which transcends existing reality more radically than the "consciousness of existing *Praxis*" to which Marx in the *German Ideology* reduces all theoretical consciousness.[63]

This profound ambiguity or incapacity in Marx's thought might have remained purely academic in significance if only history had gone according to his predictions. As it always does, however, history deviated from the eschatological course it had been assigned. The contradictions of capitalism proved less than fatal. Especially disappointing, the touted "messiah class" of the proletariat proved as "bourgeois" in its aspirations as the propertied class. The workers of the world seemed more interested in sharing power by force of numbers than in building the New Jerusalem through revolutionary praxis. Perhaps even more dismaying, they were likely to subordinate class solidarity to national loyalty, as when the German Social Democrats supported their country's war of bourgeois imperialism.

Confronted by this insubordination of history and this apostasy of the chosen people, the disciples of Marx could not avoid facing the strategic and theoretical dilemma that Marx had been able to paper over by slogans. Either they had to remain true to the interpretation of praxis that stressed its fidelity to the actual course of history or they had to remain true to the sketch of how history "ought" to unfold "rationally." To choose the former meant to abandon some of Marx's predictions and some of his revolutionary fervor. To choose the latter reduced to pure pretense the claim that praxis was a form of historical midwifery rather than an attempt to bend history to preconceived goals; it meant a clear embrace of the technocratic scheme of the "scientific" knower manipulating those who, afflicted by "false consciousness," had not attained his exalted status.

Those who took the former course have come to be known as "revisionists." They were, in fact, no more revisionist than Lenin, who took the latter course. But the entitlements of "orthodoxy" are always self-assigned by the victors of history.

Lenin's highly technocratic interpretation of revolutionary praxis appears very clearly in "What Is To Be Done?" He launches there a furious assault on what he terms "bowing to spontaneity"—that is, on according integrity and respect to the manifest wishes and desires of the real-world proletariat. He readily admits that the workers of the world do not develop "socialist consciousness" on their own; instead they incline toward enhancing their economic and political power through union organization and by participating in parliamentary democracy. But this predilection is not to be respected in the slightest, he insists, because "science" has proved it to be based on a "false" perception of the world.

The truly "scientific" socialist, he concludes, must therefore diligently strive to discipline an unruly history that fails to conform to the mandate of theory. Those enlightened few, the vanguard, themselves members of the bourgeois intelligentsia, know the truth. ("The vehicle of science," Lenin quoted Kautsky, "is not the proletariat, but the bourgeois intelligentsia.") They are thereby entitled, indeed obligated, to engage in a "fierce struggle against spontaneity," to "divert the working-class movement" from its own goals and "bring it under the wing of revolutionary Social-Democracy."[64]

Lenin thought it worth only a brief footnote to soften the blatant coerciveness of his program. In a very ultimate sense, he assures his readers, the workers really are "spontaneously" inclined toward genuinely socialist consciousness:

> It is often said that the working class spontaneously gravitates towards socialism. This is perfectly true in the sense that socialist theory reveals the causes of the misery of the working class more profoundly and more correctly than any other theory, and for that reason the workers are able to assimilate it so easily, *provided,*

however, this theory does not itself yield to spontaneity, *provided* it subordinates spontaneity to itself.[65]

On its face, this assurance is simply nonsense, a flat self-contradiction: "the working-class tends spontaneously toward socialism, but not spontaneously." And if one seeks to rescue the claim from dismissal on these grounds, as it is possible to do (by distinguishing how one *would* naturally act *if* one knew the truth from how one naturally responds to circumstances one does not understand), one does so at the price of making the claim radically incorrigible. Not only is the claim impervious to falsification by means of any empirical evidence, since any piece of data is capable of being construed in accordance with the theory. Even more importantly and more radically, no contrary judgment or testimony can be deemed competent; to the extent that anyone, however proletarian his credentials, might disagree, he thereby and to that extent is dismissed as suffering from "false consciousness."[66] Lenin's position, then, reduces to a piece of flat dogmatism that could safely be ignored were it not the ostensive grounds for some of the most massively destructive political actions ever wreaked upon the world.

The technocratic paradigm, it is clear, continues to play an important role in the legitimacy myth of official Marxist-Leninist regimes. The passage in the "New Program" of the Communist Party of the Soviet Union depicting the party's role and authority, for example, is a compact and explicit technocratic claim:

> The Communist party, which unites the foremost representatives of working people and is closely connected with the masses, which enjoys unbounded authority among the people and understands the laws of social development, provides proper leadership in Communist construction as a whole, giving it an organized, planned and scientifically based character.[67]

This technocratic conception is what serves as the warrant for the whole array of repressive measures enforced by communist regimes. It has sanctioned the elimination of the millions of kulaks who did not fit into the "scientific" plan; they were designated as anachronisms, hence legitimate "victims" of Reason in History. It has mandated the purge of countless Soviet citizens who were "objectively" guilty even if "subjectively" innocent. It has warranted the creation of those Panopticons, the gulags, in which the "experimental physics of the soul" has received such an inhumane fruition. It has justified the incarceration of numerous dissidents in asylums; they were clearly "irrational" not to appreciate their blessings. It has served to legitimize cranks like Lysenko, to corrupt the arts, and to stifle the social sciences.

The technocratic ideal, in tandem with historicism, has, in short, generated the vicious cycle of corrupted idealism that afflicts the career of modern Marxism. The Marxist promise is the attainment of Absolute Justice throught the agency of Absolute Knowledge, yet it leads, perhaps unavoidably, to the displacement of all justice by the purest expediency and to the Kafkaesque systematizing of irrationality. For historicism, by elevating a putative future Utopia to be the source of all value in the world and by its corollary denial of all transcendence, systematically justifies any and all acts presumed contributory to this final goal. And technocratic epistemology gives the "scientific vanguard" sole and unlimited authority to "make" the world "organized."

Albert Camus' marvelous parable captures the irony of this metamorphosis:

> Here ends Prometheus' surprising itinerary. Proclaiming his hatred of the gods and his love of mankind, he turns away from Zeus with scorn and approaches mortal men in order to lead them in an assault against the heavens. But men are weak and cowardly; they must be organized. They love pleasure and immediate happiness; they must be taught to refuse, in order to grow up, immediate rewards. Thus Prometheus, in his turn, becomes a master who first teaches and then commands. Men doubt that they can safely attack the city of light and are even uncertain whether the city exists. They must be saved from themselves. The hero then tells them that he, and he alone, knows the city. Those who doubt his word will be thrown into the desert, chained to a rock, offered to the vultures. The others will march henceforth in darkness, behind the pensive and solitary master. Prometheus alone has become god and reigns over the solitude of men. But from Zeus he has gained only solitude and cruelty; he is no longer Prometheus, he is Caesar. The real, the eternal Prometheus has now assumed the aspect of one of his victims. The same cry, springing from the depths of the past, rings forever through the Scythian desert.[68]

The decisive question for contemporary Marxism is whether it is doomed continually to corrupt itself in this fashion or whether it can escape this cycle and create socialism "with a human face," as the slogan goes. The reflections and efforts of those who are striving to salvage the ethical core of Marxism are certainly to be welcomed and encouraged, for Marx's insights into the destructive features of the market society are important to the agenda for all postindustrial societies. Moreover, any steps toward softening and humanizing regimes already committed to Marxist ideology are surely to be welcomed, most of all by those who live under them.

It remains, however, a very fair question, and one I shall not attempt to answer here, whether a genuine humane socialism would be genuinely Marxist. It could hardly be Leninist, for at the very heart of the deadly and ironic logic of totalitarian closure that has aborted Marx's promises lie the myths, the motifs, the assumptions of the technocratic model. To humanize Marxism it would be necessary above all to exorcise the man-become-*deus-faber,* who acknowledges no limits to his praxis and claims unbounded authority over other men because of his "scientific" grasp of Absolute Knowledge.

Empiricist Technocracy: Positivistic Therapy

Technocrats have never achieved the unrestrained success in our own, Anglo-American, politics that they have attained under the aegis of Marxism. The persistence of the older natural-rights version of liberalism (and of older natural-law ideas), together with its embodiment in the practices of constitutionalism, has prevented such a triumph. Our "social engineering"—a modest doctrine that, generally respecting the limitations nature imposes on social contrivance, does not attempt to transform nature itself—has been Madisonian rather than Marxist or Saint-Simonian.

Nevertheless, technocratic ideas and assumptions constitute a very significant cultural force in contemporary Western culture. Many influential schools of thought are permeated with technocratic premises. They, in turn, often find a ready audience in a society deeply committed to the authority of science, usually conceived positivistically. As a result, technocratic premises have often shaped social practices and institutions that in one way or another lie beyond the reach of constitutional restraints or authority.

In our society the assumptions and aspirations of technocracy have received their most forthright theoretical expression in the ideas of some academic social scientists. Not all social scientists, of course, are technocratic. The nature of social science generally—its premises, purposes, and practical utility—continues to be hotly disputed among its practitioners, but in their philosophically polyglot world the legacy of Saint-Simon and Comte continues. The times and language may have changed, but the message remains essentially the same: constitutionalism and conventional politics are anachronisms that should be superseded by the rule of a scientific elite.

Technocratic preconceptions and prescriptions can be found in various schools of psychology, in the ideas of some leading sociologists, in the views of distinguished political scientists. In varying degrees and in different combinations their theoretical models exhibit the fundamental features of the techocratic view of politics. First, they reduce human behavior to the dimensions of *res extensa*. Second, they ascribe the epistemological status of a Cartesian subject to the social scientist. Third, on that basis, they perceive the possibility and desirability of extending into the human realm the Baconian program of mastering and possessing nature. Fourth, this achievement requires the abolition or transcendence of politics in the usual sense, which is seen as a kind of prescientific anachronism. Finally, authority in the postpolitical era is delegated to the social scientist, who assumes the role of utopian demiurge.

The most relentless and explicit reduction of human life to the dimensions of Cartesian *res extensa* occurs in the claims and conceptual models of psychological behaviorism. B. F. Skinner specifically mentions that Descartes was a forerunner of behaviorist ideas because of his intimation that the automata of the Royal Gardens of France provided a suggestive model of animal behavior. Descartes's only failure, Skinner suggests, was his timid reluctance to subsume the human organism under this model.[69] Other behaviorist theorists similarly recommend a wholly mechanistic framework for the interpretation of human behavior, objecting only to Cartesian dualism.[70] In this respect, the behaviorists are very much the intellectual heirs of Hobbes, who in precisely the same way extended the automaticity of *res extensa* into the human realm. For the behaviorists, like Hobbes, "life is but a motion of limbs." They insist that "life's most complicated acts are but combinations of these simple stimulus-response patterns of behavior."[71]

In this view, the traditional image of the human self is a myth devised to fill our temporary lack of scientific explanatory capacity. The destruction of this myth is therefore a welcome development, for it signifies the advance of our understanding.[72] The whole notion of purposive agency is similarly abandoned as a piece of outworn prescientific confusion. "Careless" references to purposes in interpreting human action are tantamount to a reliance on "occult qualities," Skinner suggests.[73] In its more severe versions, behaviorist psychology even banishes consciousness as an inadmissible concept. The notion of consciousness is "speculative" in form, "intangible" in content, and, as such, has no proper role in reliable scientific accounts of the world.[74] If not an illusion, consciousness is at best an epiphenomenon, a peripheral by-product of "objective reality" of bodies in motion, something that merely accompanies the process of behavior rather than enters into it.

Consequently, human behavior is purely passive. It is a determinate result of specifiable causes. And these causes lie "outside" of and prior to the behaving organism. The remarkably amorphous concept of the "environment" serves as a covering term for all of these exhaustively determinate external contingencies, and it then becomes a truism that all behavior is "a product of the environment."

Because all causal agency is attributed to "the environment," and because the metaphor of environment carries with it the presumption that it is amenable to intervention and control, it follows that the Cartesian and Baconian aspiration to "master and possess" nature extends to the mastery and control of human behavior as well. The "environment" is "nature." It is accordingly amenable to domination. But human behavior being in turn exhaustively the product of this natural realm, it may itself, in turn, be "mastered." In Skinner's words, "all control is exerted by the environment." But the "environment can be manipulated."[75] Hence it logically follows that human beings can be manipulated and controlled via the environment.

The passivity and plasticity of "objective" human "behavior" thus tacitly underwrite the possibility and the legitimacy of manipulation and control. Nothing is being violated when human behavior is mastered in this fashion, the behaviorist contends, for freedom and autonomy are illusory. It is simply, in the behaviorist's technocratic outlook, a matter of substituting rational and scientific control for the random and arbitrary controls that have grown up and that bind us willy-nilly.

Like Hartley and Priestley centuries before, the contemporary technocratic behaviorist translates epistemology into politics. As we understand man better, we shall render him increasingly amenable to our control. The advance of knowledge carries with it the corollaries packed in the clearly political metaphors of power and domination. And, also like Hartley and Priestley, the contemporary technocrat contemplates the prospect with enthusiasm. The "conquering of the human mind," we are told, should be "a national goal at parity with conquering of poverty or landing a man on the moon."[76]

There is nothing new, of course, in the prospect of controlling human behavior by mastering the environment. If you pull the chair out from under someone, he will "behave" by falling. Nor is the control of human behavior via intervention in its bodily substratum anything new. Moslem justice does that when it cuts off the hand of a thief. What is new is simply the subtlety, sophistication, and extent of control, together with the classic technocratic assumption that the banner of "science" renders the whole process "rational" and beneficent. The "conquering" of "nature" and of the human "behavior" it "produces" is envisioned through the conceptual prism of Saint-Simon: it is seen as bringing order out of chaos by the imposition of scientific patterns of organization. It is the transcendence of anarchy, the leap from the realm of necessity into the realm of freedom.

Nonreflective Epistemology and the Distortion of Social Science

The technocratic social scientist does, however, exempt himself, as a knowing subject, from the bondage of "objective" and wholly determined "nature." Indeed, he must logically claim such an exemption if his own claim to knowledge is not to be undermined. His adherence to the canons of "scientific method" lifts him, as a mind, out of this world. The contemporary version of the Cartesian and Baconian *regulae* constitutes a gnostic escape hatch, permitting the scientist qua scientist to claim transcendence of all the radical contingency he ascribes to the existence of other men. His claim to special knowledge warrants his admittance to an altogether different class of beings.

Because positivist epistemology is nonreflexive (paradoxically enough for what should be an intrinsically reflexive mode of inquiry) on principle, this claim on the part of technocratic social scientists to the status of wholly transcendent knowing subject is rarely explicit. Skinner, to be sure, does indulge himself with a few semiserious metaphors of the scientist-as-divinity. And Karl Mannheim, who was keenly aware of the problem here, developed a theoretically plausible (though empirically questionable) account of how the intelligentsia's knowledge was singularly reliable because of that group's "free-floating" sociological status. For the most part, however, the technocratic social scientist simply converts the wholly admirable *aspiration* of the scientist to transcend idiosyncratic biases and perceptual distortions into the highly suspect and dangerous claim to have *achieved* Laplacean "objectivity." This is more a presumption than an explicit claim, but it is clearly manifest in several ways: first, in the presumed status of the normative criteria the technocratic social scientist deploys in his account of social order; second, in his blindness to or disavowal of the power relationship intrinsic in the knowing of one human being by another; and third, in the privileged role he feels entitled to assume.

The technocratic social scientist proceeds, for example, as though normative (or "value-laden") concepts like "equilibrium,"[77] "rational organization," "anomie," "developed," and "mental illness" were dispassionate inferences from perceptions unsullied by the habits, interests, and partialities that govern the political perceptions of the nonscientific. He may be highly sensitized to the "irrational" sources of ideological bias in the people he writes about. Indeed, he may engage in a kind of de facto debunking of political orientations he finds suspect by the simple expedient of treating the ideology in question as a dependent variable and looking for subrational independent variables—i.e., sociological and psychological traits or characteristics. This tack is taken in good faith, for it is the methodological approach dictated by his "scientific" determinism. Nonetheless, it constitutes a highly effective ideological ploy. The ideological claims of one's opponents are reduced to irrational products of social causes. By contrast, of course, the normative orientation of the technocrat is exempted from similarly reductive explanation. Indeed, it is considered "scientific."

Comfortably misled by his tacit epistemology, which "proceeds as if knowledge arose out of an act of purely theoretical contemplation,"[78] the technocratic social scientist is blind to the fact that reductive explanation is, logically, a two-edged sword. It would seem apparent, for example, that if "authoritarian" political "attitudes" are properly explicable by social and psychological correlates, the same should be the case for the technocrat's own "attitudes." But this inference is rarely made. Instead, the clear implication is that the technocrat's perspective (and perhaps that of his own reference group) is of a different order altogether. (It may well be, I hasten to add, that the social scientist's political values *are* more "rational" than those of the man-on-the-street he studies. It is simply that this issue must be decided by rational argument. It cannot be settled by the methodological expedient of treating sociological causal factors as exhaustively explanatory of one set of ideas and wholly irrelevant to another set.)

His adherence to a subject-object model of knowledge, embodied in his particular understanding of and allegiance to "scientific method," in effect fixates the technocratic social scientist at the stage of what Mannheim terms the "special formation of the total concept of ideology."[79] That is, he "does not call his own position into question but regards it as absolute, while interpreting his opponents' ideas as a mere function of the social positions they occupy."[80] The social scientist does not usually, like the Marxist, brandish his analysis of "false consciousness" as a systematic political weapon. However, his inadequate appreciation of the contingencies and limitations of knowledge allow him to slide into the comforting attribution of scientific status to his own perspective while undermining other positions by depicting them as socially determined. In effect, this stance of the social scientist relies on a schizophrenic and self-serving answer to the question whether human behavior should be explained by reference to *causes* or to *reasons*. His answer depends on whether one is a "subject" or an "object." He, as a scientist, claims the former role and with it the status of rational actor; those he studies are assigned the latter role and with it the status of causally determined behaver. He dwells in the realm of freedom; those he describes inhabit the realm of necessity.

The profoundly political dimension of this radically asymmetric account of knower and known might seem readily apparent, and it may be so to the outsider—perhaps painfully so to those cast in the object role; but the social scientist often seems innocently unaware of it. In his passive role as pure observer, the Cartesian "subject" is wholly above politics, totally "detached" from worldly concerns or intentions, since he is totally distinct from *res extensa*. And since he genuinely conceives of his own role in this fashion, the social scientist is systematically blinded to the political implications of his real-world role as investigator into and describer of the social lives of other men.

The result is that the social scientist, who might otherwise be supposed peculiarly skilled in perceiving political realities, sometimes commits remarkable blunders in conducting his research. A striking example of this kind of blunder, committed by social scientists who utterly failed to anticipate the rather predictable anger their intrusion would arouse, was the ill-fated "Project Camelot."[81] In this case, an interdisciplinary team of social scientists undertook a large-scale study, sponsored by the Army's Special Operations Research Office, to determine the cause of "internal war" in Latin America. The director of SORO described the project as "a study whose objective is to determine the feasibility of developing a general social systems model which would make it possible to predict and influence politically significant aspects of social change in the developing nations of the world."[82]

Understandably, this project was barely off the ground before outraged protests were heard from some of the Latin American countries to be studied, eventually causing the project's cancellation. As Senator Fulbright noted, "any sensible observer might have anticipated" this result.[83] The fact that the social scientists involved did not do so led others to remark on their peculiar obtuseness. As Johan Galtung said: "that social scientists, systematically trained in seeing an issue from many angles, should fail to grasp the immense political implication of the project is strange."[84] And M. C. Kennedy wrote: "what is the real knocker-upper is the bottomless stupidity of most sociologists. They all talk about taking the role of the other, but few of them indeed seem capable of doing so."[85] This interesting phenomenon seems less strange and inexplicable, however, when the logic of the tacit epistemology at work is considered.

For the logic of the model implies that the scientific knower utterly transcends such mundane political considerations as these. "Taking the role of the other" is part of human identify formation but not, on this view, a part of scientific knowing. A genuine "subject," as a passive, "detached," outside observer, need not (and perhaps cannot) resort to such techniques of sympathetic projection.

Indeed, some of the participants in the project seemed righteously indignant that the "objects" in this particular case had been so uppity. The negative response to Camelot represented, in their view, one of those unfortunate technical problems that can plague scientific research. The problem for them lay in the irrational resistance of the objects, not in the arrogant obtuseness of the subjects. As one defender of the project expressed it:

> Some people still resist. They reject the idea of being studied: they do not like to be observed. They refuse to fill in questionnaires, they slam the door in the pollster's face, they do not show up in laboratory experiments. They are "anal" types. . . . Some countries also resist research by outsiders. They identify it with espionage. They are, we sometimes say, "xenophobic." Their culture breeds secretiveness.[86]

There may, of course, be strands of irrationality in a resistance to serving as the "object" of social scientific research—even in the resistance to Camelot, where the Latin Americans had reasonable grounds for suspicion. But what continues to be missing in this kind of statement is any appreciation of the profound political dimension inherent in knowing and being known. What continues to be missing is an awareness that, in the words of Roberto Unger,

> knowledge changes the object by placing it in the state of subordination that being an object implies. When, therefore, the object is another man, every claim by the subject to know him involves a struggle for power. There is no situation of life in which individuals do not have and show the desire to be hidden, alongside the wish to be known. Men want to resemble the God who is seen through a glass darkly, never face to face.[87]

Many social scientists do appreciate this reality.[88] But the technocrat (and, for that matter, his resolutely "value-neutral" brother) remains oblivious to the existence of any legitimate problem here. For him, the scientist has a rightful claim to see all, and any prospective object who resists is resented as one who doesn't know his place.

This claim to the epistemological status and role of what might be termed a "passive deity" is shared by the technocrat with many other social scientists. What distinguishes the true technocrat is his deliberate extension of this role from the passive to the active voice. On the basis of his claim to quasi-divine insight, he claims the role of a quasi-divine political agent. He intends not simply to predict but to control. His "science" grants him not just an avenue to knowledge but also a warrant to rule.

The specifics of the contemporary technocratic program vary with the focus and expertise of the individual advocate. What is constant is the image of an engineered society "beyond politics," a society manipulated by a scientific elite through the application of techniques based on causal laws in the service of often rather nebulous but appealing goals of social "harmony," "progress," "happiness," or "efficiency."

The technocratic psychophysicist envisions a "psychocivilized society"[89] in which the physical instrumentalities of human behavior are directly manipulated to produce the desired results. By means of such devices as electrodes implanted in the brain, the controller can make the controlee respond in ways determined not by natural sources of motivation but rather by artificially activated "internal" stimuli. Chemical means of altering behavior could also be employed.

The psychobehaviorist advocates a less direct plan of attack. Rather than physically or pharmacologically altering the human organism itself, he recommends changing behavior by manipulating the environment. This "technology of operant behavior" would proceed by changing the contingencies of reinforcement, which in turn are the motivators of human behavior. The pathway to a society that "will work" is "cultural design."

For some enthusiastic technocrats, both of these techniques should be employed in the appropriate combinations to procure the desired results. For example, Professor James McConnell writes:

> the day has come when we can combine sensory deprivation with drugs, hypnosis and astute manipulation of reward and punishment to gain absolute control over an individual's behavior. It should be possible then to achieve a very rapid and highly effective type of positive brainwashing that would allow us to make dramatic changes in a person's behavior and personality.[90]

Secure in his benevolent intent to utilize psychological force on behalf of praiseworthy goals—in this case, the rehabilitation of convicted criminals—McConnell seems unconcerned that his technology might be employed for questionable ends. Nor does he seem to be dismayed by the radical political asymmetry inherent in a process of this kind. The total subservience of the controlled individual is not seen as problematic or undesirable. Apparently the designation of the individual as "criminal" by the larger society is considered sufficient warrant to consign him to the category of experimental "object."

Positivistic Metapsychology and the Corruptions of Therapy

Even Freudian psychoanalysis, which in many respects broke the reductionist mold, lends itself to corruption by the logic of technocracy. Very much like Marxism, Freudian doctrine is susceptible to this kind of derangement in large part because of profound ambivalences and ambiguities in the thought of the tradition's founder. In his practices and his sensibility Freud clearly transcended the framework of technocracy rather dramatically: he grasped and explored the mythical and dramatic dimension of human existence; his specific explanations of psychic disorders implicitly abandoned the simple physicalism of some of his predecessors; he manifested a profound sensitivity to the mysteries and tragedies of life that systematically escape the convinced technocrat. Moreover, the enterprise of analysis itself seems anomalous to the technocratic program. The scientist as social engineer need not converse reflectively with the "objects" of his manipulation; he simply pushes them around to put them in proper order. Freud, in contrast, centered his entire therapeutic technique around precisely the kind of encounter that takes the human integrity of the patient for granted. The therapeutic goals of liberation and enlightenment are properly attainable only through the active participation of the patient; moreover, the therapeutic self-understanding must be validated by his personal acceptance and affirmation. As long as these aspects of psychoanalytic practice retain their centrality, the therapeutic process can neither be reduced to a technocratic program nor be captured interpretively by technocratic concepts.

And yet, Freud himself was heavily committed to a crudely positivistic self-characterization. He explicitly considered psychology to be a natural science; and natural science, in his mind, entailed a rather crude physicalism, both in its implicit ontology and in its forms of explanation. His ultimate theoretical goal, he wrote, was "to represent psychical processes as quantitatively determined states of specifiable material particles and so to make them plain and void of contradictions."[91] Hence, he was determined to conceptualize the psychological phenomena of his experience in terms that adhered to the limitations inherent in such a project. Psychological relationships, for example, he described in quasi-electrical-engineering terms like "cathexis." And he labeled character orientations by physiological reference points, calling them "oral," "anal," and "genital" personality types.

The result was that Freud had to bridge the gap between the dogmatically truncated conceptual universe he appropriated and the psychological universe he apprehended, and he did so, as Jürgen Habermas has pointed out, largely by adopting a strategy that "retains the neurophysiological language of the original [program] and makes its basic predicates accessible to a tacit mentalistic reinterpretation."[92] That is, the language he speaks conforms to the dimensions of his scientistic metapsychology, but the meanings he conveys are of a totally different order.

The danger, of course, is that this metapsychological failure and its attendant terminological obfuscation tend to push the therapeutic enterprise back into technocratic channels. The humanistic and reflective practitioner will resist and possibly thwart this tendency, but the pressure to yield to it (conceptual and institutional pressure, not political pressure) is clearly there. As Michel Foucault observes: "As positivism imposes itself upon medicine and psychiatry, this practice becomes more and more obscure, the psychiatrist's power more and more miraculous, and the doctor-patient couple sinks deeper into a strange world."[93]

This "strange world" of the "doctor-patient couple" is closely akin to the strange world of Jeremy Bentham's Panopticon, in which a quasi-divine authority figure dominated his client through his absolute and asymmetric power of total observation. The therapist, in short, assumes the role, status, and functions of the Cartesian "subject." Foucault describes this pattern, assigning (whether fairly or not) part of the blame for it to Freud himself. Freud, he writes,

> exploited the structure that enveloped the medical personage; he amplified its thaumaturgical virtues, preparing for its omnipotence a quasi-divine status. He focussed upon the single presence— concealed behind the patient and above him, in an absence that is also a total presence—all the powers that had been distributed in the collective existence of the asylum; he transformed this into an absolute Observation, a pure and circumspect Silence, a Judge who punishes and rewards in a judgment that does not even condescend to language; . . .[94]

At the same time, the imposition of a positivistically conceived medical framework on the proceedings tends to consign the patient to the status of object. An excessive passivity and dependence on the therapist (who becomes a "father figure" by "transference"), potentially implicit in the situation, may at times even be encouraged as an analytic device. The self-certitude of a positivist metapsychology, moreover, stands as an open invitation to short-circuit the reflective, autonomous, participatory qualities of legitimate therapeutic inquiry. Instead of seeing himself as a kind of Socratic midwife, aiding the patient toward a self-illumination previously inaccessible to both parties, the therapist is permitted to consider himself in possession of predetermined truths in need only of application to the particular case. The acquiescence of the patient in the interpretation becomes much more a pro forma matter. Indeed, the Freudian concept of "resistance" may be abused as an excuse for imposing a largely preconceived dogmatic framework over the legitimate protestations of the patient, who ultimately succumbs to the authority figure's superior knowledge and confidence.[95]

In like manner, a psychiatric practice corrupted by the logic of technocracy may lead the patient to perceive himself as a "dependent variable" not really responsible for his actions; for these actions are systematically traced back to childhood conflicts that he did not initiate and for which he cannot be held accountable. In other words, not only may the patient be treated as an object; he may also be implicitly encouraged to regard himself as an object.[96]

What happens, in short, is the systematic truncation and disfigurement of the complete cycle of genuinely therapeutic and reflective self-understanding by the imposition of a positivistic framework that badly misconceives the dynamics of the process. Self-objectification is a necessary stage of therapeutic reflection, but it is not and cannot be a final resting place. The reflective subject must confront himself as object in order to ascertain the sources of his disturbance. This step is essential. Once the necessary causal insight is attained, however, the patient must then go on to reintegrate himself as a subject. Reflection, that is, abrogates the appropriate relationship of tacit and explicit awareness in selfhood. It does so as a necessary analytic stratagem for therapeutic purposes. Once this purpose has been achieved, however, it is essential that the self-as-object return to its appropriately tacit role in the functioning psyche; otherwise the patient becomes fixated at an intentionally contrived stage of narcissistic infantilism. Reflection must be temporary—a pathway toward a more satisfactory reintegration of the self—or it is not therapeutic at all. In fact, it becomes crippling.

This is the essence, then, of the corruption of the therapeutic enterprise when it becomes assimilated to the logic of technocracy through positivist misinterpretation. Because the technocratic framework cannot render intelligible the full dialectic of genuinely therapeutic self-understanding, it allows the patient to become stranded in the middle of his journey. It does so because the technocratic mentality sees the role of "object" not as a limited stage of self-awareness but as a permanent mode of being. Abandoned in this untenable position, the patient may be worse off than before. It is as though a surgeon removed a diseased appendix but then neglected to sew the patient back up or bring him out from under the anesthetic.

The patient who is abandoned at, or frozen into, the role of "object," then, is left with the afflictions of his servitude—unless he can complete the process of healing reintegration on his own. He may display a morbid self-consciousness, suffer from alienation or a sense of defeat, and incline toward the "ethical disease" of fatalism. These perils are not the natural and inevitable consequence of psychiatric treatment or therapeutic analysis considered in their own right. They are instead dangers resulting from the distortion of the psychiatric and psychoanalytic enterprise by the immensely destructive impact of technocratic concepts, practices, roles, and institutions. For in this area, as in all others, to be a patient under a technocratic regimen is worse than almost any ailment.

Psychiatrists and Sociologists as Philosopher-Kings

The examples cited so far have been mostly at the micro level rather than the macro level. They have been psychological rather than sociological, elaborating programs for controlling individual behavior rather than manipulating the social order more broadly conceived. The application of the technocratic model to these large-scale phenomena, however, has also been a persistent theme in American political thought. The influence of Comtean positivism and the political prescriptions of Saint-Simon, whether directly appropriated or simply replicated through acceptance of their understanding of the social role of science, can easily be discerned in many quarters. Technocratic ideas have been crucial in what Bernard Crick has characterized as a "derangement in the wider thought of American liberalism, a derangement that has made plausible the confusion of science with technology and thus the generalization of this confusion, away from the proper boundaries and the logical coherence of science, to subsume all politics."[97]

Those sociologists and political scientists who have articulated technocratic ideas have arrived at this conclusion in a variety of ways. Some have been avowedly persuaded by the Comtean dream of a "scientifically ordered" society. Some have been inspired to transform psychotherapy into social philosophy. Others have hoped to remove power from the hands of politicians and give it to "rational" administrators. The normative models of politics they have espoused differ in substantial detail, but they share the common hope of attaining a society in which scientific authority, rendering politics obsolete, will govern according to its truths.

That giant of American sociology around the turn of the century, Lester Frank Ward, was openly influenced by Comtean positivism. "The rising school of philosophy," he wrote, "is that which for want of a better name is styled the Positive. Deriving its principles from the teachings of Bacon, Galileo, Newton, Franklin, and Humboldt, it had an illustrious founder in August Comte, and is today illuminated and adorned by the intellects of John Stuart Mill and Herbert Spencer."[98]

Like Comte, Ward saw sociology as, in the first place, essentially identical with the positive natural sciences. It shared their methods: precise observation and calculation. It shared their goals: prediction and control. It also dealt with a subject matter that was basically the same.[99] Sociology, therefore, as the most comprehensive and complex of the positive sciences, should be seen as the capstone of the sciences:

> The place of sociology among the sciences has been definitely fixed. It stands at the summit of the scale of the great sciences arranged in the ascending order of specialty and complexity according to the law of evolutionary progress.[100]

The positive knowledge that sociology ascertains, Ward held, in good Comtean fashion, is certain knowledge. Sociology, he said, includes nothing "dogmatic or visionary," but is instead "liberal and exact." "Taking nature as its only source of information, and the phenomena of the universe as the material for its deductions," Ward continued, sociology

> seeks in the observation of their uniformities in the present, to trace all things back to their true origin in the past, and calculate their true destiny in the future. In this two-fold view it passes in review all the systems and institutions of man upon the earth, follows them back to their natural source in his remote history, and predicts with all necessary certainty their ultimate collapse or triumph.[101]

This "review" of "all the systems and institutions of men," as Ward put it, was not simply a causal account. It was also a normative review. It judged the social patterns it observed by the implicit (Comtean, again) standards of order and progress. Therefore, sociology is implicitly evaluative and appropriately prescriptive. It was "established as a pure science" but "is now entering upon its

applied stage, which is the great practical object for which it exists."
Ward elaborated this entitlement and this project in this way:

> With the light shed by social dynamics on the spontaneous
> modification of social structures and the consequent progress of
> society in the past, and further guided by the established law of
> social uniformitarianism which enables us to judge the future by
> the past, sociology has now begun, not only in some degree to
> forecast the future of society, but to venture suggestions at least
> as to how the established principles of the science may be applied
> to the future advantageous modification of existing social struc-
> tures.[102]

In short, sociology for Ward was formally identical to the "posttheoretical practice" of the young Hegelian technocrats. It possessed the certainty and dispassionate quality classically ascribed to
theoretical contemplation, though obtained, of course, by the
methods of modern science. Theoretical in status, it was nonetheless
properly practical in its functions. Ward expressed this understanding of social science in several ways. The new philosophy, he said, is
"scientific in its methods and rational in its doctrines [but] eminently
practical in its objects and results."[103] And elsewhere: "This is a
true science. It is constructive. Like every other true science, it aims
to utilize the forces operating in its domain."[104]

The sociologist, therefore, should become a "master builder" like
the Hegelian tradition's *Werkmeister*. His social physics should be
translated into a social mechanics. He should not simply describe
"conditions" but "remove" them when he has deemed them undesirable.[105] The sociologist should "plunge boldly" into the area of
"social control."[106] As befits the eminent practitioner of the new
philosophy, the sociologist's task is none other than to reform humanity.

> Premising a reign of law as absolute and certain over the affairs of
> men and nations as over the movements of the celestial spheres,
> the new philosophy grapples as successfully with the questions of
> human society, law, government, morals, and religion as with
> those of astronomy, chemistry or physics. To reform humanity is
> the grand object of this system. Its expounders realize their
> power, by this method, of accomplishing this object; and if his
> followers do not all avow it as openly and repeatedly as Comte
> did, they certainly practice it since his death with equal sincerity
> and far greater results.[107]

Several decades later, another leading sociologist, George
Lundberg, argued a similar position in his aptly entitled *Can Science
Save Us?* The political problems besetting humanity, said Lundberg,

might be overcome if we would simply abandon our "prescientific modes of thought."[108] These obsolescent modes of conceptualizing social phenomena include "a legalistic-moralistic, 'literary' orientation" and "the brutish abyss of the animistic and supernaturalistic conception of [man] and the universe."[109] They breed ignorance and vindictiveness and lead to social disaster. Instead, we must turn to the "positive knowledge" produced by the scientific method in order to develop "sciences of human social relations."[110] If this change of orientation is accomplished, if the capability and authority of social science are but recognized, there will be "no reason why the methods of science cannot solve social problems."[111]

Like Ward and his predecessors, Lundberg conceives of scientific knowledge as possessing the status of theoretical contemplation but the role of practical wisdom. Social science provides us with verifiable generalizations that are objective truths ascertained by dispassionate analysis. But these generalizations are then depicted as regulative "principles." Social science is analogized to physics in its methods but to practical disciplines in its utility. It can provide the solution to political problems by giving us "scientific knowledge of the kind today possessed by engineers and physicians."[112] By this kind of applied social science, Lundberg concludes, a "workable world order" may be constructed and administered.[113]

Other sociologists and political scientists have been led toward the technocratic vision of a scientifically ordered society by the example of psychotherapy. If scientists can identify and treat pathologies of individual behavior, the argument runs, why can't they do the same for society? If psychotherapy is valid, why not "societal therapy"?

In 1938, for example, Harold Lasswell wrote an article in *Psychiatry* that sought to explore the potential interaction between political science and psychiatry. It was the political scientist's dawning awareness of the importance of symbol manipulation (i.e., propaganda) and leadership in politics, he wrote, that had "led the political scientist to the door of the psychiatrist."[114] If Lasswell's own conclusions are taken as representative, what the political scientist learned at that door was to see democratic persuasion among rational individuals as an ideal so far removed from reality as to be virtually illusory. Political behavior was governed to so great an extent by irrational motives and by symbolically contrived misperceptions that this classical democratic norm could no longer seem compelling.

What psychiatry can learn from students of politics, Lasswell continued, is less clear. However, political scientists could provide psychiatrists with a "sharpened sense of context." Political science could help psychiatry to recognize that "the reduction of mental disorder depends upon extensive modifications of important features of the general context of community interrelations."[115]

This insight, in turn, issued into the remarkable invitation with which Lasswell concluded his article. Armed with his scientific grasp of the norms and dynamics of mental health and prompted by his new insight into the social sources of mental disease, the psychiatrist was invited to consider becoming a modern-day philosopher-king:

> The most far-reaching way to reduce disease is for the psychiatrist to cultivate closer contact with the rulers of society, in the hope of finding the means of inducing them to overcome the symbolic limitations which prevent them from utilizing their influence for the prompt rearrangement of insecurity producing routines.
>   So the psychiatrist may decide to become the advisor of the "king." Now the history of the "king" and his philosophers shows that the king is prone to stray from the path of wisdom as wisdom is understood by the king's philosophers. Must the psychiatrist, then, unseat the king and actualize in the realm of fact the "philosopher-king" of Plato's imagination?
>   By grace of his psychiatry, of course, the modern philosopher who would be king knows that he may lose his philosophy on the path to the throne, and arrive there empty of all that would distinguish him from the king whom he has overthrown. But, if sufficiently secure in his knowledge of himself and his field, he may dare where others dared and lost before.[116]

Writing for the *American Sociological Review,* Professor Read Bain similarly looked forward hopefully to the institutionalization of what he termed "societal therapy." "Let us suppose," he wrote,

> that the social sciences become reputable natural sciences; that they create a large body of valid principles and applied techniques based upon verified hypotheses; that citizens learn to put as much trust in the diagnoses and prescriptions of social scientists as they now do in the recommendations of physicians. Under such conditions, it would not be meaningless to speak of societal pathology and societal therapy. The disease and the remedy and the art of applying it would be as objective, as scientific, as the present practice of immunology. It is evident that such societal knowledge would be more like individual psychiatry than like chemical diagnosis and therapy.... The etiology, diagnosis, prognosis, and cure [of societal neuroses and psychoses] may be as simple for social science of the future as the control of smallpox is for medical science today.[117]

Like Lasswell, Bain is led by this supposition to the vision of a scientifically based politics of manipulation and prevention. The only difference is that he looked to the sociologist (inspired by psychiatry) rather than the psychiatrist (inspired by sociology or political science) as the logical candidate for the ruler's throne:

> Already sociology has made considerable progress toward creating an objective scientific body of knowledge. With the more general acceptance of a purely naturalistic point of view and the development and use of statistical, comparative, experimental and other sound methods of investigation, we may expect enormous strides in the near future, so that we may soon be able to define pathologic societal organizations and activities so objectively that we will run no more risk of being called "God-sakers" than medical men do in a similar case. If we can determine the mechanisms of societal behavior, we may also be able to devise techniques for manipulating them. We shall be able to predict the course of societal development, as well as the results of our therapeutic and preventive prescriptions.[118]

It would be possible to continue offering illustrations of the technocratic perspective in American social theory. However, enough has been said to document the central contention here, namely, that the presuppositions, the concepts, the role patterns, and the prescriptions of technocracy are not confined to other political cultures or to other traditions of political thought. They have, instead, received widespread and prominent articulation in our own society.

It is important to make clear at this point that there is nothing whatever the matter with utilizing the insights of the social sciences or the natural sciences in the context of public policy. A concern with the dangers of technocracy does not imply the necessity for an antiscientific know-nothingism. No one should dispute the legitimacy of recourse to scientific insight or the use of scientific techniques where these are relevant and appropriate. Sound public policy in our complex and interdependent technological society in fact clearly requires recourse to these insights and techniques.

For example, there is no affront to the norms of humane liberalism in the attempt to persuade people that certain social dynamics are "pathological." The affront comes when the attempt is made to manipulate people on the basis of that claim. There is no affront to the norms of humane liberalism even in the practice of frontal lobotomies or placing electrodes in the brain—as long as the patient chooses to undergo the treatment on the basis of a clear understanding of the consequences. (We might think such practices very unwise and the choice to submit to them terribly imprudent. And we might, as a society, want to institutionalize very stringent safeguards to guarantee the genuineness of informed consent to such drastic measures. The society might even consider it legitimate to prohibit such operations if the consequences for the general welfare—Milton Friedman's "neighborhood effects"—were considered sufficiently destructive.) The affront comes only if the attempt is made to impose the treatment on the grounds of scientific authority.

The problem with technocracy, then, is not its insistence on the relevance of social science to public policy. The problem is with the *way* it is deemed to be relevant. The danger is not in the idea of applied science per se; the danger is in *how* technocracy would apply it. The convinced technocrat subverts humane liberalism by his substitution of a politics of expert manipulation for a politics of informed consent. And he legitimizes this crucial displacement not simply by due respect for the scientific enterprise but by his adherence to the following beliefs: first, that science produces "positive" knowledge; second, that norms of social order, such as "harmonious functioning," "equilibrium," "sanity," "development," or whatever, fall within the scope of this positive knowledge; third, that the scientist, as the possessor of this knowledge, has a warrant to rule that supersedes or transcends the traditional warrant of consent of the governed.

It is safe to say, I think, that the strands of social theory reviewed above clearly qualify as technocratic in this sense, just as they clearly rely on the traditional technocratic framework of a politicized positivism. At the very least, these writers and others like them display a marked indifference to the important lines of demarcation that distinguish technocracies from constitutional democracies.

The Ambiguities, Tensions, and Problematic Assumptions of Social Scientism

Marx's thought, it was noted earlier, avoided explicit capitulation to technocracy by means of a crucial ambiguity and a crucial assumption. The ambiguity centered around his notion of revolutionary praxis, and the assumption was that history would follow the course Marx had charted for it.

In exactly the same fashion, the totalitarian implications of the ideas held by Western technocrats are considerably muffled and obscured by very important ambiguities, unresolved tensions, and empirical assumptions. Careful review of some of these ambiguities, tensions, and assumptions might in fact lead to the conclusion that these thinkers provide a theoretical counterpart to Italian fascism; for if the latter, as some wag once observed, was tyranny tempered

by incompetence, these thinkers generate totalitarian fantasies miti-
gated by profound confusion.

The most important ambiguities and unresolved tensions in the
thought of the American technocrats tend to center around (1) the
nature of salutary scientific *control* of behavior and the relation of
such control to democratic norms and institutions and (2) the status
and source of the social norms in applied science. The technocrat's
dilemma is that he wants to make it plausible that his program is
efficacious without being tyrannical and is objective without being
neutral about the democratic ideal. Needless to say, the attempt to
accomplish these goals ends by requiring considerable feats of conceptual legerdemain or else a willingness to let contradictory claims
stand side by side without resolution.

(Marx's concept of revolutionary praxis, to follow up the parallel
suggested, served precisely this function in his thought. That is, it
stood as a symbol of the claims that the revolution would engage in
radical social change without being unspontaneous and that revolutionary activity was both morally imperative and based entirely on
objective scientific prediction. The difficulties with this attempt
to paper over some crucial issues were mentioned earlier in the
chapter.)

Consider the issue of control first. Skinner tries to deal with this in
the following way. On the one hand, when he argues for the radical
potential efficacy of his program, he presents a picture of
straightforward manipulation of behavior based on a mechanistic
cause-and-effect model. All behavior is caused by external contingencies. The environmental conditions are subject to manipulation by the behavioral scientist. Hence, he can shape behavior in the
desired direction. He is the independent variable. On the other hand,
Skinner tries to blunt the clear totalitarian implications of this model
by recourse to the notion of "reciprocal control." "The relationship
between the controller and the controlled is reciprocal," he writes.

> The scientist in the laboratory, studying the behavior of a pigeon,
> designs contingencies and observes their effects. His apparatus
> exerts a conspicuous control on the pigeon, but we must not
> overlook the control exerted by the pigeon. The behavior of the
> pigeon has determined the design of the apparatus and the proce-
> dures in which it is used.[119]

Similarly, Skinner tries to fend off charges that the behavioral
engineer's discretion in designing a culture would be unlimited and
arbitrary—hence tyrannical—by insisting that "nature" sets limits.
"It's no mean achievement to build satisfaction in any way whatsoever," says the behavioral designer in *Walden Two;* "but we want

the real thing. Walden Two must be *naturally* satisfying."[120] And, along the same lines, he writes: "The Designer of a culture is not an interloper or meddler. He does not step in to disturb a natural process, he is part of a natural process."[121] On the other hand, his argument for the radically transformatory powers of his manipulative interventions in society relies on the assumption that these natural limits are minimal and insignificant; in fact, as he volunteers elsewhere, "the difference between contrived and natural conditions is not a serious one."[122]

In essence, Skinner tries to avoid embarrassment by having it both ways. But he achieves only the illusion of success in his attempt to conjure visions of potent social interventions while avoiding the onus of condoning totalitarian controls. If there is no serious distinction between the natural and the contrived, the "natural limits" are no limits at all on the discretion of the behavioral engineer. Similarly, if "reciprocal control" is really that, then the power of the controller to effectuate the vast changes Skinner envisions must be severely limited. On the other hand, if the controller really does have this degree of power, then "reciprocal control" is a term of rhetorical force but no real meaning. One rather suspects that the latter alternative is the case when one reads Skinner's assertion that "in a very real sense, then, the slave controls the slave driver."[123] Somehow it is hard to imagine that any slave would be greatly consoled by this assurance.

The internal tensions and ambiguities in Harold Lasswell's thought on the same issues of power and control have been pointed out by several commentators. The basic difficulty here is the complacency with which Lasswell juxtaposes his call for political manipulation and his insistence on "human dignity." Surely this apparent contradiction should receive some careful explanation, but it is never forthcoming—in part because the concrete meaning of "human dignity" is never specified. Floyd Matson gets right to the heart of the problem when he writes of

> the remarkable innocence with which an eminent political semanticist, for all his preoccupation with linguistic clarity and conceptual rigor, embraces the most nebulous and recondite of moral norms: that of "human dignity." All of the elaborate and exacting paraphernalia of modern scientific research is to be placed at the service of a concept so mutilated by rhetorical abuse as to be not merely dubious but actively dangerous until it has received at least the minimum degree of attention and specification which derives from what Hocking has called "ethical common sense." But such specification Lasswell, by what seems an opportune oversight, does not provide. Since he is not concerned to know the heritage

and character of his ultimate goal-value, there is no evident uneasiness in Lasswell's persistent conjunction of "human dignity"
with "manipulation," as carried out by the techno-sciences of
political prevention and behavioral reform.[124]

The analogous unresolved tension in the thought of Lester Frank
Ward surfaces when he discusses the authority of his emergent
sociocracy. Presumably the authority of this sociological elite would
clash with the authority of the democratic sovereign majority in
some cases. If it did not, if the sociocracy simply replicated the
judgments of the majority, then it is hard to see how its advent would
produce any great changes or advances. Instead of confronting the
potential clash of two different authority systems, however, Ward
simply embraced them simultaneously. He even suggested that scientific legislation is possible only in a democracy.

> When the people become so intelligent that they know how to
> choose as their representatives persons of decided ability, who
> know something of human nature, who recognize that there are
> social forces, and that their duty is to devise ways and means for
> scientifically controlling those forces on exactly the same princi-
> ples that an experimenter or an inventor controls the forces of
> physical nature, then we may look for scientific legislation.[125]

The other central area of ambiguity, unresolved antinomies, and
philosophical question-begging in these technocratic theories is the
question of the nature and source of the normative criteria that will
guide the social engineer's activities. Each of the theorists in question implies that these norms are, somehow, scientifically derived.
But when they try to specify the norms and how they derive from
"objective" scientific observations, they become extremely vague
or even commit simple logical errors.

Skinner, for example, at times falls back, as do many technocrats,
on a very vague pragmatism. What is good is whatever "works."
"In an experiment," he writes, "we are interested in what happens,
in designing a culture with whether it will work."[126] Presumably this
standard is also in effect when Skinner asserts that various issues
about the nature of the good society will be decided "experimentally." This, however, amounts to giving a secondary answer to
a fundamental question. We can all subscribe in the abstract to a
culture that "works," but the relevant issue is what standards are
deployed to distinguish "working" from "not working"—and what
the grounds are for these standards. It seems clear, for example, that
different people—say, a Marxist and a Muslim traditionalist—might
look at the same experimental results and appraise them quite differ-

ently; if one felt the experiment had been a success, the other would surely deem it a failure.

It might be supposed, then, that the de facto criterion of social good becomes the "values" (which Skinner identifies at some points, in good positivist fashion, with "feelings")[127] of the behavioral engineer. And Skinner in fact at times provides us with this kind of empirical answer to our normative question: "If a scientific analysis can tell us how to change behavior, can it tell us what changes to make? This is a question about the behavior of those who do in fact propose and make changes."[128]

On its face, this argument (if it is not a simple logical blunder) represents the Thrasymachan doctrine that what is right is determined by the will of the powerful. And perhaps this is Skinner's answer, but probably it is not. For he seems clearly to suppose that the choices the behavioral scientist makes will not be determined simply by his own arbitrary whims (although he does suggest that "to some extent he will necessarily design a world *he* likes").[129] Instead, Skinner suggests that the behavioral engineer will be guided by criteria of utilitarian efficiency and survival value. He writes, for example, that the question posed by "experimental ethics" is: "what are the techniques, the engineering practices, which will shape the behavior of members of a group so that they will function smoothly for the benefit of all?"[130] And elsewhere he writes, "Survival is the only value according to which a culture is eventually to be judged, and any practice that furthers survival has survival value by definition."[131]

These criteria, in turn, are replete with dangers, difficulties, and ambiguities. For example, are they fully compatible? Is "smooth functioning" really a persuasive overriding goal? Do the realities of life permit both smooth functioning *and* pursuit of the benefit of all? If they do, need the behavioral engineer really do anything at all beyond making this possibility known? How does reliance on the test of survival avoid the conservative logic of a Herbert Spencer? And so on. The ambiguities and problems are profound ones, indeed, but Skinner never resolves them. He seems satisfied to have provided these abstract, vague, and conflicting but ostensively "scientific" answers to the concrete political questions: what should be done, and why?

Ward's answer to the problem of the criteria that should guide his applied sociology is less convoluted than Skinner's. It is, indeed, an extremely simple answer but one that is both questionable and problematic. Applied sociology, for Ward, should be guided by the Comtean norm of "social progress." And this progress Ward characterized in terms of a straightforward hedonism. "The moral realm," he wrote, "is the realm of sensation, and all that comprises sensation is moral. Moral progress comprises only that form of sensation that is called pleasure and pain. Everything that increases pleasure or diminishes pain is moral progress."[132] Ward's standard for progress was both amiable and democratic. However, he seemed quite innocently oblivious to the potential problems of simple utilitarianism—the kinds of problems, for example, that John Stuart Mill sought to confront in his political essays. Moreover, he seemed to suppose that his stipulated ethical norms were somehow entitled to "scientific" status because they had their origins in philosophical naturalism and were sustained by sensationist imagery.

Lasswell's approach to the problem is also replete with ambiguities and unresolved tensions. In the first place, Lasswell tries, as one critic has noted, to "have his value-cake and eat it too."[133] Social science is to be purged of its metaphysical and normative components. It is to be "value-neutral." Yet, at the same time, it is somehow to be a committed and activist "value science." Social science should be "explicitly preferential."

The "values" to be "preferred," however, are not only rather vague and rhetorical; they are also inconsistent. Sometimes the ruling values are characterized in virtually the same classical terms of therapeutic utilitarianism used by Helvetius. The language of Lasswell's *Psychopathology and Politics* especially bespeaks this orientation. The ruling standards are there declared to be "harmonious social relations" and "reducing the level of strain and maladaptation in society." In *Power and Society,* the ruling norm is alleged to be the "democratic ideal." At other times and places, various suprademocratic virtues are invoked.

The reader who wishes to understand and assess Lasswell's normative stance is therefore left with two problems: first, the multiple normative standards are never reconciled with one another; second, they never receive explicit philosophical justification.

The apparent inconsistency in the "end values" Lasswell stipulates in different places might conceivably be explained as different stages of evolution in his thought. There is some evidence, for example, that his earliest works are most unadulteratedly utilitarian, his middle works more guided by democratic norms, and his later works more oriented toward broader standards of human virtue. It is also true, however, that these alternative orientations at times appear in close juxtaposition in the same source.[134] So Lasswell may conceivably believe that the democratic ideal in some fashion incorporates a naturalistic utilitarianism on the one hand and all human virtue on the other. Such a faith would indeed be appealing to our culture, which would like to be resolutely scientific, un-restrainedly democratic, and exhaustively virtuous all at the same time. The implied synthesis, however, is never specifically defended—and with good reason; for such an attempted synthesis could never withstand close logical scrutiny, however much one might like it to do so.

Whatever Lasswell's position on the relationship of the various standards he avows, they remain severally or together quite un-grounded philosophically. They are never rationally justified. Be-cause of his commitment to the idea that "facts" are "value-neutral," Lasswell cannot ground the goals he cherishes in the re-alities he depicts. (In fact, he clearly does so at an intuitive level, but he cannot do so in any open way, since he is devoid of the philo-sophical resources to suggest how this might be a legitimate possi-bility.) Instead he can only state them as his "preferences." And if that is all his values are, then it is wholly unclear why they should command the allegiance of anyone else. *De gustibus non est dis-putandum.*

Several reasons suggest themselves to account for the apparent willingness of these technocratic theorists to tolerate the profound ambiguities and antinomies in their thought. In the first place, they may be quite unaware of some of them. The technocrats as a group are not markedly distinguished by acute analytical capabilities. Moreover, the tensions in their thought are often equally present in American liberal culture, which therefore does not offer the kind of challenge that could force them to examine their claims more closely. Second, they are in some respects without the philosophical resources to resolve the tensions in their thought, because these are rooted in the deeper contradictions of the intellectual tradition they represent. But finally, and what is more important, they do not appreciate the *practical* significance of their theoretical ambiguities because their understanding of politics is informed and surrounded by some highly optimistic empirical assumptions. These assump-tions about human nature and the potentialities of the political order, if sustainable, would conceivably make the issues of manipulation and authoritative "values" largely academic. And, in their op-timism, these assumptions suggest that the technocrats are very much the heirs of the Enlightenment at its most hopeful.

Like Kant, who declared that even a race of devils could live together in peace if their constitution was well-designed, Skinner argues that "under a 'perfect' system no one needs goodness."[135] It is possible, he believes, to organize society in such a way that men will behave well "automatically." They need no superego, dissuad-ing them from selfishly antisocial behavior. The incentive structure of the system will bring about the socially desired ends.

Moreover, and this is Skinner's crucial assumption, this society of "automatically good" citizens can be achieved entirely by positive incentives. His behavioral and cultural technology can achieve its ends "based on positive reinforcement alone."[136] The scientific governor of society need appeal only to appetite, not to aversion, only to pleasure, not to pain. The citizens of the behaviorist utopia "are doing what they want to do."[137] And, so long as this is true, it is also fair to argue that the behaviorist utopia relies in no way on force, in the sense of impeding or thwarting what people desire. Thus the problem of control is relegated to the status of a purely academic and theoretical issue, of little practical consequence.

This set of assumptions as to the possibility of creating the good society entirely through positive incentives, then, is central to Skinner's utopianism. It is also a belief that rests on faith—i.e., on undemonstrable theoretical premises—rather than on hard evidence. It is, in fact, simply an updated version, in scientific jargon, of the identity-of-interests argument: the requisites of social order and the desires of men are such that there is no real collision between them. On this view, any apparent strain between public good and individual desire is only the product of bad design. The natural interests of the self are believed to be such that they can be gratified without expense to the interests of other selves or of society.[138]

Lester Frank Ward similarly relies on the assumption that positive incentives alone are sufficient for building the good society. Ward's terminology is slightly different; he speaks of "attractive legislation" rather than "positive reinforcement," but the basic point is exactly the same: the desires of men and the requisites of social order are such that the scientific legislator can achieve his goals solely through laws that incorporate appeals to positive self-interest. Ward elaborates this hopeful vision in discussing the "principle of attraction." That principle, he says, reveals

> that mandatory and prohibitory laws are highly expensive and largely ineffective, and that the only cheap and effective way to control the social forces and cause men to perform the acts beneficial to society is to offer such inducements as will in all cases make it to their advantage to perform such acts. It is probable that nearly or quite all the socially advantageous action could be secured through attractive legislation. . . . The goal toward which [the scientific legislator's] efforts would tend would be a state of society in which no one should be obliged to do anything that is in any way distasteful to him, and in which every act should be so agreeable that he will do it from personal preference.[139]

The political analysis that underlies and sustains this optimistic account is very clearly an updated version of the identity-of-interests argument. Ward makes this quite explicit in the context of his criticism of party government. Contention among political parties, he insists, is a kind of ridiculous and socially counterproductive "child's play." "A very slight awakening of the social consciousness," he asserts, "will banish it and substitute something more business-like." And the reason this is so, he continues, is that the real interests of all members of society are basically the same:

> Once get rid of this puerile gaming spirit and have attention drawn to the real interests of society, and it will be seen that upon nearly all important questions all parties and all good citizens are agreed, and that there is no need of this partisan strain upon the public energies.[140]

Ward's vision of "sociocracy," in short, is a cross between Mandeville and Fourier (private vice is transmuted into public virtue through the law of passionate attraction) expressed in the language of an abstract sociology. Ward sustains his faith in the vast potential efficacy of social design based solely on positive incentives by his acceptance of the identity-of-interests theory. This acceptance, in turn, as in Skinner's argument, relies on a very benign view of the passions and the potentialities of human nature—the former being very moderate, the latter very great—and it is this optimism that enables Ward, again like Skinner, to rest comfortably with the supposition that the "control" exerted by a scientific legislator would be that in name only. The burden of his rule would be light indeed, for he would always be providing rewards, never enforcing restrictions or imposing deprivations.[141]

George Lundberg relies on an equally sanguine assessment of human nature to transform a Hobbesian understanding of social knowledge into a very un-Hobbesian social doctrine. Like Hobbes, Lundberg depicts science as a system of causal propositions.[142] These causal propositions, projected into the future, give predictions, which in turn endow us with the capacity of foresight.[143] Again this replicates Hobbes's account. But in Hobbes's view, the reasonable man who possesses this foresight will be prompted to join in the establishment of a very authoritarian political regime. Lundberg's vision of the social consequences of better foresight is much rosier, resembling Condorcet's picture of a future peaceful world order of free peoples more than Hobbes's politics of containment. Why? Because, in Lundberg's view, human passions are not the inordinate and socially disruptive desires Hobbes depicted. Human desires are, he assures us, moderate and peaceable unless distorted by "fantastic" ideas. "The broad general wants of people, he writes, ''are perhaps everywhere highly uniform. They want, for example, a certain amount of physical and social security and some fun. It is disagreement over the means toward these ends, as represented by fantastic ideologies, that results in conflicts and chaos.''[144]

This section of our analysis can be summarized as follows:

1. An influential tradition within American social thought is properly characterized as technocratic.
2. This tradition replicates the views of Saint-Simon and Comte as to the possibility and desirability of a ''scientifically managed'' society in which the governing of men is superseded by the rational administration of things.
3. These contemporary technocratic programs rely with varying degrees of explicitness on a positivist epistemology and its political correlates.
4. These contemporary technocratic theories are characterized by profound ambiguities and unresolved tensions, especially regarding the crucial problem of power and control.
5. These theoretical weaknesses remain unalleviated in part because the technocrats' acceptance of highly optimistic assessments of human nature and its social potential makes these problems seem relatively inconsequential to them.

The social theory of figures like Skinner, Lundberg, Lasswell, and Ward is, then, neither consistently nor intentionally totalitarian. Instead, it suspends totalitarian images in a jellied aspic of conceptual assumptions. These contemporary technocrats are less culpable, therefore, than cynical advocates of tyrannical expediency. But their thought is nonetheless misleading, naive, and potentially dangerous—perhaps more so than a straightforward Machiavellianism. For the most effective totalitarian rationales are not cynical avowals of power hunger; they are much more commonly utopian projects that alternatively disguise their coerciveness and/or justify it as a temporary means to greater ends.

The problem with the political analyses and recommendations the contemporary technocrats make lies in their confusion. Their ambiguities and internal tensions obscure the real conflicts, hard choices, and genuine costs that attend most significant political issues. Rational choices require clear distinctions between conflicting ends and a careful appraisal of costs. In technocratic thought these costs and conflicts are repressed and obscured by images of a never-never land where scientific manipulation does not infringe human dignity, where sociocracy coexists with democracy, where behavioral control requires no coercion, and where scientific value-neutrality somehow sustains democratic commitments.

The formulations of technocratic theory betray the linguisitic corruption whose political consequences were analyzed so incisively by George Orwell. The coercive features of the technocratic program are systematically obscured by the strategic use of vague abstractions—it is always "social forces" that are being controlled in Ward's accounts, never concrete groups or individuals—or of rhetorical wordplay, as where Skinner tells the slave that he exerts "reciprocal control" over his master. These claims may be wholly sincere. They nonetheless betray a curious blindness to the real power struggles and real deprivations of politics.

As Reinhold Niebuhr observed in a somewhat different context,[145] those who are most innocent of the realities of power are those most prone to its unchecked use when problems arise. Adherents of a theory that represses conflict are likely to suppress those who conflict with them in the real world and then explain away the suppression with their semantic shell game: "Those aren't chains, my boy; they're the jewelry of our utopia."

Technocratic Practices in Constitutional Democracies

The influence of technocratic theories on actual political institutions and practices has obviously not been as great in the West as it has under Marxist regimes. Under the latter, technocratic ideas constitute the official canon of society, and self-appointed *Werkmeister* have arrogated plenary power to themselves. Non-Marxist countries have never succumbed so completely to the blandishments of their technocrats, in part, no doubt, because most versions of technocracy have not given the attention Marxists have to the strategy of gaining power. They have largely been content to recommend themselves by describing the wonders they could perform if given power. In the Marxist as well as the conventional sense, they have been utopians.

The tradition of Western constitutionalism has been an especially formidable obstacle to technocratic aspirations. The entire logic of constitutionalism, and of the natural-law and natural-rights ideas embodied there, is at loggerheads with the logic of technocracy. Constitutionalism speaks the language of juridical persons, not the language of "objects" and "subjects." It speaks the language of rights and obligations, not of determinism. And it speaks of liberties and justice, not of adjustment or harmonious functioning. Moreover, constitutionalism is hostile to any claims of absolute power, whether of kings (who were, theoretically at least, beneath the law), of presidents, or of scientific saviors of society. Accordingly. the tradition has developed a refined system of procedural safeguards to protect the rights and liberties of the governed and to limit the powers of the ruling elite.

These concepts and practices, though far from perfect, systematically frustrate those who would entrench themselves to tyrannize over others. In that most odious American departure from the principles of liberty and justice, the practice of slavery, it was necessary to circumvent the entire constitutional framework by the cynical expedient of legally categorizing slaves as property rather than as persons. Only in this way could the institution of slavery be preserved without radical amputations from the fundamental law of the land.

Moreover, in this country at least, and presumably in most other advanced constitutional societies, an informal "constitution" has developed that governs the social role of science. As Don K. Price describes this unwritten constitution in his excellent study, *The Scientific Estate*,[146] it has established a working relationship between the scientist and the politician that recognizes and restricts the legitimate authority of each—the former to technical knowledge, the latter to democratic consensus-building. Price suggests that the scientific establishment under our system functions rather like a medieval "estate." It has carved out for itself a realm in which it can function with great autonomy as it pursues truth. But when it turns operational, when it contributes to the formulation of public policy, the scientific establishment operates within "a lively system of checks and balances"[147] in which ultimate political responsibility vests in democratically elected officials.

One might therefore conclude that our own political system is relatively safe from technocratic incursions and that technocratic theories can be shrugged off as harmless academic treatises. It is not quite that simple. The social scientists reviewed above are not isolated cranks but eminent and influential leaders in their field.[148] And, as Price observes, there are those within the scientific establishment who regard the checks and balances of the unwritten constitution as both temporary and illegitimate.[149]

Moreover, our culture is remarkably receptive to scientistic social programs. Skinner's fictional behaviorist utopia, *Walden Two*, published in 1948, sold a million copies, and, three decades later, his nonfiction version was serialized in popular magazines and picked up by the Book-of-the-Month Club. Not only do many in our own political culture respond to these visions; many are also highly pliant to claims of authority that clothe themselves in the mantle of science. This, at least, seems to be the real lesson of Stanley Milgram's famous experiments concerning obedience to authority. The remarkable willingness of Milgram's experimental subjects to subject another human being to what they believed to be painful and dangerous electrical shocks was not elicited by the orders of ostensively *political* authorities but by the orders of ostensively *scientific* authorities. As Milgram notes, "the idea of science and its acceptance as a social enterprise" played a crucial role in eliciting the observed results. "If the experiment were carried out in a culture very different from our own—say, among Trobrianders—it would be necessary to find the functional equivalent of science in order to obtain scientifically comparable results."[150]

In this context of influential advocacy of and widespread receptiveness to technocratic ideology, significant pressures can arise on behalf of technocratic practices. These pressures have not been successful in displacing the logic of constitutionalism from its hold over the central political institutions and procedures of our system, but it can be argued that technocratic ideas, and the pressures they generate, have exerted a distorting and corrupting influence on social institutions and political practices that for one reason or another lie beyond the scope of effectual constitutional guarantees. In some cases, indeed, technocratic arguments have been employed to roll back and circumscribe the traditional requirements of due process. These efforts, as always, are beneficially conceived, but the actual policy consequences are often disastrous.

The essence of the technocratic impact is its corruption and distortion of policy by the central misconception that transforms political and moral issues into allegedly medical or engineering problems. Political roles and statuses are thereby reinterpreted as medical or engineering roles: the political world is believed to be populated not by men, with contending interests, but by patients and healers, by "social forces" and social physicists. Political stratagems—such as persuasion, compromise, threats, and coercion—are transformed into or displaced by ostensively medical and engineering procedures—such as therapeutic intervention and behavior modification. Policies conceived and undertaken in this fashion are considered to be beyond the scope of ordinary or "prescientific" politics. They are believed neither to require the justification commonly requisite for political actions nor to be appropriately subject to controls normally brought to bear on political actions.

The follies and derangements that have plagued this country's foreign policy since World War II may owe as much to technocratic misconceptions as to the "legalism-moralism" criticized by George Kennan or to the bourgeois acquisitiveness blamed by leftist critics. The "arrogance of power" Senator Fulbright discerned in our beneficent welfare imperialism was a product of our technocratic belief that we could "manage" the "social forces" in other countries, especially Third World countries, by the dextrous application of political technology. We could help these countries "develop," in the way we deemed fit, by the judicious infusion of funds and the application of rational administrative methods. This hopeful belief was in no way cynical, but it betrayed the technocratic tendency to assume the validity of one's "scientific" standards of good political "functioning," to belittle the integrity of the "objects" of one's benevolent manipulations, and thereby to overestimate the efficacy of purely technical expedients in achieving one's goals.

The corruption of domestic social policy by the perverse logic of technocracy is even clearer. The principal derangement in this respect concerns policies directed toward society's "deviants." Simply put, technocratic premises lead to interpreting departures from the norms of society—whether by the "mentally ill," by criminals, by delinquents, or even by clients of the welfare bureaucracy—as manifestations of some underlying engineering defect in the social order. Accordingly, the appropriate response is a form of remedial engineering to repair these defects and allow society to function smoothly. This way of conceiving things, however, does not simply lead to policies that are ineffectual. It also tends to compound the problems by engendering social roles and procedures that corrupt reformer, reformee, and the social system as a whole.

In a superficial sense, of course, the technocratic analysis of the nature and sources of crime—to take one example—is neither wrong nor corrupting. Clearly the phenomenon of crime indicates that something is less than ideal in the "way society works." And, conservative fatalism to the contrary, there is nothing wrong with the insistence that some social "reforms" are likely to be helpful. However, these unexceptionable claims take a perverse incarnation when interpreted through the categories of technocratic thought, for the deviants become classed and interpreted as "objects" whose "maladjusted" behavior should be refashioned—"re-formed" in a radical way indeed—by psychiatrists, wardens, welfare workers, or whoever is appointed to fill the role of *deus faber*.

It sounds remarkably beneficent, as well as enlightened, of course, to declare that "there are no criminals, only sick people who need to be healed," and the intent of those who say this is, generally, quite humane and benevolent; indeed, it seems rather clearly to be in many respects a secular equivalent of the evangelism of "saving souls."[151] But good intentions do not by themselves constitute good social policy, and under the scientistic aegis of technocracy they are easily subverted into coercive and destructive deeds.

For "therapy," as conceived by technocrats, is almost inevitably reductive, demeaning to the recipient, and coercive. Technocratic "treatment" is not freely sought help. The will of the patient is not determinative, for it is in fact conceived to be part of the "sickness." Similarly, "health" is not defined by the patient, who cannot be presumed competent to judge, but by the authorities who know these things. And, given the intellectual genealogy of technocracy, social "health" tends to be defined in the terms of a collectivist utilitarianism. Note, for example, the governing norms in the following account of changing sentencing practices in the law:

> The last 50 years have witnessed a critical evaluation of the *utility to society* of these successive systems [of deterrence]. . . . There has evolved from this experience the thesis that a more workable *way to protect society* is to fit the treatment to the individual, not the punishment to the crime; to attempt to learn the causes of his offense by skillful and experienced study and judgment, by re-education where that is possible so that his skills and talents can be *utilized in the interests of society* instead of toward its destruction, with the purpose that as a result of the treatment he receives he may become *useful to society*. The concept of "treatment" has replaced the concept of "punishment."[152]

The individual so "treated" is placed in a most unenviable position. Whether an involuntarily committed mental patient or a prisoner in a program of compulsory rehabilitation, he is under a coercive regimen that systematically denies its coerciveness. His keepers present their commands as being wholly in his interest. The procedural restraints that govern admitted adversary situations may therefore be dispensed with.[153] The "patient" is likely to be subject to confinement for an indefinite period of time, his release contingent on the judgment of his keepers that he is "cured."[154]

He is, in short, subject to a system of total control. His jailers define his status in such a way as to rob him of his integrity. They determine the length of time he shall remain subject to them, and they determine the criteria, de facto, by which he shall be deemed "cured." Since the whole system is avowedly benevolent, moreover, the inmate finds himself in a Catch-22 world. If he resists his captors, rejects their benevolence, refuses his "therapy," or insists on the simple fact that he is being coerced, this confirms his "sickness" and extends his subjection. Such recalcitrance is a sign of his continued insanity or his failure to be rehabilitated.

Numerous cases can be cited to illustrate the bankruptcy of a system of social control that is based on these technocratic premises. Particularly apt is the case of Edward Lee McNeil. McNeil was convicted, without a jury trial, of assault on a police officer and assault with intent to rape. It was 1966, and he was nineteen. The judge sentenced him to imprisonment for a term of "not more than five years." Under Maryland law, he would ordinarily have been eligible for parole after fifteen months, but the judge, on the advice of a court-appointed medical officer, sent him to the Patuxent Institution, established as a "total treatment facility" under the Defective Delinquent Statute of 1955 and hailed as a great step forward by many reformers. Once there, McNeil languished for *six* years, without any prospect of release, because he refused to cooperate with his therapists. It took an order from the Supreme Court to get him out. The brief of the state's attorney general in the case provides a remarkably candid expression of technocratic arrogance:

> The state's right to compel cooperation is based upon the state's need for diagnosis. If the state has a right, it cannot be without means of vindicating it. The means chosen—an indeterminate stay in the diagnostic area of Patuxent until cooperation is obtained—is a necessary and proper means to defeat the desire of undiagnosed defective delinquents to evade treatment by sitting out their sentences.[155]

Other cases can be cited. West Virginia committed a fourteen-year-old youth to the state training school until he was twenty-one, a seven-year term, for an offense (phoning a school and falsely reporting a bomb) that would have cost an adult no more than thirty days in jail.[156] This drastic sentence was apparently considered justified because it was "treatment," not "punishment." In England, a magistrate invoked the Mental Health Act of 1959 to order Eric Wills, a twenty-one-year-old ice-cream salesman, committed to a mental hospital to have a leucotomy (brain operation). His crime was larceny and obtaining property under false pretenses, but he had been diagnosed by mental health authorities as a compulsive gambler and a psychopath, thereby prompting the magistrate's order. Adverse public reaction caused this order to be rescinded.[157] In the District of Columbia, Frederick Lynch, charged with passing bad checks, was ordered committed to a mental hospital for an indeterminate period for treatment. Lynch did not use an insanity defense, and indeed he strenuously objected to being so labeled and treated. The court felt justified in overriding his objections and ordered him confined for a time that would almost undoubtedly substantially exceed any criminal term he could have received. "Hospitalization," the court explained, "bears no relation to a jail sentence. A jail sentence is punitive.... Hospitalization is remedial."[158] Lynch did not appreciate this distinction. He committed suicide.

These are admittedly not average or typical cases, as any adherent of the therapeutic faith would hasten to insist; but the principles and assumptions that led to and provided the rationale for these incarcerations were not distortions of the technocratic viewpoint, nor were they peripheral to it. For it is the very essence of technocracy to insist that standards of right behavior (whether sanity, "social harmony," or whatever) are part of the "positive knowledge" accessible to the experts in human behavior and that the "remedial" "treatment" by society that this epistemological warrant justifies need not be subject to the limitations placed on ordinary "political" acts, such as punishment.

The Conceptual Suicide of Liberal Humanism

The tide may well have turned against the excessive therapeutic zeal manifested in these cases. The Supreme Court has ruled that the standards of criminal due process cannot be wholly waived in juvenile cases. Many psychiatrists have become acutely aware that their mission is corrupted when they are cast in the role of wardens of the Panopticon, and federal corrections officials seem to have become disenchanted with compulsory rehabilitation and indeterminate sentences, together with the ideas that sustained these practices.[159]

The crucial and fascinating question in the present context, however, is how such practices could have been considered the apogee of liberal reform. Understanding what has gone wrong here takes us very close to the heart of the ironic self-evisceration of liberal humanism we are examining. First, the politicized epistemology of the technocratic tradition provided the positive rationale for this conception of how to control social deviance: it gave rise to the idea that these matters were appropriately left to the authority of experts—the experimental physicists of the soul. Second, the same orientation undermined the very concepts that provide the natural basis for criticizing technocratic policies.

The positive rationale has been examined in some detail, but the latter process—conceptual undermining—is worth some elaboration as a conclusion to this section of our analysis, for what it represents is, quite simply, the conceptual suicide of liberal humanism under the aegis of technocratic epistemology. (Perhaps conceptual fratricide is a better term. Condorcet wrote that the "battle cry" of the new philosophy was "reason, tolerance, humanity."[160] But as the logic of technocracy unfolded, "reason" banished tolerance and humanity as prescientific encumbrances, obstacles to its enlightened despotism.)

The crucial concepts here are: justice, liberty, responsibility, and power. These standards, and the framework they provide, would have been the normal basis for criticizing the technocratic corruption of politics; that is, the abuses reflected in the cases cited above appear *as* abuses by reference to exactly these centrally important standards. The cases were affronts to justice, infringements on freedom, abridgements of human responsibility, and assertions of arbitrary power. It is these very standards, furthermore, that provide the normative basis of liberal humanism. Liberty and justice are the twin goals most dear to the liberal tradition, as reflected in the closing words of our pledge of allegiance: " . . . with liberty and justice for all." Responsibility is both a goal and a premise of liberal policy, and the historical task of liberalism has largely been defined as the placing of restraints on the exercise of political power—especially on its inevitable tendency to abridge human rights: thus the ideal of the rule of law, the Bill of Rights, checks and balances, and all the rest. But the thrust of technocracy and its underlying understanding of knowledge is precisely that these central goals, standards, and benchmarks are meaningless.

The technocratic attack on the norms of liberty, justice, and responsibility is an interesting (and not fully coherent) mixture of moral and philosophical criticism. The technocratic critic usually begins with some moral insight that is for the most part valid, but he then goes on to distort this insight and his prescriptions by placing them in the context of his conceptually impoverished philosophy. What begins as valid moral critique thus ends, paradoxically, in prescriptions that are corrupted by their rejection of the very moral standards that were tacitly but powerfully at work in the original critique.

The attack on the norm of liberty, for example, begins typically with the insight that an empty and mindless liberty is not a sufficient moral goal for either the individual or society. From Saint-Simon and Hegel to Durkheim and up to the present day, technocratic critics have pointed out that liberty by itself tends to be empty and counterproductive. It becomes license, it degenerates into anarchy, it leads to anomie, it fails to provide meaning, order, and happiness. These arguments are, on the whole, valid and a helpful corrective to those who believe that *laissez-faire* exhausts the meaning of liberalism and provides a sufficient touchstone for all social policy.

But then the technocratic critic shifts his gears, trundles in his metaphysic, and engages in critical overkill. Not only is liberty not an exhaustive standard for social policy, he suggests; it is not even a meaningful concept. Human freedom is an illusion. Human behavior is part of *res extensa* and is therefore wholly determined by prior and external causes. Freedom is just a name for lacunae in scientific explanation; it should therefore ultimately disappear. No one is free; people are simply subject to controls from different sources. As a result of this line of argument, liberty is not only not the sufficient end of social policy; it is not even a necessary goal of policy. It is not only not a necessary goal, it is not even a meaningful goal. Human freedom can therefore be ignored in social policy. And to criticize a policy by saying that it infringes human freedom is deemed no criticism at all. It is seen merely as the commission of a metaphysical error unworthy of an enlightened man.

The attack on the idea of justice proceeds along the same lines. The pattern of argument has remained roughly constant from the early days of the technocratic tradition down to the modern reformer who would replace criminal jurisprudence by a system of therapeutic social controls. It is instructive, in this context, to compare the arguments of Jeremy Bentham and Dr. Karl Menninger.

Both Bentham and Menninger begin by pointing out the cruelty, destructiveness, and manifest unfairness of many of the practices carried on in the name of criminal justice. This is rarely difficult to do. Certainly it was an easy task for Bentham, given the remarkably Draconian quality of the British criminal law of his day. But even Menninger can convincingly suggest that "much of the laborious effort made in the noble name of justice results in its very opposite.... [It] results in its exact opposite—injustice, injustice to everybody."[161]

So far, so good. In the best tradition of social criticism, Bentham and Menninger alert their readers to the corrupt and hypocritical use of a noble ideal to dignify morally indefensible social practices. In violation of the principle of proportionality, which is essential to the concept of justice, the British criminal code provided the death penalty for dozens of rather petty crimes. In violation of the principle of equity, the sentencing practices of our own criminal system seem systematically to discriminate against the poor and black. The argument so far is therefore both sound and salutary. No self-respecting society should tolerate practices that institutionalize and perpetuate such injustices committed in the name of justice.

But then the technocratic argument shifts its ground and enters a new phase that carries radical consequences. The technocrat first makes the unwarranted assumption that the corrupt *practices* he criticizes are in fact a representative embodiment of the *concept* of justice—and the concept itself therefore must be corrupt and indefensible. This is not only an unwarranted assumption (surely it is obvious that the name of any noble ideal can be taken in vain; as the

Scriptures observe, "not all who say 'Lord, Lord' will enter the Kingdom of Heaven"); but in extending his attack from the practices to the concept, the technocrat is involving himself in a striking inconsistency. He is repressing his earlier evident reliance on the "sense of injustice"—both his own and his readers'—as a basis for condemning the nefarious practices he has criticized.[162] This reliance may have been tacitly embodied in the sense of moral outrage evoked by the earlier critique, or it may have been quite explicitly invoked: the first chapter in Menninger's book is entitled "The Injustice of Justice."

Ignoring the moral basis of his original argument, the technocrat incoherently (in the technical sense) brings in his scientistic metaphysics to undercut the very conception of justice. Having begun by arguing the injustice of the practice carried on in the name of justice, he now suggests that the notion of justice is meaningless altogether. The world of *res extensa* has no place for "justice." It is simply a world of "facts" connected by efficient causal forces. And since this is what "science" tells us the world is, it is unscientific to speak of justice at all. As Menninger puts it:

> The very word "justice" irritates scientists. No surgeon expects to be asked if an operation for cancer is just or not. No doctor will be reproached on the grounds that the dose of penicillin he has prescribed is less or more than "justice" would stipulate.
> Behavioral scientists regard it as equally absurd to invoke the question of justice in deciding what to do with a woman who cannot resist her propensity to shoplift, or with a man who cannot repress an impulse to assault somebody. This sort of behavior has to be controlled; it has to be discouraged; it has to be *stopped*. This (to the scientist) is a matter of public safety and amicable coexistence, not of justice.[163]

This does not mean, as Menninger hastens to add, that the "scientific" approach rejects all norms just because it rejects the concept of justice. It is simply that an acceptable norm must possess some kind of "scientific" status or meaning. For Bentham, of course, this meant the displacement of the norm of justice by the norm of utility. Menninger nominates some rather vaguely scientific-sounding standards—e.g., "protection of the environment"—that in fact also add up to a collectivist utilitarianism:

> I do not mean that science discards value systems. . . . But the question doctors might ask is not what would be just to do to this dangerous fellow, this dishonest woman, but, as in the case of a patient with compulsions, *what would be effective in deterring them!* That he or she has broken the law gives us a technical reason for acting *on behalf of society* to try to do something that will

lead him to react more acceptably, and which will *protect the environment in the meantime.*[164]

This displacement of the norm of justice by allegedly more scientific "values," however, is subject to several significant objections. In the first place, the suggested norms are at least as vague and relative as the technocrats reproach "justice" for being.[165] Clearly, different people and different cultures would have widely variant ideas as to what might "protect the environment" or what might be "acceptable" behavior. Unless "utility" implies a simple sensationalist hedonism, the criterion of "usefulness" only delays the normative question Useful for what? If, on the other hand, the utility standard does imply a simple sensationalist hedonism, it opens itself to the standard reproaches against that position.

Second, these substitute standards are no more "scientific" than any other norms. They may appear to be so because they are in fact more compatible with the modern version of philosophical naturalism that is often associated with science. The standards are couched in terms, that is, whose referents are not distinctively human—e.g., pleasure, pain, and the environment. But it still takes an act of commitment to give these standards normative force; they are not *merely* "descriptive" in the positive sense.

Finally, and most important in practical consequences, the new ostensively scientific standards suggested by the technocratic critics of justice would clearly permit some unconscionable actions. (And this weakness reflects a clear contrast with the discarded concept of justice. For, as I suggested above, the concept of justice has the resources within itself to condemn corrupt practices carried on in its name and therefore legitimately criticized by the technocrats—it contains, e.g., the standards of proportionality and equity. But the technocratic norms do not in this way contain resources to condemn the questionable practices associated with them.) For example, the treatment accorded Edward McNeil and Frederick Lynch clearly was "effective" in "protecting the environment." Their indeterminate commitments for minor offenses really kept the streets clean. Likewise, the compulsory leucotomy the British courts wished to inflict on Eric Wills would likely have been highly "successful" in "leading him to react more acceptably," to employ Menninger's standard. (Dr. Menninger, as a man with a keen sense of justice and compassion, surely does not intend to promote policies of this sort, but he speaks not of justice and compassion—except to discredit the former, as noted. And the relevant question is not what he would intend but, rather, what his deficient philosophy would condone.)

The critical failing of all these actions, of course, is not that they are useless or ineffective. It is not that they don't "protect the environment" or lead people to "behave acceptably." The problem is that they are manifestly unjust. They violate human dignity. They are disproportionate. They are inequitable. They are unfair. They unduly sacrifice the human rights of the individual to the comfort of society. They violate, in short, some of the crucial norms of a liberal and humane society. But the technocrat, because he has already dismissed these criteria and their parent concept of justice as meaningless residues from a prescientific era, leaves himself and those who heed him bereft of the very standards needed to save them from their errors.

The positivist and utilitarian technocrat, in short, follows the same slippery slope as does his historicist counterpart. Both of them "pseudo-objectify" the fundamental norm of their social order. That is, they attack the idea of justice as vague and "transcendental" or "metaphysical." They undermine the philosophical basis for the concept of justice. They then substitute for it a standard of order that is wholly immanent, claiming "scientific" status for it. For Marx this standard was the predicted immanent *telos* of history. For the utilitarians it was the interest of society measured in pleasure and pain. Both end the same way: having discarded the standard of justice, they wind up with an ethics of expediency that can sanction and has sanctioned the trampling of human rights.

The concept of human responsibility is undermined in the same way. The technocrat begins within the frame of reference of legitimate moral discourse. He properly and magnanimously wishes to exculpate the disadvantaged and defective for crimes or derelictions to which they were driven by forces beyond their control. As he insists, it is a sadly deficient kind of morality that would unreservedly condemn the destitute for petty theft or the schizophrenic for actions governed by his delusions. Our knowledge of psychological or sociological dynamics allows us to see the extenuating circumstances surrounding these deeds, and our judgments should be tempered accordingly.

So far, so good. This is a significant moral argument that takes the form, to borrow J. L. Austin's characterization, of a "plea for excuses."[166] As Austin observes, one very important area of moral discourse concerns claims to be excused from bearing full responsibility for acts normally deemed culpable: "I didn't mean to do it"; "I did it in self-defense"; and so on. The language of the law, of course, is similarly concerned. Acts done "with malice aforethought," for example, are distinguished from acts committed in the heat of passion and from acts done solely from negligence. Any moral or legal code worthy of the name must give careful attention to arguments of precisely this kind.

But the technocrat's metaphysic turns the exception into a universal rule. To be "responsible for" a given deed, he argues, means to have been the cause of that deed. And the universe of the technocrat is an infinite chain of cause and effect that leaves human beings in the role of dependent variables. No one "causes" himself to be. No one, then, "causes" his own actions. And no one, therefore, can legitimately be held "responsible" for what he does. The very conception of personal responsibility is depicted as a prescientific anachronism. Men are not "responsible" for what they do; it is outside or prior agencies that are "responsible." Thus, Robert Owen wrote in his *New View of Society:*

> The will of man has no power whatever over his opinions; he must, and ever did, and ever will, believe what has been, is, or may be impressed on his mind by his predecessors, and the circumstances which surround him. It becomes therefore the essence of irrationality to suppose that any human being, from the creation to this day, could deserve praise or blame, reward or punishment, for the prepossession of early education.[167]

A century and a half later, B. F. Skinner writes in a similar vein that "it is the environment which is 'responsible' for the objectionable behavior, and it is the environment, not some attribute of the individual, which must be changed." "Responsibility" in the conventional sense, he continues, is not being "destroyed" by such a view, since it is only an "occult quality."[168]

One might suppose that the logical outcome of this view would be a form of political fatalism: no one can do anything because everyone is in the deterministic embrace of outside forces. But the technocrat, like liberalism in general, is activist in orientation; so, like liberalism, he short-circuits the infinite causal regress that might seem implicit in his diagnosis. No individual is deemed genuinely responsible for his actions, but the abstract aggregate of individuals, "society," is responsible. More specifically, it is the knowledgeable and powerful segments of society who may be considered responsible for what goes on in society. Their knowledge lifts them out of the realm of necessity into the realm of freedom, and hence they—the knowers—are the only ones appropriately subject to the normal expectations and demands made of responsible persons. Indeed, they are subject to more than the normal demands and expectations, for they are deemed responsible not simply for their own actions but for the actions of the whole society.

In effect, the politicized subject-object distinction comes into play in the technocratic analysis of social responsibility—as it does in much of liberalism. Insight into the nature of sociological causality serves to exculpate the "objects" of inquiry from being held responsible for themselves, but it does not similarly excuse those who attain this insight. They in fact become burdened with, or entitled to accept, responsibility for the entire society. There is, of course, a great deal to be said for the idea that one becomes free and responsible only to the degree that one can attain some understanding of the forces that have made one what one is. What is distinctive and peculiar to the technocrat's analysis is its radical either/or quality. The many are caused—in toto—and the few are free—radically.

It is this diagnostic peculiarity that accounts for the superficially paradoxical corruption embedded in one important strand of modern liberal thought—a strand present in almost pure form in the technocrat. On the one hand, the liberal whose social analysis is governed by technocratic premises tends toward moral masochism: anytime anyone does something wrong, it is "we" who are to blame. Modern liberalism has produced all sorts of thoroughly benevolent and public-spirited people who seem willing to confess guilt for all sorts of social problems they did not create. (The obverse of this orientation—self-pity—is equally unattractive. Those who feel themselves powerless, consigned to the realm of necessity, may turn to aggressive scapegoating. Then it is "they" who are to be condemned for all the evils that beset the world.)

On the other hand, this moral masochism, in seeming paradox, rapidly leads to a claim of total power in the society. Self-abnegation turns into a radical self-arrogation of authority. The technocratic liberal who seemed so self-effacing as to accept the burden of guilt for all the sins of his society at one moment wants to take complete control of it in the next. *Mea culpa* is followed by *Obey me*. In fact, this development is quite logical, the paradox only superficial. For both the moral masochism and the claim of power are simply alternative forms of the same thing: "taking full responsibility." The politicized Cartesian subject carries an enormous burden of responsibility—hence his potential for moral masochism. But power must go with responsibility if the responsibility is not to be spurious. These two superficially contrasting aspects of liberalism-as-infected-by-technocracy have their roots, then, in the same deficient analysis of the problem of social responsibility.

The same basic paradox occurs on the other side of the subject-object divide as well. This time, however, the paradox runs in the opposite direction. Instead of beginning with an apparent burden that eventuates in extraordinary privilege, it begins with an apparent privilege and ends by exacting an extraordinary price.

For the "object" in the technocratic scheme is first of all granted a blanket pardon for all his misdeeds. The technocrat conceives a deviant from prevailing social norms to be captive to outside forces that—as a denizen of the realm of necessity—he is utterly incapable of transcending. The "object" is really a victim (of "circumstances") in transgressor's clothing. Accordingly, the technocrat treats him with extraordinary magnanimity, absolving him from sin more freely than the most charitable of prelates. Though their deeds be scarlet, they shall be white as snow, for they were but helpless pawns.

As remarkably benevolent as this complete absolution sounds, it carries with it an equally remarkable cost. The forgiveness of a *deus faber* is not free, for the "object" can accept the technocrat's "plea for an excuse" on his behalf only by forfeiting his staus as a responsible agent; in other words, to obtain his release from guilt, he must acquiesce in his status as "object." He is not guilty only because he is without responsibility. But to concede his ability to be responsible is to concede his humanity; for it is precisely by affirming that one will be responsible for one's actions that one lifts oneself out of nature and becomes a human being. Conversely, to renounce this affirmation amounts to relinquishing one's claim to personhood, and, with the abandonment of this claim to the status of responsible agent, one forfeits the integrity of one's will and with it the entitlements of autonomy. One's freedom and desires no longer warrant respect, and they can be overlooked or overriden without qualm.

The moral bargain offered to the "object" is tempting but ultimately disastrous for him. It is a Faustian kind of pact, though promising more meager rewards. He is enticed by the prospect of excuse from the burden of responsibility and the potential for guilt that comes with it. But, like Faust, he must pay with his soul. Just as the technocrat's humility, his accepting guilt beyond rational measure, turns quickly into the arrogant grasp for power, so his benevolent exculpation of those who do not qualify for the realm of freedom quickly turns into a radical disenfranchisement. The latter transmutation, like the former, is only superficially paradoxical; for both exculpation and disfranchisement are forms of "relieving someone from the burden of responsibility." As the many victims of technocratic pride have discovered, it is a poor bargain indeed. The burden of responsibility is perilous but precious. It is the cost and the seal of our humanity.

Power is the last of the four concepts crucial to humane liberalism that technocratic premises undermine. We have noted repeatedly that the technocrat makes some extraordinary claims to power, and we have also had occasion to note his curious vagueness about and blindness to the problem of power. This failure to appreciate and to understand the realities and the dangers of political power is peculiar on its face, considering liberalism's historic sensitivity to excess and abuse of power and its consequent attention to institutional devices that would prevent power concentrations; yet nothing is more characteristic of the technocratic tradition than this curious innocence. The socialist technocrat, as Frank Manuel has observed, is similarly afflicted: "The simplicity with which socialist theory turned its head away from the realities of power was the great blind spot of its outlook."[169]

There are several reasons for this notable "blind spot" in the technocratic outlook. In the first place is the universal difficulty of perceiving one's own actions as exercises of power. The power of one person is experienced and therefore easily perceived from the outside—by those whose lives are constrained and altered by its exercise. For his own part, from inside, the possessor of power is more likely to experience its exercise as a form of freedom— "absence of impediment," as Hobbes put it. Or, especially in the case of the technocrat, any strictures laid down are perceived as simply the structural requisites of the grand design.

A second contributing factor is the technocrat's utopianism. His sanguine estimation of human nature and the potentialities of social order lead him to see power as a temporary feature of collective life—a feature soon to be rendered obsolete by the scientific rationalization of society. As Manuel observes: "however much Marx differed from Saint-Simon in analyzing the historical process, there was agreement between them that the new society emerging from the last conflict of systems or classes would witness the twilight of power *and the cessation of power conflict.*"[170] As our earlier review should have made clear, this belief that we are living in the "twilight of power" is not confined to socialist thinkers. "Liberal" technocrats like Skinner, Lasswell, Ward, and Lundberg share that same hopeful expectation—or perhaps one should say they are afflicted by the same naïveté.

These are important sources of the technocratic obliviousness to the realities of power. Equally significant, however, is yet another instance of the process of conceptual deterioration that leads the technocrat to discard the fundamental norms of liberty, justice, and responsibility. The result is that he cannot perceive power, in large part, because his conceptual poverty leaves him bereft of the resources required to identify it.

Power is a relational concept. Power has been exercised when a political outcome is brought about that is different from what it otherwise would have been. This means that anyone who wishes to measure power must have some standard for determining "what otherwise would have been." Obviously, such an assessment is not easily or certainly made, requiring, as it does, an estimation of hypothetical results that might have occurred but did not. Now all sorts of things might occur hypothetically. What is needed to keep the measurement of power from becoming wholly arbitrary, therefore, is some reasonably reliable guidepost for determining what "normally" would have happened apart from the intervention of outside force.

Historically and logically, three principal possible axis points recommend themselves as plausible and nonarbitrary standards for determining what "otherwise would have been" and thus for determining the extent and direction of the exercise of power. (These three possible standards, moreover, overlap. How great the overlap is depends on certain other assumptions.) In the first place, we might identify A's power over B by distinguishing what B actually did from what B would have done "of his own free will." Alternatively, we might measure power by assessing the distance between what actually happened and what the "natural tendency" would have been. This is the way, for example, that Aristotle identified "violent motion": a motion is "violent" to the extent that what is being moved deviates from the pathway toward its natural *telos*. Finally, we might measure the exercise of power—specifically, of illegitimate power—by reference to the standard of natural right. The relevance of this standard was emphasized, for example, by de Tocqueville in *Democracy in America:* "It was the idea of right which enabled men to define anarchy and tyranny."[171]

The technocrat's failure results from the fact that his metaphysic has obliterated each of these three possible benchmarks. There is no room in his conception of the world for a genuinely free will—a will possessing the integrity and autonomy to distinguish it from a condition of repression or coercion. If all human desires are the product of external controlling conditions, then no expressed desire or intention is distinguished by its freedom and autonomy from any other. The question whether someone is under duress is no longer meaningful; the only meaningful question concerns the nature and sources of the particular controls that govern him.

Similarly, the technocrat's Newtonian cosmology has discarded all conceptions of natural teleology. The claim that human beings have certain natural ends that govern their actions, that they have certain intrinsic needs that demand fulfillment, is ridiculed as a piece of "Scholasticism" on a par with the idea that falling bodies accelerate because of their jubilation at returning to their natural home. And the idea of natural right, which depends in great part on the accreditation of some form of these prior concepts, has understandably been likewise abandoned by the technocrat as a mere residue that liberalism mistakenly took over from an earlier time.

It is not simply fortuitous, then, that technocrats are blind to power realities and heedless of the claims of justice, liberty, and responsibility. Technocratic political programs override these crucial standards of humane liberalism in practice because technocratic philosophy discredits them in theory. Technocrats can violate the most cherished values of humane liberalism and do so in good conscience because they literally see nothing to violate. The logic of the very conception of reason that the early liberals believed would nourish, even guarantee, the success of their ideals has instead cannibalized those ideals. It has turned upon them and destroyed their credibility, legitimizing in their place political conceptions that seem more akin to those that liberalism challenged in the first place.

Liberalism used reason as the cutting edge of its assault on repressive authority that demanded blind obedience. Technocracy turns reason itself into the ostensive justification for political ideas and institutions more authoritarian than anything found in medieval times.

Liberalism attacked entrenched class distinctions in the name of fundamental human equality. Technocracy creates and legitimizes a class distinction between rulers and ruled more rigid and more radical than the distinctions among the eighteenth-century French estates.

Liberalism denounced a political regime that valued order above liberty and justice. Technocracy debunks liberty and justice and seeks to impose its ideal of organization.

Liberalism attacked paternalistic restraints in the name of human dignity and responsibility. Technocracy discards human dignity and responsibility as meaningless clichés and aims at establishing a highly paternalistic secular theocracy staffed by a scientific "priesthood."

Liberalism attacked the concentration of power as a source of corruption and tyranny. Technocracy deplores the diffusion of power as an inefficient anachronism and seeks to reconsolidate power in the hands of a new elite.

As we noted in chapter 4, technocracy is no simple reversion to the status quo ante. It is not counterrevolutionary in the strict sense at all. In the first place, it relies on ideas that did not hold sway until liberalism had triumphed both intellectually and historically. It depends on concepts, methods, and ideals that are thoroughly modern. Moreover, technocratic programs are in many respects the heirs of the reform tradition in Western politics. Indeed, they are often—perhaps even characteristically—fueled by the same reformist moral passions that technocrats tend to disavow in theory.

Because it undermines, discredits, and then discards the fundamental and irreplaceable humanitarian norms of liberalism, however, technocratic ideology profoundly corrupts this reformist tradition. At the very best, it tends to suppress the humane concerns of the reform tradition in favor of its own putatively "scientific" ideals of order. At the worst, it generates a peculiarly modern form of fanaticism grounded in the coupling of its homeless moral passions with its alleged scientific certainty.

Either way, it is we and the cherished goals of humane liberalism that lose. We find ourselves threatened and our humane ideals assaulted by those who confidently assert themselves to be the legitimate heirs of liberal reformism. Until we can gain the intellectual leverage to understand and escape the tragically ironic logic of technocracy, we are doubly damned. Not only are our lives and liberties under siege from within the camp, so to speak, but we also may suffer intellectual vertigo from so disturbing an anomaly. Like the deeply chagrined Diderot confronting the doctrines of Helvetius, we may easily be as baffled as we are dismayed to see ideas that seemed so bright and promising turned upon us so destructively.

6   The Origins of Political Irrationalism

The optimism of the early liberals was grounded, as documented in chapter 3, in their conflation of old and new intellectual traditions. These early liberals anticipated that the revolution in epistemology would establish the foundations of a new "moral science," and this nascent "moral science" was in turn expected to be an extremely potent force on the side of the dramatic political reforms they desired.

This hopeful belief in an imminent and inexorable social progress rested on three interrelated assumptions about the new moral science. The first concerned the scope of the new reason, the second concerned its content, and the third related to its impact. All three reflected the persistence of epistemological conceptions carried over from the classical tradition.

The scope of the new reason, was, in the first place, assumed to be very broad. The range and competence of the new methods of inquiry, it was presumed, were essentially coextensive with the range and competence of classical *logos*-rationality. The new scientific knowledge, like the Augustinian hierarchy of knowledge, was a unity whose highest reach extended to the discovery of moral truth. Technical reason could, like classical *nous*, apprehend the order of Being and give mankind guidance for the conduct of life.

The content of these moral truths that the new reason would ascertain was likewise not expected to be novel or revolutionary. It was anticipated that the new moral sciences would basically validate the humane values of the classical tradition; these traditional norms of human conduct would be clarified and sustained, not displaced or transformed. Locke and Descartes both felt confident that the revelations of the emerging sciences would be fully consonant with their Christian faith, and the more secular classical liberals, deists such as D'Alembert and Jefferson, for example, clearly assumed that the "natural light" of the new methods of inquiry illuminated clear and distinct moral precepts that were fundamentally in accord with the tenets of the natural-law tradition.

Finally, the impact of the new moral science was expected to be profound and beneficial in large part because of the carryover of another basic idea from the classical tradition: the idea that knowledge leads directly to virtue. The assumed moral content of knowledge was, of course, one necessary foundation of this belief. But equally important was the early liberals' retention of the assumption, widespread in classical philosophy, that moral truth possesses the power to motivate those who perceive it. This carryover of the belief in the motivating power of moral knowledge sometimes took the form of a neo-Platonism, as when Colin McLaurin interpreted the Newtonian order as a kind of *agathon*. The cosmic order and beauty Newton had revealed was like a vision of the Good compelling the affections of the viewer. (In McLaurin's words, anyone contemplating the Newtonian cosmos "cannot but be himself excited and animated" by it.) Alternatively, this assumption could take the neo-Aristotelian form it did in Descartes's explanation to Mersenne: the will pursues only what it perceives as good, so the clear and distinct perception of what is good provided by the new moral science should lead directly to virtuous conduct.

The new reason, in short, was expected to replicate the old *logos*-rationality in these crucial respects: it would ascertain moral truths; the content of these truths would be essentially the same; and these truths would possess erotic (in the classical sense) power. Add to these holdover assumptions what was presumed to be the distinctive and novel features of the new reason, and the grounds for the optimism of the early liberals become quite evident. For the new reason was presumed to make good the deficiencies of the older *logos*-rationality. It would provide the clarity, the certainty, and the simplicity that the older tradition never possessed. It would place the truths of the moral order on secure foundations once and for all and make them accessible to all people. This was something the older *logos*-rationality never was able to do in fact or even claimed in theory to be able to do. The liberal reformers, as it were, came not to destroy the old law but rather to fulfill it and to make it known beyond challenge to all who possessed the natural light of reason—and that included all but the immature and the defective. It was as if Plato had suddenly stumbled on a learning machine that would allow—nay, guarantee—even those souls made of brass to become philosophers.

Old Wine in New Wineskins:
The Dissolution of "Moral Science"

There was only one major problem with this optimistic hope: the mixture of old and new philosophical premises that produced it was logically unstable. The new epistemology could not—logically could not—fulfill its crucial role in the reformers' political program. The new reason did not, on careful examination, possess the competence to establish and clarify traditional moral ideas as it was supposed to do. Instead, it incorporated premises that logically had to undermine or at least radically transform the normative conceptions of the classical tradition. Some of the most fundamental conceptions that underlay the new model of human cognition were simply incompatible with other conceptions essential to the traditional conception of moral knowledge.

The basic dilemma was not immediately apparent to most of the seventeenth-century reformers. If it had been, it would have substantially clouded their optimism. There were some unusually rigorous and perceptive thinkers, to be sure, who realized relatively quickly that the revised philosophical premises brought with them some radical implications. Foremost among these prescient intellects was Hobbes, who saw quite early that acceptance of the new philosophy made morality and politics newly problematic: it required establishing a conception of human order on a thoroughgoing nominalist and materialist footing. The overwhelming reaction to Hobbes's attempt to do just that was, however, shock and revulsion. His ideas were universally reviled from the pulpit and almost uniformly rebutted by academicians. The hunting of Leviathan became a popular late-seventeenth-century British preoccupation.

However, the more astute among his critics realized that the challenge he presented to established truths was a very real one, for in its basic outline it did not reflect the idiosyncratic excesses of a single eccentric thinker but was instead a serious attempt to deal with the moral and political implications of philosophical assumptions that were achieving widespread acceptance among Europe's intellectual elite. If Hobbes's answer was not persuasive, the questions he had confronted could not be shunted aside so easily.

The recognition began to dawn among serious thinkers, in short, that some of the original, largely tacit, assumptions of the early liberal reformers were not really tenable. Old truths and new truths did not blend so unproblematically and so productively as they had assumed. Some of the old truths would therefore have to be abandoned or significantly refashioned if the new epistemology were to be deemed authoritative. Especially, some of the received truths of morals and politics were at minimum not fully compatible with the new conception of reason, and, since the new idea of reason seemed to be becoming relatively impregnable, it was the old truths rather than the new truths that would have to give way.

Those who had looked forward enthusiastically to the fruition of a "moral science" that would firmly ground old moral truths on new, firmer foundations had relied on the assumption that the moral order was a part of the natural order, broadly conceived. This was the basic understanding that had undergirded the idea of "natural law." It followed from this assumption that moral truth could be known and validated by the same rational procedures that had so effectively opened the gateway of natural philosophy. However, it was equally possible to read this implicit equation of moral and natural order the other way around. That is, instead of assuming that the newly illuminated natural order would have the dimensions of the traditional moral order, the moral order might have to be reduced to the dimensions of the natural order. As the gap between the content of the moral tradition and the dimensions of the new view of nature widened, this latter way of reading the equation became dominant. For the new conception of nature seemed so wholly justified by the explosive progress it permitted the natural sciences that it was beyond reproach. If the traditional moral truths could not be compressed into the bounds of resolutely nominalist naturalism, that was simply too bad for them. They would either have to be whittled down somehow to fit into nature or they would have to seek new grounding altogether.

It seemed that this conclusion could be avoided only by philosophical schizophrenia or philosophical incoherence. That is, one might, like Descartes, try to keep critical reason on a short leash, permitting it to transform the understanding of the subhuman world but keeping it from transgressing into moral and political issues. One would be a skeptical, inquiring rationalist when considering the principles of the natural sciences but would become a credulous fideist vis-à-vis the principles of human conduct. Alternatively, one might, like Locke, simply affirm both the new rationalism and the old moral tradition without taking sufficiently seriously the tensions between them.

To those aware of the problem, however, neither of these philosophical avoidance mechanisms could appear satisfying or honorable. The resort to schizophrenia seemed morally corrupt: it was not a principled position so much as it was an expedient of timidity or cowardice. The other tack, of simply embracing apparent incompatibles, was intellectually indefensible: the principle of non-contradiction could not be simply ignored.

Once the logical instability of the original expectations about the "moral sciences" was appreciated, then, and assuming that the new model of human knowing was accepted as authoritative, the only real alternatives seemed to be these: either normative conceptions might be retained within the ambit of genuine knowledge by refashioning them as naturalistic "scientific" concepts; or normative discourse might be regarded as incapable of meeting the preconditions for real knowledge and on these grounds be excluded from the realm of reason. The standards of clarity and certainty, together with what I earlier termed the "epistemological manicheanism" of the new theory of knowledge, left no other apparent choice.

The first tack was followed by those whose ideas were examined in chapters 4 and 5. These thinkers—Helvetius, Marx, Saint-Simon, Skinner, et al.—persevered with the original belief that positive knowledge possessed normative competence. The criteria of order that might legitimately serve as guideposts for human action were, to their minds, within the scope of scientific reason. Moral truths fell within the circle of light circumscribed by the new epistemology. Thus far these thinkers maintained continuity with the hopes of the early liberal reformers.

They departed from the expectations of the early liberals, however, when it came to the content of these normative conceptions. They might agree with Locke, Descartes, Condorcet, et al. about the scope of the new reason vis-à-vis moral truths, but they had a very different notion about the substance of these norms. The norms ascertained by scientific reason were not the traditional values of the classical and Christian tradition. They were instead conceptions of order that had been trimmed down substantially—conceptions of majority interest rather than common good, of pleasure rather than happiness, of utility or equilibrium or smooth functioning rather than justice. This watering-down of the content of traditional moral notions, together with the persistence of the belief in the objectivity of these standards, plus the recognition that the scientific competence necessary to ascertain these truths was much more limited than the early liberals' "simple-truths" model had suggested—these three ideas, taken together, constituted the matrix of the technocratic tradition.

The other, more radical, solution to the perceived instability of the original moral-sciences idea was to push moral conceptions outside the circle of reason altogether. Those who took this route realized that no normative conceptions could, in the first place, ever measure up to the stringent standards the new epistemology had set for "real knowledge." Beliefs about what is right and good could not be made certain. They were not all that simple. They could not be grounded on secure and unshakable foundations. Whatever the Declaration of Independence might claim, these truths were not genuinely self-evident. Despite the protestations of Tom Paine, common sense was not so common or unanimous and therefore not all that reliable when it came to moral and political issues. Both experience and logic suggested that these early hopes were the effusions of enthusiasts or the psuedo-certainties of the dogmatic.

But the problem ran even deeper than that. The more careful and critical philosophical minds began to realize that normative concepts could not really fit into the dimensions of the new epistemology at all. Moral ideas not only were unclear and uncertain. They were frankly anomalous. The new epistemology suggested that knowledge was built up by logical computations out of sensations. These sensations, in turn, were deemed to be the passive "impressions" made on the human mind by the outside world. Since final causes and substances had been purged from the outside world, and since no other conceptions had been devised to replace them, all the passive impressions in the world could never add up to a normative order.

The real problem, in short, was that a thoroughgoing empiricist epistemology—given the implicit model of sensation—was incapable of coming up with any moral "facts." A truly positive science could never apprehend moral truths because its own premises had eliminated their ontological foundations. In a world of primary qualities, "is" and "ought" simply fell apart. And despite talk of an experimental moral science, which even Hume engaged in, all the empirical investigation in the world could not overcome this fundamental problem. No matter how many trips you make to the well, you won't bring up water with a sieve.

What happens, given this line of thought, is a complete dissolution of the concept of "moral knowledge." Given the standards of the new epistemology and given its underlying premises, it followed that moral claims, whatever they might be, were not genuinely cognitive. This is the essential feature of the "value noncognitivist" tradition, which, in parallel with the techocratic tradition, is a second-generation offspring of liberal reason. It is "neutralist" in the sense that it depicts real knowledge as "value-neutral." It is "irrationalist" in the sense that it accords no role to reason (i.e., cognition) in the ascertainment of standards or guidelines for moral and political action. Paradoxically, it is a tradition that sometimes is called "rationalist" because of its devotion to the stringent demands of its conception of knowledge—to "scientific rigor." But it is "irrationalist" beyond the narrow confines of its conception of science, a conception that limits science to discrete "factual" claims plus "if . . . then" propositions. This is a "rationalism" so stringent in its demands and so limited in its conception of facticity, then, that it consigns vast areas of human inquiry and concern to the unfathomable reaches beyond the grasp of the human mind. Ethics, aesthetics, jurisprudence, political philosophy—all disciplines with an irreducible normative dimension—are shoved out "into that abyss of darkness where we have not eyes to see, nor faculties to perceive anything." (This phrase is Locke's, from *Essay IV. 3. 22.* Locke would have been chagrined, however, to find this abyss growing so wide.) These are held to be pseudo-disciplines, for their subject matter is "something which our understanding is unable to intuit sufficiently well," and they therefore constitute "useless labor." (These phrases are from Descartes's *Rules for Direction of the Mind,* though he, like Locke, would not have expected or desired his principle of exclusion to be applied so drastically.) Anyone who tries to speak rationally about ultimate normative issues is considered to be speaking nonsense; he is failing to heed the young Wittgenstein's admonition to keep silent about what can't be said.

Once it became reasonably clear, then, that the new epistemology, with its sensationism and stringent standards, could not accommodate the substance of traditional moral ideas, only two options seemed to be left. Either one accorded rigorous objectivity to normative concepts, qualifying them as part of science while rendering them as "naturalistic" as possible. This was the technocratic path. Or else one simply discredited the whole idea of moral knowledge, focused one's efforts on the narrow "factual" or purely logical domains, and abandoned ethical and political norms to demonic caprice, to the passions, or to other extrarational determinants. This was the "value noncognitivist" approach.

The strength of the technocratic interpretation, apart from its optimism and its intrinsic appeal to any power-seeking intelligentsia, is that it gives a more adequate account of the empirical social sciences in one important respect. Specifically, the technocratic accreditation of "scientific" normative truth removes the puzzlement from the inexorable tendency of social science macrotheories to "secrete values," as Charles Taylor has put it.[1] If social scientific theories seem to generate normative models of equilibrium, development, functionality, sanity, or whatever, that is not an embarrassment to the technocrat. He need only accord the mantle of science to these conceptions. His "value noncognitivist" sibling, on the other hand, must always find such tendencies in social science to be a scandal. By his lights, any normative dimension to a social theory is scientifically illicit. He is therefore perpetually engaged in the arduous endeavor to purge social science of any "value" taints. This he can do by placing any social theory on his Procrustean bed of abstract logic and amputating any part of it that does not fit. His problem is that what will fit is often so "pure" as to be virtually empty.

The strength of the noncognitivist position, conversely, is its logical force. The noncognitivist is correct in asserting, on the basis of the standards and premises of the new (nowadays the regnant) epistemology, that norms *ought* not to appear in any scientific theory. If they do crop up, they are like weeds in a formal garden. A lot of weeding may be needed to keep things proper, but it must be done. The rules clearly demand it. If the technocrat can account for the *presence* of norms in social theory, he cannot give a convincing account of their legitimate *origin;* and here the noncognitivist has him licked. So far as the noncognitivist is concerned, since there is no legitimate origin for the intrusion of "values" into social science, the only sources are illegitimate: stupidity or bias. Hence the noncognitivist critic's fervor in his quest to expose and excise all these values and to discredit those who have allowed them to contaminate "real knowledge."

This pattern of opposing strengths and attendant weaknesses of the technocratic and the noncognitivist positions helps to explain the rather widespread oscillation back and forth between them, often by the same individual. This is the pattern referred to earlier as "having one's value-cake and eating it, too." When speaking critically and in the abstract, these individuals adhere to the noncognitivist position: it makes an excellent critical weapon, and its abstract logic is impeccable. When speaking affirmatively and concretely, however, the same individuals may accord scientific status to the normative content of their own theories. Those who are "value-neutral" may thus also be for democracy or may intersperse calls for value-neutrality with demands that mankind "grow up."

There is a biblical parable that warns against pouring new wine into old wineskins. The old wineskins, weakened by age or past use, might burst, spilling the new wine irretrievably. It might be said that the politics of liberal reason suffered from a reversed version of the same kind of problem. The liberal reformers who adhered to the new epistemology tried to pour the old wine of traditional moral wisdom into the shiny new wineskins of the new science. They thought that the transfer would better secure their treasure. Instead, the new wineskins proved porous receptacles for the claims of practical reason. And the inherited tradition began to seep away.

The Disintegration of Locke's Moral Cognitivism

This process of seepage is strikingly and poignantly apparent in Locke. Locke began his philosophical career confident of the basic verities of the natural-law tradition. He incorporated these beliefs into his fundamental political principles. But as he worked out the implications of his sensationist empiricism, he found the basis for these beliefs increasingly problematic. His later reflections on the problem tended to be fragmentary and inchoate, some of them even exposing him to charges of "Hobbism." In the end, in perplexing asymmetry with his basic rationalism, he seemed content to rely on the testimony of the Gospels for insight into moral truths.

In his youthful *Essays on the Law of Nature*, Locke addressed the question: "Is there a rule of morals, or law of nature given to us?" He answered with an unequivocal yes. He denied, in answer to his own rhetorical question, that "man alone has come into the world altogether exempt from any law applicable to himself, without a plan, rule, or any pattern of his life."[2] "The nature of good and evil," he continued, "is eternal and certain, and their value cannot be determined either by the public ordinances of men *or by any private opinion*."[3] He contemplated the consequences of denying the existence of natural law with alarm. Without natural law, he wrote, "it seems that man would not be bound to do anything but what utility to pleasure might recommend, or what a blind and lawless impulse might happen perchance to fasten on. The terms 'upright' and 'virtuous' would disappear as meaningless or be nothing at all but empty names."[4]

The natural law consists, Locke said, of "duties" that "necessarily follow from [man's] very nature."[5] The fulfillment of these duties is depicted as intrinsically unavoidable by anyone who would fulfill his essential humanity. One's obligation to observe the law is tantamount to the lawfulness of logical implication:

> It seems to follow just as necessarily from the nature of man that, if he is a man, he is bound to love and worship God and also to fulfill other things appropriate to the rational nature, i.e., to observe the law of nature, as it follows from the nature of a triangle that, if it is a triangle, its three angles are equal to two right angles.[6]

The content of these obligations imposed by the law of nature Locke conceives in quite traditional terms. He draws some of his central arguments from classical sources, such as Cicero and Aristotle, and from Christian sources, such as Aquinas and Hooker, and he clearly believes that the natural law embodies the basic moral truths conveyed in these traditions. Already the obligation "to love and worship God" has been noted; in addition, Locke affirms that

> we can equate with that law [i.e., natural law] that moral good or virtue which philosophers in former times (and among them especially the Stoics) have searched for with so much zeal and adorned

with so many praises; we can equate it with that single good which
Seneca says man ought to be content with, to which appertains so
much dignity, so much glory, that even those among mortals who
are corrupted by vice recognize it and while shunning it approve
it.[7]

The law of nature is not innate. It is not, in Locke's words, "inscribed in the minds of men."[8] And it is not known "from the
general consent of men."[9] Assertions to the former effect conflict
with Locke's basic understanding of the nature of mind and the
origins of knowledge. And both claims, Locke argues, are con-
tradicted by experience. Nevertheless, he avers, the law of nature is
"sufficiently known to men because it can be perceived by the light
of nature alone."[10] By the metaphor "light of nature" Locke means
not some mystic inner light. He means, he explains, "nothing else
but that there is some sort of truth to the knowledge of which a man
can attain by himself and without the help of another, if he makes
proper use of the faculties he is endowed with by nature."[11]

This essentially traditional conception of a law of nature discernible by right reason played a significant role in Locke's political
theory. It was not merely a speculative philosophical claim that was
left aside when he gave his attention to the practical issues of politics. Very early in the *Second Treatise* he reiterates his firm belief in
the law of nature:

> For though it would be beside my present purpose to enter here
> into the particulars of the law of nature, or its measures of
> punishment, yet it is certain there is such a law, and that too as in-
> telligible and plain to a rational creature and a studier of that law
> as the positive laws of commonwealths, nay, possibly plainer; as
> much as reason is easier to be understood than the fancies and in-
> tricate contrivances of men.[12]

Locke trades repeatedly on this assumption at many crucial places
in the pages that follow. It is the presence of the law of nature, for
example, that distinguishes liberty from license. For that reason, its
presence in the state of nature serves to distinguish the state of
nature from a state of war:

> The state of nature has a law of nature to govern it, which obliges
> every one, and reason, which is that law, teaches all mankind who
> will but consult it, that being all equal and independent, no one
> ought to harm another in his life, health, liberty, or possessions.[13]

The rights and privileges of citizenship, the status of "free man"
under the law, are depicted by Locke as attendant on the possession
of right reason. Citing "the judicious Hooker" freely, he says that

if through defects that may happen out of the ordinary course of nature, any one comes not to such a degree of reason wherein he might be supposed capable of knowing the law, and so living within the rules of it, he is never capable of being a free man, he is never let loose to the disposure of his own will.[14]

(The immediately preceding sentence clearly suggests, also, that the law that a man must be capable of knowing includes the law of nature as well as positive laws.)

Most important of all, the premise that right reason can discern the reality and basic substance of natural principles of justice undergirds Locke's discussion of the nature and extent of legitimate power. The principle of constitutionalism that legitimate power is limited power is incorporated into Lockean liberalism in this way. Natural law sets limits on the scope of legislative power:

A man, . . . having in the state of nature, no arbitrary power over the life, liberty, or possession of another, but only so much as the law of nature gave him for the preservation of himself and the rest of mankind, this is all he doth, or can give up to the commonwealth, and by it to the legislative power, so that the legislative can have no more than this.[15]

The positive laws of a commonwealth, moreover, are to be deemed valid only insofar as they are compatible with the natural law, and they are properly to be interpreted and understood in light of the natural law.[16] The criterion of natural law is also invoked to explain the illegitimacy of despotic power: "this is a power which neither nature gives, for it has made no such distinction between one man and another, nor compact can convey."[17]

In Locke's own formulation, in short, much that is considered characteristic, distinctive, and influential in his political theory hinges on the moral cognitivism he takes over from the traditional sources and affirms anew. The reality of natural law and the capacity of right reason distinguish his contract theory from the radically nominalist theory found in Hobbes, for example. Similarly, it is his natural-law ideas that serve to sustain his belief in man's capacity for self-governance; it is natural law that provides a basis for distinguishing his legitimate regime from a majority tyranny; it is natural law that invalidates all despotic power; and it is natural law that both establishes and sets limits on the obligations of citizenship. Removing the moral cognitivism from Lockean liberalism would not be like deleting the olive from a martini; it would be like forgetting the gin.[18]

In his later philosophical endeavors, however, Locke's moral cognitivism seems to disintegrate. Or, at the very least, it becomes highly problematic, seemingly at variance with the general tendency of his thought. Not only did he never respond to the urgings of many to work out the demonstrative ethical theory whose possibility he had suggested; he never completed any further study of "natural morality," nor did he elaborate further the philosophical foundations of the claims he made in the *Essays on the Law of Nature*.

In fact, the "natural morality" that seemed implied by much of Locke's later thought was essentially hedonistic. This hedonistic drift in his ethical reflections apparently bothered Locke himself, for he deleted from his writings or never published some of his more forthright utterances along these lines.[19] Even with this degree of reticence, or perhaps of discretion, Locke's account in the *Essay* opened him to charges of Hobbism. Locke genuinely, it seems, felt such accusations to be both unfair and inaccurate. He genuinely retained his early belief in some sort of objective moral principles, and he therefore was not really in Hobbes's camp, politically or philosophically. But it is safe to say that the charges were not wholly unfounded. At the least, they pointed up the hedonistic tendencies in his later thought and his failure—perhaps his incapacity—to reconcile these tendencies with his professed belief in natural law.

Abstract Sensations and the Paradox of the Age of Reason

The tensions and difficulties in Locke's thought go right to the heart of the logical and political dilemma the liberal philosophers faced as they sought to work out the details of rational politics. The more they tried to specify the relationship of the new conception of reason to the supposedly allied directions in politics, the more problematic that relationship became. Instead of unveiling the reciprocity of their epistemology and their politics, these philosophers uncovered their incongruence. Where they expected to find a clearly demarcated pathway to the good society, they found instead a paradox. As Isabel Knight has aptly characterized it, they stumbled into

> the paradox of the Age of Reason, in which reason unexpectedly turned upon itself and, by its own rigorous application, struck at the very foundations on which it rested—an intellectual development of baffling circularity and continuing relevance.[20]

Locke's basic difficulty—and the paradox that beset his fellow liberals—was not, as is often suggested, any contradiction between his affirmation of objective moral truths and his denial of innate ideas. That interpretation of his difficulty is either based on Cartesian premises, hence begging the issue between Locke and Descartes, or, more probably, is based ex post facto on the Kantian assumption that moral claims must be categorical and a priori. Locke's problem emerges most accurately and clearly, however, not by contrasting him with Descartes and Kant but by comparing both his early and his mature ideas with corresponding Aristotelian conceptions.

When these comparisons are made, it should become evident that Locke's dilemma arises not from his rejection of innate ideas but rather from his doctrine of sensation. Ernst Cassirer gets very close to the nub of the liberals' problem in his *The Philosophy of the Enlightenment:*

> The philosophy of the Enlightenment at first holds fast to this apriority of law, to this demand for absolutely universally valid and unalterable legal norms. Even the pure empiricists and the philosophical empiricists are no exception in this respect. Voltaire and Diderot scarcely differ from Grotius and Montesquieu, but they fall indeed into a difficult dilemma. For how can this view be reconciled with the fundamental tendency of their doctrine of knowledge? How does the necessity and immutability of the concept of law agree with the proposition that every idea is derived from the senses and that, accordingly, it can possess no other and no higher significance than the various sense experiences on which it is based?[21]

The problem, then, as Cassirer's statement makes clear, is the tension between the liberals' belief in objective norms and their sensationism. What Cassirer's formulation does not make sufficiently clear is that the dilemma arises, not from the claim that "every idea is derived from the senses" per se, but from the relatively new conception of what these sensations are. The problem is not formal but substantive. It stems from the alleged *content* of sensations, as conceived by the empiricist philosophers.

For if our senses reveal to us patterns of order, meaning, and purpose—if they register gestalts of potentiality striving to become actualized—then they may in fact provide us with norms to govern our actions. These norms, considered by themselves, would be hypothetical imperatives rather than categorical demands. (Attributing these teleological patterns to a divine Creator, whose will that they be actualized possesses the force and status of law, makes it possible, of course, to regard these patterns as commands rather than simply the basis for counsel.) But anyone who desired fulfillment rather than destruction, life instead of death, would find these norms persuasive. This was the logic of classical natural law. It was based on a conception of a teleological order of Being—imperative for one who wished to participate in that order and obligatory, strictly speaking, only when adapted to theology—that was discernible to the mind of man through the evidence of his senses.

The important thing in this conception, epistemologically, was the idea that *forms* are impressed on the mind through sensation. In Aristotle's (and Plato's) rendition, these forms are the essences of a finite cosmos, and herein lay the opening wedge for the disintegration of the entire formulation; for central to the whole intellectual revolution of the seventeenth century was the complete rejection of all essences, substances, "quiddities," and the like, and this rejection in turn necessitated a transformed notion of what a sensation was. Sensations could no longer be "of" substances, for there were none. Sensations could, therefore, only be impressions of corpuscular "data," since that was all there was out there for them to register.

What happens to the liberal reformers, then, is that this profound transformation in the presumed content of the sensations erodes the basis of their belief in a rationally cognizable normative order. Had the older conception—that the senses are competent to perceive dynamic patterns of becoming—remained viable, Enlightenment epistemology and politics might have retained their coherence. But this older doctrine of sensation was incompatible with the basic premises of the new ontology. The new image of sensations had to square with the new image of the world. The data of the senses, accordingly, came to be conceived in a highly abstract fashion as discrete and static little bits and pieces of things.

This highly significant conception of sensations as abstract, discrete "simple ideas" or "impressions" (as Locke and Hume, respectively, called them) was the epistemological counterpart of what Whitehead termed the seventeenth century's "fallacy of misplaced concretion." It is, as numerous commentators have observed,[22] a conception remarkably distant from the real, concrete, experience of everyday life, but it is nevertheless presented as what, at bottom, "experience" really is. The empiricist account of experience, and of its constituent sensations, is not itself an empirical account. It is not a description of experience; it is instead an interpretation of what experience must be, given the corpuscular constitution of the world.

In this respect, then, Engels's criticism of the empiricist tradition as "metaphysical" is justified formally—as it is essentially accurate substantively. The empiricist philosophy was metaphysical—despite its professed abhorrence of metaphysics—in the sense that it was an account of knowledge and of nature clearly arrived at by working out the implications of basic presuppositions it did not question.[23] The result was, as Engels wrote, the habit of observing natural objects and processes in isolation, apart from their connection with the vast whole; of observing them in repose not in motion; as constants, not as essentially variables; in their death, not in their life. And when this way of looking at things was transferred by Bacon and Locke from natural science to philosophy, it produced the narrow, metaphysical mode of thought peculiar to the last century.[24]

Here, as elsewhere, the assumptions and the weaknesses of one of the two opposing heirs of liberal reason (the technocratic and the noncognitivist) are acutely depicted and criticized by the other. Engels is insisting that his own equally metaphysical and defective Hegelian conception of reason is "concrete" and "scientific" and hence the only reasonable alternative to a reductive, abstract, and static empiricism.

Locke, as Engels suggests, can be examined as a locus classicus of this phenomenon of the erosion of objective norms via the abstractification of sensation. To illustrate this, it is only necessary to refer once again to his *Essays on the Law of Nature,* this time not simply to substantiate Locke's belief in the existence of natural law but to examine his account of how this law is known.

Locke tells us there that the knowledge of natural law comes through "sense-experience." It is not "inscribed" in the minds of men: "It has only been an empty assertion and no one has proved it until now, although many have labored to this end, that the souls of men when they are born are something more than empty tablets capable of receiving all sorts of imprints but having none stamped on them by nature."[25] And, after raising several objections to any such claim, he concludes: "Thus it appears to me that no principles, either practical or speculative, are written in the minds of men by nature."[26] Nor, he continues, can either tradition or the "general consent of men" be taken as valid and reliable sources of the knowledge of the law of nature. Consistent with his later thought, he argues that "the foundations . . . on which rests the whole of knowledge which reason builds up and raises as high as heaven are the objects of sense-experience."[27]

However clear is Locke's insistence that the law of nature is apprehended by sense experience, his account of how, exactly, this comes about is neither clear nor convincing. His basic argument is an argument from design, with all its attendant difficulties. He argues that a rational being will infer from the evidence of his senses the existence of a "wise and powerful creator of all things," and it follows from his divine status that the commands of this creator are obligatory as well as just. As Locke states it: "Hence it appears clearly that, with sense-perception showing the way, reason can lead us to the knowledge of a law-maker or of some superior power to which we are necessarily subject."[28]

The crucial thing about Locke's argument, in the context of this study, is not the argument from design itself. The crucial point is that Locke could entertain such an argument only because his conception of "sense experience" had not yet been pruned of its capacity to apprehend form and order in the world. One does not infer the existence of God from little bits and pieces of data. If that were all there were to "sense experience," Locke's argument would make no sense at all. It is clear that he trades tacitly on an older notion of sensation, decisively richer and more complex than the mature empiricist conception. Sense experience, he writes, can discern "the visible structure and argument of this world."[29] It can perceive this structure to be "in every respect...perfect and ingeniously prepared."[30] And again, "It is evident from sense-experience that...this visible world is constructed with wonderful art and regularity."[31]

Locke can consider sense experience competent to ascertain this kind of normative order in the world, this beauty and perfection and design, because he also, it seems, retains some of the classical assumptions about "nature." Specifically, although he does not expatiate on the subject, he seems to endow nature with some of the teleological structure accorded to it in the Aristotelian tradition. At least he can speak of "that height of virtue and felicity whereto the gods invite *and nature also tends.*"[32]

Locke thus sets himself up for his own downfall. He relies on sense experience as the only persuasive possible basis for moral knowledge—as it is, for that matter, the only basis he sees for any kind of knowledge. But this reliance can be plausible only because he incorporates into his presuppositions ideas about sensation and nature that come from an earlier philosophical tradition, one that he and his contemporaries were in the process of replacing. As his thought develops and matures, therefore, these older attributes of sensation and nature begin to appear anomalous and unsupportable. "Nature" he came to envision with increasing consistency as, in Basil Willey's words, "a collection of invisible atoms varying in their figure and motion."[33] Sensations accordingly had to be understood in like fashion, since they were reflections of this reality: "This to him, as to Hobbes, Descartes, and the Cartesians, was the real world; and when he pondered the phenomenon of sensation it was always this that he visualized acting upon our senses."[34]

Sensations of this kind, unlike the essence-reflecting Aristotelian sensations, could never add up to a normative order. However they might be put together, they could add up only to a heap of particles. Locke finally could not explain how reason, now in the narrow sense of logical inference, could, as he had alleged in the *Essays on the Law of Nature,* construct normative patterns of order out of sensations that he now regarded as abstract, discrete, atomistic. He could not do so, quite simply, because it is impossible. And so, Locke understandably became increasingly vague, reticent, and vacillating on the topics of natural law and moral knowledge. On the one hand, his philosophical speculations tended to drift into utilitarian and hedonist channels, prompting the charges of "Hobbism," which he resolutely denied. On the other hand, he seems at times to have taken refuge in revelation. It is "too hard a task," he wrote in *The Reasonableness of Christianity,* "for unassisted reason to establish morality in all its parts, upon its true foundation, with a clear and convincing light." But that was not really necessary, he averred, for "there needs no more but to read the inspired books to be instructed: all the duties of morality lie there clear, and plain, and easy to be understood."[35]

To summarize, then: Locke began with the firm conviction that objective norms exist that (1) are not reducible to utility or to pleasure and (2) are accessible to the natural light of the human mind. He incorporated this conviction into his public—and highly influential—political theory. But he never made good on his early implied promise that he could establish moral truths with quasi-mathematical certainty. Indeed, he was never able to specify at all how moral knowledge might be established within the parameters of his mature epistemology, and this inability was due primarily to his having clarified his doctrine of sensation to render it consistent with his underlying corpuscular model of nature.

Locke's philosophical difficulties merit close attention because they anticipate the fundamental irony of liberalism in the empiricist tradition. Liberalism based much of its original optimism on the conviction that autonomous critical reason would—after discrediting repressive superstitions and decadent Scholasticism—establish its humanitarian premises on luminous and secure foundations. Instead, the new reason proved to have a much greater appetite for critical debunking than the liberal reformers had anticipated. After discrediting beliefs the liberals disdained, it turned on beliefs they cherished. By rendering the whole notion of moral knowledge anomalous, by pushing moral claims beyond the pale of reason into the realm of pseudo-propositions, the empiricist conception of human understanding finally undermined the very humanitarian standards it was supposed to have secured for all time. Epis-

temological revolutions, like their political counterparts, sometimes
devour their own children.

Hume's Epistemological Skepticism

The next important step in the disfranchisement of reason in moral
matters was taken by the amiable Scottish skeptic, David Hume.
Hume fully accepted Locke's corpuscular sensationism. He recognized much more clearly than Locke, moreover, that this doctrine led to the conclusion that reason alone was incompetent to
provide men with normative guidelines for the conduct of their lives.
Very much the Enlightenment man in so many respects—in his
tolerance, his worldliness, his disdain for enthusiasm and superstition—Hume demonstrated that the premises of the new philosophy were incompatible with one of its adherents' fondest professed
hopes: namely, to build the society of the future on the precepts
of reason. No wonder that a careful reading of Hume's speculations should produce, in Carl Becker's words, the sensation of
"a slight chill . . . at high noon of the Enlightenment."[36]
Hume, however, did not draw relativist conclusions from his
skeptical premises. He did not reject the enterprise of developing a
moral theory applicable to all men of good will. In fact, he devoted
some of his most diligent inquiry to the goal of "introducing the
experimental method of reasoning into moral subjects," as the sub-
title of his *Treatise* avowed. Nevertheless, rather like Locke's,
Hume's ethical theory rested precariously on the ontological and
epistemological principles he espoused. When the latter were more
rigorously developed in the empiricist tradition, therefore, Hume's
ethical theory was itself undermined. Against his own intent and
belief, consequently, the final issue of his thought has been the reduction of all moral claims to mere expressions of individual taste.
Hume was a phenomenalist rather than, like Locke, a physicalist.
That is, having taken Berkeley's critique to heart, Hume regarded it
as unprovable whether our sensations arise directly from and correspond to external physical objects. That may be the case, or it may
not, he says. But it doesn't really matter. We can simply begin our
account of human knowledge with the impressions considered as the
phenomena of experience. There is no need to inquire beyond this.
In Hume's words:

> As to those impressions, which arise from the senses, their ulti-
> mate cause is, in my opinion, perfectly inexplicable by human rea-
> son, and 'twill always be impossible to decide with certainty,
> whether they arise immediately from the object, or are produced

by the creative power of the mind, or are derived from the author of our being. Nor is such a question in any way material to our purpose. We may draw inferences from the coherence of our perceptions, whether they be true or false; whether they represent nature justly, or be mere illusions of the senses.[37]

In other respects, Hume's account of the origins and basic constituents of human knowledge is essentially an extension and consolidation of Locke's sensationist principles. All of our knowledge originates in perceptions. Perceptions, in turn, are either "impressions" or "ideas," and, since ideas are really only the "faint images" of impressions, all knowledge ultimately arises from impressions.[38]

Hume's characterization of these impressions is very similar to Locke's account of "simple ideas." In the first place, as the metaphor of impression suggests, the "impressions" are conceived as wholly passive. They are the docile registration of stimuli upon the recipient mind. Second, the impressions are believed by Hume to possess the clarity, the simplicity, the unassailability, of clear and distinct ideas. There is nothing vague or uncertain about them. "All impressions are clear and precise," he writes; and therefore "the ideas, which are copied from them, must be of the same nature, and can never, but from our fault, contain anything so dark and intricate. An idea is by its very nature weaker and fainter than an impression; but being in every other respect the same, cannot imply any great mystery."[39] Finally, the impressions are conceived, atomistically, as fully discrete and separable integers: "Every distinct perception, which enters into the composition of the mind, is a distinct existence, and is different, and distinguishable, and separable from every other perception, either contemporary or successive."[40]

Hume, we can say, constructed his entire world, in a philosophical sense, out of these passive, discrete, clear, and precise impressions. The fundamental premise of his thought was a subjectivized version of Hobbes's dictum that "the universe . . . is . . . body and that which is not body is no part of the universe."[41] Hume could easily have expressed his own vision in parallel language. All the human universe, he could have said, is an aggregation of impressions, and anything not formed of impressions is no part of the human universe.

A quick survey of Hume's basic conceptions makes this view of things quite clear. Ideas are but copies of impressions. The passions, desires, and emotions are but "impressions of reflexion."[42] The memory and the imagination are simply different modes of repeating impressions.[43] A belief is simply a peculiarly forceful or "vivacious" idea.[44] "All probable reasoning," moreover, "is nothing but a species of sensation."[45] Both the cogitative and the affective sides of the mind, in short, are various configurations of impressions.

It is not too surprising, then, that Hume's general account of the mind and his account of the self add up to nothing but more of the same thing: impressions, impressions, nothing but heaps of impressions. Of the mind, he writes: "what we call a mind is nothing but a heap or collection of different perceptions."[46] Personal identity suffers the same fate:

> When I enter most intimately into what I call *myself*, I always stumble on some particular perception or other, of heat or cold, light or shade, love or hatred, pain or pleasure. I never can catch *myself* at any time without a perception, and can never observe any thing but the perception. . . . I may [thus] venture to affirm of the rest of mankind, that they are nothing but a bundle or collection of different perceptions, which succeed each other with an inconceivable rapidity, and are in a perpetual flux and movement.[47]

Hume's philosophical writings are essentially an attempt to elaborate this account of the world, to consider its implications, and to render it plausible. His goals are both critical and constructive. Critically, he deploys his basic premises to undermine traditional accounts of knowledge and morals. Constructively, he tries to demonstrate the utility and adequacy of his own concepts for understanding the same phenomena.

The central problem Hume faced in his constructive efforts was posed by his atomistic nominalism. If the basic constituents of all experience are deemed to be the discrete, separable, corpuscular bits and pieces of things that Hume describes, then the obvious question arises: how do these bits and pieces hang together in the ways that they do? What are the principles behind the patterns and relationships that obtain among them? In short, in his accounts of both science and morals Hume was faced with the need to provide some principle or principles of coherence.

Regarding knowledge, Hume's fundamental critical claim is very simple and straightforward: namely, there is nothing in impressions or ideas considered in themselves that necessarily connects them with any other impressions or ideas. Observing that a full appreciation of this principle, inherent in his premises, undermines the usual accounts of knowledge, Hume expresses his critical principles (in language not fully respecting his ostensive phenomenalism) and their corrosive impact on traditional epistemology in the following way:

> Let men be once fully persuaded of these two principles, that there is nothing in any object, considered in itself, which can afford us a reason for drawing a conclusion beyond it; and that even after the observation of the frequent or constant conjunction of objects, we have no reason to draw any inference concerning any

object beyond those of which we have had experience; I say, let men once be convinced of these two principles, and this will throw them so loose from all common systems, that they will make no difficulty of receiving any, which may appear the most extra-ordinary.[48]

What then is the basis of knowledge? How and why are simple ideas related and aggregated into the complex ideas, generalizations, and causal claims that characterize scientific and philosophical discourse? Our simple and essentially discrete ideas, Hume declares, are related by the operation of an ultimately inexplicable attractive force whose operations in the mental world are analogous to the cohesive force of gravitation in the physical world:

Here is a kind of *Attraction*, which in the mental world will be found to have as extraordinary effects as in the natural, and to show itself in as many and as various forms. Its effects are every where conspicuous; but as to its causes, they are mostly un-known, and must be resolved into original qualities of human nature, which I pretend not to explain.[49]

This source of intellectual coherence, this "gentle force, which commonly prevails," Hume concedes, is simply a mental habit. Custom, and custom alone, is the real basis of human knowledge. We link up our impressions in the way we do solely because we are accustomed to do so:

Now as we call every thing *Custom*, which proceeds from a past repetition, without any new reasoning or conclusion, we may establish it as a certain truth, that all the belief, which follows upon any past impression, is derived solely from that origin.[50]

Elsewhere Hume expands somewhat on this characterization, but he does so consistent with the general claim that the association of ideas is, as he puts it concerning cause-and-effect claims, "more properly an act of the sensitive, than of the cogitative part of our natures."[51] Our reason, he says in one place, is "nothing but a wonderful and intelligible instinct in our souls,"[52] and elsewhere he asserts that our beliefs are essentially matters of taste:

'Tis not solely in poetry and music, we must follow our taste and sentiment, but likewise in philosophy. When I am convinced of any principle, 'tis only an idea, which strikes more strongly upon me. When I give the preference to one set of arguments above another, I do nothing but decide from my feeling concerning the superiority of their influence.[53]

If our knowledge, if one can call it that, is just a customary or habitual way of linking ideas, what provides it with any justification?

Why should anyone acquiesce in one set of habits rather than another? Why should our beliefs, being expressions of mere taste, not be absolutely arbitrary? Why not be a fanatic rather than a philosopher?

Hume gives several answers, at different levels, to these questions that his skeptical principles raise. His first-level response arises directly from his contention that belief is simply a peculiarly forceful or vivacious idea. I can give no ultimate grounds for preferring my own philosophical ideas, he says, other than the very strength with which they impinge upon me. Here I stand; I can't believe otherwise:

> After the most accurate and exact of my reasonings, I can give no reason why I should assent to it; and feel nothing but a *strong* propensity to consider objects *strongly* in that view, under which they appear to me.[54]

For Hume to be fully consistent, that is where the matter must stand. However, to someone not sufficiently impressed by the mere strength of Hume's personal beliefs, he offers two lines of proximate justification that might be more persuasive. Even apart from his own strong propensity to believe in the validity of his own mental habits, Hume says, these habits are by no means arbitrary. In the first place, following up on a notion that reason is a kind of "wonderful instinct," he suggests, in several key places of his argument, that these habits are "natural"—almost in a Scholastic sense of that term. "Nature," he tells us, "may certainly produce whatever can arise from habit: Nay, habit is nothing but one of the principles of nature, and derives all its force from that origin."[55] Then, when introducing his supposition about the "gentle force" of association of ideas, he suggests that it, too, is grounded in nature. It is "nature," he writes, that "in a manner points out to every one those simple ideas, which are most proper to be united in a complex one."[56] Should anyone object that superstitions and other sorts of discredited beliefs are also natural, Hume responds that these ideas are natural only "in the same sense, that a malady is said to be natural; as arising from natural causes, though it be contrary to health, the most agreeable and most natural situation of man."[57]

Hume's other line of proximate justification for assenting to his principles picks up from this health/malady distinction. This second line of argument is pragmatic, conventionalist, and (to borrow an execrable phrase) "value-oriented." Acceptable habits of mind, he argues, are those that are in a practical sense necessary. Without them—for example, without the habit of reasoning about cause and effect—human life would be practically impossible. The principles

that philosophy receives are "permanent, irresistible, and universal"; the principles it rejects are those that are "neither unavoidable
to mankind, nor necessary, or so much as useful in the conduct of
life."[58]

The principles accepted by philosophy, then, are those that are
useful and agreeable. They are justified, as pragmatists would later
say, because they "work." In a remarkable passage at the conclusion of Volume One of the *Treatise,* moreover, Hume makes it clear
that the pragmatic criteria that recommend philosophy are not
merely academic. That is, the principles of philosophy are preferable
to other principles not simply because they are more intellectually
useful; they are preferable also because of their superior political
and social consequences. "Concerning the choice of our guide," he
writes, we

> ought to prefer that which is safest and most agreeable. And in this
> respect I make bold to recommend philosophy, and shall not
> scruple to give it preference to superstition of every kind or de-
> nomination. For as superstition arises naturally and easily from
> the popular opinions of mankind, it seizes more strongly on the
> mind, and is often able to disturb us in the conduct of our lives and
> actions. Philosophy on the contrary, if just, can present us only
> with mild and moderate sentiments; and if false and extravagant, its
> opinions are merely the objects of a cold and general speculation,
> and seldom go so far as to interrrupt the course of our natural pro-
> pensities.[59]

Thus, though Hume is commonly known for his insistence on the
"logical gap" between "is" and "ought," he is by no means above
connecting them intimately—though not deductively. That is, one of
his major recommendations for his view of what "is" refers to its
normative consequences: accept philosophy, he argues, because it is
safe and agreeable. And conversely, we shall see, his moral theory is
very closely tied to what "is." Indeed, the whole point of his constructive inquiry in ethics is to base the principles of human action
on "fact and observation."

Hume's Displacement of Moral Reason

Hume's moral theory, to which we now turn, runs in close parallel to
his account of theoretical reason. His account of "science," as we
have seen, began with a critical skepticism that undermined traditional realist accounts of knowledge. Having demolished these traditional bases for accrediting human knowledge, Hume substituted a
conventionalism allegedly rooted in "natural" necessity and utility.
Knowledge was depicted as a product of mental custom or habit; but

these habits were justified by their productivity (political as well as intellectual) and by their apparent unavoidability in the conduct of human life. Hume's views on ethics are formally very similar. He begins with a critical argument that eventuates in the rejection of traditional moral theory and in a profound skepticism about the role of reason in arriving at moral norms. He then tries to reestablish moral distinctions on a conventionalist foundation, depicted as grounded in the circumstances and necessities of human life.

Hume's moral theory is commonly and quite correctly viewed as a milestone in the growth of contemporary moral noncognitivism. What is not so widely appreciated is that he is by no means an ethical relativist, nor is he an adherent of the "emotive theory of ethics" in the contemporary sense. He indeed denied that reason is the source of moral distinctions, but he nevertheless believed that moral distinctions exist that are universally applicable and not arbitrary. This important side of Hume's moral theory is easily obscured, and he is consequently misconstrued by those who, taking some of his more striking and memorable skeptical utterances out of context, interpret them according to subsequent philosophical premises foreign to Hume himself. This misconstruction highlights a very important truth about the import of Hume's views, but it is nonetheless a half-truth.

The content and the ultimate impact of Hume's moral theory cannot be adequately understood unless we realize, first, that his critique of previous moral theory is not singular but plural and that its different strands need to be analytically disentangled; second, that his critique is not so destructive of traditional moral theory as is commonly supposed or as he himself supposed (because he misconstrued this theory); third, that his constructive moral theory is not so radical or entirely novel as he presents it and as is therefore often supposed, even though it does contain some significant new departures; and fourth, that even allowing for these reservations about the radicalism and novelty of his ideas, it is nonetheless entirely appropriate to see Hume as providing the framework for the radical moral subjectivism and relativism of a later day.

There are several distinguishable dimensions in Hume's attack on the long-standing characterization of moral rules as precepts of reason. These different dimensions, or components, of Hume's critique overlap in some respects, and they are formally complementary. Though together they add up to a relatively coherent whole, the various parts of the critique need to be kept analytically distinct, for they stand on somewhat different foundations, and changes in the premises on which these foundations stand would affect them unequally. Moreover, identifying the different dimensions of Hume's critique helps to clarify how he avoided the complete moral subjectivism that eventually issued from his ideas.

The first level of his critique was purely logical. It is the simplest and most straightforward part of his attack, and it is also one of the most commonly cited. Hume simply points to the logical distinction between "is" and "ought" statements. Given this logical gap, he observes the impossibility of deducing the latter from the former. Scrupulous observation of this simple and fundamental logical precept, he suggests, would by itself lead to the disqualification of most previous moral doctrines—especially those that purported to base morals on reason. The classic statement of this criticism comes as an apparent concluding afterthought, though one clearly deemed to be of profound moment, in the opening section of Volume Three of the *Treatise*.

> I cannot forbear adding to these reasonings an observation which may, perhaps be found of some importance. In every system of morality, which I have hitherto met with, I have always remarked, that the author proceeds for some time in the ordinary way of reasoning, and establishes the being of a God, or some observations concerning human affairs; when of a sudden I am surprised to find, that instead of the usual copulations of propositions, *is*, and *is not*, I meet with no proposition that is not connected with an *ought*, or an *ought not*. This change is imperceptible; but is, however, of the last consequence. For as this *ought*, or *ought not*, expresses some new relation or affirmation, 'tis necessary that it should be observed and explained; and that a reason be given, for what seems altogether inconceivable, how this new relation can be a deduction from others, which are entirely different from it. But as authors do not commonly use this precaution, I shall presume to recommend it to the readers; and am persuaded, that this small attention would subvert all the vulgar systems of morality, and let us see, that the distinction of vice and virtue is not founded merely on the relations of objects, nor is perceived by reason.[60]

It is often implied, especially by contemporary positivists, that this is the sum and substance of Hume's critique. Moreover, it is also suggested that this is all that need be said on the subject—that by itself this very simple argument suffices to settle the issue of the moral competence of reason by denying it altogether. An "ought" cannot be deduced from an "is," the argument runs; therefore moral assertions must be considered ventings of emotions rather than claims about reality.

This interpretation is understandably appealing to some noncognitivists, since it seems to ground their position on a very uncomplicated and unassailable foundation. It is, however, afflicted with several very substantial weaknesses—weaknesses that adversely affect our comprehension of both Hume and the issue at hand.

In the first place, this interpretation carries with it a patently ludicrous account of intellectual history. It implies that all premodern philosophers, including and perhaps especially Aristotle, were incompetents unable to distinguish imperatives from declaratives and incapable of recognizing invalid syllogisms. Hume, in his youthful arrogance and polemical enthusiasm, might indeed have wished to convey that impression, and there are today those who are sufficiently parochial, credulous, and philosophically illiterate to entertain such a view. This rather astonishing account of the classical tradition in philosophy, however, does not merit a serious hearing, and any interpretation that implies or relies on such an account has to be suspect from the very beginning.

Next, this interpretation makes it rather unclear why Hume, as the discoverer of the fundamental logical disparity of "is" and "ought," goes on to develop a serious and elaborate moral theory of his own. Instead of now simply dusting his hands of moral inquiry, he attempts in fact to provide an "experimental" (today we would say "empirical") foundation for moral judgments. That is, he himself tried to create a system of morality grounded on "fact and observation."[61]

Finally, this attempt to reduce the whole issue to a simple logical distinction overlooks, or at best fails to deal adequately with, the fact that many moral claims are embodied in declarative language—e.g., "This is good," "He is a just man," and so on. Moral claims so expressed clearly cannot be set aside *solely* on the basis of the distinction between "is" and "ought" statements. The standard response to this problem is that these claims are "pseudo-propositions," improperly and misleadingly cast in descriptive form. To dismiss the meaningfulness of propositions like these, however, clearly requires some principle of discrimination and disqualification that goes beyond mere syntax or pure logic. This supplementary principle is the distinction between "fact" and "value." However, this important distinction cannot itself be reduced to the logical distinction between "is" and "ought" without becoming a worthless redundancy. Instead, this distinction between fact and value, which is necessarily called into play to render the is/ought distinction nontrivial, must rest on some other foundation. Specifically, it must rely on some substantive premises that contain within them the criteria for ascertaining and delimiting the category of "facts."

Many of Hume's philosophical descendants—for example, the

garden variety of positivists who heavily populate the social sciences—fail to appreciate this problem. As a result, they try, inadmissibly, to have it both ways: they rely on the fact/value distinction when the results of the straightforward is/ought distinction are not acceptable to them, but they think that the fact/value distinction is reducible to, and hence requires no justification beyond, the simple is/ought distinction.

Hume himself, whatever polemical overkill he may have indulged in, was clearly aware that the matter was not that easily settled. Accordingly, the major part of his critique of traditional moral realism is concerned with an elaboration of the premises that make the is/ought distinction nontrivial. It is an account of the world, reason, and man that explains why most previous moral theories are unacceptable and then suggests an alternative approach. The major portion of his critique is therefore devoted to his complementary claims about ontology, anthropology, and epistemology proper. These may be considered in any order, since it is neither clear nor crucial which comes first, either logically or temporally. Each is compatible with the others, and they are all mutually reinforcing.

Hume's central epistemological claim is that reason is "perfectly inert," "wholly inactive," and therefore "utterly impotent."[62] Reason is a faculty that does two things: it registers impressions and compares ideas derived from these impressions. "Moral distinctions, therefore, are not the offspring of reason," he concludes, because they can arise directly and solely neither from the comparison of ideas nor from the "inferring of matter of fact."[63]

Hume has an easy time proving that moral distinctions cannot arise purely from the comparison of ideas. His argument is quite simple. As he puts it, "If you assert, that vice and virtue consist in relations susceptible of certainty and demonstration, you must confine yourself to those four relations, which alone admit of that degree of evidence; and in that case you run into absurdities, from which you will never be able to extricate yourself."[64] The hope that was ofttimes expressed but never fulfilled, that morality might be "geometricized," that it might become a demonstrative science based on undeniable axioms, was simply a chimera.

The second part of Hume's thesis about the incompetency of reason to provide moral distinctions is more complicated, and it trades on the ontological component of his thought. Moral distinctions cannot arise from the second operation of understanding—the recording of matters of fact—Hume argues, because "matters of fact" do not possess any properties from which these distinctions could arise. The heart of his argument on this issue occurs in the following passage:

But can there be any difficulty in proving, that vice and virtue are not matters of fact, whose existence we can infer by reason? Take any action allowed to be vicious: wilful murder, for instance. Examine it in all lights, and see if you can find that matter of fact, or real existence, which you call vice. In which-ever way you take it, you find only certain passions, motives, volitions, and thoughts. There is no other matter of fact in the case. The vice entirely escapes you, as long as you consider the object. You can never find it, till you turn your reflection into your own breast, and find a sentiment of disapprobation, which arises in you, towards this action. Here is a matter of fact; but 'tis the object of feeling, not of reason. It lies in yourself, not in the object.[65]

In this very important argument, Hume's ontology comes out of the shadows to make its presence and significance felt. The world, he presumes, is isomorphic with the impressions, on the whole. Like the impressions, the world is an aggregate of separate, discrete, static bits and pieces of things. These are the "objects" or "real existences" that constitute "matters of fact." Given this account of "objective reality," of what is "out there" in the world, it is clear that a lot of things previously considered real and objective cannot possibly be objective. Instead, if they exist at all, they must exist in the "interior space" of the mind ("it lies in yourself"). And, as Hume insists, the referents of moral terms like vice and virtue must be among these internal phenomena. Try as you may, you cannot put your finger on some discrete, static thing out there in the world that corresponds to "vice" or "virtue." Since, then, there are no moral entities, moral terms must denominate a species of feeling rather than a species of external reality. Therefore, "When you pronounce any action or character to be vicious, you mean nothing, but that from the constitution of your nature you have a feeling or sentiment of blame from the contemplation of it."[66]

The correlate of this ontology and epistemology—this conception of the world and the operations of the understanding—in Hume's philosophical anthropology, his model of man, is his notable reassessment of the relationship between reason and passion. Hume's conception of the world and of the understanding results in the depiction of reason as a purely passive faculty. His "reason," one might say, amounts to a retina linked with a computer: impressions impinge on it from the external world of objects, and it compares the ideas copied from these impressions. That is all.

A great many of the features assigned by an earlier philosophical tradition to reason—i.e., to *logos*-rationality—therefore had to be reassigned by Hume if he was not to deny their existence altogether. The account of the formation of general terms, for example, was not problematic for this earlier tradition. *Logos*-rationality was simply deemed to be capable of perceiving essences. For Hume, of course, there were no essences out there, and general terms could therefore not be perceptions of reason. Their origin and status thus become rather problematic and mysterious for Hume. General terms arise from the collection of discrete individual ideas, and these ideas "are thus collected by a kind of magical faculty in the soul, which, though it be always most perfect in the greatest geniuses, and is properly what we call a genius, is however inexplicable by the utmost efforts of human understanding."[67]

If the capacity of reason to perceive essences, a capacity claimed for *logos*-rationality, must be denied by Hume and the capacity for induction rendered mysterious, the self-activating quality of *logos*-rationality is also denied. *Logos*-rationality was axiological. It was rooted in the *conatus* of a rational contingent creature toward Being. It had an "erotic" dimension of its own. Hume's retina-plus-computer model of reason and his exteriorized model of "Being" leave this conception, too, quite unintelligible. But here Hume has no need for recourse to some "magical faculty in the soul." The motives behind knowing are simply reassigned to the category of the passions. All motives are varieties of passions. The "eros" of *logos*-rationality is no longer the distinctive self-activating principle of reason; instead it becomes "curiosity"—one passion among many—which is explained by Hume in characteristically utilitarian fashion.[68]

Since all the wellsprings of human action lie in the passions, Hume concludes that the traditional appeal to reason to control the passions is based on a hopeless misconception. Nothing wholly inactive can govern or control anything. In fact, being completely inert, reason cannot even conflict with the passions, much less govern them. "We speak not strictly and philosophically when we talk of the combat of passion and of reason," he writes. "Reason is, and ought only to be the slave of the passions."[69] The familiar phenomenon of internal conflict between competing inclinations is not a clash between reason and passion but a clash between different passions. Specifically, it is the warfare between the "calm" and the "violent" passions.

This clash is still a real and important one for Hume. The calm passions are necessary to the creation of a viable social order (playing here for Hume the sobering and civilizing role Hobbes accorded to the fear of violent death). Reason, however, is banished from the seat of governance. The chariot of Plato's *Phaedrus* is driven no longer by reason but by calm appetites.

Hume's Experimental Morality

Hume's apparent demolition of traditional moral theory, it should be noted, is not as complete or as devastating as he seems to think or as others following him have sometimes assumed. He demolishes one type of moral rationalism, but it is not the classical understanding of practical reason and its role in moral conduct; instead, it is something of a straw man produced by the unreflective use of established terms in a radically different philosophical context, which changes their meaning. It should be fairly clear, for example, that Hume is getting this kind of straw man in his sights when he says of classical moral rationalism: "All these systems concur in the opinion, that morality, like truth, is discerned merely by ideas, and by their juxtaposition and comparison."[70] There is little resemblance between this characterization and, let us say, Aristotle's account of *phronēsis*.

Since Hume's critical efforts are not as destructive of classical ideas as he imagines, it is not too surprising that his constructive moral theory is not quite so totally novel as he suggests, despite its terminological radicalism. There are indeed some important new departures in Hume's view of ethics. Other parts of his doctrine, however, are innovative more in language than in content. The furniture in Hume's ethical theory is not all new; some consists of older pieces that have wound up in different rooms because of changes effected in the floor plan of the cosmos by the philosophical revolutionaries of the seventeenth century. Slipcover an old couch, move it from the living room into the den, call it a "daybed"; it may look different in the new surroundings, but still does some of the same old things. Thus, in Hume's theory, the reflective capacities of reason reappear in the time-delayed passions of a "calm" mind. "Ought" and "is" may be logically divorced, but norms of conduct are adduced from fact and observation and deemed valid for all human beings. Even the much-maligned laws of nature show up in a new guise.

The content of Hume's moral theory is hedonistic and utilitarian. Herein lies his principal substantive departure from the Christian and Platonic-Aristotelian traditions. This aspect of his ethics is itself, of course, not wholly without precedent. Had Epicurus been a public-spirited English gentleman of the eighteenth century, he would greatly have resembled the genial Mr. Hume. Hume is no relativist, however. Moral tastes he conceives to be common in normal human beings. They are not idiosyncratic and individual. Like traditional moralists, therefore, Hume believes that he can identify universal standards of good and evil. What is different here from the conventional view concerns the origins of these standards and the proper means of discerning them: where conventional moral theory depicted these norms as originating in the external world, Hume grounds them in "internal" sentiments; and where conventional theory thought they were found by reason, Hume wants to find them "experimentally."

Moral distinctions, Hume argues, not being precepts of reason, are a species of feeling or taste. "Since vice and virtue are not discoverable merely by reason, or the comparison of ideas, it must be by some impression or sentiment they occasion, that we are able to mark the difference betwixt them."[71] These defining sentiments, he suggests, are not at all difficult to identify. Virtue makes us feel good; it is an "agreeable" sensation. Vice makes us feel bad; it is a sensation of "uneasiness." Hence the moral distinction between good and bad should properly be conceived as one particular species of the difference between pleasure and pain. "An action, or sentiment, or character is virtous or vicious; why? because its view causes a pleasure or uneasiness of a particular kind."[72]

In saying that the pleasure and pain that distinguish good and bad are "of a particular kind," Hume means not that moral tastes are sui generis or that they transcend the ordinary sources of pleasure and pain. He means to point to the peculiarly general quality of the moral sensations. It is their public character that makes the moral pleasures and pains distinctive. Moral distinctions are not peculiarly self-referring. Linguistically, they do not reverse themselves, like the pronouns "me" and "you," depending on the speaker. The claim that moral distinctions are a variety of pleasure and pain does not, then, entail for Hume the consequence that they are merely another name for self-interest. The logic of moral discourse requires that they refer to general interests.[73]

Since moral terms are expressions of approbation and disapprobation arising from pleasure and pain, and since they refer to general rather than uniquely individual interest, Hume is logically required to identify some self-transcending sentiment able to lend these general interests their pleasurable quality. This sentiment he finds in what he calls "sympathy." Sympathy for Hume is a close kin to Rousseau's "natural pity." It is a natural tendency to participate vicariously and with like affect in the experience of fellow human beings. Sympathy "takes us so far out of ourselves, as to give the same pleasure or uneasiness in the characters of others, as if they had a tendency to our own advantage or loss."[74] Sympathetic sentiments are to be found "even in persons the most depraved and selfish." And even though the intensity of sympathy "is much fainter than our concern for ourselves,"[75] it nonetheless, as a universally active sentiment, is an adequate motivational base for moral distinctions that refer to public good.

We can summarize Hume's theory of ethics in this way: moral distinctions are terms that represent the perception of usefulness or agreeableness of persons or actions either to particular persons or, through the power of sympathy, to mankind.

Although he characterizes moral distinctions as expressions of "taste," "sentiment," or "feeling," Hume is by no means an ethical relativist or nihilist. His version of emotivism does not imply, for him, that moral distinctions are not real and meaningful. At the beginning of his *Enquiry Concerning the Principles of Morals* he writes:

> Those who have denied the reality of moral distinctions may be ranked among the disingenuous disputants; nor is it conceivable, that any human creature could ever seriously believe, that all characters and actions were alike entitled to the affection and regard of everyone. . . . Let a man's insensibility be ever so great, he must often be touched with the images of Right and Wrong; and let his prejudices be ever so obstinate, he must observe, that others are susceptible of like impressions. The only way, therefore, of converting an antagonist of this kind, is to leave him to himself. For, finding that nobody keeps up the controversy with him, it is possible he will, at last, of himself, from mere weariness, come over to the side of common sense and reason.[76]

The theoretical basis for this conclusion of "common sense and reason" as to the meaningfulness of moral distinctions lies in a crucial basic assumption Hume retains from the earlier philosophical tradition that he rejects in other respects; namely, he remains secure in a belief that human nature is "constant and universal." The tastes, sentiments, or feelings that lead to the concepts of vice and virtue are not random or idiosyncratic. They arise from "the original fabric and formation of the human mind, which is naturally adapted to receive them." Moral distinctions stem from "some internal sense or feeling, *which nature has made universal in the whole species*."[77]

Recall, then, for a moment, Hume's concise formulation of his ethical emotivism: "so that when you pronounce any action or character to be vicious, you mean nothing, but that *from the constitution of your nature* you have a feeling or sentiment of blame from the contemplation of it."[78] For a contemporary emotivist who sees moral statements as nothing more than expressions of individual "preference," the phrase "from the constitution of your nature" is a useless intrusion; his understanding of morals is aptly expressed without its presence in the sentence. For Hume, however, the phrase is far from being a meaningless redundancy. It stands there to represent his underlying conviction, which has significant consequences for his ethical theory, that moral distinctions "express those *universal* sentiments of censure and approbation, which arise from humanity."[79]

Fundamental moral principles, such as the principle of justice, Hume therefore can assert, are the product of feeling and convention, but they are certainly not arbitrary, dispensable, or significantly variable. The needs and inclinations arising from human nature being constant, all human societies are, in a sense, naturally—i.e., unavoidably—led to establish these standards of behavior. These virtues are universally valid, then, in the sense that they arise from "the circumstances and necessity of mankind."[80] So long as one clearly understands what one is saying, Hume allows that it is not even inappropriate to refer to these unavoidable moral norms as laws of nature. "Mankind is an inventive species," he writes,

> and where an invention is obvious and absolutely necessary, it may as properly be said to be natural as any thing that proceeds immediately from original principles, without the intervention of thought and reflection. Though the rules of justice be *artificial,* they are not *arbitrary.* Nor is the expression improper to call them *Laws of Nature;* if by natural we understand what is common to any species, or even if we confine it to mean what is inseparable from the species.[81]

The belief that human nature is constant and universal, together with the companion claim that certain standards of behavior are absolutely necessary and inseparable from the species, provides the basis for Hume's project of placing morality on an "experimental" footing. Just as he can adduce principles of justice that are tantamount to laws of nature even after he rejects the concept of natural law, so also he intends to find valid moral principles by empirical investigation even after insisting on the logical gap between is and ought.

Hume conceives his experimental method as follows. Good is what men praise and esteem; evil is what men blame and condemn. Therefore, in order to discover what is good and what is evil, we should simply conduct a general survey to find out what attributes and actions are universally praised and condemned. Because human nature is uniform, Hume assumes that these findings will be consistent, regardless of variations in time, place, and culture. "The quick sensibility, which, on this head [i.e., which assigns praise and blame], is so universal among mankind, gives a philosopher sufficient assurance, that he can never be considerably mistaken in framing the catalogue [of virtues and vices]."[82] If any doubt or ambiguity arises, moreover, the philosopher can even consult his own feelings on the matter, since these feelings presumably arise not from his personal whims but from the constitution of his universally constant human nature.[83]

When this survey is completed, when the philosopher has finished "collecting and arranging the estimable or blameable qualities of men," he need only analyze these two empirically ascertained lists in order to arrive at a correct theory of morals. To understand the foundation of good and evil, that is, the student of morals need only identify what the items on the list of virtues all have in common and do the same with the items on the list of vices. These common properties will then be "those universal principles, from which all censure and approbation is ultimately derived," and the theory of morals thus derived will be "founded on fact and observation."[84]

On the basis of his own survey of estimable and blameable qualities, and after looking for the common properties of these conventionally acclaimed virtues and vices, Hume concludes that good qualities are those "useful or agreeable to ourselves or others." Vices are qualities that, on the contrary, are "pernicious and dangerous." Thus, suggests Hume, his hedonistic utilitarianism is confirmed experimentally. Virtue is revealed in all her loveliness as the gentle mistress of the *dulce* and the *utile*, not as the stern taskmaster depicted by some.

> The dismal dress falls off, with which many divines, and some philosophers, have covered her; and nothing appears but gentleness, humanity, beneficence, affability; nay, even at proper intervals, play, frolic, and gaiety. She talks not of useless austerities and rigors, suffering and self-denial. She declares that her sole purpose is to make her votaries and all mankind, during every instant of their existence, if possible, cheerful and happy.[85]

A critic might well protest that this acknowledgment that "many divines and some philosophers" hold views of what is virtuous quite different from Hume's raises a real problem for his theory of morals. Hume claims to be presenting a view of morals based on "fact and observation," i.e., on a straightforward report of universally praised and condemned qualities. Yet he then turns around and tries to discredit some of the same empirically existing moral sentiments from which he allegedly derived his own hedonist utilitarianism. How can he have it both ways?

To this reproach Hume would have supplied a characteristic Enlightenment response. Superstitions, unenlightened prejudice, and false religion can all create a kind of "false consciousness" that distorts and corrupts the sentiments of people who are afflicted by these evils. Moral sentiments distorted by such superstitious misconceptions are therefore not properly deemed to be natural and hence are not to be included in the "experimental" survey of moral feelings upon which the theory of morals should rest. Hume's Gallup Poll of men's agreeable and uneasy feelings is not based on a random sample; it is a sample of only uncorrupted moral tastes.

Hume's method, then, is not, strictly speaking, circular. However, it does clearly rely on a prior premise that there are such things as false beliefs, that adherence to them can corrupt the moral sentiments, and that the philosopher can identify those whose sentiments are thus corrupted and exclude them from his "experimental" survey. Only "men of sense" are to be asked for their views. When this nonrandom survey is carried out, Hume is convinced, his claim that "virtuous" means "useful or agreeable to ourselves or others" will be vindicated. No other quality will be accepted as a real basis of merit, he writes,

> where men judge of things by their natural, unprejudiced reason, without the delusive glosses of superstition and false religion. Celibacy, fasting, penance, mortification, self-denial, humility, silence, solitude, and the whole train of monkish virtues; for what reason are they everywhere rejected by men of sense, but because they serve to no manner of purpose; neither advance a man's fortune in the world, nor render him a more valuable member of society; neither qualify him for the entertainment of company, nor increase his power of self-enjoyment? We observe, on the contrary, that they cross all these desirable ends; stupefy the understanding and harden the heart, obscure the fancy and sour the temper. We justly, therefore, transfer them to the opposite column, and place them in the catalogue of vices; nor has superstition force sufficient among men of the world, to pervert entirely these natural sentiments. A gloomy, hair-brained enthusiast, after his death, may have a place in the calendar; but will scarcely ever be admitted, when alive, into intimacy and society, except by those who are as delirious and dismal as himself.[86]

The substance of Hume's ethical theory, whatever its legitimate virtues and insights, is rather mundane, parochial, and reductive. He construes moral norms as precepts that enable an individual or a group to get along well in the world. Though it would not be wholly fair to Hume to see his ethics as tantamount to the nostrums of, say, a Dale Carnegie self-improvement text, it is nonetheless clear that his conception of virtue barely exceeds being a set of precepts conducive to prosperity and happiness. He makes virtue such a gentle mistress that she seems little more than the handmaiden of calm and reflective self-interest. Modes of behavior and institutional arrangements deemed generally useful to society are pretty much beyond reproach by Hume's account. The concrete applications of his theory are thus, not too surprisingly, marked by complacency and conservatism. Justice, for example, becomes reduced essentially to useful property relationships, and, by this standard, Hume sees no problem whatever with the established pattern of property distribution in eighteenth-century England.

Even by his own professed standards for testing a moral theory, Hume's reduction of the good to the useful produces some problems. A convincing account of morals must, on his view, conform to the actual moral feelings of men of sense. There should, then, if his theory is to be acceptable, be no great difference between our emotive responses to virtue and to utility. But that is generally not true. We may value what is merely useful or convenient; we do not, however, accord to the merely functional the kind of esteem we feel for the morally right. Hume, who is often his own best critic, recognizes this difficulty at the conclusion of his *Treatise* and simply confesses his inability to deal with it:

> On the other hand, a convenient house, and a virtuous character, cause not the same feeling of approbation; even though the source of our approbation be the same, and flow from sympathy and an idea of their utility. There is something very inexplicable in this variation of our feelings; but 'tis what we have experience of with regard to all our passions and sentiments.[87]

Despite its substantive deficiencies, the formal structure of his theory is remarkably ingenious. The formal account of ethics he offers may be, in fact, the only possible constructive response to the philosophical problem he faced. Once the axiological dimension is removed from reason and once nature is turned into *res extensa,* a theory of morality must turn into a phenomenology of the passions. There is nothing else left for it to be, unless it can be, as Kant thought, a set of imperatives based on a priori principles. Hume at least recognized this necessity, had the courage to affirm it, and tried to carry out the project as he understood it.

Hume's Philosophical Incoherence

In this respect, Hume escapes the philosophical bankruptcy concerning normative knowledge that so dramatically afflicted John Locke. Locke continued to affirm the conventional wisdom that reason had the capacity to ascertain moral truths, and he relied on this presumed capacity of the natural light of reason in his social theory. Yet he could not, given his simultaneous acceptance of empiricist sensationism as an epistemological doctrine, explain how reason could possibly possess this competence. Hume avoids this philosophical incoherence and solves Locke's immediate problem by disavowing the moral competence of reason and locating morality in the anatomy of human emotions.

In another sense, however, Hume does not really solve Locke's problem so much as he transfers it to another plane. For Hume's thought suffers from the same kind of tensions that wracked Locke's philosophy. They simply appear at a deeper level. Hume's moral theory relies as much as Locke's belief in natural law on assumptions carried over from traditional philosophy—assumptions that are in dissonance with the newer philosophical ideas that serve as their integument. There is still, to recall an earlier metaphor, some old wine that Hume tries to pour into his new wineskins.

The tension in Locke's thought is especially apparent because it occurs internally, within his epistemology: one of his professed beliefs about the range of knowledge conflicts head on with his basic premises about knowledge. In Hume's case, this is no longer a problem; his account of moral phenomena no longer conflicts directly with the sensationist epistemology that he, like Locke, embraces, because he locates these phenomena in the presumably noncognitive realm of the passions. The incoherence found in Locke's epistemology nonetheless recurs with equal gravity between Hume's philosophical anthropology and his ontology. That is, Hume's account of human nature is hardly supportable by his account of reality.

The fundamental problem for Hume's anthropology can be formulated this way: his account of reality leads logically to his characterization of the human person (either as "self" or as "mind") as a "heap of impressions," but it seems altogether inconceivable that a mere heap of passive, discrete impressions could possibly possess the characteristics Hume ascribes to human nature. He simply relies on his reader's, and his own, common-sense recognition that human beings do in fact have certain passions and moral feelings, such as pride, sympathy, and so on; no one, therefore, would think to challenge the assumption that these phenomena exist. Whenever Hume does not simply assume the reality of these human attributes, however—when, instead, he tries to account for them or even to describe them in terms of his underlying ontology—the incapacities and incoherences of his thought become almost painfully obvious.

These problems surface both in Hume's attempt to characterize certain passions in terms of his basic world view and in the moral theory he bases on his theory of the passions.

The passions of pride and humility, for example, play an important role in Hume's psychology, yet his account of them in the *Treatise* is surely one of the most curious and ineffectual in all of philosophical literature. Pride and humility are, like all "mental" phenomena in Hume's theory, types of impressions. Specifically, they are "indirect" and "violent" "impressions of reflexion," or "secondary" impressions, Hume tells us. The mind, which is a "heap of impressions," feels one of these passions when it takes as an object its own self in association with its perception of some other quality that causes pleasure or pain. If the mind perceives itself in relation to a pleasurable quality, pride occurs. If the self is perceived in relation to a painful quality, humility occurs.

The self, however, is "that succession of related ideas and impressions of which we have an intimate memory and consciousness" (Hume never explains in what sense ideas and impressions are "related" or how "consciousness" is not a redundancy in his scheme once "impressions" are mentioned). Hence pride, once the full definitions are inserted, becomes a secondary impression, occurring in a heap of impressions, that somehow reflects on that same heap of impressions in concurrence with an immediate impression of pleasure from a related object. Surely, if we refrain from supplementing it by everyday experience, this account loses all plausibility. Considered strictly on its own terms, it is hardly conceivable how a heap of impressions, related in an unspecified (and probably, in Hume's philosophical vocabulary, unspecifiable) way, could have the capacity to accomplish such a feat or, equally, could have the capacity to be so affected by it. As if that difficulty were not enough, Hume compounds the problem in his attempt to make the whole phenomenon explicable:

> That we may comprehend this the better, we must suppose that nature has given to the organs of the human mind a certain disposition fitted to produce a peculiar impression or emotion, which we call pride: To this emotion she assigned a certain idea, *viz.* that of *self,* which it never fails to produce. . . . All this needs no proof. 'Tis evident we never should be possessed of that passion, were there not a disposition of mind proper for it.[88]

As a philosophical argument, this recourse to some peculiar agency of nature that needs no proof because its effects are evident is about on a par with saying that opium makes us sleepy because of its dormative properties and that the existence of these dormative properties needs no proof because it is evident that otherwise opium wouldn't make us sleepy. Hume's account renders these passions, in short, inexplicable as well as inconceivable.

The remarkably strained, even ludicrous, quality of this important part of the *Treatise* is no accident. Nor is it the product of simple ineptitude on Hume's part. Instead, it is the unavoidable consequence of trying to account for a complex passion of reflective consciousness on the basis of a reductive and static ontology like that of modern empiricism.

The same problem afflicts Hume's moral theory, although in a somewhat less evident fashion. Here the Humean claim that seems inconceivable on Humean premises is the contention that there is a constant and universal human nature, possessing a fixed constitution and perennial needs. If this claim cannot be supported, the whole force and logic of Hume's constructive moral theory collapses with it.

The "experimental method of reasoning" Hume commends to us as the fitting approach to moral theory depends on the presumption of a fixed human nature. It is a search to discover "empirically" those qualities that are universally approved and disapproved by an uncorrupted human sensibility. These universally approved and disapproved qualities are, then, the experimentally ascertained "good" and "bad," and the only remaining task for a moral theory is to identify the common properties of the various items on the inventory lists of good and bad qualities. But if human nature is not constant and universal, if the emotive responses of undeluded men are not fundamentally unanimous, the whole project makes no sense. Hume has to assume, as he does, that moral taste is, beneath superficial diversity, essentially the same in all men—that beneath the babble of human voices there is some constant refrain.

The assumptions that sustain this faith, and therefore sustain also the whole project of an experimental moral theory dependent upon it, actually amount to a barely submerged quasi-Aristotelian streak in Hume's thought. As a result, his allegedly novel understanding of moral theory in fact relies on ideas that are not at all new, that are ostensively abandoned, and that are not really compatible with his own fundamental philosophical perspective.

These assumptions surface in a casual but decisive way whenever Hume talks about the relationship between human nature and the origin of the moral virtues. It becomes clear in this context that Hume's "virtues" are qualities universally approved because of their relationship to the *essence* of man. Hume may conceive all the world, in the abstract, as a congeries of impressions, but when he speaks of human nature he is talking in terms of an Aristotelian substance—that is, a teleological pattern of order peculiar to and definitive of a given species of being. How else can one make sense of certain of his phrases that arise in this context, such as the "internal frame and constitution of animals" or the "peculiar nature" of the "several classes and orders of existence"?[89] What else could be the "humanity" he alludes to when he writes that, "Whatever conduct gains my approbation, by touching my humanity, procures also the applause of all mankind, by affecting the same principle in them"? And what other than essential properties, in the Aristotelian sense, are those traits "common to" or "inseparable from the species"?[90] Hume likewise smuggles in a quasi-Aristotelian notion of potentiality, particularly in accounting for the origin of the moral passions. For example, he assigns as the reason for the affections underlying the concepts of vice and virtue "the original fabric and formation of the human mind, which is naturally adapted to receive them."[91] In the concept of "necessity," which he rather offhandedly but significantly deploys when accounting for an artificial virtue such as justice, he again imports a latent teleology at a crucial point in his argument. The virtue of justice, he tells us, arises from "the circumstances and necessity of mankind," and the rules of justice are an invention that is both "obvious and absolutely necessary."[92] One might ask, what kind of necessity is this? Clearly, the existence of rules of justice is not a logical necessity: no rule of logic is violated by the empirical absence of rules of justice. It is not a causal necessity: one can easily find instances where men have existed with only the law of the jungle—sheer force—to govern their relationship. What Hume is really saying is that rules of justice are "necessary" in the sense that mankind cannot fulfill its potential apart from them—that man, apart from justice, is not really man but only the worst (Aristotle) or most miserable (Hobbes) of animals. Under the cover of his cryptic notion of "necessity," then, Hume virtually translates into his new idiom Aristotle's contention that man is by nature a political animal. Man produces the social institutions of law and property not "naturally" in the strict sense, Hume would say; but man does so "artificially, *though necessarily*."[93] On the basis of the teleology that is implicit here, Hume can then, just like Aristotle, go on to base his social ethic on what he deemed necessary for the fulfillment of man's natural end.

This slightly adapted Aristotelian (or Stoic or Christian) notion of an "essence of humanity," common to all times and places, then, provided the rationale for Hume's "experimental method" in moral subjects. The experimental data for moral theory were to be provided by a survey of historical experience. This survey was not conceived as a simple narrative. Instead, as Carl Becker has ably suggested, it was to be a "new history," having philosophical and didactic significance.[94] Historical experience was to provide the storehouse of examples that could be compared and culled to find "man in general." And this essential man's (i.e., "humanity's") needs and tastes would then provide the norms for moral judgment and political action.

This conception of historical inquiry as the source of data for the discernment of the essence of man turns out to be in fact not all that different from the Aristotelian account of how an essence is discerned by induction. The language has been altered, the ideological intent is different, and the arena of relevant examples is more broadly conceived; but the form of inquiry is fundamentally the method Aristotle outlines in the last chapter of the *Posterior Analytics*. That is, you begin with sense perception, acquire memory, develop experience from a number of memories, and then, from this experience, you identify the common and essential features you are looking for—"the one beside the many which is a single identity within them all."[95] Like Aristotle, moreover, the practitioner of the new history (and the new ethics founded on it) does not simply arrive at a lowest common denominator. He must, and is entitled to, in Rousseau's words, "distinguish between the variety in human nature and that which is essential to it."[96] He should disregard mere "accidents" and should also discard particular examples he has warrant to consider deformed either by a "mistake" of nature (Aristotle) or by malicious social artifice. As Rousseau puts it, "disfigured" examples—"monsters, giants, pygmies and chimeras"— are to be excluded from the selected particulars out of which the universal essence is discriminated. In Hume's account, "hairbrained enthusiasts," "gloomy and dismal men," and those deluded by "superstition and false religion" are specifically to be set aside as perverted cases, which distort rather than embody the essential, the "natural," sentiments of "humanity."

Very much like Copernicus,[97] to whom he likened himself, Hume could thus backslide into reliance on traditional concepts and methods to help himself out of trouble when he ran into problems he could not handle adequately within his own new framework. This backsliding is particularly important in his moral theory, where it provides the implicit teleology and the assumption of a universal human nature necessary to underwrite the significance of his "experimental method of reasoning."

The Slide into Relativist Emotivism

A theory constructed in this fashion is clearly very vulnerable. Indeed, those who would attack it can find sufficient ammunition in its own conceptual arsenal. How, one might ask, can these mere heaps of impressions possess the intrinsic needs Hume ascribes to them? Why can't they be heaped one way as well as any other? Why should any one heap be considered any more natural or normal than any other? And, if these questions can't be answered, why should anyone's moral feelings or tastes, being mere accidents rather than essential properties, possess any normative force whatever? Why, that is, should one heap's emotions be significant or persuasive to another heap if they are not conceivably expressions of a common essence, which unites them? Hume would seem to have no very good answers to protect his moral theory from these questions, which are generated from within his own thought.

Simply from its inner tensions, then, Hume's moral theory is a very precarious one. Its footing in his atomistic empiricism is extremely shaky at best. Therefore, it was not sufficiently strong to withstand the profound doubt that later theories, discoveries, and interpretive biases cast upon it.

These later assaults on the coherence of Hume's ethical theory had one common theme: relativity. Hume was neither a relativist nor an emotivist in the contemporary sense because he saw nothing random or essentially variable about human passions. Given his covertly traditional view of human nature, he believed that the fundamental emotional economy of human beings was eternally fixed (apart from those "unnatural" distortions produced by socially created delusions). Within his premises, this belief was only partly anomalous: it rested uneasily on his atomism, but his Newtonianism at least warranted the motif of fixity. The Newtonian cosmos was mechanistic and therefore not well adapted in some respects to a theory of human nature, but it was nonetheless an "eternal" cosmos, and this made the assumption of constancy and universality in nature (including human nature) seem plausible. It was this surviving element of plausibility in Hume's theory that disappeared with the disappearance of Newtonianism.

Darwin is probably the crucial figure in this conceptual change that completed the undermining of Hume's moral theory; for the Darwinian cosmos retains the mechanistic features of Newtonianism that made Hume's theory suspect, but it abandons the assumption of a fixed and eternal nature that sustained Hume's theory. The world is atomistic, but the forms composed of these atoms are in flux. Everything is mutable, including human nature. Hence, Darwinian cosmology seems to lead to cultural relativism in anthropology: differences among cultures are not construed as the result of "accidents" (in the Aristotelian sense) or as perversions. There is no fixed human nature to distinguish from accidents or to contrast with perversions. Different cultures are simply different; none is any more natural or normative than any other; therefore, the different feelings and ethical tastes produced by these different cultures are also all on a par.

(Alternatively, Darwinian evolutionism could lead to glorification of laissez-faire on the grounds that it guarantees the "survival of the fittest." This outcome would have been equally foreign to Hume's viewpoint.)

Hume could not have anticipated this shift to relativism in both cosmology and anthropology. It is safe to say, however, that he could not have defended against it on his own premises. And, with this shift, his moral theory turns into contemporary emotivism. The human sentiment that in his thought had the dignity of constancy and essentiality becomes *mere* sentiment—an expression of accident instead of essence. The hope that an "experimental" survey of existing human sentiments would reveal constant standards of value—warranted by a consensus of informed taste—accordingly appears illusory. Deprived of universality by Darwinian principles, the feelings become *mere* feelings, moral tastes *mere* tastes. They are not only conventional; they are what Hume expressly denied them to be—namely, arbitrary.

Hume's moral theory, in short, when undermined by a consistent application of his own basic philosophy and transformed by post-Newtonian relativism, turns into the view that normative claims are not only extrarational but also trivial. The allegation that something is good not only conveys nothing "objective": its "subjective" import is also limited. The expression of approval embodied in such a pseudo-proposition represents no more than the random configuration of appetites produced by chance in the single individual who makes the utterance. Strictly speaking, no one is entitled to claim that something is good. He should, to avoid misleading others, say only, "I prefer X."

This doctrine received paradigmatic form, of course, in the emotivist theory of logical positivism. This theory is well enough known not to need recounting here.[98] It is also a view of ethics—or lack of ethics—that has become widely disseminated in popular culture: norms governing human conduct are held to be idiosyncratically personal, a matter of individual taste, based on "opinion" and not on "fact," judged by no test other than sincerity. The invitation to rational discourse on questions of "value" is deemed to be grounded either in primitive misconception or outright fraud.

This widespread orientation in contemporary sensibility—embodied explicitly in philosophical positivism and tacitly in vulgar subjectivist relativism—represents, then, the central ironic reversal produced by the dissolution of liberal rationalism into value-noncognitivism; for the whole thrust of the classical liberal program presumed the definitive moral competence of reason. This presumption was crucial both critically and constructively. Critically, all the political institutions and all the social practices of the world were to be hauled before the judgment of reason. As Engels put it, everything had to "justify its existence before the bar of reason or give up existence." Constructively, reason was to be the foundation of the good society that would be built to supplant those it had condemned. The world was to stand, in Hegel's metaphor, on its head.

Precisely the epistemological doctrines that gave rise to this rationalistic enthusiasm, however, have led, ironically, to exactly the opposite conclusion by the unfolding of their own logic in the way we have recounted. Reason is not the "sole measure of everything" (Engels again). Reason can measure nothing. Reason cannot judge; it can only provide flat statements of "value-neutral" "facts." Reason cannot criticize irrational practices; instead, it declares all human behavior and institutions to be equally and indifferently nonrational. Reason does not simply transcend particular interest to identify common interest; it transcends human interest altogether.

The rationalism of pride therefore turns into a rationalism of despair. Incapable of discerning norms for human conduct, value-noncognitivist reason is also unable to provide motives for human action. Both motivation and "guidance," such as it is, must be resigned to the arbitrary emotions of blind appetite. The world that was to be stood on its head is left to crawl on its belly. Such is the ironic disintegration of liberalism's political rationalism within the empiricist tradition.

Kant's Salvage Operation:
Cartesian Dualism as Moral Parable

This disintegration is paralleled in Continental European philosophy. In that tradition, just as in British philosophy, reason begins as king and ultimate arbiter and ends by being wholly divested of any influence in moral and political affairs. The slide into political and moral irrationalism that we observed in the movement from Locke through Hume to logical empiricism can be seen most clearly, perhaps, in the moral philosophy of Immanuel Kant and its eventual outcome. Just as Hume's passions, rendered "arbitrary" by later emendations, turn into the sovereignty of random appetite, so Kant's rational and lawful will, divested of its tacit assumptions, becomes the sovereign and "demonically" free will of Weber and Sartre.

Kant was a Cartesian and Newtonian who became alarmed by the rapid growth of moral skepticism under Enlightenment auspices. In this he resembled closely the temperamentally very different Rousseau, who had likewise reacted with dismay to what he saw as the drying-up of the wellsprings of good morals and good citizenship in the corrosive critical rationalism of the Parisian salons. Like Rousseau, moreover, Kant was convinced that this destructive tendency could be checked by paying appropriate attention and respect to the "heavenly voice" of the "moral law within." What he tried to do in his moral philosophy, then, was to provide the philosophical grounding and explanation for this inner law of conscience.

Kant was particularly concerned by and profoundly opposed to attempts, such as Hume's, to turn moral philosophy into an empirical or "experimental" discipline. Not only did he believe that these attempts fundamentally misconceived the very essence of moral action; he also believed that, however well intentioned they might be, they could end only in the complete dissolution of morality. An "experimental" approach to moral doctrine makes the mistake of trying to find a "heteronomous" basis for moral commands—i.e., of trying to locate the source of these commands in the contingent passions of empirical human nature. The only possible ultimate outcome of such a tactic, Kant believed, is self-interested hedonism. He rises to eloquence in his condemnation of this "lax and low" approach to morals:

> We cannot repeat our warning too often against this lax and even low habit of thought which searches empirical motives and laws for principles. Human reason when weary likes to rest on this cushion and in a dream of sweet illusions it substitutes for morality a bastard made up of limbs of quite different origin which appears as anything one chooses to see in it, save as virtue to one who has once beheld her in her true form. . . . Every empirical element is not only quite incapable of aiding the principle of morality, but is even highly prejudicial to the purity of morals. For the proper and inestimable value of a genuine good will consists just in the principle of action being free from all contingent causes.[99]

Empiricism's relegation of reason to the role of slave of the passions is a sure pathway to disaster, in Kant's view. The only way to prevent this outcome, the only way to salvage genuine morality, is to recognize the determinative and the constitutive role of reason, a priori, in making moral judgments. In this respect, Kant's answer to moral skepticism paralleled his answer to the skeptical reduction of the sciences to merely convenient mental habits. It is the organizing power of pure reason that gives order to what otherwise would be a chaos—a chaos of percepts, scientifically, or a chaos of impulses, morally. The reestablishment of the sovereignty of reason is the sine qua non in both cases. In the creation of scientific knowledge, reason rules a priori as the transcendental unity of apperception. In the creation of a moral order, reason rules a priori through the dictates of the categorical imperative.

Reason is, for Kant, once again to be the sovereign arbiter in moral questions. In this respect, he reasserts an essential claim of the classical tradition. The way in which he conceives this rationality, however, is markedly different from that tradition. His pure practical reason stands closer to the Cartesian *cogito* than it does to classical *nous*. Pure practical reason Kant conceives as that part of the human self that cannot be compressed into *res extensa,* accounted for by purely external causation. Practical reason is man's "interior" consciousness of himself as a free will. It is the free ghost that resides in the determined machine. It is the aspect of man that makes him a spiritual being.

In this respect also, Kant seems to take the lead from Rousseau, who conceived man in a similarly dualistic way metaphysically—and who drew a similar moral lesson. Rousseau put it this way:

> I see nothing in any animal but an ingenious machine. . . . I perceive exactly the same things in the human machine, with this difference, that in the operations of the brute, nature is the sole agent, whereas man has some share in his own operations, in his character as a free agent. . . . Nature lays her commands on every animal, and the brute obeys her voice. Man receives the same impulsion, but at the same time knows himself at liberty to acquiesce or resist: and it is particularly in his consciousness of this liberty that the spirituality of his soul is displayed. For physics may explain, in some measure, the mechanism of the senses and the formation of ideas; but in the power of willing or rather of choosing, and in the feeling of this power, nothing is to be found but acts which are purely spiritual and wholly inexplicable by the laws of mechanism.[100]

Kant's conception of pure practical reason proceeds directly from this basis. Man exists in two realms. The first realm is the sensible realm—the "mechanism of nature"—in which he is implicated along with all other contingent beings. But man also inhabits the intelligible realm, in which he experiences himself as a free spirit. As Kant explains:

> The concept of a world of the intellect is only a position outside the phenomena which reason finds itself compelled to take in order to conceive itself as practical, which would not be possible if the influences of the senses had a determining power over man,

but which is necessary unless he is denied the consciousness of himself as an intelligence; that is, as a rational cause acting freely and through reason. This thought certainly involves the idea of an order and a system of laws different from that of the mechanism of nature which governs the sensible world, and it requires the concept of an intelligible world; that is to say, of a whole system of rational beings as things in themselves.[101]

Man's moral self, then, is himself as free *cogito*. It is his "invisible self," his "personality," his self "within." It is a self that "reveals a life independent of animality and even of the entire world of sense."[102] It is man's noumenal self rather than his phenomenal self, his self as agent rather than as determined dependent variable; it is the self of spirit rather than the self as body.

In Kant we have Cartesian dualism turned into a moral parable. The tension that characterizes morality—the source of "oughtness"—lies not within Being, as in classical thought. It lies, that is, not between actual and potential but between the two substances of Descartes—between the world of sense (*res extensa*) and the world of intellect (*res cogitans*). The dictates of the latter transcend the inclinations of the former morally because they in fact transcend them ontologically. As Kant puts it, "the world of the intellect contains the basis of the world of sense, and consequently of its laws."[103]

Thus man is uniquely the being subject to moral tension because he is uniquely the being who inhabits both worlds. Animals, who inhabit only the sensible world, are devoid of moral tension; they simply obey blindly the voice of instinct, the causal forces that impinge upon them. The divine will, on the other hand, is wholly pure and transcendent. Its perfection renders it devoid of the "empirical" qualities that require moral control. Only man is both sensible and intelligible being, and the moral tension to which he is subject is the war between these two realms, which he unites within him. Says Kant,

> If I were only a member of the world of the intellect, all my actions would conform perfectly to the principle of the autonomy of pure will; if I were only a part of the world of sense they would be assumed to conform wholly to the natural law of desires and inclinations, i.e., to the heteronomy of nature. . . . The moral "ought" is then the necessary "will" of a member of an intelligible world and he conceives it as an "ought" only to the same extent that he considers himself a member of the world of sense.[104]

Kant turns his Cartesian ontology into a moral parable because he also uses it as an anthropological metaphor. He sees the dualism of the sensible and intelligible realms not only as the source of moral tension but also as the framework of the human psyche: the two realms of being are seen as manifested in two levels of the soul. Kant's model of man bears some resemblance to the Platonic conception of the soul as composed of *nous,* spirit, and appetite and the properly ordered self as one in which reason, the highest faculty, controls the other two. Kant, however, compresses the Platonic tripartite soul into two levels: reason and appetite. These two levels are similar in some respects to Plato's noetic and appetitive parts of the soul, but there are also some significant changes that arise from the different philosophical context and from the compression of three levels into two.

The psychology of Kant's "sensible" self—the self implicated in the "mechanism of nature"—is essentially the Platonic appetitive self. It is driven from the outside by a welter of desires, impulses, and inclinations. But Kant's conception of what he calls the "lower desires" is much broader than the Platonic conception. The lowest level of the Platonic psyche was modeled basically on the grossly physical desires of hunger and sex. Other desires, for Plato, might be seen as arising from higher levels. He saw the desires of honor and ambition as a product of the spirited self, for example. Even more, Plato saw *nous* itself as characterized by desire—by the erotic attraction to Goodness, Truth, and Beauty. Kant is much more radical, and much more reductive, in his account of the appetitive self. Virtually *all* desires, *all* pleasures, *all* "empirical" motives are lumped together into this single category. Here Kant is very "puritanical" in the vulgar sense. *All* human wants and inclinations are "lower." Some motives, some desires, may be better than others in a utilitarian sense, but none has any moral worth whatever.

Kant directs the rigorously critical ethical judgment implicit in this psychology principally at utilitarian and hedonistic conceptions of morality. Basing ethical values on pleasure of any kind, he feels, leads inevitably to a debasement of morals. "If we follow Epicurus and assume that virtue only determines the will by means of the pleasure it promises, we cannot blame him afterwards for considering this pleasure to be of the same kind as those of the coarsest senses."[105] In his critique, however, Kant also undermines other very important and much less vulgar conceptions of morality. By insisting that all human interests and all human pleasures are on a par, he does away with distinctions crucial to classical and Christian conceptions of the good will and of right action.

"Prudence," for example, has for Kant none of the ennobling overtones of Aristotelian *phronēsis.* It is no longer the practical knowledge of what is good for man but simply the skill of calculating accurately the best means to one's own self-interest. (Kant writes: "Now a man's skill in choosing the means to his own greatest well-being may be called prudence in the most specific sense.")[106] The prudent man is not, then, the man of moral wisdom venerated by Aristotle; he is the Benthamite petty shopkeeper despised by Marx. Similarly, the regenerate Christian soul, the man who acts out of the love of God and out of *caritas* for his fellow man, is morally devalued by Kant. *Amor sui* or *amor Dei*, what's the difference? They are both forms of love, hence are both inclinations, hence are devoid of true moral significance. "There are many minds," Kant tells us,

> so sympathetically constituted that without any other motive of vanity or self-interest, they find a pleasure in spreading joy [about them] and can take delight in the satisfaction of others so far as it is their own work. But I maintain that in such a case, however proper, however amiable an action of this kind may be, it nevertheless has no true moral worth, but is on a level with other inclinations.[107]

The Lord may love a cheerful giver, but Kant would be suspicious of the cheer: it might signify the presence of the gross alloy of pleasure behind the outwardly moral act. Truly moral actions, Kant insists, are done not simply *as* duty requires but *because* duty requires.

The sole surviving "higher desire" in Kant's Cartesian-puritan psychology, then, is conformity to the dictate of pure practical reason. The "purity" of practical reason is twofold. It is pure both ontologically and morally, in both cases for the same reason: namely, it allegedly utterly transcends the merely sensible world of phenomena. Ontologically, practical reason is depicted as wholly distinct from the material realm. It is a feature, indeed the defining feature, of the world of "intelligence." Morally, practical reason is "pure" because it is devoid of determination by the lower desires that belong to the world of sensation and pleasure. Kant thus identifies the moral nobility of practical reason with its wholly abstract and a priori nature. Its very lack of empirical content is what guarantees its moral purity. Kant expresses the connection this way:

> It is clear from what has been said that all moral concepts have their seat and origin completely *a priori* in the reason, and have it in the commonest reason just as truly as in what is speculative in the highest degree. Moral concepts cannot be obtained by abstraction from any empirical and hence merely contingent knowledge. *It is exactly this purity in origin that makes them worthy of serving as our supreme practical principle [for right action]* and, as we add anything empirical, we detract in proportion

from their genuine influence and from the absolute value of actions.[108]

The voice of pure, a priori, practical reason, then, is the command of duty in the abstract. It is the injunction to act in conformity to the wholly formal principle of volition, to "the concept of law in itself." This formal essence of the concept of law in itself Kant then identifies with *generality:* since it is wholly devoid of empirical content, the idea of law in itself must transcend all particularity. Thus Kant asserts that "conformity to law in general" implies that one must act only in such a way that one could will one's maxim "to become a general law."[109] By transcending particularity via its formal abstractness, the idea of law thus triumphs, in Kant's view, over selfishness. Since "the point of view of reason" has no concreteness, it has no particularity; by having no particularity, it cannot be determined by any selfish motive. Kant's "rational will" therefore attains a kind of formalistic sainthood via its fidelity to logical consistency. Any man who acts in such a way that his maxim could not become a general law of nature contradicts himself as a rational being. Transgressing the moral law, having a bad will, and reasoning poorly are all rolled into one thing.

Kant's intent is clearly to consolidate and justify Rousseau's "general will" by giving it a metaphysical basis. His "realm of ends," in which all rational beings treat each other with complete respect as moral equals, is a universalized version of Rousseau's ideal polity. But in turning Rousseau's sociologically grounded concept into a logician's norm, Kant sacrifices more than he gains. He gives the general will universal status only at the price of rendering it wholly abstract and thus highly vulnerable.

Kant's moral theory is a Platonic ethics and psychology run amok under the influence of Cartesianism. Reason is put back into the driver's seat of the chariot of the soul, but it is only a shadow of its former self. With no *logos* in Being, reason perceives only form with a small "f." It perceives only the general rather than the Good, and it must make the former do for the latter. Wholly abstract, the voice of reason therefore loses its power to impel by the force of *erōs*. It must govern through a thin and watery substitute. "Respect" is the ghost of *erōs* that Kant hopefully relies on to make pure reason practical:

> To behold virtue in her proper form is but to contemplate morality divested of all admixture of sensible things and of every spurious ornament of reward or self-love. To what extent she then eclipses everything else that charms the inclinations one may readily per-

ceive with the least exertion of his reason, if it be not wholly
spoiled for abstraction.[110]

Kant was indeed a man of faith!

The Neo-Kantian Slide into Subjectivism

Kant's strategy for salvaging a normative role for reason was bold
but dangerous. He built his temple of pure reason on the ruins of the
classical conceptions of virtue. Indeed, he contributed to the destruction of these classical conceptions through his relentless and
crude reduction of all "empirical" human motives to the status of
undifferentiated "lower desires." Conceiving his destructive critique as but the necessary prelude to his constructive efforts, he ran
the risk of suffering the same fate as Hume: his destructive work
might be accepted but his constructive theory spurned.

This, indeed, is what seems to have happened. Kant's determined
attempt to maintain the constitutive role of reason in moral questions within the framework of a Cartesian ontology was both noble
and ingenious, but it has been unconvincing. Many of his successors
seem to have accepted his contention that "whoever considers
morality real, and not a chimerical idea without truth, must likewise
admit its principle as discussed here."[111] However, they have
bought the alternative rather than the thesis. Finding Kant's constructive claims unacceptable but acquiescing in his critique, they
have concluded that moral claims are in fact "chimerical ideas without truth."

For the truth is that Kant, much like Locke and Hume, was sustained in his constructive efforts by some of the "old wine," as we
have called it, of the classical tradition. In his critique of theoretical
reason, Kant was indeed thoroughly modern. In his moral thought,
however, he was not. He was, instead, very much a man of traditional faith, one who took for granted the dignity, worth, and ultimate moral equality of all human beings. His constructive moral
theory clearly betrayed, and depended on, these uncritically held
assumptions—assumptions which, to a truly skeptical mind, would
seem ill at ease within his ostensive doctrines.

The presence of the "old wine" in Kant's moral theory is betrayed both in the substantive identifications he makes within it and
in the warrants he adduces for it. He refers repeatedly, for example,
to "common sense" as a touchstone for his moral doctrines. He
believed that the "heavenly voice" of the moral law was "clear,
irrepressible, and distinctly audible even to the most ordinary
man."[112] "So sharply and clearly defined are the boundaries of
morality and self-love," he wrote, "that even the most ordinary eye

cannot fail to distinguish whether a thing belongs to one or the other."[113] He was not intent on substantive innovation in morality; that kind of novelty would have been, in his view, its own refutation. He was concerned simply to explain and to justify the plain moral truths that all men, to his mind, instinctively apprehended. He considered it an important test of his moral theory, then, that it was allegedly in full agreement with these clear truths of good common sense. He considered it an essential recommendation of his views that they arguably accorded with what "people say" or with "the judgment of common sense."[114] He could include his own moral "can't helps" among these touchstones. When he looked "within himself," he had no trouble perceiving the "wonder of the moral law," and he presumed that everyone else saw it with the same clarity.

These truths of "common sense," however, were neither so clear nor so immutable as Kant supposed. Similarly, they were not so immaculately conceived "within" selves bereft of a coherent moral tradition. The presumed truths of morality found in the conventional wisdom and within Kant's own earnest breast were a fruit of the classical and Christian tradition, and they could, and would, seem considerably less clear and distinct as this tradition lost its hegemony over the cultural and intellectual life of the West. Kant's uncritical appeal to prevailing moral assumptions, therefore, did not have the power he attributed to it. As a tactic, moreover, it revealed not so much the indisputability of his moral premises but rather their dependence on his own moral culture.

In like fashion, the presence of the uncritically held assumptions that Kant took from his tradition and packed into his theory shows up rather clearly when he articulates the nature and content of the categorical imperative and the realm of ends. In the first place, he reads the attributes of personhood into the category of "rational being." Or perhaps one might say that he reduced the nature of personhood to rationality as he understood it. In either case, he claimed for his spare noumenal selves the dignity and status that had been attained by full human persons within the Western tradition. ("Rational beings," Kant says, in making this potent identification, "are called persons.")[115]

Having made this identification, Kant then makes a rather gratuitous leap in stipulating that rational beings possess the status of "ends-in-themselves." (That is to say, this is a gratuitous leap within the limitations of Kant's own account of rationality. It made more sense within the context of the tradition within which Kant was raised and upon which he relied; but, strictly speaking, he was not entitled to any philosophical purchase derived from that tradition, since he was leaving it behind.) This move is, of course, an essential intermediary step before Kant can formulate the categorical imperative as demanding that a human being must always be treated as an end and never merely as a means.[116] This crucial step to one of his more impressive formulations of the categorical imperative, however, is logically very suspect. Kant seems simply to accord rational beings the status of ends-in-themselves by outright fiat. He reasons that only something that was an end-in-itself could be the basis of a true practical law; he then simply confers that status by his own say-so:

> Supposing that there were something whose existence was in itself of absolute value, something which, as an end in itself, could be a ground for definite laws, then this end and it alone, would be the ground for a possible categorical imperative, i.e., a practical law. *Now I say that man, and generally every rational being, exists as an end in himself,* not merely as a means for the arbitrary use of this or that will; he must always be regarded as an end in all his actions whether aimed at himself or at other rational beings.[117]

When he tries to justify this seemingly rather arbitrary grant of great dignity, moreover, Kant is still in trouble. He tells us that the "very nature" of persons-as-rational-beings "constitutes them as ends in themselves." And in explicating this very cryptic claim, he says the following:

> Now there are in mankind capacities for greater perfection which belong to the end of nature regarding humanity. . . . To neglect these capacities might at best be consistent with the survival of humanity as an end it itself, but [it is not consistent] with the promotion of nature's end regarding humanity.[118]

Had Kant been more rigorously true to his basic premises, I suggest, he would have been forced to see this argument in the light in which it would appear to many modern critics: as a commission of the "naturalistic fallacy" or even of the "pathetic fallacy." Instead, he could offer this argument as a plausible explanation because he was in some respects still an adherent of the classical tradition. What he was trying to do here is understandable if not legitimate: he was trying to confer on his practical *cogito* the teleological attributes of human nature as conceived by the classical tradition. His argument was terse and not very strong, because it is not at all clear how such a disembodied ego could manifest the tension of potentiality-becoming-actuality. His recourse to this argument, with all its apparent precariousness within the confines of his basic philosophical project, once again simply offers profound testimony to the significant presence of much "old wine" in his moral theory.

Kant likewise showed his tacit grounding in older conventional normative assumptions when he offhandedly suggested that the order of pure intelligence encompasses the order of charity.[119] In parallel fashion, he seemed to conflate the Golden Rule with the law of non-contradiction; for rationality, he argued, implies obedience to law in general, and law in general implies general laws, and general laws imply laws that are generally—i.e., impartially—applied. In juris-prudential terms, he was in essence contending that the form of law in itself encompasses the requirement of "equal protection of the laws." In this argument for a kind of substantive due process, Kant puts his finger on one key facet of the "rule of law" embraced by liberal constitutionalism. His attempt to justify this moral norm by reference to logical necessity, however, is equally well accomplished by reference to the requisites of moral language as a form of discourse. Hume had made that point earlier: moral terms, to be a part of a medium of general discourse, have to be general terms. The really important question relates to who is included in the relevant "general" community—whether the community of discourse or the realm of rational beings. And, as suggested above, Kant's liberal universalism in this respect trades heavily on assumptions about the moral dignity of all men that had been instilled in him from traditional sources.

In sum, it seems very clear that Kant relied heavily on older moral and anthropological verities in formulating his conception of practical reason and its role in human life. These older ideas influenced the content he attributed to practical reason; they contributed to the evidence he adduced as warrants for his account; and they contributed to his account of the force of reason—i.e., to his account of how pure reason could be practical. His "pure" reason was not so "pure" after all, in a philosophical sense. Instead, it was shaped profoundly and sustained significantly by the very "heteronomous" elements that Kant so roundly contemned. Without these features, tacitly imported from traditional sources, Kant's theory turns out to be the "dream of sweet illusions" he considered "empirical" accounts of morals to be.

This dependence of Kant's moral doctrine on traditional and a posteriori ideas for its content, its warrants, and its force is borne out by its subsequent history. Just as his a priori theoretical categories could become perceived as hypostasized Newtonian axioms, so his a priori practical imperatives could become seen as a hypostasized Lutheran conscience. More critical mentalities—morally speaking—steeped in Kant's rationalism but not in his pietism, would drain his philosophy of its "old wine." This would be a logical advance but a moral and political loss, for the vitality of Kant's theory was a function of its confusions and prejudices. Indeed, when his prejudices (in Burke's nonpejorative sense) are omitted, the import of his system seems to be quite the opposite of his intent. The bare framework of his intended moral rationalism becomes a foundation of contemporary irrationalism.

When the content of Kant's philosophical version of substantive due process is drained away, what is left is an empty legalism. This drift into a rather barren formalism was precisely what most characterized neo-Kantian jurisprudence. The more rigorously the neo-Kantians tried to carry out Kant's project of identifying the pure a priori nature of law, the more devoid of substance it became. "Pure" form was empty form. Such a conclusion was only logical, but lost in the process were the very guarantees of human dignity and integrity Kant considered crucial. He would surely have been dismayed by the formalistic claim of the neo-Kantian Hans Kelsen that "any content whatsoever can be legal; there is no human behavior which could not function as the content of a legal norm. A norm becomes a legal norm only because it has been constituted in a particular fashion, born of a definite procedure and a definite rule."[120] Kelsen's conclusion, however, was more consistent with Kant's stated project of abstracting law from all empirical content than was Kant's categorical imperative.

As the a priori demands of the law become increasingly empty, Kant's "rational will" becomes correspondingly more free—in the conventional sense of not being bound by restrictions. The intimate but problematic connection he posited between being a "free will" and being a law-bound "rational being"[121] simply dissolved. To be a truly free will, then, no longer means to be free from the control of a posteriori "empirical" impulses but subject to the a priori laws of rationality; it means to be free from any externally derived law whatsoever.

Schopenhauer was very quick to take this fundamental step in the conception of the will. Kant's practical *cogito* became in his hands Dionysian rather than Apollonian. The noumenal self, the self as agent, he depicted as irrational will. As Korner observes, "this modification of Kant's philosophy by one who considered himself Kant's only true heir, turns the crowning achievement of the great European movement known as the Enlightenment into one of the foundations of irrationalism."[122]

Perhaps the clearest example of what happens, however, anthropologically and morally, when Kant's practical *cogito* is genuinely "purified" is found in the philosophy of Jean-Paul Sartre. Strip away the intrinsically lawful rationality from Kant's noumenal self and you will find Sartre's "consciousness." This consciousness is the "nothingness" that, existing outside the mechanism of nature, must create itself out of its own spontaneity. It is wholly free, bound by no restraints except its own freely made commitments. "Existence precedes essence" means, anthropologically, that man creates himself ex nihilo, at every moment, according to no preconceived plan, subject to no a priori obligations.

The ethical consequences of this true "purification" of the ego—this cleansing it of any essence and of any predetermined content whatever—are enormous. The ego is wholly transcendent (i.e., "being-for-itself," human consciousness, is wholly other than "being-in-itself," causally determined nature) and therefore totally unshackled. The defining experience of the authentic *cogito* is existentialism's "dreadul freedom." This is Kierkegaard's "fear and trembling" without God. (Indeed, as Sartre insists, it is man's fundamental project to become God.) In creating himself gratuitously, as it were, man gives himself the law. To be a free will and a will subject to moral law, Kant said, were "one and the same." With the dissolution of the a priori moral law, to be a free will (and an authentic man) means, in Sartre's world, to be subject only to the law of one's own choosing or indeed of one's own making. As Sartre puts it: "My freedom is the only foundation of values, and nothing, absolutely nothing, justifies me in adopting this value rather than that, this hierarchy of values rather than another."[123]

In the skeletal remains of Kant's universe, moral man emerges as the Orestes of Sartre's *The Flies*. "Suddenly," says Orestes, repudiating Zeus's claim upon him,

> out of the blue, freedom crashed down on me and swept me off my feet. Nature sprang back, my youth went with the wind, and I knew myself alone, utterly alone in the midst of this well-meaning little universe of yours. I was like a man who's lost his shadow. And there was nothing left in heaven, no right or wrong, nor anyone to give me orders. . . . Outside nature, against nature, without excuse, beyond remedy, except what remedy I find within myself. But I shall not return under your law; I am doomed to have no other law but mine.[124]

In the social sciences proper, a very similar conclusion is reached in the methodological and ethical views of the great Max Weber. Weber clearly stands in the neo-Kantian tradition, and the philosophy he articulates on that basis has led one astute commentator (Raymond Aron) to classify him as an existentialist. A very brief look at Weber's views makes clear his indebtedness to Kant, on the one hand, and the affinities of his ethics with "dreadful freedom" on the other.

Methodologically, Weber begins with the Kantian distinction between the causally determined but meaningfully chaotic phenomenal world and the transcendent world of consciousness. The phenomenal world is a "vast chaotic stream of events, which flows away through time."[125] Order is brought, descriptively, into this chaos only by the application of concepts from the outside—concepts that are themselves "value-oriented." As Weber puts it, "Order is brought into this chaos only on the condition that in every case only a part of concrete reality is interesting and significant to us, because only it is related to the cultural values with which we approach reality."[126] These ordering concepts, Weber asserts, with explicit reference to Kant, are "primarily analytical instruments for the intellectual mastery of empirical data and can be only that."[127]

The social scientist, then, serves methodologically the function that Kant assigned to the transcendental unity of apperception. He bestows order on the chaos of data by the application of his theoretical concepts. Weber's social scientist is differentiated in an important way from Kant's theoretical ego, however, because he no longer inhabits a Newtonian cosmos. His value-orientation is not a single a priori universal set of categories. It is one *Weltanschauung* among others. The Kantian unity of apperception applied an allegedly universal viewpoint, but Weber relativizes this conception. Knowledge in the social sciences, he tells us, is a function of the "unremitting application of *viewpoints* of a *specifically particularized character*, which, in the last analysis, are oriented on the basis of evaluative ideas."[128] The social scientist chooses among these, apparently on an "instrumental" rather than an ideological basis. Thus, as Weber concedes, because our knowledge depends on the application of "a priori" theoretical categories, and because these categories derive from one value-orientation or *Weltanschauung* among many, science is separated only by a "hairline" from faith.[129]

Just as Weber's social scientist is a relativized Kantian theoretical ego, so is his moral man a relativized version of Kant's practical *cogito*. The meaning of life, and the norms for action implicit therein, he tells us, cannot be *found* "empirically." One cannot discover order and significance in the given world of historical events. Reality "in-itself," as Sartre would say, is meaningless—or, what amounts to the same thing, it offers a potential multitude of conflicting meanings. As Weber says: "Life with its irrational reality and its store of possible meanings is inexhaustible."[130]

Human consciousness must therefore *impose* meaning on this irrational chaos of the phenomenal world. Order and significance are brought to the empirical world from the outside—from the noumenal world to the phenomenal world, from "being-for-itself" to "being-in-itself." Man *creates* his own meaning. "The fate of an epoch which has eaten of the tree of knowledge is that it must know that we cannot learn the meaning of the world from the results of its analysis, be it ever so perfect; it must rather be in a position to create this meaning for itself."[131]

Weber thus places man in general in the role of Hobbes's sovereign: he is a nominalist deity who is entitled or doomed, depending on how you look at it, to confer meaning upon and establish order within the world by the application of defining concepts. The difference is that Weber's political world is pluralistic and therefore filled with the unending conflict that Hobbes hoped to eliminate. Hobbes's goal, Weber believes, was utopian.

> Conflict cannot be excluded from social life. One can change its means, its object, even its fundamental direction and its bearers, but it cannot be eliminated. . . . "Peace" is nothing more than a change in the form of the conflict or in the antagonists or in the objects of the conflict, or finally in the chances of selection.[132]

The moral life is accordingly depicted by Weber in very "existentialist" terms. The individual has no given essence. He creates himself by the free choices he makes. He may conceivably "permit" life to "run on as an event in nature." This option would be tantamount to Sartre's "bad faith." The individual who sinks into being-in-itself is renouncing his freedom and seeking a moral excuse. The moral man must affirm his freedom and make his choices. This is what moral responsibility is all about. The moral life, therefore, is "a series of ultimate decisions through which the soul—as in Plato—chooses its own fate, i.e., the meaning of its activity and existence."[133]

The difficulty here, however, is that these "ultimate decisions" seem to be arbitrary. Plato's soul chose its own fate, but only within the context of *logos*-ordered reality. The options faced by the Platonic soul were not on a par with each other. One could not equally happily or equally legitimately choose to be tyrant or philosopher—slave to the dark *erōs* or lover of the Good. The rational structure of the world made some choices ultimately productive and others destructive. The freedom of the soul to choose did not supplant or abrogate the moral order of Being. The choices of Kant's practical *cogito* were similarly subject to rational guidance. The "autonomy" of rational will, Kant held, was constrained by the a priori moral law. Kant did not depict this as external constraint, strictly speaking, since he saw obedience to the dictate of pure practical reason as an *expression* of man's essential nature—his status as "rational being"—not as a limitation on it. Nevertheless, the choice of Kant's moral man was clearly a limited one. It was a profound yea or nay, neither a random choice among fully equivalent alternatives nor a creation ex nihilo.

The self-determination of Weber's soul, in contrast, seems to be radically free in just this sense. Weber does not depict each single decision as arbitrary, to be sure. He fully recognizes the way that *Weltanschauungen* serve to determine and constrain conceptions of what should be done in specific instances. These *Weltanschauungen* themselves, however, he sees as radically individual and "subject- ive." They are, at best, matters for "speculation" and for "faith." They amount to a "personal view of the world."[134] The individual's choice of a *Weltanschauung* is not only "subjective" and "per- sonal"; it is apparently wholly undetermined and unconstrained by "objective" knowledge. What scientific reason tells us about the world has no bearing on our ultimate choice, Weber says explicitly (though other specific claims of his seem inconsistent with this theoretical contention), because the "establishment of empirical facts" and the making of "practical evaluations" are "entirely het- erogeneous problems."[135] The choice of "ultimate standards" is not a matter for reason. It is a "personal affair" that "involves will and conscience, not empirical knowledge."[136]

The distinction that Weber is concerned to make between spe- cialized, technical knowledge and practical evaluation is, of course, a valid and important distinction—one that was not sufficiently re- spected, one might add, by some of his academic contemporaries. By grounding this distinction within the skeletal remains of Kant's neo-Cartesian dualism, however, he arrives, despite his protests,[137] at a relativistic dead end. In a sense, he abandons altogether the notion of practical reason. Evaluation is "practical" but not ra- tional. It is, as he says, a matter of "will and conscience"; but his will is not rational and there is no objective grounding for—and therefore no "science" in—his "con-science."

Weber's version of the categorical imperative thus becomes, as Leo Strauss has suggested, "Thou shalt have ideals."[138] In politics and practical affairs, the moral man, in Weber's words, "should do what his God or daemon demands."[139] The moral life seems to be distinguished, as in Sartre, not by its content but by its passion and sincerity. The fundamental norm is not goodness but authenticity. There is nowhere else for Weber to go: he can find no substantive criteria for right action because his "phenomenal" world is a chaos and his "noumenal" world is protean.

Weber's concrete image of moral man obviously differs from Sartre's. His moral hero is not an Orestes but an Atlas. He is the responsible political actor who takes the burden of an "ethically irrational" world upon his shoulders. This responsible man is not a conventional saint; he must, in fact, "contract with diabolical powers" to fulfill his responsibilities. But he is also not "Saint" Genet, for his overriding concern is with the consequences of his action, not with the purity of his self-affirmation.

In a purely philosophical sense, however, it is hard to understand the rational basis for the concrete ethical models of the two thinkers—or to understand why they should differ. Sartre would be very hard pushed to explain why the specific content of Genet's behavior should be valued any higher than the behavior of, let us say, a truly "authentic" fascist. He can, on his own terms, justify a preference for someone like Genet over someone corrupted by "bad faith." It seems clear, however, that many very divergent moral orientations can be adopted in good faith. This being the case, Sartre's exaltation of Genet and other "bastards," as he puts it, seems more explicable as a function of Sartre's psychobiography than as a function of his philosophy. It is likewise hard to see why, on strictly logical grounds, Weber should value the ethical stance of his "mature man" above the fervor of the fanatic, since each is doing "what his God or daemon demands." No doubt Weber chose wisely; but he gives us no basis for knowing what a "wise" choice might be or why it might be so.

In their different idioms, Sartre and Weber both represent the denouement and the ultimate failure of Kant's tactical attempt to reclaim for reason sovereignty over morality and politics. Both of them depict human action as a dance against the backdrop of a cosmos that is absurd, irrational, chaotic. It is not clear who calls the tune or what sets the beat for this dance, but one thing does seem clear: it is not reason.

In the technocratic tradition, the sovereignty of reason turns into the sovereignty of power. Reason the Liberator becomes Caesar the King. In the value-noncognitivist/irrationalist tradition, sovereign reason abdicates to become a slave of the passions. Reason no longer serves, like Dante's Virgil, as a divine guide. Instead, like Sophocles' Oedipus, it blinds itself in despair. What then shall show the way?

7 Custom, Preference, and Will: The Several Faces of Modern Political Irrationalism

In another of the many superficial paradoxes in the strange career of liberal reason, then, a political and moral irrationalism develops directly out of a tradition that sought to make reason sovereign in human life. Rationalism as a general perspective generates its opposite in human affairs. And since, at its outset, this rationalist orientation aimed very directly at explicitly political outcomes, this process amounts to self-immolation. Liberal humanism suffers yet another ironic reversal, but one different from the reversal it suffered from the unfolding logic of technocracy.

The logic of this process is not all that mysterious, despite its apparently self-contradictory nature. What happens, quite simply, is that the skepticism of liberal reason, a marvelous weapon when turned on one's adversaries—and a central one in the arsenal of Enlightenment liberalism—turns destructively upon the deepest affirmative convictions of the same tradition.

Though not mysterious, this pattern is beset by some very real semantic difficulties and attendant confusion. One commentator is likely to call this "value noncognitivist" (or "value neutralist") tradition "rationalism." Another may term it an "irrationalist" tradition, as I have done. Despite the apparent contradiction, there is not necessarily any real disagreement here. The tradition is both rationalist and irrationalist, depending on the focus. Its adherents are irrationalists in the sense that they renounce the competence of reason in morals and politics. They consider "normative knowledge" a contradiction in terms. But they reach this renunciation of the normative competence of reason precisely because of their supreme commitment to reason as they understand and interpret it. Put another way, because they see all genuine exercise of reason as theoretical, they are led to consider the very notion of practical reason to be spurious.

The strongest suit of the irrationalist tradition in political theory is, for obvious reasons, its function as critique. All the various sub-schools of the irrationalist tradition devote a great deal of attention to, and are especially powerful in, the debunking of rival orientations. The very stringent standards for legitimate knowledge embraced by the positivist tradition provide it with a very potent skeptical thrust against any claims that bear on political life. If it is not possible to move from descriptive premises to a normative conclusion, no one should claim to have done so. Anyone who, on the basis of his beliefs, purports to impose normative demands can therefore be justifiably considered a fraud and a charlatan. It is precisely in ex-posing such intellectual fraud and charlatanry—along with the political demands based on them—that skeptical rationalism excels.

It is possible, of course, to argue that the positivist, as a strict "value neutralist," has no legitimate warrant to engage in such de-bunking. If he is truly neutral to all values, one might suggest, he has no reason to prefer truth to falsehood, honesty to fraud, the genuine authority to the infamous quack. In fact, of course, the value non-cognitivist or neutralist in his role as social critic is not so completely and reflexively consistent. In this one respect, at least, he is not neutral or indifferent. As much as, and probably more than, the generality of men, he values the truth. Indeed, fidelity to the truth, intellectual honesty, and "objectivity" are the great and un-questioned values underlying his whole enterprise. Any criticism of these fundamental, orienting "value premises" he dismisses as quibbling, unworthy of serious response, and he is, of course, right to do so in human terms if not in purely logical terms.

The paradox of a rationalist irrationalism thus possesses its ethical corollary. In ethical terms it is a tradition ostensively and explicitly amoral that is at the same time fiercely moralistic in its utter devotion to the norm of truthfulness. The zeal with which the contemporary positivist seeks to expose his ideological adversaries stands as tes-timony to this profound but tacit moral dimension of positivism. The critiques are not cool and dispassionate because they are not morally indifferent. Instead they are fueled by the kind of righteous—and often self-righteous—wrath that is appropriately directed at those who are believed to have violated what is sacred. The ideologue who grounds his political demands on spurious knowledge claims is, for the positivist, both a heretic and a blasphemer. He has defiled the holiness of truth by taking its name in vain.

The special *bêtes noires* of the skeptical rationalist are philosoph-ical "enthusiasm," superstition, and "metaphysics." In each of these, in his view, fraudulent and insupportable claims of knowledge are put forward which are in fact effusions of passion and interest rather than products of the mind. Fear, anxiety, hatred, cupidity, and the lust for power, among other nonrational motivating forces, generate lies, fairy tales, and myths. These in turn obscure the true face of the world, mislead those who fall prey to them, and cause the generality of mankind to suffer at the hands of charlatans.

Here again the paradoxes mount up. The skeptical rationalist's animus against enthusiasm is itself an enthusiasm; his anti-metaphysical doctrine has a dogmatic metaphysics of its own; and he relies on a credulous interpretion of scientific reason that has become the principal superstition of modernity. Moreover, as we shall argue, this philosophical orientation tends to produce significant ideologies in the very process of trying to eliminate or transcend ideology.

In its fidelity to truth and its consequent passion for philosophical debunking, skeptical rationalism is an authentic heir of the Enlightenment. It seeks to carry on Bacon's destruction of the "idols" of the mind, to continue the battle of Reason against Authority and Superstition that Condorcet described in epic terms, to persist in Voltaire's mission of eradicating the "infamy" of religion. Equally constant is the political and ethical grounding for these critiques: the conviction that philosophical error almost invariably leads to human slavery and folly. The basic weapon remains the same, as well: it is autonomous reason that has the power and the right to haul impostors before its tribunal and pronounce judgment on them.

The value-noncognitivist rationalism that has been one of the principal heirs of liberal reason, then, has produced a very powerful tradition of social criticism. This tradition begins with Hume himself and his attacks upon "dismal" divines, "enthusiastic" sectarians, and rationalistic liberals. It then continues into the twentieth century, where it becomes especially strong with the dominance of a basically positivist empiricism in Anglo-American thought. Representative important examples of this critical tradition in recent decades include Karl Popper's criticism of Plato, Hegel, and Marx, Bertrand Russell's dismissal of intellectual "rubbish," the Vienna Circle's assault on metaphysical social dogmas, and Hans Kelsen's critique of natural-law doctrines. In this country, Thurman Arnold's critique of pre–New Deal liberal verities, Jerome Frank's and Oliver Wendell Holmes, Jr.'s, assaults on legal "idealism," and the "realistic" revisions of democratic theory by empiricist social scientists are all significant examples of the same genre. In all of them the critical power of a stringently rigorous and reductive empiricism is deployed against political doctrines based on transcendentalist, idealist, or teleological philosophies. "Exposing" and attacking these ideas by holding them up to methodological dictates or to "common sense" realism, the empiricist critics debunk the political theories and the political claims based on them.

When it comes to upholding, creating, or defending a political theory or political practice, the situation of the value noncognitivist turns highly problematic. The very critical power of the tradition converts directly into constructive impotence. If one rejects the competency of practical reason, how can one produce any political theory—a form of knowledge clearly belonging to that proscribed domain? If "ought" is separated from "is" by an unbridgeable logical gap, how can one who respects the implied prohibition pretend to connect the two in the coherent fashion requisite for political theory? If normative utterances are mere expressions of emotion, one may indeed declare one's own idiosyncratic "preferences" but can never justify them. In short, skeptical rationalism, by its renunciation of the very idea of normative knowledge, leaves itself incapable of affirming on rational grounds any constructive political ideals whatsoever. Herein lies its great difficulty. And herein lies its great departure from the Enlightenment orientation it perpetuates in other respects. For the classical liberal rationalist looked to Reason for positive vision as well as for critical might. He expected Reason to rebuild on foundations of its own after it had demolished the pretensions of vain philosophy. In contrast, the rationalism of the modern skeptic exhausts itself in criticism. When it comes time to ask "What is to be done?" he receives no sustenance from reason.

Prevented by their own self-imposed limitations from developing any coherent and explicit political theory, the rationalistic irrationalists cannot desist, as they rise to comprehensive accounts of politics, from arriving at and relying on certain understandings of the political order that carry practical implications for "reasonable and proper" action. Relentlessly objective and descriptive though they may be, these accounts will suggest that some goals are impossible or illusory while others are important, that some policies are imprudent or ill-conceived while others are necessary to human welfare.[1]

These "implications," in the loose sense, are one source of the constructive theory, such as it is, of the irrationalist tradition. Another significant way in which this tradition arrives at its political orientations resembles the way winners are produced in a demolition derby. This is the winner-by-default approach: after everything else has been demolished by the onslaught of critical reason, whatever is left standing wins the day. It then is recommended to us as the counsel of "realism" and "common sense." "Reasonable" action is the action that is least palpably unreasonable.

Like its technocratic sibling, the irrationalist tradition has produced political orientations of widely divergent ideological hue. The common thread they share is the rejection of reason as the appropriate ordering principle for political life. Having agreed on that wholly negative principle of exclusion, however, the members of this tradition confront a considerable range of pretenders for the vacant throne of reason. A whole host of nonrational, subrational, or extrarational forces might conceivably claim to be the appropriate ordering principle for politics. Particular irrationalists, then, may fall into quite different conventional ideological categories, depending upon which of these extrarational touchstones they select.

One species of irrationalism is clearly conservative in its orientation. The conservative irrationalist begins by debunking the philosophical pretensions and political demands of legalism and idealism. He demonstrates to his satisfaction that the normative framework of these legalists and idealists is a mythical abstraction masquerading as concrete reality. He further concludes that the political demands based on these faulty ideas are unrealistic and utopian, in the pejorative sense of that term. Partly by simple default, partly by obeying his own implicit counsel of realism, and partly by his conviction that what has survived must have some utility, the conservative irrationalist finds his own norms in established patterns and practices. His touchstone, then, is custom. What reason cannot provide—namely, positive governing principles for the ordering of political society—convention, habit, and tradition can provide. The conservative irrationalist could say of society what Holmes said of the law: its life is experience, not logic.

The liberal irrationalist directs most of his skeptical fire at philosophical holism and transcendentalism. Holistic notions such as the state or rational will he derides as dangerous mythology. Similarly, transcendental or communitarian conceptions of natural law, natural right, common good, and public interest he sees as misleading hypostasizations. Reproaching these illusory misconceptions, the liberal irrationalist sees the only reality in politics as appetite or desire. Depicting these as relatively modest and limited, he exhibits his tacit embrace of the "enlightened self-interest" model of "rational" man. The only real, hence legitimate, ordering principle in politics for him, then, is individual preference or specific group interest. His interpretation of politics accordingly tends to resemble "bourgeois individualism," and Marxist criticisms to that effect mean little to him, since he considers Marxism to be the height of philosophical humbug and political madness.

The rejection of reason as a political guide can also lead to various forms of radicalism, ranging from fascism to anarchism. The radical irrationalist is typically a romantic who is frustrated by the sterility he finds in the counsel to "be reasonable." What is presented to him as rationality he sees, with some justification, as barren in principle and repressive in fact. Like his liberal-skeptic counterpart, he tends to see the rational discourse allegedly central to classical parliamentarism as a glossing-over of pure and simple interest, but he evaluates this game of political bargaining much more negatively, seeing it as both crass and ineffectual. Disenchanted with existing institutions and without recourse to discredited reason, the radical irrationalist looks to imaginative fantasy, to passion, to will, or even to instinct for political inspiration. Since these sources of guidance are protean, this kind of radicalism may have widely divergent outcomes. The radical irrationalist may turn out to be anything from a relatively amiable absurdist to a furious nihilist—from a Yippie to a terrorist. The dilemma, and the ultimate futility, of the radical skeptic is that he is by choice cut off from the status quo and is by philosophical incapacity bereft of any rational alternative.

These subschools of political irrationalism, clearly differentiated by and dispersed along the conventional ideological spectrum, may at times link up or interact in some interesting ways. In particular, it is quite possible for conservative and liberal irrationalism to merge rather comfortably under the appropriate sociological conditions. Whenever basically liberal institutions become well established, they can be defended not only by the liberal skeptic but by his conservative counterpart as well. The former defends them because of their content, the latter because of their acquired status as custom. Radical irrationalism, moreover, tends to be linked both causally and logically with its more moderate siblings. The relationship here is not one of assimilation but rather an opposition of alter egos. The radical shares the logic and factual perceptions of the others, but he inverts the value sign. He agrees that conservatism is largely an attachment to the status quo, but he sees that as static rather than stable. He agrees that liberalism is the politics of interest, but he sees this as swinish rather than as inevitable and normal. Finally, he agrees that reason is impotent as a corrective to liberalism or conservatism so interpreted; but he takes this as an invitation rather than a prohibition.

Critical Conservative Irrationalism:
Empiricism as Debunking Methodology

The model of the conservative skeptic was set very early on by David Hume himself. In the preceding chapter we examined his attempt to establish a new kind of experimental ethics after he denied the authority of reason in that area; we saw some of the problems and tensions arising from this attempt; and we noted the way that the direction he took has led, without his intending it, to contemporary ethical relativism and positivist emotivism. Here we want to observe the way in which he turned these ethical and epistemological doctrines into the service of a conservative utilitarianism in politics.

To begin with, Hume deployed his skeptical principles to undermine and condemn the "enthusiasm" and the "fanaticism" he saw as the product of philosophical sophistry and religious superstition. A "considerable part of metaphysics," he averred, is "not properly a science but [arises] either from the fruitless efforts of human vanity, which would penetrate into subjects utterly inaccessible to the understanding, or from the craft of popular superstitions, which, being unable to defend themselves on fair ground, raise these intangling brambles to cover and protect their weakness." These pretenders to knowledge Hume then likens to "robbers" because of the costs they exact from those who fall prey to them. These robbers, he writes,

> lie in wait to break in upon every unguarded avenue of the mind, and overwhelm it with religious fears and prejudices. The stoutest antagonist, if he remit his watch a moment, is oppressed. And many, through cowardice and folly, open the gates to the enemies, and willingly, receive them with reverence and submission.[2]

The therapeutic function of true philosophical inquiry, then, is to prevent these maladies of the mind and the follies and oppression they occasion:

> Accurate and just reasoning is the only catholic remedy, fitted for all persons and all dispositions; and is alone able to subvert that abstruse philosophy and metaphysical jargon, which, being mixed up with popular superstition, renders it in a manner impenetrable to careless reasoners, and gives it the air of science and wisdom. [The aim, then, is to] undermine the foundations of an abstruse philosophy, which seems to have hitherto served only as a shelter to superstition, and a cover to absurdity and error.[3]

Hume clearly feels that his careful examination of the nature and the limits of human understanding exposes as groundless some of the major claims of the fanatics and sophists. At the very least, these claims are demonstrated to be absolutely beyond the scope of valid perceptions and rational inferences. The belief in miracles, the argument from design, even the idea of causation are shown to be either indemonstrable or clearly dubious. Any political claims based on these doctrinal grounds, therefore, could have no legitimate claim on the loyalties of rational men.

Because of his own historical context, Hume tended to identify these unwarranted claims of philosophical enthusiasm with the political left. In this respect his concern for the disrupting influence of vain philosophy coincided with the similar concerns and with the parallel criticisms emanating from the slightly differing perspectives of Hobbes and Hooker. Hobbes's criticism was similar to Hume's, although he thought the solution lay in a theoretical rather than an experimental political science. Hooker, as a good Anglican, understandably attributed the problem to heterodoxy rather than to religious faith itself. In each case, though, the concern was with the way the beliefs of the republican sectarians led them to challenge and disturb the social order. Hence, unlike Enlightenment skepticism in France, which was principally directed against superstitions deployed in support of the established regime, Hume's skepticism was from the beginning conservative in its concrete political orientation.

Hume's skeptical onslaught on popular political arguments did not stop with his dismissal of "dismal" and "fanatical" divines. He also deployed his critical debunking techniques against some of the most fundamental philosophical claims of Lockean Whiggism and of rationalistic liberalism in general. Reason could not accredit the idea of natural law or the idea of natural justice generally, Hume argued. Similarly, the justification of property by the labor theory of value and the derivation of political authority from the consent of the governed—at least in the way that consent was depicted in contractarian theory—he declared to be insupportable. In each case, these faulty doctrines were based, as he saw them, on abstract philosophical systems rather than on empirical examination of the nature and grounds of the actual practices in question.

The practical goal of Hume's "experimental" science of politics was essentially the same as the goal of Machiavelli's "new way" in understanding politics. Like Machiavelli, he sought to arrive at persuasive prudential maxims for sound public policy. When he criticizes Machiavelli, it is on the grounds that, to use contemporary parlance, he overgeneralized from a limited sample. Machiavelli, he writes, did not fully appreciate the imperfections inherent in his young science; hence some of his conclusions have been proved defective.[4] Hume does not criticize the goals or basic approach of Machiavelli, however, because they are virtually identical to his own. Like Machiavelli, he looked to the record of history for his materials. Like Machiavelli, moreover, he went to history for the purpose of finding there a storehouse of examples from which he could garner enough evidence to warrant his experimental maxims. Careful and knowledgeable historical study could provide vicarious experience to supplement dramatically the limited materials of a man's own immediate experience. Hence, even more reliably, it could "instruct us in the principles of human nature, and regulate our future conduct, as well as speculation."[5]

Hume's argument that history could serve as the principal source of his experimental science rested on another important assumption he shared with Machiavelli—namely, his belief in the fundamental constancy of human nature. Hume was not oblivious of cultural differences, of course, and he cautioned that "we must not expect that the uniformity of human actions should be carried to such a length as that all men, in the same circumstances, will always act precisely in the same manner, without making any allowance for the diversity of characters, prejudices, and opinions."[6] Nevertheless, human nature was sufficiently uniform, in his view, to give adequate warrant for maxims based on it.

Hume's declaration of the uniformity principle and its bearing on his experimental science are sufficiently clear and revealing to quote at some length. "It is universally acknowledged," he writes,

> that there is a great uniformity among the actions of men, in all nations and ages, and that human nature remains still the same, in its principles and operations. The same motives always produce the same actions: The same events follow from the same causes. Ambition, avarice, self-love, vanity, friendship, generosity, public spirit: these passions, mixed in various degrees, and distributed through society, have been, from the beginning of the world, and still are, the source of all the actions and enterprises, which have ever been observed among mankind. Would you know the sentiments, inclinations, and course of life of the Greeks and Romans? Study well the temper and actions of the French and English: you cannot be much mistaken in transferring to the former *most* of the observations which you have made with regard to the latter. Mankind are so much the same, in all times and places, that history informs us of nothing new or strange in this particular. Its chief use is only to discover the constant and universal principles of human nature, by showing men in all varieties of circumstances and situations, and furnishing us with materials from which we may form our observations and become acquainted with the regular springs of human action and behavior. These records of wars, intrigues, factions, and revolutions, are so many collections of experiments, by which the politician or moral philosopher fixes the principles of his science, in the same manner as the physician or natural philosopher becomes acquainted with the nature of plants, minerals, and other external objects, by the experiments which he forms concerning them.[7]

Besides sketching the theoretical rationale for his experimental science, Hume offers some positive contributions to its corpus. These lessons—or maxims of prudence—that he draws from history are to be found principally in his essays and in his historical writings.

Like Machiavelli, Hume must, in order to gain normative direction from the patterns of historical recurrence, stipulate some value to serve as his major premise. Historical fact provides the minor premises from which he can draw the conclusions of his maxims, but he needs some normative touchstone in his major premise. Lacking such normative content in his premises, his historical findings could produce only descriptive conclusions—not directives and counsel.

This normative touchstone he finds in "public interest or utility." "In all determinations of morality," he tells us,

> this circumstance of public utility is ever principally in view; and wherever disputes arise, either in philosophy or common life, concerning the bounds of duty, the question cannot, by any means, be decided with greater certainty, than by ascertaining, on any side, the true interests of mankind.[8]

The touchstone, then, is the "common good" of the classical tradition—but now reinterpreted and revised to accommodate Hume's metaphysical reductivism, his anthropological hedonism, and his ethical irrationalism.

Hume would insist that this stipulation of a normative *axis mundi* for his practically oriented, experimentally derived maxims was in no way an arbitrary fiat. Indeed, it was quite the opposite. It was a respectful acquiescence in the "general sentiments of mankind"— sentiments he considered to be quite uniform. His fundamental normative principle of utility, in short, he conceived to be ratified by a form of *jus gentium*. It received its status and validity from its affirmation by the general and uncorrupted opinion of men everywhere. This uniformity of opinion he believed to be ascertainable by empirical observation, once the distorting influence of superstition was properly discounted. And it was both predictable and explicable on the basis of his theoretical beliefs as well: moral distinctions are "founded on" pleasure and pain; these pleasures and pains are the natural reactions of the human constitution and disposition; this basic constitution and disposition is everywhere the same. Ergo, unanimity of moral judgment among the undeluded is only normal; and this unanimity of response provides moral judgments with the only kind of validation to which they are subject.[9]

This conception of an "experimental" science of politics, it is important to understand, is not ideologically neutral. It is often supposed that the choice of methods is an antiseptically technical one, but that is not the case. One may indeed select one's methodology without any conscious normative bias or ideological intent. Even then, however, the choice may easily favor one ideological perspective over another. Methodological criteria and procedures do not leave the "data" to speak for themselves—which in any case is impossible. Instead, they determine what is "relevant" and what is not. Hence they provide a principle of inclusion and exclusion. They govern what shall count as "valid" argumentation and what shall not, and they provide interpretive categories that shape, divide, and relate the subject matter in significant ways. Rarely are any of these choices wholly neutral in their ideological implications. Cumulatively, they may be very potent indeed. In Hume's case, it is safe to say, the bias of his methodology was conservative. Before he ever reached substantive questions, his conception of a valid "experimental" science, together with the underlying assumptions that sustained it, pointed him in a conservative direction.

In the first place, Hume's skepticism about the moral competency of reason and the static, reductive ontology that went with it led him into a principled obtuseness concerning rational ideals. Ideals and standards of this kind simply dissolve when he examines them because he has no interpretive categories that would make them intelligible. The most important specific examples here are standards of justice, the labor theory of property, and the contract theory of obligation. In each case Hume rejects the arguments, not by meeting them on their own terms, but rather by changing the terms of the argument altogether. And he does this not simply out of expediency—because it is effective—but because these arguments are fallacious in their very form by reference to Hume's philosophical principles. He has to find the arguments meaningless on their own grounds, and he also finds them faulty on his own, "experimental," grounds.

What Hume does, in effect, is to translate arguments about legitimacy in the normative sense into questions about legitimacy in the Weberian descriptive sense. An ethical question is transposed into an empirical question. The question of right becomes a question of fact. Given Hume's understanding of the "tension-less" quality of the world—i.e., its lack of transcendent essences or immanent potentialities—and given his understanding of ethics, that is the only meaningful kind of question. "What is right?" must in principle really mean "What do men take to be right?" "What is the justifiable basis for property or obligation to the state?" is similarly translated into "What is the actual nature of these institutions as established and accepted?"

This reinterpretation of normative questions into empirical ones, dictated by Hume's "experimental" methodology, is his version of what might be called the "Thrasymachan ploy" in such matters. In *The Republic*, it may be recalled, Thrasymachus answers Socrates' question "What is justice?" with the formula "The interest of the strongest." This response did not mean that Thrasymachus considered the interest of the strongest to be normatively valid. It meant that he denied the notion of normative validity itself. Saying that justice was the interest of the strongest was his de facto response to a de jure question. And his answer was a radical rejoinder precisely because its formal eccentricity was not a result of any misunderstanding on his part. By answering the question in the way he does, Thrasymachus indicates that he does not simply disagree with Socrates about what is right but that he dissents from the very premise of Socrates' question that there is such a thing or standard as "right" at all. Thrasymachus, in short, does not merely think Socrates' answer is wrong; he thinks his question is meaningless. He therefore translates the question into the only terms in which he can accredit it and then answers it; and his answer, though not on a par with Socrates' answer, is nonetheless as pregnant with "moral" consequences.

Hume's approach to the questions of justice, property right, and obligation is formally very similar. He refuses acceptance of the very terms of the questions and translates them into "experimental" issues. The result is that he does not so much sever "is" and "ought" as associate them in a different—and fundamentally conservative—way. "Is" is simply elevated to the place of "ought"—not as a moral "ought" but as a practical and utilitarian "ought." Like Thrasymachus, Hume answers how men *should* act by pointing out how they *do* act. His version is decidedly less nihilistic in tone and in consequence than that of Thrasymachus, however, because his reading of how men *do* act is decidedly less cynical. In Hume's hands, what is legitimate descriptively comes to seem normatively legitimate as well.

This assimilation—the elevation of fact to the status of a somewhat reinterpreted norm—is justified by Hume on two grounds. First, what men accept can claim "moral" status because, as noted earlier, the very meaning of ethical terms for Hume is "what men find agreeable and useful." Therefore, the acceptance of a practice or an institution is at the same time its warrant of validity. Second, Hume makes accepted practices appear justified in a utilitarian sense by pointing out their *function*. Established institutions owe their existence to their serviceability on behalf of the interests of society. In observing how this is the case for specific practices, e.g., property rights, Hume demonstrates their utility and thus their rationale. Thus what "is," for Hume, may not be able to claim "goodness" in the classical sense, but it can claim *acceptance* and *utility*. And, on his hedonistic and utilitarian premises, that is all that "good" should really mean.

The conservative cast of Hume's methodology is further intensified by the presumptive validity it accords to history. His understanding of history leads him to see it as both a valid *record* of human nature and as a validating *process*. In each of these two senses of "accepting history" the existing order receives a kind of justification or a kind of protection against certain forms of criticism.

Hume's "experimental" science assumes, first, that history is a valid record of human nature. As he argued, in the long passage cited above, history is a valid record in this sense because of the constancy of human nature. To the extent that this is the case, the pattern of recurrence and imperfections evident in the past indicate that the same should be expected today and in the future. The historical record, in short, could for Hume legitimately serve as a reproach to any political program or ideology that depended on the emergence of any fundamental novelty in human affairs. Particularly insupportable by Humean premises, then, were the promises and prospects of revolutionaries or progressives who claimed that mankind could be perfected or that governmental authority could be abolished. No examples of such enviable states of affairs could be found in history. To the extent that history was a valid experimental record of political tendencies and possibilities, these claims had to be seen as utopian fantasies. This kind of use of the historical record as a test of plausibility (and Hume's own historical writings, predicated as they were on this belief) became, then, a very formidable resource for French opponents of the Revolution.[10]

Hume's methodology tended to validate history—and existing institutions—in another way, as well. History was not only a valid record but also a valid process of selection. Current practices, on this view, were justified, in a rough, pragmatic sense, on the grounds that they had passed the "test of time." Historical dynamics were seen as a kind of "experimental" science of their own very practical sort, in which some "artifices" survived and others were eliminated on a trial-and-error basis.

This understanding of history tends to be conservative because it accords to the status quo at least a prima facie validity. What exists may not be perfect, but its very existence suggests that it must have proved itself of some real value. As Sheldon Wolin has suggested, Hume's approach leads to "the blending of fact and utility" in the concept of historical time.

> It followed that there was no necessary opposition between what was useful and what existed; the desirable and the factual were not out of joint. In this way Hume indicated to later conservatives that the strongest arguments for the existing order were to be found within the facts of that order; that under an empirical approach utility could be located as an immanent value dwelling

within the interstices of actual social arrangements, not as a grim measuring rod contrived to reveal the shortcomings of institutions.[11]

Constructive Conservative Irrationalism:
The Utilitarian Case for Custom and Stability

Hume's conservativism is also grounded in, or reflected by, the substantive interpretation he gives to the very crucial notion of "interest." Public interest and utility, as we noted above, were the determinative norms of Hume's experiential maxims. Having said that much, it still remained for him to attribute some substance to the "public interest." Even if one grants his stipulation *that* the public interest should govern policy choices, Hume must or inevitably will provide some interpretation of *what* is most fundamental to that interest. Public "happiness" is the end, by the criteria of Hume's hedonistic utilitarianism; but *what* does he see as making men happy?

The "liberal" or radical move at this point might be to claim that freedom—defined, perhaps, in various ways—lies at the heart of human interest. Men are happy by virtue of their liberation. Hume sees things differently. He assumes, or alleges, in good conservative fashion, that what men most want from the social order is "peace and security." The heart of the public interest is law and order. The overriding concrete standard of public utility, then, is political stability.

Hume does not really argue for this interepretation as if it were a normative choice of his own. Instead, consistent with his basic view of the source of valid ethical norms, he claims that this is the natural, normal choice dictated by the human constitution. Peace and security are not what should be desired in a moral sense; peace and security are instead what are in fact desired. Indeed, Hume tells us, it is from the instinctive approbation of actions that contribute to social stability that the moral sentiments arise in the first place:

> The mind of man is so formed by nature that, upon the appearance of certain characters, dispositions, and actions, it immediately feels the sentiment of approbation or blame; nor are there any emotions more essential to its frame and constitution. *The characters which engage our approbation are chiefly such as contribute to the peace and security of human society;* as the characters which excite blame are chiefly such as tend to public detriment and disturbance: Whence it may reasonably be presumed, that the moral sentiments arise, either mediately or immediately, from a reflection of these opposite interests.[12]

Just as Hobbes finds a civilizing passion in the fear of violent death, which in turn is rooted in the "natural tendency" to persevere, Hume believes that men's natural sentiments favor social stability and the security it brings. In keeping with the "experimental" cast of his political theory, he does not so much deduce this sentiment theoretically, as Hobbes claimed to do in accordance with his demonstrative science; he claims instead to have found it as an empirical constant, which he speculatively assumes to reflect some innate disposition in "the mind of man." In either case, however, the political implications run in the same direction: authority, stability, law and order, are depicted as the political ends most consonant with the natural desires of mankind and, accordingly, with the public interest.

Hume's treatment of the specifically political topics in his moral theory fully reflects the conservative orientation of his methodological postulates and his reading of human interests and inclinations.

Justice, he tells us, cannot be defined in the classic formula of giving every one his due. Such a definition, in his view, is fallacious because it is circular. One's "due" is established by the rules of justice, he says. Hence we cannot turn right around and say that the rules of justice are determined by what is due. Justice is an artificial virtue, not a natural one. The rules of justice, in other words, are artificial conventions that men establish out of their common interest. The "well-being of men" depends on the peace and security of society; and rules of justice are, in turn, essential to the support of society. That—the furtherance of the common interest in social order and stability—and that alone, is the reason for the rules of justice: "The necessity of justice to the support of society is the sole foundation of that virtue."[13]

In Hume's psychology, contention over property is virtually the sole source of human conflict. Apart from that, he seems to believe, mankind might have been able to subsist peaceably in a state of nature. Quite absent from his account is Madison's bleak suspicion that mankind's propensity to factionalism is so strong that it will seize almost any pretext for manifesting itself. Explicitly rejected, moreover, is the Hobbesian account of the divisive impact of human vanity. "No one can doubt," writes Hume,

> that the convention for the distinction of property, and for the stability of possession, is of all circumstances the most necessary to the establishment of human society, and that after the agreement for the fixing and observing of this rule, there remains little or nothing to be done towards settling a perfect harmony and concord. All the other passions, beside this of interest, are either easily restrained, or are not of such pernicious consequence, when

indulged. Vanity is rather to be esteemed a social passion, and a bond of union among men. Pity and love are to be considered in the same light. And as to envy and revenge, though pernicious, they operate only by intervals, and are directed against particular persons, whom we consider as our superiors or enemies. This avidity alone, of acquiring goods and possessions for ourselves and our nearest friends, is insatiable, perpetual, universal, and directly destructive of society.[14]

When this diagnosis of the causes of social strife is put together with Hume's analysis of the reasons for establishing rules of justice, the result is to identify justice with property rights. Hume refers to this close connection when he says in the *Treatise* that "the origin of justice explains that of property" and when he writes in the *Principles of Morals* that property is "the object of justice."[15] The "laws of nature" recognized by Hume—and "laws of nature" means for him general rules whose observance is absolutely necessary for society—are therefore all closely related to the regulation of property. These "fundamental laws of nature" are "the stability of possession, its transference by consent, and the performance of promises" (i.e., of contracts).[16]

What, then, are the concrete rules of property that amount to social justice? By what measure are they to be established? Not by virtue of "mixing one's labor" with raw materials, as Locke, among many others, had claimed. To create a property right in this way, Hume observes, one must already have control over, have exclusive access to, and therefore have an antecedent property right in the raw materials. Therefore, the labor theory begs the fundamental issue. Moreover, he says, it cannot account for other kinds of property "where we cannot be said to join our labor to the object we acquire: As when we possess a meadow by grazing our cattle upon it."[17]

The standards for legitimate property right, and hence for justice, that Hume offers in lieu of the labor theory turn out to be essentially a benediction of the status quo. The four "circumstances," as he puts it, that "may give rise to property after society is once established" are "occupation, prescription, accession, and succession."[18] Of these four circumstances, occupation is "first possession"; prescription is "long possession"; and accession and succession are both derivative from the first two. Hume's criteria for justice and property right therefore have no critical force whatever. Possession apparently is, for him, ten-tenths of the law. Or, in practical terms, his conclusion seems to be that those who have should keep. The whole rationale for the institution of property is for him its utilitarian contribution to the peace and security of society, and, in his judgment, this constitutive end is best served by respecting established patterns of possession. What is, in this case, is also what "ought" to be.

Hume's treatment of the grounds of political allegiance, or obligation, runs in exactly the same channels. The "fashionable" contract theory, which attributes the origin of governmental authority to the consent or promise of the governed, Hume asserts, "is entirely erroneous."[19] His denial of this theory is warranted, he asserts, by the

> universal consent of mankind that the obligation of submission to government is not derived from any promise of the subjects. It being certain that there is a moral obligation to submit to government, because every one thinks so; it must be as certain, that this obligation arises not from a promise; since no one, whose judgment has not been led astray by too strict adherence to a system of philosophy, has ever dreamt of ascribing it to that origin.[20]

By the principles of Hume's moral philosophy, this judgment alone is quite sufficient to invalidate the consent theory, wholly apart from any practical defects it may have.[21]

Although express consent may play some part in the establishment of political obligation, Hume says, the principal warrant for legitimate authority is precisely the same as the grounds for legitimate rules of justice. Specifically, obedience to constituted authority is properly demanded because such allegiance is requisite to social stability, which in turn is indispensable to human well-being. Interest and utility, in short, are the basis of obligation to government, just as they are the basis of justice and property.

By this standard, the demand by a government that it be obeyed is justified by the same kinds of "circumstances" that justify claims to property. The sources "of all public authority" Hume lists in the *Treatise* as long possession, present possession, conquest, succession, and positive law.[22] The interests that dictate the requirement of political allegiance, he concludes, basically dictate obedience to whatever regime is established. The regime's very existence, its de facto power, gives it its best claim to legitimacy at the same time: by virtue of its current hold on power, it is protecting the very human interest in peace and security that is the best, most fundamental reason for instituting any government.

Hume's argument does not go so far as to proscribe any right of disobedience or revolution whatever. If nothing else, so extreme a "law-and-order" position would have been impolitic in a society that celebrated its "Glorious Revolution" as the source of its constitutional settlement. "In the case of enormous tyranny and oppression," he allows, "'tis lawful to take arms against supreme power; [for,] as government is a mere human invention for mutual advantage and security, it no longer imposes any obligation, either natural or moral, when once it ceases to have that tendency."[23] Hume's argument on behalf of constituted authority is thus not un-qualified. No divine right, certainly, sanctifies governmental author-ity. It must be justified by its contribution to human interests.

Nonetheless, in his application of this principle—a fairly con-servative principle to begin with—Hume tends to weight his judg-ment rather strongly on the side of the powers-that-be, whatever they are. In part, this tendency was undoubtedly based on the very close tie Hume saw between human interest and social stability. In part, it was due to his distrust of "dangerous novelties" in public affairs. In any case, his view that the better part of wisdom almost always lies with obedience to established authority was evident both in his historical narratives (which, for instance, were very favorable toward the Stuarts) and in his explicit counsel. "No maxim," he writes, "is more conformable, both to prudence and morals, than to submit quietly to the government, which we find established in the country where we happen to live, without enquiring too curiously into its origin and first establishment."[24] His advice is, then, a fully secularized version of Saint Paul's often cited admonition in *Ro-mans:* Obey those who are in power. Do so, however, Hume says, not out of piety but out of prudent self-interest.

Burke without Reverence

David Hume, in sum, provides us with an early model of the mod-ern, skeptical, secular, utilitarian conservative. A review of the major political conclusions he drew from his irrationalist "experi-mental" science suggests, in fact, that he might be appropriately styled "Burke without reverence." The practical substance, the concrete recommendations, and the basic strategic orientation of Hume's politics were almost identical to Burke's. If the content is largely the same, however, the mood, the attitude, and the rationale are quite different. Burke is the believer, both intellectually and morally. His counsel consists of what he believes to be moral im-peratives incumbent on man as a contingent creature of God. Hume is the skeptic, both intellectually and morally. His counsel consists of what he believes to be sound advice to prudent men of the world.

Like Burke, Hume insisted on deference to political authority. Where Burke based this demand at least in part on the intrinsic moral legitimacy of constituted authority, however, Hume is content to rest his case entirely on utilitarian considerations. Civil society simply cannot subsist without authority, he argues; and civil society is in turn absolutely essential to the well-being of humanity. One need not rely on any transcendental considerations, therefore, to insist that authority be given first place in the hierarchy of social values. Any prudent man who understands the facts of life will do so. "It may be owned that liberty is the perfection of civil society," Hume concedes, "but still authority must be acknowledged essential to its very existence; and in those contests which so often take place between the one and the other, the latter may, on that account, challenge the preference."[25]

Like Burke, Hume looked for guidance to the past, to history. Burke looked to history for its tradition, and he venerated tradition for its moral worth as, in effect, the pattern of a human pilgrimage. Historical tradition encompassed and passed on to the present generation the blood and tears, as well as the accumulated wisdom, of its ancestors. Hume's respect for history was every bit as great as Burke's, but it, again, appeared in the more mundane form of a prudent regard for custom.

In this respect, Hume's politics paralleled his epistemology. The only source of knowledge was experience. The only record of experience was historical. And the "lessons" deriving from historical experience came embodied in the habit patterns it produced. As in science, so in public affairs: "Custom . . . is the great guide of human life. It is that principle alone which renders our experience useful to us."[26] The prudent man, therefore, will give due respect to history as the only available repository of the experience he needs if he is to act wisely. And he will similarly respect those practices and institutions now established, for these are themselves products of the accumulated experience of past generations. Once again the message largely replicates Burke's message, but the spirit is much more calculating and less "spiritual." Established customs come equally well recommended by Hume, but out of his Baconian experimentalism rather than out of any sense of the majesty and dignity of tradition.

Like Burke, moreover, Hume was a determined opponent of abstract rationalism in politics. An excessive reliance on the claims of speculative, theoretical reason was regarded by both thinkers as dangerous folly. Here again, however, the specific analysis of the problem, and the preferred alternative, has a very different flavor in the two cases. Burke saw the excesses of Enlightenment rationalism as the fruit of extreme secularism and as a form of impiety as well as foolishness. They were a product of "insolent irreligion," which transgressed its proper bounds not only by its relative disregard for experience but also by its denigration of belief and by its failure to understand the proper place of emotion and "prejudice" in human life. The concrete reason he extolled in contrast to the presumption of an abstract and "metaphysical" rationalism was essentially Aristotelian prudence set in a context of religious humility.

Hume fully shared Burke's distrust of abstract rationalism and his fear of its political consequences, and, like Burke, he viewed the problem as the result of a failure to mark the limits of the human understanding and its grounding in concrete experience. Hume, however, saw this faulty presumption not as the product of impiety or of disregard for the emotional side of human life. Indeed, looking at the English republicans rather than, like Burke, at the French *philosophes*, he saw the problem as positively linked with religious credulity and fueled by emotional zeal. "Metaphysical" sophistry was to his mind the fruit of pious superstition rather than irreligious insolence, the folly of enthusiasts rather than the frigidity of economists and calculators. The concrete reason Hume commended as the proper antidote for the distempers so engendered was a different kind of respect for proper limits than Burke's concrete reason. He prescribed a prudence more utilitarian than Aristotelian and a worldly moderation rather than humility and veneration for what is sacred and sublime. (Burke, we might recall parenthetically, wrote an essay entitled "On the Sublime and Beautiful." Hume had little conception of either. Beauty he reduced in remarkably philistine fashion to an efflorescence of utility—e.g., "the conveniency of a house, the fertility of a field, the strength of a horse, the capacity, security, and swift-sailing of a vessel, form the principle beauty of these several objects."[27] And the concept of "sublime" was for him essentially a mere subspecies of the larger and more general notion of "agreeableness.") As the opposite of abstract rationalism, Hume counseled empiricism, not piety, and "experimental" science, not religion. He saw the healthy and realistic approach to be one of cautious skepticism and "common sense." The truly reasonable man was like Hume himself: skeptical, tolerant, moderate, governed by the calm passions, and devoid of any unsettling manias or, we might add, of any sublime ideals.

"Empiricism" in politics means at least two things for Hume—as it in fact means at least two things in the philosophical tradition. It means an unwillingness to rely heavily on any knowledge claims— whether moral or explanatory—that depart significantly from "simple" and "hard" perceptual "data." Failure to respect this cautionary rule leads in Hume's view to metaphysical absurdities in theory and to equally delusionary but more dangerous "fancies" in practice. The rule of empiricism also means a reliance on "trial and error" as the only rational test for both theories and practices. This meaning of empiricism is an ancient one; in fact, it is central to the word's etymology: the Greek word *peira*, "trial." "Experimentalism," then, is the only correct approach in politics, as in science. Innovations in practice, as in theory, must be accredited only by how they actually work out, not by how good they look on paper. Existing, accepted practices must for the same reason be accorded great respect. Their continued existence suggests that they have performed at least passably well in the experimental crucible of time.

Hume's empiricism, then, leads him once again to a very Burkean-sounding conservatism in his basic orientation toward political change. His cautious skepticism in epistemology turns into an equally cautious incrementalism in politics. He counsels extreme care in introducing innovations. He can even describe the proper attitude toward the ''ancient fabric'' as one of ''reverence,'' though his argument makes clear that what he means by this is simply a high utilitarian regard.

> An established government has an infinite advantage, by that very circumstance of its being established; the bulk of mankind being governed by authority, not reason, and never attributing authority to anything that has not the recommendation of antiquity. To tamper, therefore, in this affair, or try experiments merely upon the credit of supposed argument and philosophy, can never be the part of a wise magistrate, who will bear a reverence to what carries the marks of age; and though he may attempt some improvements for the public good, yet will he adjust his innovations, as much as possible, to the ancient fabric, and preserve entire the chief pillars and supports of the constitution.[28]

Hume's skeptical and empiricist conservatism has its very real virtues, both moral and intellectual. His hardheaded realism and his respect for the limitations of human knowledge enable him to provide acute and salutary criticism of those charlatans who demand too much on the basis of inflated claims of authority. His appreciation of the organic qualities of institutional development and his modest willingness to accept the attitudes and desires of other people lead him to a politics that is moderate, tolerant, benign, and safe. In a world where great crimes are committed and destructive upheavals are precipitated by those who contemn realism and tolerance, these are qualities of no little value.

Still, there are equally real flaws and incapacities in Hume's political philosophy—weaknesses that are in large part a function of his inability to understand and unwillingness to accredit rational ideals. With his skepticism, Hume can warn of the dangers of drastic innovations. But without any rational norms, he can give no positive guidance or inspiration. He can explain why some things should not be done, and he can provide reasons for appreciating the present. But he cannot tell us what should be done, and he can provide no vision for the future. Without any constructive norms that transcend the status quo, in fact, he tends to assign excessive value and permanence to the established order. As Frederick Watkins fairly concludes,

> Hume did not wholly escape the conservative tendency to ascribe permanent value to temporary institutions. This danger was, indeed, implicit from the beginning in the attempt to derive norms from empirical experience. Observation of the facts of social life may reveal the nature of currently operative social standards, but provides no clue to the nature of standards which may prove to be operative in the future.[29]

His brand of skeptical empiricism, in short, tends to breed an excessively complacent attitude toward the established order because it has no philosophical resources for identifying and transcending the shortcomings of that order. An insistence on "trial and error" is all right as far as it goes, but some criteria have to be supplied to suggest what needs to be tried and what is to distinguish error from success.

Liberal Irrationalism:
Value Relativism as Social Theory

If the conservative irrationalist promotes custom and habit as the appropriate heirs to deposed reason in politics and morals, the liberal irrationalist's candidate for the throne is individual or group *preference*. Or, to put it in slightly more elaborate form, the only proper touchstones in politics for him are particular *interests;* and interest is interpreted in such a way as to make expressed preferences the exhaustive and unchallengeable measure of interest.[30]

The liberal version of political irrationalism centers around "value relativism," its derivation from scientific naturalism, and its alleged political counterpart of liberal democracy. This perspective on politics begins in epistemology, with a defense of—or, more usually, a simple declaration of—"scientific" empiricism; this empiricism is interpreted in light of an underlying ontology of "facts related by causality"; the argument thence moves to a relativist doctrine of ethics, which is a product of this conception of reason and nature; and, finally, the basically liberal political norms of tolerance, freedom, and compromise are suggested as the appropriate correlates of this philosophical orientation. This configuration of epistemological, ethical, and political ideas may also be called the "relativist theory of democracy."[31] Its leading representatives include figures like Bertrand Russell (at least at one point in his career), Oliver Wendell

Holmes, Jr., and Thomas Vernor Smith. These thinkers are a product of Anglo-American skeptical and empiricist traditions. However, the same basic political orientation can equally as logically grow out of the Continental brand of value noncognitivism; indeed, one of the ablest and most systematic exponents of the relativist theory of democracy is the neo-Kantian legal and social theorist Hans Kelsen.

The relativist democrat insists that there can be no rational standards of right and wrong, good and evil. Rational justifications of any action, writes Kelsen, make sense only in the context of ends and means: "A rational justification is justification as an appropriate means; and an ultimate end is—by definition—not itself a means to a further end."[32] Rationality is purely technical, in short. It does not and cannot extend to the apprehension of "real," "objective," or "natural" values. "Ultimate values" are not potentially cognizable because the "objective" world has no place for them to be:

> Nature, as a system of facts, connected with one another according to the law of causality, has no will and hence cannot prescribe a definite behavior of men. From facts, that is to say, from that which is, or actually is done, no inference is possible to that which ought to be or ought to be done.[33]

It follows that the notion of justice cannot be a meaningful one, since it purports to be an objective norm of this sort. "Absolute justice," writes Kelsen, "is an irrational ideal or, what amounts to the same, an illusion—one of the eternal illusions of mankind."[34] In his debunking of justice, therefore, the liberal irrationalist is at one with his technocratic counterpart and with his conservative-skeptic brother. The parallel with Hume is especially close. Kelsen's argument against the formulation that justice means giving everyone his due, for example, is virtually identical with Hume's argument. This definition, Kelsen writes, "is an empty formula, because the decisive question, what is that which is everybody's own, is not answered, and hence the formula is applicable only under the condition that his question is already decided by a social order—legal or moral—established by custom."[35] And, therefore, also like Hume, Kelsen reduces justice to "social happiness." It is whatever men find agreeable and useful, as Hume would say, except that Kelsen does not share Hume's belief in a basic uniformity of human nature. Therefore Kelsen pluralizes Hume's reduction of justice to the useful and agreeable into whatever a particular individual finds to be so—judged by his own desires and taste:

> I do not know, and I cannot say what justice is, the absolute justice for which mankind is longing. I must acquiesce in a relative justice

and I can only say what justice is to me. Since science is my profession, and hence the most important thing in my life, justice, to me, is that social order under whose protection the search for truth can prosper. "My" justice, then, is the justice of freedom, the justice of peace, the justice of democracy, the justice of tolerance.[36]

The analysis of ethical judgment that follows this rejection of any "objective" basis for moral notions, then, closely resembles the analysis of Weber and Sartre—who stand in the same Cartesian, neo-Kantian tradition as Kelsen. A "value judgment," Kelsen holds, is emotive rather than rational. It is a function of will or feeling, not a matter of cognition. The parallel with the logical empiricist account is evident here. It is impossible, Kelsen tells us, to decide between conflicting judgments of value "in a rational scientific way. It is, in the last instance, our feeling, our will, and not our reason; the emotional, and not the rational element of our consciousness which decides this conflict."[37]

Emotive rather than rational, value judgments are also "subjective" rather than "objective" and radically individual rather than universal. It is the combination of these three characteristics, in turn, that adds up to the "relativity" of these judgments. Kelsen ties together all of these constituent aspects of normative judgments in his theory when he writes: "The answer to these questions is a judgment of value, determined by emotional factors, and, therefore, subjective in character—valid only for the judging subject, and therefore relative only."[38]

Like Weber and Sartre, Kelsen depicts the individual as radically free in his moral choices and hence radically burdened with responsibility for them. He must make choices wholly on his own, without any outside help or rational basis. Kelsen's positivistic relativist finds himself in the role of Sartre's Orestes: he is the determinant of what shall count as good and bad. And the choice, as Weber would have put it, is ultimately "demonic."

> Thus relativism imposes upon the individual the difficult task of deciding for himself what is right and what is wrong. This, of course, implies a very serious responsibility, the most serious moral responsibility a man can assume. Positivistic relativism means: moral autonomy.[39]

Those who claim to find objective grounds for their moral choices, Kelsen charges, are guilty of what Sartre would have called "bad faith." They are guilty of both a kind of arrogance—by attributing a larger significance to what are in reality their own individual preferences—and a kind of irresponsibility—by seeking to place the burden of choice beyond their own shoulders. They "try to shift" this burden, Kelsen writes, "from their own conscience to an out-side authority competent to tell them what is right and wrong, to answer their question, what is justice?"[40] These questions, then, are purely a matter of individual "conscience." However, this "con-science" is a very peculiar faculty and one that is ill labeled by that term; for, since it is radically individual, it has no "con," and, since it is radically subjective and emotive, it has no "science." It is in fact the disposition of an individual will, pure and simple. And the determinations of individual wills are "preferences," each equally as valuable and equally groundless as any other.

Philosophical value-relativism of this kind, liberal irrationalists contend, correlates quite directly with the politics of liberal democracy. Sometimes the claim is simply one of formal parallelism, at other times of a logical and causal connection between the two. Sometimes it is empiricism that is held to be philosophically crucial; sometimes it is relativism. The accounts of what is crucial to democracy, moreover, also have different emphases, but tolerance and liberty are relatively constant principles, deemed to be linked with democracy on the one hand and with relativism/empiricism on the other. Bertrand Russell's view of the relationship is stated in the following terms:

> The only philosophy that affords a theoretical justification of democracy, and that accords with democracy in its temper of mind, is empiricism. Locke, who may be regarded, so far as the modern world is concerned, as the founder of empiricism, makes it clear how closely this is connected with his views on liberty and toleration, and with his opposition to absolute monarchy.[41]

Kelsen argues not only for the connection of relativism and democracy but also for a similar connection between their philosophical and political opposites. He claims that

> there exists . . . not only an external parallelism but an inner relationship between the antagonism of autocracy and democracy, on the one hand, and philosophical absolutism and relativism, on the other, that autocracy as political absolutism is co-ordinated with philosophical absolutism and democracy as political relativism with philosophical relativism.[42]

The essence of democracy, in Kelsen's view, is captured by the principles of freedom—including toleration and civil liberty—and equality. Relativism and empiricism are in turn, it is argued, related logically to these norms, in several ways. In the first place, a thoroughgoing relativism seems to suggest the parity of all values. All values are on an equal footing. Hence, a political order proceeding on the basis of this assumption has no grounds for giving priority to any particular values or to the individuals holding them. Such a relativist-inspired political order must therefore proceed on the basis of a principle of equality.

An ethical world of morally indifferent preferences translates into a political world of morally equivalent interests. Politics can "rationally" be considered not a clash of good and bad, or better and worse, but only a conflict of relative and particular individual desires. "From the point of view of rational cognition," says Kelsen, "there are only interests of human beings and hence conflicts of interests."[43] Recognition of this fact is held to be a precondition of legitimate—in the sense of candid and nonfraudulent—political action. Political acts and claims allegedly based on cognitive moral grounds are necessarily fraudulent, and they are dangerous as well—inimical to stability, moderation, and compromise because of their insistence on absolute "principles." A realistic avowal of politics as only the clash of particular interests by contrast conduces both to political equality and to political moderation.

The recognition that all "values" are relative, hence equal, should further suggest the propriety of a certain humility about one's own desired ends, the relativist argues. The political result of this humility seems logically to be tolerance and respect for the liberty of others. If one understands that one's own preferences have no transcendent or objective status entitling them to priority over others' preferences, one must then respect the right of these opposing preferences to exist—and of opposing views to be expressed. Kelsen even goes so far as to suggest that "sympathetic understanding" of these opposing views is called for on relativist grounds:

> The particular moral principle involved in a relativistic philosophy of justice is the principle of tolerance, and that means the sympathetic understanding of the religious or political beliefs of others—without accepting them.[44]

Kelsen also suggests, in essence, that his relativizing of Kant does not do away with the Kantian demand that every moral being be treated as an end in himself. Instead, it retains this demand in the form of the norm of toleration and respect for freedom. Each self is still depicted as autonomous; indeed, the self is even more radically autonomous, since it is not bound by some universal rationality. Even if the expectation, in a relativist and irrational setting, will now be a plurality rather than an identity of moral judgments, the autonomy and dignity of the constituting subject remains intact. And this autonomy suggests by analogy, Kelsen believes, the propriety of political freedom and respect.

The political norms of liberty, moderation, and tolerance can be derived, it is also argued, from empiricism as well as from relativism. In this line of argument, the crucial attribute of liberal humility is derived not so much from an appreciation of the *parity* of one's preferences with all other values as it is from an apprehension of the inescapable *uncertainty* of one's views. The spirit of democracy, or, more specifically, of liberal democracy, is the spirit that, as Learned Hand once wrote, is not too sure that it is right. The recognition that all ideas inescapably rest on a tentative and precarious epistemological footing should prevent anyone appreciative of that fact from pressing his own claims too far. Hence, he will be tolerant, moderate, and a defender of civil liberty.

Bertrand Russell exemplifies this line of argument in his defense of what he terms "empiricist liberalism." The empiricist's theory of knowledge, he writes, "is half-way between dogma and skepticism. Almost all knowledge, it holds, is in some degree doubtful, though the doubt, if any, is negligible as regards pure mathematics and facts of present sense-perception."[45] A good empiricist, accordingly, is always concerned to make people aware "that they may be mistaken, and that they should take account of this possibility in all their dealings with men of opinions different from their own."[46] This emphasis of philosophical empiricism is in turn identical with "the essence of the liberal outlook," which "lies not in *what* opinions are held, but in *how* they are held: instead of being held dogmatically, they are held tentatively, and with a consciousness that new evidence may at any moment lead to their abandonment."[47] The political correlate of this outlook "is one of live-and-let-live, of toleration and freedom so far as public order permits, of moderation and absence of fanaticism in political programmes."[48]

What both relativism and empiricism rule out in politics is the imposition of any political order or political claim on "absolutist" or "dogmatic" grounds—on the grounds that any pattern of order or claim is "right" in any absolute or certain sense. Politics is nothing but the interaction and conflict of contending interests, each partial, each equal, and each without any certain "objective" basis. The problem now remains: How is political order to be established? How are these various contending interests to be reconciled into a tolerable harmony? In short, what decision rule should be followed now that the rule of selecting the right or just solution is not only not adequate but not even meaningful? On this score the relativists diverge among themselves, and their different positions relate closely to some of the most important axes of ideological and partisan disagreement within the camp of liberal democracy.

One answer is to rely on the mechanism of the market. Liberal relativism herewith issues into laissez-faire liberalism: let everyone choose his own goals and set his own priorities and let these be worked out by the operation of the invisible hand. This solution to the problem of contending interests maximizes both freedom and efficiency. The problem for many liberals here, of course, is first, that (contrary to the hopeful expectations of Condorcet, for example) this decision rule does not seem to give results acceptable to an egalitarian temperament and, second, that the resulting inequalities leave the disadvantaged less free, in a real sense. The cause of justice, then, by some standards at least, might also seem to be ill served. For the laissez-faire relativist, however, this is not a defensible reproach. Distributive justice is one of those philosophical illusions that is in reality simply a gloss covering special interest or envy. Hence Milton Friedman always dismisses the relevance of fairness or justice to economic transactions, and Hayek writes, "the question as to whether the resulting distribution of incomes is fair has no meaning."[49]

A second expedient for reaching decisions in the context of contending interests is the "democratic" rather than the "liberal" device: majority rule. Since no one is right in any profound sense, the reasonable thing to do seems to be simply to count noses. As Herman Finer puts it, "in a democracy right is what the majority makes it to be."[50] If the market-oriented liberal advocates the market as a means of producing "order without commands" (Hayek's characterization), then Bertrand Russell can offer majority rule as a counterpart. It is the only way of achieving "order without authority"—which, he says,

> might be taken as the motto of both science and of liberalism. It depends, clearly, upon consent or assent. In the intellectual world it involves standards of evidence which, after adequate discussion, will lead to a measure of agreement among experts. In the practical world it involves submission to the majority after all parties have had an opportunity to state their case.[51]

Kelsen argues, in addition, that relativism implies the propriety not only of the principle of majority rule but also the respect of minority rights.

> It may be that the opinion of the minority, and not the opinion of the majority, is correct. Solely because of this possibility, which only philosophical relativism can admit that what is right today may be wrong tomorrow—the minority must have a chance to express freely their opinion and must have full opportunity of becoming the majority.[52]

A last, and most hopeful, expedient of relativist conflict resolution is that of compromise. When conflicting interests and "principles" of equal status collide, the best thing to do is to work out some intermediate bargain that assigns some satisfaction and some sacrifice to all parties. In the eyes of T. V. Smith, in fact, the willingness to submit to compromise is a paramount ethical principle of democracy. The political broker is the mundane hero of democratic government, the political embodiment of the blessed peacemaker of the Beatitudes. And Kelsen, in somewhat less exalted terms, seems to suggest not only that compromise is the appropriate lesson of relativism but that only his relativism can legitimate compromise. The solution to conflicts of interests, he says,

> can be brought about either by satisfying one interest at the expense of the other, or by a compromise between the conflicting interests. . . . Only if it is not possible to decide in an absolute way what is right and what is wrong is it advisable to discuss the issue and, after discussion, to submit to a compromise.[53]

In brief, such is the political theory of democratic relativism and empiricist liberalism: Relativism and/or empiricism tells us that all values are equal or at least uncertain. Appreciation of this truth should lead to the rejection of all "absolutism" and to an acceptance of the liberal democratic practices and norms of toleration, liberty, moderation, and—to some degree—equality. Contending interests can and should be reconciled by reliance on the market, by compromise, by acquiescence to majority will, or by some combination of these. This is a negative, if sometimes impassioned, defense of liberal democracy: liberal democracy cannot be said to be a positive good, but it seems to be the decent and proper way to conduct affairs in a world where nothing can really be said to be good.

Locke without Reason, Hobbes without War

The relativist and empiricist theories of democracy have their very real virtues, at least in practical terms. Those who subscribe to the humane values of liberal humanism can be grateful, of course, for the democratic relativists' commitment to the norms of toleration and liberty. The value of compromise and moderation in maintaining the fragile fabric of a free society is also very great, fully worthy of the attention given them by the relativistic theorists. And the reminder that one may be mistaken in one's most cherished beliefs is a welcome reinforcement to the democratic spirit praised by Learned Hand. However, after all due appreciation is rendered, it must be said that the relativist theory of democracy, first, is afflicted with some very real logical problems and ambiguities and, second, is sustained in its conclusions only by relying on a moral tradition it disclaims.

The strongest part of the relativist and empiricist justifications of liberal and democratic institutions is their common focus on epistemological fallibilism. If the truth about what is good for human fulfillment were clearly and definitively knowable, the warrant for an absolutist politics, creating and enforcing that good, would be quite strong. That warrant might still be overridden by an analysis of the dynamics of freedom in the context of self-knowledge or by other competing considerations; nonetheless, in this circumstance the prima facie case for absolutist politics would be a good one. This logic is a crucial part of the rationale for technocracy, for example, and for some of the totalitarian models criticized by Popper, Talmon, and Russell. On the other hand, if the limitations of the human mind are such as to render all moral beliefs somewhat uncertain, then the case for the politics of freedom and toleration improves dramatically. Hence, the relativists' and the empiricists' emphasis on the fallibility of human knowledge is important and right on target.

The problem, however, is that if the relationship between fallibilism and liberal democracy is relatively clear, the relationship between fallibilism and both relativism and empiricism is considerably more suspect. Russell has no difficulty in linking empiricism and fallibilism because he equates them virtually by definition. "The empiricist's theory of knowledge," he writes, "is half way between dogma and skepticism."[54] If this equation is accepted, then Russell's argument is made. In fact, however, empiricism has tended not so much to avoid dogma and skepticism as to produce both; specifically, it has tended toward extreme skepticism in ethics and extreme dogmatism in metaphysics. The only way it can be made to fall "half way" between dogma and skepticism, then, is by averaging its divergent tendencies.

The identification of fallibilism with relativism is even more problematic. Fallibilism presumably suggests a situation in which there is something to know that can be only imperfectly apprehended. A thoroughgoing relativism, as in Kelsen's paradigmatic formulation, suggests that there is nothing to know. This difficulty afflicts some of Kelsen's most central philosophical terms with profound and systematic ambiguity. He speaks of "values" but makes it clear that there can be nothing real or objective about these curious entities: they are not "immanent in nature." Similarly, it is equally confused or misleading to speak of these "values" as being "relative." In fact, as Kelsen makes clear in his more lucid and candid moments, what his philosophy in fact suggests is that "values" is a cover term for interests ("From the point of view of rational cognition, there are only interests of human beings and hence conflicts of interests") and that value claims are "relative" only in the sense that they are equally meaningless in any cognitive sense.

Kelsen perpetuates this semantic and conceptual confusion in some of his crucial formulations of the relationship between relativism and democratic practices. For example, he says:

> It may be that the opinion of the minority, and not the opinion of the majority is correct. Solely because of this possibility, which only philosophical relativism can admit—that what is right today may be wrong tomorrow—the minority must have a chance to express freely their opinion and must have full opportunity of becoming the majority. Only if it is not possible to decide in an absolute way what is right and what is wrong is it advisable to discuss the issue and, after discussion, to submit to a compromise.[55]

On the contrary, it would in fact seem that the very notions of "correct," "right," and "wrong" are not really permissible within the context of Kelsen's kind of philosophical relativism, in which "there are only interests." This whole formulation dissolves into absurdity, then. What could it even mean, to one of Kelsen's persuasion, to say that a minority might be "correct"? Only that they might succeed one day in becoming the majority, we might presume. And, if that is the relevant measure, one could then guarantee, by the simple expedient of forcible suppression, that the minority would never be "correct." It is equally unclear what the "discussion" Kelsen sees as "advisable" would consist of. If value claims are cognitively empty—or at best are utterly not subject to rational adjudication—then the parties could not really discuss anything, in the usual sense of that term. They could only "declare their interest" or perhaps identify their (Weberian) "demon." Kelsen's brief for minority rights, for civil liberties, and for parliamentarism, then, seems unable to survive the resolution of his semantic confusion.

The fact is that the relativist democrats draw liberal conclusions from their philosophical premises only because tacitly they trade on a tradition they in theory reject: the tradition of civility, as Ernest Barker and Walter Lippmann call it. Hume interpreted his skepticism as grounds for moderation and humanity not so much because of strictly logical reasons as because he was himself moderate and humane. Similarly, Russell, Smith, and Kelsen were all liberal and tolerant men of very real moral sensitivity. Any of these moral skeptics, Hume as well as the twentieth-century thinkers, might equally well have said what Leslie Stephen wrote: "I now believe in nothing, but I do not the less believe in morality.... I mean to live and die like a gentleman if possible."[56]

Consider, for example, the relativist derivation of the democratic norm of equality. It does indeed follow from relativist premises that all human beings and all human values stand on a par. All values are equal. What logic cannot say, however, is that this is a parity of worth rather than worthlessness. Only because the relativist tacitly incorporates the tradition of civility's assumptions about human dignity and individual worth can he suggest the positive reading of his equation. Apart from these tacit assumptions, one might just as easily conclude that all men and all values are equally meaningless and inconsequential and thus equally unworthy of respect. It is relativism's tacit dimension, then, that makes it liberal rather than nihilistic.

The relativist derivation of the norms of liberty and toleration is subject to the same qualification. It follows logically from relativist premises that no one has rational justification for imposing his own values on anyone else. Stated in this way, the relativist argument seems in fact to imply the propriety of toleration, since it undercuts any attempt to legitimize domination. Drawing again on the tradition of civility, the relativist democrats choose to interpret the practical import of their doctrines in just this way. The culture of relativism is depicted as a negative version of a culture of civility. However, one could with equal logic come to quite different conclusions. For if relativist premises undermine any attempt to legitimize political domination, they also provide no basis for *prohibiting* domination. An aspiring dictator can, on relativist premises, claim no rational support for his *libido dominandi,* but his opponents can claim no rational grounds for declaring his tyranny unacceptable. These "good reasons" for the rule of law and limited government must come from something like the tradition of constitutionalism, with its positive moral assumptions.

Beneath the surface humility of relativistic toleration, moreover, lies a kind of arrogance. Relativism is tolerant in that it does not presume to question anyone's behavior. Indeed, its toleration in this respect must be total and undiscriminating: everyone has a right to act as he will without challenge of any sort. It is in reference to the relativist's *own* choices that the arrogance appears, for on his premises he is exempt from the normal human obligation to give "good reasons" for his actions when requested to do so. However, the expectation that one can and will "explain oneself" is an important part of the mutual accountability of a human community. Because most of my acts inevitably impinge on others, I owe them an accounting of my reasons if these acts seem problematic. The relativist, however, feels entitled to reject out of hand any requests for good reasons, since he deems moral choices to be arbitrary and radically autonomous. Carried to its logical conclusion, the tolerance *cum* arrogance of relativism would tend both to disintegrate the bonds of human community and to dissolve the rational discourse of a politics of civility.

The democratic relativist argues, in sum, that his relativism will lead, and should logically lead, to a politics of liberty, equality, toleration, and even altruism. A relativist philosophy is said, indeed, to produce a "democratic personality," depicted as moderate, tolerant, and charitable. Russell sees this democratic personality as tentative and conciliatory, unlikely to oppress anyone else and willing to abide peaceably by the will of the majority. T. V. Smith envisions him as public-spirited, benevolent, and willing to compromise. And Kelsen describes the relativist democratic personality as an "altruistic type" who "does not experience the other as his enemy but is inclined to see in his fellow-man his friend. He is the sympathizing, peace-loving kind of man."[57]

One would like to accept these sanguine estimates of "relativist man" as descriptively accurate and theoretically sound. Both empirical evidence and logic suggest, however, that these accounts are remarkably optimistic and predictively unreliable. Our democratic relativists, it seems, have simply generalized their own good will—without giving a very persuasive account of its origins, even in their own case. Their optimism therefore rests on an interpretation of the relationship between relativism and liberal humanism that is a reversal of the actual facts. They argue that relativism produces toleration and altruism, whereas the truth is that only someone who is already tolerant and altruistic will read the implications of relativism that way.

The empiricists' liberalism is traced, as Russell explicitly acknowledges, to John Locke. It is a Lockeanism divested, however, of the natural-law beliefs and the faith in moral reason that Locke defended in his early thought and incorporated in his political premises. Empiricist liberalism gives us, therefore, what we might call "Locke without Reason"—without noetic rationality, that is. Locke so interpreted, however, looks a great deal like Hobbes, as indeed the anxieties of some of Locke's own contemporaries indicated. Similarly, the world of philosophical relativism is virtually identical with the world of Hobbes. The account of reality, of science, and of ethics is the same in both.[58] Here, as elsewhere, the empiricist's version of liberalism and the relativist's version of democracy tend to coalesce. They differ with Hobbes's account of the likely political consequences of his doctrines, however. Whereas he depicted a moral chaos held together only by the power of a strong sovereign, the empiricist-relativist prognosis is for "order without authority" (Russell's phrase).

We might justifiably characterize the political theory of empiricist liberalism and democratic relativism, accordingly, as tantamount to "Hobbes without war." Kelsen, Russell, et al., that is, depict the universe in basically Hobbesian terms but avoid his bleak political conclusions by interposing a hopeful conception of human nature that, philosophically, is largely free-floating. One would like to accede to their optimism. It seems more reasonable, however, to conclude that in this instance the Enlightenment's unrealistic political optimism has somehow survived the demise of its equally untenable philosophical optimism.

The Absolutist-Relativist Controversy: A Brief Digression

This account suggests some tentative conclusions concerning the lively and sometimes bitter debate between the adherents of relativist and "absolutist" conceptions of liberal democracy. This debate raged most furiously during the 1930s and 1940s, when the unexpected challenge of modern totalitarianism forced the reexamination of some fundamental principles. This debate, moreover, was never really resolved. It simply subsided as political and intellectual circumstances changed, only to reemerge in somewhat different form in the 1960s, when the ideological complacency of the 1950s was disturbed. The basic claim of the relativists in this encounter was Kelsen's claim, cited above, that liberal democracy is correlated with and justified by the premises of philosophical naturalism and relativism and that, conversely, political absolutism, including modern totalitarianism, is a function of belief in philosophical absolutes. The absolutist democrats held just the contrary: liberal democracy, they argued, is based on certain fundamental moral principles, such as the dignity of the individual, which are "absolute" and inviolable; conversely, modern totalitarianism, especially Nazism, is a function of a complete philosophical relativism, which permits the cynical use of absolute power to manipulate and eliminate political opponents.[59]

Concerning philosophical "absolutism," we can say that the relitivists were correct in arguing that the belief in absolute values can and has led in the past to political absolutism. Political absolutism follows from the philosophical belief in absolute values, however, only if it is also believed that some particular group of savants, experts, or philosophers can legitimately claim to know that truth with certitude. This kind of political absolutism based on philosophical absolutism must also possess some grounds for overriding the value of freedom or the realities of free will. (Indeed, one can make a very good case that the decisive argument for toleration in

Locke's *Letter concerning Toleration* is not epistemological empiricism so much as it is the theological notion of "justification by faith." As Locke took pains to observe, if salvation comes only from a free and internal act of faith, then it follows (*a*) that others cannot be saved by constraining their external actions and (*b*) that the heterodoxy of others cannot threaten one's own salvation.)[60] Finally, an immanentist absolutism is more likely to be politically absolutist than a transcendentalist absolutism, since it envisions the *eschaton* as a present or future this-worldly possibility. It is for all these reasons that Hegelian philosophy has been so potent a stimulant of political fanaticism.

The "absolutists" are right, however, in arguing that the accreditation of "objective" values can contribute and has contributed to the ethos of liberal democracy, especially when this absolutism is transcendentalist (or at least sees perfection as an unreasonable expectation for historical existence) and includes an appreciation of the contingencies of human knowledge—if, for example, it realizes that these absolute goods are perceived "through a glass darkly." In this form, philosophical absolutism is quite compatible with the democratic practices of civil liberty and toleration. Indeed, the argument for toleration may be based on theological grounds, as in Locke's argument just noted or in the contention that the claim to know God's will is a sinful presumption. While it respects the pluralist element in democracy, moreover, this kind of philosophical "absolutism" can also provide the basis for insisting on the justice, the human dignity, and the intrinsic limits on the legitimate scope of government that are the essence of political constitutionalism— which is, in turn, a crucial element in Western liberal democracy.

Concerning relativism, the democratic relativists are justified in their contention that this philosophical orientation can and has led to liberal and democratic political standards, especially those of liberty, equality, and toleration. Humane skeptics from Democritus to T. V. Smith have drawn precisely these kinds of inferences from their philosophical premises. On the other hand, the absolutists are quite correct in pointing out that a thoroughgoing relativism offers no grounds for principled opposition to tyrannical and oppressive political practices and that it can be read by those so inclined as a warrant for cynicism and nihilism. As perhaps is appropriate for a philosophy of moral irrationalism, the determinative factor in the political outcome of relativism seems to be personal predisposition or political culture rather than logic. Relativism does not necessarily or even usually lead to totalitarianism, then, but it is, by the same token, a very weak foundation for the liberal and humane norms of constitutional democracy.

Positivist Pluralism: The Contemporary American Amalgam

The positivist pluralism that has become a leading, perhaps even dominant, perspective on contemporary democratic politics is heir to both Humean skeptical conservatism and relativist liberalism. Indeed, it is the genius of contemporary positivist pluralism to have combined these two traditions into a compelling amalgam highly congruent with the realities and inclinations of a conservative liberal society. (The United States, as Gunnar Myrdal once wrote, is a profoundly conservative nation, but the principles it conserves are liberal ones.) In addition, the pluralists have contributed some "experimental" ammunition that would have pleased Hume, and they have provided some nice theoretical embellishments as well.

By "positivist pluralism" I mean the public philosophy that is a vulgarized and ideologized version of the descriptive pluralism of recent political science. This public philosophy, called "interest-group liberalism" by Theodore Lowi (who has given one of the most influential accounts of its nature and origins), also bears affinity to what has been called the "end-of-ideology" ideology.[61] The pluralists and the end-of-ideology theorists have described contemporary American politics in the same general light. For both, American politics—and sometimes, by implication, modern democratic politics or the politics of postindustrial society—is in its essence the piecemeal accommodation of contending group interests. Although these descriptions were ostensibly purely "empirical," "scientific," and descriptive of just the facts, it seems clear that the investigators both (*a*) found the situation they depicted to be generally healthy and proper and (*b*) made several interpretive judgments that tended cumulatively to give a favorable cast to the workings of pluralism.[62] From the relatively sanguine accounts given by the pluralist political scientists, then, it did not require too great a leap to convert the descriptive interpretation into a model with prescriptive force.

The ideology of positivist pluralism, then, can be adumbrated in the following way: Democratic politics is not the story of any grand ideological vision. It is not even the story of a quest for justice or for the common good, both of which are rhetorical concepts of no cognitive meaning anyway. Instead, democratic politics is a story of conflicting plural interests. Around these interests, which are normatively equivalent preferences, groups are formed. These groups then contend for dominance or at least for the attainment of their own interest. Since none of the groups can in fact dominate or secure all of its goals, public policy is formulated by compromise and piecemeal "muddling through." The vector of forces that results from this interest-group struggle is a kind of equilibrium. And this equilibrium represents the "public interest," insofar as that is a meaningful term. This kind of pluralist polity is neither grandiose nor perfect, but it does satisfy the democratic norms of liberty and equality—interpreted in one way, at least. And it seems also to satisfy the utilitarian norm of success and stability. It is a form of politics, therefore, that is "no negligible contribution to the art of government''; and any profound problem with the system is more likely to be resolved by its extension—i.e., by greater inclusion of affected interests or groups within the system—than by its displacement or fundamental revision.

The affinity between positivist pluralism and democratic relativism should be fairly easy to appreciate. It is not, I think, that the pluralists are explicitly or directly influenced in their ideology by writers such as Kelsen or T. V. Smith so much as that they are simply another branch of the same tree. Both the relativists, who are explicitly normative in their intent, and the more covertly or subtly normative pluralists are a product of the same intellectual and political culture. Therefore it is not surprising that they should overlap a great deal in their political outlook, which is in fact a blend of these two cultures: positivism and established democratic liberalism.

Like the democratic relativists, the positivist pluralists subject some of the classic norms of democratic politics to skeptical analysis and then jettison them as "operationally" meaningless. Especially important among these discarded concepts are the notions of the public interest and natural right, for it is these touchstones that have traditionally served to give limits and meaning to the free-for-all of democratic pluralism. Apart from these notions, and the derivatively identified hazards of injustice, tyranny, and anarchy, there is little to distinguish the democratic process from a (perhaps sublimated) war of all against all. Undeterred by these considerations, the pluralists are adamant in their dismissal of these ideas. The public interest, they insist, is purely mythical or nonexistent. At best it is so lacking, by empiricist criteria of significance, that any right-thinking man must do without it. In like fashion, the idea of natural right is adjudged to be a residue from a bygone era, whose assumptions are no longer compelling to scientific moderns. "The assumptions that made the idea of natural rights intellectually defensible have tended to dissolve in modern times," Robert Dahl suggests.[63] For that reason, he concludes, the Madisonian concepts of "tyranny" and "faction" must also be set aside as cognitively useless, since they are identified by reference to natural rights and the public interest.[64] As de Tocqueville said in *Democracy in America,* "it was the idea of right which enabled men to define anarchy and tyranny."[65] Conversely, when the pluralists are led by their positivist standards to discard the notion of right, they also lose the power to discriminate when a regime becomes tyrannical or when a society dissolves into anarchy.

Like the democratic relativists, the pluralists, once they have dismissed the anachronistic debris of the normative tradition, take "interests" as their starting point. These interests are generally conceived as the interests of a group, since purely individual interests are not likely to reach a level of public significance. Any suggestion that something other than group interests is present as the "stuff" of politics is dismissed as "metaphysical." Any attempt to rank, distinguish, or discriminate different types or levels of "interests" is likewise dismissed as a scientifically unacceptable or morally presumptuous intrusion. Interests are interests, all "relative" and all "equal."

Like the democratic relativists, the positivist pluralists see the policy process that arises on this basis as a politics of logrolling or bargaining among the various interested parties. The broker is the democratic hero. Compromise is the motto and overriding norm of the system. And the outcomes or "outputs" of the system are not so much approximations of justice or approximations of rational policy as they are simply the vector that results from the conflicting interests. This feature of the democratic policy process, moreover, is not only a fact; it is a positive virtue, for comprehensive plans are likely to be unworkable or counterproductive.

Finally, the pluralists borrow the optimistic assumption that the outcomes of this process amount to some kind of equilibrium. Laissez-faire economics is in essence turned into a political model. It is broadened from a model of how the economy does—and should—work into a model of how a free and democratic political system does—and should—work. Pluralist logrolling, it is held, produces "peaceful adjustment" rather than deadlock or coercion, and it is the most reliable means of obtaining this felicitous resolution of conflict. As Lowi suggests, in this respect pluralism—and democratic relativism as well, one might add—represents a "transformation of capitalist ideology," together with its blindspots, its consequent complacency, and its consequent conservatism.[66]

The ideology of positivist pluralism is also remarkably similar in many respects to Hume's skeptical conservatism. As in the parallels between pluralism and the relativist democrats, these similarities are more likely the result of shared basic presumptions than of any conscious borrowing. Hume is not widely read today as a political theorist or, for that matter, as a guide to social scientific methodology. The lack of explicit indebtedness makes only more remarkable the extent to which contemporary American pluralists have replicated the pattern of Hume's eighteenth-century British utilitarian conservatism.

Like Hume, the contemporary positivist pluralist relies heavily on his epistemological skepticism as an ideological weapon. Just as Hume deployed his skepticism against the very principle of rational or transcendental norms that might give leverage to revolutionary critiques of the status quo, the pluralists attack their opponents on methodological grounds, utilizing the very stringent standards of their positivist empiricism. By these standards, it proves rather easy to dismiss, for example, the stratification theory that underlies Marxist and many progressive ideologies as being "unscientific."[67]

As in Hume, moreover, there is a curious element of asymmetry and overkill in these debunking methodological critiques. The standards deployed are so stringent that they could destroy almost any kind of social theory if consistently applied. As Terence Ball wrote recently, the application of these standards is tantamount to going duck-hunting with antiaircraft guns.[68] Given the extremely destructive capacity of this kind of methodological critique, therefore, the positivist pluralist rarely devotes to his own theories the same degree of critical scrutiny he gives to opposing theories. As William Connolly says:

> It is a bit difficult to find a recent study in political science in which the author explicitly claims to conform to a stringent version of operationalism. The doctrine is most often invoked by political scientists when they criticize the work of others, especially those others who advance ideological orientations with which the political scientist disagrees. In this way the doctrine of operationalism is supported less by displaying its merits in concrete studies than by the repeated charge that others do not live up to it.[69]

This asymmetry of application of the requirements of a stringent operationalism leaves the positivist social theorist in a somewhat exposed position, however. Astute critics have come to learn that he can be hoist with his own petard—even if he can justifiably claim to violate his criteria of scientific respectability somewhat less drastically than many others. In this respect, the positivist's position is formally on a par with that of the Marxist whose debunking use of the sociology of knowledge is highly effective but also capable of being turned against him. When that happens—in both instances—the time is ripe to move the argument to a somewhat higher level of sophistication and subtlety.[70]

(In Hume's case, this asymmetrical application of rigorous skeptical standards led him into some outright contradictions as he sought to escape being boxed in by his own criticism. He insists on the one hand, for example, that it is wholly fallacious to adjudicate theoretical issues on practical grounds: "when any opinion leads to absurdities, it is certainly false; but it is not certain that an opinion is false, because it is of dangerous consequence."[71] Yet he escapes succumbing to Pyrrhonism on just such practical grounds: "For here is the chief and most confounding objection to excessive skepticism, that no durable good can ever result from it; while it remains in its full force and vigour.")[72]

As in Hume, moreover, the pluralists' positivism tends to lead them into the "conservative" habit of elevating current realities into de facto norms. When the pluralists look at the "functions" of existing institutions and practices, these receive an implicit justification—just as Hume's conservatism was based in large part on his demonstration of the immanence of utility in the historical process. When a great gap is revealed between existing fact and conventional ideal, the tendency then is to assume that it is the ideal rather than the reality that needs revision. Thus, for example, the contemporary democratic "revisionists" point out the "functionality of apathy" and seek to revise downward many of the classic standards and expectations of democratic theory.[73]

It is not that either Hume or the positivist pluralists simply construe what "is" as being ideal. Neither is so naïve. The bias of their skepticism, however, leads them both to be very dubious about the validity of important concepts, such as "potentiality" or "objective interest," that give empirical footing to somewhat more demanding normative criteria of political order. Consequently, there is a tendency on the part of both to assume that, since any convincing potentialities or interests must have concrete and "operational" manifestations, realistic possibilities must be tangibly reflected in, if not wholly exhausted by, current realities. Thus the positivist pluralist or democratic revisionist, much like Hume, finds it easy to slide from the finding that something is not now the case into the supposition that it cannot be the case. The famous conclusion to Berelson, Lazarsfeld, and McPhee's *Voting*,[74] for example, slides from the finding of present fact that voters do not presently behave like John Stuart Mill's ideal citizen to the claim that "individual voters today seem *unable* to satisfy the requirements for a democratic system of government outlined by political theorists."[75] Now if it is genuinely true that voters are not even potentially competent to be "rational voters," some long-standing democratic ideals need some review. "Ought" implies "can." But one cannot justifiably draw such a conclusion about long-run possibilities simply on the basis of the current state of voter rationality. One can make the move from "is not now" to "cannot be" only on the basis of further assumptions and judgments—assumptions and judgments, it should be added, that are hard to fit into a positivist framework, whatever their content. In parallel fashion, the pluralist dismissal of "false-consciousness" notions on principle leads to the assumption that real interests are exhaustively expressed in explicit policy preferences. This assumption, in turn, tends to be "conservative" in its implications insofar as it narrows the gap between existing policy outcomes and the fulfillment of real interests. And, whether it is warranted or not, this rejection of false-consciousness claims and the consequent conservative interpretive bias depends on the acceptance of working assumptions not justifiable by positivist standards: it may be more modest, but it is no more provable, to assume that everyone understands and manifests his real interests than to assume that some people do not.

Positivist pluralism falls into the Humean tradition of skeptical conservatism in other ways as well. Like Hume, pluralist ideology puts a premium on order and stability in its hierarchy of political values. Perhaps simply because stability in the sense of regime maintenance is more unproblematic to "operationalize" than justice, freedom, or effectiveness, perhaps because of some tacit judgments or valuations in their own minds, pluralists have tended to focus in their research on the dependent variable of stability, and pluralist ideology has tended to celebrate the utilitarian virtue of stability. The pluralists, like Hume, may have very good reasons for their judgments; but, also like Hume, they have tended to assume the validity of their valuations more than to justify them. The pluralist bias here has been largely innocent and unintentional, I think. It has been more the reflection of the prevailing political culture in America than an attempt to impose debatable values surreptitiously. Like Hume, the pluralists might have found it rather easy to assume that their concern with stability was justified on the basis of its widespread acceptance by enlightened men.[76]

Democratic revisionists have also tended to deprecate the political capabilities and rationality of the general populace. With one eye on the specter of McCarthyism and the other on the dismally poor levels of political perception revealed by survey data, the revisionists might well have echoed Hume's dictum that "popular rage is dreadful, from whatever motive derived; but must be attended with the most pernicious consequences, when it arises from a principle which disclaims all control by human law, reason, or authority."[77] With this fear lurking in the background, it might indeed seem reasonable to see the relative apathy of the majority quite positively. Instead of representing a weakness or failure of democratic performance, apathy represented a significantly stabilizing ballast for the ship of state. Rather than strive with Mill to enhance the lives of the democratic citizen through encouraging political participation, it was better to second Hume's wary recommendation to let sleeping potential fanatics lie.

For the pluralists, finally, as for Hume, this skeptical conservative perspective issues into the prescription of a cautious incrementalism. Rapid political change is dangerous and unsettling, especially if it is dictated by sweeping ideological imperatives or by grand rational abstractions. The prudent pluralist joins Hume in his call: "Let us cherish and improve our ancient government as much as possible, without encouraging a passion for such dangerous novelties."[78] Policy innovation is in the pluralist system just what it properly should be in pluralist ideology: a series of piecemeal and pragmatic adjustments to reflect specific pressures and to ameliorate specific problems. The pluralist's motto for his conservative interest-group liberalism is "Muddle through."

The Inversion of Madisonian Democracy

The philosophical core of pluralism, therefore, is an ingenious amalgam of liberal relativism and conservative skepticism, at once encouraged by and adapted to its setting within a conservatively liberal society. To this amalgam pluralism adds its own distinctive contribution, namely, its inverted Madisonian analysis of the American political system.

Madison's analysis of the nature and potential dangers of republican polities was structured by a definite normative framework, and it was somewhat pessimistic about the likely natural—i.e., formally unregulated—outcome of factional strife in republican regimes. The pluralists follow Madison in his focus on the "group process" as the central determining feature of democratic—or, to use Robert Dahl's term—"polyarchal" politics. However, the pluralist model transforms Madison's perspective via both normative and empirical criticism. The contemporary version of pluralism "relativizes" the Madisonian model, on the one hand, and derives a more optimistic prognosis from it on the other.

First, the contemporary pluralist deploys his positivism to strip away the normative context of Madisonian theory. Madison's analysis of democracy was dedicated to certain rather clear—if not fully specified—normative goals. A good democratic regime, the kind of system he wanted to see established, would promote justice, protect liberty, guarantee natural rights, and produce policies aimed at the common good, i.e., at "the permanent and aggregate interests of the community.'' Negatively, the desired system would avoid the pitfalls of both tyranny and anarchy. The problem of group politics, in this context, was that groups are "factions": their own particular interests are different from and often adverse to the common good. These factions, therefore, would very likely tyrannize over others if they were able to do so; and the strife among contending factions could also tear asunder the body politic and produce anarchy.

From the point of view of positivism, such an analysis has to be seen as miscast from the very beginning. Its entire meaning, point, and vocabulary are contingent on the presupposition that certain norms may be assumed to be cognitively meaningful and valid. The most fundamental of these norms are the notions of natural right, justice, and common good. But, the positivist pluralist objects, these premises are unacceptable to him or to "anyone of positivist or skeptical predispositions."[79] It follows, therefore, that the terms "faction" and "tyranny" must also be rejected—or at least be re-defined in such a way as to strip them of their normative content— for they are defined by reference to the previously discredited con-cepts. If natural right has no meaning, then tyranny likewise has no meaning insofar as it is defined, as by Madison, as a severe trans-gression of natural right. And if a faction is defined, as Madison defines it, as a group interest adverse to the public interest, then it loses its meaning with the loss of the notion of public interest.[80]

For the positivist pluralist, then, the reality of democratic politics consists not of selfish factions whose warfare carries with it the constant threat of tyranny or anarchy. Instead, the reality must be seen "objectively"—i.e., without the allegedly illicit and encum-bering normative assumptions—as simply the interaction and con-flict of "interest groups," which must be viewed as morally equiva-lent, moreover, since they each presumably feel their cause is right—and who is to say? In methodological terms, each "interest" is on a par because it is impossible to give "operational meaning" to any criterion that would distinguish them. This is a route, via methodological positivism, to the same end as philosophical rela-tivism: "from the point of view of rational cognition, there are only interests of human beings."[81]

The application of positivist value noncognitivism to Madison's model, then, results in its reduction to the dimensions of the rel-ativist world view. The conceptual models and verbal formulations of positivist pluralism, in consequence, are not only morally "neu-tral"; they are also, for the same reason, peculiarly amorphous. Intent on respecting the "scientific"—i.e., positivist—proscription against normative discrimination, the pluralist models are left in principle without the capacity to discriminate adequately the different types of "interest groups" in society; they can discriminate them only by reference to overt and nonnormative characteristics such as numbers, tactics, and resources. Black people struggling for minimal rights and businessmen fighting to retain the three-martini-lunch tax deduction, for example are both "interests." Admirable "neutrality" of conceptualization? Perhaps. But also, clearly, rather insufficient cognitively as well as perverse morally.[82]

If the pluralist view of the dynamics of group struggle in a democracy is relativist rather than—as in Madison—interpreted from a normative point of view, it is also more optimistic in certain key respects. Or perhaps it is more accurate to say that the contemporary pluralist tends to assess the potential causes of democratic instability somewhat differently than Madison did. The contemporary pluralist sees the principal threat to democratic stability to be an excessive ideologizing of political issues and excessive politicization of society. Unlike Madison, however, he tends to depict the group struggle itself as unproblematic. Madison saw factional strife as sufficiently divisive to constitute a very real danger to the health of any democratic republic. The contemporary pluralist is more sanguine. He sees interest-group battles as simply the normal policy process of democracy—a process that leads to relative "equilibrium" through bargaining and compromise.

Part of this optimism about the nature of the group process is brought about "automatically," as it were, by the semantic force of relativizing Madison's terms. "Interest group" is a more benign term than "faction," and the shift to it, or to some such term like it, is dictated by the dismissal of natural right and public interest. Likewise, the fear that democratic politics might lead to majority tyranny can be dismissed by simple recourse to the semantic imperatives of relativism. If "natural right" and "public interest" are meaningless, then "tyranny" is also meaningless. And, as Dahl says, "if tyranny has no operational meaning, then majority tyranny has no operational meaning."[83] So, happily, Madison's fear of majority tyranny seems to have been simply a bogeyman created by his unscientific semantics.

Dahl is quite aware, of course, that this kind of argument—however influential it has been, tacitly, in shaping positivist pluralism's benign account of group politics—is not a very satisfactory answer to Madison's concern. It might be a reasonable worry, Dahl realizes, that one group might succeed in dominating all other groups, whatever term might be applied to the situation. (Dahl in fact later uses the word tyranny without putting it into inverted commas.) The real answer the pluralist gives to the problem of tyranny—or group domination—within a democracy, then, is empirical rather than merely semantic and conceptual. Madison, it is argued, "underestimated the importance of the inherent social checks and balances existing in every pluralistic society."[84] A minority cannot tyrannize over other groups, for it lacks the numerical weight to do so. And a majority cannot tyrannize, for it cannot attain sufficient coherence to do so.[85] The real situation is one of "minorities rule." And that means that no single group is able to obtain complete dominance over the others.[86]

Madison's preoccupation with formal constitutional checks and balances, then, is adjudged to have been misdirected.[87] It is the informal social balance of power that instead is determinative, and the pluralist seems reasonably assured that contemporary American society is indeed pluralistic enough to satisfy this criterion.

If formal institutional checks and balances are downplayed in the pluralist program for a reasonably balanced and stable democratic system, another Madisonian theme also seems to be largely ignored. A republic was likely to survive, Madison suggested, only if "the people" did not become the kind of "mob" or aggregation of mobs depicted and feared by classical political theorists. Some degree of moral sensibility, some "capacity for justice," as Reinhold Niebuhr has termed it, some "republican virtue," was deemed necessary to keep Plato's account of democratic degeneration from unfolding. Madison stated his hope that these qualities were indeed present in human nature and also stated in *Federalist* #55 his conviction that they were essential to the success of the democratic venture:

> As there is a degree of depravity in mankind which requires a certain degree of circumspection and distrust, so there are other qualities in human nature which justify a certain position of esteem and confidence. Republican government presupposes the existence of these qualities in a higher degree than any other form.[88]

An astute pluralist like Robert Dahl is aware that the "democratic ethos" plays a significant role in sustaining the viability of a democratic polity. "Even if universal belief in a democratic creed does not guarantee the stability of a democratic system," he writes, "a substantial decline in the popular consensus would greatly increase the chance of serious instability."[89] Within the confines of positivism or philosophical relativism, however, this ethos has to appear as something of an irrational phenomenon. Or, especially under relativist auspices, it is watered down in content to "live and let live"—the ethos of Kelsen's "democratic personality." In some of the cruder versions of interest-group liberalism, moreover, this demand for (or awareness of the systematic need for) the element of self-restraint embodied in the notion of republican virtue disappears altogether. In this respect the liberal optimism behind contemporary pluralist ideology is evident in the lack of any concern about the "character" of the people. It represents something of a cross between Mandeville and Jackson: either private vice is transmuted into public virtue, or the character of the people can simply be assumed to be good.[90]

If, as I am suggesting, contemporary positivist pluralism shares the basic orientation of Hume's skeptical conservatism, operates within the fundamental parameters of liberal democratic relativism, and embodies an inverted form of Madisonian theory, then it might be summarized in the following terms: it is Burke without reverence, Locke without reason, Hobbes without war, and Madison without right, the threat of tyranny, or the need for republican virtue. It is an interpretation of politics that is secular, utilitarian, and relativistic in its moral orientation; and it is skeptical about unrealized ideals while relatively sanguine about currently established political institutions and practices. Hence it represents a positivist interpretation and conservative defense of secularized American liberalism.

It can justifiably be viewed, then, as a leading "irrationalist" ideology, and perhaps, as critics such as Lowi, Crick, and Connolly suggest, it is the dominant public philosophy of our time and place.[91]

The Inadequacies of Positivist Pluralism

When assessing the merits and defects of positivist pluralism as an ideology, it is only fair and proper to observe the many credits that can be entered on the positive side of the ledger. It has given us added empirical insight into the workings of a modern democratic system, and it possesses some very real moral and political virtues as well. We owe to the pluralists a greatly refined understanding of the actual informal dynamics and processes that go on behind democratic legal and institutional formalities. We understand, thanks to them, the positive functions of interest groups in making government more responsive. We have been led to a better understanding of the presence and role of elites in a polyarchal system. We have been made aware of some of the differences between the democratic citizen's ideal image and his actual current capacities and forms of behavior. The list could be extended further. No responsible theory of contemporary democracy can fail to be indebted to these discoveries, even where it wishes to interpret the evidence in somewhat different ways than the pluralists did.

Normatively, the pluralist can legitimately claim commendation for his hardheaded realism—for his unwillingness to let social theory be based in wishful fantasies and idealized misconceptions rather than on the facts of life. The pluralist's sense of the limitations of knowledge, even if misconceived, has also given him, like Hume, an ability to expose charlatans dealing in inflated claims. For like reason, pluralism has been characterized by a modest willingness to accept the feelings and desires of others as entitled to some legitimacy. The pluralist's conception of democratic politics is moderate, tolerant, and accommodating. These are no mean virtues, especially in a world that still produces its share of fanaticism and oppression.

Largely because of its philosophical value noncognitivism, however, positivist pluralism has some very substantial liabilities. Its conservative and relativistic interpretation of liberal democracy produces significant empirical distortions, it suffers from genuine normative deficiencies, and it consequently carries with its ascendancy very real potential dangers.

In the first place, it has contributed to a reductive interpretation of liberal democracy in general and American democracy in particular that is simply inaccurate historically. Reading their own philosophical prejudices into the past, democratic relativists have implied that the philosophical rationale and motivation behind the growth of liberal democracy has been a rejection of the belief in "absolute values." One instance of this ex post facto reductivist interpretation of democratic reforms and practices, for example, is the rendering of Locke as a modern empiricist whose embrace of toleration stemmed from this source. (The distance between this account and the reality may be measured by, among other things, the surprise and dismay evinced by today's student when he reads the last few pages of Locke's *Letter concerning Toleration*.) Contemporary pluralist democracy, of course, did indeed develop out of the breakdown of the moral and religious unanimity of medieval society, but that is quite another thing than suggesting that it developed from a conviction that "all values are relative."

The contemporary pluralist understanding of democracy also contributes to a falsely optimistic account of the democratic prospect and of American realities. Contemporary democracy is depicted in pluralist theory as both more stable and more just than in fact it is.

Because of its interpretive bias—e.g., because of its narrow interpretation of interest, its attribution of political inactivity to apathy and apathy in turn to relative contentment, its focus on a narrow range of issues—the pluralist model tends to obscure the tensions, forced inequities, and economic constraints that are one part of the current internal balance of power in American politics. Marxist-inspired critiques may greatly exaggerate these aspects of the system, for obvious reasons of intellectual bias and political motivation, but the pluralist conception of contemporary democracy seems consistently and unnecessarily to hide the fact that, as E. E. Schattschneider once put it, the flaw in the pluralist heaven is that the heavenly chorus sings with a distinctly upper-class accent.

Similarly, perhaps because of a careless use of the notion of "equilibrium" and because of its historical reductivism, the pluralist model may impute more stability to contemporary secular democracy than it in fact possesses. Once he has interpreted American democracy as an embodiment of interest-group liberalism, the pluralist takes note of the relative continuity and stability of American democracy and concludes by imputing stability to interest-group liberalism. In fact, it may well be that, the more fully the American polity approximates the pattern of interest-group liberalism, the more unstable it may become. To the extent that the policies of such a system are increasingly perceived as the product of purely self-interested logrolling, the more that system will be subjected to intensified demands and afflicted by loss of support. The system loses support because it loses its moral legitimacy, and intensified demands are placed on it as each group seeks to compensate for the real or imagined influence of its rivals. For both reasons, the system suffers from an erosion of its authority and, with it, a diminution of its capacity to govern effectively. The system thus becomes progressively less stable. This analysis is undeniably somewhat speculative and impressionistic. However, it seems at least as persuasive hypothetically as the pluralist's optimism, and recent events can reasonably be interpreted as lending credence to an alternative, and less sanguine, set of expectations.[92]

If it is subject to empirical question in some respects, positivist pluralism is also open to charges of normative deficiency. Because of its relativism, it is largely sterile. It has no energizing appeal, no capacity to inspire much in the way of commitment or dedication on the part of anyone. It is, as Bernard Crick has written, "not a humanistic view of society but a gelded view, something so over-civilized and logically dogmatic as to deprive many of any feeling that anything, let alone free institutions, is worth while."[93] A thoroughgoing skepticism regarding all political and moral values may indeed be useful in quenching the flames of fanaticism, but its pyrrhonism may equally effectively extinguish the candles of passion and loyalty requisite to sustain even moderate and tolerant regimes.

Similarly, if it is without the power to inspire, positivist pluralism is equally devoid of the capacity to illuminate and liberate. Insofar as its normative incrementalism is based on an appreciation of the un-avoidable complexities and imperfections of policymaking in a free and pluralistic society, that is one thing. But insofar as this in-crementalism is simply a function of positivist incapacity to suggest any rational goals or directions for policy, that is entirely another matter. At that point, "muddling through" ceases to be a counsel of realism and becomes an attempt to make a virtue of a complete lack of creative political imagination and moral vision. Not only are any existing systemic problems repressed as a result, but ineffective procedures and destructive policies may simply be perpetuated and intensified rather than corrected. At its best, incrementalism may produce policymakers who are competent, effective, "realistic" technicians, and the policies they produce may result in piecemeal progress, as advertised. At its worst, however, it can amount to a pragmatic and instrumentalist rationale for making a political hero out of Nietzsche's "last man"—the one who "forgot why he ever had begun." It may also contribute to disasters like Vietnam and the Bay of Pigs, where technical virtuosity and precision function in the context of acute political and moral shortsightedness.[94]

The positivistic version of pluralism, moreover, not only obscures but positively contributes to the debasement of the legitimate—and perhaps even necessary—sustaining ideals of republican govern-ment. With its remarkably undiscriminating reduction of all the very disparate passions, aspirations, and commitments that actuate de-mocracy into a set of fundamentally homogeneous "preferences" or "interests," for example, relativist theory erases the conceptual distinctions between a democratic moral community and the anar-chism of selfish individualism. Like Madison's preoccupation with the dangers of democratic brands of tyranny, the concern that most penetrating observers of democracy have shared—that democratic individualism might degenerate into a rapacious and destructive general egoism—is set aside by simple semantics. Since all the dog-matic relativist can conceive is individual interests anyway, he would be unable to see or describe a process of cultural disintegra-tion if it unfolded before his very eyes.

In *Democracy in America,* de Tocqueville pondered this problem aloud.

No power on earth can prevent the increasing equality of con-ditions from inclining the human mind to seek out what is useful or from leading every member of the community to be wrapped up in himself. It must therefore be expected that personal interest will become more than ever the principal if not the sole spring of men's actions; but it remains to be seen how each man will understand his personal interest. If the members of a community, as they become more equal, become more ignorant and coarse, it is difficult to foresee to what pitch of stupid excesses their selfishness may lead them; and no one can foretell into what disgrace and wretchedness they would plunge themselves lest they should have to sacrifice something of their own well-being to the prosperity of their fellow creatures.[95]

Furthermore, as others have suggested, this threat is made even more acute by the momentum and bias in a democratic "market" society toward this kind of selfishness. The problem is, in the words of William Lee Miller, "that twentieth-century democracy requires a civic responsibility that its own characteristics discourage." Specifically,

collaborative, democratic government requires a recognition of the principle of government, and of the public good. American political culture has been strongly imbued with the opposites of these qualities: a considerable anarchistic feeling . . . and an excessive trust that the pursuit of private interest will serve the common good.[96]

To the extent that moral conduct, including Madisonian "republican virtue," depends on an adequate moral imagination, the impact of positivist pluralism only intensifies these difficulties. As William Connolly has argued, the tacit assumptions of this ideology collapse the "important distinction sanctioned in ordinary discourse between one's support for a policy because of a perceived moral obligation and one's support for it solely on the grounds of self-interest." The "pernicious effects of such an assumption, both for political inquiry and for the considerations governing the political commitments of citizens," Connolly concludes, "can hardly be exaggerated."[97]

The Debasement of Democratic Ideals

The positivistic interpretation of politics in general and of democratic politics in particular also contributes to the debasement or erosion of the ideals of liberty, equality, right, and common good. Liberty, for example, must become—in the context of positivism's unidimensional conceptualization of the passions—just what it was for Hobbes: mere "absence of impediment." Or, to put it another way, the distinction between liberty and license is lost. Given the very real abuses that seem to surround many theories of "positive liberty," especially in the Hegelian tradition, this particular oversimplification may be quite preferable even in its reductionism. At the very least, such a conceptualization of liberty has the virtue of relative precision and clarity, and it leaves those who like to "force others to be free" where they belong—namely, without justification. In the context of Anglo-Saxon liberalism, however, which tends to exalt liberty above all other political values and to leave it without "other ends which might temper the passion for liberty,"[98] the loss of the distinction between liberty and license produces its own corruptions. The understanding of the nature, the justification, and the appropriate limits of the institutions of private property and free speech, for example, tends to be corrupted by this reductivist conception of liberty. Stripped of the assumptions about the reality of common good and moral truth that provided part of their rationale and gave them limit and structure, the claims on behalf of both property rights and rights of free speech easily slide into assertions of an inviolate privatism and subjectivism.[99]

A purely relativistic notion of equality is similarly flawed. The fundamental components of democratic equality are moral equality and equality before the law. Democratic equality also means at least equality of opportunity and—by some standards of justice and prudence—a limit on permissible inequality of condition in economic affairs. What it does not properly mean is that every individual desire or every performance is to be accorded equal value. But the reductivist "toleration" of positivist relativism, consistently applied, leads toward this conclusion. Since there are no objective criteria of good and bad, the assumption runs, there are also no such things as better and worse. There are only *different* actions, choices, desires, and accomplishments, all of which possess equal worth. This kind of amiable nihilism may have its value as a corrective to the excesses of a status-conscious adversary culture. However, in its democratic majoritarian incarnation it tends to enshrine mediocrity, philistinism, and the delusion that right and truth are determined by popular vote, and in its liberal individualist formulation it tends toward harmless eccentricity or toward a more somber unleashing of destructive energies—as, for example, in the counterculture's slide from Woodstock to Altamont.

It is almost as if the positivistic interpreters and defenders of democracy were in covert alliance with antidemocrats like Plato. With respect to the norms of democratic liberty and equality, these apparent political and philosophical opposites are in curious agreement, for both see these standards and democratic norms in general as intrinsically relativistic and philosophically reductivistic. It is simply that Plato condemns them and the positivists embrace them. Neither seems willing to envision or to accredit a conception of democracy grounded in the equal moral dignity of all men and in the quest for ordered liberty under law—Plato because he could not accredit the common man, the relativists because they cannot accredit moral truths. One wonders, with concern, whether the relativists' embrace of Plato's interpretation of the meaning of democracy might not also help to validate his sociological pessimism about its fate.

Positivist reductivism also transforms the notion of natural right in a curious way. If the concept of natural right is dismissed on principle, it does not simply die outright in a culture that has embraced that idea. Instead, it is reincarnated in "empirical" and subjectivist form. All preferences are equal. They do not, on positivist premises, differ in merit or essentiality to human fulfillment. They do, obviously, differ in intensity. The obsolescent notion of natural right, the positivist pluralist will allow, may have some cognitive significance in this context: "natural right" means, in a sense, "intense preference."[100]

This formulation is the best the positivist can do, since he has renounced any principles of legitimate interest, any normative understanding of human nature, that would allow natural right to be more than a decibel rating of appetite. There is, of course, some real overlap between rights and needs and between needs and intensity of desire, but there is some important slippage as well. Mighty preference, like objective might, does not make right, as even a cursory survey of possible examples might suggest. Lester Maddox undoubtedly had a more "intense preference" for keeping black people out of his fried-chicken emporium than they had to enter it, but that consideration didn't, and shouldn't, give him the right to act as he did. Intensity and essence are not always identical.

Finally, the constitutive goals of justice and the common good also lose their meaning and force under the aegis of positivist pluralism. One of the reasons why interest-group liberalism "cannot achieve justice"[101] is that it cannot conceive of justice. Just as right is reduced to intense preference, so "justice" is reduced to balance-of-power and the outcome of bargains based on it.[102]

Once again, as in the case of right, a partial truth has been converted into an untenable claim by the excision of normative criteria. No tolerable relative justice has ever been achieved or is achievable in power politics apart from some grounding in a balance of power, but that does not mean that a balance of power is therefore just. Indeed, as circumstances change, an established balance of power must be adjusted by some mediating standards of justice or it will become increasingly corrupt, unjust, and delegitimized. This might be called a moral version of the Marxian analysis of contradictions.

Denying the validity of the mediating standard on principle only accentuates the conservatism inherent in the balance-of-power approach and hastens its corruption.

Likewise, the skeptical debunking of the common good may be a justifiable rejection of holistic myths about some metaphysical fusion of state and *Geist*, but, by its disaggregation of all common interests into their individual constituents, such an analysis mistakenly suggests that the common good is nothing but a concatenation of individual egocentrisms. The mutual interest in the self-transcending aspects of community is either obscured or is denied by implication. The result is, in Grant McConnell's well-chosen words, an "attribution of almost all virtue to the institutionalization of what another era might have seen as narrow selfishness."[103]

In all of these ways, then, the impact of positivist pluralism—our contemporary fusion of Hume with Hans Kelsen—substantially erodes and transforms the constitutive ideals of liberal democracy. Liberty turns conceptually into license; equality means denial of merit; common good is reduced to a collection of individual ends; right is measured by mere subjective intensity; justice is dismissed as a not genuinely meaningful end of government.

Although advanced by advocates who are themselves generous and public-spirited, and although it has acknowledged strengths, it is a conception of liberal democracy that is historically distortive, philosophically primitive, morally crude, and politically deleterious. To the extent that it is accepted as the valid public philosophy—the definitive self-interpretation of the meaning of liberal democratic society—it tends not only to distort the institutional and procedural norms of the system, as Lowi has demonstrated; it also tends to undermine the tacit tradition of civility that is the sustaining core of the democratic ethos.

As a result, positivist pluralism invites a slide into the disintegrative narrow particularism described—at an extreme—by Hobbes and feared by de Tocqueville, and it erodes the system's authority and legitimacy by grounding its right to govern exclusively in its ability to satisfy the egocentric demands that pluralist theory itself encourages.

Irrationalism and Radical Romanticism: Alter Egos under the Skin

As a final potential danger, the positivist pluralist conception of liberal democracy fosters the growth of an explicitly irrationalist radicalism. This alter-ego relationship between a rather complacent pluralism and an almost indiscriminately indignant radicalism may seem peculiar on the surface, but it is neither unprecedented nor illogical. All it takes to shift from one to the other is a change of heart, not a change of mind. The complacent relativist has already declared reason defunct as a political guide, and he falls back on his moderate (in Hume's case, "calm") passions and his "reasonable" interests. The radical irrationalist accepts this verdict on the moral incompetency of reason, but his passions and aspirations are not moderate, and his "interests" are not so "reasonable" or pedestrian.

The restrained and civilized skepticism of the liberal or conservative irrationalist may lead, on the one hand, to a much cruder and much less restrained amoralism. This might be called the Ivan Karamazov–Smerdyakov connection, after Dostoyevsky's depiction of the relationship between the cerebral, passive amoralism of the former and the active amoralism of his crude acolyte. Or, alternatively, the same complacent and scientistic amoralism may produce by reaction a romantic, antiscientific hypermoralism, which can be almost equally nihilistic in practice. An arid technicist "rationalism" *cum* value irrationalism leaves the moral passions homeless when it leaves moral claims groundless. In complacent "common-sense" skepticism these moral passions tend to become stunted; in outright amoralism they are obliterated; and in irrationalist hypermoralism they regain or retain all their natural fervor—and more—but in problematic disjunction with reality.

Thus, Hume's skeptical campaign against political enthusiasm paradoxically "cleared the way for political romanticism."[104] The sterile, positivistic "liberalism" of Germany contributed to the moral vacuum that Nazi romanticism could fill and to the narrowly legalistic jurisprudence it could subvert,[105] and, in the 1960s in this country, the complacent skepticism of middle-aged "pragmatists" established both the occasion and the argumentative terms for a youthful and often romantic rebellion. As Alasdair MacIntyre has observed, this conflict was not simply a "generational conflict":

> For such a characterization misses the symbiotic character of the phenomenon; the pragmatism of the attitude involved in the end-of-ideology thesis leaves precisely those whom it seeks to educate vulnerable to almost any ideological appeal by its failure to criticize social wholes. . . . The implicit nihilism of so much student attack on institutions is the natural outcome of the defense of the institutions of the status quo as the only possible ones.[106]

You have convinced us of the impotence and irrelevance of reason in ethical and political affairs, the rebels might well have said; now don't turn around and tell us to "be reasonable."

The mutual incomprehension and the polemical incompetence of these alter-ego opponents, moreover, is almost total. Rational criticism, not to mention rational dialogue, is impossible because neither party considers it meaningful. The politics of "confrontation," as barren as it is mindless, is all that is left. Without the resources to understand, to illuminate, to criticize, to adjudicate normative perceptions, each side can only presume the other guilty of perversity of will. The romantic radical sees his opponent as irredeemably corrupt, while his adversary in turn views him as simply demented.[107]

The irrationalism of feeling embodied by the romantic rebel is a very understandable response. His complacently positivistic culture has rejected the competency of reason concerning the ends of human life and has then offered the inertia of habit or the promptings of individual interest as substitutes. The rebel, with some justification, perceives the recourse to habit as mere reactionary stodginess and perceives the recourse to interest as the petty selfishness of bourgeois materialism. Without recourse to reason to criticize and transcend these weaknesses, he can only look to yet another species of unreason as a corrective. He naturally looks, then, to "feeling," to "instinct," to "will" for the warmth and substance he finds lacking in his increasingly sterile culture.

In a sense, of course, the romantic radical is looking in the right direction. As Theodore Roszak insists, the romanticism of the counterculture has the virtue of opening dimensions of human life that have been drained and constricted by the imperatives of secular, technology-oriented modernity.[108] The problem is that "feeling" tends to dissipate into mindless and random sensation when it is devoid of noetic structure. Kenneth Keniston says it well:

> If reason is seen as powerless to discover men's purposes, then what is left is of course instinct, passion, and feeling. Yet, separated from reason, these potentially benign and liberating forces have been more and more reduced to blind animal drives. In an individual, when the basic instincts are separated from controlling intelligence, they tend to become crude and bestial; and so, in intellectual history, the cleavage between the apostles of passion and the advocates of mind has brought an abasement of our conception of passion to an equation with the forces of destructiveness, self-seeking, the call of the blood, and the imperatives of lust.[109]

The positivistic rationalist has grounds for concern, then, about a renascent "irrationalist" barbarism. What he does not appreciate, however, is that his own impoverished philosophy is a major cause of what he fears.

8 The Quiet Demise of Liberal Reason

Our critical analysis of the ironic career of liberal reason can now be brought to a conclusion. We saw, in the first two chapters, how a new and optimistic epistemological program developed out of a diagnosis of Scholasticism's failure, and we saw how this conception of human reason produced several programs, sometimes overlapping, sometimes insufficiently differentiated, depicting the political benefits the advance of reason would confer on mankind.

We argued, however, that these optimistic political prognoses were logically flawed. They depended, in various ways, on the persistence of premises carried over uncritically from the classical tradition—premises whose compatibility with the new philosophy was insufficiently considered. Especially important in this respect was the widespread assumption that the new conception of reason would retain the scope and content of *logos*-rationality as it acquired its geometric precision and its new empiricist foundations.

The untenability of this expectation—and consequently the unpersuasiveness of the political hopes based on it—gradually became apparent under critical examination. At first these difficulties surfaced in the tensions and inconsistencies afflicting the philosophical systems of transition figures, such as Locke, who could renounce neither the old assumptions nor the new ideas. Later, something had to give way to provide escape from the manifest philosophical incoherence thus produced. The "normative truth" of *logos*-rationality had either to be scaled down to the dimensions of scientific naturalism—at least in outward appearance—or to be abandoned altogether.

The framework was thus set for the dual disintegration of the original hopes of liberal reason. On the one hand, technocratic visions emerged, which assigned to the nascent scientific elite the task of "finding the laws" of "rational" political development. On the other hand, a stringent scientific asceticism abjured all rational inquiry into "values" and assigned them to the ostensively "demonic" realm of random passion.

The political implications of these alternative second-generation offspring of liberal reason, we have seen, ran directly counter to the humane hopes and aspirations of that tradition. The early liberals' goal was to establish a political order that avoided the polar dangers of tyranny and anarchy. They looked forward to a politics of "ordered liberty." When their philosophical center gave way, the logical impetus of their heirs' ideas was away from this difficult but crucial middle ground and toward the feared extremes. By encouraging new versions of the fanaticism and skepticism that seventeenth-century rationalism had sought to transcend, the offspring of liberal reason have nourished the tyrannical and anarchistic derangements the early liberals hoped to put behind them forever.

Technocratic philosophies have proliferated "prison fantasies" that have all too often been converted into practice, either in the all-encompassing oppression of totalitarianism or in more specific and limited corruptions within liberal societies. The tyranny of scientistic rationalism comes in different forms and is sanctioned by language different from that employed by the tyrannies of premodern times, but it is every bit as real and every bit as destructive—perhaps more so, because of its technological efficiency and because of its ironclad exculpations and justifications. "Heretics," "barbarians," and "traitors" are at least worthy foes; recalcitrant "objects" are merely part of the terrain that must be leveled for the building of utopia.

Value noncognitivist philosophies, on the other hand, lead toward anarchism, whether that of the amiable relativist or the impassioned nihilist. They obscure the light of practical reason and fall back on complacent habit, bourgeois interest, or the potential primitivism of feeling and instinct. The empty throne of reason is filled by displaced moral passions, by dionysiac deities, or by simple appetites. The unrestrained selfish individualism of corrupted democracy or the unbounded passions of romanticism flourish in the vacuum these philosophies create. In cultures where they were well established, the institutions, beliefs, and attitudes of an earlier tradition of civility may "suspend the logic" (as Michael Polanyi puts it) of political disintegration. But it makes one nervous, to say the least, to observe the essentially residual and subrational status of these bases of order. We are left to wonder with de Tocqueville "what pitch of stupid excesses" might result if these residues were to vanish.

The first, technocratic, orientation and its ideologies lose sight of the *contingency* of practical reason. The latter, irrationalist, orientation and its ideologies lose sight of the very *possibility* of practical reason. In both cases, the problem arises at bottom from the identification of all knowledge with theoretical science—or, more precisely, with a specific understanding of theoretical science that arose from the modernization (i.e., accommodation to seventeenth-century ontological premises) of that Aristotelian epistemological category. The technocrat accredits normative truths as a valid part of the corpus of this theoretical "real knowledge," while the irrationalist applies the same test and reaches the opposite conclusion. In either case, the result is disastrous to the enterprise of humane politics. Camus may be guilty of hyperbole, but he has a point when he writes:

> Those who rush blindly to history in the name of the irrational, proclaiming that it is meaningless, encounter servitude and terror and finally emerge into the universe of concentration camps.
> Those who launch themselves into it preaching its absolute rationality encounter servitude and terror and emerge into the universe of the concentration camps.[1]

In this country we may have been spared, mercifully, the political upheavals that led Camus to this somber conclusion. Honesty requires that this good fortune be attributed, however, not to our superior acumen or, even less, to any superior virtue but rather to historical and sociological accident.

The question now becomes: so what? Suppose that the account offered here of changes in the idea of reason and attendant shifts in political conceptions is essentially accurate? What then? How are we to understand and respond to our current situation?

It is perfectly conceivable a priori, for example, that these philosophical developments represent a straightforward intellectual advance. The original liberal understanding of reason and its constructive relationship to politics was, as we have seen, fundamentally confused, philosophically incoherent, and ultimately untenable. The disintegration of this epistemology *cum* political theory, therefore, would seem on the face of it to have been inevitable and—intellectually, at least—salutary. The original outlook may have been a humane and hopeful doctrine, but it was an erroneous one. It offered a faulty assessment of human understanding; and, insofar as its social theory was based on this assessment, its political program was a lullaby of illusion.

The disappearance of this lullaby might be regretted, then, in the sense that one regrets the loss of comfortable childhood illusions, but it could hardly be deplored. The truth will come out, and we must embrace it or else sacrifice our intellectual probity. Perhaps, then, we must simply accept and learn to live with the technocratic or the value noncognitivist conception of reason and politics? These might be hard truths, but, if they are truths, they can hardly be set aside simply because we do not like their consequences. As Hume wrote, it is a wholly fallacious form of argument to leap from a demonstration of a doctrine's pernicious effect to the conclusion that it is false.

It might well be, then, that the technocratic or the value noncognitivist view of human understanding must be accredited even if we do not happen to like its consequences. We similarly have to adjust to these consequences if we are not to abandon our grip on reality. On this account, however, we must at least adjudicate the dispute between the two second-generation paradigms. They cannot— logically cannot—both be right. Rational norms of human action cannot be both "objective" and nonexistent. Since technocracy presumes the former and value noncognitivism presumes the latter, we must choose between them. Recognition that one cannot have it both ways, and a concomitant recognition of the political stakes involved, manifests itself in the "methodological" focus of much recent and contemporary controversy between opposing ideological camps. Lenin's critique of Mach and the pluralist debunking of Marxist sociology are examples of this genre. In each case the disputants deploy their own epistemological criteria to malign the opposition as "ideological" and "metaphysical" in contrast with their own allegedly scientific bona fides.

Our choice, however, may not be so limited. Other alternatives are conceivable. We are not bound to choose between technocracy and irrationalism simply because they carried out the logical critique of the original version of liberal rationalism and because they are logically more coherent than the tradition they superseded. If it is fallacious to reject a theory purely because of its presumed pernicious consequences, it is also fallacious to presume the validity of a theory solely because it grew out of a valid criticism of some previous theory. In philosophy and in politics, as well as in science, theoretical models built on the ruins of models they supplanted are in turn succeeded by others superior to them. The appropriate response to our current situation, accordingly, may not be to face up to choosing between technocracy and irrationalism but rather to examine possible alternatives.

Renford Bambrough has suggested that persistent and apparently irresolvable philosophical battles, such as those between realism and nominalism or between idealism and materialism, are often the product of a particular kind of intellectual situation. In many of them, he suggests, each adversary has grasped one horn of an apparent dilemma arising from a fundamental presupposition they hold in common. Both parties to the dispute cling tenaciously to an important, but partial, valid insight. In order to do so, however, they are forced into the error of denying the equally valid part of their opponent's position, since to concede the opponent's point would apparently require them to relinquish their own valid insight. The culprit in cases like this, Bambrough suggests, is usually the common tacit presupposition shared by both sides. This underlying presupposition is never subjected to close examination because it seems not to be at issue, practically speaking. Both sides, that is, happily and perhaps quite unconsciously accept it. The best way to proceed in such cases is to try to uncover the common assumption that has forced a choice between impalatable alternatives and to see if it may not itself be flawed or untenable.

Whether or not this analysis is widely generalizable, it does, I would argue, provide us with a good approach to the family quarrel between technocrats and irrationalists. The technocrat is right to insist that our interpretations and explanations of human behavior generate conclusions about what a rationally ordered society would look like. In that sense, moral and political norms have their roots—at least partly—in cognition and not merely in spontaneous, autonomous emotion. On the other hand, the value noncognitivist is quite correct in his equally adamant insistence that this kind of normative "knowing" does not measure up to the prevailing criteria of "scientific" knowledge: it is not wholly explicit, verifiable, "objective" knowledge. (Alternatively, the value noncognitivist may fall back on the claim that the technocrat's conclusions are simply the result of logical error—of a failure to stick to "facts" and to respect the "logical" gap between "is" and "ought" statements. This argument depends on auxiliary semantic and metaphysical assumptions that will be noted in the next chapter.)

The common error in the technocratic and value-noncognitivist arguments, which forces each to deny the other's valid claim in order to maintain its own insight, is their common adherence to the basic epistemological program of liberal reason. Whatever criticisms the second-generation schools of liberal reason have leveled against their common ancestor, whatever amendments they have made, they have remained true to its basic conception of human knowledge. Other claims and expectations of the original liberal rationalists have been rejected as either logically flawed or empirically untenable, but the fundamental model of human understanding has remained largely intact and unquestioned.

The issue dividing the technocrat and the irrationalist can thus be put into syllogistic terms. The technocrat argues as follows: If all genuine cognition is "scientific," and if normative perceptions are cognitive, then these norms must be "scientific." The irrationalist argues, on the other hand: If all genuine cognition is "scientific," and if normative models are not "scientific," then normative models must not be cognitive. In each of these syllogisms, I wish to suggest, the minor premise is sound but the conclusion is not. Suspicion, then, should be focused upon the common major premise, which the parties do not debate because they share it. Their neglect is understandable in practical terms, but, if our analysis is correct, it is inappropriate and unfortunate theoretically. For if the parallel minor premises are both correct and the apparently opposing conclusions are both wrong, then the problem must lie with the major premise. Something must be amiss with the conceptions of cognition and science that lead to their equation.

If this is so, then what we are faced with is not a choice between technocracy and irrationalism but a quite different task. We need to effect a more radical and fundamental reform, one that can resolve the deadlocked polarity of these two options. We need, that is, to reexamine and to revise the basic epistemological program that has produced the deadlock in the first place. If we do so, we shall not reconcile the two antagonists; rather, we shall transcend them. The valid insights of each position can survive if we do our job well; but neither of the two positions will remain tenable as a whole, since both depend on premises that must be abandoned.

The construction of an alternative conception of human understanding, transcending the limitations of the orientations previously surveyed, is not only a possibility; it is also rapidly becoming something of a necessity. This task is not simply a political "necessity"—although it is that, too—but it is philosophically and intellectually a necessity. Radical revision of the most fundamental postulates of "liberal reason" is indicated on theoretical grounds, and not just for practical reasons. For the conception of human understanding we received from the seventeenth century and the epistemological program based on it have now fallen into a state of grave disrepair.

There are many, to be sure, who insist that all the particular problems and difficulties encountered by the received tradition can be resolved through progressive amendments. On the other side are those who insist that these profound and persistent difficulties cannot be met short of a fundamental reassessment of the nature and scope of human reason. In the remainder of this chapter I wish to place this argument in the context of the larger political and philo-

sophical issues addressed in this book; to sketch a case on behalf of
the more radical interpretation of the present situation—the claim
that fundamental epistemological revisions rather than minor
amendments of detail are in order; and to suggest the bare outlines of
what seems to me to be an emerging conception of human understanding that is both more plausible than the received conception
and more salutary in its effects.

In the final chapter we can then consider the potential implications
of the revised conception of human reason for our understanding of
the nature and demands of a "rationally ordered" society—i.e., one
whose institutions and practices take appropriate account of the
powers and the limitations of the human mind.

Before we plunge into the substance of the argument, a word of
caution is in order concerning its intrinsic ambiguities and contingencies. Any account of the meaning and significance of recent or
contemporaneous historical patterns is notoriously risky, inherently
judgmental. This risk characterizes intellectual history as well as
other kinds. To understand the import of any historical event requires some understanding of its context, and part of the relevant
context of any historical event is its future. We can, for example,
characterize Copernicus as a landmark figure in the history of science only because we know the eventual outcome of his theoretical
conjectures. Someone writing very soon after the fact, however,
when very relevant considerations led some authorities to continue
to prefer the Ptolemaic model, would have had to take a real chance
in rendering that same judgment. For all he could know, Copernicus
might eventually be seen as a minor curiosity who had hazarded an
interesting—but quite mistaken—hypothesis about the earth's
movement. In short, in order to interpret any trends in contemporary intellectual history—as contrasted with the easier task of providing a flat report of contending ideas—one must inescapably
hazard some guesses about likely future outcomes.

It should also be evident that, in any case like this, the predictive
estimations that shape the interpretation are themselves, in turn,
very likely to be partially a function of prescriptive judgments. That
is to say, any interpreter is likely to gauge the future direction of an
intellectual controversy partly on the basis of his own beliefs as to the
"right" outcome. There is nothing at all improper about this intrusion of the interpreter's own judgment: unless he has specific reasons for supposing otherwise, the normal supposition is that it is the
better, more convincing, viewpoint that will eventually emerge victorious.

This methodological warning can be made specific to the present

argument. I shall characterize the fundamental epistemological program of "liberal reason" as being in irreversible decline and disrepair in part because I believe it is being superseded by another
epistemological program, one that proceeds on substantially different premises as to the nature of human knowledge, its foundations,
its warrants, and its methods. And I believe that this will happen
because the newer account is a better one—one that provides a
much more convincing and illuminating account of the actual conduct of rational enterprises. My interpretation is thus open to dispute, based as it is on a series of interlocking judgments. But anyone
who does dispute it must do so on the basis of formally equivalent, if
substantively conflicting, judgments that are equally as hazardous as
my own.

That warning having been entered on the record, we can return to
the argument.

The central claim of this chapter can be stated in this analogy: the
positivistic tradition of "liberal reason" has become the Scholasticism of the twentieth century. The basic conception of human knowledge it has espoused and the epistemological program it has engendered have fallen into radical disrepair. Simply on autonomous
intellectual grounds—i.e., wholly apart from any political considerations—the fundamental assumptions of that tradition are
no longer compelling, its distinctive forecasts, expectations, and
explanations are no longer convincing. The common ground that
sustained the original hopes of the early liberals, the aspirations of
technocracy, and the accounts of the irrationalists seems to have
given way. The particular assumptions and goals most distinctively
characteristic of this tradition have either been abandoned outright
or else transformed in quite profound ways.

To the extent that this claim, to be elaborated here, is warranted,
and to the extent that the previous argument as to the political effects of the tradition is also warranted, the comparison with
Scholasticism is fully appropriate. We have saddled ourselves with a
decadent epistemology that has been immensely destructive in its
political consequences. And though the philosophical foundations of
this tradition have now been eroded, the oppressive political practices it has produced continue to flourish. Political organisms do not
always follow all the rules that apply to biological organisms: a
political tradition, unlike a plant, can bear fruit long after its roots
have gone rotten.

All of the diagnostic language deployed by the seventeenth- and
eighteenth-century reformers in their attempts to break the hold of
an oppressive tradition is therefore applicable to our own situation.
We have been "bewitched" by our own faulty ideas, "enchanted"

and "entrapped" by the "spell" of words. We have succumbed, in Kant's phrase, to "self-incurred tutelage." We have fallen victim to dreams and delusions created by our own mistaken and inordinate aspirations. And the starting point for escape from this predicament is the recognition that our problems are in large part produced by "realities" that are real only in their burdensome consequences.

Hobbes's acerbic metaphors of potent illusion may be especially apt. Just as he depicted the papacy as "no other than the ghost of the deceased Roman Empire, sitting crowned upon the grave thereof,"[2] so we need to see the autocrats and would-be autocrats of technocracy as "ghosts" sitting crowned on the grave of a primitive form of scientific rationalism. And just as Hobbes decried the "vain philosophy of Aristotle," which "would fright men from obeying the laws of their country, with empty names; as men fright birds from the corn with an empty doublet, a hat, and a crooked stick,"[3] so we need to dismiss the modern irrationalist scarecrows who would fright men from using the resources of practical reason to shed light on their political predicament.

Our current intellectual task, then, is a threefold one of recognition, exorcism, and reconstruction. We must recognize the intellectual sources of the powers that bind us. We must then break the spell with which these illusionary "demons" have kept us in thrall. Finally, we must examine anew the genuine achievements and limitations of the human mind in order to reshape our image of reason.

Logical Positivism as Updated Liberal Reason

A good place to look in order to appreciate the decay of the epistemological program of "liberal reason" is to reflect on the fate of logical positivism—or, more broadly, logical empiricism—as a theory of knowledge and a philosophy of language over the past several decades. This is an appropriate place to look, I would suggest, because the positivist program amounted to a contemporary and vigorous restatement of the most fundamental assumptions and goals of liberal reason (in its value noncognitivist incarnation). On its "logical" side, it was an updating of Cartesian rationalism via Frege and Russell. On its "empiricist" side, it was an updating of Hume via Mach. Like the French Enlightenment figures examined by Vartanian, the positivists fused the Cartesian ideal of a clear and distinct, mathematicized science with the assumptions of British empiricism, which grounded knowledge in discrete sense data. The positivists' classificatory scheme for categorizing knowledge claims, moreover, embodied the dichotomizing framework we earlier termed "epistemological manicheanism": on the one hand were "real knowledge" and hypotheses deemed meaningful aspirants to that status; on the other hand was the utterly empty and meaningless verbiage of pseudo-knowledge, epitomized by "metaphysical" nonsense and including ethics.

The positivists' principal philosophical *bête noire* was not medieval Scholasticism so much as it was nineteenth-century German idealism. Their diagnosis of the causes of philosophical error and vanity, as epitomized for them by this tradition, was nonetheless the same diagnosis rendered by the seventeenth-century reformers. Let us examine the parallels.

Like the original advocates of liberal reason in the seventeenth and eighteenth centuries, the positivists focused a great deal of their critical attention on the misuse of language and the effects of this misuse. A great deal of literal nonsense, they contended, was spoken in philosophy because proper rules governing the use of language were ignored. Especially was this the case in metaphysics, which was an intrinsically vain enterprise. The emptiness of metaphysical discourse was held to be produced by and obscured by reliance on "pseudo-concepts" and "pseudo-statements"—pseudo because they had the outward appearance of meaningful speech without meeting the real requirements of meaningful speech. Just as Hobbes endeavored to show that much of the vocabulary and many of the contentions of the Scholastics were literally nonsensical, so Carnap contended that much of the discourse of a metaphysician like Heidegger was simply meaningless.[4]

Like the seventeenth- and eighteenth-century epistemological reformers, moreover, the positivists believed that prior philosophical efforts had foundered because of their lack of clear, firm, and certain foundations. Earlier philosophy had also come to grief, the positivists contended, because it failed to adhere to explicit and rigorous methods, based on canons of formal logic. It had also been subverted by its entrapment in false complexities.

The positivists' epistemological program, which followed from this analysis, was similarly an updated version of the goals of the original liberal rationalists. It embodied, just as the original program of liberal reason did, a search for "simple truths and infallible methods," an attempt to specify the "sure foundations" of knowledge, and an attempt to purify knowledge by cleansing it of all "metaphysical" taint and by specifying the means of its verification. Like the program of liberal reason, moreover, the positivist program aimed at establishing a "unified science" expressed in a language modeled on mathematics.

The first requisite for philosophical advance, as the positivists' saw it, was the elimination of metaphysics. The halls of philosophy had become a kind of academic Augean stables, needing to be purged. All the metaphysical dung that had cluttered and corrupted the philosophical enterprise needed to be entirely swept away.

The elimination of metaphysics would simultaneously accomplish a second major goal: namely, the purification, if not the perfection, of language. Cleansed of the metaphysical refuse that had clung to and obscured it, language could become a clear and sharp means of wholly meaningful and fully intelligible inquiry and communication. Wittgenstein's *Tractatus* was interpreted and acclaimed by positivist philosophers as a significant step toward that goal. As Bertrand Russell wrote in his introduction to the *Tractatus:*

> Mr. Wittgenstein is concerned with the conditions for a logically perfect language—not that any language is logically perfect, or that we believe ourselves capable, here and now, of constructing a logically perfect language, but that the whole function of language is to have meaning, and it only fulfils this function as it approaches to the ideal language which we postulate.[5]

Through application of newly refined techniques of logical analysis, the dichotomizing program of epistemological manicheanism was to be given new force. In the first place, the line of demarcation between sense and nonsense, knowledge and pseudo-knowledge, was to be drawn with precision and definitively applied to specific cases. The "horizon" described by Locke, which "sets the bounds between the enlightened and dark parts of things; between what is and what is not comprehensible by us,"[6] could be delimited by a logical and linguistic Occam's razor. The meaningless utterances of metaphysics could therefore be finally banished beyond that horizon. What men could not (meaningfully) say, they should not try to say at all. In other words, as Stephen Toulmin has written, Wittgenstein's admonition ("Wovon man nicht sprechen kann . . .") was interpreted as meaning: "Metaphysicians, shut your traps!" On the other side of the line, within the circle of light, meaningful claims could be given new clarity and precision, again by the application of the new logical methods. Just as that which could not be known would be cast into total darkness—by showing that it could not properly even be said—so that which could be known would be fully illuminated—by specifying exactly what was being said and how it could be accounted true or false. This dual process was what Carnap described as the "positive" and "negative" results the positivist program would yield:

> The development of modern logic has made it possible to give a new and sharper answer to the question of the validity and

justification of metaphysics. The researches of applied logic or the theory of knowledge, which aim at clarifying the cognitive content of scientific statements and thereby the meanings of the terms that occur in the statements, by means of logical analysis, lead to a positive and to a negative result. The positive result is worked out in the domain of empirical science; the various concepts of the various branches of science are clarified; their formal-logical and epistemological connections are made explicit. In the domain of metaphysics, including all philosophy of value and normative theory, logical analysis yields the negative result that the alleged statements in this domain are entirely meaningless.[7]

The crucial tools to be used in accomplishing this feat of discrimination between the meaningful and the meaningless and the clarification of the meaningful were the rules of logical syntax and the verification criterion of meaning. Together, these tools would identify pseudo-concepts and pseudo-statements for exclusion while they specified the exact sense or meaning of genuine concepts and statements. A complete system of logical syntax, which Carnap hoped to construct, would serve as the measure of meaningful statements. The requirement that the method of verification be specified for any concept would serve as the measure of meaningfulness for concepts, as well.

The verification principle was to serve a dual function. Not only was it a criterion of demarcation, i.e., between the meaningful and the meaningless; it was also the means of giving meaning to empirical concepts or claims. These two functions, moreover, were linked, in the sense that the former significance of the criterion depended for its utility on its success in the latter function. For as a demarcation criterion it excluded statements and concepts whose meaning could not be operationally defined; and, to accomplish this exclusion legitimately, it had to be successful in its role as a specifier of meaning.

In its latter role as the specifier of meaning in individual cases, the verifiability principle was dependent on two further procedures: reductive analysis and ostensive definition. The close connection between the verifiability criterion and reductive analysis, in fact, made it possible for Carnap to refer to the latter procedure rather than the former principle in his account of meaning-giving.[8] The process of "reduction" was essentially the same as Hobbes's process of "resolution"—a process Hobbes likewise saw as essential to scientific and philosophical rationality. Meaning-giving through reduction was basically a process of defining "complex" terms by resolving them into "simple" terms, or, in Carnap's formulation, into words that occur in "observation sentences" or "protocol sentences." These latter simple or observation terms, in turn, were presumed to be unproblematically definable by pointing to the "given"—i.e., by ostension. The positivists saw the process of reduction as "logical" in the sense that each complex sentence was deducible from the particular sentences into which it was resolved. They took inspiration from Russell's use of such reductive analysis to resolve apparent philosophical puzzles, such as the "meaning" of a sentence like "The present King of France is bald." And they had little doubt that similar clarifying reductions could be carried out both to reveal the illusory quality of philosophical pseudo-problems and to clarify genuinely meaningful words and sentences, such as those of empirical science. (As Carnap expressed this conviction: "The analysis of the concepts of science has shown that all these concepts, no matter whether they belong, according to the usual classification, to the natural sciences, or to psychology or the social sciences, go back to a common basis. They can be reduced to root concepts which apply to the 'given', to the content of immediate experience.")[9]

Just as the verification principle as a criterion of demarcation depended on the plausibility of the same principle as a theory of meaning, and just as the latter depended on the universal applicability of reductive analysis, so the program of reduction depended logically on the existence of "simples" that were unproblematically "given." These simple "data" were held to be both unambiguous and uninterpreted. They constituted a pretheoretical "observation language," which was to be conveyed in "protocol" sentences. These simple, uninterpreted protocols, then, amounted to the bedrock floor of real knowledge. They were the "firm foundations" deemed essential by the tradition of liberal reason since its inception. They were the measuring rod of objective truth. They were thus the final fixed point of our knowledge of the world.

Schlick's account of the nature and role of the protocols, or "observation statements," reflects this understanding. The protocol statements, he wrote, "are those statements which express the *facts* with absolute simplicity, without any molding, alteration or addition, in whose elaboration every science consists, and which precede all knowing, every judgment regarding the world." The protocols "serve to mark out certain statements by the truth of which the truth of all other statements comes to be measured, as by a measuring rod." They represent "the unshakeable point of contact between knowledge and reality." Therefore, "*finality* is a very fitting word to characterize the function of observation statements. They are an absolute end.... They are really the absolute fixed points."[10]

At bottom, then, the positivists' epistemological program was tied to a Humean doctrine of sensation. The origin and the final points of knowledge were presumed to be simple and unambiguous blips of discrete sense data. The members of the Vienna Circle differed among themselves as to whether the protocols should be interpreted in phenomenalist fashion—i.e., as the sensa of an individual—or in physicalist fashion—i.e., as reports of objective physical "givens." Each interpretation had its drawbacks: the former account seemed to fall into solipsism; the latter seemed to cloud the requisite indubitability. They were at one, however, in relying on this corpuscular sensationism and its *esprit simpliste*, and they accordingly reembodied in a refined form the expectations and aspirations of D'Alembert. Like him, they believed that "there are but few arts or sciences whose propositions or rules cannot be reduced to some simple notions and arranged in such a close order that their chain of connection will nowhere be interrupted."[11]

Relying on these premises, the positivists developed a distinctive, though by no means wholly novel, account of scientific theory. This account, once again, neatly tied together an empiricist rendering of the concrete bases of knowledge and a rationalist account of its structure. Moreover, it should be added, this account served as a model for all valid theoretical knowledge, since the scope of empirical science and empirical knowledge was the same. A scientific theory, it was held, consists of a formal calculus, a closed logical system whose components are tied together by deductive inference. This formal-logical structure, itself empirically empty, gained its empirical significance by linking some of the terms of the system with "observables." This linkage once made, the "empirical juice" (Herbert Feigl's phrase) could then "seep upward" to give substantive meaning to the other constituents of the formal system.

This process of upward seepage of meaning might at first seem rather mysterious. (It is in fact as problematic as it is crucial, as should be apparent when the issue is framed in terms of concrete scientific concepts rather than in terms of abstract concepts of pure logic. How, for example, do any number of sensory "data" of the form "red here now" add up to a theoretical concept like "electron"?) For the positivists, however, it allegedly occurred with the automatic rigor of logical inference. Once some observational content was "hooked" onto the system, calculation did the rest. This process thus replicated the process of "composition" in Hobbes's nominalist version of scientific theoretical demonstration, and in both cases rather remarkable feats of constructing complex theoretical wholes out of simple sensory parts were presumed to be accomplished by straightforward ratiocination.[12]

Equally problematic, it might seem, would be the process of linkage itself—that is, the process of linking sensory data to terms of the theory. Here again, however, the positivists saw no difficulty because of their corpuscular sensationism and their radically nominalist conception of (ostensive) definition. The linkage, as they saw it, was simply an association of an unproblematic, unambiguous observational primitive with a purely nominal, hence equally unproblematic, logical primitive. The linkage process was thus conceived to be nothing more than stipulating identities of one-to-one correspondence, as in: Let "x" equal "this here red."

Philosophy, on this view, was reducible to the theory of knowledge. And the theory of knowledge was nothing more than applied logic. As Carnap put it:

> Logic is no longer merely one philosophical discipline among others, but we are able to say outright: Logic is the method of philosophizing. Logic is understood here in the broadest sense. It comprehends pure, formal logic and applied logic or the theory of knowledge.[13]

And science was just as Hobbes had said: the "reckoning of consequences." The goal—and the warrant—for scientific theory was accurate prediction. Hence it followed that scientific explanation and prediction were logically equivalent: read the deduction forward, from theory to consequence, and you have prediction; read it backward, from observed consequence to theory, and you have explanation.

In sum, the positivist epistemological program was an attempt to give rigorous form to the three-centuries-old quest for a unified science of demonstrable theoretical knowledge—the quest begun by Descartes and Locke. It believed that knowledge was a unity, not only in its common substantive basis in the "simples" but in its logical form. (Carnap: "There are not different sciences with fundamentally different methods or different sources of knowledge, but only *one* science. All knowledge finds its place in this science and, indeed, is knowledge of basically the same kind.")[14] Knowledge could be given solid foundations—the protocols or observation statements—whose simplicity and indubitability would guarantee the validity of any claims rigorously grounded upon them. Knowledge also had a ceiling, which could be specified with precision—the verifiability criterion. Anything falling within this house of science could be explicitly stated and (at least potentially) confirmed. Anything not falling within it could be definitively dismissed as literal nonsense. Philosophical disputes could thus be definitively resolved, either by elucidation of their absurdity or by turning them into questions of empirical science or logic. Linguistic confusion could likewise be dispelled by rigorous logical analysis. The long-cherished aspirations to end the chaos of contending philosophies and to put in its place the sure path of science could thus be realized.

Schlick therefore could summarize the import of the positivist program in millennial terms:

> I am convinced that we now find ourselves at an altogether decisive turning point in philosophy, and that we are objectively justified in considering that an end has come to the fruitless conflict of systems. We are already at the present time, in my opinion, in possession of methods which will make every such conflict in principle unnecessary. What is now required is their resolute application. . . . Everything is knowable which can be expressed, and this is the total subject matter concerning which meaningful questions can be raised. There are consequently no questions which are in principle unanswerable, no problems which are in principle insoluble.

And, Schlick adds, with what in retrospect appears as unintended irony, that Ludwig Wittgenstein, in his *Tractatus*, "is the first to have pushed forward to the decisive turning point."[15]

The Vienna Circle thus gave new force and new rigor to the claims and aspirations of the revolutionary epistemological program whose origins were recounted in the opening chapter. The fundamental assumptions and goals of the seventeenth-century reformers and the twentieth-century reformers were very much the same. They differed in only two major respects. First, the arguments of the twentieth-century positivists were able to take on a sharpened linguistic and logical form, thanks in large part to the achievements and the inspiration of mathematical logicians like Russell, Frege, and Hilbert. Second, the twentieth-century positivists recognized what many of their early counterparts did not, namely, that the ideal of wholly explicit theoretical knowledge of deductively linked atomic "facts" had no place within it for normative truths. The sure path of science did not lead, logically could not lead, to the alleged insights of the old *logos*-rationality or of practical reason. (Even here there are a few complications. Neurath, for example, might legitimately be held to be a technocrat—since he found rational political norms within science—rather than a value noncognitivist. He was ostensively the most adamant opponent of "metaphysics" in the Circle, but he was also a Marxist of sorts who apparently believed that the physicalist sociology he envisaged would somehow converge with scientific socialism. Since Neurath was more a scientistic visionary than an analyst, however, the way this convergence was going to occur has to remain something of a mystery.)

The Vicissitudes of Positivism

This sharpened rearticulation of the positivist conception of knowledge has indeed proved to be a turning point in philosophy, but not in the way that Schlick had in mind. The positivists performed a valuable service by specifying the tasks that should be accomplished in order to fulfill their epistemological program. Instead of these tasks moving toward successful completion, however, important and intractable difficulties have seemed to arise at almost every crucial point. In reflecting on these difficulties, and in seeking to escape them, the philosophy of language and the philosophy of science have been stimulated to develop in some quite promising and quite unexpected directions. In the process, moreover, our understanding of the fundamental nature of language, of scientific theory, and of scientific progress have been transformed. Finally, these developments seem to suggest both the need and the basis for revising our most basic notions concerning knowledge and human understanding.

The role of Ludwig Wittgenstein has indeed been pivotal, as Schlick intimated, but, once again, not at all in the way that Schlick had in mind. For Wittgenstein began to realize that the ideal model of language he had constructed in the *Tractatus* was not the basis for a concrete and realizable reformation of language. He then came to see it as a kind of myth—one that had actually misled him in several ways by its esthetic appeal. Accordingly, he began to reflect in a radically different fashion on the way words acquire meaning and on the relationship of language to the world. These reflections, in turn, have played a strategic role in the rejection of the positivist conceptions of both language and scientific theory. Wittgenstein thus did not produce the framework for ending philosophical confusion, as Schlick and the other positivists anticipated; rather, he helped to stimulate new conceptions of philosophical perplexity and new ways of trying to deal with it by reflecting on the inadequacies of his earlier views.

The difficulties the positivist program encountered can best be sketched by focusing on the fate of the verification principle and its corollary doctrine of operationalism, the fate of reductive analysis, and the fate of the quest for an interpretation-free observation language. These components of the positivist program, as we have noted, were logically closely related, and each had a crucial part to play in the fulfillment of positivist goals. Each of them, however, ran into problems very quickly.

The verification principle, first, proved impossible to formulate in such a way that it would do what the positivists wanted it to do, namely, to separate the "meaningful" from the "meaningless" by a clear dividing line that coincided with a line between empirical science and metaphysics.[16] The attempt to remedy this problem by succeeding amendments and alterations to the principle not only proved unsuccessful but also made it rather clear that the principle was not truly an autonomous principle. That is, it was not a standard, set up on autonomous logical or linguistic grounds, whose consequences were henceforth to be accepted as unassailable. Quite the contrary. When the principle did not lead to the desired outcomes, the "principle" was to be revised rather than the outcomes accepted. The conclusion was not, in other words, "Well, this metaphysical claim is meaningful after all" or "Who would have thought it, this theory of nuclear physics is simply meaningless." Instead, the conclusion was "Well, we'll have to change the principle, since it didn't produce the results we wanted." In short, the verification principle was not a rule but a rationalization. It was not conceded the right to adjudicate outcomes; it was instead intended to explain and give a rationale for a set of results already decided on in advance. The truly relevant question, then, seems to be: What are the nature and substance of the intellectual judgments whose authority is in fact determinative?

The logical status of the verification principle, moreover, raised some very interesting questions—and vexing ones for the positivists. The situation was really the same one that Hume had faced. Hume, recall, stipulated that all significant assertions were either tautologies or claims about matters of fact. His stipulation to that effect, however, along with a great number of the assertions in his *Treatise* and *Enquiry*, was clearly neither. Did he, then, really mean that his own work should be "committed to the flames" as nothing more than "sophistry and illusion"?

The verification principle, like Hume's parallel stipulation, is also neither tautological nor empirical. Some positivists tried rather half-heartedly to maintain that it was indeed merely an empirical generalization about the use of language, but that desperate expedient was not at all convincing. If the principle was merely a claim about ordinary discourse, it seemed false. Moreover, it clearly was intended to have regulative force, not merely empirical accuracy. It was a claim about the "proper" use of language, although it was not simply a logical clarification in the sense of being *analytic* and *a priori*. The status of the principle thus seemed highly problematic and paradoxical. If it was acceptable, then it must be nonsensical by its own stipulation. If one tried to save its meaningfulness, on the other hand, then one had to find it unacceptable. The only third choice seemed to be to "swallow the camel," as it were, and accept the mystical or perhaps even magical status for the principle that Wittgenstein had accepted for his *Tractatus*. That is, in Wittgenstein's analogy, it was like a ladder that one climbs up and then discards. It was "nonsense," strictly speaking, but "important nonsense." But this conclusion was also, clearly, unattractive, both to the positivists, who were distinctly uncomfortable with such a status for the central principle of their common-sense realism, and to those who, like Ramsey, considered the notion of "important nonsense" to be a philosophically unacceptable evasion.[17] Finally, it might be held that the verification principle was merely a proposed convention for the use of language—i.e., "Let us mean this by 'meaningful'." If that was all it was, though, then clearly it was binding on no one: if it was purely conventional, anyone who pleased could refuse to be bound by it without being subject to reproach.

Verificationism as a means for determining the concrete meaning of specific terms, as contrasted with its role as a criterion of meaningfulness in general, turned out to be rather unsatisfactory in its attempted application, also. If the requirement of complete and explicit definition by reference to observable "data" or to specific "operations" were to be rigidly applied, a great many theoretical terms and concepts of empirical science would seem to be excluded. In its strong form, the doctrine turned out to be excessively restrictive. On the other hand, if the requirement were loosened in order to make room for these terms and concepts—e.g., by permitting "partial" definitions or "indirect" reduction to observations or "symbolic" operations—then the alleged precision-inducing capabilities of the standard would be severely compromised. Moreover, its exclusionary rigor would become significantly attenuated, since even a Heidegger, say, might claim "indirect" or "partial" operationalizability for his most metaphysical concepts. Finally, loosened in this fashion, operationism also seemed to lose a great deal of its utility as a procedural guideline. As Abraham Kaplan has written, once these emendations are introduced,

> the operationalist principle is so watered down that it no longer provides methodological nourishment. To find what a scientific concept means, examine how you apply it, or how you apply other concepts related to it. But what else has anyone ever done? Indeed, what else is there to do?[18]

Furthermore, the program of reductive analysis quickly reached its limits, and with a very great deal less to its credit than had been anticipated. The original expectation, following Russell's example, had been that language could be clarified and that metaphysical pseudo-questions and concepts could be exposed by reductive logical analysis. That is, problematic formulations could be resolved by substituting for them more basic propositions, which could either be verified or else eliminated. This expectation proved, however, chimerical.

At first, the problem seemed to arise simply as an "empirical" embarrassment. As Urmson puts it, "nobody was producing any satisfactory analyses."[19] This indisputable shortage of results, moreover, seemed not to be caused by any lack of effort or technical skill on the part of philosophers. Gradually, therefore, the very same philosophical analysts who had welcomed "the pleasure of a dance beneath the brilliant lights of *Principia Mathematica*"[20] realized that an intrinsic misconception was at work here. It was not simply an accident that Russell's successes in mathematics were not being replicated in philosophy. Rather, the hope that this would happen was premised on a faulty conception of language and a faulty conception of what produced metaphysical puzzles. To accomplish the goals of reductive analysis, as Wisdom wrote,

> it seemed essential to find sentences not of sort X which meant neither more nor less than sentences of sort X. But these translations could not be found. And this was not because of the accidental paucity of the English, French, or German language. It was no accident at all . . .; in other words, a typical metaphysical difficulty about what is expressed by sentences of sort X cannot be met by translating those sentences into others.[21]

The positivist presuppositions that suggested that such translations could and would be found likewise lost much of their persuasiveness with this realization. As Urmson put it,

> philosophers could not go on maintaining seriously that ordinary language was even a very inexplicit and untidy version of a truth-functional calculus provided with a vocabulary; nor was it possible to regard it as an inexplicit version of any other calculus.[22]

The reductivist program intrinsic to verificationism—and the allied notion of an observation language, to which complex and theoretical terms were allegedly to be reduced—suffered similar setbacks in the context of scientific language. Telling criticism of the positivist account of scientific theory as a logical calculus that received "interpretation" and empirical meaning by having some of its terms hooked to "observables" by correspondence rules came from two principal quarters.

First, some philosophers of science were decisively influenced by Wittgenstein's reflections on what was involved in "observing" and in giving meaning to linguistic symbols. Wittgenstein's objections to the "picture" theory of language, a theory that informed the notion of an unproblematic observation language as the basis of meaning-giving, were, they decided, telling objections. They also realized that, insofar as these objections were persuasive, they undermined the positivist account of scientific theory, scientific language, and scientific observation. The real-world language of science and real scientific "observations" simply did not square with the idealized and dichotomized account that the Vienna Circle and its allies wanted to offer. Genuine scientific theories are never autonomous and self-subsistent logical calculi; they are intrinsically bound by and dependent on their basis in concrete perceptions. Apart from their "interpretation" they are not scientific theories at all but simply empty mathematical formulas. As Norwood Hanson put it:

> To take the interpretation out of optics is to take the optics out of optics. The *theory* of geometrical optics (in the positivists' sense) is simply geometry, not optics at all. To put my position more generally, if you extract the physical interpretation from a physical theory, the result will not be physics, but algebra, pure and simple.[23]

Just as there are no such things as observation-free scientific theories, moreover, there are no such things as wholly theory-neutral "observations." (If the positivists were neo-Humeans in their account of scientific knowing, these critics were, in a sense, neo-Kantian in their objections. Like Kant, they suggested that in science, as elsewhere, concepts without percepts—i.e., "theories" without "observations"—are empty and that percepts without concepts—i.e., "observations" without "theories"—are blind. Unlike Kant, however, they neither wanted to nor could suggest the permanence and necessity of specific concepts.)[24]

Hanson makes this point with an explicit nod to Wittgenstein:

> Most philosophers now realize that Wittgenstein carried the day. It was his analysis of complex concepts such as *seeing, seeing as,* and *seeing that* which exposed the crude, bi-partite philosophy of sense datum versus interpretation as being the technical legislation it really is. By means of philosophy he destroyed the dogma of the immaculate perception.[25]

In any case, Hanson continues, the positivist account of observation (which, no doubt because of a Humean belief in discrete and clear sensations, was considered to be unproblematic)[26] is not an acceptable account of observation as it actually occurs in scientific inquiry.

The atypical signal registrations of inebriates, idiots, and infants may constitute *de facto* interpretation-free sense encounters with phenomena. But these certainly are not observations—not in any sense that the last five hundred years of scientific inquiry would recognize as an "observation." The sharp, bipartite decomposition of *observation* into sense-data awareness as against interpretation does *not* constitute a valid analysis of the *concept* of observation in science, past or present. It is, rather, the substitution of a technical, prescriptive recipe—useful for certain varieties of philosophical cookery—for the concept of observation as it sustains scientific discourse, thought, and theory.[27]

In another angle of attack, W. V. Quine argued that the program of reductionism depended on the theory-observation dichotomy and that this distinction in turn depended on the belief in a fundamental cleavage between analytic and synthetic truths; but the latter belief, he argued, was not sustainable. The category of analytic truths is impossible to draw with precision and finality. "Any statement," he wrote, "can be held true come what may, if we make drastic enough adjustments elsewhere in the system. . . . Conversely, by the same token, no statement is immune to revision." Therefore, "it becomes folly to seek a boundary between synthetic statements, which hold contingently on experience, and analytic statements that hold come what may."[28] The epistemological program of reductionism, accordingly, turns out to be equally hopeless and mistaken for exactly the same reason.[29]

In short, the most central tenets of the positivists' epistemological program—which was, in turn, a sharpened, "value-neutral" version of the program of liberal reason—have turned out to be implausible. The most central projects of the program have turned out to be unworkable. The most central expectations have turned out to be unfulfillable or, at the very least, remarkably resistant to completion. Logical positivism in its classical and original strong version, therefore, is no longer tenable. Not even Carnap and Hempel held to the original form of their position, eventually leaving it very far behind in some respects.

Revolution or Evolution?

There is, however, no consensus among philosophers of science or among philosophers generally as to the cumulative impact of the various setbacks and difficulties that brought about positivism's demise. Therefore, there is also no consensus as to the full significance of the intellectual changes that have taken place during the past several decades. Instead of consensus, we have a quite broad spectrum of viewpoints.[30]

At one end of this spectrum are those who see the various criticisms as less than fatal to the basic intent of the positivist program. In their view, some of the criticisms are less than fundamental and the others are at least in principle capable of being defused by modifications, revisions, refinements, and additions to the program. The present task of philosophy of science, on this account, is largely that of proposing and considering those modifications and revisions that are tenable and that would further the basic purposes pursued by the tradition of logical empiricism—for example, the specification of criteria for genuine cognition, the exposure of claims that do not meet these criteria, the determination of what constitutes acceptable confirmation of a scientific theory, the clarification of these theories via logical formalization, and so on.

At the level of epistemology proper, the appropriate task, on this view, is to work out the dimensions of a tenable neoempiricism. The most informed and candid proponents of this approach, however, concede that their task is not an easy one and that its prospects are considerably more modest than those envisaged at the outset of the empiricist project. Israel Scheffler, for example, acknowledges that

> we have traveled a long way from the conception of empiricism as a shiny new philosophical doctrine for weeding out obscurantism and cutting down nonsense wherever they crop up. We have, furthermore, seen that even if we take empiricism as the proposal of a general meaning-criterion in terms of translatability into a chosen artificial language, we run into trouble. We have thus come to restrict the empiricists' job to providing merely an adequate sufficient condition of significance on an observational basis in the form of an observational system capable of housing our scientific beliefs. Even this restricted task has, however, turned out to have quite difficult obstacles before it. . . . It appears, in sum, that even a modest empiricism is presently a hope for clarification and a challenge to constructive investigation rather than a well-grounded doctrine, unless we construe it in quite a trivial way.[31]

At the other end of the spectrum are those who see the cumulative impact of all the incapacities and problems of the positivist program as thoroughly devastating. In their view, the appropriate task of philosophy of science is to construct an altogether different understanding of scientific theory, its logic and warrants, and the way in which it changes and develops. At the level of epistemology, correspondingly, it follows that a new model of human cognition is called for, one that will have to depart substantially from the premises of the long-established viewpoint in order both to overcome that viewpoint's incapacities and to account for the actual "empirical" conduct not only of scientific enterprises but of other forms of knowing as well.

One of the consequences of this wide spectrum of judgments is a divergence in interpretation of the meaning and significance of recent developments in epistemology and philosophy of science. Those at one end of the spectrum, quite naturally, are inclined to emphasize the continuities that exist between past and present accounts of knowledge and of science. For them, any changes that have occurred are properly seen as "evolutionary."[32] Those at the other end of the spectrum, in contrast, are naturally inclined to emphasize the discontinuities between past and present doctrines and therefore to characterize the significance of the changes as more "revolutionary."

Disputes over whether the changes in question are "revolutionary" or "evolutionary" have sometimes been very hotly argued because they grow out of and reflect these divergent perceptions. One important factor in these arguments is, to be sure, largely semantic. That is, our vocabulary for characterizing patterns of change is an impoverished one. Change, whether political or intellectual, comes in a very wide variety of patterns and degrees. It requires, therefore, to put it mildly, a considerable oversimplification and hence distortion to lump all instances of change into one of only two categories: revolution or evolution. Depending on how tightly one establishes one's criteria, moreover, conceivably any change can be properly seen as evolutionary, since total and complete discontinuity is practically never found in nature or in history.

These contrasting accounts of recent changes in epistemology and philosophy of science therefore need to be understood in part as exercises in "persuasive definition." The opponents may in fact be in agreement on many more particulars of the case than is at first readily apparent in light of their overriding and explicit argumentation as to whether the changes have been "evolutionary" or "revolutionary." The interpretive categorization, however, becomes a matter of heated contention because it carries connotations that are significant vis-à-vis some of the larger, usually tacit, moral and metaphysical commitments of the disputants. Those, for example, who sympathize with the monistic naturalism that underlay many of the positivist formulations and who sympathize with the moral and political thrust of the positivist critique are almost surely going to characterize postpositivist developments as "evolutionary" in order to suggest, both to themselves and to the world, the continued tenability of these underlying commitments. On the other hand, those who operate from different metaphysical and moral positions, and who therefore are interested in discrediting the substratum of positivism as well as questioning specific points of doctrine, are almost surely, for similar strategic considerations, going to characterize the same changes as "revolutionary."

In order to adjudicate these alternative interpretations, one must at a minimum (1) try to overcome the distortions induced through our limited vocabulary of change by focusing on particular questions and issues; (2) recognize the bearing that contrasting normative and interpretive positions have on the characterizations offered; and (3) keep in mind the element of "persuasive definition."[33] Having done these things, we must then go on to reach our own conclusions. It would be wholly illusory under the circumstances to write as if any interpretation were unambiguously correct or indisputably authoritative. Keeping this reservation in mind, we must nonetheless lay our bets and make our judgments, for the issues at stake have a profound bearing on political questions that will not lie down or go away while awaiting some definitive consensus that may not soon arrive.

Implicit in the thesis that positivism has become the Scholasticism of the twentieth century is the corollary judgment that we are entitled to view the cumulative setbacks of the positivist program as amounting to at least the negative half of a revolution. That is to say, the positive outcome of the intellectual transformation that is going on has not been fully developed or settled; however, the previously dominant account of knowledge has lost most of its explanatory power and its persuasive appeal. The principal claims and assumptions of the model have been either abandoned, transformed beyond recognition, or patched up by increasingly convoluted amendments.

The changes that have taken place have for the most part been generated internally, and each step has been a small one, each new position continuous in many respects with what preceded it. In this sense, the "evolutionist" account is quite correct. However, it is quite possible by a series of small steps to turn around completely or to head off in entirely different directions. Simply to insist on the gradualism of the process is thus not sufficient to determine the cumulative effect and extent of the changes. This issue is either not reached or is positively obscured by the "evolutionist" account.[34]

We must, then, compare preponderant current opinion—or, where consensus is lacking, the current opinion we find most persuasive—with the corresponding original assumptions with respect to a series of particular questions. Especially when contemporary ideas are viewed from a long-term perspective and compared with the basic tenets of the tradition, the depth and extent of change become apparent. It is the most fundamental and distinctive conceptions, assumptions, and goals—the ones that informed the program of liberal reason and thereby also the technocratic and irrationalist orientations—that have been abandoned or radically altered. By ordinary standards of intellectual persuasiveness and by more explicit standards, such as those suggested by Imre Lakatos as indicative of research programs in decline,[35] the conclusion would seem to be that the basic model is in need of replacement.

To be specific, let us consider the following aspects of the traditional epistemological program: the quest for "simples"; the notion of an "observation language"; the quest for a principle of demarcation; the goal of eliminating metaphysics; the notion of ostensive definition; the program of reductive analysis; the notion of scientific theory as a formal calculus. We have already observed some of the difficulties encountered in the attempt to carry out these tasks or to clarify these notions. We shall now suggest that these tasks and notions have either been abandoned outright or else have been reformulated into quite different ones.

The hopeful aspirations of the *esprit simpliste* now seem altogether unrealistic. The "simples," whether conceived as discrete and unambiguous sense data, atomic facts, or whatever, just aren't there. Or at least they cannot be identified and utilized in such a way as to perform the irreducible epistemological function assigned to them. In the context of scientific theory, it is now generally recognized that the "complexity" of many concepts is intrinsic and indissolvable. They cannot be "reduced" or "translated" or "resolved" into discrete constituent simples without being destroyed.[36] In philosophical analysis of language, similarly, the idea that the goal is to isolate the simple reports of experience that lie at the basis of all meaningful use of language is no longer compelling.[37]

The associated quest for a wholly pretheoretical and unambiguous "observation language" has likewise proved chimerical. Not only is such an account of observation irrelevant to the real-world "observations" of scientists, which are inescapably and productively theory-laden from the start; it represents a practical impossibility. Such a language would not be a realm of "pure" meaning; instead, having no shape and organization, it would have no meaning or empirical significance whatever. Wholly pretheoretical observations would not be pristine and uncluttered so much as they would be absolutely unintelligible. Even the examples usually offered of such observation statements, such as "this-here-red," moreover, are not in fact unstructured but "reflect a complex achievement of abstraction and appraisal."[38] As Michael Scriven concludes, "there is no 'ultimate observation language' any more than there is an ultimate sense datum language."[39]

It is possible, of course, as some logical empiricists now do, to distinguish between a "basic language" (or "antecedent vocabulary") and a given theoretical vocabulary. Such analytical distinctions, which are the successors to the discredited theory/observation dichotomy, may have their legitimate uses in the analysis of scientific theories as logical structures. Once the notion of a genuine observation language has been discarded, however, the subsequent distinctions no longer have any profound epistemological significance. They may, in short, have analytic utility, but they do not have the epistemological force of the original claim.

With the obsolescence of the quest for primitive "simples" and for an unsullied observation language, the whole notion of an ideal language as a truth-functional calculus hinged on atomic facts turns out to be not so much a genuine ideal as a reductio ad absurdum. The *Tractatus,* in short, is to be understood, not—as the positivists and Russell understood it—as the norm for which language should strive, but as Wittgenstein came to see it later: as a set of demands that, if seriously levied against speech, would end by silencing us altogether. Marjorie Grene says it well:

> Logic, and the wholly precise speech of logically governed exact science, would mirror the universe if the universe were composed of atomic facts; but they are nowhere to be found, nor, *a fortiori,* are there any atomic sentences with which to begin such a construction.... If we can speak only exactly, using an aggregate of wholly precise atomic statements to build our discourse; if, of all not thus exactly articulated, we must be silent, then we must be silent altogether. All discourse, even that which has led to this conclusion, becomes absurd.[40]

The goal of specifying the meaning of all genuinely cognitive terms by "ostensive definition," therefore, must also be abandoned as misconceived. We do not relate our language to the world in that way, nor could we do so without reliable "simples" to refer to. That is the background of the current philosophical admonition: "Don't ask for the meaning, ask for the use." Words do not "picture" facts. Rather, they perform a variety of functions, some descriptive, some not. And even the descriptive functions of words cannot be adequately accounted for or clarified so simply as the notion of ostensive definition suggested. Instead, as Wittgenstein was fond of showing through myriad examples, we have to "catch on to" the use of words by a complex and partly tacit process of learning to play the "language games" in which they function.

All of the foregoing changes imply the need for a reassessment of the causes for breakdown and confusion in the use of language. For we do indeed "bewitch" ourselves by our words; we do become entrapped in our own linguistic "fly-bottles." The older conception of knowledge had a ready explanation for this very real and central problem—an explanation predicated on its theory of meaning. The diagnosis was that the offending terms and expressions which misled us did so (*a*) because their meaning was unclear or (*b*) because they were in fact meaningless. This meant that they either (*a*) were not clearly tied down to a hard basis in clear and unambiguous simple terms or (*b*) were not able to be so tied down. With the abandonment of the "clear foundations" assumptions, however, this diagnosis no longer carries any force. You cannot convincingly pin the blame for the breakdown of language on its failure to accomplish something now conceded to be impossible. In place of the now defunct ploy of blaming linguistic bewitchments on the presence of terms that are meaningless—i.e., are not ostensibly definable by reference to simple data—some new diagnosis must therefore be offered.

Wittgenstein's substitute diagnosis is that the problem arises when language "goes on a holiday." Alternatively, he says that problems arise when language is "idling," as in an engine running without getting us anywhere. Words and languages, as distillates of forms of life, develop to perform certain functions in the language games they play within. When they are taken out of context, when we try to put them to work in other settings, they may cause us difficulty. They do so by carrying with them all the unspecifiable "meanings" of their old context, which may not fit at all well in strange surroundings.

Like the positivist program, contemporary linguistic analysis continues, then, to be "therapeutic" in its intent. It continues to seek to break the "spell of words," to lead the "fly out of the fly-bottle," to clarify our thought by improving our discourse. It seeks, however, not so much to "cleanse" our speech—as if it could potentially be purified and made wholly clear, distinct, and explicit—as to set it functioning aright. Linguistic analysis, therefore, is no longer reductive in its methods or its goals. Reductive "translations" are still conceivably useful therapeutic devices, but they are seen to be only one of many possible ways of "displaying the use" of our language and one that, moreover, has utility only in limited areas.[41]

The vicissitudes of the verifiability principle have led to another conclusion of profound significance vis-à-vis the epistemological program of liberal reason. It is now generally recognized, that is, that it is simply not possible to provide any clear and straightforward principle of demarcation between "meaningful" and "meaningless" speech, terms, or theories.[42] If the scope of "meaningfulness" is narrowly defined on the basis of stringent criteria, whole clusters of ideas, concepts, and explanatory principles that play an important role in even the "hardest" of sciences are excluded—as in "dispositional" terms and nondirectly observable theoretical constructs. If the line is drawn more loosely, however, whole classes of very suspect ideas seem to qualify as meaningful. Hence, as Carl Hempel concedes, in remarks written in 1958 and appended to a reprint of his article on the empiricist criterion of meaning:

> much like the analytic-synthetic distinction, the idea of cognitive significance, with its suggestion of a sharp distinction between significant and non-significant sentences or systems of such, has lost its promise and fertility as an explicandum, and . . . it had better be replaced by certain concepts which admit of differences in degree, such as the formal simplicity of a system; its explanatory and predictive power; and its degree of confirmation relative to available evidence.[43]

It remains possible, of course, to attempt to define lines of demarcation that can serve to distinguish one kind of discourse or one kind of intellectual enterprise from another. Such boundaries may be useful for various reasons. Once again, however, as in the shift from ascertaining an observation language to stipulating a "basic" language, the epistemological import of the enterprise is no longer what it was originally intended or believed to be. That is, these lines no longer can presume to mark *the* line between meaningful and meaningless speech, much less do so in such a way as to coincide with the line between science and metaphysics; instead, they simply mark conceptual or logical or functional distinctions that may be highly serviceable for particular purposes. The "line" one chooses to draw between " science" and "metaphysics," then, is a somewhat blurred line that may in fact move (with good reason) over time. Drawing the line is, in part at least, a matter of sound strategic judgment rather than a matter of applying some neutral logical test. Finally, the *status* of some of the usually included scientific concepts—as well as the *grounds* for including them—must therefore be seen as, in a sense, "pragmatic."[44]

To sharpen the irony here, it might be added that the enterprise of drawing these lines of demarcation might best be characterized as "metaphysical" in a new and nonpejorative sense. That is, the act of distinguishing relevant distinctions among types of speech and recommending observance of categorial distinctions based on them is a "reclassificatory move," and "reclassificatory moves" such as this are the appropriate province of a descriptive and therapeutic metaphysics. Such an understanding of the nature and function of this kind of linguistic boundary-drawing lies behind Wisdom's conclusion in his article "Metaphysics and Verification":

> Well, shall we accept the verification principle? What is it to accept it? When people bring out with a dashing air the words "The meaning of a statement is really simply the method of its verification," like one who says "The value of a thing is really simply its power of exchange," in what sort of way are they using words? What is the general nature of their theory? The answer is "It is a metaphysical theory."[45]

To summarize, so far: the particular components of the changes I want to characterize as "revolutionary" in their cumulative impact are these:

1. The inherited epistemological program urges us to find and to specify the simple, unambiguous, and discrete "foundations" of all our ideas; but it is now recognized that nothing meeting these standards is available to serve as the definitive basis of knowledge.
2. All genuine knowledge was alleged to be specifiable in a fully explicit, final, and certain way; but that is now conceded to be unrealistic.
3. The line between sense and nonsense, between the unambiguously knowable and the absolutely unknowable, was supposed to be specifiable on this basis; but it is now recognized that no line of this sort can be drawn.
4. "Metaphysics" was slated for elimination as the example par excellence of insignificant speech; instead, metaphysics has been reinterpreted and revitalized in a linguistic mode, prompted in part by reflections on the status of the very claims lodged against "metaphysics."
5. Language was slated for purification, on these grounds, into a unified quasi-geometrical calculus whose terms pictured the "facts" of the world; but language is now conceded to be sui generis and plural—a variety of language games, whose terms take their meaning from the roles they play within the system.

New Directions in Philosophy of Science and Epistemology: Relinquishing the Geometric Ideal

The inherited tradition envisaged the house of knowledge as a solid and finite structure grounded on a firm floor (the "observables") and covered by a clear ceiling (the line of demarcation between sense and nonsense). Because these architectural specifications have proved to be chimerical and utopian, it has followed that the presumed nature of the knowing activities that took these specifications for granted also requires reexamination.

This reexamination has led to a series of interrelated shifts of focus and interpretation that, taken together, compose the basis for a comparable shift of similar magnitude in our whole conception of "knowledge" and the human understanding. These changes of focus and interpretation can be characterized as including, most centrally: (1) a shift from a focus on logic to a focus on concepts; (2) a breakdown of the sharp distinction between the "context of justification" and the "context of discovery," with an associated shift of interest toward the latter; and (3) a shift from a static analysis of scientific theories or other knowledge artifacts as finished products to a dynamic analysis of the judgments that produce them. To the extent that these shifts of focus are compelling, moreover, the philosophy of science and epistemology both become properly construed as less abstract and idealizing in their approach and more concrete and empirical. "Rationality," in turn, is properly defined not simply by a priori stipulation but by generalizing from the features of the intellecual enterprises we deem to have been successful.

The positivist epistemological program defined knowledge by its finished products. It did so, at least in part, because of the status it ascribed to these products. Genuine knowledge, that is, was conceived *in fact* to be "finished" in the sense that it was subject to verification. It should, then, be described by reference to the process by which it was *justified*, not by reference to the process through which it had been originated. The latter process, indeed, was deemed to be both hopelessly unspecifiable and irrelevant to the status of the finished product. Hence it—the "context of discovery"—was wholly written off, being regarded as a subject fit only for "empirical" disciplines, such as sociology or psychology. The results of the latter were, in turn, deemed irrelevant to epistemology, which was a priori and normative. (These ground rules and associated judgments ran quite parallel, for example, to Kant's dismissal of the merely heteronomous facts of anthropology as irrelevant to the normative science of ethics. Whenever *validity* is presumed to be ascertainable on a priori grounds, the a posteriori becomes insignificant to normative criteria, whether of knowledge or of action.)

Knowledge could be conceived in this fashion because of its presumed content. That is, knowledge was supposed to be composed of observations—which were unproblematic because they were unambiguous—and of logical calculi—which were also unproblematic because they were automatic. 'Knowing," then, was an ex post facto activity (of validating rather than discovering, of confirming rather than learning) that was also static in the sense that both of its components were basically nontemporal processes in anything other than an accidental sense: neither passive, discrete "observations" nor logical calculations require temporal extensionality. This might be denominated the "retina-computer" model of knowing. If a sensitive and accurate receptor of sensations could be linked with a powerful computer, you would have the ideal model for a genuine theoretical knower. "Practical" considerations kept this from being a genuine empirical possibility, of course. But this was not a significant problem, since the linkage process was also deemed to be unproblematic—i.e., the "pointing" operations of "ostensive" definition.

Knowledge, in short, was depicted as an amalgam of observation and logic. Either by implication or by specific declaration, a number of mental activities were then held to be justifiably ignored by epistemology. Among these were learning, conceptualization, and judgment. It was not deemed essential to give an account of any of these processes because they were seen as either logically irrelevant or functionally trivial. Learning, or discovery, was believed to be too amorphous to lend itself to disciplined characterization because it was not "logical." Herewith, the whole creative aspect of inquiry was excised from epistemology. This excision, however, was not considered crippling insofar as questions of validity could be sharply distinguished from questions of origin, and insofar as the former could be settled in isolation from the latter. That is, as long as questions of justification were deemed to be definitively determinable by criteria of logical sufficiency (supplemented by one-to-one simple linkages of the logical calculus to "observations"), an account of knowledge could be given without any reference to the processes of discovery. "Knowing" was not a matter of the "logic" (and, strictly speaking, there was none) of making conjectures; it was a matter of definitive procedures of refutation and validation.

The roles of conceptualization and judgment in knowing activity were justifiably ignorable on the retina-computer model because they were in this account very trivial and unproblematic intellectual processes. The role of conceptualization in knowledge was simply squeezed out. The logical-empiricist depiction of scientific theory-construction exemplifies this trivialization of the role of concepts very nicely. On the one hand, concepts were not seen to be necessary to "seeing" the data: "observations" were depicted as self-organizing in their discrete purity. "Immaculate perceptions" needed no concepts to father them. If concepts were not essential to making observations, on the one hand, they were also trivial in the context of theory. "Concepts" were depicted as purely formal, like mathematical concepts, and therefore as specifiable from within the calculus—i.e., as determined fully by their relationship to the other terms of the logical system. The role of concepts in structuring the data, making them intelligible, interpreting them—all this received little attention within the idealized and formalized account of the logical empiricist's model. As Thomas Nickles puts it, this view can justifiably be termed "the *conceptual vacuum account* of theories."[46] And, as Toulmin writes:

> By declining to admit into philosophical discussion any intellectual relation that is not amenable to formal analysis, the Viennese empiricists eliminated from philosophy the whole subject of "conceptual change"—the whole question of how conceptual problems of a nonformal kind arise and are dealt with rationally within scientific enterprises.[47]

It followed that the element of judgment in knowledge was also minimized. "Adjudication" among theories, which was the only relevant potential task for judgment within the "context of justification," was depicted as a relatively automatic exercise of matching up "facts" with hypotheses—rather like the myth of wholly "objective" judicial review, in which the statute in question is allegedly simply "laid side by side" with the Constitution.

These three aspects of the standard view, it should be noted, since they are intimately related to the basic assumptions of the model, have been relative constants since its inception. The exclusion of learning and discovery from the account of knowing—because they were inexplicable as well as inessential—was very clear in Hume's empiricism, for example. The mind's capacity to organize discrete data under general categories that embody their patterns of similarity—the conceptual power of the imagination—Hume left utterly mysterious. Individual ideas, he wrote, "are thus collected by a kind of magical faculty in the soul, which though it be most perfect in the greatest geniuses, and is properly what we call a genius, is however inexplicable by the utmost efforts of human understanding."[48] The "conceptual-vacuum account" of theoretical understanding, similarly, was already implicit in Hobbes's account of science as the "reckoning of consequences of general names," where reckoning meant "addition and subtraction" and naming was ostensive "marking." And, as Helvetius suggested in his extension of Condillac's empiricism, judgment was an inconsequential factor in human understanding. "All judgment," he wrote, "is nothing more than a recital of" or "nothing more than the pronouncing upon" sensations.[49]

Contemporary accounts of "knowing" and of scientific theory

embody challenges to all of these features of the received view. These challenges, moreover, are systematically related, just as the several features of the received view were parts of a single whole. The notion that a theory is produced by the wedding of "observations" with logical calculation loses its persuasiveness when knowledge is denied its solid foundations and its unambiguous ceiling—i.e., with the demise of the dogma of immaculate perception and the relativization of the verifiability principle. The "retina-computer" model of knowing thereupon loses its force, and the notion of "ostensive definition" begins to appear quite mysterious. These developments, in turn, begin to focus attention on the previously trivialized or ignored aspects of knowing: on conceptualization, judgment, and discovery.

In the first place, the sharp distinction between the "context of justification" and the "context of discovery," together with the associated exclusive focus on the former, has broken down. I think it was always possible to protest against this restriction of epistemology to questions of justification on the same grounds that led Locke to complain of the Scholastic emphasis on a syllogistic—i.e., logico-deductive—account of knowledge. Both the positivist account and the Scholastic account (and the former inherited its ideal of demonstrative certainty from the latter) were limited to being ex post facto "reconstructions." And, as Locke wrote, these have utility in some respects but little utility in other, equally important, respects. Both accounts are "but the art of fencing with the little knowledge we have, without making any addition to it."[50]

Thus, Norwood Hanson could protest that

> these positivistic rewritings of the history of physics too often stand unchallenged because of the clarion call that they constitute *analysis* and have nothing to do with the "context of discovery." But philosophy of science may differ in this respect from "pure philosophy"; it *does* have a subject matter. If a profferred analysis fitted no science whatsoever—neither its history nor its present state—if it illuminated nothing problematic within research and resolved no perplexities found therein, then philosophy of science would be an arid, worthless, logic-chopping discipline indeed.[51]

The utility of enforcing the distinction, plus the admonition to concentrate solely on the "context of justification," would nonetheless retain prima facie plausibility so long as the process of justification could be depicted in accordance with the retina-computer model. So long as "justification" could be seen as unambiguous, final, and definitive, that is, a full accounting of this process could seem to be a satisfactory account of knowledge—and to be the essence, indeed, of scientific rationality. Not only could it seem a satisfactory and sufficient account; it could seem to be the only possible account, since the intellectual dynamics involved in discovery seemed clearly unable to measure up to the criteria allegedly applicable to the procedures of justification. The distinction and its associated exclusive focus on the "context of justification" lose a great deal of force, however, when it turns out that the process of justification cannot meet the standards it was supposed to meet. When the criticisms levied against the postivist assumptions noted above took hold, it became evident that the process of justification—e.g., in choice among competing theories—involves the same kinds of relative conceptual judgments that characterize the "context of discovery." With that recognition (which followed from the breakdown of the theory-observation dichotomy and its corollary doctrines) the sharp line between the "context of justification" and the "context of discovery" began to dissolve, and, at the same time, the "context of discovery" began to assume more significance, not simply as historical, psychological, or sociological curiosity but as a resource for understanding what scientific rationality was all about.

This blurring of the "justification/discovery" dichotomy has brought with it a new concern with the problems and processes of concept formation, comparison, and acceptance not only in science but in knowledge generally. The same renewed focus on concepts is also a consequence of the abandonment of the "theory/observation" dichotomy. The former development leads to a focus on concepts for practical or "empirical" reasons; the latter leads to the same focus for theoretical reasons.

The latter, theoretical, source of the new salience of concepts was suggested earlier, when the revisionist philosophy of science was characterized as "neo-Kantian." Once one has insisted that there is no such thing as a meaningful, genuine, neutral "observation language"—i.e., once one has rejected the "theory/observation" dichotomy—one is saying with Kant that "percepts without concepts are blind." The revisionist philosophers of science were, therefore, logically faced with the Kantian task of accounting for the nature, functions, and warrants for these indispensable concepts—though in our post-Newtonian cosmos Kant's proposed answer to this question was no longer available to them.

The practical stimulus for elevating concepts to the front and center of philosophy of science was simply a matter of empirical fact: when one looks at the actual practice of scientific inquiry instead of imposing on it a set of a priori demands, one has to be struck with the centrality of conceptual development and change. Dudley Shapere draws the appropriate conclusion when he writes:

Despite the fact that the history of science contains a multitude of cases in which the introduction of new concepts, or the abandonment of old ones, played a crucial role in developments, little attention has been devoted to this problem of the acceptability of concepts. Presumably the reason for this was a belief, often tacit, that that problem would be solved automatically with the problem of the acceptablity of statements. This belief, however, is highly questionable, and a close examination of reasons for introducing new concepts and abandoning old ones is needed in science.[52]

These considerations have led to a rather substantial reorientation of philosophy of science in the past decade or two. An excellent short account of this reorientation is provided by Stephen Toulmin in an article entitled "From Form to Function: Philosophy and History of Science in the 1950s and Now,"[53] which is well worth consulting in its entirety. Toulmin writes:

By the mid-fifties, it was becoming clear to some younger philosophers of science that certain crucial questions on the subject could not be tackled with any hope of success, unless they set aside all formal or "logical" issues, and paid attention instead to the processes of historical change out of which the basic concepts, theories, and methods of science have emerged, and to which they are continually subject. The rationality of science cannot depend solely on the formal validity of the inferences drawn within the scientific theories of any given time. (By itself, that can do little more than protect scientists from inconsistency and incoherence.) We can recognize the source of science's explanatory power only if we come to understand also what is involved in processes of conceptual change: in particular, how the character of these processes can give authority to new concepts, new theories, even new methods of thought, inquiry, and argument. The current content of a science can be represented as a system of "propositions" linked by "formal inferences" only when we have at our disposal a common, agreed-upon vocabulary of terms and concepts to serve as the "subjects" and the "predicates" of all those propositions; and, manifestly, all really profound changes in scientific thought and theory have brought with them correspondingly profound changes in the basic vocabulary of scientific terms and concepts. Once we turn to the really basic level of theoretical interpretation and conceptual variability, as a result, a formalist approach is *necessarily* insufficient, and the architectural metaphors of formal logic—"structure" and the rest—must be set aside in favor of some other analysis of scientific work.
    It had been all very well for the logical empiricists to develop a purely formal and abstract organon of "inductive logic" for the natural sciences, so long as nobody asked how that set of formal canons was to be given specific applications to real-life scientific

practice. But it now began to be called in question, not merely whether the formal algorithms of "confirmation theory" and the rest were capable of being applied in practice as they stood—few of the logicians concerned had ever made that claim—but also whether there was any possibility, even in principle, of reframing them in terms relevant to the conceptual issues that actually face working scientists in the context of their professional activities. That now became the crucial question for the philosophy of science, and it was a question that could be settled only by taking the record of history seriously. By the early 1970s, as a result, public debates in the philosophy of science were repeatedly turning into analyses of key episodes in the historical evolution of science; and the scholarly burden of proof had shifted so far that these historical issues had to be faced and dealt with, even by those who still wished—like Imre Lakatos, and other associates of Karl Popper—to keep alive the ideal of a timeless and universal "rational organon" for all genuine natural science.[54]

Although there are those who continue to conduct sophisticated studies of the formal-logical components of science, therefore, and although there is clear disagreement as to how crucial and how definitive these formal aspects are for scientific inquiry, it is now probably safe to say that philosophy of science—as a result of the critiques and changes noted here—can no longer persuasively be characterized, as the logical empiricists did, as "applied logic." Instead, it has become the critical study of "scientific jurisprudence." Its task is

> not so much to establish and exemplify the formal and universal Ten Commandments of the scientific method, as to map out the historical development of its jurisprudence: showing how, as we move from one age or branch of science to another, the progressive changes in the standards of "good argument" and "rational inquiry" have been functional responses to the changing problematics of the different sciences in different milieux. What is characteristically rational about scientific inquiry, from this point of view, will then no longer be the conformity of scientific argument to permanent formal canons, but rather the manner in which scientists have changed their procedures and patterns of argument, in any particular area of theory, investigation, or debate, so as to adapt them better to the demands of its changing problems.[55]

The Return of Practical Reason

This reorientation within the philosophy of science has not, for the most part at least, been motivated by any overarching program of epistemological reform. Instead it has been the cumulative result of a number of gradual and piecemeal changes, each of which was prompted by specific needs and problems of the enterprise at hand. Nevertheless, implicit in this reorientation, when one reflects on it as a whole, is a fundamental reassessment of the nature and scope of human understanding. The picture of scientific inquiry it offers us suggests—even demands—that we reconsider our most basic assumptions about "reason."

Specifically, the changes recounted here call into question the whole "geometric ideal" of human reason, at least insofar as it purports to embody the essential features of rationality. The geometric model of knowledge, it would appear, must be seen as a kind of "limiting case" that is never in fact attained or attainable in any empirical discipline. As a norm, it can at best be very imperfectly achieved by any inquiry into the real world. Since, moreover, the reasons it can be only imperfectly achieved are quite *essential* reasons, the sense in which this falling-short can properly be considered under the heading of "imperfection" must also be questionable.

Insofar as the geometric model of reason is held up as a genuine account of any empirical knowledge—including that of the "hardest" natural science—it is an illusion, and a distortive one.[56] Insofar as it is set up as a legitimate norm, in the sense that any falling-short of its standards is deemed culpable, it is a mistake—and a destructive one. Insofar as it is used to set an agenda for epistemology that seeks to find ways of bringing concrete fields of inquiry up to its standards, it is misconceived and futile—a will-o-the-wisp.[57]

The modern epistemological program initiated in the seventeenth century was premised on the belief that all genuine knowledge could be and should be held to the geometric ideal. The stunning success of Galileo—and then, later, of Kepler, Newton, and others—served as an "exemplar" for the scientific reformers. They thought that the advances achieved in these cases through mathematicizing methods were the proper model for all intellectual advance. They identified the power of reason with these methods. They rejected Aristotle's "verbalizing" approach and discarded his distinction between theoretical and practical knowledge. Plato, with his Pythagorean embrace of the mathematical conception of knowledge, was greatly preferred.[58]

All real knowledge, then, was "scientific." And all science was theoretical in its form and status. The contents of the old category of practical knowledge had either to be "upgraded," as it were, to conform to these standards, or else be "demoted" to some lesser status. This basic imperative eventually led, as we have seen, toward technocratic conceptions of politics, in which the norms of practical reason were deemed genuinely theoretical, or to wholly relativistic conceptions of politics, in which the same norms were interpreted as expressions of will or emotion masquerading as knowledge.

The contemporary reorientation in both philosophy of science and epistemology suggests a quite different conclusion. Perhaps the premises and the program associated with the "Cartesian delusion" need to be stood on their head. Instead of all knowledge aspiring to meet an unattainable standard of geometric clarity, certainty, and precision, all knowledge should be seen as potentially ambiguous and open-ended, corrigible, and groping. Instead of all real knowledge being theoretical, in short, all knowledge is incurably and indelibly "practical."

Contrary to the confident expectations of the epistemological revolutionaries who initiated the program of "liberal reason," there are neither "simple truths" nor "infallible methods." There are no certain foundations to knowledge, nor is there a clear and sharp horizon separating the knowable from the unknowable, the unsayable, the nonsensical. The very best efforts to specify these "simple truths," to formalize these "infallible methods," to find these "foundations," and to delineate this "horizon" have proved unavailing.

More than that, it now seems clear that these several centuries of sustained effort, running from Descartes and Locke through the logical positivists, have been unavailing for good reason. It is no lack of effort, no failure of intellect, that is to blame. The problem is, quite simply, that these goals have all along been quite literally unattainable. "Reason" is not amenable to being fully codified, finalized, and purified—either in its processes or in its products—for it is simply not that kind of capacity. Nor could it ever be that kind of capacity so long as it inhabits the kind of world it does—so long, that is, as it is a human capacity in a world whose most basic properties are subject to change.

What Hobbes said of Aristotelian natural philosophy we can now say of the whole enterprise of liberal reason: it was "rather a dream than science." In some ways it was a noble and ennobling dream—this quest for perfect knowledge, transcending all human limitations and imperfections. In other ways, however, it has been a peculiarly destructive dream, quite the opposite of what was expected of it. As long as we can preserve its legitimate ideals—and that should not be impossible—we should not mourn its passing.

The claim that all exercise of reason is in some respects "practical" is based on several specific features of the emerging picture of rationality. In the remainder of this chapter I shall try to describe some of these practical aspects of rational enterprises, noting, in the process, the contrasts with the ideal of "theoretical" reason. The point of this section is *not* to *make* the argument. To do that would far exceed the scope of this study. Instead, I intend simply to specify more fully what is *meant* by the claim that all reason has "practical" aspects. To get a full sense of the argument, and of the evidence for it, the reader has no choice but to look at some of the literature for himself.[59]

Stated in very summary fashion, the claim that all knowledge of the world is in some sense "practical"—and that it can never measure up to the demands of theoretical reason—entails that all knowledge of the world is: (1) a form of problem-solving activity; (2) irreducibly contingent; (3) always subject to change; and (4) "organic." It is not, and cannot be: (1) contemplative; (2) absolute, autonomous, and certain; (3) final and eternal; and (4) mechanical and/or divine.

All knowing is a form of *problem-solving*. Knowledge, if we may amend Aristotle, begins in a kind of "puzzled concern." It is a form of intelligent adaptive behavior that originates from a need to make one's environment intelligible in order to interact more satisfactorily with it. It is active, not passive. It is neither static nor contemplative and can be made to appear so only by a process of great abstraction—an abstraction that excises, among other things, both the dynamic structure and the "point" of knowledge. Even the basic perceptions underlying knowledge are things that one does, not things that happen to one. To perceive anything, in a sense relevant to knowledge, requires attention; and attending to anything is already an active process of orienting oneself to one's surroundings. In this respect, both the Aristotelian image of contemplation and the empiricist account of sensation tend to be misleading abstractions because they depict the origins of knowing as much more passive than they in fact are—or could be.

If the motivations and the constituent percepts of knowledge are both types of problem-solving activity, the same pattern characterizes the most advanced and sophisticated exercises of the scientific intelligence. Both "normal" and "extraordinary" science, to borrow Kuhn's terms (and it now appears that this distinction is more one of degree than of kind, in any case) are enterprises that are practical in this sense. "Normal" science, which for the moment can take its basic concepts for granted, engages in "puzzle-solving" of various forms. This mode of scientific activity is an attempt to improve the precision, or extend the range of applicability, of existing concepts and theories.[60] "Extraordinary" science is still a kind of problem-solving activity, only here the depth and extent of the problem are greater. It is a kind of crisis management rather than the more circumscribed task of "puzzle-solving," for here the scientist is faced with the larger task of transforming or replacing fundamental concepts or theories in order to eliminate anomalies produced when regnant concepts or theories are at work. Here, more dramatically, the essence of the task is to reestablish some kind of equilibrium between the knower and his environment by refashioning the concepts that mediate between them.

Toulmin's account, however much he may criticize Kuhn for overemphasizing the element of discontinuity in scientific "revolutions" and for failing to address the problem of "good reasons" for accepting suggested conceptual changes, is in this respect very similar. Science is a "rational enterprise" whose most fundamental concern is to improve and revise our common conceptual equipment by attending to scientific problems. These problems are constituted, in turn, by the gap between the "explanatory ideals" and "current capabilities" of the particular science. The extent to which science is a form of intelligent adaptation to the environment is in fact sufficiently profound, in Toulmin's view, to warrant a very extensive analogy between the "adaptivity" of rational enterprises on the one hand and the "adaptivity" of the process of evolution on the other.[61]

Polanyi similarly insists that scientific knowledge can be properly understood only by seeing it as a very sophisticated form of a "skilled performance"—much more akin in basic structure to, say, the practical activity of riding a bicycle than to theoretical contemplation.[62]

All knowledge of the world is, moreover, *contingent* knowledge. It is not final, absolute, or certain. However compelling any particular theory, or even a belief, may be with respect to a matter of fact, it is always sustained by and dependent on an act of rational assent for its affirmation. All genuinely intelligible "facts" are interpreted. All theories could conceivably be supplanted by alternative explanatory models; they therefore require judgment for their acceptance. Further, both interpretation and judgment require "fiduciary" backing, to borrow Polyani's term.[63] To put it another way, anything can be doubted. There is no self-evident and certain core of knowledge upon which all else rests. The Aristotelian claim that the first principles of science are known "with certainty" is either mistaken or else it simply refers to a quality of belief—to strength of conviction. The Cartesian program of critical doubt cannot, as claimed, find an indubitable basis for knowledge. "Protocols" are either dubitable or solipsistic.

The contingency of all knowledge claims on the assent and judgment of a knower, who is himself a contingent being, is not escapable, moreover, by confining ourselves to the "context of justification." The element of judgment may be less visible in replicating theories and in reconstituting factual claims than in originating them, but it is still present and still essential epistemologically. One makes judgments even in "testing" or "verifying" the results of previous inquiry; one may know the answer already, but one must decide whether the evidence warrants one's assent, even ex post facto.

At times, in simple cases, these judgments may be so straightforward as to appear utterly nonproblematic. In assessing more fundamental concepts and claims, however, the role of judgment is more clear and profound, for now competing considerations may well have to be weighed against each other. As Toulmin writes:

> Typically, then, the task of evaluating conceptual changes in science requires us to consider implications of half a dozen kinds; and this calls for the exercise of judgment, in two separate respects. Not only are the relevant considerations frequently incommensurable—not only may we lack any simple index for comparing the respective "values" of (e.g.) accuracy, scope, and degree of integration—but, in addition, the decisions frequently involve striking a balance between a profit of one kind and a loss of another. . . . Even in straightforward situations, then, the task of selecting between conceptual variants involves scientists in a complex kind of intellectual accounting.[64]

To insist on the contingency of all knowledge, its dependence on affirmation, and the dependence, in turn, of affirmation on complex judgments and "rational bets" is not to imply that there is anything arbitrary, idiosyncratically "subjective," or irrational about this "practical" account of knowledge.[65] Good reasons—legitimate warrants—do exist, which serve to make the acceptance of particular theories, the accreditation of particular "facts," and the choice of particular research programs "reasonable." These include simplicity, elegance, heuristic fertility, explanatory power, coherence with other generally accepted theories, and so on.[66] However: (1) these warrants are neither self-validating nor self-applying; (2) they may run in conflicting directions at given times in given cases; and (3) what seem to be appropriate warrants may themselves change, at least in relative priority, in the course of a scientific enterprise. The existence of these warrants therefore fully justifies the characterization of science—among other organized intellectual traditions—as a rational enterprise (so long as rationality is not equated with mere logicality) and as subject to "objective" constraints. This structure and these constraints, however, are not

sufficiently automatic and certain to justify characterizing even the
natural sciences as legitimate examples of "theoretical science" by
the criteria of Aristotle, or Descartes, or Laplace, or the Vienna
Circle.

Scientific claims are indeed "testable" and "confirmable." But
they are "tested" and "confirmed" not by reference to some unchanging neutral algorithm but by the rational judgment of those
who have the relevant experience and intellectual capacities. Truth
claims are "verified" or "falsified" "intersubjectively." What we call
"knowledge," then, is not some eternal and changeless body of
indubitably ascertained truths. In this sense, there is no "positive"
knowledge. And there is nothing that answers to Aristotle's dictum
that "anything science knows scientifically must exist by an unalter-
able necessity . . . and must therefore be eternal."[67] What we call
knowledge is our current stock of "warranted beliefs," accredited
by and dependent on the reasoned judgments of appropriate authorities.

There is an important ontological correlate of this recognition of
the "practical" dimension of all rationality. To see reason as a practical activity suggests that reason is a property of "organic" life.
"Knowing" is neither the automatic functioning of a mechanism,
nor is it the contemplation of a wholly transcendent subject. It is,
instead, the cognitive power of living beings who are striving to
make their life and their world intelligible. It follows that epistemology must be reintegrated with biology—or perhaps, more
specifically, with anthropology—with consequences for each part-
ner to the merger. And this reintegration in turn can be made possible only by refashioning our conceptions of "mind" and of "nature," for "knowledge" is life reflecting upon itself and upon its
environment. Our understanding of nature must permit what our
understanding of knowledge requires.[68]

Anthropologically, the ideal of theoretical reason tended to generate images of gods or machines rather than persons, and this happened by system rather than by accident. Man, considered as a
knowing subject, took on elements of divinity insofar as he embodied the utter transcendence of "knowledge": eternal, dispassionate, absolute, pure, wholly free. Descartes's and Laplace's
omniscient spectator, Kant's pure rational being, Sartre's being-
for-itself, Bentham's warden, Hegel himself, Skinner's founder of
Walden Two: in one way or another, each of these claimed some
divine status as a consequence of his perfect knowledge. On the
other hand, when reason was wholly immanentized in a monistic
ontology—reduced to "reckoning"—man became depicted as a
"thinking machine." (Even in the latter case, images of quasi-divine

"master builders" tend to appear, perhaps because someone has to program the computer. Hobbes established the model for this paradox when, despite his monistic ontology, he provided for man as "artificer" of the state and thereby left open the way for his sovereign to be a nominalist deity, entrusted with absolute power to confer names.)

In contrast, the knowing subject of "practical" reason is neither divine nor mechanical. He is neither wholly free nor wholly programmed, neither wholly "above" nature nor wholly submerged within it. He is a part of nature, but he transcends it in that he can become conscious and reflect on both nature and himself. He is bound by his physicality, by his biology, and by his humanity, but he is a distinctive historical person, able to act on his environment as well as be subject to it. He can rise above the world far enough to "know" something about it, but he can never claim to know what he knows with finality, certainty, or perfection. He can vastly expand his historical perspective, but he can never eliminate it entirely. He is, in short, a "rational animal."

From the ideal standpoint of theoretical reason, the "organic" footing and "practical" quality of reason have to appear as gross imperfections. To insist on the inexpungeability of the practical dimension of knowledge seems to involve a potentially disastrous failure of nerve. Critics of Toulmin and Polanyi, for example, fearing they have opened a Pandora's box, are quick to charge them with the crimes of "irrationalism" and "subjectivism."[69]

It is easy to sympathize with these misgivings. No one wants to give a carte blanche to scientific quackery or to ideological charlatanry. In this respect, the instincts and goals of the Enlightenment are every bit as valid today as they ever were. Perhaps, however, these critics are unduly harsh as well as misguided in their reactions because they set up an either/or choice premised on standards set so unrealistically high as to be mythical. Their demands on "science," on "knowledge," and on "reason" seem to be unattainable. Recent philosophy of science and analytical history of science, as we have suggested, seem unable to find any real-world scientific inquiry that answers to the ideal description. If we accredit the real-world practice of modern natural science as exhibiting "rationality"—and certainly we should—then the empirical record of its intellectual history and the structure of its actual practices are a problem for, rather than a vindication of, the idealized model of reason.

Even more than that, the kind of knowledge depicted by the tradition of liberal reason pays for its perfection by being literally inconceivable. If, as a philosophy of science, it is afflicted by empirical inaccuracy, it is, as epistemology, afflicted by persistent and grievous incapacities at very crucial junctures. Considered in light of these difficulties of the idealized account, insistence on the "practical" dimension of all knowledge is not so much an infirmity as an overdue corrective. The "practical" dimension of reason, that is, is no mere imperfection; it is instead a necessary precondition for there being such a thing as knowledge at all.

The ideal of fully explicit, final, "theoretical" knowledge, that is, has always been sustainable only by ignoring or giving absurd answers to such questions as (1) what, where, and who is the knowing subject; (2) how does the knowing subject contact the known; and (3) how does knowledge arise in the first place—i.e., what is the nature of learning and discovery. Alternatively, the same ideal demands have forced the most rigorous and candid thinkers who tried to put it to work into a potentially solipsistic idealism (e.g., Berkeley or the positivist phenomenalists) or into a profound skepticism tempered by recourse to such subrational considerations as custom and strength of belief (e.g., Hume). Either the knowing subject has—as in materialistic sensationism—been so immersed in matter-in-motion as to make his capacity to rise to knowledge very problematic, or else he has been left above and outside the world so completely as to make his acquaintance with his subject matter quite a mystery. In the first instance, attempts to remedy the problem have led to conceptions of ineffable processes and inexplicable or arbitrary achievements (e.g., Hume's "magical faculty," the "problem of induction," Hobbes's stipulative definitions, Popper's apparently random "conjectures"). In the second instance, attempts to remedy the difficulties lead to such desperate expedients as Descartes's speculations about the pineal gland and Wittgenstein's "ladder" in the *Tractatus*.

It was these incapacities in epistemology, moreover, that by implication produced the nonhuman anthropological conceptions of the godlike "scientist" and the artifact-like "behaver" that have populated the technocratic and irrationalist corruptions of the liberal tradition. In this case, as in others, ideals that are too high exact a significant price when the myths they generate are mistaken for realities.

To abandon as misguided the most fundamental premises and aspirations of the program of liberal reason has its costs. In doing so, one must accept somewhat "lower" ideals for knowledge, learn to tolerate ambiguity and uncertainty, and rely on less than definitive measures for assessing intellectual progress on the one hand and for discrediting pseudo-science on the other.

The benefits, however, seem well worth the price. For accepting as inexpungeable the "practical" dimension of human reason allows us to give a much more honest and accurate account of real-world "rational enterprises," including the natural sciences. It opens up the possibility of remedying some of the glaring gaps in the received tradition of epistemology. It offers the prospect of surmounting the ontological weaknesses of rationalism's subject/object dualism—which excises mind from the world—or empiricism's objectivist monism—which renders mind altogether anomalous. Finally, it offers the means of demythologizing technocratic tyrants, or would-be tyrants, and suggests the possibility of rehabilitating practical reason as a contributor to humane politics.

9 Picking Up the Pieces: Rational Enterprises and Humane Politics

If the basic argument of the preceding chapter is sound, we may be experiencing in the twentieth century a philosophical revolution that compares with the philosophical revolution of the seventeenth century. Like the seventeenth-century revolution, this philosophical transformation centers on epistemological issues. Like that revolution, too, its implications are wide-ranging: it necessitates changes in ontology, in philosophical anthropology, and in political theory.

This contemporary philosophical revolution is quieter, less visible, and less spectacular than its seventeenth-century counterpart. It is also, perhaps, less universally accepted. (I say perhaps, because only time will tell for sure. Even the seventeenth-century revolution was far from being universally accepted—something we tend to forget, since history is written by the victorious in philosophy as in politics. Today we read Voltaire much more than we do Bossuet, Hobbes more than Cudworth. In doing so, however, we are selecting on the basis of what is significant in retrospect; we are not selecting a statistically representative sample.)

The relative quietude of the transformation, by comparison with the seventeenth-century revolution, has several causes. First, it has largely been internally generated. Philosophical "outsiders" have indeed attacked the dominant tradition, ever since Vico and Pascal dissented from Cartesianism, but the more decisive contemporary changes have come from within: it is the adherents of the tradition who have done the most to undermine it in the process of attempting to repair its specific weaknesses. Wittgenstein is an outstanding case in point. And while defections from within are ultimately more devastating than criticisms from those wholly unsympathetic to the cause, this pattern tends initially to obscure the extent of the change involved.

Second, the changes have in some respects been subtle ones. For example, philosophers are still greatly involved in "linguistic analysis," and it may therefore not be readily apparent what a difference in goals and underlying assumptions there is between the "analyses"of a J. C. Austin, for example, and the earlier reductive analyses of a Bertrand Russell. In this particular case, moreover, the changes in question tended to come to fruition almost in private, as it were, during a period of time—World War II—when philosophical issues were understandably not in the forefront of people's attention.[1]

Third, the larger import of the changes that have occurred is rarely addressed directly, since epistemology in the grand style has largely gone out of fashion. Both in philosophy and in philosophy of science, current discussions tend to be highly concrete, specific, and particularlistic. Linguistic analysts focus on "resolving" specific puzzlements rather than developing a "philosophy of language," even though their enterprise seems rather clearly to depend on substantially different premises about the nature of language than did the positivists' reductivist program.[2] Similarly, philosophers of science, with occasional exceptions, tend to be concerned at present with problems of formalization or with rather specific questions about concepts, procedures, and warrants in the context of historical case studies. In both fields, this particularism has distinct merits and is probably an appropriate methodological emphasis, given the current situation. Nevertheless, once again, the larger bearing of recent changes tends to be obscured or ignored.

A third form of contemporary particularism not only blurs the overall import of specific changes but actually impedes perception of the extent of change. I am referring here to the institutional pattern of relatively autonomous disciplinary divisions within contemporary academia. In the seventeenth century the European *illuminati* were conversant with a wide range of "disciplines." They were aware of developments in the theory of knowledge, in "natural philosophy," and in social theory, and they recognized some of the common premises and mutual influences found within these different fields. As a result of today's disciplinary particularism, this kind of recognition is much more difficult. It is quite possible to be well aware of changes in one's own area of expertise without having much awareness of cognate developments in other fields—or, perhaps, of the larger potential significance of the changes one does perceive. Once again, the consequence is that very substantial shifts in the overall intellectual landscape may take place very quietly because they occur piecemeal.[3]

The philosophical revolution in question is also relatively quiet because of the relatively inchoate condition of the new view of knowledge, nature, and man. That the inherited tradition is inadequate is substantially clearer than what, exactly, the substitute should be. In contrast, the seventeenth-century revolutionaries came armed with a relatively clear and simple epistemological program, even if it turned out to be not at all clear and simple in its elaboration and even if there was a great deal of confusion about its larger implications.

Finally, the significance of contemporary alterations in the philosophical landscape is hidden to some degree by the continuing vitality the inherited view retains as a metaphysical myth. A culture steeped in positivistic premises and committed to positivistic aspirations for science and for society will not easily relinquish these attachments. Here there may be more parallel than contrast with the seventeenth century, since the intellectual and emotional commitments to Scholastic cosmology were never entirely dispelled, even though the triumph of a determinedly anti-Scholastic philosophy was generally conceded.

Despite all these intellectual, emotional, and institutional factors that cloud the picture, it is nonetheless my contention that the intellectual developments cited in chapter 8 amount to at least the negative half of a substantial philosophical transformation. Moreover, as I suggested there, at least the broad outlines of newer and more adequate conceptions of knowing and being—i.e., a newer and more adequate epistemology and ontology—are discernible.

The essentials of this transformation in epistemology, ontology, and anthropology can be briefly summarized as follows.

Epistemologically, we must recognize that there is no such thing as "positive" knowledge. None of the formulations of the human mind in its attempts to comprehend reality amount to final, certain, fully explicit, demonstrable, "clear and simple" truths. However successful, accurate, profound, persuasive, and fruitful these formulations may be, they are inescapably "fiduciary." That is, they fall appropriately under the general heading of "warranted beliefs," produced and accredited by the responsible judgment of those whose training, experience, and capabilities equip them to make these judgments. There is nothing arbitrary or "subjective" about these knowledge claims. They are warranted by their explanatory power, their coherence, their exactitude of fit to accepted data, their intellectual beauty or "simplicity," and their heuristic fertility. They are, nonetheless, potentially corrigible to the core, subject to revision or rejection as circumstances change, and never wholly devoid of dependence on suppositions that are themselves indemonstrable.

Another way of putting this is to say that even the hardest science cannot wholly cut itself off from some kind of metaphysical base. All rationality, then, has a "practical" dimension in the sense that it is a "problem-solving" kind of activity carried on by contingent beings.

Ontologically, this epistemological transformation undermines any attempt to divide the world between thinking substance and extended substance—between wholly transcendent subject and wholly immanent and inanimate object. It suggests, in short, the utter untenability of the "subject/object dichotomy." On the one hand, the knowing mind is "naturalized." As Merleau-Ponty has put it, consciousness is reincarnated in the envelope of being. On the other hand, nature is, by the same token, "mentalized." To the degree that it is capable of generating and sustaining consciousness and intentionality, the world cannot be justly characterized as mechanical and lifeless.

Anthropologically, these changes intimate that man is not the problematic union of "purely spiritual" consciousness and "ingenious machine" described by Rousseau in good Cartesian fashion. He is not a curious amalgam of "autonomous" rational will and "heteronomous" creaturehood, as described by Kant. He is neither a "ghost in a machine," nor is he the pure undetermined ego of Sartre's "being-for-itself." The *sapiens* in *Homo sapiens* is not divine contemplation; neither is it the world-creating transcendence of a *deus faber*. It is the intelligent activity of a "rational animal."

It also follows, therefore, that just as no individual man may be divided into spirit and mechanism, so mankind as a whole cannot legitimately be divided into quasi-divine knowing "subjects" and quasi-bestial known "objects." Anyone capable of intelligible speech participates to some extent in rationality, is capable of some transcendence of subtemporal matter. Anyone bound by the limitations of speech, conversely, cannot claim to live or think beyond the timeful contingency of historical existence. Men may differ—and differ rather dramatically—in the degree of their "rationality," but no genuine human being is completely "heteronomous," in Kant's sense, and no real human being is wholly "autonomous," either.

In the context of this study, the remaining question concerns the political significance of these philosophical changes. As earlier conceptions of reason did in their time, our altered view of human understanding should tend to preclude some political arrangements as unrealistic, inappropriate, or illegitimate, and it should provide some positive guidelines for the definition and design of a "rational society." By a "rational society," I should add, I mean not some millennial incarnation of Reason but simply a society whose patterns of authority, whose institutions, and whose procedures embody a sufficient understanding of the real powers and the real limitations of the human mind and an appropriate respect for them as well.

Philosophical doctrines, of course—and this includes the doctrines of philosophical anthropology, i.e., theories of human nature—never generate political conclusions on a simple one-to-one basis. They merely delimit what might be called a "range of propriety and legitimacy." Within the boundaries of this range of propriety and legitimacy, prudential considerations and compromises between contending goods will determine specific choices of policies and institutions. Political policies and programs falling beyond this range of propriety and legitimacy lose their warrant for accreditation by rational men; but even here there will be ambiguities surrounding the outer limits of the spectrum. Any attempt to determine the "political implications" of philosophical changes such as those we have examined must, accordingly, be considered in this light.

Subject to these reservations, the gradual dissolution of the premises of "liberal reason" would seem to have significant implications for our understanding of a "rational society."

In negative terms, it provides the grounds for a critique of both of the second-generation offspring of liberal reason. The case for technocracy, on the one hand, and the renunciation of reason as a political guide, on the other, are each weakened by the demise of the epistemological program that sustained them. Each of these conceptions of politics might conceivably survive, but only in a revised and attenuated form.

Constructively, the contemporary account of "fiduciary rationality," and of the "rational enterprises" in which it is institutionalized, provides a model for a conception of political rationality that is neither technocratic nor limited to a rationality of means-to-"demonically"-preselected-ends. This conception of a rational society bears real resemblance to the political ideals of early "integral" liberalism, purged, however, of the utopian cast they sometimes assumed. In a final ironic twist, then, the humane core of the liberal tradition may be salvaged most effectively precisely by abandoning the epistemological conceptions that were originally thought to guarantee its success.

Exorcising Technocracy

The philosophical changes that have occurred in recent years substantially undermine the argument for technocracy. The warrant for investing complete authority in the members of some "scientific" elite was their claim to possess an absolute kind of knowledge. These experts were alleged to know, "positively," the laws of human behavior or social dynamics or history. Absolute political power, in short, was predicated on "absolute" knowledge. Anyone who differed with the dictates of the technocratic elite, conversely, had no legitimate claim whatever. The elite, secure in their "science," were simply right; the dissenter was simply wrong.

If, however, all human knowledge is, as we have claimed, indelibly contingent, corrigible, and fiduciary, the technocrat's warrant to govern in this fashion is invalidated. No absolute power can be claimed or granted on the basis of some absolute knowledge, because the latter simply does not exist. When Enlightenment rationalism deprived the ruling divines of their epistemological "keys of the kingdom," they allowed positivist "divines" to retrieve these keys and claim them for themselves—a possibility Condorcet foresaw but thought unlikely. But now the illegitimacy of this coup is apparent. In light of the frailty of human knowledge, the prophets and practitioners of technocracy are shown up as the charlatans they really are.

On the one hand, the entitlement of the technocratic "divine" is eliminated when the absolute transcendence of the knowing subject is denied. On the other side of the subject/object dichotomy, moreover, a complementary revision undermines the technocrat's alleged entitlement to shape and manipulate the "behavior" of other men. The technocrat cannot play God, because he cannot escape the contingencies of nature. By putting mind back into "nature," it also follows that "nature" cannot be depicted as the wholly plastic, passive matter upon which the sovereign "artificer" was able to practice his feats of social engineering. The "class" gulf between ruling "subject" and ruled "object," which is the hallmark of technocracy, is broken down from both sides.

From both sides of the knower/known relationship, the new conception of rationality offers precisely what was distinctively and disastrously missing in the technocratic tradition: namely, principles of limitation. "Expertise" has its legitimate claims on our respect and our obedience, but these claims have irreducible limits. They are limited, first, by what all knowers *lack* and, second, by what all "knowns"—at least if they are human "objects" of knowledge— *possess*. All human knowers, specifically, lack certainty, and all human "knowns" possess their own intrinsic structure and hence their own integrity.

On the side of the knower, at least two limitations are implied by the recognition of the "practical" dimension of all rationality. The first relates to the substance of the claims of expertise: all such claims, whatever the strength of their warrants, are dubitable. They are not entitled to absolute credence; therefore, no political claims based on them are entitled to absolute obedience. The second limitation is procedural: in order to count as rational, the claims of expertise must be the result of an open process of critical discussion, and they must remain subject to change and revision by the continuation of the same process. The "court of reason" is never closed.

On the side of the known, the recognition that the human "objects" of knowledge are themselves "organically" structured and at least partly "rational" suggests other limitations on the legitimate authority of expertise. It suggests the untenability of the presumption of Helvetius and his technocratic descendants that they are able, and entitled, to indulge in the legislative refashioning of human beings. Because the human behavioral "objects" of the legislator's intervention were depicted as part of *res extensa*, and because *res extensa* was plastic and passive, the technocrats argued that to re-shape the political landscape in this way did not involve "violent motion" (in Aristotle's sense). That is, it did not involve the coercive imposition of restraint on a form of motion—i.e., "organic" strivings—that had its own integrity. The new conception of rationality, together with its ontological and anthropological correlates, calls into serious question this convenient enabling supposition.

What is really involved here is the recovery of the rather well-worn notion that there is such a thing as "human nature." The technocrats denied this, always implicitly, often explicitly. For them, there was human "matter" but not human "nature"—not some intrinsic and organic dynamic of human growth and development.[4]

The theory that man is wholly malleable must be recognized as a metaphysical myth that imposes itself on some avowedly scientific theories. It is not, and logically cannot be, an uninterpreted "finding" of any empirical discipline. It is, moreover, a myth that has had pernicious consequences, deluding some social reformers into believing they were entitled to a carte blanche in their relationship to their subject matter and depriving the unwilling subjects of the appropriate grounds for resistance to these arrogant incursions. Recall, for example, the plight of those prisoners who wished to refuse compulsory "rehabilitation" or those populations who wished to reject "liberation."

Kenneth Keniston states the point succinctly: no human nature, no limits: "If human nature *is* infinitely malleable, then of course no one society can be said to 'violate' human nature more than any other, for men can mold themselves into whatever forms the society provides."

But, he continues, men are *not* infinitely malleable, and there *are* limits:

> The theory of infinite human plasticity, however, errs by confusing the ability of men to adapt *somehow* to overwhelming pressures with their ability to adapt *successfully* to these pressures; its confuses the ability to survive with the ability to flourish. Though "human nature" is indeed shaped differently by every society, and though men and women are indeed flexible in adapting to their society's demands, there are limits beyond which they cannot be safely pushed.[5]

The epistemological critique of technocracy has as its corollary in political ethics what Peter Berger has aptly termed the principle of "cognitive respect."[6] The technocratic elevation of the subject and its complementary reduction of the object legitimated an almost total disregard for the "object's" ideas and perceptions. The technocrat's ideas allegedly possessed the certainty of "positive" truth; the "ideas" of the unenlightened, in sharp contrast, were but the subrational "attitudes" of wholly determined creatures and therefore not entitled to be taken seriously—except perhaps as obstacles to the technocrat's projects. Epistemological presumption, in short, fed political and ethical presumptuousness.

If, however, all knowledge is contingent and limited, distinguished only in degree from the consciousness of the known, this philosophical legitimation of domination is discredited. The would-be social engineer loses his warrant to consider his understanding of the situation to be incorrigible and definitive. He also loses his justification for his contemptuous disregard of the perceptions and beliefs of the "objects" he would save through his beneficent interventions. Any legitimate policymaker ("legitimate" in our sense of operating within the "range of propriety and legitimacy" determined by philosophy) must take all empirically ascertainable worlds of consciousness with the utmost seriousness and respect. The fruit of technocratic epistemology was an almost unrestrained arrogance. The lesson of the new epistemology is one of humility.[7]

In moral terms, all of this may sound pedestrian, even banal. "Do unto others...," "Walk a mile in my shoes...," etc. And perhaps it is. Nevertheless, even the best-established moral truisms seem to be easily set aside when the *libido dominandi* is fueled by high aspirations and is sanctioned by sophisticated philosophical rationales. Accordingly, it is a happy consequence of the emerging conception of rationality that it discredits the philosophical beliefs that in our modern world have performed this dubious function.

Transcending Irrationalism

The impact of the obsolescence of positivistic epistemology on irrationalist conceptions of politics is somewhat less direct and less definitive than its impact on the rationales for technocracy. Simply because all reason has a "practical" dimension in the sense we have noted does not necessarily mean that reason's competence to ascertain political and moral standards is thereby established. It is perfectly coherent to say that all rational judgments are corrigible, contingent, and fiduciary—and therefore never "positive"—but that these judgments are still confined to matters of "fact," which are distinct from questions of "value." The "irrationalist" relegation of normative judgment from the court of reason to the control of the passions rests on several arguments. These arguments overlap and are mutually reinforcing, but rejection of one of them does not prevent the others from being used to the same ends.

Nevertheless, the recent changes in epistemology do have implications that bear on the irrationalist argument. They suggest the untenability of one of the strongest arguments against the normative competence of reason. They raise some doubts about other bases of the same position. And they suggest some analogies and continuities between the functions of reason in science and in politics.

The irrationalist argument is grounded on three dichotomies that are, respectively, epistemological, logical or syntactical, and ontological. The first of these is the epistemological distinction between meaningful and meaningless propositions. The second is the distinction between "is" and "ought" statements. The last, ontological, distinction is that between "facts" and "values." These dichotomies are grounded in a coherent world view and are mutually reinforcing. On the one side of the metaphysical divide are *factual* claims, which are expressed in descriptive ("*is*") language and are *meaningful*. On the other side are "*value*" statements, which are expressed in "*ought*" language and are cognitively empty or *meaningless*.

The first of these dichotomies that sever cognition from evaluation—i.e., the meaningful/meaningless distinction—is the only one that seems to be *directly* obviated by the demise of positivism. In this case, as we saw in chapter 8, the presumed basis for drawing so clear and specifiable a line between the (scientific) knowable and the (metaphysical and ethical) unknowable-because-cognitively-empty was lost with the failure of the verifiability principle as the criterion of demarcation. If ethical claims are not meaningful, this must be so for some other and more complex reason than because they are not verifiable.

The proponent of irrationalism can, however—and readily does—fall back on the other dichotomies as grounds for denying normative cognition. Even if genuinely cognitive claims are not verifiable, and even if ethical claims are therefore not dismissable because they are likewise not verifiable, he insists that cognitive claims are both logically and ontologically distinguishable from normative "claims." Cognitive statements are "descriptive"— expressed in "is" syntax; ethical claims are "oughts," which are logically underivable from "is" statements. And cognitive claims are about "facts," which are different from "values." The question is, then, whether the philosophical shift we have described affects these grounds for denying reason any "practical" (in the Aristotelian sense of *phronēsis*) end-discerning ability. I think it does.

First, it seems to me rather easy to see that the is/ought distinction is, by itself and speaking strictly, a rather trivial one. The logical gap—the syntactical distinction—is clear and unbridgeable enough. However, it does not coincide with the distinction between appraisive and descriptive statements. Ethical imperatives and prudential recommendations may indeed be expressed in "ought" terms, but the claims on which these counsels are based are themselves characteristically 'is" statements: e.g., this is fair, that is good, this is sane, that is alienating, this is corrupt, that is liberating, and so on. In order to keep the category of "is" statements normatively "neutral," these claims have to be reinterpreted and invalidated as somehow constituting "pseudo-statements." This feat is accomplished by declaring them to be dependent on terms that are "value-laden."

Now these claims may indeed be distinguished and excluded on these grounds. However, the exclusion can obviously not be represented as merely syntactical or logical in its justification. Instead, the syntactical or logical distinction is made to perform its desired function—i.e., to fall in the right place—only by the application of a further, supplementary, distinction employed to invalidate normative concepts—concepts that can function, and do function in everyday discourse, perfectly well in the declarative mode.

In other words, the is/ought distinction can be very clear and unbridgeable; but then it is trivial vis-à-vis the issue at hand—the cognitive status of political and moral norms. On the other hand, it may not be trivial in this context—that is, it may in fact sever "is" statements and normative statements; but it can do so only because it is supplemented by an auxiliary distinction—namely, the distinction between "fact" and "value"—which serves to exclude terms that give "is" sentences normative content.

The question then is: does the philosophical obsolescence of "liberal reason" and its associated doctrines have some bearing on the fact/value dichotomy? Is so, what? And here I think the answer is that it does have some bearing and that the effect is to call the sharp distinction between fact and value into question.

The line of demarcation between fact and value was part of the epistemological distinction between subject and object. Values were peculiar emotive reactions that somehow were characteristic of *res cogitans*. The same conscious "substance" that knew things also placed "value" on things. In both cases, the act—of knowing or of valuing—took place in some sense "outside" "the world," which was *res extensa*. And just as the nexus of subject and object in knowledge was highly problematic ontologically, so—for the same reason—the source of the act of "valuing" was highly problematic: it seemed somehow inescapably arbitrary. "The world" of "facts," meanwhile, was depicted as an ontologically "flat" landscape of matter in motion. Within such a world, all events or outcomes were structurally on a par.

As the new epistemology breaks down the dualism of subject and object, therefore, it also breaks down the ontological dualism of fact and value. If "the world" of "facts" contains feats of conscious knowledge and intentionality, then "facts" are to that extent not "flat" or static. Since "facts" must encompass feats of knowledge, they must be more than inert bits of matter in motion. "Facts" must include "organic" patterns of growth and decay, order and disintegration, achievement and failure. Correlatively, the "valuing" of "subjects" need not be left as some random and inexplicable introjection of emotion into this value-free landscape. Instead, "valuing" can be seen as the empathic apprehension by conscious creatures of the patterns of growth and decay, achievement and failure within which their lives take place. "Value judgments" so conceived have a distinctive "emotive" dimension to them, reflecting the emotional economy of the beings who make them. At the same time, however, they are profoundly cognitive, inescapably involving, as they do, the intellectual apprehension of the organic patterns of success and failure that generate them.

"Value judgments," empirically speaking, may in fact be nothing more than cognitively ungrounded emotive expostulations—verbal expressions of "attitudes" the speaker has simply absorbed somewhere. But these are degenerate shadows of genuine value judgments and are easily recognized as such by those who engage in the relevant evaluative disciplines, whether these are ethical, political, physiological, or aesthetic. The man who says "This is good" and can give no reasons—who can provide no cognitive grounds for his claim—is expressing his likes and dislikes, but he is not making a genuine value judgment. The failure of value noncognitivism lay precisely at this point: in identifying these two very different acts, in seeing no difference between the corrupt and empty form of a value judgment and the real thing. And this failure was systematically induced by the underlying ontological bifurcation that makes the real thing so inexplicable.

The fiduciary conception of rationality therefore undermines the philosophical bases of both technocracy and irrationalism. Vis-à-vis technocracy, the new conception of human understanding eliminates the basis for the absolute status technocrats accorded to their theoretical claims and, *pari passu*, to their political claims. At the same time, it provides the basis for principles of limitation—i.e., the intrinsic "organic" structure of human nature and the principle of "cognitive respect"—that set bounds to the legitimate scope of social engineering. Vis-à-vis irrationalism, the new conception of human understanding prevents the consignment of normative discourse to the dark areas beyond the pale of reason on the grounds that its claims are "unverifiable," and it provides a basis for questioning the fact/value dichotomy, which is the principal alternative grounds for denying any normative competency to reason.

More constructively, moreover, the revised conception of human understanding, together with an empirical investigation into its real-world operations, provides us with grounds for the reentitlement of "practical reason" in the traditional sense. That is, the understanding of a "rational enterprise" it gives us provides analogies through which the functioning of reason as a political guide becomes intelligible. And this understanding, in turn, suggests to us a new model of what is involved in the construction of a truly "rational society."

Rational Enterprises

In looking for the constructive political implications of the new conception of human reason, the most appropriate place to begin is with the notion of a "rational enterprise."[8] The preeminent examples of "rational enterprises" are the scientific disciplines, and it is to them we should primarily look to find what is essential to such enterprises. We can add, however, that scientific disciplines are not the only enterprises that are rational. Other human enterprises, including those devoted to the pursuit of the arts, to the refinement of crafts, and to the ordering of social relationships, can and do exemplify rationality.

The scientific disciplines—and I refer here particularly to the natural sciences—can appropriately be taken as the best model of rational enterprises simply because of their extraordinary success. The warrant for accrediting them, I would argue, is pragmatic. We look to them for inspiration not for the a priori reason that they embody some theoretical epistemological ideal but rather for the a posteriori reason that they have produced compelling results. It is not that the natural sciences satisfy the geometric ideal, for example, because, as we have seen, they in fact do not. It is rather that they have been successful in rendering nature increasingly intelligible.[9]

To what can we attribute this success? It is not because the natural sciences are rational in the sense of logical. They are that, certainly. But that is no satisfactory explanation. Logicality is necessary, in the natural sciences as elsewhere. But logicality is causally quite insufficient to account for the achievements of modern natural science. Aristotle, after all, was a supreme logician, and Scholasticism, however sterile its content became, epitomized syllogistic rigor. Moreover, by itself, logical rigor suffices merely to keep a science from falling into inconsistency and incoherence. Or, alternatively, logical calculation may serve to spell out further implications of what is already known. The process of conceptual advance that marks scientific progress, however, is itself no matter of simple logic. Logic, in short, plays a very important role *within* scientific enterprises, but it is not the source of their productivity because it is neither unique to them nor sufficient for their accomplishments.

Neither is the productivity of natural science accounted for by the demonstrability of its theories. On the one hand, the clear ideas, unambiguous perceptions, and simple definitions that were variously depicted as the solid basis for the allegedly "demonstrated" truths of science have been shown to be philosophical fictions. On the other hand, the kinds of "demonstrations" actually employed in the natural sciences are forms of persuasive argument used in human discourse generally.

Finally, the success of modern natural science cannot be attributed to its adherence to some set of unique "methods." This explanation is a myth based on Cartesian and Baconian delusions as to the possibility of prescribing a series of quasi-automatic *regulae* for the pursuit of scientific inquiry. The fact is that in their general and abstract form such methods amount to, in the words of James Conant, "hardly more than a description of trial-and-error procedures which have been employed in the practical arts ever since our distant ancestors became tool makers."[10] In their concrete application, on the other hand, these very vague rules of method require so sophisticated an understanding and so much experience as to render them almost superfluous.

In short, the remarkable success of natural science is not attributable to the demonstrability of its theories, for they do not possess such definitive certainty. It is not attributable to their logicality, for logical rigor, though it is important and necessary in science, is clearly an insufficient cause of scientific advance. And it is not attributable to the existence of some cookbook set of scientific methods, for these are not only insufficient but trivial. What else, then, might be important determinants of scientific advance?

First, a brief digression is necessary concerning the notion of scientific advance, or progress, or productivity, or achievement itself. In looking for the causes of the success of natural science, we are not looking for causes of the ascertainment of some form of Real Knowledge, some kind of absolute and definitive Truth. Natural science is a form of human knowledge; and, as we have seen, human knowledge is incapable of attaining so exalted a content, whether it is conceived in Platonic, Hegelian, or positivist fashion. Instead, the success of natural science is embodied in its apparent capacity to improve our understanding of nature through the step-by-step refinement of our concepts in the context of specific scientific problem-situations. This pattern of progress may be conceived in highly instrumental and pragmatic terms, as Toulmin, Conant, and Quine tend to conceive it. Or it may be conceived in somewhat more philosophically "realistic" terms—as approximations and intimations of the shape and dynamics of an intelligible world of reality—as Polanyi does. In either case, the crucial point is that the progress is achieved through the piecemeal solution of concrete problems and that the results of this process are always somewhat tentative and corrigible "warranted beliefs." In Toulmin's words:

> Galileo and Descartes liked to talk of the scientists' task as being to decipher, once and for all, the secret cipher in which the Book of Nature was written, and so to arrive at the "one true structure" of the natural world. Yet that was always a Platonist ideal or aspiration, rather than a plain description of the task facing scientific research, as it is in fact done. Speaking less portentously, we might rather say that the task of a science is to improve our ideas about the natural world step by step, by identifying problem areas in which something can now be done to lessen the gap between the capacities of our current concepts and our reasonable intellectual ideals.[11]

To return to our question, then: What accounts for the great success of natural science in achieving this kind of progress? The answer, we have argued, lies not so much in logic and methodology. Instead, the more important causal forces in scientific achievement have been (1) ontological, (2) conceptual, (3) technological, and (4) political. It is the last of these factors—the organizational and procedural characteristics of a "rational enterprise"—that constitutes our principal concern in the context of this study. But let us mention the other contributing factors in passing.

The first causal factor, the one I have termed "ontological," is in a sense almost too trivial to deserve mention, but it is essential. It might best be termed an "enabling condition" of natural science. This "enabling condition" is simply that nature is so ordered as to be, apparently, accessible to mind. Nature is not the simple "open book" depicted by the more enthusiastic Enlightenment figures, but it is also not inherently mysterious throughout, intrinsically opaque to the understanding. Nature is a form of being that is marked by order and regularity discernible to one who knows where and how to look for it. Obviously, if nature were not so ordered, natural science would be an impossibility; and there are cultures that have not recognized it to be so ordered.

The second causal factor behind the development of modern natural science is conceptual, and here we begin to see why modern natural science has been essentially the product of Western culture. All science and all knowledge are of course "conceptual," so this may sound like a truism. But I am referring here to two or perhaps three partly related conceptual breakthroughs that permitted and then stimulated the scientific "takeoff" that occurred in Western Europe in the seventeenth century. The first of these conceptual necessities was the disentangling of the category of "nature" from other categories—especially from that of the divine. From the other direction it was also necessary that "nature" be recognized as real and worthful—not a shadow world of illusion. "Nature," in short, had to be recognized as a distinguishable category of being that was valorized but not divinized: it had to be real and valuable to be worthy of exploration, and it had to be less than divine to be amenable to exploration without blasphemy. Greek thinkers largely accomplished this conceptual feat, and it was extended and radicalized under the aegis of the Judeo-Christian tradition, with its radically transcendent God.[12]

Having discriminated the category of "nature," the next crucial conceptual achievement concerned the phenomenon of motion. Aristotle himself had designated the proper understanding of motion as the key to understanding nature, but he had botched the job, at least as far as physical motion was concerned. Before physics and astronomy could really get off the ground, it was necessary that the faulty Aristotelian doctrine of impetus be replaced by the modern notion of inertia. Profoundly connected with this conceptual transformation—one that Herbert Butterfield has called "the most amazing in character and the most stupendous in the scope of its consequences . . . in the last fifteen hundred years"[13]—was the recognition that mathematical and geometrical abstractions provided the appropriate models and explanations for bodies moving in space. Galileo's discoveries can stand as the pivotal exemplars of this conceptual revolution; the later achievements of Kepler and Newton followed in the pathway thus opened up.

Galileo can also stand as a significant example of the next important source of the development of modern natural science. This time, however, it is his tools rather than his concepts that are significant, for part of the stimulus for his cosmological theories was what he learned by looking through his new-fangled contraption, the telescope. Requisite for the investigation of nature, of course, are observation and measurement, and it is technological proficiency that has vastly expanded our ability to gather data. Technological inventions and scientific discoveries prove to be mutually reinforcing: new technological breakthroughs permit new theoretical discoveries, and the theoretical discoveries may then provide the basis for additional technological accomplishments. The causal dialectic thus set in motion has been absolutely central to the dramatic achievements of modern natural science.

Finally, and this is our principal concern here, the success of natural science has been due much more than is widely appreciated to the "politics" of the scientific enterprise—to its organizations, procedures, and behavioral norms. The image of the solitary great scientist, alone with his thoughts and autonomous in his discoveries, is a myth or, at best, a vast oversimplification. Science is and always has been a profoundly communal enterprise. Even the great individual geniuses, such as Galileo and Newton and Einstein, have been inspired and sustained by a complex network of other individuals and institutions. The scientific revolution of the seventeenth century would almost surely never have got off the ground—and it certainly would not have achieved what it did—apart from formal institutions like the universities at Padua and at Paris and informal institutions like the communications network centering around Mersenne, which linked the European *illuminati* in a common enterprise.

Important in this respect are both external and internal political considerations. By "external" political forces I mean the larger social setting within which the scientific enterprise must operate; by "internal" politics I mean the manner in which the enterprise governs itself. External political forces can stimulate and sustain the scientific enterprise by granting it—above all—its essential autonomy and by providing material support, or the larger polity can, on the contrary, rather easily cripple or destroy science by imposing intolerable constraints, whether ideological or financial. The internal self-governance of a scientific enterprise must also, apparently, embody certain features if it is to be genuinely successful. The internal and external political requisites of successful scientific enterprises, moreover, tend to be overlapping and mutually reinforcing in some fundamental respects; for both sets of political norms involve and embody what Charles Frankel has called the "faith of reason"—the belief in the reality and importance of truth and in the capacity of the free mind to discern this truth more satisfactorily than any other agencies.

The internal politics of a rational enterprise is a dialectic of consensus, authority, and freedom. The presence, operative force, and institutional embodiment of each of these three political features is necessary to the success of the enterprise. Moreover, the political structure of a rational enterprise is not simply accidental. It is not a purely fortuitous integument, one that could be exchanged equally well for another set of arrangements, for another pattern of behavior. Rather, the politics of a rational enterprise is essential to its functioning. The political interplay of consensus, authority, and freedom is one of the defining characteristics of human "rationality" in action.

The consensus of a scientific rational enterprise arises in the first place from the dedication of each individual scientist to the truth, however defined. Although considerations of personal interest may play their part in motivating the scientist—the need to earn a living, the desire for recognition, an unnatural attachment to Bunsen burners, or whatever—it is understood by all involved that these individual ends are subordinate to the overriding end of improving our understanding of nature. More proximately, some consensus is also necessary on the most important current explanatory goals of the enterprise and, correlatively, on what major current "problems" presently confront the discipline.

The more abstract and general of these consensual commitments finds embodiment in the rhetoric of the scientific credo—the professed obligation to be "dispassionate," "objective," candid in the reporting of one's work, and so on. (One of the reasons for resistance to acknowledging the fiduciary grounding of all knowledge, in fact, is that this fundamental consensual commitment of the scientific enterprise is expressed in some of the same words used by positivistic epistemology. The fear of denigrating the credo is a fully legitimate fear. The fear that the overarching scientific commitment to the truth somehow loses its force with the abandonment of belief in "clear and distinct ideas" or their equivalent, however, is a mistake.) The more specific consensus of a scientific discipline as to its constituent problems and explanatory goals receives concrete embodiment in the "research program" of that discipline.

The rational pursuit of scientific knowledge also requires the constitution of legitimate authority and submission to appropriate restraint. Every scientific enterprise recruits, tests, and establishes a number of leaders whose judgment on matters of scientific concern is accorded special weight. The recognition of these "authorities" and the vesting in them of the powers of governance of the discipline represent a recognition of the just claims of experience, competence, and past achievement in rational conduct. This same recognition leads to a further constraint on the actions of the members of the enterprise—that is, the demand for warrants. Any scientist is entitled to his "opinion," but he is so only insofar as he is able and willing to support that opinion by argument and evidence. The deliberations within a court of reason—by definition, perhaps, but certainly in practice—demand "reasons."

These principles of restraint, discipline, and authority receive expression throughout the day-to-day functioning of a scientific enterprise. The discourse of the scientific community is permeated by—indeed, it is predicated on—the provision of "good reasons." Depending on the nature of the claims being put forward, these good reasons may vary from straightforward "supporting data" to much more complex and subtle arguments about appropriate research strategy or explanatory tactics; in either case it is taken for granted that, to gain a hearing, relevant warrants are required. The influence of recognized "authorities" is likewise embodied in the network of academic governance that regulates the attention and direction of the discipline through passing judgment on grant proposals, selecting papers for publication, recommending appointments for specific individuals, and so on.

Equally important are the freedoms accorded to the participants in the enterprise. A rational enterprise is based on a faith in the power and the legitimacy of the free mind. This faith in the free mind does not entail the licensing of every opinion as just as good as any other, nor does it imply the denigration of tradition, training, and experience. It does entail the belief that no legitimate authority is entitled to dictate the conclusions of a rational enterprise a priori or to suppress criticism of established doctrine, and it also implies the existence and protection of the procedural means for giving a hearing to innovative and critical claims.

The freedoms of the scientific republic are institutionalized in a number of ways. These institutions are intended to guarantee the autonomy of the individual scientist and to permit—even encourage—responsible criticism, dissent, and discussion. The principle of academic freedom, together with the various institutional devices intended to protect it, represents the attempt to keep the work of each scientist as free as possible from the incursions of outside political authority or from unduly burdensome restriction by internal authorities—such as dominant senior figures within the academic discipline itself. Moreover, a scientific discipline in various ways fosters and maintains a wide number of established forums for the free communication of new ideas and for the free criticism of both old and new doctrines. Scholarly journals and disciplinary conferences are examples of these forums.

Each of these three organizational features—consensus, authority, and freedom—is necessary for the success of a rational enterprise. Indeed, each of the three features is essential to its being "rational"—and the success of the enterprise is a function of its rationality. It could not be successful, other than by some wild stroke of luck, were it not rational; and it would not be rational were it structured differently.

The essentiality of consensus, authority, and freedom—of the sort indicated—to a rational enterprise is manifested in the consequences that follow if any of them is lacking. Without a crucial minimum of consensus—both the basic consensus as to the reality and value of truth and the more specific consensus on current problems and explanatory ideals—the enterprise would never get off the ground. It would lack the minimal coherence necessary for a communal human enterprise in which goals are set noncoercively. Apart from mutual dedication to the truth, the mutual accreditation of the participants would disappear. In short, no one would trust anyone else. In the absence of that trust, the enterprise would simply dissolve.[14] At a different and somewhat less exalted level, a parallel disappearance of some consensus regarding the problems and explanatory ideals of the discipline would have a similar result. Each scientist would go his own way. Each would consider the other's research "irrelevant," and no cross-fertilization of experimental results or explanatory hypotheses could occur until such time as some consensus could be reestablished.

In the same way, an absence of authority in the conduct of a rational enterprise would severely hamper it and might lead to its dissolution. Apart from the recognition of scientific authorities and the vesting in them of the right to perform some adjudicatory functions in winnowing out articles for publication, evaluating aspirants for positions of leadership in the discipline or for positions of control over the discipline's resources, and so on, the work of the discipline would tend to disintegrate. The legitimacy of both scientific papers and position-holders would become suspect; valuable contributions to the discipline might easily become lost in piles of relatively inconsequential and incompetent reports. In the absence of accredited internal authority, moreover, the integrity and autonomy of the enterprise would become much less resistant to incursions from the outside. To the extent that any opinion was considered to be as good as any other, legislatures or university administrators might feel not only inclined but properly entitled to impose their own opinions on the academic enterprises under their control. If authority is not constituted and respected from within, it will not be listened to from without.

The freedoms, finally, are equally essential. Without the practice of toleration, without the maintenance of open forums for criticism and discussion, without guarantees of scholarly autonomy, the scientific enterprise would lose its sources of creativity and innovation. It would tend to stagnate and rigidify. Despite myths to the contrary, individual scientists are generally as tradition-bound and as reluctant to abandon ideas they have lived and worked by as anyone else. Indeed, their ways of thinking may become sufficiently ingrained that they are unable to participate imaginatively in important conceptual changes.[15] Unless a scientific enterprise permitted its members their freedom of inquiry and gave them a hearing, therefore, it would cease to be "rational." Its ideas and conduct would become governed not by reason but by encrusted tradition and entrenched power—every bit as much as in a traditionalist and dictatorial political system.

Each of these three organizational features of a rational enterprise—consensus, authority, and freedom—in sum, is intrinsic to the rationality of the enterprise and essential to its success. Moreover, each must be understood and defined by reference to the others.

The self-orienting consensus of a rational enterprise, for example, must be freely achieved. It cannot be imposed from above or from outside if it is to be a genuine consensus rather than merely a stipulated goal. And if it is not genuinely a consensus, it will not perform its orienting functions properly and effectively. The authority structure of a scientific enterprise likewise depends on an underlying consensus for its legitimacy—indeed, for its very possibility. The exercise of this authority is, moreover, contingent on and limited by the freedom and autonomy of the discipline's members. These freedoms are themselves contingent, at the same time, on the other essential organizational aspects of the enterprise: they are predicated on the consensus permeating the enterprise, and they are disciplined by the self-constituting authority structure within which they arise and are protected.

Politics and Rational Enterprises

The question then becomes: Does it make sense to suggest that politics can be a "rational enterprise"? And, if politics can be a rational enterprise, should it be?

A classical rationalistic liberal like Condorcet would have answered both of these questions with an enthusiastic yes. The early liberals' account of rationality, however, combining features of the old *logos*-rationality with features of the new technical rationality, was philosophically incoherent, and the political prognosis based on it was utopian.

A prototypical technocrat like Saint-Simon would also have responded to these questions with an enthusiastic affirmative. But the technocratic account of rationality was primitive and reductive, and the political program based on it was, as a consequence, similarly primitive and humanly destructive.

The value noncognitivist—for example, a classical positivist—would answer the first of these questions in the negative, and the second question would lose its enabling premise. "Politics," on this view, is by definition an irrational enterprise in the sense that its ends are determined by will rather than knowledge and its means are characterized by force rather than suasion.

My own answer to both of these questions is a qualified yes, an affirmative conclusion that, it should be kept in mind, is dependent on the preceding account of rationality and "rational enterprises."

Our model for a rational enterprise has been the conduct of a scientific discipline. The applicability of this model to politics depends, therefore, on the validity of analogies between the two kinds of pursuits—the scientific and the political. If there are no analogies, then the applicability of the norm of rationality to politics loses its plausibility. And even if there are some analogies, the disanalogies must not be so profound as to render suspect the allegiance to a common norm.

The obvious disanalogies between scientific and political enterprises, accordingly, need to be openly acknowledged at the outset. The most important distinction between scientific and political enterprises is that the former is directed toward explanation and the latter toward "regulation." Science seeks to improve knowledge; politics exists to improve behavior and/or its consequences. This difference will be examined in more detail later on. Second, the substance of politics is human interests, desires, wants, needs. The focus of scientific inquiry is, in some sense, on "objective" truth, and therefore the interests of the individuals involved are not so intimately related to the goals of the enterprise.

Even in these respects, scientific and political enterprises are not, however, wholly discontinuous. Scientific enterprises must perform regulative functions in the service of their explanatory goals. It is perfectly intelligible to speak of the "governance" of scientific inquiry, since the scientific establishment allocates resources, promulgates rules, distributes benefits, and runs organizations. Moreover, individual scientists have their own distinctive interests vis-à-vis these resources and benefits—interests that potentially conflict with each other and can also exist in some tension with the common interest of the discipline.

Nevertheless, these two disanalogies between scientific and political activities are intrinsic and significant. There is also a third difference of circumstance that warrants mention because of its consequences: namely, the scientific luxury of suspended judgment. Scientific decisions, that is, may be postponed when relevant evidence is unavailable or when theoretical development is inadequate for further reliable progress. Political actors do not have this luxury. Political decisions often—perhaps characteristically—come with deadlines attached; and it is probably the rule rather than the exception that the policymaker must act with less information at his disposal than he really needs.

Finally, the membership of a scientific enterprise is different from the membership of a political society. Participation in a scientific enterprise is a matter of choice and vocation. "Citizenship" in such an enterprise comes through self-selection to some extent. In contrast, political citizenship is generally an accident of birth. The "republic of science" is a "sect" in the sociological sense (as defined by Weber and Troeltsch). It is a voluntary association of true believers, bound together by shared convictions. Political society is, in contrast, not a sect but a church; that is, it is a social affiliation into which one is born.

All of these disanalogies between scientific societies and political societies suggest inexpungeable differences between the exercise of authority in the two enterprises. Political authorities must reach specific conclusions in choosing between policies; they cannot rely, as scientific authorities often do, on simply laying down general presuppositions. They must often decide issues "prematurely"—by comparison with an ideal standard. And they must, ultimately, utilize force or the threat of force as part of their enforcement arsenal. Polanyi's belief that "the cooperation of independent scientists'' may provide ''a highly simplified example of a free society,'' therefore, is surely overly optimistic, at least insofar as their respective structures of authority are concerned.[16]

Once this difference between science and politics is conceded, however, the larger normative conception of the ''rational enterprise'' has significant utility in understanding political societies and legitimate force in evaluating them.

The purpose of politics, like the purpose of science, is to establish a progressive, productive, and harmonious equilibrium between human beings and their environment. This continuing equilibrating process is accomplished in science by the progressive adaptation and refinement of concepts to solve scientific problems. The analogous process in politics involves the progressive adaptation and refinement of institutions and practices to solve political problems. The notion of rationality in the context of scientific enterprises, accordingly, has applicability to politics to the extent that political problems are analogous to scientific problems and to the extent that institutions are analogous to concepts.

The latter analogy—between concepts and institutions—is not difficult to sustain. Both concepts and institutions are patterns of order that structure and regulate behavior—explanatory behavior in the first instance, political behavior in the second. Concepts amount to ''micro-institutions,'' as Toulmin puts it, controlling and directing the activity of knowing; institutions, conversely, are ''macro-concepts.''

> Like concepts, institutions find behavioral expression through changing constellations of ''standard operating procedures.'' They preserve their self-identity through change by selective innovation in response to changing situations, in the name of collective social goals, and in this, too, they display an unremarked parallel to concepts and conceptual evolution. So regarded, indeed, the historical evolution of social institutions would simply become the process of conceptual evolution writ large.[17]

The crucial issue thus becomes the extent to which political problems may be appropriately analogized to scientific problems. This issue is tantamount, more or less, to the question whether behavioral problems have a cognitive dimension. To the extent that political and scientific problems are alike, we may speak meaningfully of ''practical reason'' in Aristotle's sense. And, in like fashion and to the same extent, we can speak meaningfully of rational political activity and of a rationally ordered society.

Political problems and scientific problems are not identical, quite obviously. Nevertheless, I would argue, they are analogous in a number of important respects.

Scientific problems are defined (to borrow again from Toulmin) by the gap between the explanatory ideals and the current capabilities of a discipline. Ultimately, the goal of a scientific discipline could be said to be attainment of the truth; the ultimate achievement would be to make its subject matter utterly and wholly intelligible, explicable, and (possibly) predictable. This is, to all evidence, an unattainable goal, perhaps even in principle. It is, however, a valid "Utopia" toward which a science may strive. More proximately and probably more productively, the "problems" of a scientific enterprise are defined by more immediate and specific goals. These goals are identified largely by contrast with the particular gaps, flaws, incapacities, and anomalies discernible in the discipline's available repertory of theories and concepts. The task of attacking these problems, together with the strategy employed in the attack, constitutes the "research program" of a scientific discipline.

Are scientific goals and ideals "objective," or are they constituted by the "subjective" judgments of the members of the discipline? The only reasonable answer is: both. At the ultimate level, belief in the reality and accessibility of truth is just that—a belief; and dedication to its pursuit is a matter of will—of commitment. However, truth seems to be an "objective" reality—a potentially attainable "objective" relationship between knower and known. Similarly, the more proximate goals of a science are determined by the judgments of the discipline's members, and they are "subjectively" defined in the sense that they are so determined. However, there is nothing arbitrary or irrational about these determinations of appropriate specific goals. Rather, they are a projection of future productive possibilities made on the basis of the discipline's collective experience and past achievements.[18]

Political problems are of a different order (living is more than knowing). Structurally, however, they are quite similar to scientific problems.

Like scientific problems, political problems may be identified and defined by the gap between ideals and current capabilities. Political ideals are regulatory rather than explanatory. Like scientific ideals, however, they arise from the need to achieve a productive equilibrium between human needs and the constraints of their environment. If the ultimate goal of scientific endeavor can be said to be attainment of the truth, the ultimate goal of political endeavor can be said to be attainment of the good. And as attainment of the truth amounts to satisfaction of the human desire for intelligibility, so attainment of the good would be the satisfaction of the human desire for fulfillment. Like scientific problems, moreover, political goals can be given a less "idealized" and more proximate formulation: they can be defined by the particular gaps, flaws, incapacities, and anomalies in the society's available repertory of institutions and procedures.

Political ideals and the regulatory "problems" they identify, like scientific ideals and the explanatory "problems" they identify, are both "objectively" and "subjectively" established. Human needs and therewith the demands of human fulfillment are "objective" realities. They are a function of the organic economy of human beings, which is a pattern of created reality that must be taken as a given. Likewise, the flaws and incapacities of a society's current institutions and procedures are also real and objective: the pain, deprivation, inequity, and frustrations they cause are neither created by nor eliminable by nominalistic definitions imposed by the mind. At the same time, there is a process of collective judgment involved in identifying these goals and problems, just as there is a process of collective judgment essential to the definition of scientific problems. As in science, similarly, these "subjective" judgments are not thereby arbitrary. They are projections into the future based on the collective experience of the society.

It is meaningful, then, to speak of politics as a rational enterprise—at least potentially rational. A political society, to be sure, is not likely to be able to display the "compactness" of a scientific discipline. Its goals and its problems are more extensive and diffuse and therefore more difficult to codify. Nevertheless, it is possible for politics, like other human enterprises, to be conducted in a rational manner. A political society, that is, can proceed rationally to identify its problems and to establish its goals by mobilizing its collective experience, its understanding of human nature, and its grasp of the environmental constraints it faces. Having thus acted rationally to identify its current weaknesses with respect to allowing or assisting its citizens to satisfy their needs and to fulfill their human potentialities, a political society can then devise its strategy and tactics accordingly. These rational determinations parallel the determination of goals, problems, and associated research strategy by a scientific enterprise. And then, just as a scientific enterprise displays its rationality by identifying and selecting those conceptual adaptations and innovations most likely to be productive, so a rational political society can move reflectively to identify and select the institutional adaptations and innovations most conducive to its own goals.

Does this mean that politics can be turned into a science? Not at all. That would be a most misleading claim, especially given the widespread misconceptions about the "objective" certainty of scientific conclusions. Instead, it would be both accurate and less misleading to say that politics is capable of being conducted as a rational practical art—as science is in fact conducted. Politics cannot be "scientific," but it can, like science, be "rational."

Would politics conducted as a "rational enterprise" supersede "politics" in the usual sense? Would rational political behavior make obsolete, to be specific, the form of life praised by Bernard Crick in his *In Defense of Politics*? Again, the answer is: not at all. That conclusion is a characteristic technocratic misconception based on a misunderstanding of science and/or on a failure to respect the limitations of rationality in politics. The real point is quite different. Rationality cannot replace politics. It is, instead, what makes politics "political" rather than "military." It is the leavening of practical reason that can make a society Lockean rather than Hobbesian. Human beings united by the common discipline of reason can rely on that "natural" resource to construct a society governed by representative parliamentary institutions and characterized by extensive civil liberties. Human beings devoid of the common discipline of reason (or "rational" only in the narrow sense of "ratiocination") begin in a military situation rather than in a partially political situation: they begin in the war of all against all. And they escape this military anarchism only by substituting for it the essentially military hegemony of sovereign power. Reason, then, does not transcend or supersede politics. Reason permits politics to transcend or supersede warfare.

The Structure of a Rational Society

The structural requisites for a rational society are basically the same as those incumbent on rational enterprises generally. A society that wants to be a rational enterprise must possess some consensus on its basic goals so that it can, in turn, identify the problems it wishes to overcome. It must permit and promote the freedom of its citizens to discuss these problems. It must insist that the parties to this discussion of its problems present warrants for their views. And it must recognize and respect the legitimacy of authority duly constituted by these rational means. In short, a rational society is characterized by the same procedural and organizational hallmarks as our exemplary scientific enterprise—the same dialectic of consensus, freedom, and authority.

Does the consensus necessary for a rational society itself have predetermined substance? Is it more than a purely formal necessity, which could be compatible with any content at all? At the abstract level, at least, I think the answer is: yes, there is a fundamental core to the consensus of any rational society.

In the first place, the consensus of a rational society must incorporate the basis of scientific consensus: it must include the spontaneous commitment of its citizens to respect the truth. Why is dedication to the truth a necessary part of the consensus of a rational society? First, because the truth is a *telos* of any rational enterprise whatever—by definition. No enterprise, political or otherwise, could claim rationality if it were indifferent to or contemptuous of the truth. Second, commitment to truth is essential because apprehension of the truth is contributory to—conceivably, essential to—the pursuit of human fulfillment. The truth may not "set you free" as unproblematically as either the biblical claim or the Enlightenment faith suggested, but it is difficult to imagine that a society could be good in the long run if it were grounded on lies, delusions, or superstitions. Attainment of the common good means the satisfaction of human needs and achieving the best possible modus vivendi between these needs and the limitations of the environment; the successful pursuit of the common good therefore demands a reasonably accurate perception of human nature and of its environment. In this way, then, it seems safe to say that a commitment to the good society is contingent on a commitment to the truth.[19]

Why is a dedication to the common good the other constitutive element in the consensus of the rational society? Simply because that is the *telos* of politics by definition. It is hard to improve here on Aristotle, who observes that the purpose of politics "can only be the good for man."[20] A survey of all attempts to provide rational justification for any specific political regime, potential or actual, reveals virtual unanimity on this point, for, in the history of politics and political theory, even highly stratified and dictatorial regimes have rested their claims to legitimacy on their alleged benefit to the general welfare. Plato recommended vesting political authority exclusively in an elite class of philosophers, but he justified his recommendation by reference to the common good. Hobbes recommended the establishment of an absolute power above the citizenry "to overawe them all," but he alleged that step to be necessary for the general welfare. Even slavery, when hauled before the court of reason, has been defended on the grounds that it was in the best interests of the whole society, including those enslaved. And, to take the most extreme example, when violence or repression has been explicitly justified against some specific social grouping—as in Hitler's "final solution" for the "Jewish problem,"

in communism's "excision" of "reactionary forces," or in
Machiavelli's calculated brutalities—either the targets of the repression had to be denied their humanity (e.g., "Saujuden") or else the
repression had to be argued to be for the common good in the long
run. Rationality is inescapably "general" in its force and therefore
cannot lend itself to claims of special preferment. This is the feature
of rationality Kant captured in his definition of "rational beings" as
citizens of the "kingdom of ends" and in his dictum that a rational
being had to "act as if the maxim of his action were to become by his
will a general law of nature."[21] In short, to "rationalize" is to generalize. Therefore, if politics is aimed at achieving some good, "rational" politics must be directed at the general good.

Hume made the same basic point in a slightly different way. As he
observed, rational discourse about values inevitably converges on
the common good. This happens simply because of the requisites of
a common language. Anyone who wishes to speak rationally about
values must use a generally intelligible language to do so, and this
requirement forces a general and impartial standpoint on him. As
Hume wrote:

> When a man denominates another his enemy, his rival, his an-
> tagonist, his adversary, he is understood to speak the language of
> self-love, and to express sentiments, peculiar to himself, and
> arising from his particular circumstances and situation. But when
> he bestows on any man the epithets of vicious or odious or de-
> praved, he then speaks another language, and expresses senti-
> ments, in which he expects all his audience are to concur with
> him. He must here, therefore, depart from his private and par-
> ticular situation, and must choose a point of view, common to him
> with others; he must move some universal principle of the human
> frame, and touch a string to which all mankind have an accord and
> symphony. If he mean, therefore to express that this man pos-
> sesses qualities, whose tendency is pernicious to society, he has
> chosen this common point of view.[22]

A rational society, then, is marked by a consensus directed toward the truth and the common good. Each of these commitments is
an essential feature of its rationality. Commitment to the truth is
essential because rationality is by definition oriented toward the
truth. Commitment to the common good is essential because politics
is by definition directed toward the good for mankind and because
rationality demands universality.[23] These commitments constitute
the rational society's necessary consensus on a general and abstract
level, just as the dedication to truth provides the basis of scientific
consensus on the same plane. But what about the more concrete and
specific consensus of the rational society? What, if anything, is the

nature and source of the political analogue to the "research program" of a scientific discipline?

The "faith of reason" suggests that a society rationally ordered in all other respects could be expected to reach some rough consensus on this level as well. That is, a society that is informed by a general dedication to truth and to the common good, that protects and promotes free political debate, and that respects rationally constituted authority might reasonably be expected to be able to achieve some working consensus about its major pressing problems, weaknesses, and incapacities. The "rational" political strategy of the society would emerge out of the recognition of those problems in the same way as the research strategy of a scientific discipline emerges from that discipline's explanatory problems.

It should be recognized, however, that a specific consensus on a political working agenda may be unattainable under certain circumstances, however "rational" a society may be in other respects. For example, there may be so little reliable information or understanding about crucial issues that they cannot be rationally discussed. Or the needs and problems of the society may be so many and so profound that they overwhelm any attempts to impose rational order upon them. In circumstances like these, politics may not be able to be conducted as a rational enterprise; instead, it would revert to a "military" or anarchistic situation. (The same kind of organizational fragmentation eventuating in a failure of rationality can also happen to a scientific discipline, although a coherent research program can usually be reestablished after one of the resulting "fragments" of the discipline proves itself more productive and promising than the others.) The hard fact is that "rational" politics may be something of a luxury item—a possibility only for societies that have reached a certain minimum level of knowledge and affluence.

If consensus is one structural requisite of a rationally ordered society, civil liberty is another. Civil liberty is necessary for political rationality for essentially the same reasons that freedom of inquiry is essential to scientific rationality. Refinement and improvement of regulative institutions, like the refinement and improvement of explanatory concepts, requires creative innovation. Established practices, like established concepts, are tested by rational criticism. Even ideas and institutions that were originally rationally conceived may lapse into irrational and maladaptive rituals when not subjected periodically to critical evaluation. Apprehension of what is right to do as well as what is right to believe is much more likely when alternative viewpoints can receive a hearing. There is nothing particularly novel about this argument; it is given its classic formulation in Chapter Two of Mill's *On Liberty*, and anyone who wishes to pursue it further can return to that source.

A rational society must, therefore, cherish and foster the institutions that promote open discussion and inquiry. Toleration must be practiced. Freedom of the press must be protected. Academic institutions must be guaranteed their autonomy and integrity. A rational society is dependent on the viability of its "courts of reason," the forums in which ideas and proposals are evaluated by the standards of rational discourse.

The justification of civil liberties, so far as a rational society is concerned, is not based on the intrinsic virtue of "free expression." There may be virtue, to be sure, in freedom of expression per se, on the grounds that individual spontaneity, diversity, and autonomy are good things. (Mill makes the argument in Chapter Three of *On Liberty*). Free expression, moreover, may reasonably be considered a necessary condition of genuinely representative government, and it can be valued on that basis as well. From the standpoint of a rational society, however, the crucial justification of free speech is its essential contribution to the society's grasp of what is true and what is good.

Accordingly, a rational society will insist that its forums not be abused. It will insist on the presentation of warrants by those who would receive a serious hearing. It will demand argument, justification, and good reasons, not license mindless diatribes or sanction any idea as "just as good as any other." These sanctions on behalf of competent rational argument and against ungrounded opinion (Plato's *doxa*) must, of course, be largely imposed informally. They must, that is, be a function of the norms and expectations of the political culture rather than a matter of law. The law may be able to discriminate some categories of speech that are baneful in certain respects and are clearly of no use in revealing what is true or good (libel, "fighting words," yelling "Fire!" in a crowded theater, and so forth) and so leave them without protection. Most of the discrimination between rational discourse and mere words, however, must be accomplished by more informal social institutions. Warrantless "arguments" need not be censored or repressed, but they also need not be given "equal time." Any rational enterprise has its standards and must apply them. Without this selectivity, the enterprise would suffer—and indeed would be less than rational.

If the freedom of a rational society is not license, it is also not incompatible with authority. Indeed, as the example of scientific enterprises indicates, a rational enterprise would not be viable without the constitution and exercise of authority. Rational conduct, in politics as well as in science, means to govern one's actions by reference to the best available knowledge. Given the complexities of this knowledge and the realities underlying the division of labor, a rational society must possess mechanisms for the recruitment and identification of competent authorities. A rational society knows how to accredit—and is willing to obey—those who know what they are doing.

It is crucial here to distinguish authority and power, a distinction systematically blurred under the sway of positivism. Both power and authority involve the capacity to govern, but they are in other respects quite different—even opposites. Authority is a function of assent based on legitimacy; power is a function of force. The former rules by the recognition of its competence, the latter by coercion. Obedience to authority is premised on rational consent; subjection to power is a sometimes unavoidable misfortune. Given a constant level of regulative control within a society, power and authority are thus inversely related: the decline of authority increases the need for governmental power; the vitality of authority minimizes the need for the exercise of power.

Authority is not an intrinsic good, by any means. It is a device to cope with the incapacity of any human being to know everything relevant to his activity. In an epistemological utopia, where everyone knew everything essential, intellectual authority would be redundant. In the real world, our best strategy—indeed, the only rational one—is to rely on competent authority when our own knowledge runs out. It is only because individual scientists are able to rely on institutions that accredit authorities in adjacent fields, for example, that they are able to do their own work properly and to coordinate it with the larger scientific enterprise. If these mechanisms were to break down, modern science as we know it would be impossible; at the very least, its productivity would be slowed to a crawl.

The Enlightenment rationalists who, like Condorcet, depicted Reason and Authority as arch-antagonists therefore misconstrued the real battle. They defined authority as intrinsically subrational and thought a rational society could do entirely without it. That belief, however, depended on their conviction—not wholly implausible by their premises but clearly untenable in retrospect—that the simplicity of truth would ultimately enable everyone to know the essentials of virtually everything. In point of fact, of course, the knowledge explosion of modern science has done nothing of the sort. Instead of making everyone his own expert about everything, it has made even the most learned scientific experts relative tyros outside their own field. So far from making everyman a "philosopher," a Renaissance man of knowledge, it has turned that allegedly attainable ideal into a virtual impossibility.

The real battle, accordingly, is not between Reason and Authority but between rationally constituted authority on the one hand and either subrational authority or outright power on the other. A rational society, then, does not do without authority because it cannot. Instead, it constitutes a whole range of authorities, legitimated by their ability and competence, and then accords them due respect. Due respect is not slavish submission. Rational authority is always a contingent and limited affair, and the particular incumbents of positions of authority are continually subject to displacement by those who are better qualified.

If it is descriptively meaningful to speak of a rational society, then, as a society that embodies the fundamental structural features of a "rational enterprise," is the conception normatively valid? Or, to put it another way, why should a society aspire to "rationality"? These are perfectly legitimate questions, because reason is not a god; it does not carry intrinsic moral weight. Moreover, it is quite possible for societies to be relatively stable, efficient, or just without measuring up to the criteria of a rational enterprise.

The answer here is basically an argument from prudence, in the largest sense of that term. A society that can do so should organize itself as a rational enterprise because it will in that way improve its prospects for success. Its rationality will help it to be progressive, productive, and fair. Its rationality will help it adapt to changing circumstances. Its rationality will enhance the lives of its citizens, better enabling them to satisfy their needs and to fulfill their potentialities.

Conversely, departures from rationality exact their price. A traditionalist society, for example, will, almost surely, never be able to attain the dynamism of a society organized in accordance with the faith of reason. In many respects it will remain "underdeveloped." The ideologues of development may very well have parochially overestimated the virtues, and underestimated the costs, of "modernizing" traditional societies. Nonetheless, it seems hard to deny that "modern" societies have been able to improve the standard of living of their citizens in a wide variety of ways—or to deny that these improvements have been intimately dependent on the process of "rationalization."

A society that misconstrues reason in a closed and technocratic fashion will be subject to penalties of another kind. Dogmatism in the name of reason produces its own curious and profoundly destructive irrationalities. Communist countries tend to manifest these irrationalities most markedly, since they are the leading examples of officially imposed technocratic delusions. The strange phenomenon of Lysenkoism in the Soviet Union, with its destructive scientific and social consequences, was not an accident. It was simply one rather striking example of the kinds of irrationality endemic in a society that prohibits the freedoms essential to a truly rational society. Equally destructive are the crippling effects on the social sciences and the arts. Whatever its other achievements, a society that refuses to recognize the autonomy of reason—and therefore refuses to institutionalize the liberties implied by that recognition—will inevitably pay the price. By stifling the sources of creativity, innovation, and criticism essential to a rational enterprise, this kind of society will suffer from social and spiritual arteriosclerosis. The constraints it imposes will be "repressive" in the specific Freudian sense; and, as Freud explained, repression is not only painful but it eventually exacts its revenge.

Finally, a society that denigrates the discipline essential to a rational enterprise also suffers the costs of its folly. Contempt for reason's justified claims and restraints is the perennial temptation of libertarian democracies. Egalitarianism may be taken to imply that every person's ideas are as good as anyone elses, no matter how untutored they may be. Or the need for "good reasons"—for warrants—in political discourse may be ignored, with the result that the politics of the society is turned into a mere game of threat and bluff among adversaries. Whatever the achievements of such a society—and they may be substantial—the departure from the requisites of a rational enterprise again exacts its penalty. A contempt for good reasons and for the due respect appropriate to rationally constituted authority—like contempt for the freedoms essential to reason—creates delusions of its own. If technocratic closure is repressive, a libertarianism and egalitarianism contemptuous of the restraint of reason tends toward a kind of social schizophrenia. It will tend to mistake its myths and desires for realities, and it will find it increasingly difficult to retain the coherence necessary for a rational approach to its problems.

It should be emphasized that the "rational society" is not an all-encompassing normative model. In politics as in private life, rationality is not the only human virtue. In other words, the rational society is not necessarily the equivalent of the good or ideal society. Considerations of courage, compassion, altruism, conviviality, and so on, go beyond rationality as we have defined it, and each has a role to play in the good society.

Moreover, it should also be clear that the ideal of a rational society is one that will never be fully attained. The practical difficulties that stand in the way are almost insuperable. The model of the rational society, in this respect, is a regulative ideal rather than a realistic possibility. To borrow a phrase from Reinhold Niebuhr, it is one of those "impossible possibilities" of human life—an ideal within man's potential reach but not within his grasp.

The significance of the normative model of a rational society, therefore, is limited but nonetheless important. It signifies that, once the incoherence of early liberal rationalism and the mistaken pretensions of technocracy are set aside, it still makes sense to speak of "rationality" in politics and that the "rational" approach to politics can still be accorded normative validity on the basis of its contribution to the success of political enterprises embodying its procedures and abiding by its standards.

The Rational Society: Some Comparisons

This sketchy and abstract model of a rational society can perhaps, in conclusion, be given some further definition—and its normative thrust may be further illuminated—by some comparisons with other normative political models.

This conception of political rationality, for example, incorporates in some respects Hegel's notion about the "cunning of reason." It suggests that reason is in fact a progressive force in political development. It is in accord with the Hegelian notion of the "dialectic" in seeing this process of rational development as one in which new and more adaptive social practices continually evolve out of the critical confrontation of differing viewpoints. At the same time, however, our notion of "reason in history" not only departs from but is specifically hostile to Hegel's metaphysical hypostasizing of Reason and to his epistemological arrogance. Reason is properly seen as a tool of man; man is not the tool of some absolute Reason-as-Geist. History never loses its contingency, never becomes a finished product. Above all, no one can ever legitimately claim to have attained Real Knowledge, as Hegel alleged; that kind of *hubris* is not only delusionary but potentially catastrophic.

This conception of a rational society also incorporates the fundamental idea behind Kant's model of the "kingdom of ends." The participants in a rational enterprise are subject, as Kant perceived, to the discipline inherent in the universalizing impetus of reason. A "rational being," accordingly, must be oriented to considerations of the common good, since he has no rational claim to special preferment; when he enters the world of rational discourse, he must abandon his individual particularity to that extent. The conception of practical reason I have outlined is not so "pure" as Kant's, however. It neither entails nor relies on the metaphysical dualism implicit in Kant's formulation. Nor is it so narrowly legalistic; for it sees practical reason as an attribute of "heteronomous" humanity rather than its antithesis.

Similarly, the consensus that undergirds a rational society has features in common with the political ideal that inspired Kant—namely, Rousseau's conception of the General Will. A rational society, like Rousseau's society of the *Social Contract,* is actuated by a common dedication to principles that transcend the particular self-interest of the individuals. The consensus of a rational society is more than the "will of all," in Rousseau's phrase—more than a mere aggregate of the particularistic individual wants of the society's members. As Rousseau suggested, moreover, this consensus plays an important role in maintaining the coherence and integrity of the society. The consensus of a rational society, however, makes no claim to the "infallibility" or the mystical "indivisibility" of Rousseau's General Will. It is likewise not hostile, like the General Will, to "partial associations" within the society. Therefore, it is devoid of the collectivist implications of the General Will, and it is also devoid of the unjustifiable pretense that it can be used as grounds for "forcing someone to be free."

The idea of a rational society incorporates the pragmatists' focus on concrete "problem-solving" as the essence of rational action. Rationality, as the pragmatists insisted, is not the idle contemplation of detached minds; it is a style of behavior characteristic of an intelligent animal's response to challenging circumstances. However, whether necessarily or not, "pragmatism" has come to be identified with a rather mundane instrumentalism. My conception of the rational society does not imply such a reductivist account of social "problems." The problems of politics are not simply matters of tinkering with techniques; they may well involve, and usually do involve, problems of the spirit, problems of the equitable distribution of goods, and other problems that cut far deeper than difficulties of merely technical contrivance.

The model of the rational society happily concedes Plato's insistence—and for that matter the insistence of the technocrats—that good politics depends in part on sound knowledge. Competence, moral wisdom, technical know-how, are all important to a successful political enterprise. To that extent, a rational society will cultivate and cherish its intellectual elites. Where the ideal of the rational society takes its leave of both Plato and the technocrats, however, is where they assume that the relevant knowledge is the exclusive property of a single elite group. The conception of a rational society is both more pluralistic and more democratic than either Plato or the technocrats supposed, because it recognizes varieties of expertise and because it sees both the information and the moral wisdom requisite for sound political decisions as more widely dispersed than they thought. Moreover, both Plato and the technocrats, misled by their overmathematicized image of cognition, overestimated the finality and certainty with which valid social norms can be apprehended. The rational society I have sketched is much more modest in this respect. Although it is predicated on the belief that the common good is a matter for rational inquiry, it sees this common good as an evolving "better-for-the-time-being" that can be only imperfectly known.

The rational society is democratic, then, in contrast with the radical distinction between governors and governed in Platonic and technocratic rationalism. The principle of "cognitive respect" grants a hearing to all who subscribe to the rules of rational discourse. All "rational beings" are considered equal and as ends rather than means—as in Kant. Representative institutions are valued by the rational society because they embody these principles, because they provide a framework for the rational confrontation of different perspectives, and because they therefore are instrumental in rational decision-making. A rational society, however, is not democratic insofar as democracy entails a mindless obeisance to vox populi. To the extent that "public opinion" is unknowledgeable—and, in the aggregate, it always will be so to a considerable extent—it is not an absolute touchstone. Representation in a rational society, therefore, has a Burkean dimension to it: the representative is not free to substitute his own will or opinion for that of his constituents, but he is obligated to mediate their will by the exercise of his experienced rational judgment.

My conception of politics as a rational enterprise also has a point of tangency with the conservatism of a Burke, a John Adams, or a Michael Oakeshott. The meeting ground with this form of conservatism comes at the point where a rational society seeks to define its ideals and thereby to establish its agenda. For a rational society must rely here, as an Oakeshott would consider proper, on its tradition. It establishes its ideals, that is, by projecting into the future the intimations of human fulfillment it has encountered in its collective experience. The goals of a rational society, like the goals of a scientific discipline, are not in actual practice the product of abstract a priori dictates. Instead, they arise as specific and concrete a posteriori extensions of what the enterprise has achieved in the past. From this perspective, Oakeshott's polemic against "rationalism in politics" must, like Burke's strictures against the "speculative designs of "metaphysical" rationalism, be understood not as a rejection of reason's role in politics per se but rather as a critique of a distorted style of politics based on a misconception about reason.[24]

A rational society, however, would not be in sympathy with the conservative's tendency to glorify "prejudice"—perhaps as a desperate expedient. Established prejudices may indeed embody profound truths, as Burke insists; but they may also be little more than encrusted myths, crippling in their consequences. It is reason that must judge. Moreover, the rational society is not hidebound or reactionary. Where the institutions of a rational society are healthy, innovations should not be feared but welcomed as potential improvements subject to experimental test. The new is not necessarily better than the old, but neither is it necessarily worse. Again, reason must be the judge.

Because the rational society is directed toward the common good, it implicitly shares the assumption of the natural-law tradition that there is a real "objective" good that the mind may comprehend and that men should try to attain as a condition of their fulfillment. Because the rational society understands the determination of the good to be a product of a concrete problem-solving intellect, it shares Hume's belief in an "experimental" morality. In point of fact, there is more convergence between the natural-law tradition and Hume's ideas on public morality than is generally realized. Understandably, these two viewpoints are usually seen as quite different, not only because of their radically different ontologies, but because of Hume's insistence that moral judgments are a function of the passions rather than of reason and because of his famous "gap" between is and ought. These are real and important differences. Nevertheless, Hume's conception of an objectively—i.e., experimentally—determined social good is strikingly similar in basic outline to the natural-law tradition's conception of the public interest. Thus, for Hume the good is what men would naturally desire as a function of their "human constitution" if they had all the relevant information and if their minds were unclouded by superstition. The definition of the public interest provided by an adherent of the natural-law tradition, such as Walter Lippmann, is not all that distant. The public interest, he wrote, is "what men would choose if they saw clearly, thought rationally, acted disinterestedly and benevolently."[25]

The idea of the rational society, as we have defined it, shares this assumption—that is, the assumption that there is an "objective" public interest potentially if imperfectly ascertainable by the collective judgment of rational men. As a philosophical model, however, it is free of Hume's cultural parochialism and his anthropological hedonism, and it departs very definitely from his corpuscular ontology—an ontology that had so reductive an impact on his moral theory that, as we have seen, it eventually undermined it altogether. In like fashion, the rational society's commitment to the premise of "objective values" does not depend on—indeed, it rather clearly departs from—the static ontology of the usual natural-law formulations. One need not believe in eternal essences to accredit the idea that human beings have their distinctive potentialities, needs, and natural ends.

Conclusion: The Rational Society and Liberal Ideals

Finally, how does the rational society as I have conceived it compare with the classical liberalism of the Enlightenment? What happens to the high hopes and the humane ideals that were pinned to liberal reason from its first inception? The answer, I believe, is that the high hopes must be modified considerably but that the humane ideals are preserved and strengthened.

The utopian expectations entertained by many of the early liberals must be abandoned. They were premised, we can now recognize, on philosophical assumptions that could not stand up and on empirical predictions that have not been borne out. The truth is not simple. Every man cannot become a "philosopher." Reason will not necessarily triumph, nor will it necessarily lead to perpetual peace, international harmony, universal good will, and continual progress.

Nevertheless, the normative model of politics as a "rational enterprise" gives genuinely realistic embodiment to liberalism's basic goals, aspirations, and moral ideals. The rational society sustains, protects, and encourages the humane heart of liberalism. Its philosophical basis makes human dignity once again intelligible and human integrity once again defensible. The institutions of a rational society protect Liberty; they presuppose and promote Equality; they require and nourish Fraternity.

Above all, the philosophical beliefs that inform the rational society delegitimize the technocratic tyranny and the irrationalist anarchism that were latent alternatives in the original conception of liberal reason. These revised philosophical beliefs bring new meaning and respectability to the fundamental project of liberal politics: the quest for a regime of ordered liberty established through the "natural light" of reason.

The transformed and chastened brand of rationalism made possible by contemporary philosophical trends offers the prospect of healing the rift between ideals and beliefs that has plagued the liberal tradition from relatively early in its career. It provides to contemporary liberalism a means of deliverance from Diderot's dilemma: from entrapment in a logical progression of ideas that its heart cannot accept but that its head cannot reject.

The irony of liberal reason has so far been disturbing and destructive. The unfolding implications of liberal epistemology have run counter to liberal ideals and have provided ammunition for profoundly illiberal political enterprises. Perhaps, however, the final ironic twist to the career of liberal reason may be hopeful and constructive. Perhaps nothing will improve the liberal prospect more than the final abandonment of the very epistemological premises that were originally thought to be liberalism's surest resource. Perhaps a revised appraisal of human understanding will permit us to escape the strange oscillation between pride and despair that has characterized political life in the modern West—to replace that unhappy pattern with a more felicitous dialectic of hope and humility. Perhaps the "party of humanity" will one day be able to borrow Eliot's words and say: "the end of all our exploring [has been] to arrive where we started and know the place for the first time."

Notes

Preface

  1. Harold J. Laski, *The Rise of Liberalism* (New York: Harper, 1936), pp. 2–3.
  2. Charles Frankel, *The Faith of Reason* (New York: King's Crown Press of Columbia University, 1948), p. 2.
  3. Reinhold Niebuhr, *The Irony of American History* (New York: Scribner's, 1962), p. viii.

Chapter One

  1. Hans J. Morgenthau, *Scientific Man versus Power Politics* (Chicago: University of Chicago Press, 1946), p. 222.
  2. Edmund Stillman and William Pfaff, *The Politics of Hysteria* (New York: Harper, 1964), p. 26.
  3. Kenneth Keniston, *The Uncommitted* (New York: Dell, 1970), p. 300.
  4. Ibid., p. 301.
  5. Cf. Kingsley Martin, *French Liberal Thought in the Eighteenth Century* (Boston: Little, Brown, 1929), p. 3: "In the twentieth century, new knowledge and bewildering experience have once more brought disillusion, scepticism, and a paralyzing sense of impotence."
  6. See, for example, Charles Frankel, *The Case for Modern Man* (New York: Harper, 1955). "The great problem," says Frankel, "is to reconstruct the liberal tradition to make it applicable to an age of technical specialization, bureaucratized power, and mass movements" (p. 205).
  7. Paul Tillich, *The Protestant Era* (Chicago: University of Chicago Press, 1957), p. 153.
  8. Carl Becker, *The Heavenly City of the Eighteenth-Century Philosophers* (New Haven: Yale University Press, 1932).
  9. See John Dillenberger, *Protestant Thought and Natural Science* (New York: Doubleday, 1960), p. 26.
  10. Cf. Stillman and Pfaff, *The Politics of Hysteria*, pp. 2 and 13: "To be a man of the modern West is to belong to a culture of incomparable originality and power; it is also to be implicated in incomparable crimes.... There is a tradition of excess—of violence for transcendental and essentially unattainable goals—that is as much a part of the West as our tradition of regard for individual

destiny and worth. They are, indeed, tragically related beliefs."

11. Morgenthau, *Scientific Man and Power Politics*, p. 122.

12. The liberal modern West is still predisposed to deprecate the worth of traditional social orders. This bland incomprehension, at bottom a form of arrogance, has been one contributing factor to the destructive impact of Western culture and policy on the countries of the Third World. As J. William Fulbright has observed, "American government officials, technicians, and economists have been strikingly successful in breaking down the barriers to change in ancient but fragile cultures. Here, however, our success ends. Traditional rulers, institutions, and ways of life have crumbled under the fatal impact of American wealth and power but they have not been replaced by new institutions and new ways of life, nor has their breakdown ushered in an era of democracy and development" (*The Arrogance of Power* [New York: Vintage Books, 1966], pp. 18–19). Cf. my *Dilemma of Contemporary Political Theory* (New York: Dunellen, 1973), pp. 85–95.

13. See Robert A. Nisbet's *The Quest for Community* (New York: Oxford University Press, 1953).

14. Keniston, *The Uncommitted*, p. 208.

15. Sheldon Wolin, *Politics and Vision* (Boston: Little, Brown, 1960), pp. 314–25.

16. John Locke, *Second Treatise of Civil Government*, Everyman's Library ed. (London: J. M. Dent, 1924), chap. 9, pt. 128.

17. Laski, *The Rise of Liberalism*, p. 236.

18. Niebuhr, *The Irony of American History*, p. 76. To deepen the irony still further, radical critics of American liberalism often assail it on the basis of its own premises. That is, it is offered as proof of liberalism's bankruptcy that the system is not utterly without its coercive aspects. Even such subtle alleged coercion as "repressive desublimation" is decried. Both the libertarian right and the radical left are truly the children of liberalism; they simply are more consistent than most "moderates" in pursuing the implications of the tacit anarchism in the liberal attitude toward power. Moreover, the radical myth of revolutionary violence to rid the world of its corruption is simply a slightly altered version of the liberals' "war to end all war." Marx said that a morbid society produced its own morbid gravediggers. Similarly, naïve liberalism produces its own naïve antagonists.

19. As Robert Nisbet has written, "In large part, the present crisis of liberal thought in the West comes, I believe, from the increasing loss of correspondence between the basic liberal values and the prejudgments and social contexts upon which the historic success of liberalism has been predicated" (*The Quest for Community*, pp. 218–19).

20. Herbert Marcuse, *One-Dimensional Man* (Boston: Beacon Press, 1966). p. 125.

21. Niccolò Machiavelli, *The Prince and the Discourses*, trans. Luigi Ricci (New York: Random House, 1950), p. 103.

22. Ibid., p. 104.

23. Ibid., p. 56.

24. See my *The Politics of Motion: The World of Thomas Hobbes* (Lexington: University Press of Kentucky, 1973), esp. chap. 5, and Michael Oakeshott, Introduction to Hobbes's *The Leviathan* (Oxford: Blackwell, 1947).

25. Marcuse, "One-Dimensional Thought," pt. 2 of *One-Dimensional Man*.

26. John Stuart Mill, *Autobiography* (New York: Columbia University Press, 1924), p. 74.

27. Walter Lippmann, *The Public Philosophy* (Boston: Little, Brown, 1955).

28. Nisbet, *The Quest for Community*, p. 213.

Chapter Two

1. Jean D'Alembert, *Preliminary Discourse to the "Encyclopedia" of Diderot*, trans. Richard N. Schwab (Indianapolis: Bobbs-Merrill, 1963), p. 85.

2. Ibid., p. 76.

3. Ibid., p. 83.

4. Ibid.

5. See Voltaire's *Philosophical Letters*, no. 13 (*Lettres philosophiques* [Paris: Hachette, 1924], vol. 1, p. 166).

6. Paul Hazard, *La Pensée européenne au XVIIIème siècle* (Paris: Boivin, 1946), vol. 1, pp. 54–55.

7. Ernst Cassirer, *The Philosophy of the Enlightenment*, trans. Fritz C. A. Koelln and James P. Pettegrove (Boston: Beacon Press, 1955), p. 99.

8. Aram Vartanian, *Diderot and Descartes* (Princeton: Princeton University Press, 1953), p. 9.

9. Charles Frankel, who generally credits Locke as providing "the philosophical source-book of the Enlightenment," goes on to note that "Locke was sufficiently like Descartes so that the advantages of Descartes, the revolutionary, were not lost" (*The Faith of Reason*, p. 42).

10. For an excellent discussion, see A. C. Fraser's Prolegomena to Locke's *An Essay Concerning Human Understanding* (New York: Dover, 1959), pp. lxxi–lxxiii. (All further references to Locke's *Essay* will be to this edition.)

11. Quoted by Fraser, ibid., p. lxxii.

12. Ibid., pp. lxxii–lxxiii.

13. Vartanian, *Diderot and Descartes*, p. 198.

14. Quoted by Fraser, Prolegomena, p. xx.

15. Quoted by John W. Yolton, *John Locke and the Way of Ideas* (London: Oxford University Press, 1956), p. 4.

16. René Descartes, "Discourse on Method," in *Philosophical Writings*, ed. and trans. Norman Kemp Smith (New York: Modern Library, 1958), p. 137.

17. Ibid., pp. 136–37.

18. Thomas Hobbes, *Leviathan* (New York: Dutton, 1950), p. 589. For an account of Hobbes's relationship to the Aristotelian tradition, see my *The Politics of Motion: The World of Thomas Hobbes*.

19. Locke, of a more charitable disposition than the contentious sage of Malmesbury, was even willing to call Aristotle "one of the greatest men among the ancients; whose large views, acuteness, and penetration of thought and strength of judgment, few have equalled" (*Essay*, IV. 17. 4).

20. Descartes, *Philosophical Writings*, p. xi.

21. Hobbes, *Leviathan*, p. 588.

22. Ibid., pp. 598 and 597.

23. Locke, *Essay*, "Epistle Dedicatory," p. 14.

24. Hobbes, *English Works,* ed. William Molesworth (London: John Bohn, 1839), vol. 1, p. viii.

25. For discussions of the conceptual revolution turning around the axis of the altered view of motion, see Herbert Butterfield, *The Origins of Modern Science,* rev. ed. (New York: Collier, 1962); Basil Willey, *The Seventeenth Century Background* (New York: Columbia University Press, 1934); E. A. Burtt, *The Metaphysical Foundations of Modern Science* (Garden City, N.Y.: Doubleday, 1954); and my *The Politics of Motion: The World of Thomas Hobbes.*

26. Marie Jean Antoine Nicolas Caritat de Condorcet, *Sketch for a Historical Picture of the Progress of the Human Mind,* trans. June Barraclough (London: Weidenfeld & Nicolson, 1955), p. 97.

27. Locke, *Essay,* IV. 20. 4. See also IV. 20. 7–17.

28. Condorcet, *Progress of the Human Mind,* p. 97.

29. Friedrich Engels, "Socialism: Utopian and Scientific," in Lewis Feuer, ed. *Marx and Engels: Basic Writings on Politics and Philosophy* (Garden City, N.Y.: Doubleday, 1959), p. 68. Cf. Locke, *Essay,* IV. 19. 14: "Reason must be our last judge and guide in everything."

30. The Marquis de Chastellux, quoted by Frankel, *The Faith of Reason,* p. 67.

31. Immanuel Kant, "What Is Enlightenment?" in *The Philosophy of Kant,* ed. and trans. Carl J. Friedrich (New York: Random House, 1949), p. 132.

32. Locke, *Essay,* III. 10. 2.

33. Hobbes, *Leviathan,* p. 604.

34. Ibid., p. 26.

35. Ibid., p. 27.

36. Locke, *Essay,* III. 10. 1. Note that the incapacity of language to attain the precision of mathematics is expressed as a kind of failure, even here.

37. Claude Helvetius, *A Treatise on Man,* trans. W. Hooper (New York: Burt Franklin, 1810), vol. 1, p. 207.

38. John Aubrey, cited by A. D. Lindsay in his Introduction to Hobbes's *Leviathan,* p. viii.

39. D'Alembert, *Preliminary Discourse,* p. 26.

40. Hobbes, *Leviathan,* p. 588.

41. Ibid., p. 32.

42. Descartes, "Rules for Direction of the Mind," *Philosophical Writings,* p. 19.

43. Ibid., p. 7.

44. James Gibson, *Locke's Theory of Knowledge and Its Historical Relations* (Cambridge, Eng.: At the University Press, 1960), pp. 4–5.

45. Fontenelle, quoted by Cassirer, *The Philosophy of the Enlightenment,* p. 16. For an excellent study of Condillac, see Isabel Knight, *The Geometric Spirit: The Abbé de Condillac and the French Enlightenment* (New Haven and London: Yale University Press, 1968).

46. Cassirer, *Philosophy of the Enlightenment,* p. 16. For a superb examination of Pascal in this context, see William H. Poteat, "Pascal's Conception of Man and Modern Sensibility" (Ph.D. dissertation, Duke University, 1950).

47. Hobbes, *Leviathan,* p. 26.

48. Descartes to Mersenne, November 20, 1629, in Descartes, *Philosophical Letters,* trans. and ed. Anthony Kenny (Oxford: Clarendon Press, 1970), p. 6.

49. Descartes, "Rules for Direction of the Mind," *Philosophical Writings*, pp. 2–3.

50. D'Alembert, *Preliminary Discourse*, p. 29.

51. As Pierre Bayle wrote: "I do not know whether one could say that the obstacles to a good examination do not come so much from the fact that the mind is void of knowledge as that it is full of prejudice" (quoted by Cassirer, *Philosophy of the Enlightenment*, p. 162).

52. Quoted by Vartanian, *Diderot and Descartes*, p. 191. For an excellent exploration of the interaction of the poetic and scientific imaginations, see Elizabeth Sewell, *The Orphic Voice* (New York: Harper & Row, 1971).

53. Locke similarly contrasts "wit and fancy" with "dry truth and real knowledge," for example (*Essay*, IV. 10. 34).

54. Trublet, quoted by Paul Hazard, *The European Mind* (New Haven: Yale University Press, 1953), p. 340.

55. Leclerc, quoted ibid., pp. 340–41. Hazard comments: "Whence comes this hostility on the part of one of the most representative of the rationalists? It comes from the conviction, firmly implanted, that poetry is just another name for falsehood. And, after all, that was the view held, albeit unconsciously, by the great majority of people in those days" (p. 341). Needless to say, poetry did not flourish in this intellectual environment. Hazard writes: "When they did write verse, it was merely a vehicle for their ideas on geometry. And so poetry died; or at least seemed to die" (p. 336).

56. Hume, *Treatise*, I. III. 10.

57. Descartes, "Discourse on Method," *Philosophical Writings*, pp. 97–98.

58. "Often, however, it does happen that this or that house is pulled down with a view to rebuilding; and sometimes this is due to their being in danger of themselves falling, their foundations being insecure" (ibid., pp. 102–3).

59. Descartes, *Philosophical Letters*, p. 53.

60. "I thought . . . that I ought to reject as downright false all opinions which I could imagine to be in the least degree open to doubt—my purpose being to discover whether, after doing so, there might remain, as still calling for belief, something entirely indubitable" (Descartes, "Discourse on Method," p. 118).

61. Ibid., p. 116.

62. Ibid., p. 132.

63. Ibid., p. 120.

64. Locke, *Essay*, IV. 18. 13. Descartes wrote that "God has given each of us a light for the distinguishing of the true from the false" ("Discourse on Method," p. 115).

65. Descartes, "Meditations," *Philosophical Writings*, p. 183.

66. Descartes, "Discourse on Method," p. 122.

67. Descartes, "Meditations," p. 229. Elsewhere he wrote that "the fundamentals of my physics are almost all so evident that they have only to be understood to be believed" ("Discourse on Method," p. 135).

68. Locke, *Essay*, IV. 9. 2.

69. Locke, *Essays on the Law of Nature*, ed. W. von Leyden (Oxford: Clarendon Press, 1954), p. 149.

70. Locke, *Essay*, II. 2. 1 and II. 31. 2.

71. Abbé de Condillac, *An Essay on the Origin of Human Knowledge*, trans. Thomas Nugent (Gainesville, Fla.: Scholars' Facsimilies and Reprints, 1971), pp. 8–9.

72. Locke, *Essay*, II. 30. 2. It is a very short step from Locke's "nothing

can be plainer to a man than the clear and distinct perception he has of those simple ideas" (ibid., II. 2. 1) to Condillac's "it is very certain that nothing is more clear and distinct than our perception when we experience sensations" (*Origin of Human Knowledge*, I. 2. 11). All that happens is the translation of the equivocal Lockean "idea" into the unequivocal "sensation." There was, indeed, plenty of warrant in Locke himself for taking this step, although other things he said could be taken as warrant for taking the very different step that Berkeley took. In the *Preliminary Discourse*, Condillac's move is accepted as authoritative. As one commentator has written, "In D'Alembert's exposition the clear and distinct sensation replaced the clear and distinct *a priori* idea of Descartes as the basis of all truth or certain knowledge" (Richard N. Schwab, Introduction to D'Alembert's *Preliminary Discourse*, p. xxxiii).

73. Vartanian, *Diderot and Descartes*, p. 156.

74. Descartes, "Rules for Direction of the Mind," *Philosophical Writings*, p. 67.

75. Condillac, *Origin of Human Knowledge*, p. 26 (emphasis in original).

76. D'Alembert, *Preliminary Discourse*, pp. 22 and 31.

77. Helvetius, *Treatise on Man*, 1:228 (emphasis in original).

78. Frankel, *The Faith of Reason*, p. 16.

79. Descartes, *Philosophical Writings*, pp. 191, 123.

80. Helvetius, *Treatise on Man*, 1:14–15.

81. Condillac, *Origin of Human Knowledge*, p. 8.

82. Ibid., pp. 8–9. Cf. D'Alembert, *Preliminary Discourse*, pp. 6–7.

83. Descartes, "Discourse on Method," p. 105.

84. Descartes, "Rules for Direction of the Mind," p. 43.

85. Descartes, *Philosophical Letters*, p. 30.

86. See Alexandre Koyré, *From the Closed World to the Infinite Universe* (Baltimore: Johns Hopkins University Press, 1957), and Burtt, *The Metaphysical Foundations of Modern Science*.

87. See Marjorie Grene, *A Portrait of Aristotle* (London: Faber & Faber, 1963).

88. Descartes, "Discourse on Method," pp. 106–7.

89. Although it is an oversimplification to depict the leading philosophers of the seventeenth century and the eighteenth century as wholly of one mind, they nevertheless were basically united on the fundamental issues we are examining here. Differences of emphasis are certainly present, and they are significant in some contexts. Considered as a whole, however, it is the intellectual continuity of the period rather than the changes that are most striking. As Cassirer has written: "Thus it is evident that, if we compare the thought of the eighteenth century with that of the seventeenth, there is no real chasm anywhere separating the two periods. The new ideal of knowledge develops steadily and consistently from the presuppositions which the logic and theory of knowledge of the seventeenth century . . . had established" (*Philosophy of the Enlightenment*, p. 22). It is this essential and profound continuity that warrants using the terms "the Enlightenment," "the seventeenth century," and "the proponents of the new rationalism" as largely overlapping.

90. Frank E. Manuel, *The Prophets of Paris* (New York: Harper & Row, 1965), p. 86.

91. John Stuart Mill, *On Liberty* (Indianapolis: Bobbs-Merrill, 1956), p. 53.

92. Descartes, "Rules for Direction of the Mind," pp. 4, 57, 7.

93. Locke, *Essay*, IV. 16. 4.

94. Ibid., IV. 3. 29.

95. Locke, Second Letter to Stillingfleet, cited by Gibson, *Locke's Theory of Knowledge*, p. 2.

96. Locke, Third Letter to Stillingfleet, cited by Gibson, ibid., p. 123.

97. Locke, *Essay*, IV. 16. 3.

98. Ibid., I. 3. 24.

99. Ibid., IV. 17. 16.

100. Ibid., IV. 3. 22.

101. Ibid., Introduction, sec. 7.

102. Voltaire wrote in his *Treatise on Metaphysics* that "when we cannot utilize the compass of mathematics or the torch of experience and physics, it is certain we cannot take a single step forward" (*Traité de métaphysique* [Manchester, Eng.: University of Manchester Press, 1937], p. 23). Helvetius wrote that "Philosophy cannot advance without the staff of experience: it does indeed advance but constantly from observation to observation, and where observation is wanting it stops" (*Treatise on Man*, 1:99). Hume's famous passage in section 12 of the *Enquiry Concerning Human Understanding* expressed his resolution to "commit to the flames" everything except "abstract reasoning concerning quantity or number" or "experimental reasoning concerning matter of fact and existence."

103. Locke, *Essay*, Introduction, sec. 4.

104. Descartes, "Rules for Direction of the Mind," p. 33.

105. Cf. Locke, *Essay*, IV. 12.

106. Marjorie Grene, *The Knower and the Known* (New York: Basic Books, 1966), p. 17. Chapters 1 and 2 of this study are full of insight on this issue. Dewey's views appear in his Gifford Lectures of 1929, *The Quest for Certainty* (New York: Putnam's, 1960).

107. Hobbes, *Leviathan*, p. 588.

108. Condorcet, *Progress of the Human Mind*, p. 163.

109. Hobbes, *Leviathan*, p. 594.

Chapter Three

1. D'Alembert, *Preliminary Discourse*, p. 80.

2. Charles Frankel, *The Faith of Reason*, p. 20.

3. J. B. Bury, *The Idea of Progress* (London: Macmillan, 1924), p. 67. See also R. V. Sampson, *Progress in the Age of Reason* (Cambridge, Mass.: Harvard University Press, 1956), p. 27.

4. Vartanian, *Diderot and Descartes*, p. 17.

5. Descartes, "Discourse on Method," *Philosophical Writings*, p. 99.

6. Descartes, *Philosophical Letters*, p. 28.

7. Descartes, "Rules for Direction of the Mind," *Philosophical Writings*, p. 3.

8. Locke, *Essay*, "Epistle to the Reader."

9. Ibid., IV. 20. 3.

10. Ibid., I. 1. 5.

11. Condorcet, *Progress of the Human Mind*, p. 117.

12. Hobbes, *English Works*, 1:7.

13. Sigmund Freud, *Civilization and Its Discontents*, trans. James Strachey (New York: Norton, 1962), p. 23.

14. Descartes, "Discourse on Method," pp. 130–31.

15. See Bacon, *Advancement of Learning*, II. 7. 1. (*The Advancement of*

Learning and New Atlantis, ed. Arthur Johnston [Oxford: Clarendon Press, 1974].)

16. Condorcet, *Progress of the Human Mind*, p. 200.

17. Ibid., p. 163.

18. Ibid., p. 102.

19. Ibid.

20. Ibid., p. 100.

21. John Stuart Mill, *Considerations on Representative Government* (Chicago: Regnery, 1962), p. 61.

22. In public opinion, Condorcet said, "we now have a tribunal, independent of all human coercion, which favors reason and justice, a tribunal whose scrutiny it is difficult to elude, and whose verdict it is impossible to evade" (*Progress of the Human Mind*, p. 100).

23. Locke, *Essay*, Introduction, sec. 5.

24. Frankel, *The Faith of Reason*, p. 22. Fontenelle was later to salute Descartes for introducing in physics *and* in morals "a precision and accuracy which, until now, had not been known" (ibid., pp. 105–6). See also Sampson, *Progress in the Age of Reason*, p. 27.

25. Hobbes, *Leviathan*, p. 318.

26. Ibid., p. 319.

27. Locke, *Essays on the Law of Nature*, p. 123.

28. Locke, *Essay*, I. 2. 13.

29. Locke, *Essays on the Law of Nature*, pp. 199 and 201.

30. Locke, *Essay*, IV. 3. 18.

31. Ibid., IV. 12. 8.

32. Condillac, *Origin of Human Knowledge*, p. 2.

33. Helvetius, *Treatise on Man*, 1:11.

34. Holbach, *La politique naturelle*, cited by Frankel, *The Faith of Reason*, p. 70.

35. Marquis de Chastellux, *De la félicité publique*, vol. 1, p. 135, cited by Frankel, *The Faith of Reason*, p. 70.

36. Harold Laski, *The Rise of Liberalism*, p. 208.

37. Elie Halévy, *The Growth of Philosophic Radicalism*, trans. Mary Morris (Boston: Beacon Press, 1960), p. 184.

38. D'Alembert, *Preliminary Discourse*, pp. 44–45.

39. Ibid., p. 45, n. 56.

40. Locke, *Essay*, IV. 3. 18.

41. Gibson, *Locke's Theory of Knowledge*, p. 159.

42. Locke, *Essay*, IV. 3. 18.

43. Helvetius, *Treatise on Man*, 1:261.

44. Hobbes, *Leviathan*, p. 328.

45. Hobbes, *English Works*, 1:82–83.

46. Helvetius, *Treatise on Man*, 1:261.

47. Hobbes, *English Works*, 1:8.

48. Hobbes, *Leviathan*, p. 154.

49. Hobbes, *English Works*, 2:xvii.

50. John Stuart Mill, *Autobiography* (London: Longmans, Green, Reader, & Dyer, 1874), pp. 165–66.

51. Manuel, *The Prophets of Paris*, pp. 43–44.

52. Descartes, "Discourse on Method," p. 111.

53. Ibid., p. 112.

54. Descartes, *Philosophical Letters*, p. 26.

55. Ibid., p. 19.

56. Karl Stern, *The Flight from Woman* (New York: Farrar, Straus, & Giroux, 1965), p. 95.

57. Descartes, "Discourse on Method," pp. 103–4.

58. Locke, *Essay,* IV. 10. 6.

59. Locke, *Essays on the Law of Nature,* p. 113.

60. Ibid., p. 111.

61. Ibid., p. 27, n. 3.

62. Richard S. Westfall, *Science and Religion in Seventeenth-Century England* (New Haven: Yale University Press, 1958), p. 32.

63. Cassirer, *The Philosophy of the Enlightenment,* p. 241.

64. These ideas, he said, rested "on the harmonizing sentiments of the day, whether expressed in conversation, in letters, printed essays, or in the elementary books of public right, as Aristotle, Cicero, Locke, Sydney, etc." (*The Life and Selected Writings of Thomas Jefferson,* ed. Adrienne Koch and William Peden [New York: Modern Library, 1944], p. 719).

65. D'Alembert, *Preliminary Discourse,* p. 14.

66. Catherine Drinker Bowen, *Francis Bacon: The Temper of a Man* (Boston: Little, Brown, 1963), p. 49.

67. Condorcet, *Progress of the Human Mind,* p. 127.

68. Locke, *Essay,* I. 3. 25.

69. Descartes, "Discourse on Method," p. 93.

70. Descartes, "Rules for Direction of the Mind," pp. 37–38.

71. Helvetius, *Treatise on Man,* 1:232.

72. D'Alembert, *Preliminary Discourse,* p. 31.

73. Quoted by Cassirer, *The Philosophy of the Enlightenment,* pp. 268–69.

74. Descartes, *Philosophical Letters,* p. 6.

75. Theodore Roszak, *Where the Wasteland Ends* (Garden City, N.Y.: Doubleday, 1973), p. 187.

76. Condorcet, *Progress of the Human Mind,* p. 192.

77. Lester G. Crocker, *Nature and Culture* (Baltimore: Johns Hopkins University Press, 1963), p. 510.

78. Quoted by Cassirer, *The Philosophy of the Enlightenment,* p. 169.

79. Quoted by Isidor Schneider, *The Enlightenment* (New York: Braziller, 1945), p. 45.

80. Descartes, *Philosophical Letters,* p. 32 (italics signify Latin phrases in the original French context).

81. Colin McLaurin, *An Account of Sir Isaac Newton's Philosophical Discoveries,* quoted by Becker, *The Heavenly City of the Eighteenth-Century Philosophers,* p. 63.

82. Quoted by Kingsley Martin, *French Liberal Thought in the Eighteenth Century,* p. 144.

83. Carl Becker, *The Declaration of Independence* (New York: Random House, 1942), pp. 24–26.

84. Quoted by Frankel, *The Faith of Reason,* p. 73.

85. Quoted by Daniel Boorstin, *The Lost World of Thomas Jefferson* (New York: Holt, 1948), p. 164.

86. Kant, *Perpetual Peace,* First Supplement.

87. Condorcet, *Progress of the Human Mind,* p. 119.

88. Halévy, *The Growth of Philosophic Radicalism,* p. 184.

89. Ibid., p. 186.

90. Halévy uses the phrase ''identity of interests,'' which was employed by some of the principals themselves. However, ''reconciliation of interests'' captures the idea somewhat better, since it was not really held that different individuals had wholly *identical* interests; rather, it was thought that their distinct individual interests were not ultimately incompatible and hence could be combined, reconciled, into an overarching pattern without frustrating or doing violence to the original interests.

Chapter Four

1. Cassirer, *The Philosophy of the Enlightenment*, p. 25. See also Blair Campbell, ''Helvetius and the Roots of the Closed Society,'' *American Political Science Review* 68 (March 1974): 153–68, where he remarks: ''Thus Helvetius differs from the more humanitarian *philosophes* neither in intention nor orientation; his departure is confined to the 'extreme' conclusions he draws from common premises'' (p. 159).

2. Halévy, *The Growth of Philosophic Radicalism*, p. 18.

3. Cassirer, *The Philosophy of the Enlightenment*, p. 25.

4. Halévy, *The Growth of Philosophic Radicalism*, p. 19.

5. Baron Paul d'Holbach, *The System of Nature*, trans. H. C. Robinson (New York: Burt Franklin, 1970), p. 79.

6. Locke, *Essay*, II. 1. 2 and I. 1. 15.

7. Ibid., II. 1. 4.

8. Ibid., II. 2. 2.

9. Condillac, *Origin of Human Knowledge*, p. 8.

10. Ibid., pp. 8–9.

11. Ibid., p. 9.

12. Ibid., p. 10.

13. Claude Helvetius, *De l'Esprit, or Essays on the Mind* (New York: Burt Franklin, 1970), pp. 8, 10.

14. Claude Helvetius, *De l'Homme, or A Treatise on Man*, trans. W. Hooper (New York: Burt Franklin, 1970), vol. 1, p. 96.

15. Locke, *Essay*, II. 1. 17–25.

16. Helvetius, *De l'Esprit*, p. 7.

17. See Helvetius, *Treatise on Man*, 1:287: ''Man is born without ideas *and without passions*'' (emphasis added).

18. Ibid., p. 31.

19. Locke, *Some Thoughts Concerning Education* (Cambridge, Eng.: At the University Press, 1902), p. 187.

20. Ibid., p. 2.

21. Ibid., p. 1.

22. Helvetius, *Treatise on Man*, 1:4.

23. Ibid., pp. 149–50.

24. David Hartley, *Observations on Man* (Gainesville, Fla.: Scholars' Facsimiles and Reprints, 1966), p. 82.

25. Helvetius, *Treatise on Man*, 1:287.

26. Ibid., p. 3.

27. Hartley, *Observations on Man*, pp. 81–82.

28. Ibid., pp. 84, 81.

29. Rousseau, ''A Discourse on the Origin of Inequality,'' in *The Social Contract and Discourses*, trans. G. D. H. Cole (New York: Dutton, 1950), p. 189.

30. For both an explicit account of the necessity and utility of the ''state

of nature" construct and a clear manifestation of the emerging identification of essential with original, see the Preface and the opening pages of Rousseau's "A Discourse on the Origin of Inequality."

31. Rousseau, "Discourse on the Origin of Inequality," p. 214.

32. Ibid., p. 193.

33. Ibid.

34. Ibid., p. 223, n. 2.

35. Ibid., p. 192.

36. Ibid., p. 227.

37. Ibid., p. 210.

38. Ibid., p. 200.

39. Helvetius, *Treatise on Man*, 2:4.

40. Ibid., p. 24. Helvetius does say elsewhere (1:279) that the passion of "love of ourselves" might be considered innate, as he believed it to be implicit in corporeal sensibility.

41. Rousseau, "A Discourse on the Origin of Inequality," p. 207.

42. Ibid.

43. Helvetius, *De l'Esprit*, pp. 31–32.

44. Holbach, *The System of Nature*, p. 40.

45. Ibid., p. 41.

46. Aristotle, *Metaphysics* 1.3.984b.

47. Jeremy Bentham, *Collected Works*, ed. John Bowring (New York: Russell & Russell, 1962), vol. 1, p. 193.

48. Helvetius, *Treatise on Man*, 2:386.

49. Helvetius, *De l'Esprit*, p. 126.

50. Cf. Irving Horowitz, *Claude Helvetius* (New York: Paine-Whitman, 1954), p. 65.

51. Rousseau, *The Social Contract*, bk. 2, chap. 7.

52. Helvetius, *Treatise on Man*, 1:4.

53. Ibid.

54. Ibid., 2:148.

55. Ibid., p. 156.

56. Ibid., p. 117.

57. Ibid., p. 148.

58. As much as I would like to claim this phrase, it is John Passmore's. See *The Perfectibility of Man* (New York: Scribner's, 1970), p. 175.

59. Helvetius, *De l'Esprit*, pp. 280–81.

60. Helvetius, *Treatise on Man*, 1:316.

61. Jeremy Bentham, "A Critical Examination of the Declaration of Rights," in *Bentham's Political Thought*, ed. Bhikhu Parekh (London: Croom Helm, 1973), p. 269.

62. Jeremy Bentham, quoted by Halévy, *The Growth of Philosophic Radicalism*, p. 84.

63. John Locke, *Some Thoughts Concerning Education* (Woodbury, N.Y.: Barron's, 1964), p. 103.

64. Helvetius, *Treatise on Man*, 2:406–7.

65. Robert Owen, *A New View of Society*, 3d ed. (London: Longman, Hurst, Rees, et al., 1817), p. 34.

66. Helvetius, *Treatise on Man*, 2:410.

67. Ibid., 2:17.

68. Ibid., 1:318.

69. Helvetius, *De l'Esprit*, pp. 172, 178.

70. David Hartley, *Observations on Man*, p. 419.

71. Helvetius, *Treatise on Man*, 2:279.
72. Helvetius, *De l'Esprit*, p. 251.
73. Rousseau, *The Social Contract*, bk. 2, chap. 7.
74. Robert Owen, *A New View of Society*, p. 115.
75. Auguste Comte, "Plan of the Scientific Operations Necessary for Reorganizing Society," in *Auguste Comte and Positivism*, ed. Gertrud Lenzer (New York: Harper & Row, 1975), p. 49.
76. John Passmore, *The Perfectibility of Man*, p. 149.
77. Michael Polanyi, *Personal Knowledge* (Chicago: University of Chicago Press, 1958), p. 230.
78. Mary Peter Mack, Introduction to *A Bentham Reader* (New York: Pegasus Books, 1969), p. xviii.
79. Quoted by Mack, ibid., p. xix.
80. "Panopticon Papers," ibid., p. 195.
81. Ibid., pp. 194, 196.
82. Quoted by Halévy, *The Growth of Philosophic Radicalism*, p. 83.
83. Quoted by Mary Peter Mack, *A Bentham Reader*, p. 36.
84. Gertrude Himmelfarb, *Victorian Minds* (New York: Knopf, 1968), p. 59. The essay in this book entitled "The Haunted House of Jeremy Bentham" is well worth consulting for a more detailed account of Bentham's project.
85. Helvetius, *Treatise on Man*, 2:164.
86. Ibid., pp. 180–81.
87. For the important logical role that the belief in a nascent universal language played in the hopes of the democratic liberals, see the Tenth Stage of Condorcet's *Progress of the Human Mind*.
88. René Descartes, Preface to *The Principles of Philosophy* (from *The Essential Descartes*, ed. Margaret D. Wilson, trans. Elizabeth S. Haldane and G. R. T. Ross [New York: New American Library, 1969], pp. 305–6).
89. These phrases come from Mary Peter Mack's characterization of Bentham in *A Bentham Reader*, p. xxvii. As a devotee of Bentham, Mack seems either innocent of or unconcerned about the coercive potential implicit in these metaphors.
90. Friedrich A. Hayek, *The Counter-Revolution of Science* (Glencoe, Ill.: Free Press, 1952).
91. Quoted by Crocker, *Nature and Culture*, p. 372.
92. D. W. Smith, *Helvetius: A Study in Persecution* (Oxford: Clarendon Press, 1965), pp. 165–66.

Chapter Five

1. Wolin, *Politics and Vision*, p. 358.
2. I have commented on some of these elements of unresolved tension in Skinner's thought in *The Dilemma of Contemporary Political Theory*, p. 49.
3. Eric Voegelin, *From Enlightenment to Revolution*, ed. John Hallowell (Durham, N.C.: Duke University Press, 1975), p. 165.
4. For reflections on this loose form of "logic," see Michael Polanyi, "The Logic of Tacit Inference," in *Knowing and Being*, ed. Marjorie Grene (Chicago: University of Chicago Press, 1969), pp. 138–58. See also Roberto M. Unger, *Knowledge and Politics* (New York: Free Press, 1975), pp. 107 ff.
5. David Braybrooke and Alexander Rosenberg, "Comment: Getting the

War News Straight: The Actual Situation in the Philosophy of Science,"
American Political Science Review 66 (September 1972): 818.

6. The gap between positivist and historicist traditions in contemporary philosophy is widened in part, it should be noted, because the clearly dominant version of philosophical positivism is "value noncognitivist"—i.e., accords no cognitive status to normative statements—whereas the most visible wing of historicism believes in "objective," rationally discernible "values." Hence, what appears as a clash between positivism and historicism is partly a clash between the dominant wings of each tradition, which take opposing sides on this central issue of political philosophy.

7. Comte, "Plan of the Scientific Operations Necessary for Reorganizing Society," in *Auguste Comte and Positivism*. (Unless otherwise specified, all citations of Comte's works will be to this edition.)

8. Ibid., p. 11.

9. Ibid.

10. Ibid., pp. 40, 18.

11. Ibid., p. 42.

12. Ibid., p. 12.

13. Auguste Comte, *Cours de philosophie positive*, p. 222.

14. Ibid., p. 223.

15. Ibid., p. 222.

16. Comte, "Operations for Reorganizing Society," p. 46.

17. Ibid., p. 42.

18. Ibid., p. 47.

19. Ibid., p. 46.

20. Comte, *Cours*, p. 236.

21. Comte, "Operations for Reorganizing Society, pp. 31, 15.

22. Ibid., p. 23.

23. Comte, *Cours*, p. 84.

24. Ibid., p. 227.

25. Ibid., p. 212.

26. Ibid., p. 264.

27. Comte, "Operations for Reorganizing Society," p. 50.

28. Comte, *Cours*, p. 243.

29. Ibid., pp. 204–5.

30. Comte, "Operations for Reorganizing Society," p. 51.

31. Ibid., p. 54.

32. Ibid., p. 67 (my emphasis).

33. Mary Peter Mack, Introduction to *A Bentham Reader*, p. xxvii.

34. Comte, *Cours*, p. 244.

35. Ibid., p. 238.

36. Ibid., pp. 214, 269.

37. Comte, *Système de politique positive*, p. 356.

38. Comte, *Cours*, p. 214; *Système*, p. 359.

39. Comte, *Cours*, p. 268.

40. Comte, *Système*, p. 355.

41. Gustave d'Eichthal, quoted by Hayek, *The Counter-Revolution of Science*, p. 193.

42. Alexandre Kojève, *Introduction to the Reading of Hegel*, trans. James H. Nichols, Jr., ed. Allan Bloom (New York: Basic Books, 1969), p. 44.

43. Ibid., pp. 148–49 (emphasis in original).

44. Ibid., pp. 33–34.

45. Quoted by William J. Brazill, *The Young Hegelians* (New Haven: Yale University Press, 1970), p. 10.

46. Comte, *Cours*, p. 257.

47. Comte, "Operations for Reorganizing Society," p. 46.

48. G. W. F. Hegel, *Reason in History*, trans. Robert Hartman (Indianapolis: Bobbs-Merrill, 1953), p. 40.

49. Comte, "Operations for Reorganizing Society," pp. 42–43.

50. Quoted by Hayek, *Counter-Revolution of Science*, p. 193.

51. Hegel, *Reason in History*, pp. 52–53.

52. Comte, *Cours* and *Système*, pp. 451, 301, and 280–81.

53. Comte, "Operations for Reorganizing Society," pp. 44–45.

54. Hegel, *Reason in History*, p. 53.

55. Lobkowicz elaborates: "Hegel's sophism consists in his describing social restraints as restraints which man imposes upon himself. There is a certain truth in his statement when it is put in a general way, for social restraints undoubtedly differ from restraints imposed by nature in that they are due to man. But what Hegel (and after him Marx) overlooks is that it is not *I* who imposes these restraints upon myself but *other men* who impose them upon me. In short, Hegel confuses a mythical self-restraint of a Man with a capital 'M' with the fact that men impose restraints upon each other, that *other men* impose restraints upon *me*." (Nicholas Lobkowicz, *Theory and Practice: History of a Concept from Aristotle to Marx* [Notre Dame: University of Notre Dame Press, 1967], p. 337).

56. Quoted by Lobkowicz, ibid., p. 193.

57. Quoted ibid., p. 198.

58. Comte, *Cours*, p. 227.

59. Quoted by Lobkowicz, *Theory and Practice*, p. 230.

60. Ibid., p. 197.

61. Ibid., p. 198.

62. Ibid., p. 241.

63. Ibid., p. 421.

64. V. I. Lenin, "What Is To Be Done?" in *Selected Works*, vol. 1 (New York: International Publishers, 1967), pp. 129–31.

65. Ibid., pp. 131–32.

66. Positivist writers tend to see the former difficulty—i.e., nonfalsifiability—as the decisive and sufficient grounds for denying that such claims are genuinely scientific or even meaningful. In fact, this criterion alone has proved to be either overly stringent or overly inclusive, depending on its formulation. It is the latter difficulty, I would argue, that is really decisive here. Any genuinely scientific claim is at least open to criticism by an authority accredited as competent on grounds that are not circular—i.e., not on the grounds that the authority agrees with the conclusions.

This Leninist claim, and the Marxist theory of ideology that lies behind it, is unscientific, then, not so much because it cannot meet the impossible criteria of positivism but because it remains at the level of a "specific" rather than a "general" theory (in Mannheim's sense of these terms in *Ideology and Utopia*). That is, it is logically unstable because it cannot be generally (including reflexively) applied without self-destructing.

67. "The New Program of the Communist Party of the Soviet Union" (1961), reproduced in *Essential Works of Marxism*, ed. Arthur P. Mendel (New York: Bantam Books, 1971), p. 481.

68. Albert Camus, *The Rebel*, trans. Anthony Bower (New York: Vintage Books, 1956), pp. 244–45.

69. B. F. Skinner, *Beyond Freedom and Dignity* (New York: Bantam Books, 1971), pp. 14–15.

70. For the embrace of mechanist models, see Clark L. Hull, *Principles of Behavior: An Introduction to Behavior Theory* (New York: Appleton-Century, 1943), pp. 24 ff., and John B. Watson, *The Ways of Behaviorism* (New York: Harper, 1928), p. 42: "The behaviorist is a mechanist? Yes, utterly." For the criticism of Descartes's exclusion of thinking activity from the realm of "objects," see Watson, pp. 14, 79, and 84: "Thought then is a form of general bodily activity."

71. Watson, *The Ways of Behaviorism*, p. 3.

72. See Skinner, *Beyond Freedom and Dignity*, p. 191.

73. Ibid., pp. 6–7.

74. See Watson, *The Ways of Behaviorism*, p. 3.

75. Skinner, *Beyond Freedom and Dignity*, pp. 77, 16.

76. José Delgado, *Physical Control of the Mind* (New York: Harper & Row, 1969), p. 259.

77. See Cynthia Russett's excellent study, *The Concept of Equilibrium in American Social Thought* (New Haven: Yale University Press, 1966).

78. Karl Mannheim, *Ideology and Utopia* (New York: Harcourt, Brace, & World, 1936), p. 31.

79. Ibid., p. 77.

80. Ibid.

81. See *The Rise and Fall of Project Camelot*, ed. Irving Louis Horowitz (Cambridge, Mass.: MIT Press, 1967).

82. Ibid., p. 47.

83. Ibid., p.199.

84. Ibid., p. 289.

85. Ibid.

86. Jessie Bernard, ibid., p. 132.

87. Unger, *Knowledge and Politics*, p. 204.

88. Johann Galtung's essay in *The Rise and Fall of Project Camelot*, for example, exhibits a nice sensitivity to this dimension of knowledge and to some of its implications.

89. This phrase is Delgado's. See his *The Physical Control of the Mind*, cited in n. 76.

90. James McConnell, "Criminals Can Be Brainwashed—Now," *Psychology Today*, April 1970. Cited by Theodore Roszak, *Where the Wasteland Ends*, p. 243.

91. Freud, *The Origins of Psychoanalysis: Sigmund Freud's Letters*, ed. Marie Bonaparte, Anna Freud, and Ernst Kris, trans. Eric Mosbacher and James Strachey (New York: Basic Books, 1954), p. 355.

92. Jürgen Habermas, *Knowledge and Human Interests*, trans. Jeremy Shapiro (Boston: Beacon Press, 1971), p. 248. Habermas' chapter "The Scientistic Self-Misunderstanding of Metapsychology" is an excellent analysis of some of the fundamental tensions in Freud's thought.

93. Michel Foucault, *Madness and Civilization*, trans. Richard Howard (New York: Random House, 1965), p. 275.

94. Ibid., pp. 277–78. For a contrary suggestion, that Freud was aware of the dangers of medical authoritarianism, consider Erik Erikson: "Freud judged some of his patients to be outstanding in character and talents, rather than degenerate. He began to let himself be led by the sequence and the

nature of their communications. With amused surprise he would admit that a hypnotized patient, in suggesting to him that he should stop interrupting her with his authoritative suggestions, had a point. . . . He realized that habit and convention had made him and his fellow physicians indulge in an autocratic pattern, with not much more circumspection or justification than the very paternal authorities who he now felt had made the patients sick in the first place'' (Erik Erikson, *Insight and Responsibility* [New York: Norton, 1964], pp. 28–29).

95. For comment on the authoritarian dimension of Freud's therapeutic posture, see Philip Rieff, *Freud: The Mind of the Moralist* (Garden City, N.Y.: Doubleday, 1961), pp. 107 ff. As Rieff observes, although ''Freudianism involves analyst and patient in a cooperative search for insight . . . there is every theoretic encouragement for the analyst to assume a monopoly of insight and responsibility for moral direction.'' In this context, consider also the words of James Agee: ''Psychiatry, and for that matter psychoanalysis still more, interest me intensely; . . . But I would somewhere near as soon die (or enter a narcotic world) as undergo a full psychoanalysis. I don't trust anyone on earth that much; and I see in every psychoanalyzed face a look of deep spiritual humiliation or defeat, to which I prefer at least a painful degree of spiritual pain and sickness. The look of 'I am a man who finally could not call his soul his own, but yielded it to another''' (*Letters of James Agee to Father Flye* [New York: Bantam Books, 1963], p. 116).

96. Erikson, again, expresses his awareness of and chagrin at this destructive tendency: ''We were dismayed when we saw our purpose of enlightenment perverted into a widespread fatalism, according to which man is nothing but a multiplication of his parents' faults and an accumulation of his own earlier selves. We must grudgingly admit that even as we were trying to devise, with scientific determinism, a therapy for the few, we were led to promote an ethical disease for the many'' (*Young Man Luther* [New York: Norton, 1958], p. 19).

97. Bernard Crick, *The American Science of Politics* (Berkeley: University of California Press, 1959), p. 209. One of my few quibbles with this excellent, if acerbic, study is that it seems to me to be slightly off center in its diagnosis of the sources of these derangements. Crick seems to find the principal cause of the problem in the liberal unanimity of most American thought—as suggested, for example, by Louis Hartz. Clearly this peculiarity of American intellectual and social history plays an important role here; but I think it is best perceived as an *enabling condition* that permits the culture's pervasive scientism to receive expression in this way.

98. Lester Frank Ward, ''The Rising School of Philosophy,'' from *Lester Ward and the Welfare State*, ed. Henry Steele Commager (Indianapolis: Bobbs-Merrill, 1967), p. 16. (Page numbers in subsequent references to Ward's works are to this volume.)

99. ''Social phenomena are produced by the action of true natural forces, which, when abstraction is made of all perturbing elements, are found to be as regular and reliable as are the forces of gravitation, chemical affinity, or organic growth'' (Ward, ''The Establishment of Sociology,'' p. 375).

100. Ibid., p. 374.

101. Ward, ''The Rising School,'' pp. 16–17.

102. Ward, ''The Establishment of Sociology,'' p. 376.

103. Ward, ''The Rising School,'' p. 16.

104. Ward, ''Ethical Aspects of Social Science,'' p. 245.

105. For example: ''Now it is precisely the function of social science to

do away with this state of things, not by allowing free vent to catabolic impulses, but by removing the conditions under which they arise" (Ward, "Ethical Aspects of Social Science," p. 247).

106. Ward, "The Establishment of Sociology," p. 375.

107. Ward, "The Rising School," p. 17.

108. George A. Lundberg, *Can Science Save Us?* (New York: Longmans, Green, 1961), p. 5.

109. Ibid., pp. 5, 70.

110. Ibid., pp. 8, 1.

111. Ibid., p. 40.

112. Ibid., p. 140.

113. Ibid., p. 142. For a fine review and critique of technocratic optimism in the realm of international politics, see Hans J. Morgenthau, *Scientific Man versus Power Politics*.

114. Harold Lasswell, "What Psychiatrists and Political Scientists Can Learn from One Another," *Psychiatry* 1 (February 1938): 33–39.

115. Ibid., pp. 38–39.

116. Ibid., p. 39.

117. Read Bain, "Sociology and Psychoanalysis," *American Sociological Review* 1 (February 1936): 209–10.

118. Ibid., p. 216.

119. Skinner, *Beyond Freedom and Dignity*, p. 161.

120. B. F. Skinner, *Walden Two* (New York: Macmillan, 1948), p. 175 (emphasis in original).

121. Skinner, *Beyond Freedom and Dignity*, p. 172.

122. Ibid., p. 151.

123. Ibid., p. 161.

124. Floyd Matson, *The Broken Image* (Garden City, N.Y.: Doubleday, 1966) p. 96.

125. Lester Frank Ward, "Applied Sociology," p. 367.

126. Skinner, *Beyond Freedom and Dignity*, p. 146.

127. "A value judgment is a matter not of fact but of how someone feels about a fact" (ibid., pp. 98–99).

128. Ibid., p. 97.

129. Ibid., p. 156.

130. Skinner, *Walden Two*, p. 145.

131. Skinner, *Beyond Freedom and Dignity*, p. 130.

132. Lester Frank Ward, "Social Progress," p. 426.

133. Matson, *The Broken Image*, p. 83.

134. For example, the introduction to Harold Lasswell and Abraham Kaplan, *Power and Society* (New Haven: Yale University Press, 1950), articulates the need to be "value-neutral," the need to be guided by the "democratic ideal," and the need to pursue "the realization of human capacities"—all at once.

135. Skinner, *Beyond Freedom and Dignity*, p. 62.

136. Skinner, *Walden Two*, p. 216.

137. Ibid., p. 218.

138. Skinner's optimistic assumptions about the natural propensities and inclinations of human beings are never systematized into a coherent philosophical anthropology. However, some of the components of his view surface sporadically. For example, he has a belief in enlightened self-interest that incorporates conscience (*Walden Two*, p. 45). He believes, like Aristotle, in the natural desire to know (ibid., p. 101). He believes, like all

utopians, that man is possessed of great "potentialities" that have been thwarted by bad conditions (ibid., p. 241), and so on. He clearly sees man as a creature of moderate passions that can be satisfied without infringing on the needs of society or the rights of others. The socially disruptive passions, such as desire for great wealth, eminence, or power over others, are assumed (contra Hobbes, Freud, Saint Augustine, et al.) to be perversions arising from poor social design.

139. Lester Frank Ward, "Applied Sociology," pp. 367–68.

140. Ward, "Psychic Factors of Civilization," p. 174.

141. Ward's optimistic view of human nature shines through most of his copious writings. He viewed men the way he viewed plants. Each man, like each plant, "may be regarded as a reservoir of vital force, as containing within it a potential energy far beyond and wholly out of consonance with the contracted conditions imposed upon it by its environment" ("Broadening the Way to Success," p. 102).

Ward's charitably enthusiastic view of human potentialities is actually one of his most engaging qualities. It certainly was a welcome contrast to the socially defeatist fatalism of the Darwinian social theorists who preceded him. As an antidote to this fatalism, as a call to needed social reform, Ward's optimism was all to the good. It becomes problematic only when it leads to a dangerous blindness to the realities of power and conflict in society. Then it tends to engender arrogantly obtuse criticism of existent political actors and institutions (e.g., his utter lack of appreciation of the functions of political parties in a free society) and to foster, paradoxically, extreme coerciveness—however benevolently characterized and motivated—in social policy.

142. "The sole function of scientific work is to grind out and publish systematically related and significant 'if...then' propositions which are demonstrably probable to a certain degree under given circumstances" (Lundberg, *Can Science Save Us?*, p. 35).

143. Ibid., pp. 38, 63.

144. Ibid., p. 39.

145. Niebuhr noted that the liberal-bourgeois tradition tends to be largely "unconscious of the factor of power in political life" and that a business society, when thrust into power politics, "is inclined to exchange the sentimentalities and pretensions of yesterday...for the cynicism of today" (*The Irony of American History*, p. 76).

146. Don K. Price, *The Scientific Estate* (London: Oxford University Press, 1968).

147. Ibid., p. 153.

148. This is not to say that their ideas are representative. But Lundberg and Ward were both presidents of their national professional associations, and Skinner and Lasswell have been influential figures in their respective fields of psychology and political science.

149. Those "who read Congressional hearings," he writes, "may get the impression that scientists now think that science may some day, even if it cannot now, provide the answer to any question of policy. Many scientists feel obliged to assert their potential jurisdiction in this way; they believe that science, for more than three centuries, has been winning its intellectual battle against theology and traditionalism, and do not see why it should accept any limits on its victory except as a temporary tactic" (*The Scientific Estate*, p. 102). Price believes, however, that this view is usually foreign to the "working natural scientist," but he adds that "some philosophers of

science" and "certain types of social scientist or political theorist" find it very appealing (ibid., p. 116).

150. Stanley Milgram, *Obedience to Authority* (New York: Harper & Row, 1974), p. 142.

151. See, for example, the rehabilitative goal expressed by the keynote speaker of the first Congress of the National Prison Association in 1870: to "work that reformation in the soul of the man that will restore him to society regenerated and reformed" (quoted by Jessica Mitford in *Kind and Usual Punishment* [New York: Knopf, 1973], p. 33).

152. F. Bergan, "The Sentencing Power in Criminal Cases," *Albany Law Review* 1 (1949): 3, cited by Nicholas Kittrie, *The Right to Be Different* (Baltimore: Penguin Books, 1973), pp. 30–31 (emphasis added).

153. For example, an advocate of the therapeutic approach to juvenile justice asserts: "The delinquent . . . is not the enemy of society. He is society's child, and, therefore, the interests of the state and the child do not conflict but coincide. Since the interests coincide there is no need for the criminal adversary adjudicatory procedure" (Joel Handler, "The Juvenile Court and the Adversary System," *Wisconsin Law Review* 7 (1965): 10, cited by Kittrie, *The Right to Be Different*, p. 155).

154. For the hazards of the indeterminate sentence, see Jessica Mitford, *Kind and Usual Punishment*, chap. 6.

155. Ibid., pp. 111–12.

156. *State* vs. *Mills*, 144 W. Va. 257, 107 S.E. 2d 772 (1959).

157. This case occurred in the late 1960s. It is reported by Kittrie, *The Right to Be Different*, p. 354.

158. *Overholser* vs. *Lynch*, 288 F 2d, 393 (D.C.Cir. 1961), at 394. See Kittrie, *The Right to Be Different*, pp. 43–44.

159. See, respectively: (1) *In re Gault*, 387 U.S. 1 (1967); (2) the writings of Dr. Thomas S. Szasz; (3) the introduction to the 1976 federal prison system handbook, written by Norman Carlson, director of the Bureau of Prisons. In the latter, Carlson writes: "Medical terms such as 'treatment' have been dropped since they imply that offenders are sick, that we know the causes of their crimes and we know how to effect cures, none of which is true."

160. Condorcet, *Progress of the Human Mind*, p. 137.

161. Karl Menninger, *The Crime of Punishment* (New York: Viking Press, 1968), p. 11.

162. For an excellent essay on the sense of injustice, see Edmond Cahn's book with that very title: *The Sense of Injustice* (Bloomington: Indiana University Press, 1964).

163. Menninger, *The Crime of Punishment*, p. 17.

164. Ibid., p. 18 (emphasis added). This line of argument closely replicates that of the early technocrats. In volume 1 of his *Treatise on Man*, Helvetius:

1. Belabors traditional moral standards for their vagueness: "The word Virtue, equally applicable to prudence, courage, and charity, has, therefore only a vague significance" (p. 318)
2. Debunks "justice" as the interest of the stronger: "What in fact is injustice? The violation of a convention or law made for the advantage of the majority" (p. 302)
3. Subsitutes the standard of utility: "Every action conformable to the interest of the greatest number is just and virtuous" (p. 316)

4. Ends by concluding that in this "government of all," which is "always cited as the best," the collectivity is all-powerful ("The nation is then the despot") (p. 316)

165. Menninger says of the concept of justice: "Any word that can elude precise usage by metamorphosis into scores of shades of meaning is apt to be more inspirational and rhetorical than scientifically useful" (*The Crime of Punishment*, p. 11).

166. "A Plea for Excuses," reprinted in Austin's *Philosophical Papers*, ed. J. O. Urmson and G. J. Warnock (Oxford: Clarendon Press, 1970), pp. 175–204.

167. Owen, *A New View of Society*, pp. 107–8.

168. Skinner, *Beyond Freedom and Dignity*, p. 70.

169. Manuel, *The Prophets of Paris*, p. 137.

170. Ibid.

171. Alexis de Tocqueville, *Democracy in America*, ed. Richard D. Heffner (New York: Mentor Books, 1956), p. 105.

Chapter Six

1. Charles Taylor, "Neutrality in Political Science," in Peter Laslett and W. G. Runciman, eds., *Philosophy, Politics, and Society*, 3d ser. (New York: Barnes & Noble, 1967), pp. 25–57.

2. Locke, *Essays on the Law of Nature*, p. 109.

3. Ibid., p. 121 (emphasis in original).

4. Ibid.

5. Ibid., p. 201.

6. Ibid., p. 199.

7. Ibid., p. 109.

8. Ibid., p. 137.

9. Ibid., p. 161.

10. Ibid., p. 113.

11. Ibid., p. 123.

12. Locke, *Second Treatise of Civil Government*, chap. II, par. 12.

13. Ibid., II. 6. See also III. 19.

14. Ibid., VI. 60.

15. Ibid., XI. 135.

16. The "municipal laws of countries," says Locke, "are only so far right as they are founded on the law of nature, by which they are to be regulated and interpreted" (ibid., II. 12). And he approvingly cites Hooker's insistence that human laws "have also their higher rules to be measured by, which rules are two—the law of God and the law of nature" (ibid., XI. 136, ftn.).

17. Ibid., XV. 172.

18. Although I have some reservations about Leo Strauss's view of Locke, expressed in his *Natural Right and History* (Chicago: University of Chicago Press, 1953), my argument is not necessarily incompatible with his claim that "Locke cannot have recognized any law of nature *in the proper sense of the term*" (p. 220; my emphasis). Strauss is accurate and helpful in noting the several ways in which Locke's natural-law ideas were an attenuation of traditional natural law into a much more individualistic and secular vein. Strauss's standards for a "proper" conception of natural law, however, are higher than—or at least different from—mine. The crucial issue in

the context of my argument is whether Locke asserted a belief in the existence of objective ethical norms discernible by the human mind. Clearly, he at least *said* that he did, and he accorded this belief a significant role in his most important political treatises. Strauss tends to dismiss Locke's explicit protestations of and reliance on this belief as merely a "prudent" or "cautious" concession to popular prejudice. My response to this interpretation is twofold. First, I am content to take the written documents at face value. Historically speaking, at least, what Locke said in the *Treatise* cannot be dismissed as irrelevant to liberalism's self-understanding. Second, I am not fully persuaded that Locke is as completely consistent in his beliefs or so hypocritical in his written statements as Strauss claims. (It may be "prudent" to withhold potentially unpopular claims. It is hypocritical to avow beliefs one does not hold. And Strauss's interpretation of Locke insists that he did the latter as well as the former.) At the very least, certainly, there is tension and inconsistency between Locke's early ideas concerning natural law and its accessibility and his later fragmentary speculation about moral knowledge. To claim otherwise would require construing the Locke who wrote the *Essays on the Law of Nature* to be an utter fraud.

19. See von Leyden's Introduction to the *Essays on the Law of Nature*, pp. 72–73.

20. Knight, *The Geometric Spirit*, p. 89.

21. Cassirer, *The Philosophy of the Enlightenment*, p. 243.

22. Marjorie Grene, for example, writes: "Consider even the so-called 'empirical' philosophies: the atomism of the ancients and the associationism of the British tradition, which thought themselves close to good, honest, obvious things. Consider their conception of human life as put together of distinct little bits of red, round, sweet, hard, pleasant, painful, etc. Try really to take it literally, even for a moment. Surely it is fantastically apart from what concretely in its vague half-meaningless confusion of something and nothing, of direction and indirection, our experience at most times is" (*Dreadful Freedom: A Critique of Existentialism* [Chicago: University of Chicago Press, 1948], pp. 24–25).

23. See R. G. Collingwood's account in his *An Essay on Metaphysics* (Oxford: Clarendon Press, 1940).

24. Friedrich Engels, "Socialism: Utopian and Scientific," in Mendel, ed., *Essential Works of Marxism*, p. 58.

25. Locke, *Essays on the Law of Nature*, p. 137.

26. Ibid., p. 145.

27. Ibid., p. 149.

28. Ibid., p. 155.

29. Ibid., p. 133.

30. Ibid., p. 153.

31. Ibid., p. 151.

32. Ibid., p. 147 (emphasis added).

33. Basil Willey, *The Seventeenth Century Background*, p. 285.

34. Ibid.

35. John Locke, *The Reasonableness of Christianity* (Stanford: Stanford University Press, 1958), p. 67.

36. Carl Becker, *The Heavenly City of the Eighteenth-Century Philosophers*, p. 68.

37. David Hume, *A Treatise of Human Nature* (London: Longmans, Green, 1898), vol. I, pt. III, sec. 5.

38. Ibid., I. I. 1.

39. Ibid., I. III. 1.
40. Ibid., I. IV. 6.
41. Hobbes, *Leviathan,* pp. 591–92.
42. Hume, *Treatise,* I. I. 2.
43. Ibid., I. I. 3.
44. Ibid., I. III. 5 and 7.
45. Ibid., I. III. 8.
46. Ibid., I. IV. 2.
47. Ibid., I. IV. 6.
48. Ibid., I. III. 12.
49. Ibid., I. I. 4.
50. Ibid., I. III. 8. See also I. III. 9, where Hume speaks of "custom, to which I attribute all belief and reasoning."
51. Ibid., I. IV. 1.
52. Ibid., I. III. 16.
53. Ibid., I. III. 8.
54. Ibid., I. IV. 7 (emphasis in original).
55. Ibid., I. III. 16.
56. Ibid., I. I. 3.
57. Ibid., I. IV. 4.
58. Ibid. Here, as in other crucial passages in Hume's writing, it is easy to see where Kant found the opening wedge for conceiving Hume's subjectivist principles in quite a different way: these "necessary" and "unavoidable" ideas that are "in the mind and not in the objects" become construed as a priori concepts constitutive of all possible knowledge.
59. Ibid., I. IV. 7.
60. Ibid., III. I. 1.
61. Hume, *Principles of Morals* (Oxford: Clarendon Press, 1975), sec. I.
62. Hume, *Treatise,* III. I. 1.
63. "As the operations of human understanding divide themselves into two kinds, the comparing of ideas, and the inferring of matter of fact; were virtue discovered by the understanding; it must be an object of one of these operations, nor is there any third operation of the understanding, which can discover it" (ibid.).
64. Ibid. The four relations alluded to are "resemblance, contrariety, degrees in quality, and proportion in quantity and number."
65. Ibid.
66. Ibid.
67. Ibid., I. I. 7.
68. See ibid., II. III. 10.
69. Ibid., II. III. 3.
70. Ibid., III. I. 1.
71. Ibid., III. I. 2.
72. Ibid.
73. "Every man's interest," Hume writes, "is peculiar to himself, and the aversions and desires, which result from it, cannot be supposed to affect others in a like degree. General language, therefore, being formed for general use, must be moulded on some more general views, and must affix the epithets of praise and blame, in conformity to sentiments, which arise from the general interests of the community" (*Principles of Morals,* V. II).
74. Hume, *Treatise,* III. III. 1.
75. Hume, *Principles of Morals,* V. II.

76. Ibid., I.

77. Ibid. (emphasis added).

78. Hume, *Treatise*, III. I. 1 (emphasis added).

79. Hume, *Principles of Morals*, IX. I (emphasis added). See also the first appendix to the same work, where Hume writes that moral taste arises "from the internal frame and constitution of animals" and therefore "is ultimately derived from that Supreme Will, which bestowed on each being its peculiar nature, and arranged the several classes and orders of existence." Given Hume's skepticism in theological matters, the reference to a "Supreme Will" might be presumed more of a rhetorical flourish than a serious contention. The attribution of moral taste and the standards it generates to the "internal frame and constitution" of a universally fixed species—i.e., a constant human nature—is, however, quite in keeping with other similar statements he makes elsewhere.

80. Hume, *Treatise*, III. II. 1.

81. Ibid.

82. Hume, *Principles of Morals*, I.

83. The philosopher, Hume says, "needs only enter into his own breast for a moment, and consider whether or not he should desire to have this or that quality ascribed to him, and whether such or such an imputation would proceed from a friend or an enemy" (ibid.).

84. Ibid.

85. Ibid., IX. II.

86. Ibid., IX. I.

87. Hume, *Treatise*, III. III. 5. Hume does not suggest the possibility that in the long run a theory like his could solve this problem for itself; that is, that it could by its own influence destroy those feelings that stand as an apparent reproach to it. In a thoroughly utilitarian culture, no one may be left capable of discriminating between moral and utilitarian considerations; hence the discrepant response to the virtuous and to the merely useful that Hume observes might disappear. The very notions of justice and morality as distinct from narrowly utilitarian calculations might then be deemed among those "superstitions" of "gloomy, hair-brained enthusiasts."

There is evidence suggesting that our own culture has gone a long way down this path. See, for example, the report of one English professor that many of her students seem almost blind to the clear moral issues at the heart of many pieces of literature: Susan Resneck Parr, "All's Not Well Aboard the 'Indomitable': Teachers who challenge their students to think about values are fighting an entire culture," *Chronicle of Higher Education* 15 (3 October 1977): 40.

88. Hume, *Treatise*, II. I. 5.

89. Hume, *Principles of Morals*, Appendix I.

90. Hume, *Treatise*, III. II. 1.

91. Hume, *Principles of Morals*, I.

92. Hume, *Treatise*, III. II. 1.

93. Ibid., (emphasis added).

94. Carl Becker, *The Heavenly City*, chap. 3.

95. Aristotle, *Posterior Analytics*, 2. 19. 100a.

96. Rousseau, cited by Becker, *Heavenly City*, p. 87.

97. For example, Copernicus, when it was objected to his system that a spinning earth would fly apart, answered by saying that rotation was a "natural" movement for the earth and that the natural movement of any

body could never have the effect of destroying the nature of that body. See Butterfield, *The Origins of Modern Science,* esp chap. 2, "The Conservativism of Copernicus."

98. The interested reader can consult A. J. Ayer's *Language, Truth, and Logic,* 2d ed. (New York: Dover, 1946), or "On the Analysis of Moral Judgments" in his *Philosophical Essays* (London: Macmillan, 1954).

99. Immanuel Kant, *Metaphysical Foundations of Morals,* trans. Carl J. Friedrich, in *The Philosophy of Kant: Immanuel Kant's Moral and Political Writings,* pp. 174–75.

100. Rousseau, "Discourse on the Origin of Inequality" in *The Social Contract and Discourses,* pp. 207–8.

101. Kant, *Metaphysical Foundations,* pp. 202–3.

102. Kant, *Critique of Pure Practical Reason,* in Friedrich, ed., *The Philosophy of Kant,* p. 262.

103. Kant, *Metaphysical Foundations,* p. 199.

104. Ibid., pp. 198–200.

105. Kant, *Critique of Pure Practical Reason,* p. 217.

106. Kant, *Metaphysical Foundations,* p. 164.

107. Ibid., p. 145.

108. Ibid., p. 159 (emphasis added).

109. Ibid., p. 150.

110. Ibid., p. 175 (in footnote).

111. Ibid., p. 191.

112. Kant, *Critique of Pure Practical Reason,* p. 228.

113. Ibid., p. 229.

114. Ibid., p. 259.

115. Kant, *Metaphysical Foundations,* p. 177.

116. "Accordingly," Kant writes, "the practical imperative will be as follows: Act so as to treat man, in your own person as well as in that of anyone else, always as an end, never merely as a means" (ibid., p. 178).

117. Ibid., p. 176 (emphasis added).

118. Ibid., pp. 177, 179.

119. "Even the most consummate villain," Kant tells us, would want to exhibit "honesty of purpose, steadfastness in obeying good maxims, sympathy, and charity," assuming only that he "is accustomed to the use of reason" (ibid., p. 199).

120. Hans Kelsen, "The Pure Theory of Law," trans. C. H. Wilson, *Law Quarterly Review* 51 (1935): 517.

121. Kant held that "a free will and a will subject to moral laws are one and the same" (*Metaphysical Foundations,* p. 192).

122. S. Korner, *Kant* (Baltimore: Penguin Books, 1955), p. 68.

123. Jean-Paul Sartre, *L'être et le néant* (Paris: Gallimard, 1943), p. 76.

124. Jean-Paul Sartre, "The Flies" in *No Exit and Three Other Plays,* trans. S. Gilbert (New York: Random House, 1949), pp. 121–22. For further comments on the way in which Kant's practical ego, minus the a priori law, turns into the radically self-constituting ego of romanticism and nontheistic existentialism, see Lewis White Beck, *A Commentary on Kant's "Critique of Practical Reason"* (Chicago: University of Chicago Press, 1960), p. 125, and Alfred Stern, *Sartre,* 2d ed. (New York: Dell, 1967), p. 75.

125. Max Weber, "'Objectivity' in Social Science," in *The Methodology of the Social Sciences,* ed. and trans. Edward Shils and Henry Finch (New York: Free Press, 1949), p. 111.

126. Ibid., p. 78.

127. Ibid., p. 106.

128. Ibid., p. 111 (emphasis added).

129. Ibid., p. 110. Weber writes: "We are now at the end of this discussion, the only purpose of which was to trace the course of the hairline which separates science from faith and to make explicit the meaning of the quest for social and economic knowledge. The objective validity of all empirical knowledge rests exclusively upon the ordering of the given reality according to categories which are subjective in a specific sense, namely that they present the presuppositions of our knowledge and are based on the presupposition of the value of those truths which empirical knowledge alone is able to give us."

130. Ibid., p. 111.

131. Ibid., p. 57.

132. Max Weber, "The Meaning of 'Ethical Neutrality,'" ibid., pp. 26–27.

133. Ibid., p. 18.

134. Weber, "'Objectivity' in Social Science," p. 53.

135. Weber, "The Meaning of 'Ethical Neutrality,'" p. 11.

136. Weber, "'Objectivity' in Social Science," p. 54.

137. See Weber, "The Meaning of ' Ethical Neutrality,'" p. 18.

138. Strauss, *Natural Right and History*, p. 44.

139. Weber, "The Meaning of 'Ethical Neutrality,'" p. 5.

Chapter Seven

1. For elaborations of these connections between interpretative vision and prescriptive suggestion, see Charles Taylor, "Neutrality in Political Science," in Laslett and Runciman, eds., *Philosophy, Politics, and Society*, 3d ser., pp. 25–57, and chap. 5, "Prescription," in my *Understanding Political Theory* (New York: St. Martin's Press, 1976).

2. David Hume, *Enquiry concerning Human Understanding* (Oxford: Clarendon Press, 1975), p. 11.

3. Ibid., pp. 12–13, 16.

4. See Hume's essay, "Of Civil Liberty," in *Theory of Politics*, ed. Frederick Watkins (Edinburgh: Nelson, 1951), p. 176.

5. Hume, *Enquiry*, p. 84.

6. Ibid., p. 85.

7. Ibid., pp. 83–84.

8. Hume, *Principles of Morals*, II. II.

9. "The distinction of moral good and evil is founded on the pleasure or pain, which results from the view of any sentiment, or character; and as that pleasure or pain cannot be unknown to the person who feels it, it follows, that there is just so much vice or virtue in any character, as every one places in it, and that 'tis impossible in this particular we can ever be mistaken" (Hume, *Treatise*, III. II. 8).

10. For an excellent account, see Lawrence L. Bongie, *David Hume: Prophet of the Counter-Revolution* (Oxford: Clarendon Press, 1965).

11. Sheldon S. Wolin, "Hume and Conservatism," *American Political Science Review* 48 (1954): 1007.

12. Hume, *Enquiry*, p. 102 (emphasis added).

13. Hume, *Principles of Morals*, III. II. See also *Treatise*, III. II. 6.

14. Hume, *Treatise*, III. II. 2.

15. Ibid. *Principles of Morals*, III. II.

16. Hume, *Treatise*, III. II. 5.

17. Ibid., III. II. 3 (in footnote).

18. Ibid.

19. Ibid., III. II. 8.

20. Ibid.

21. "Though an appeal to general opinion may justly, in the speculative sciences of metaphysics, natural philosophy, or astronomy, be deemed unfair and inconclusive, yet in all questions with regard to morals, as well as criticism, there is really no other standard by which any controversy can ever be decided" (Hume, "Of the Original Contract," *Theory of Politics*, pp. 213–14). This appeal to "general opinion" as a valid test for ethical claims, moreover, is not arbitrary in Hume's case; it is quite consistent with his skepticism and hedonism in moral theory.

22. Hume, *Treatise*, III. II. 10. In his summary list, Hume adds "original contract" to these, and in his essay "Of the Objects of Allegiance" he drops "conquest" from his list.

23. *Treatise*, III. II. 10.

24. Ibid.

25. Hume, "Of the Origin of Government," *Theory of Politics*, p. 157.

26. Hume, *Enquiry*, p. 44.

27. Hume, *Treatise*, III. III. 1.

28. Hume, "Idea of a Perfect Commonwealth," *Theory of Politics*, p. 228.

29. Frederick Watkins, Introduction to Hume's *Theory of Politics*, p. xxii.

30. For an excellent account of different understandings of "interest" and an analysis of some of the assumptions and implications of each, see William E. Connolly, *The Terms of Political Discourse* (Lexington, Mass.: Heath, 1974), chap. 2.

31. See, for example, the very useful historical account of the interplay between scientific naturalism and democratic theory in twentieth-century America provided by Edward A. Purcell, Jr., *The Crisis of Democratic Theory: Scientific Naturalism and the Problem of Value* (Lexington: University Press of Kentucky, 1973).

32. Hans Kelsen, *What Is Justice?* (Berkeley: University of California Press, 1957), p. 10.

33. Ibid., p. 20.

34. Ibid., p. 21.

35. Ibid., p. 13.

36. Ibid., p. 24.

37. Ibid., p. 5.

38. Ibid., pp. 4–5.

39. Hans Kelsen, "Foundations of Democracy," *Ethics* 66 (October 1955): 97.

40. Ibid., p. 40.

41. Bertrand Russell, "Philosophy and Politics," in *Basic Writings*, ed. Robert Egner and Lester Denonn (New York: Simon & Schuster, 1961), p. 462.

42. Kelsen, "Foundations of Democracy," p. 14.

43. Kelsen, *What Is Justice?*, pp. 21–22.

44. Ibid.

45. Bertrand Russell, "Philosophy and Politics," *Basic Writings*, p. 465.

46. Ibid., p. 462.

47. Ibid., p. 463.

48. Ibid.

49. Friedrick A. Hayek, *The Constitution of Liberty* (Chicago: University of Chicago Press, 1960), p. 99. Hayek, of course, is not a philosophical relativist across the board. He is a critic of legal positivism, for example, and a defender of the "rule of law." Perhaps because he believes that accreditation of the notion of distributive justice inevitably leads to an all-powerful, coercive, and arbitrary central government, however, he is led to dismiss the claims of justice altogether in this area.

50. Herman Finer, *Road to Reaction* (Boston: Little, Brown, 1946), p. 60.

51. Bertrand Russell, "Philosophy and Politics," p. 464.

52. Kelsen, "Foundations of Democracy," p. 39.

53. Kelsen, *What Is Justice?*, p. 22, and "Foundations of Democracy," p. 39.

54. Russell, "Philosophy and Politics," p. 465.

55. Kelsen, "Foundations of Democracy," p. 39.

56. From *The Life and Letters of Leslie Stephen,* quoted by Gertrude Himmelfarb, *On Liberty and Liberalism: The Case of John Stuart Mill* (New York: Knopf, 1974), p. 300.

57. Kelsen, "Foundations of Democracy," p. 26.

58. See, e.g., Marjorie Grene, "Hobbes and the Modern Mind," in *The Anatomy of Knowledge,* ed. Grene (Amherst: University of Massachusetts Press, 1969).

59. This debate is well summarized in Purcell's *The Crisis of Democratic Theory,* cited earlier. The relativist position was forcefully and explicitly argued by Kelsen and T. V. Smith, among others. The absolutist position was ably argued by such figures as Emil Brunner, John Hallowell, and John Wild.

60. Locke writes concerning (*a*): "It is in vain for an unbeliever to take up the outward show of another man's profession. Faith only and inward sincerity are the things that procure acceptance with God.... In vain, therefore, do princes compel their subjects to come into their church communion, under pretense of saving their souls." And, concerning (*b*): "If any man err from the right way, it is his own misfortune, no injury to thee" (*A Letter concerning Toleration* [Indianapolis: Bobbs-Merrill, 1955], pp. 34 and 24).

61. For Lowi's analysis, see his *The End of Liberalism* (New York: Norton, 1969). Lowi's study is clearly inspired in its theoretical orientation by Grant McConnell's *Private Power and American Democracy* (New York: Knopf, 1967). See also Henry Kariel's *The Decline of American Pluralism* (Stanford: Stanford University Press, 1961), David Ricci, *Community Power and Democratic Theory* (New York: Random House, 1971), esp. chap. 8, and William Connolly, ed., *The Bias of Pluralism* (New York: Atherton Press, 1969).

62. For example, the interpretation of political interest as exhaustively revealed by express and explicit policy preference; the interpretation of political uninvolvement as a function of inertia or apathy, which in turn reflected satisfaction more than alienation; and the focus on the value of stability—all of these contributed to giving prevailing pluralist practices the visage of relative harmony and success.

I am here not interested in trying to adjudicate the merits of these interpretative judgments as compared with some of the contrasting interpretations offered by the pluralists' critics. I am rather inclined to see some truth in both sides to this debate.

63. Robert A. Dahl, *A Preface to Democratic Theory* (Chicago: University of Chicago Press, 1956), p. 45.

64. Ibid., p. 25.

65. Alexis de Tocqueville, *Democracy in America*, p. 105.

66. See Lowi, *The End of Liberalism*, chap. 2.

67. See, for example, Nelson Polsby's *Community Power and Democratic Theory* (New Haven: Yale University Press, 1963), and Robert A. Dahl, "Critique of the Ruling Elite Model," *American Political Science Review* 52 (1958): 463–69. Many of the specific criticisms in these sources and in others like them, I hasten to add, are very persuasive. One need not be a positivist, however, to find suspect arguments in which data and conclusions are at odds, empirical claims are decided by definitional fiat, and biased questions are posed to respondents.

68. Terence Ball, "From Paradigms to Research Programs: Toward a Post-Kuhnian Political Science," *American Journal of Political Science* 20 (February, 1979): 172.

69. Connolly, *Terms of Political Discourse*, p. 41.

70. For the classic analysis of this situation with respect to Marxist debunking, see Karl Mannheim, *Ideology and Utopia*. Mannheim writes, for example: "Such a revealing insight into the basis of thought as that offered by the notion of ideology cannot, in the long run, remain the exclusive privilege of one class. But it is precisely this expansion and diffusion of the ideological approach which leads finally to a juncture at which it is no longer possible for one point of view and interpretation to assail all others as ideological without itself being placed in the position of having to meet that challenge. In this manner we arrive inadvertently at a new methodological stage in the analysis of thought in general" (p. 74).

71. Hume, *Enquiry concerning Human Understanding*, p. 96.

72. Ibid., p. 159.

73. See, for example, the selections in Henry Kariel, ed., *Frontiers of Democratic Theory* (New York: Random House, 1970).

74. (Chicago: University of Chicago Press, 1954).

75. Quoted in Kariel, *Frontiers of Democratic Theory*, p. 70.

76. This would certainly not be the first or only time that models and assumptions prevalent in American social science have taken their coloration from America's Lockean consensus. See Crick, *The American Science of Politics*.

77. Hume, "Of the Coalition of Parties," in Watkins, ed., *Theory of Politics*, p. 226.

78. Hume, "Of the First Principles of Government," ibid., p. 152.

79. Dahl, *Preface to Democratic Theory*, p. 45.

80. See Dahl's critique, ibid., pp. 22–27.

81. Hans Kelsen, *What Is Justice?*, p. 21.

82. The basic problem here is that a great deal of our "descriptive" vocabulary of human affairs is formulated from a normative "point of view." Cf. Julius Kovesi, *Moral Notions* (London: Routledge & Kegan Paul, 1967). Therefore, when the resolute attempt is made to purge the social scientific vocabulary of all its tacit normative dimension, the result is not so much the achievement of clarity as the loss of content and discriminative capacity.

83. Dahl, *Preface to Democratic Theory*, p. 24.

84. Ibid., p. 22.

85. "If majority rule is mostly a myth, then majority tyranny is mostly a myth too" (ibid., p. 133).

86. A fair question still remains, which the pluralists have tended to gloss over: could not a ruling coalition of minorities still cohere enough on certain specific issues to tyrannize over others? Couldn't different white interest groups, to take an obvious example, which differed profoundly on many issues, nonetheless find it in their common interest to keep racial minorities "in their place"?

87. "The Madisonian argument exaggerates the importance, in preventing tyranny, of specified checks to governmental officials by other specified governmental officials" (Dahl, *Preface to Democratic Theory*, p. 22).

88. James Madison et al., *The Federalist Papers* (New York: New American Library, 1961), p. 346.

89. Robert Dahl, *Who Governs?* (New Haven: Yale University Press, 1961), p. 325.

90. The relativizing and optimistic revising of Madisonian theory by contemporary pluralists is paralleled, if Irving Kristol is right, in similar blindspots of American historians. "It really is quite extraordinary," Kristol says, "how the majority of American historians have, until quite recently, determinedly refused to pay attention to any thinker, or any book, that treated democracy as problematic"—that is, as having any problems "organically connected with the political system" rather than being merely "external or adventitious" (Irving Kristol, "American Historians and the Democratic Idea," *On the Democratic Idea in America* [New York: Harper & Row, 1972], p. 52).

91. It is a side issue here whether the academic pluralists, such as Robert Dahl, Nelson Polsby, et al.—and, for that matter, older pluralists, such as Arthur Bentley—can accurately be described as ideologues themselves or be held identical to or responsible for interest-group liberalism as a prescriptive model.

These academic social scientists, I think, have good warrant for rejecting these charges when they are made without careful qualification. Although they clearly sought to combat certain ideological orientations they believed had distorted our accurate perception of the realities of American politics, they did not consciously intend to erect any other ideology in its place. They sought quite diligently, in fact, to live up to the standards and to pursue the goals mandated for social scientists by Max Weber. That is, they sought to bring to light some "inconvenient facts" that should disconcert those who adhered to a priori ideological convictions, but they did not deem it proper for them or for any man of science to "carry the marshal's baton of the statesman or reformer in his knapsack."

On the other hand, it is also fair to say (1) that there is more interpretative judgment in their descriptive accounts than they have generally acknowledged and (2) that the interpretative bias of their descriptions is such as to lead to a favorable attitude toward the pluralist system; i.e., most of us would be favorably disposed toward a system that is stable, free, and nontyrannical. It is probably also fair to say, for whatever it is worth, that the interpretative bias of the pluralists' theories correlates relatively closely with their characteristic political and philosophical orientation. Therefore, the academic pluralist can be wholly sincere in his claim that he was trying only to be objective, neutral, and purely descriptive; at the same time, his critic may also be justified in suggesting that there is an ideological dimension and import to these pluralist models. For one discussion concerning this problem, see the exchange between Robert Dahl and Jack Walker in the *American Political Science Review* 60 (1966): 285–305.

92. See Lowi's case studies in *The End of Liberalism,* for example. See also Irving Kristol's argument in ''When Virtue Loses All Her Loveliness,'' chap. 6 of his *On the Democratic Idea in America.*

93. Bernard Crick, *In Defense of Politics,* rev. ed. (Baltimore: Penguin Books, 1964), p. 154.

94. For some excellent commentary on these weaknesses and their impact on recent American politics, see William Lee Miller's *Of Thee, Nevertheless, I Sing* (New York: Harcourt, Brace, Jovanovich, 1975), esp. chap. 4, ''On the Limitations of Tough-Minded, Technical, Realistic, Hard-Nosed, Pragmatic Liberalism,'' and chap. 15, ''The Moral Comedy of an Operational Society.'' See also Alasdair MacIntyre's comments on the end-of-ideology thesis in his *Against the Self-Images of the Age* (New York: Schocken, 1971), esp. p. 10.

95. Alexis de Tocqueville, *Democracy in America,* ed. Philip Bradley (New York: Random House, 1945), vol. 2, p. 132.

96. William Lee Miller, *Of Thee, Nevertheless, I Sing,* pp. 8, 10.

97. Connolly, *Terms of Political Discourse,* p. 49.

98. This phrase is Gertrude Himmelfarb's in *On Liberty and Liberalism,* p. 321. The concluding chapter of her book includes some provocative thoughts on the problematics of the enshrinement of liberty conceived in overly simple terms.

99. See Walter Lippmann's analysis in *The Public Philosophy* (New York: New American Library, 1955), pp. 90–101.

100. ''What if the minority prefers its alternative much more passionately than the majority prefers a contrary alternative? Does the majority principle still make sense? This is the problem of intensity. And, as one can readily see, intensity is almost a modern psychological version of natural rights'' (Robert Dahl, *A Preface to Democratic Theory,* p. 90).

101. See Lowi, *The End of Liberalism,* p. 289.

102. See ibid., esp. chap. 5, ''Liberal Jurisprudence.''

103. Grant McConnell, *Private Power and American Democracy,* p. 353.

104. Sheldon Wolin, ''Hume and Conservativism,'' p. 1004.

105. See Fritz Stern, *The Politics of Cultural Despair* (Berkeley: University of California Press, 1961), and John H. Hallowell, *The Decline of Liberalism as an Ideology* (Berkeley and Los Angeles: University of California Press, 1943).

106. Alasdair MacIntyre, *Against the Self-Images of the Age,* p. 11.

107. For a thoughtful analysis of this dimension of 1960s confrontations, see Wayne C. Booth, *Modern Dogma and the Rhetoric of Assent* (Notre Dame: University of Notre Dame Press, 1974).

I do not suggest that a better understanding of normative discourse would have eliminated the political differences at issue. Among other things, choices among competing goods and among different readings of crucial empirical questions would clearly have remained to be decided by exercise of political will rather than moral reason. However, the relevant choices would have been clarified rather than distorted, and the bonds of community and civility would have been left somewhat more intact.

108. Theodore Roszak, *The Making of a Counter Culture* (Garden City,

N.Y.: Doubleday, 1969), and *Where The Wasteland Ends.*
    109. Keniston, *The Uncommitted,* pp. 285–86.

Chapter Eight

1. Camus, *The Rebel,* p. 246.
2. Hobbes, *Leviathan,* p. 614.
3. Ibid., p. 594.
4. Compare Carnap's analysis in "The Elimination of Metaphysics through Logical Analysis of Language" (trans. Arthur Pap, reprinted in A. J. Ayer, ed., *Logical Positivism* [New York: Free Press, 1959]) with Hobbes's analysis in *Leviathan* (esp. pt. 1, chap. 5 and pt. 4, chap. 46) and also in *De Corpore.* Carnap suggests (and J. O. Urmson apparently concurs; see pp. 102–3 of his *Philosophical Analysis*) that the logical positivists' attack was novel and radical in its claim that "metaphysical" language was literally meaningless rather than merely false, uncertain, or sterile. A close look at the relevant passages in Hobbes would suggest, however, that this claim for novelty is at least overstated if not wholly mistaken. Hobbes clearly rejects certain Scholastic concepts on the grounds that they are quite literally meaningless pseudo-concepts. They are, Hobbes says, "names that signify nothing"; they are "senseless" words; they are "insignificant"; they are "absurd"; they are "nonsense." "If a man should talk to me of a round quadrangle; or accidents of bread in cheese; or immaterial substances; or of a free subject; a free will; or any free, but free from being hindered by opposition, I should not say he were in an error; but that his words were without meaning; that is to say, absurd" (*Leviathan,* p. 34).
    Carnap's analysis of pseudo-statements (which violate the rules of empirical meaningfulness) is somewhat novel. At least it is a formally more advanced argument. Even here, however, Hobbes's analysis of the syntactical error of turning the copulative *est* into a noun—which he saw as the source of Scholastic notions of "essence"—could have taken this form.
    5. Russell, Introduction to Ludwig Wittgenstein, *Tractatus Logico-Philosophicus* (New York: Harcourt, Brace, 1933), p. x. This interpretation was a quite plausible one at the time, I think, although most authorities on Wittgenstein now believe it to have been mistaken.
    6. Locke, *Essay concerning Human Understanding,* Introduction, sec. 7.
    7. Rudolf Carnap, "The Elimination of Metaphysics," in *Logical Positivism,* pp. 60–61.
    8. E.g., "It is through this reduction that the word acquires its meaning." Also, "a word is significant only if the sentences in which it may occur are reducible to protocol sentences" (Carnap, ibid., p. 63).
    9. Carnap, "The Old and the New Logic," in Ayer, ed., *Logical Positivism,* pp. 143–44.
    10. Moritz Schlick, "The Foundations of Knowledge," trans. David Rynin, ibid., pp. 209–10, 213, 226, 223 (emphasis in original). As Carnap put it, the positivists regarded the "system of knowledge" as "a closed system in the following sense. We assumed that there was a certain rock bottom of knowledge, the knowledge of the immediately given, which was indubitable. Every other kind of knowledge was supposed to be firmly supported by this basis and therefore likewise decidable with certainty" ("Intellectual Autobiography," in *The Philosophy of Rudolph Carnap,* ed. Paul Schilpp [La Salle, Ill.: Open Court, 1963], p. 57).
    11. D'Alembert, *Preliminary Discourse,* p. 31.

12. For an account of Hobbes's conception of science, see chapter 5 of my *The Politics of Motion*. For a good summation of the many ways in which Hobbes's account and the logical empiricist account coincide, see Grene, "Hobbes and the Modern Mind," cited earlier. Grene writes: "it is precisely the supplementation of verbal calculation by reference to sensation that gives Hobbes, three centuries in advance of Schlick or Carnap, the model in which the chief contemporary conception of science has come to rest" (p. 7).

13. Carnap, "The Old and the New Logic," p. 133.

14. Ibid., p. 144.

15. Moritz Schlick, "The Turning Point in Philosophy," trans. David Rynin, in Ayer, ed., *Logical Positivism*, pp. 54, 56.

16. See Carl Hempel's appraisal in "The Empiricist Criterion of Meaning," reprinted ibid., pp. 108–29.

17. "Philosophy must be of some use and we must take it seriously; it must clear our thoughts and so our actions. Or else it is a disposition we have to check, and an inquiry to see that this is so; i.e. the chief proposition of philosophy is that philosophy is nonsense. And again we must take seriously that it is nonsense, and not pretend, as Wittgenstein does, that it is important nonsense" (Frank P. Ramsey, from *The Foundations of Mathematics*, excerpted ibid., p. 231).

18. Abraham Kaplan, *The Conduct of Inquiry* (San Francisco: Chandler, 1963), p. 42. A strict adherence to operationism, moreover, seemed to run afoul of the fact that different sets of operations are often used in science to measure the same thing. The various ways of dealing with that problem—e.g., Bridgman's acceptance of the conclusion that a different concept is in fact being used in each individual case—all seemed very strained, at best. See, e.g., Frederick Suppe, *The Structure of Scientific Theories* (Urbana, Ill.: University of Illinois Press, 1974), pp. 19–20.

19. J. O. Urmson, *Philosophical Analysis* (London: Oxford University Press, 1967), p. 149. Urmson's book, especially chapter 10, provides one of the best available brief accounts of the logic, vicissitudes, and eventual transformation of the program of reductive analysis in philosophy.

20. John Wisdom, "The Metamorphosis of Metaphysics," in his *Paradox and Discovery* (Oxford: Basil Blackwell, 1965), p. 61.

21. Ibid., pp. 64–65.

22. Urmson, *Philosophical Analysis*, p. 160.

23. "What then *is* the interpretation-free theory within, for example, contemporary microphysics? It is little more than a motley combination of classical matrix algebra, non-commutative operator calculus, and sundry mathematical inelegancies that never would have been introduced into the algorithm of quantum electrodynamics had they been in any way avoidable" (Norwood R. Hanson, "Logical Positivism and the Interpretation of Scientific Theories," in Peter Achinstein and Stephen F. Barker, eds., *The Legacy of Logical Positivism* [Baltimore: Johns Hopkins University Press, 1969], p. 75).

24. Cf. Stephen E. Toulmin, "From Logical Analysis to Conceptual History," in *The Legacy of Logical Positivism*, esp. pp. 41 and 44.

25. Hanson, "Logical Positivism," p. 74.

26. "In later writings, advocates of the Received View typically took the notion of being directly observable as nonproblematic and generally understood, giving little in the way of characterization of the distinction other

than examples" (Suppe, *The Structure of Scientific Theories*, p. 46).

27. Hanson, "Logical Positivism and the Interpretation of Scientific Theories," in *The Legacy of Logical Positivism*, pp. 74–75. Other "revisionist" philosophers of science made the same point. Thomas Kuhn, for example, wrote that attempts to make an empiricist epistemology viable "through the introduction of a neutral language of observations now seem to me hopeless" (*The Structure of Scientific Revolutions*, 2d ed. [Chicago: University of Chicago Press, 1970], p. 126). And Michael Polanyi concurred: "If, therefore, the ideal of a virgin mind is pursued to its logical limit, we have to face the fact that every perception of things, particularly by our eyes, involves implications about the nature of things which could be false." If one could in fact eliminate all the theoretical and quasi-theoretical contexts that organize percepts, he continued, "I would not feel assured of gaining access thereby to a core of indubitable virgin data. I should merely be blotting out my eyesight" (*Personal Knowledge*, p. 296).

28. W. V. Quine, "Two Dogmas of Empiricism," *Philosophical Review* 60 (January 1951): 40.

29. It has been argued, however, that a revised and somewhat softened version of the analytic-synthetic distinction is not so flawed and can perform some of the same functions. See, e.g., G. Maxwell, "The Necessary and the Contingent," in Herbert Feigl and Grover Maxwell, eds., *Minnesota Studies in the Philosophy of Science* (Minneapolis: University of Minnesota Press, 1962), vol. 3, pp. 398–404.

30. For a good characterization of these divergent outlooks in the philosophy of science regarding the focal question of scientific theories, see Suppe, *The Structure of Scientific Theories*, p. 116.

31. Israel Scheffler, "Prospects of a Modest Empiricism," *Review of Metaphysics* 10 (1957): 624–25. See also Scheffler's *The Anatomy of Inquiry* (New York: Knopf, 1963) and *Science and Subjectivity* (Indianapolis: Bobbs-Merrill, 1967) for further constructive suggestions along the lines of his proposal.

32. See, for example, the repeated insistence to that effect by Richard S. Rudner, "Comment: On Evolving Standard Views in Philosophy of Science," *American Political Science Review* 66 (September 1972): 827–45.

33. These suggestions, for example, should help anyone interested in sorting out some of the divergent claims found in a recent dispute of this kind. See Eugene F. Miller, David Braybrooke, Alexander Rosenberg, Richard S. Rudner, and Martin Landau, "Positivism, Historicism, and Political Inquiry," ibid., pp. 796–873. This particular symposium, while both useful and a good example of the problem at hand, suffers somewhat because of the limited representation of possible positions.

34. Consider, for example, Carnap's change of position from the view that "there was a certain rock bottom of knowledge, the knowledge of the immediately given, which was indubitable" and that "every other kind of knowledge was supposed to be firmly supported by this basis and therefore likewise decidable with certainty" to the view that there was "an important difference between our views and that of those traditional philosophical schools which look for an absolute knowledge" (both quotes are from Carnap's "Intellectual Autobiography," published in Schilpp, ed., *The Philosophy of Rudolf Carnap*). It is misleading in cases like this one, I would suggest, to say that Carnap's views "evolved." It would be more candid and accurate simply to say that he changed his mind.

35. See, for example, Lakatos, "Falsification and the Methodology of Research Programmes," in Imre Lakatos and Alan Musgrave, eds., *Criticism and the Growth of Knowledge* (London: Cambridge University Press, 1970).

36. "Complexity never constitutes a good argument for reluctance to undertake analysis. We can all grant that. But complexity is not confusion. When analysis results in destroying complexity in the name of clearing up confusions, to that extent it destroys the concept in question. It slices it out of existence" (Hanson, "Logical Positivism and the Interpretation of Scientific Theories," p. 77).

37. "The ancient doctrine of British empiricism that all non-simple concepts are complexes of simple concepts must finally go" (Urmson, characterizing the changing understanding of philosophical analysis, in *Philosophical Analysis*, p. 161).

38. Grene, *The Knower and the Known*, p. 164.

39. Michael Scriven, "Logical Positivism and the Behavioral Sciences," in *The Legacy of Logical Positivism*, p. 199.

40. Grene, *The Knower and the Known*, p. 165.

41. See Urmson, *Philosophical Analysis*, pp. 180–87.

42. "One can sum up the results that emerge from such a discussion quite simply: it is not possible to state a principle that will sharply demarcate meaningful (or 'scientifically meaningful') statements from others. One must concede that there is a matter of degree involved" (Scriven, "Logical Positivism and the Behavioral Sciences," p. 196).

43. Carl Hempel, in Ayer, ed., *Logical Positivism*, p. 129.

44. Thus Quine argues that two major consequences of the inability to give precise expression to the analytic-synthetic distinction are "a blurring of the supposed boundary between speculative metaphysics and natural science" and "a shift toward pragmatism." Concerning the "pragmatic" status of scientific theoretical concepts, he adds that these are "convenient intermediaries, . . . comparable, epistemologically, to the gods of Homer" and warranted because they "have proved more efficacious than other myths as a device for working a manageable structure into the flux of experience" (Quine, "Two Dogmas," pp. 20, 41).

45. Quoted by Urmson, *Philosophical Analysis*, pp. 169–70.

46. Thomas Nickles, "Heuristics and Justification in Scientific Research," in Suppe, ed., *The Structure of Scientific Theories*, p. 572.

47. Stephen Toulmin, "The Structure of Scientific Theories," ibid., p. 611. Toulmin adds that this omission "ended by giving a misleading picture of the intellectual content of a natural science."

48. Hume, *Treatise*, I. 1. 7.

49. Helvetius, *Treatise on Man*, 1:112, 114.

50. John Locke, *Essay concerning Human Understanding*, IV. 17. 6.

51. Hanson, "Logical Positivism and the Interpretation of Scientific Theories," p. 78.

52. Dudley Shapere, "Notes Toward a Post-Positivist Interpretation of Science," in *The Legacy of Logical Positivism*, p. 116.

53. *Daedalus* 106 (Summer 1977): 143–62.

54. Ibid., pp. 147–48, 152.

55. Ibid., pp. 156–57.

56. As Hanson puts it, the use of this model to interpret particular cases of modern physical theory is a "procrustean analysis," which simply "cuts away the living parts that do not fit the logical analysis" ("Logical

Positivism and the Interpretation of Scientific Theories," p. 83).

57. Cf. Toulmin: "Perhaps the idea of timeless, eternal standards, applicable to arguments-in-general in abstraction from their practical contexts, was always (as Vico claimed) a Cartesian delusion. Over-reliance on the model of Euclidean geometry has led philosophy into dead ends before now; since the mathematicians themselves have reappraised the status of their knowledge, philosophers too should reconsider their own standards of certainty" (Stephen Toulmin, *Human Understanding*, [Princeton, N.J.: Princeton University Press, 1972], vol. 1, p. 23).

The "General Introduction" (to a proposed three-volume work), from which this quotation is taken, is an excellent statement of the basic situation and fundamental tasks of a contemporary epistemology that would take seriously the untenability of the premises that informed the origins of the modern epistemological tradition. How far Toulmin succeeds in his constructive attempt to fulfill this task is another question, and one that lies beyond the scope of this study.

58. Plato, said Hobbes, "was the best philosopher of the Greeks" because he "forbade entrance into his School to all that were not already in some measure Geometricians"—geometry being "the Mother of all Natural Science" (*Leviathan*, p. 588).

59. A complete study would be almost coextensive with recent philosophy of science and epistemology. The most directly useful sources, however, are the accounts of scientific inquiry provided by Stephen Toulmin, Michael Polanyi, Norwood Hanson, Thomas Kuhn, and Imre Lakatos. These commentators by no means speak with one voice. On some issues, indeed, they are in explicit disagreement or exhibit some contrasts. Toulmin, for example, is critical of what he sees to be Kuhn's fumbling of the question of the warrants for conceptual change in science and for what he sees to be an exaggeration of the discontinuities of this conceptual change. Toulmin gives a rather "instrumentalist" account of truth and of the nature of scientific theory; Polanyi gives a "realist" account. I would argue that they nonetheless converge in their accounts of science as the fruit of a rationality that is "practical" in the ways to be specified.

60. See Kuhn, *The Structure of Scientific Revolutions*, chaps. 3 and 4.

61. See esp. *Human Understanding*, vol. 1.

62. See *Personal Knowledge* and *The Tacit Dimension* (Garden City, N.Y.: Doubleday, 1967).

63. "The attribution of truth to any particular stable alternative is a fiduciary act which cannot be analyzed in non-committal terms" (*Personal Knowledge*, p. 294).

64. Toulmin, *Human Understanding*, 1:227–28. These judgments, moreover, may require an element of "heuristic anticipation"—the laying of "rational bets" as to which concepts and strategies will prove to be more fruitful in the future. See, e.g. Toulmin, ibid., p. 255, and Polanyi, *Personal Knowledge*, p. 311.

65. Paul Feyerabend admittedly does go almost to this extreme in labeling himself a philosophical "dadaist" or "anarchist." See his *Against Method* (London: Humanities Press, 1975).

66. See Kuhn, *The Structure of Scientific Revolutions*, 2d ed., p. 199. See also the sections on "Intellectual Selection" and "The Objective Constraints on Scientific Change" in Toulmin's *Human Understanding*, 1:222–60.

67. Aristotle, *Nic. Ethics* VI. 3.

68. For an account of this necessity for a mutual reshaping of the notions of "mind" and "nature," see Burtt, *The Metaphysical Foundations of Modern Science*, esp. the "Conclusion," and R. G. Collingwood, *The Idea of Nature* (New York: Oxford University Press, 1960). Collingwood argues that some of this refashioning has already taken place, even if it is not yet universally accepted or understood (p. 136: "I think it is fair to say that the conception of vital process as distinct from mechanical or chemical change has come to stay, and has revolutionized our conception of nature. That many eminent biologists have not yet accepted it need cause no surprise"). Burtt sees it as still awaiting accomplishment (p. 319: "a theory of mind . . . which will be fair to all the data and meet all the basic needs clamoring to guide their interpretation is yet to be invented"). Part of this divergence of assessment may be due to the fact that Collingwood is looking at one of the pair of concepts—"nature"—whereas Burtt is looking at the other—"mind." See also Polyani's *Personal Knowledge*, pt. 4, and *The Tacit Dimension*, chaps. 1 and 2, and Grene's *Knower and the Known*, chaps. 8 and 9.

69. See, for example, May Brodbeck's review of *Personal Knowledge, American Sociological Review* 25 (August 1960): 583, and L. J. Cohen, "Is the Progress of Science Evolutionary?" *British Journal for the Philosophy of Science* 24 (1973): 41–61.

Chapter Nine

1. In his Introduction to *Philosophical Analysis,* J. O. Urmson commented on this phenomenon. "During the years of war public philosophizing was practically at a standstill in England, though a few important articles in the new style were published. Yet during these years many analytic philosophers quietly assimilated and developed these new ideas and discarded the old; and when they returned to philosophy after the war they returned to philosophize in the new style without any formal recantation or explanation" (p. vii).

2. This observation is applicable to Wittgenstein, as well. Indeed, his example may be one significant source of the deliberately particularistic form of inquiry that characterizes contemporary analysis. Even though he did not elaborate a "philosophy of language" and disclaimed having one, as one commentator notes, his ideas had significance at that level: "Wittgenstein disclaimed any intention of propounding a philosophy of language. To me it seems that he has done so whether he intended it or not" (David Pole, *The Later Philosophy of Wittgenstein* [London: Athlone Press, 1958], p. 79).

3. In fact, as Roberto Unger has observed, it is even possible as a result of disciplinary particularism that practitioners of one discipline may transform or abandon part of a larger intellectual model while continuing to believe, mistakenly, that the model is still tenable in other areas. "Each specialized science of society," he argues, "working on its own, has so enriched and revised the parts of the classical liberal theory with which it is most immediately connected as to destroy any appearance of continuing dependence on that theory. But because the deviations are partial, they must share the fate of all partial criticism: to remain enslaved by that from which it claims to be free.

Each science refuses to accept the premises of the liberal theory that bear most immediately on its chosen subject matter, while continuing to rely, unavowedly and unknowingly, on principles drawn from other branches of the system of liberalism. . . .

In all these cases, interdependent propositions are treated as if they could be accepted and rejected piecemeal. The result is that the specialized disciplines become in varying measures inadequate. Their inadequacy, however, is hidden by the illusion of their autonomy from one another and from commitments to any underlying system of thought" (*Knowledge and Politics,* pp. 9–10).

4. Historicist technocrats could not fall into this pattern, of course, since they clearly recognized a natural and normative human "essence." They simply undermined the limiting force such a notion might be presumed to exert on themselves by their sophistic derogation of "spontaneity." Once the integrity of expressed choices and desires was thus denied, they were able to stipulate, on the basis of their alleged scientific insight, what anyone else "really" wanted.

5. Keniston, *The Uncommitted,* p. 309.

6. See Peter Berger, *Pyramids of Sacrifice* (New York: Basic Books, 1974), chap. 4, "Consciousness Raising."

7. The principle of cognitive respect does not imply, any more than our model of fiduciary rationality does, complete anarchism or relativism epistemologically. Not all perceptions of a situation are all equally right, necessarily; they are not all on a par. It does imply that those allegedly mistaken must be persuaded and educated, not simply controlled and manipulated by law and propaganda. Especially when it comes to defining one's own situation, one's own needs, "informed consent" becomes a requirement that can be overridden only in the most extreme circumstances.

8. The following account is principally indebted to Toulmin's account of rational enterprises in *Human Understanding.* It also draws on Polanyi's analysis of the organizational features of scientific disciplines (e.g., in *Science, Faith, and Society* [Chicago: University of Chicago Press, 1964]) and on Imre Lakatos's account of the rise and fall of scientific "research programs." None of these writers should be held responsible, however, for the larger argument within which I am using their ideas as resources.

9. Positivism has traded heavily—but illicitly—on this record of success. The positivists' argument for extending their conceptions of knowledge and method to the social sciences, for example, was predicated on the achievements of the natural sciences. The argument was: if the natural sciences can do so well, operating according to positivist premises, then shouldn't the social sciences try to approximate their success by emulating their methods? That is, shouldn't the social sciences also be governed by positivistic rules and prohibitions? The assumption here, of course, is that the natural sciences have in fact embodied the norms of positivism and that this accounts for their success. The truth is quite different: the natural sciences have not proceeded according to positivist methods, nor have they lived up to positivist standards. They could not have done so because it is impossible. If they really tried seriously to do so, they would be crippled. They can be interpreted as having done so only by systematic ex post facto misconstrucions, which are not based on the actual conduct of natural science but instead impose preestablished interpretative categories on scientific practice.

10. James B. Conant, *Scientific Principles and Moral Conduct* (Cambridge, Eng.: At the University Press, 1967), pp. 7–8.

11. Stephen Toulmin, *Human Understanding,* vol. 1, p. 150.

12. In Theodore Roszak's view, in fact, Christianity stands guilty on precisely this account of carrying the dedivinization of nature too far. That is, once nature was denied any status as sacred, it was utterly profaned and thereby opened up to rapacious domination as well as to intellectual investigation. See *Where the Wasteland Ends*, esp. chap. 4.

13. Herbert Butterfield, *The Origins of Modern Science*, p. 15.

14. Michael Polanyi argues this point by a hypothetical speculation. "Suppose," he writes, "scientists were in the habit of regarding most of their fellows as cranks or charlatans. Fruitful discussion between them would become impossible and they would no more rely on each other's results nor act on each other's opinion. Thus their mutual collaboration on which scientific progress depends would be cut off. The processes of publication, of compiling text-books, of teaching juniors, of making appointments, and establishing new scientific institutions, would henceforth depend on the mere chance of who happened to make the decision. It would then become impossible to recognize any statement as a scientific proposition or to describe anyone as a scientist. Science would become practically extinct. Nor," he adds, "could the coherence of scientific opinion be restored by the establishment of any kind of central authority" (*Science, Faith, and Society*, pp. 52–53).

15. Toulmin provides a relevant example here in his account of the development of atomic physics by J. J. Thompson and Ernest Rutherford. As he notes, "Thompson's more conservative colleagues, who could not make this imaginative leap, began by treating his suggestion that the electron was a material object of 'sub-atomic' dimensions as some kind of practical joke" (*Human Understanding*, 1:153). Not all that many years later, it was Rutherford who confessed his inability to grasp another innovation: quantum mechanics (see ibid., 1:286).

16. See his *The Republic of Science* (Chicago: Roosevelt University Publications, 1962). The quotation is from page 5 of that essay. Conversely, Polanyi's argument that recourse to "specific" authority leads inevitably toward a centralized and absolutist regime is unduly pessimistic, ignoring other forms of checks and balances.

17. Toulmin, *Human Understanding*, 1:353.

18. Cf. Toulmin: "The subject-matter of a science is in fact 'problematic' at all, only when considered in the light of those intellectual ambitions of the scientists concerned; yet those very ambitions can be formulated realistically, only in the light of experience of the relevant subject-matter. . . . In this dialectical manner the task of defining the current ideals of a science with all the necessary precision implicitly mobilizes the whole of its historical experience" (ibid., p. 154).

19. This dependency of a good society on a commitment to the truth, incidentally, seems to me the appropriate ultimate self-justification of the academic enterprise vis-à-vis the larger political order. When a legislative body, for example, asks why it should support a public university or why it should respect academic freedom, it is only a partial answer to cite the concrete "cash-value" benefits of literacy, vocational preparation, and so on, on the one hand, and First Amendment guarantees on the other. At least equally as important is this response: that respect for the truth is essential to the good society and that this respect is best embodied, and truth is most reliably attained, in healthy academic institutions, which possess autonomy and integrity.

20. Aristotle, *Nic. Ethics*, bk. 1, chap. 2.

21. Immanuel Kant, "Metaphysical Foundations of Morals," in Friedrich, ed., *The Philosophy of Kant*, p. 170.

22. David Hume, *Principles of Morals*, sec. IX, pt. 1.

23. This conception of political rationality obviously diverges from the tendency of bourgeois individualism to equate "rational" political behavior with the maximization of self-interest. Perhaps, however, the divergence is in one sense more superficial than real—a matter of divergent focus rather than contrary meaning. For the individualist sees the rational man as maximizing his own individual good; our account of the rational society sees it as dedicated to maximizing its own (common) good. The difference is one of level. The real difference comes a step further down the road. The individualist conception of "rational man" is a generalization into politics from the "rational economic man" of classical economics. The viability of the translation depends on the tenability of the idea that there is some political equivalent of the market; it depends, that is, on the early liberal optimism that "nature" will automatically reconcile individual interests into common good. To the extent that this assumption does not hold, however, I think it could be shown that the "rational" behavior of trying to maximize individual self-interest is actually irrational. This was Hobbes's point in his analysis of the dynamics of the state of nature. Long-run rationality, as he saw, in such circumstances required a kind of enforced "altruism"—a taking of a common standpoint—in which the rights of others were accorded respect in return for the guarantee of one's own integrity. The difference between Hobbes's "rational man" and Kant's, then, may not be so great as it first appears—at least in outward behavior. The difference is more one of attitude—Hobbes's man grudgingly accepts what Kant's man willingly embraces: the "rational" restriction of particular desire on behalf of the common good.

24. Indeed, there is genuine similarity in many respects between Toulmin's conception of a rational enterprise—which derives principally from his analysis of the natural sciences—and Oakeshott's conception of rational conduct—which derives principally from his consideration of moral and political action. See Oakeshott, "Rational Conduct" in his *Rationalism in Politics* (New York: Basic Books, 1962), pp. 80–110. See also Francis Canavan, *The Political Reason of Edmund Burke* (Durham, N.C.: Duke University Press, 1960).

25. Walter Lippmann, *The Public Philosophy*, p. 40.

Index

"Absolutist" conception of democracy, 289–90
Accessibility of knowledge, 50, 82–83, 123–24
Adams, John, 392
Agathon, the, 69, 84–85, 91–92, 197
Analytic/synthetic distinction, the, 332
Aquinas, Saint Thomas, 74, 204
Archimedean point, the, 50, 108–9, 138
Arendt, Hannah, 6
Aristotle, 84, 90, 108, 193, 221, 237, 369, 383; on certainty, 47; and Hume, 234–36; on method, 41; on natural law, 74, 204; on nature, 101–2, 106, 211, 363, 371–72; on sensation, 96–98, 208–9, 211; on theory and practice, 55, 93, 124, 138, 143, 197, 225, 244, 313, 348, 350–51, 353, 366, 379
Arnold, Thurman, 258
Aron, Raymond, 251
Artificial reconciliation of interests, the, 76, 89–90, 92–93
Augustine, Saint, 118, 124
Austin, J. L., 188, 358
Authority, 53; in rational enterprises, 373–77, 386–89; in technocracy, 115–16
Autonomy of reason, 50, 81–82

Bacon, Francis: conservatism of, 76–77; on practical utility of reason, 54–57, 61–62, 90; as source of liberal rationalism, 18–19, 32, 82–83, 96, 134, 258, 369; and technocracy, 151–53, 162
Bain, Read, 165–66
Ball, Terence, 294
Bambrough, Renford, 314–15
Barker, Ernest, 286
Bauer, Bruno, 142
Becker, Carl, 5, 213, 235–36
Bentham, Jeremy, 65, 94, 126, 130, 136, 244; on the Legislator, 108–11; moral theory of, 111, 113–14, 118–19, 185; on the Panopticon, 119–21, 159, 353
Berelson, Bernard, 295
Berger, Peter, 364
Berkeley, George, 21, 37, 44, 95, 213, 355
Bonald, Louis de, 129
Bossuet, Jacques, 20
Boyle, Robert, 53
Braybrooke, David, 131
Browne, Sir Thomas, 72
Burke, Edmund, 75, 87, 120, 301; and Hume, 273–76; and the rational society, 392–93
Bury, J. B., 51

Cambridge Platonists, 53, 65, 74
Camelot, Project, 155–56
Camus, Albert, 149, 313
Carnap, Rudolf, 131, 320–25, 332
Cassirer, Ernst: on Enlightenment, 31, 33, 208; on Grotius, 74, 208; on Helvetius, 93, on Locke, 20

Certainty: quest for, 15–16; within limits, 43–47. *See also* Foundations of knowledge

Chastellux, François, marquis de, 64–65, 78

Cicero, 74, 204

Cieszkowski, August von, 142–44

Clarke, Samuel, 74

Common Good, the, 298, 307–8, 383–84, 392–93

Comte, August: compared with Hegel, 137–41, 143; influence of, 150, 161–62, 171; on progress of the mind, 33; and technocracy, 94, 117, 131–37

Conant, James, 369–70

Conceptual change: and institutional development, 379; in scientific theory, 343, 345–47, 351–53

Condillac, Abbé de: conservatism of, 77; on the geometric ideal, 31, 32, 34; on Locke, 19, 36–37, 39; on moral science, 64; on sensation, 37–40, 95–96, 343; and technocracy, 94

Condorcet, Marie Jean Antoine Nicolas Caritat de: on authority, 26–27, 72, 258, 387; and democracy, 78, 83, 92, 122–24; on the future, 5, 56–57, 175, 283, 362; on natural reconciliation of interests, 80–81; on progress of the mind, 33, 43; on public opinion, 80–81; on the relation between science and politics, 49, 54, 56–60, 84, 111, 183, 200, 377

Connolly, William, 294, 301, 305

Conscience, 247, 254, 280

Consensus in rational enterprises, 373–77

Context: of discovery, 341–45; of justification, 341–45

Copernicus, 236, 317

Crick, Bernard, 161, 301, 303, 382

Crocker, Lester, 84

Culverwel, Nathanael, 74

Cumberland, Richard, 65

Dahl, Robert, 292, 297–300

D'Alembert, Jean: on epistemology, 30, 33, 37, 38, 83; on moral knowledge, 65–66, 74–75, 197; on sources of Enlightenment, 18–19

Darwin, Charles, 85, 237–38

Declaration of Independence, 86, 201

Democratic ideas, debasement of, 305–8

Democratic relativism, 289–90, 293; problems of, 284–89. *See also* Kelsen, Hans; Empiricism; Pluralism

Democritus, 48, 290

Descartes, René, 16, 34, 104, 138, 202, 211, 355, 360; on autonomy of reason, 81; on certainty, 44, 46, 59, 353; compared with Locke, 20–22, 207–8; conservatism of, 71–73, 76–78; egalitarian implications of, 82–83; on foundations of knowledge, 35–40; on geometric spirit, 30–33; and Kant, 239–46, 254; and logical positivism, 319, 325; on method of doubt, 35, 40–42, 351, 369; on moral science, 50–52, 54, 56, 62, 64, 84, 90–91, 125, 196–200; Platonism of, 47, 370; on Scholasticism, 23–25, 35, 40–41; on simple ideas, 35–40; as source of liberal rationalism, 14, 18–23, 134, 349; and technocracy, 151–55; on unified science, 32–33

Deus faber, 115–21, 144, 150, 180, 191, 360

Dewey, John, 15, 47

Diderot, Denis: on epistemology, 30, 34, 36; on moral science, 65, 84, 87, 208; populism of, 83; reaction of, to Helvetius, 127, 195, 394

Dostoyevsky, Fyodor, 309

Durkheim, Emile, 7, 184

"Dynamo-objective coupling," 118, 136

Eichmann, Adolf, 6

Einstein, Albert, 372

Eliot, T. S., 395

Emotive theory of ethics, 61, 227, 236–39
Empiricism: neoempiricism, 333; in political theory, 261–69, 275–84. *See also* Hume, David; Sensations; Value noncognitivism; Vienna Circle
Engels, Friedrich, 27, 133, 209–10, 239
Epicurus, 225, 243
"Epistemological manicheanism," 45–47, 61, 200, 320–21. *See also* Verification, principle of
Equality, 306
Esprit simpliste. See Simple ideas
"Experimental physics of the soul," 70, 79, 93, 110, 115, 157
Experimental science of morality. *See* Hume, David, moral theory of; political theory of

Fact/value distinction, 221–23, 238, 365–68
Feigl, Herbert, 324
Feuerbach, Ludwig, 142
Finer, Herman, 283
Fontenelle, Bernard de, 31
Foucault, Michel, 159
Foundations of knowledge, 34–40, 320, 323–25, 340. *See also* Simple ideas
Fourier, Charles, 175
Frank, Jerome, 258
Frankel, Charles, ix, 51, 62, 373
Franklin, Benjamin, 162
Freedom: in irrationalism, 287, 305–6; as liberal ideal, 6–7, 81; in rational enterprises, 373–76; in technocracy, 104–5, 106, 111, 125, 184–85, 190
Frege, Gottlob, 319, 326
Freud, Sigmund, viii–ix, 6, 56, 85, 389; and positivism, 158–61
Friedman, Milton, 167, 283
Fulbright, Senator William, 155, 179

Galilei, Galileo, 14, 25, 123, 134, 162, 348, 370, 372
Galtung, Johan, 155
Genet, Jean, 255

Geometric ideal, 30–34; relinquishing the, 340–49, 369
Gibson, James, 66–67
Glanvill, Joseph, 53
Godwin, William, 65, 86
Grene, Marjorie, 47, 337
Grotius, Hugo, 65, 74, 208

Habermas, Jürgen, 159
Halévy, Elie, 65, 66, 87, 93
Hand, Learned, 282
Hanson, Norwood, 331–32, 344
Harrington, Michael, 129
Hartley, David, 94–105; on human malleability, 100–101, 152; moral theory of, 112–14, 118
Hayek, Friedrich, 126, 283–84
Hazard, Paul, 19
Hegel, G. W. F., 27, 239, 258, 290; compared with Comte, 137–41; epistemology and politics in, 12, 43, 370; on liberty, 184, 305; and the rational society, 390; on reason in history, 54–55, 137–44
Hegelians, Left-wing, 141–44, 163
Heidegger, Martin, 320, 329
Helvetius, Claude, 82, 127, 195; on epistemology, 29, 33, 37–38, 46, 96–99, 343; on Locke, 19, 36; on moral science, 64, 67, 200; moral theory of, 113–14, 118, 172; on state of nature, 102–5; and technocracy, 93–94, 100, 109–14, 120–21, 126, 130, 363
Hempel, Carl, 332, 339
Hess, Moses, 132, 143
Hilbert, David, 326
Hitler, Adolf, 383
Hobbes, Thomas, 151, 207, 211, 214, 225, 263, 270, 301, 308, 324–25, 343, 382–83; conservatism of, 76; on epistemology and politics, 12, 27, 175, 198; on freedom, 192, 305; on geometric spirit, 30, 32, 47; and irrationalism, 284, 288–89; on language, 28–32, 355; on moral science, 62, 67–69; on reductive analysis, 38, 322; on Scholasticism, 24–25, 27–30,

32, 49, 319; on the sovereign,
109, 115, 253, 354; on state of
nature, 102–4, 235
Holbach, Baron Paul de, 33, 64,
95, 105–6
Holmes, Oliver Wendell, Jr.,
258–59, 277–78
Hooker, Richard, 74, 204–5, 263
Humboldt, Wilhelm von, 162
Hume, David, 16, 39, 44, 46,
105, 246, 258, 286; and Burke,
273–76; epistemology of, 34,
48, 209, 213–18, 355; and logical positivism, 319, 324, 328,
331, 343; and Machiavelli,
263–64; moral theory of, 201,
218–39, 249, 384, 393; philosophical incoherence of,
231–39; and pluralism, 291,
293–97, 301–2, 308–9; political
theory of, 261–78; and the rational society, 393
Humphrey, Hubert, 129

Impressions. *See* Sensations
Interest-group liberalism. *See*
Pluralism
Irrationalism, 256–61; in conservative ideology, 260–77;
impact of recent philosophy
on, 365–68; in liberal ideology,
260–61, 277–89; in radical
ideology, 260–61, 308–10;
variants of, 260–61. *See also*
Value noncognitivism
Is/ought distinction, 220–23,
365–66

Jackson, Andrew, 301
Jefferson, Thomas, 74, 78, 86,
197
Justice: in irrationalism, 263,
267, 270–71, 278–79, 298, 307;
in technocracy, 125, 184–88

Kant, Immanuel, 319, 341, 353,
360; on Enlightenment, 28, 38,
81; moral theory of, 207–8,
239–55, 384; on natural reconciliation of interests, 86, 173;
and neo-Kantianism, 246–55,
281; and philosophy of science, 331, 345; and Plato, 243,
245; and the rational society,

390–92; traditionalism of,
246–50
Kaplan, Abraham, 329
Kelsen, Hans, 250, 258, 292,
300, 308; and democratic rela-
tivism, 278–89
Keniston, Kenneth, 4, 310,
363–64
Kennan, George, 179
Kennedy, M. C. 155
Kepler, Johannes, 348, 372
Kierkegaard, Søren, 109, 251
Knight, Isabel, 207
Kojève, Alexandre, 138–39
Korner, S., 250
Kuhn, Thomas, 43, 350–51

Lakatos, Imre, 336, 347
Lamettrie, Julian, 33
Language: abuse of, 28–34, 320,
338; ideal, 31–33, 321, 327–32.
336–38, 340
Laplace, Pierre, 108, 153, 353
Laski, Harold, ix, 8, 65
Lasswell, Harold, 164–65,
169–70, 172–73, 176, 192
Law of nature. *See* Natural law
Law, rule of, 117, 245, 250
Lazarsfeld, Paul, 295
LeClerc, Jean, 34, 48
Lee, Henry, 74
Leibniz, Gottfried, 32
Lenin, V. I., 129, 131, 147–50,
314
Lewis, Sinclair, 7
Liberalism: conceptual suicide
of, 183–95, 256; problems of,
viii, 5, 9–10, 13–16, 89, 212,
238–39, 256; and the rational
society, 394–95
Liberal reason: definition of, xi,
14, 22–23; disintegration of,
311–13; sources of, 18–20, 37
Liberty. *See* Freedom
Lippmann, Walter, 286, 393
Lobkowicz, Nicholas, 146
Locke, John, 8, 14, 26, 141, 263,
301, 311, 344, 383; on certainty,
44–47, 59, 321; compared with
Descartes, 20–22; on education,
112; on foundations of knowledge,
35–40, 325; on geometric spirit,
31; and irrationalism, 284, 288; on
language, 28–29, 31; on moral sci-

ence, 50–54, 61–67, 72–74, 125, 196–213, 231–32, 239; on natural law, 204–13; on political use of reason, 27, 81–82; sensationism in, 95–96, 98–99, 207–14; on simple ideas, 35–40; as source of liberal rationalism, 18–23, 349; on state of nature, 102–4, 205; and *tabula rasa*, 94–101; on toleration, 290, 302; traditionalism of, 72–74, 76, 204, 246

Logical positivism: decline of, 327–40, 370; on scientific theory, 341–43; as updated liberal reason, 319–27

Logos-rationality, 70–71, 75, 125, 197, 223–24, 311, 326, 377

Louis XIV, king of France, 126

Louis XV, king of France, 80

Louis XVI, king of France, 80

Lowi, Theodore, 291, 293, 301, 308

Lundberg, George, 163–64, 175–76, 192

Lynch, Frederick, 182, 187

Lysenkoism, 148, 388

McConnell, Grant, 308

McConnell, James, 157

Mach, Ernst, 314, 319

Machiavelli, Niccolò, 11, 132, 263–64, 384

MacIntyre, Alasdair, 309

Mack, Mary Peter, 118–19

Mackintosh, James, 65, 87

McLaurin, Colin, 85, 197

McNeil, Edward Lee, 181–82, 187

McPhee, William, 295

Maddox, Lester, 307

Madison, James, 12, 270; and artificial reconciliation of interests, 90, 150; and pluralism, 292, 297–301, 304–5

Magruder, Jeb, 60

Malebranche, Nicolas, 20

Malleability of human nature, 99–101, 110–12, 152, 363–64

Malthus, Thomas, 57

Mandeville, Bernard, 87, 175, 301

Mannheim, Karl, 153–54

Manuel, Frank, 43, 70, 192

Marcuse, Herbert, 10, 12, 131

Marx, Karl, 4, 107, 133–34, 158, 177, 192, 244, 258, 294, 314; on revolu-

tionary praxis, 143–50, 167–68, 200

Masham, Lady, 22

Matson, Floyd, 169–70

Menninger, Karl, 185–87

Merleau-Ponty, Maurice, 360

Mersenne, Marin, 32, 41, 71, 84, 197, 372

Michelet, Karl, 142

Milgram, Stanley, 178–79

Mill, James, 13, 60, 83, 122–24

Mill, John Stuart, 13, 162; on liberty, 385–86; on moral science, 69–70; moral theory of, 114, 179; and pluralism, 295, 297; on progress, 43, 59–60, 69–70

Miller, William Lee, 305

Mitchell, John, 60

Molière, Jean, 28

Molyneux, William, 66

Montesquieu, Charles Louis Secondat, baron de, 117, 208

"Moral Newtonianism," 66, 69, 85; varieties of, 75–94

"Moral sciences," 50–58, 61–66, 122–25, 138, 225–31; dissolution of, 196–201, 207–13, 231–39; problematic content of, 66–75

Morgenthau, Hans, 3

Myrdal, Gunnar, 291

Natural law, 199; in Hume, 228, 263; in Locke, 73–74, 204–13; in the rational society, 393–94

"Natural light" of reason, 27, 36, 63, 73, 197, 205, 394

Natural reconciliation of interests, 76, 86–89, 92, 174

Natural rights, 86, 89, 111, 125, 298–99, 307

Neurath, Otto, 326

Newton, Isaac, 237, 239, 249, 252; as exemplar for liberal rationalism, 14, 18–19, 123, 162, 197, 348, 372. *See also* Moral Newtonianism

Nickles, Thomas, 343

Niebuhr, Reinhold, x, 9–10, 177, 300, 389

Nietzsche, Friedrich, 304

Nisbet, Robert, 16

Nous, 55, 196, 241, 243

Oakeshott, Michael, 392

Orwell, George, 59, 177
Owen, Robert, 94, 112, 116, 189

Paine, Thomas, 78, 86–87, 92, 201
Panopticon, the, 119–21, 159, 183
Paradox of the age of reason, 39, 207
Pascal, Blaise, 31, 357
Passmore, John, 118
Paul, Saint, 88, 273
Pelagians, 118
Pfaff, William, 3
Phronēsis, 55, 93, 143, 225, 243–44,
  366, 379. See also Practical reason
Physiocrats, 65, 77
Plasticity of human nature. See
  Malleability of human nature
Plato, 11, 18, 79, 209, 224, 253, 258,
  383, 386; on certainty, 47–49, 370;
  and Kant, 243, 245; and liberal
  reason, 47–49, 84, 90, 124, 197,
  348; and pluralism, 300, 306–7;
  and the rational society, 391–92;
  and technocracy, 124
Pluralism: as an ideology, 291–301;
  inadequacies of, 301–8
Polanyi, Michael, 118, 312, 351, 354,
  370
Popper, Karl, 131, 258, 285, 347
Positivist pluralism. See Pluralism
Posttheoretical practice, 93, 142–50,
  163, 167–68
Power: liberal view of, 7–8; in
  technocracy, 168–70, 191–94
Practical reason: in Hume, 225; in
  irrationalism, 256, 259, 313, 326;
  in Kant, 24–45, 249, 253–54; in
  liberal reason, 55; return of,
  347–56, 360, 362–63; 365–68, 379,
  382; in technocracy, 93, 143–50,
  163, 167–68, 313. See also Post-
  theoretical practice; Rational en-
  terprises; Rational society
Price, Don K., 178
Priestley, Joseph, 5, 86, 152
Protocol statements, 323–25
Prussia, 141–42
Public opinion, 59–60, 392
Pufendorf, Samuel von, 65
Pythagoras, 48

Quine, W. V., 332

Ramsey, Frank, 329

Rational enterprises, 349–56, 361,
  368–77; authority in, 373–77,
  386–89; consensus in, 373–77,
  382–85; freedom in, 373–76,
  385–86; politics as, 377–95
Rational society, a, 360–61, 382–95;
  authority in, 386–89; consensus
  in, 382–85; freedom in, 385–86
Ray, John, 74
Reductive analysis. See Simple
  ideas
Reformation, Protestant, 53
Relativist theory of democracy. See
  Democratic relativism
Res cogitans, 107–9, 118, 242
Res extensa, 36, 40, 105–9, 118, 151,
  155, 184, 186, 241–42, 363, 367
Responsibility, 188–91
Rosenberg, Alexander, 131
Roszak, Theodore, 83, 310
Rousseau, Jean-Jacques, 80; on
  human nature, 106–7, 132, 226,
  236, 241, 360; and Kant, 240–41,
  245; on the Legislator, 109,
  115–16; and the rational society,
  391; on the state of nature, 103–5,
  236
Ruge, Arnold, 142–43
Russell, Bertrand, 258, 277; and
  "empiricist liberalism," 280,
  282–89; and logical positivism,
  319, 321, 323, 326, 337, 358

Saint-Pierre, Abbé de, 77
Saint-Simon, Claude Henri, comte
  de, 94, 150, 152, 161, 184, 192,
  200, 377
Sartre, Jean-Paul, 239, 250–55, 279,
  353, 360
Schattschneider, E. E., 303
Scheffler, Israel, 333
Schlick, Moritz, 323–24, 326–27
Scholasticism, 311, 318–19, 335,
  344, 359; criticism of, 23–42;
  methods of, 41, 369; on sensation,
  39–40, 96
Schopenhauer, Arthur, 250
Scientific theory: positivist account
  of, 324–26, 331–32, 341–43; re-
  visionist account of, 331–32,
  343–47
Scriven, Michael, 336–37
Seneca, 205

Sensations, 37–40, 94–98, 201, 324–25; and moral science, 201–15, 232–33, 236–37
Shapere, Dudley, 345–46
Simple ideas, 34–40, 123–24, 322–25, 329–32, 336–38, 340
Skinner, B. F., 178, 353; on control, 168–69, 192; moral theory of, 170–71, 200; and technocracy, 130, 151–53, 173–77, 189
Smith, Adam, 86–87, 114
Smith, D. W., 127
Smith, Thomas Vernor, 278, 284, 286, 288, 290, 292
Spencer, Herbert, 9, 162, 171
Spinoza, Benedict, 31, 62, 79
State of nature, 101–5, 205
Stephen, Leslie, 286
Stern, Karl, 72
Stillman, Edmund, 3
Stirner, Max, 144
Strauss, Leo, 254
Suarez, Francisco, 74
Subject/object dichotomy, 154–56, 356, 360, 362–64; as political model, 105–9, 118, 120, 190–91

Tabula rasa, 94–101, 105–8, 116
Talmon, J. L., 285
Taylor, Charles, 202
Technocracy: in American social theory, 161–77; central misconception of, 179, 313–16; comparison of, with liberalism, 121–27, 194–95; conception of reason in, 15; in constitutional democracies, 177–83; and empiricism, 150–58; hallmarks of, 128; and historicism, 131–50; obsolescence of, 361–65, 368; origins of, 93–127; and psychiatry, 158–61, 164–67; and the rational society, 391–92; relation of, to value noncognitivism, 202–3, 312–16; and social deviance, 180–83
Theoretical science: and irrationalism, 256, 313; and liberal reason, 55; and positivism, 324–26; and rational enterprises, 350–56; and revisionist philosophy of science, 348–49, 359; and technocracy, 93, 138, 256, 313. See also Posttheoretical practice

Thrasymachus, 171, 266–67
Tillich, Paul, 4
Tocqueville, Alexis de, 60, 193, 292, 304–5, 308, 312
Toulmin, Stephen: on conceptual change, 343, 346, 352, 379–80; on rational enterprises, 351–52, 354, 370, 379–80; on Wittgenstein, 321
"Tradition of civility," 15, 286–87
Troeltsch, Ernst, 378
Trublet, Abbé, 34
Turgot, Jacques, 33
Tyrrell, James, 22, 53

Unger, Roberto, 156
Unified science, 31–33, 320, 325
Urmson, J. O., 330
Utility, principle of, 89; in Hume, 229–31, 265, 267, 269; in technocracy, 111–14, 172, 186–88

Value noncognitivism, 238–39; definition of, 15, 201–3; and irrationalism, 256–59; relation of, to technocracy, 202–3, 312–16
Vartanian, Aram, 20, 22, 37–38, 51
Verification, principle of, 322–23, 328–30, 338–40, 353, 355–56. See also Epistemological manicheanism
Vico, Giambattista, 44, 357
Vienna Circle, 21, 46, 258, 324, 326, 331, 353
Virtue: conceptions of, 112–13, 229; relation of, to knowledge, 84–85, 88
Vischer, Friedrich Theodor, 139
Voegelin, Eric, 130, 138
Volney, Comte de, 86
Voltaire, 46, 87, 258; conservatism of, 77, 79, 92; on Locke, 19, 36; on moral science, 65, 84, 208

Ward, Lester Frank, 129, 162–64, 170–77, 192
Watkins, Frederick, 277
Weaver, Richard, 129
Weber, Max, 6, 266, 378; and irrationalism, 239, 251–55, 279, 286
Werkmeister, 144, 163, 177, 354. See also Deus faber
Whitehead, Alfred North, 18, 209
Wills, Eric, 182, 187